# Translation of

## Sefer zikaron le-kehilat Rozniatow, Perehinsko, Broszniow, Swaryczow veha-seviva

## Memorial (Yizkor) Book of
# Rozniatow,
## Perehinsko, Broszniow, Swaryczow, and Environs

Originally in Hebrew, Yiddish, and English

Edited by Shimon Kanc

Published in Tel Aviv, 1974

Published by JewishGen

An Affiliate of the Museum of Jewish
A Living Memorial to the Holocaust
New York

Sefer zikaron le-kehilat Rozniatow, Perehinsko, Broszniow, Swaryczow veha-seviva
Yizkor Book in Memory of Rozniatow, Perehinsko, Broszniow, Swaryczow and Environs

Translation Project Coordinator: Thomas F. Weiss
Layout: Thomas F. Weiss
Cover Design: Jan R. Fine
Publicity: Sandra Hirschhorn

Published by JewishGen, Inc.
An Affiliate of the Museum of Jewish Heritage
A Living Memorial to the Holocaust
36 Battery Place, New York, NY 10280

Printed in the United States of America by Lightning Source, Inc.

Library of Congress Control Number (LCCN): 2013932631
ISBN: 978-1-939561-00-8 (hard cover: 512 pages, alk. paper)

Cover photographs: Illustrations from the original Hebrew/Yiddish book

## JewishGen and the Yizkor Books In Print Project

This book has been published by the **Yizkor Books in Print Project**, as part of the **Yizkor Book Project** of **JewishGen, Inc.**

**JewishGen, Inc.** is a non-profit organization founded in 1987 as a resource for Jewish genealogy. Its website [www.jewishgen.org] serves as an international clearinghouse and resource center to assist individuals who are researching the history of their Jewish families and the places where they lived. JewishGen provides databases, facilitates discussion groups, and coordinates projects relating to Jewish genealogy and the history of the Jewish people. In 2003, JewishGen became an affiliate of the **Museum of Jewish Heritage - A Living Memorial to the Holocaust** in New York.

The **JewishGen Yizkor Book Project** was organized to make more widely known the existence of Yizkor (Memorial) Books written by survivors and former residents of various Jewish communities throughout the world. Later, volunteers connected to the different destroyed communities began cooperating to have these books translated from the original language—usually Hebrew or Yiddish—into English, thus enabling a wider audience to have access to the valuable information contained within them. As each chapter of these books was translated, it was posted on the JewishGen website and made available to the general public.

The **Yizkor Books in Print Project** began in 2011 as an initiative to print and publish Yizkor Books that had been fully translated, so that hard copies would be available for purchase by the descendants of these communities and also by scholars, universities, synagogues, libraries, and museums.

These Yizkor books have been produced almost entirely through the volunteer effort of researchers from around the world, assisted by donations from private individuals. The books are printed and sold at near cost, so as to make them as affordable as possible. Our goal is to make this important genre of Jewish literature and history available in English in book form, so that people can have the personal histories of their ancestral towns on their bookshelves for themselves and for their children and grandchildren.

*Lance Ackerfeld, Yizkor Book Project Manager*

*Joel Alpert, Yizkor Books in Print Project Coordinator*

Memorial Book of Rozniatow, Galicia

Title Page of Original Hebrew/Yiddish Edition

# ספר זכרון

לקהילת

# רוזניאטוב

## פרהינסקו, ברושניוב

## והסביבה

ה`,`ה העורך : שמעון קאנץ

הוצא לאור ע"י אירגון יוצאי רוזניאטוב, פרהינסקו,
ברושניוב והסביבה בישראל ובארה"ב

תל־אביב       תשל"ד       1974

Translation of the Title Page of Original Hebrew/Yiddish Edition

# Memorial (Yizkor) Book of
# Rozniatow,
## Perehinsko, Broszniow,
## Swaryczow, and Environs

**Editor Shimon Kanc**

**Published by the Organization of Former
Residents of Rozniatow, Perehinsko, Broszniow and Environs
in Israel and the USA**

1974

Tel Aviv

# JewishGen
# Yizkor Book Project

This book is presented by the
Yizkor Books in Print Project
Project Coordinator: Joel Alpert

Part of the
Yizkor Books Project of JewishGen, Inc.
Project Manager: Lance Ackerfeld

These books have been produced solely through volunteer effort
of individuals from around the world. The books are printed and
sold at near cost, so as to make them as affordable as possible.

Our goal is to make this history and important genre of Jewish
literature available in English in book form so that people can have
the near-personal histories of their ancestral towns on their bookshelves for themselves and for their children and grandchildren.

Any donations to the Yizkor Books Project are appreciated.

Please send donations to:
Yizkor Book Project
JewishGen
36 Battery Place
New York, NY 10280

JewishGen, Inc. is an affiliate of the
Museum of Jewish Heritage
A Living Memorial to the Holocaust

# Preface for the Translation

As a child growing up in New York City, I often heard my parents laughing after my step-father said to my mother in mock derision, "What can you expect from a Galitzianer?" I failed to see the humor. I knew that my mother was born in Vienna, where her parents lived and both my father and I were born in Prague. My step-father was born in Mattersdorf on the Austrian-Hungarian border. What was so funny and what was a Galitzianer? I never knew.

In 1998 at age 64, I visited Vienna for the first time in 60 years; I had also acquired "roots disease" (an unrelenting search for ancestors). In the Israelitische Kultusgemeinde Wien (Jewish Community Center in Vienna), I found my mother's birth record, her marriage record, and the marriage record of her parents. I learned that my grandfather was born in Buczacz, Galicia and my grandmother in Rozniatow, Galicia. The mystery was partially resolved. My maternal grandparents were Galitizianers and, therefore, I was a ½ Galitzianer! I still failed to see the humor in that. It took a few more years of learning about Jewish culture before I began to see the humor in the geographically-based rivalries of Eastern European Jews.

But new questions arose. Where were these towns that would hold the birth records of my maternal ancestors? The towns were found relatively easily (both were in Eastern Galicia, now in Western Ukraine). Historical accounts indicated that changing political boundaries placed both towns successively in Poland, Austria, Austria-Hungary, Poland, USSR, Germany, USSR, and currently in Ukraine. After a great deal of searching, I unfortunately discovered that the vital records of these two towns were not to be found. They may have been lost during the Holocaust or may still reside undiscovered in some Eastern European archive. What to do? I decided to travel to Ukraine and visit these sites, which I had learned contained Jewish cemeteries with some erect gravestones. Naively, I thought to find my relatives' gravestones and learn something from the inscriptions.

In 2000 and 2001, I traveled to Ukraine — together with family members and a guide/trans-

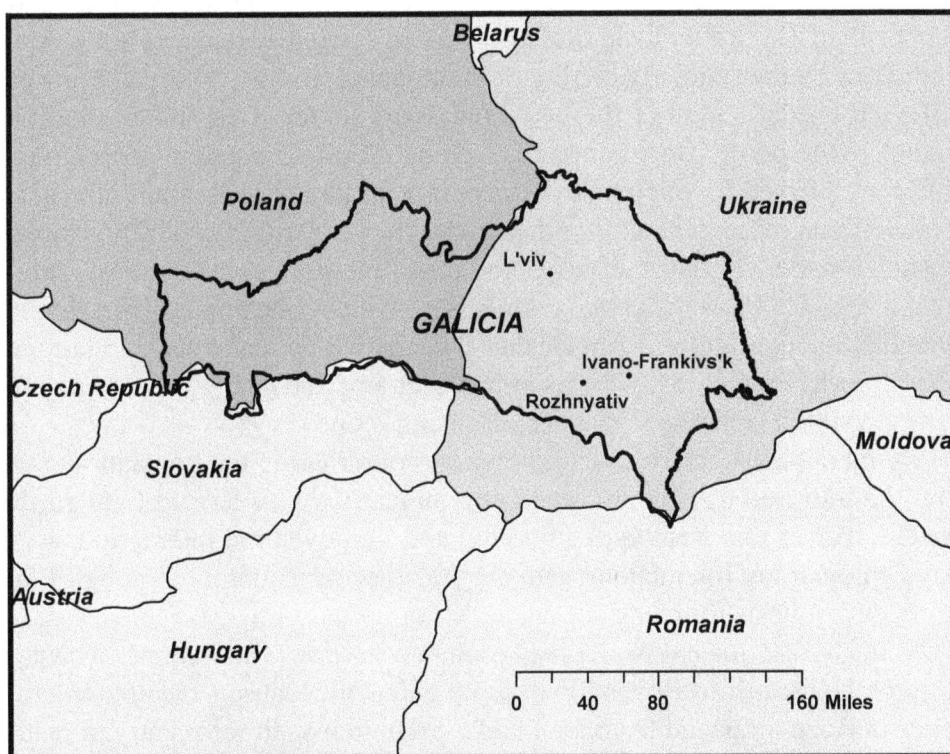

Contemporary map of central Europe on which an outline of the Province of Galicia of the Austrian Empire (thick line) is superimposed. Rozniatow (now called Rozhnyativ) is in Ukraine located just west of Stanislau (now called Ivano-Frankivsk) and south of Lemberg (now called L'viv).

lator extraordinaire (Alex Dunai) — and eventually photographed every legible gravestone in the Buczacz and Rozniatow cemeteries. Many of these photographs are available on the Internet. Unfortunately, I discovered that in both cemeteries many gravestones are missing and I was unable to find any gravestones of close family members.

What else could I do to learn about my Galician family? I learned that there were Yizkor Books for both towns and that these were filled with information about the towns and the fate of the Jewish community during the Holocaust. Using the Internet, I purchased a copy of the Yizkor Book for Buczacz from a used-book dealer. It is in Hebrew, which I do not read. However, I also discovered that this book was already being translated as a part of the Yizkor Book Translation Project of JewishGen. I then focussed on the Yizkor Book for Rozniatow, which is quite rare. I could not find a copy for sale nor was it available in many libraries. I asked on JewishGen if anyone had a copy. Fortunately, I found Alain Fallik, who lives in Brussels and whose family also comes from Rozniatow. He not only had a copy of the Yizkor Book, but copied the entire book for me. By June 2000 I had a xerographic copy of the book and resolved to coordinate its translation.

The Rozniatow Yizkor Book is written primarily in Hebrew (237 pages) and Yiddish (305 pages), neither of which I can read. The only section I could read was the brief (58 pages) English section. In seeking help with translation, I considered two methods — find volunteer translators or raise money and hire a professional translator. I tried volunteer translators initially, among whom Isak Shteyn was most helpful. Unfortunately he became ill early in the translation project. I soon decided that this job was going to be done only once and I wanted the translation to be of high quality and of uniform style. So I decided to raise money and hire a professional translator with a good record of accomplishment. I consulted Joyce Field and ultimately hired Jerrold Landau. This was a most important decision as indicated by the scholarly quality of the translation.

Based on the length of the book and Jerrold's fee, I estimated that it would cost about $6,000 to translate the book. Beginning in December 2000, I raised money entirely with solicitations over the Internet. I asked for support from people who had indicated an interest in Rozniatow but I also sent solicitations more generally to the JewishGen community. Twenty-three different people (including myself) made 57 contributions, some made multiple contributions. Individual contributions ranged from $5 to $500. When *donor fatigue* set in and it became difficult to obtain further funds from individuals, I sought grants from Gesher Galicia, which made substantial contributions to help complete the project. In total, $5,248 was raised over a period of 6½ years to pay for the translation. The main delay resulted from the slow pace of raising money.

My main tasks included raising money, coordinating the translation, scanning graphics, proof reading the translation segments, and communicating with Jerrold Landau, Joyce Field, and Lance Ackerfeld. All of this went very smoothly and I enjoyed the interactions with these dedicated people. I also enjoyed my interactions with the 22 other contributors although I am not sure they enjoyed my frequent requests for contributions.

As the translation evolved, I read each new section with interest. The poignancy of sections describing the Holocaust in Rozniatow was heightened because I recalled visiting the mentioned Holocaust sites in Rozniatow and Dolina. I had to remind myself frequently to read as a proof reader and not as a descendent of Rozniatowers.

I read translations of sections of the Yizkor Book in fits and starts as they became available from Jerrold and not necessarily in the order in which they appeared in the original book. When the translation was completed, I put all the text and graphics into desktop publishing software (Adobe InDesign) and produced a bound copy of the translation for my own use. I was then able to read the translation from beginning to end. I did the same with the Buczacz Yizkor Book when its translation was complete and posted on the Internet. When I learned about the Yizkor Books in Print Project, I contacted Joel Alpert and made both books available.

*Thomas F. Weiss Rozniatow Yizkor Book Translation Project Coordinator*
*January 16, 2013*

# Table of Contents

**Translated by Jerrold Landau**

## TRANSLATOR'S FOOTNOTES

1. There is significant overlap between these Hebrew and Yiddish sections. However, the overlap is not complete – for example, the Yiddish section has a description of the Communists which is not in the Hebrew, and the Hebrew section includes a description of Kazinu and Bnei Akiva which is not in the Yiddish. The Yiddish section's subheadings are not listed in the table of contents. They are: Achva, Hitachdut – Poale Zion, Mizrachi, Gordonia, Hashomer Hatzair, Betar, Stam Chalutz, Communists, Activists.

2. There is a significant overlap between these Hebrew and Yiddish sections, but once again, they do not seem to be exactly equivalent.

3. A Lamed-Vovnik (literally, 'one of the thirty six'), is a reference to a special righteous person who conceals his righteousness. Jewish legend has it that there are always 36 such special righteous people in the world.

4. This long chapter of Holocaust history is equivalent in Hebrew and Yiddish, with the exception of a short preface to the Yiddish chapter. The Yiddish chapter on 'Our Heroes' which begins on page 455 and forms a separate chapter in the Yiddish, is included in the single Hebrew chapter under a subheading. In the Hebrew it starts on page 201 and goes to the end. The Hebrew version does not have an entry in the table of contents.

5. There is apparently much overlap of history in these two sections, but they are not equivalent. The Yiddish section goes into much detail of events after the war.

# May G-d Remember

**May G-d Remember**

Six million Jews, of the holy nation, who were killed, slaughtered, burned, strangled and murdered with all types of cruel and unusual deaths by the Nazi enemies during the frightful years of 5600-5605 (1939-1945) for the sole iniquity of being members of the people of faith, the seed of Abraham, Isaac and Jacob.

**May G-d Remember**

And have mercy on the ashes of the slaughtered people of Israel, the nation that sanctified G-d's name, who were brought in large groups to the gas chambers and crematoria, and their bones were turned into cinders and scattered as ashes on the fields of the gentiles, without leaving a trace and memorial, or a sign of their life and activities on earth.

**May G-d remember**

And bind in the bonds of eternal life the communities of Rozniatow and environs, along with the hundreds of thousands of holy communities in the Diaspora of Europe, who were cut off and annihilated in the prime of their lives, the elderly and youths, fathers and children, mothers and infants, teachers with their students, and the destructive Satan poured out his wrath also on the synagogues of the communities of Israel. Destruction came upon everything.

**We will remember**

The simple Jews, as well as the cultured ones, young and old, upright and precious, charitable and full of good deeds; the dreams, hopes, burdens of the soul, lofty desires, love of fellow Jews and love of the Land of Israel.

**We will remember**

And lament for them with all 22 letters of the alphabet, with which they sang songs of hope.

**We will remember, and not forget!**

Engraved in memory of the martyrs of the communities of Rozniatow, Perehinsko, Broszniow and environs, by the Jewish National Fund.

**These do I remember.**

It is impossible to describe in words the destruction of our city, for it is completely impossible to find proper expression for our great grief over the loss of six million Jews, pure and holy, who were murdered during the frightful period of murder of the Jews of Europe.

We stand aghast and startled due to the holocaust, and it impossible to find a person who is able to lament properly over this destruction, and therefore the grief will not be assuaged, the tears will not dry, and our souls will be bound forever and will not be extinguished further.

It is now impossible to do anything for these holy martyrs.

It is impossible even to erect a monument over their graves, for the accursed cruel enemy who murdered them burned their bodies, and it is not known where their ashes lie.

However, we cannot forget them!

# Introduction

In this book that is before us, we unite ourselves the holy memory of our dear fellow townsmen, who were murdered in such a frightening and terrible manner, and for whom there are no words in the mouth of a person on earth to describe properly.

Many of us were troubled, and many of us hesitated before we commenced this holy work of preparing a Yizkor book for the community of Rozniatow and the adjacent communities.

We realized that this is not a common task. We knew that there would be very many questions during the preparation of this book, for we must prepare a book from ashes... Very few facts reached us about the history of Rozniatow, its inhabitants, and their activities. There were very few who survived and who were able to write about the life in our town, whether from an economic perspective, or more importantly, from the perspective of the Jewish population.

Nevertheless, after much deliberation, it was decided to take on this holy task, to perpetuate the memories of fathers and mothers, children, brothers and sisters; an entire community that was destroyed

Their souls fluttering in the grave demand of us to establish a memorial in the form of a Yizkor book; an eternal monument to the life that was cut of mercilessly. As well, this book should serve as an inerasable mark of Cain, upon the forehead of the Satan, who like wild beasts spilled the blood of the elderly and children, and even the suckling infants were not spared.

May this book serve as a memorial candle to the souls of the martyrs.

May it stand as a monument and send its cries to the heights of heaven forever.

This Yizkor book is the fruit of the collective labor of our fellow townsmen who live in Israel and the Diaspora, who survived.

All that is written in it is the fruit of the pens of average people, who are not and never aspired to be writers among the Jewish people. In this, we see the special merit of the book, for it is written with simplicity and unpretentiousness.

We also tried to encourage some of our fellow townsmen to describe to us their memories of the events that took place to them during the frightening days of the holocaust.

We gathered photographs and lists, descriptions and documents, line by line page by page, until we completed the book, full of material about the spirit and form of our community, the way of live and environment of Jewish Rozniatow.

The pages of the book are filled with teardrops. The hand of fate saved us while there was still time, but prevented us from closing the grave and reciting the final Kaddish for our dear townsmen, for relatives, and relatives of relatives whom we loved so much, and all of them are engraved on the tablets of our hearts.

This work is the final good dead, and the entire task was done with dedication and great feeling.

This is their monument – the holy monument to their eternal memory

The Book Committee

## My Town
### A poem by Yechezkel Neubauer of Petach Tikva

There once was a small town
At the foothills of the Carpathians, and near to the forests
With a large pond in main path
And a flour mill to its side.

Above the pond was a beautiful hill
With thick trees which spread out to the bottom
And also a beautiful field for walking
Where there is a school, post office and courthouse.

In the center of the city there is a large marketplace
With two ancient wells
A simple path crosses the middle of the marketplace
And twisted alleyways spread out right and left.

Three synagogues stood there together
And the voice of Torah was heard day and night.
A Beis Midrash on the right and a Kloiz on the left,
And in the center was the large synagogue that was destroyed.

Small houses stood crowded together
Like mushrooms after a rainfall
And their white roofs were spread out like a cloth
And sparkled in the sun like opals.

Around the city, to the north and the south
The turtles and bears roam around peacefully
And in the air there is the smell of flowers as well as destruction.

## The City and its Walls

Rozniatow was a typical Jewish town in Galicia, with its joys and sorrows, a dear place, where the entire spectrum of the rainbow was represented, and life was interesting and multifaceted; a life of warm Jewish content, of desire to broaden horizons, thirst for Torah and its wisdom, a hope for a better future. Everything that took place in the multifaceted Jewish life of Galicia could be seen through the lens of Rozniatow.

The town was small, and modest by nature. The natives of Rozniatow did not seek fame, and they were happy in their lot. Even during times of siege and suffering it was permeated with love and acceptance of the difficult yoke of the exile, and people would assuage their worry by reciting chapters of Psalms. The synagogue and Beis Midrash were full of people three times a day: during Shacharit, Mincha and Maariv. Along with the sounds of prayer, the sounds of Torah study could be heard from the mouths of pure and G-d fearing Jews, scholars as well as youths who frequented the house of study, who were educated and grew up with the light of Torah and the commandments.

Slowly, changes took place in the life of the city. The youth began to join various movements and factions, and became enthused with the ideas and ideals which swept across the town, from right and left, both religious and free thinking, Zionistic and Socialist.

This was the life, suffering, woes, and joys of the town of Rozniatow. Light, rejoicing, sadness, good and bad all came together, however over and above everything there was the light of Jewish life permeated with the warmth of the Jewish family, and of the large, multifaceted community.

And if someone were to ask the town of Rozniatow if it still had a name and memory in the hearts of its children, the answer would be: Certainly, just open this book and read it. Just as it exists in the recesses of the heart, it also can be found in these pages, which contain hearts that beat about the previous generations, as well as the landscapes.

Read and see that the town is remembered fondly by its children, and its power its power is engraved in our hearts, and just as the hearts of its children live, it is a sign that its memory and treasures will be carried on to future generations.

The editor

# A map of Rozniatow

## Drawn from memory by Zecharia Friedler

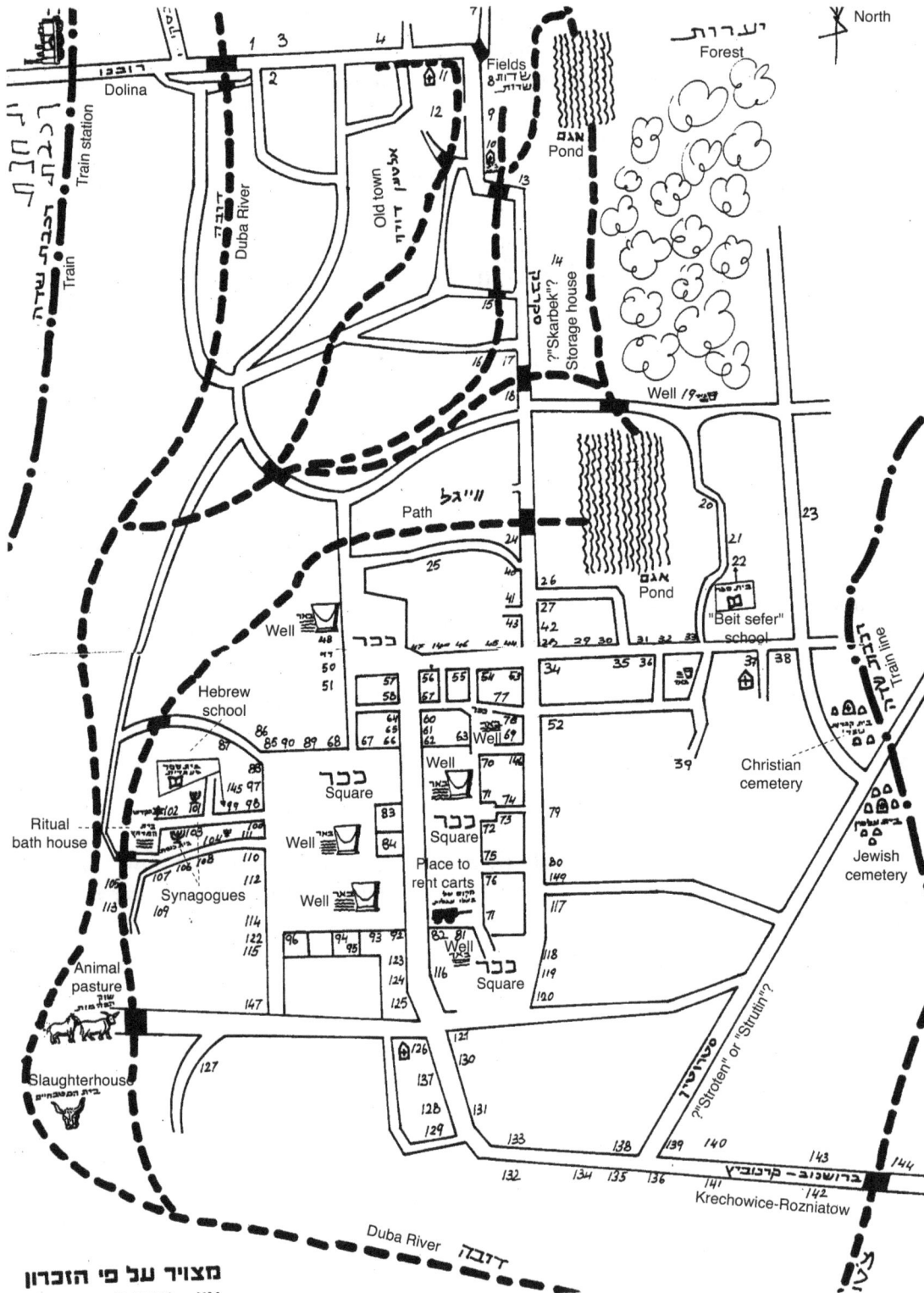

North

יערות
Forest

Fields
שדות

Dolina

Train station

Train

Duba River

Old town

אגם
Pond

"Skarbek"?
Storage house

Well 19

Path
וולגב"

אגם
Pond

"Beit sefer"
school

Well

ככר

Hebrew
school

ככר
Square

Well

Well

Square

Place to
rent carts

Well

Well

ככר
Square

Christian
cemetery

Train line

Jewish
cemetery

Ritual
bath house

Synagogues

Animal
pasture

Slaughterhouse

"Strofen" or "Strutin"?

Krechowice-Rozniatow
ברושנוב – קרנוביץ

Duba River   דובה

מצויר על פי הזכרון
Drawn from memory

Translations by Alona Amsel and Morris Halle

**Legend**

| | | | |
|---|---|---|---|
| 1 | House of Eliahu Horowitz | 76 | House of Haim Frisch |
| 2 | House of Chaye Adler | 77 | House of Aba Tanne |
| 3 | House of Nahum Artmann | 78 | Oil press Hersh Rechtschaffen |
| 4 | House of Shlomo Jungerman | 79 | House of Yehuda Weissberg |
| 5 | Sawmill of Wewe Tanne | 80 | House of Jacob Hammermann |
| 6 | Flour mill of Wewe Tanne | 81 | House of Chanina Weissmann |
| 8 | House of Sara Esther Horowitz | 82 | House of Leibcie Jaeckel |
| 9 | House of Leiblsh Friedler | 83 | House of Mordehai Gross |
| 10 | Prayer House | 84 | and Sender Friedler |
| 11 | Chapel | 85 | House of Berl Joel Rosenmann |
| 12 | House of Alter Bermann | 86 | House of Liebe Hammermann |
| 13 | House of Simon Hillmann | 87 | House of Benjamin Stern |
| 14 | House of Weinloes | 88 | House of Rabbi Hemerling |
| 15 | House of Michal Jagiellowicz | 89 | House of Josef Gelobter |
| 16 | House of Mordehai Mark | 90 | House of Debora Weitzmann |
| 17 | House of Nahman Scheiner | 91 | House of Josef Berger |
| 18 | House of Shlomo Shmerl Horowitz | 92 | House of Mlhael Weissmann |
| 19 | Warm-Water Well | 93 | House of Wolf Ber Karczman |
| 20 | The Court House | 94 | House of Israel Friedler |
| 21 | The Post Office | 95 | House of Zeinwel Soltis, Melamed |
| 22 | The School | 96 | House of Leib Friedler |
| 23 | Police Station | 97 | House of Moshe Weiser, Shochet |
| 24 | Flour mill Efraim Rechtschaffen | 98 | House of Abraham Groll |
| 25 | Municipality | 99 | Hebrew School |
| 26 | House of Josef Rottenberg | 100 | House of Kreiter |
| 27 | House of Jacob Loew | 101 | Beth Hamidrash |
| 28 | House of Moshe Weinreb | 102 | Mortuary |
| 29 | House of Leisor Itzik Loew | 103 | Big Synagogue |
| 30 | House of Zaharia David Liebermann | 104 | The Klause, Synagogue |
| 31 | House of Shmuel Fieler | 105 | House of Hersh Lelsor Waechter |
| 32 | House of Aharon Kassner | 106 | House of Haim Simon Lutwak |

| | | | |
|---|---|---|---|
| 33 | House of Mendel Waechter | 107 | House of Chana Horowitz |
| 34 | House of Hersh Mendel Artmann | 108 | House of Moshe Ziering |
| 35 | House of Leopold Adlersberg | 109 | House of Moshe Rosenbaum |
| 36 | House of Bunim Geller | 110 | House of Itzchak Katzmann |
| 37 | The Catholic Church | 111 | House of Abraham Mark |
| 38 | The SOKOL House | 112 | House of Shlomo Frost |
| 39 | Farm of Woloszynowicz | 113 | House of Zelig Stern |
| 40 | House of Wolf Horowitz | 114 | House of Efralm Rechtschaffen |
| 41 | House of Reuben Getzel Heisler | 115 | House of David Ratenbach, Melamed |
| 42 | House of Balm Kirschenbaum | 116 | House of Jacob Strassmann/ |
| 44 | House of Shlomo Widmann | 117 | House of Shmaye Goldschmidt |
| 45 | House of Haim Nussbaum | 118 | House of Azriel Wassermann |
| 46 | House of Wewe Hoffmann | 119 | House of Moshe Mirl Kornblueh |
| 47 | House of Josef Kassner | 120 | House of Moshe Jacob Lustig |
| 48 | House of Mendel Horowitz | 121 | House of Dr. Wassermann |
| 49 | House of Itzik Barnik | 122 | House of Eisik Wassermann, Melamed |
| 50 | House of Israel Trau | 123 | House of Fajge Vogel |
| 51 | House of Eliabu. Kassner | 124 | House of Philipp Ferszt |
| 52 | House of Eliehu Spiegel | 125 | House of Haim Lelsor Rottenberg |
| 53 | House of Nissan Schindler | 126 | Greek-Catholic Church |
| 54 | House of Itzik Rosenbaum | 127 | House of Shmuel Schwindler |
| 55 | House of Hersh Rechtschaffen | 128 | House of Simon Strassmann/ |
| 56 | House of Eisik Rosenberg | 129 | House of Moshe Klinger |
| 57 | House of Aharon Hersh Kopf | 130 | House of Bendet Horowitz |
| 58 | House of Haim Shlomo Meisels | 131 | The Pharmacy |
| 59 | House of Meier Frisch | 132 | House of Baron Walisz |
| 60 | House of Josef Kaufmann | 133 | Shmuel Nussbaum |
| 61 | House of Meshulam Fruchter | 134 | House of Leib Falik |
| 62 | House of Meier Fraenkel | 135 | House of Meier Kaufmann |
| 63 | House of Eisik FrIedler | 136 | House of Lipe Tanne |
| 64 | House of Moshe Artmann | 137 | House of Wolf Landsmann |
| 65 | House of Israel Hersh Londner | 138 | House of Dr. Sabath |
| 66 | House of Abraham Erdmann | 139 | House of Berl Londner |
| 67 | House of Mordehai Kriegel | 140 | House of Leisor Turteltaub |
| 68 | House of Benjamin Keller | 141 | House of Hersh Tanne |
| 69 | House of Haim Geller | 142 | House of Sisie Arye Kupferberg |
| 70 | House of Shmuel Wirt | 143 | House of Jacob Meier Lehrer |

| 71 | House of Haim Asher Jaeckel | 144 | Flour mill of Weinfeld |
|----|------------------------------|-----|-------------------------|
| 72 | House of Benzion Joeckel | 145 | House of Alter Reb Jeckele |
| 73 | House of Mordehai Tisch | 146 | House of Abraham Sauerberg |
| 74 | House of Aharon Honig | 147 | House of Itzlk Meier Waechter |
| 75 | House of Sosie Heller | 148 | House of Nachman Dornfeld |
|    |  | 149 | House of Shabse Spiegel |
| ERRATA IN MAP |||||
| 1./ instead of No. 57 (near 56) should be 59/Meir Frisch |||||
| 2./ instead of No. 71 (near 81) should be 91/Josef -Berger |||||
| 3./ instead of No. 149 (near 80) should be 148/Nachman Dornfeld |||||

## The Town and its Walls

**The great synagogue, with the Beis Midrash (House of study) to the right,
and the old Kloiz to the left.**

# Our Town

## by Zechariah Friedler

We will surely remember you, our town of Rozniatow!

You are etched in our memories with letters of fire that warm and light up our souls, from your breasts we imbibed influence, imagination and vision.

Our cradles of infancy stood on your ground, and we spent our youth in your precincts. Your soul, oh our town, accompanied us on all of our paths of life, and anointed us with a very personal and spiritual way of life.

There, we received support and assistance from our parents, brothers and sisters; we received knowledge and understanding from our teachers in its schools, and from the leaders, counselors and friends in various organizations.

All of their images are engraved, and dwell in the inner crevices of our hearts, and we find in them comfort from the cruelty on earth.

You became an orphan, oh our town, from the best of your children, and now you sit forlorn, mournful, and accursed in your heart, just like us, on account of the murderers who brought destruction upon you without mercy. You were denuded of your most vital element, of the well-rooted Jews who for generations toiled for you greatly – a toil of creativity and spirit.

I remember you, Rozniatow, your children, the Jews of various stripes: Hassidim, Misnagdim, Zionists, workers, simple people, well cultured people, upright and dear, charitable and doers of good deeds – all of them awaited the redemption, filled with love of their fellow man and self sacrifice.

I remember you, your synagogues and Beis Midrashes (study halls), your charitable and benevolent institutions, your libraries and your buildings that were dedicated to the service of the people and the land; all of the fine traits, the dreams, hopes and visions of the soul, the lofty aspirations, the love of fellow Jews and of the Land of Israel, the faith and bravery in the face of the epitome of death.

We, the survivors of your Jewish community, will remember you, in your flowering and in your desolation. We will remember all of those who were murdered and cut off by the hands of the inhuman evildoers: those who died by fire and those by water, those by hunger and those by thirst, those by sword, those buried alive, and those who perished in the gas chambers[1] – all of those who were tortured, cut off, and gave their souls in sanctification of the Name of G-d.

We will remember and bind them in the annals of history forever.

{18}

# Chapters of History

### by Pinchas Kanner

**Lines about the History of the Town**

The town of Rozniatow possesses great charm. It is situation in the foothills of the Carpathian Mountains in southeastern Galicia, in the region of Stanislawow, in the area of Dolina, about seven kilometers from the main Stryj-Stanislawow road and 7 kilometers from the Krechowice train station. It is surrounded by hills and forests, in a wide valley that is traversed by two rivers, the Czeczwa and the Duba. The rivers are supplied by the plentiful waters of the Carpathians, and they are tributaries of the Lomnica and Dniester rivers, which flow into the Black Sea.

From a historical perspective, these regions were under Polish rule for hundreds of years. They were populated by Ukrainians, or, as they were known then, Ruthenians. The name Galicia comes from the word Halicza or Halicz, which is a city on the Dniester, which in former times was the place of residence of the Ukrainian dukes. When Poland was partitioned in the 18th century between its three powerful neighbors, Russia, Austria, and Prussia, the southern portion was annexed to Austria and took on the name Galicia.

During the era of Polish rule, Rozniatow was a feudal estate, and during the era of Austrian rule, it was owned by the Polish Skarbek family, whose members were feudal barons and owners of large tracts of land in Galicia. Their connection to the Polish monarchy was known already in the 13th century. Testimony exists that a group of tenants in Rozniatow, numbering sixty people, responded to a request from the Skarbek family in the years 1835-1845, and made a donation for the building of a theater in Lvov-Lemberg, the Galician capital. There was a road in that city by the name of Skarbek.

The noblemen of the Skarbek family were the rulers until the First World War. Later leased the area to the Glesinger group, who were owners of the modern sawmill in Broszniow. Most of the income from this family's properties was dedicated to the upkeep of the dormitory in Chirow were the children of the Polish noblemen were educated, including the sons of the Baron Walisz who lived in Rozniatow.

The building, situated on the top of a hill, was adorned with turrets. The courthouse was also situated there. Previously, it served as the feudal palace of the Skarbek family. The best kept area of the estate was a splendid boulevard lined by basswood trees which led to the Catholic church which was built on that same hill, overlooking the town.

With the Austrian agrarian reforms in the years 1848-1849, the farmers were freed from the heavy feudal yoke, and there was a need to establish a courthouse in order to register properties. On November 15, 1850, a post office opened. This granted Rozniatow the status of a significant town, since it became an economic and administrative center for the many villages to the south, all the way to the Carpathians. The population of this administrative area was more than 50,000. The fact that Rozniatow served as a supply center for the Russian troops who hurried to the aid of Austria during the Hungarian revolution of 1848, and that the Russian commander resided in the town, also added to the status of the town.

There were many villages surrounding Rozniatow, including Perehinsko with a population of 10,000. Many Jewish estate owners resided in the area, including: the Weinfeld family of Swaryczow, the Mandelbaum family of Krasna, and the Lustig family of Spas. The oil wells of Dubno and Rypne, as well the large factories of Broszniow, from which two rail lines led to the vast forests of the Carpathians, contributed greatly to the development of industry and business in the region. Without these industries, the economy would have been weak and unproductive.

Rozniatow had a population of about 8,000 people, including more than 6,000 Ukrainians, known also as Ruthenians, who belonged to the Unitarian Greek Catholic church, 100 Poles, and 2,000 Jews. It had barely 20 to 30 stone houses, for the rest of the houses were build of wood, including many with straw roofs, a few with shingled roofs, and only a handful covered with metal sheets.

Since the town was situated between two rivers, which overflowed in the spring due to the melting of the snow of the Carpathian Mountains, Rozniatow suffered from floods that caused great damage. On the other hand, during the clear summers, there were fires in the town, and flames would suddenly leap from roof to roof, destroying large portions of the town. The elders of Rozniatow used to keep track of events in the city based on the large fire or the great flood.

The Jews of Rozniatow already had an organized community in the 18th century, set up according to Jewish tradition. The Jews were engaged in all manner of business, independent professions – primarily doctors and lawyers, and all manners of artisanship, communication services – which at that time consisted of wagons and carriages, local manufacturing including a water powered sawmill, three flour mills, a flaxseed press and two soft drink factories.

The generally modest lifestyle, the work and diligence which was conducted for the most part to meet the needs of the family livelihood, and over and above all, the study of Torah and fulfillment of the commandments and customs of the Torah, all joined together to form the typical Jewish character of Rozniatow, according to its fine characteristics and customs.

Testimony of such can be found on the following pages, which are dedicated to our town and its surrounding area.

Pinchas Kanner

**TRANSLATOR'S FOOTNOTES**

1. These statements are based on the Unetane Tokef prayer of Rosh Hashanah and Yom Kippur.

{21}

# Rabbis, Hassidim, and Influential People

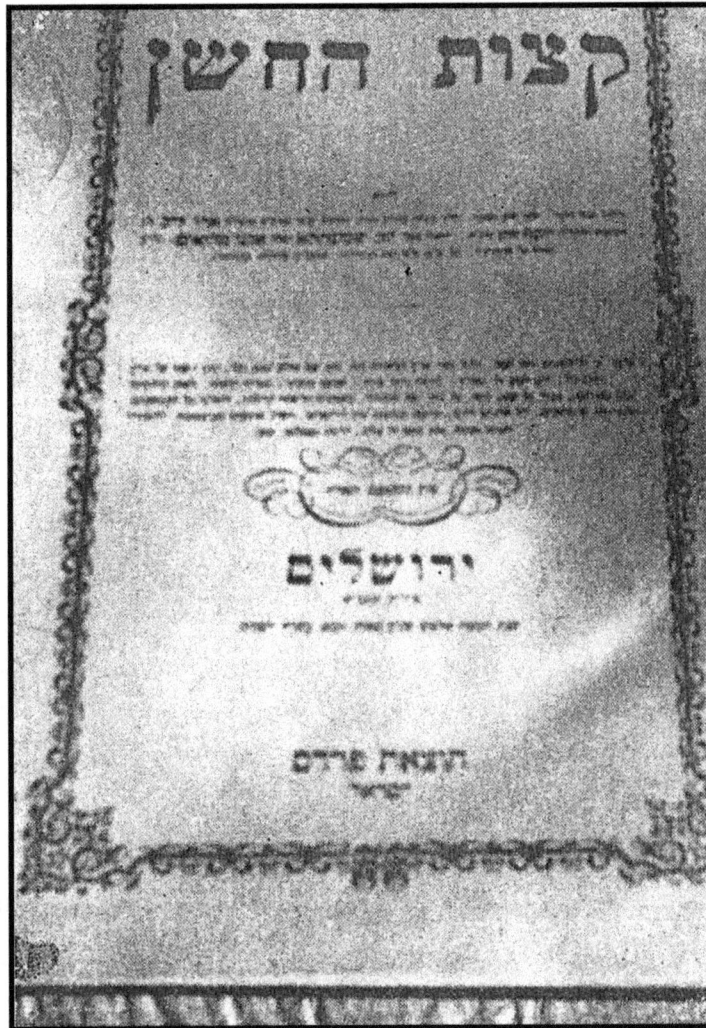

קצות החשן

ירושלים

no caption provided: The title page of Ketzot Hachoshen,
a commentary on the Code of Jewish Law.

{22}

no caption provided: Several books on a table,
including Ketzot Hachoshen, Avnei Miluim and Shav Shamata.

Who are the Kings, the Rabbis

"... But if one sees a large crowd of people, one should say: Blessed is the Knower of secrets. For just as their faces are different one from the other, their characters are also not equivalent. Rather, each individual has his own set of thoughts.

You should know that this is the way it is. For, at the time of his death, Moses requested from the Holy One Blessed Be He the following. Thus did he say: Master of the Universe, the character of each individual is known before You, and the character of one person is not the same as that of another person. Therefore, at the time that I am departing from them, I request of You: If You wish to appoint a leader over them, appoint a man who will be able to relate to each one according to his individual character."

(Midrash Tanchuma on the Torah portion of Pinchas[1])

{23}

# Rabbis

## by Yehuda Har-Zohar Zauerberg

### Reb Aryeh Leib Hakohen Heller

The author of "Ketzot Hachoshen", "Avnei Miluim", and "Shav Shamata"

(5505 – 5573, 1745-1813)

Cedars of Lebanon, mighty ones of Torah
Champions of Mishna and Gemara
Mighty of strength, who toil in purity –
Their blood was shed and their strength failed.
Oh Merciful One, look down from the heavens
At the spilled blood of the righteous, their lifeblood
Oh King Who sits on the throne of mercy
Witness from your chamber, and remove the blemishes.

(From the hymn of the Ten Martyrs, of Yom Kippur[2])

It is impossible to describe the character of a person without understanding the environment in which he existed. It is certainly impossible to describe the personality of a man of the stature of the author of "Ketzot Hachoshen"[3] without understanding the era in which he was born, raised, educated and forged. That era, the era of the 18th century, was rich in events and changes in the life of humanity as a whole, and also in the life of the Jewish people.

In the second half of the 18th century, the emancipation movement spread out throughout Europe. It also reached Germany and Prussia. In 1740, King Friedrich II decreed the "Manifest", regarding individual rights and the power of the individual through democratic rule. This marked a turn for the better in the lives of the Jews in Germany and Prussia. Slowly, the walls of the Ghetto broke down, and the sparks of haskalah (enlightenment) began to penetrate even into the Jewish community. This at first took place with the Jews of Germany and Austria, and later also with the Jewish communities of Moravia, Bohemia, Poland, and Galicia.

In the 18th century, great suffering came upon the Jews of Poland. They suffered from degradation, evil decrees, blood libels, pogroms, and attacks in cities and town in which they lived. The Ukrainian "Hydmaks" fell upon them on one side, and the Polish "Szliachta" on the other side. Both of them wreaked havoc on their places of residence, and drowned numerous communities in rivers of blood.

In 1764, the Polish government disbanded the Jewish "Council of Four Lands" that dealt with all

Jewish affairs, whether in the private judicial realm or, of course, the public realm. With the disbanding of such a large, recognized, and weighty institution as the Council of Four Lands, the autonomous security foundations that the Jews had until that time were weakened, and days of decline and somnolence came upon the Jewish community.

A decline in the spiritual life of the masses also took place on the heels of the physical tribulations. The circles of students and teachers dwindled, and the deep knowledge of Torah became the inheritance of a small number of elite. The masses were preoccupied with the concerns of livelihood. They were immersed in pain and agony, and they did not have the possibility of delving in depth into Torah and Jewish law. Worst of all was the status of the Jews in the villages, who were far from the Jewish community.

After the downfall of the various Messianic and Shabtai Tzvi[4] movements, the mysterious aspects of Torah did not find their place in the hearts of the Jewish masses. Kabbalah[5] floated around in the upper worlds. The self-abnegation and separation from worldly affairs of the masters of the mysterious no longer attracted the Jews who were satiated with tribulations. Downtrodden and persecuted, the souls of the masses were content with new spiritual food, simple faith that warmed the heart and raised the spirit, so that they could find a balm for their many difficulties.

From amongst all of these causative factors, a new movement arose in the regions of eastern Poland and the Austria-Hungary of the time. This movement raised the value of the simple man, the man of the masses who had value because he was a Jew. This is the Hassidic movement.

Reb Yisrael the son of Eliezer, or as he was known by the masses, the "Baal Shem Tov"[6] (Besht) (1700-1760), was the founder and forger of the Hassidic movement. He was born in Podolia, and was orphaned as a child. After his marriage, he settled near Brody in Galicia, and he later moved to the area of Rozniatow. He lived in one of the nearby villages until he revealed himself to the masses.

The Besht drew the simple folk, the masses, towards fear of G-d, love, brotherhood, and friendship. The masses gathered around their Rebbe, rich and poor, scholar and simple laborer. All of them were equal before G-d, and in that manner, he succeeded in gathering together and unifying the distraught nation, including the simple folk, the scholars, and the wealthy.

As time went on, the Hassidic movement moved in different directions, and divided into different segments. I have not come here to delve into the entire Hassidic movement, but rather to discuss only what relates to our topic: regarding the Ketzot Hachoshen and his era.

In the year 5505 – 1745, a son was born in the city of Kalusz in Galicia to Reb Yosef Heller, the fourth generation from the author of the Tosafot Yom Tov, Reb Yom Tov Lipman Heller. He was the third child of three sons and one daughter, and he was named Aryeh Leib. In his youth, the child excelled in his sharpness and diligence in studies. When the local teachers discovered that the lad Aryeh Leib was succeeding so well in his studies, and that they were not able to satisfy his thirst for Torah, they decided to advise Reb Yosef the Kohen to send his young son to study Torah with the well known Gaon in the nearby reason, Reb Meshulam Igra of Tysmienica. It is worthwhile for us to know who taught our rabbi Rabbi Aryeh Leib Hakohen his Torah and mannerisms that lasted for his lifetime. Therefore, I will spend a little bit of time discussing the personality of his Rebbe, Rabbi Meshulam, the rabbi of Tysmienica. Tysmienica was one of nine large communities in the region of Lvov. He was also the teacher of the following great Torah luminaries and rabbis: Rabbi Mordechai Bennet, the rabbi of Nikolsburg; Rabbi Naftali Tzvi Horowitz, the head of the Ropszyce Hassidic dynasty; Rabbi Baruch Frankel-Teomim, the rabbi of Lipnik; Rabbi Yaakov Lorberbaum, the rabbi of Lissa and later of Stryj, the author of "Chavat-Daat".

Rabbi Meshulam was a strong opponent (Misnaged) to Hassidism. Nevertheless, one of the great Hassidim of our time, Rabbi Chaim of Czernowitz, the author of "Beer Mayim Chayim", describes the strong "Misnaged" in his second book "Shaar Tefilla"[7] as "the omen of our generation, the master of the shepherds, the chariot of Israel and its horsemen, the true Gaon, the prince of Torah, the light of the world, the clear lens, the pure menorah, the crown of the glory of Israel"[8].

Legend states that when Reb Yisrael Baal Shem Tov saw the son of Reb Shimshon (the father of Reb Meshulam) in Buczacz as a boy of four years old, he looked into the face of the child and said to those gathered around:

"Look closely, this child has a new soul, noble from the heavens, of which there was none like him for several generations" (from "Sarei Meah" by Y. L. Maimon).

Rabbi Meshulam dwelled in the city of Tysmienica, which in those days was a large city. Stanislawow was close to Tysmienica. He spread Torah to the masses, and established many students. When the parnassim (communal administrators) of various communities turned to him requesting that he take upon the yoke of the rabbinate, he refused. He spread Torah for 27 years, until something took place that caused him to leave the place. He accepted upon himself the rabbinate of Petersburg.

At that time, a government edict was issued requiring Jews to enlist in the army. The Jewish community of Tysmienica, the crown of the communities of Galicia, was required to provide a certain quota of men for the army on an annual basis. The parnassim of Tysmienica were wont to turn their eyes from the Torah students and scholars, and in their place, they transmitted ordinary people and ignoramuses to fulfil the army quota. Rabbi Meshulam castigated these parnassim with all his might, and decreed in all of the Beis Midrashes in Tysmienica that "there is no favoritism in judgment. All Jews, including scholars, all of them must fulfil the law of the country and enlist in the army. If the government requests of us a certain number of people, we must cast lots among all of those who are fit to serve in the army. Whomever's lot come up, even if he is one of the leading scholars of the generation, must go to army service."

Rabbi Meshulam jumped up and took an oath: "Even if the lot falls upon my only son Yitzchak Eliahu, I swear that I will my self turn him over to the army" (from Sarei Meah by Y. L. Maimon).

Thus was the Rebbe of Aryeh Leib Heller of Kalusz, the rabbi of Rozniatow. From him did he learn and from him did he absorb.

When the parnassim of Rozniatow invited Rabbi Aryeh Leib the Kohen of Kalusz to sit upon the rabbinical seat in their community, they did not have much to offer him, for the community was small, and the members of the community earned their own livelihoods with difficulty. Most of them earned their livelihood from wine taverns and from transporting cattle and sheep from place to place. The community was small and poor, and it could not sustain the rabbi of the community in an honorable fashion. There were no Torah giants in the place, and therefore they did not bother him greatly with questions and answers, so he was able to sit in quiet and dedicate himself to his studies without interruption. He lived a life of difficulty and pain, and he accepted everything with love. It is told that once, some of the householders came to him to ask him a question, and they found him sitting upon his bed writing his essays, with the inkwell under his blanket so that the ink would not freeze from the cold in the room.

His first work was a modest book, filled with words of wisdom and philosophy on those of elite thought, the holy ones of the Most High, the masters of Kabbalah and mystery. Here we see before us not only a man of halacha (Jewish legalism) but also the master of a broad outlook in the matters of the world and its events, words of philosophy, ideas, and quotes from the words of the Holy Ari[9] of blessed memory in matters of Kabbalah and the celestial spheres.

In his introduction to his book "Shav Shamata", he writes innovations on seven sections of Talmud. This book is fifteen pages long. It begins, as is customary, with an acronym of the Tetragrammaton[10] : Yitbarach (Blessed) Haechad (is the One) Veyishtabach (and praiseworthy) Haboreh (is the Creator). This is followed by eleven chapters, ordered by the aleph beit. Each chapter begins with its ordered letter, and deals with lofty general matters, issues of ideas and thoughts on halacha. Rabbi Aryeh Leib wrote this work during his time in Rozniatow. Given that his financial situation was very dire, he was not able to publish it immediately, so he kept it in manuscript form. Only towards the end of his days did he bring it to the publishing house, with small emendations. He wrote the following as a preface to the book.

"I wrote this booklet during my younger days, when I was still in my prime. I erected its cornerstones before I was even a man. Since I have pity on the best days of my youth, and I dreamt about the greatness of my travail and toil during those days, and since I mention it in my book Ketzot Hachoshen numerous times, I had in mind to publish it. Since this work is very dear to me, it is very pleasant to me that it be added to my published works, for it is the first fruits of my labor of the designs of my heart.

Even though it is short, it is now presented to the public with the help of the L-rd, for it is based upon pathways to the Talmud, and it includes powerful, necessary material regarding deep halachot (laws). It will find favor in the eyes of the intelligent, with the help of the Blessed G-d."

From here we can see how much he valued this book himself. He describes "this work is precious in his eyes" not with regard to his monumental halachic work Ketzot Hachoshen, by whose name he is called to this day. Rather he holds in esteem this modest work, that in accordance with his words "includes powerful, necessary material regarding deep halachot. It will find favor in the eyes of the intelligent."

His own esteem of his work, which he called Shav Shamata, is sufficient for us.

He also compiled his main work Ketzot Hachoshen in Rozniatow. He began to concern himself with its publication in Lvov. To this end, he went to live for a period of time with his sister and brother-in-law, the well-known Hebrew poet and author known as Shir[11] – Shlomo Yehuda Rappaport.

From the introduction to the book Ketzot Hachoshen that he published several years after he left Rozniatow, it is possible to discern how he lived in Rozniatow in difficulty and pressure. Now that he lived in the larger city of Stryj with an ample livelihood, he reminisces about the days that he lived in poverty and lack. Thus does he write in his introduction to Ketzot Hachoshen.

"I will first bow down to my G-d, who rides upon the ancient firmament, who dwells among the Cherubs, the angels of yore, who did show great mercy upon me, the dreaming youth, on the merit of my fathers who walked before Him in purity. Those that fear you will be with the sun, and before the moon from generation to generation[12]. You led us with Your wisdom, You fed us in our hunger, You saved us from the sword, You delivered us from pestilence, and You kept us from terrible and persistent illnesses[13]. All of these I saw with my own eyes. You afflicted me with tribulations, yet You did not give me over to death[14], and You will never abandon us."

Indeed, he does not only write nicely for the sake of the rhyme, but for the sake of actuality. "All of this I saw with my own eyes". "You fed me in hunger, You saved me from the sword, You afflicted me with tribulations" were the pleasant memories from the days of his residency in Rozniatow.

He concludes his introduction, which is literally an outpouring of the soul of the author on his difficult living situation, by reverting to the topic at hand. "I called this book Ketzot Hachoshen on account of its content, and also because the Torah novellae come from its corners, and are piled up in it."

Only volume I of the book was published in Lvov in the year 5548 (1788). Due to his difficult economic circumstances, he was not able himself to publish volume II. His grandson Asher Mordechai the son of Reb David the Kohen published it in Lvov in the year 5586 (1826). At the same time, he published volume II of his second work, Avnei Miluim on the Even Haezer[15].

The grandson writes the following in his preface to the book Avnei Miluim.

"... They shall teach their statutes to Jacob, and their Torah to Israel[16], in order to attain the paths of life, even in the days of our poverty and misery You did not abandon us. From generation to generation, He sent to us saviors who guard the legacy of Torah, and who are like eyes unto us. Even at this time, when the spirit of G-d was still within us, he sent us as a savior and rabbi my honorable grandfather, the Admor, the rabbi and true Gaon, the rabbi of the entire Diaspora, our teacher and rabbi Rabbi Aryeh Leib Hakohen, may his virtue stand us in good stead[17], the world lights up from him, and people call to him from the ends of the earth. He appeared to me as the light of his wisdom, and I basked in the splendor of his honor. They referred to my grandfather of blessed memory as the author of Avnei Miluim. His name was fitting to him, for he was like the stones in the crow of the Even Haezer15, and was full of all good[18]. As well, the acronym of the word Avnei includes the name of the author, and the name of his mother and father of refined spirit, as follows: Aryeh "A" Ben "V" Nissel "N" Yosef "I"."

At the time that he compiled volume II of the book Avnei Miluim, Rabbi Aryeh Leib Hakohen includes as well the composition of his brother Rabbi Yehuda Hakohen. He wrote as follows in that book:

"... In the interests of comprehensiveness of the efforts of this work, I have included at the end "Kuntrus Hasfeikut", which was the handiwork of my brother, the proper good and wise, our Rabbi Yehuda Hakohen in the year 5548."

The brother of the author of Ketzot Hachoshen, Rabbi Yehuda Leib Hakohen was the author of the book Kuntrus Hasfeikut"[19] on the Choshen Mishpat section of the Code of Jewish law, in which he went into great depth. He possessed a sharp intellect and clear way of thinking. He left behind blessed generations of righteous descendents, children and sons-in-law, Gaonin, scholars, and wealthy individuals.

At first, he served as the rabbi and head of the rabbinical court of the community of Solusz in Hungary. Later he moved to Munkacz, and from there to Sighet, where he died in the year 5549.

As luck would have it, despite the fact that the author of Ketzot Hachoshen and his brother the author of Hakuntrus, and all of the descendents of Yosef Mordechai Hakohen and his son Feivish, and after them Meir, Yosef Mordechai, Yehuda and Chaim Leib were all strong misnagdim by their nature and education; the descendents of these people founded a new Hassidic dynasty that was centered in the small town of Spinka. They changed their name from Hakohen to Kahane, a name that remains to this day. The Admor of Spinka who lives in Bnei Brak and also the Kahane family of Kfar Haroeh and Nechalim, as well as others – are all descendents of sharp misnagdim from eastern Galicia, who originated in Kalusz. From one of them, Rabbi Chaim Kahane of Nechalim, I received a great deal of information on his family, the family of Rabbi Yehuda Hakohen of holy blessed memory.

Rabbi Chaim Kahane told me that his ancestor Rabbi Mordechai Yosef the son of Rabbi Yehuda Hakohen "went sour" towards the end of his days and became of staunch Hassid of the righteous Admor Rabbi Menachem Mendel Hager of Kosow, may his merit protect us. He left his rabbinical seat and traveled to Kosow to dwell under the shadow of the protection of that Tzadik. He died there on the 2nd of Adar 5584. His son set up an "ohel"[20] over his grave.

If only I had known this during the time of my youth, when I went on Hachsharah in the city of Kosow prior to my making aliya, I would have certainly gone to visit that grave in the local cemetery, and recorded all of the praises that were written on his gravesite. Today, not even one stone remains in Kosow. Everything was destroyed and ruined, and not one vestige remains of that Jewish community.

I have already outlined above the difficult economic situation of the author of the Ketzot, who lived a life of deprivation and poverty in Rozniatow, but loved the place and was tied to it, for there he composed the majority of his works, since they permitted him to work in peace without being disturbed. Even at the time when he had attained fame as the author of Ketzot Hachoshen, and when the parnassim of the community of nearby Stryj approached him with the request to serve in their community, a large community of scholars, and he accepted their offer; he packed up his scanty belongings and ascended the wagon to travel to Stryj, and while he was still sitting on the wagon, he turned to the leaders of the small community of Rozniatow who had come to bid him farewell, and he told them the following in these words: "Despite all this, I wish to remain with you. If you increase my meager salary, I would remain." His request to the communal administrators of Rozniatow remained unanswered.

It is told that on one occasion, Rabbi Efraim Zalman Margolis, the rabbi of Brody, went on a journey and passed through the town of Rozniatow. He told his servants: "How can I pass through the living pace of the Tzadik and Gaon, and not go to visit him?". He went to visit him in his simple house, and during the course of the conversation with Rabbi E. Z. Margolis, Rabbi Aryeh Leib sighed. The guest, the Gaon Rabbi E. Z. Margolis though that he was sighing on account of his physical situation, and he asked him: "On what account is your honor signing, and what is lacking for you?" Rabbi Aryeh Leib answered him: "I was weighing in my mind that if I were not a scholar and well known, it would certainly not have been in accordance with the honor of such a powerful rich man as yourself to visit me in such a simple house. Is this not a denigration of the honor of Torah? This is why I was sighing."

His livelihood improved when he lived in Stryj. He had hoped to live in peace and dedicate himself to his writings and novellae, however the anger of a group of local Hassidim was aroused against him. This was the era of stormy winds and fierce battles between Hassidim and Misnagdim. The ink of the "Kol Koreh" ("manifesto") of the Gaon of Vilna (Gra) of the year 1772 had not yet dried. This decree called upon the parnassim of any communities that the ban of the rabbis of Vilna reaches "to persecute the sect of Hassidim until the hand of Israel catches them", for their iniquity is couched in wisdom, and they are as difficult as a psoriatic blemish.

The war against Hassidism was at its height. From Rabbi Akiva Eiger, the rabbi of Posnan and the Chatam Soffer of Pressburg, they received support to fight "against those who cast off the yoke of Torah and who cheapen the commandments". He himself, as a man of halacha who was meticulous with both easy and difficult commandments, was not able to tolerate the behavior of the Hassidic sect whom he had no opportunity to get to know up close when he lived in peace and quiet in Rozniatow. In Stryj, they overdid themselves, and he was no longer able to tolerate their ways and customs, which cheapen the law of the Code of Jewish Law under the pretext of Hassidism. Due to his great anger and deep anguish, he, along with his court in Stryj, decided to excommunicate the local Hassidic sect.

This is what is written by the expert of Chabad Hassidism[21], the scholar and religious adjudicator Rabbi Shlomo Yosef Zevin, may he live long, in his book "Tales of the Hassidim", page 350, regarding the battle of the Ketzot Hachoshen with the sect of Hassidim.

"Why were you not afraid to speak against my servant Moses?[22]"

... "In the city of Stryj, there were many Hassidim of the Tzadik 'The Seer of Lublin' (The Chozeh of Lublin). On account of the difference of heart between the Hassidim and the rabbi, the Hassidim did not act honorably toward the rabbi of the city. The behavior of the Hassidim seemed to the rabbi as violating the Code of Jewish Law. He warned them not to behave in such a manner, but they did not listen to him, and impinged on his honor. He excommunicated them with a rabbinical ban, which, as described in the Code of Jewish Law, is in effect for thirty days. Many of the people of the city took heed not to conduct business with them during this period. The Hassidim conferred with each other, and decided that all of them should travel to their Rebbe in Lublin for the duration of this period, and in the interim, the ban would expire.

It was the custom in Lublin that the shamash would bring to the Rebbe a list of names who have come to receive greetings, and the Rebbe would tell him whom to summon to his inner chamber. When the people of Stryj arrived, the Rebbe told the shamash that they would have to wait over two weeks to receive their greetings. Indeed, this time frame was calculated exactly to fall on the day when the ban would expire.

The Rebbe said to them: Regarding the verse 'Why were you not afraid to speak against my servant Moses?', Rashi explains: 'against my servant' – even if he was not Moses, and 'Moses' – even if he was not my servant. Many raise the question: it is obvious about my servant, even if he is not Moses, but what about Moses if he is not my servant – what type of special status or greatness would he have that would inspire awe? However, the meaning is the following: There are two groups among the Jews, the group who occupy themselves with service of G-d, who hug Him and cleave to Him as a faithful servant. This cleaving is evident when they are traveling and when they are staying put, when they lie own or when they are awake, when they eat and when they drink. As it is written: 'with Moses', who is the expert in the revealed Torah – even though he is not my servant in cleaving to me at all moments, and 'my servant' – who occupies himself in the hidden aspects of Torah, and is exacting at all times, even though he is not Moses – with regards to the revealed Torah. One has to fear both aspects! If that is the case, your rabbi, who is a prince of Torah and one of the leaders of the generation in the written Torah, why were you not afraid before him?[23]

With his words, he delineated the spiritual essence of one of the giants of the Jewish world in the 19th century, who spent his first years of his career as the rabbi of Rozniatow.

During his tenure in Stryj he attracted many students, who became Torah leaders. Among the best known were: the Gaon Rabbi Aryeh Leib Lipschitz, the head of the rabbinic court of Visznicz, and the Gaon Rabbi Asher Enzil Cuzmir. His lessons that he presented publicly excelled in their great sharpness. The breadth of his knowledge was famous.

A typical example of his personality and uprightness can be seen from the following story.

As is well known, the opponent and disputant of the author of the Ketzot Hachoshen was the author of Chavat Daat, Rabbi Yaakov Lorbenbaum. However, he was younger than him by many years. He also sat on the rabbinic seat of Stryj after the Ketzot.

The author of Chavat Daat married the daughter of a very rich man, Reb Herzl of Stanislawow. After his wedding, he lived in Stanislawow, where he wrote Chavat Daat. From Stanislawow, he traveled to nearby Tysmienica to study Torah with Reb Meshulam Igra, the Torah giant of that era. At first, he conducted a business in wine, and after he found that he was not successful in business, he was forced to rabbinate of Monasteriats, and later of Kalusz, the birthplace of the Ketzot. Once the author of the Ketzot passed through Kalusz and went to the house of the rabbi to honor him, as was customary. The rebbetzin wished to honor the guest, and went down to the basement to fetch a bottle of mead for the guest. The bottle was dusty, and the rebbetzin apologized for this. A rumor had reached the ears of the Ketzot that the rebbetzin was involved in the arranging of loans for interest. He said to her "perhaps this is the dust of usury?"[24]. The rebbetzin, who was intelligent, and the wife of a trustworthy man, answered to him immediately: "No, honorable rabbi, it is the dust of the evil tongue".

The author of Chavat Daat moved from Kalusz to Lissa. That is where he picked up the nickname Reb Yaakov of Lissa. On account of the difficulties and persecutions that the local Hassidic sect suffered, he returned once again to Kalusz. Two years later, he accepted the rabbinate of Stryj. He died there in 1882.

The rabbi succeeded in establishing many students, including leaders of the Torah generation, an those who were taken by the vision of the revival of the Land and the return to Zion, Reb Eliahu Gutmacher and Reb Shmuel Kaliszer, who were later among the first of Chovevei Zion. The later two merited– on account of their vision, hope, and dedication to the return to Zion – that we, the students of their students, could sit and actualize that which they dreamed. We remember those greats and luminaries of the earlier generation with holy trembling and love, and we pray to the Blessed G-d that we should be fitting to be among those who fulfill the hopes of the dreamers and strugglers.

These are the words of Yehuda Mishel the son of Reb Moshe Zauerberg, the youngest of the brothers of that family, the only survivor of the large, wide-branched family. He gathered together all of this material that was written about the author of the Ketzot Hachoshen.

{32}

### The Last Rabbi of Rozniatow Rabbi Yosef Menachem Meczner[25]

I remember, when I was still living in my father's house during my youth, that once Reb Moshe Weiser, the shochet of Rozniatow, appeared, accompanied by my brother Avraham of blessed memory. The aforementioned Reb Moshe was his in-law, for his son Reb Zeida married Bracha, the daughter of his brother-in-law Reb Shlomo Stern. They came to consult with my father of blessed memory regarding the great controversy among the shochtim (ritual slaughterers) of Rozniatow – between the aforementioned Reb Moshe Weiser and the shochet Reb David Roth, with regards to the status of the local slaughter. Since my father of blessed memory knew our judge Reb Yechiel Alter Nebenzahl, and held in esteem as an extremely intelligent Jew, and an adjudicator of similar disputes, he advised Reb Moshe the slaughterer to approach the aforementioned judge, and to ask him to intercede for Reb Moshe the slaughterer regarding this controversy.

Since I knew that the grandson of Reb Yechiel Alter Nebenzahl, Rabbi Meczner, was later the rabbi of our town, but I did not know of all of the particulars regarding him and the choosing of him for the rabbinate, I decided to go the home of Reb Shmuel Nebenzahl, the brother-in-law of the rabbi and the grandson of the judge, in order to hear an explanation of these serious issues.

When I came to him, the only survivor of the well-known Nebenzahl family of Stanislawow, today living in Tel Aviv, in order to obtain details from him about his brother-in-law, Rabbi Meczner the last rabbi of Rozniatow; he took out a book from his bookcase entitled Minchat Yechiel, which was written by Rabbi Yechiel Alter Nebenzahl of holy blessed memory. He showed me in chapter 101 a specific answer regarding the Torah court case between the shochtim Reb Zeida Weiser and Reb David Roth In this case, the author interceded on behalf of the shochtim Reb Moshe and Zeida, and the young shochet Reb Yaakov Hochman; and on the second side the Gaon of Dikla Reb Tivele interceded on behalf of the slaughterer Reb David Roth. The third party between them was the rabbi of Przemysl Rabbi Shemayahu Sternberg.

In the above mentioned responsa book, Rabbi Nebenzahl brings three reasons and proofs to the correctness of his words, and he adjudicated to push aside the complaints of the shochet Reb David. The following is the crux of the matter.

In the above mentioned book, chapter 101, Rabbi Yechiel Alter Nebenzahl gives his answer with regards to the dispute in the form of a letter to the rabbi of Rozniatow, as follows:

Blessed is G-d, Sunday of the Torah Portion of Vayeshev, 5682 (1922)

To my colleague, the great luminary Yehuda Tzvi Korn, may he live long, the rabbi and head of the rabbinical court of Rozniatow.

Regarding the matter upon which I weighed regarding the shochtim of the community of Rozniatow, despite the fact that a legal decision has not been published for reasons that are known, between the two slaughterers Reb Yaakov and Reb Zeida, who purchased the rights of slaughter from the shochet Reb David:

The slaughter Reb David's claims are true, that he sold his rights in the city of Rozniatow to the two shochtim Reb Yaakov Hochman and Reb Zeida Weiser. He was accepted in the city of Premyslan, and worked their as a shochet from the month of Shvat 5691 (1931) until Cheshvan 5692. However, due to the fact that his wife did not want to move her home from there, his hand was forced, and he wished to retract the sale and return the money. Even though he had already left the community and submitted his resignation, he wished to be accepted there again, and that the two new shochtim would be removed from their posts, even though they had already been accepted by the community and were working as shochtim. The opinion of the honorable rabbi and Gaon favored Reb David, claiming that the law was with him due to the fact that his hand was forced, for his wife does not want to travel with him to Premyshlan. This is as is explained in Choshen Mishpat paragraph 207 that if a person sells his land in order to move to a different place, and he is prevented from moving there, the sale is nullified, for it is considered to only be a valid sale on the condition that the seller would do something specific, and that something was not done. However, in accordance to my humble opinion, our case does not resemble the case described in the previous sentence at all, for several reasons.

Here, the author brings down nine specific reasons, based on many sources, and he concludes as follows: Therefore, the law is very clear and simple, that Reb David the shochet of Premyshlan is forbidden from slaughtering in Rozniatow. If he does so, he is, Heaven forbid, violating the law that is explained in the Beit Shlomo, whose words I have brought down above. He must return to his city of Premyshlan, and all will be good.

When Rabbi Yechiel Alter Nebenzahl came several times to Rozniatow on account of this case, he took interest in the physical and spiritual situation of the town. He found that, since the passing of the previous rabbi, Rabbi Hamerling of Jaroslaw of blessed memory, there was no spiritual leader to lead the vibrant Jewish community of Rozniatow. He came upon the idea of advising his grandson, who had recently gotten married, to become the local rabbi.

However, an obstacle arose from another place, a place from where he did not expect this at all.

Suddenly, close to the time of the elections were set to choose Rabbi Meczner as the rabbi of Rozniatow, a large delegation came from the family of the preceding rabbi. They demanded the rights of inheritance, and asked that Rabbi Meczner be brought to a Torah trial.

Warnings were published in the newspapers. They were issued by the new candidate, warning the rabbi in Rozniatow to change his stance regarding "rights". There were also strong and sharp responsa in the newspaper against this, written by Rabbi Meczner.

The Torah court case between the two sides took place in front of the rabbi...

Rabbi Meczner emerged victorious in the case, and he was coronated as the rabbi of Rozniatow with great fanfare.

The origins of Rabbi Yosef Menachem Meczner were from a family of Hassidim of Tzanz and Bobov from Krakow. He was the son of the chairman of the communal council of Krakow Rabbi David Meczner, and the grandson of Rabbi Godel Meczner, who was a well-known merchant and a frequenter of the home of the Bobover Rebbe. Rabbi Meczner studied in the kloizes of Krakow, under the greatest of teachers of that city.

As is known, the Jews of Krakow, even those in religious circles, spoke amongst themselves in the language of the state. Therefore Rabbi Meczner was fluent in the Polish language. On one occasion on May 3, the day of celebration of Polish independence, the rabbi appeared as a speaker in the Great Synagogue, and he enchanted the entire audience with his clear and excellent Polish. Among those present at the celebration were the captain of the region, and several representatives of the regional government. When the captain of the region heard the brilliant speech of the rabbi, he turned to the head of the community who was sitting next to him and said that they should send the priest to the rabbi to learn how to speak Polish and how to lecture.

The rabbi spoke with Divine grace. He was also an excellent prayer leader and singer. Young and old came from all of the houses of prayer to hear his prayers, and they swallowed up every word that came from his throat.

He was pleasant in his manner, and he knew how to endear himself to the members of the community, even to those who had previously been his opponents. Slowly, his opponents made peace with him, thanks to his personal charm and great uprightness. My brother Avraham of blessed memory was among those who frequented his house. Avraham honored and appreciated him.

When Rabbi Meczner took upon himself the yoke of the local rabbinate and communal needs, he found a free-for-all situation. The shochtim and butchers were locked in a dispute. The rabbi was able to bring peace to the butchers from both sides, between those who supported the Zionist government, and those who supported Reb Zechariah Liberman.

In a meeting prior to the communal elections, called by the Zionists in the kloiz, one of the prominent members of the Zionists was supposed to speak. The opponents of Zionists gathered together, did not permit the speaker to speak, and shattered the windows of the kloiz. The next day, when Reb Zechariah Liberman was supposed to appear, the Zionist youth paid him back, and the entire town was in ferment.

Discretely and with wisdom, he was able to win over hearts, and make peace between the combatants. He tended to his flock in a peaceful manner, until the great storm broke out that swept away the entire community, with their rabbi at the head. A portion of the community was exiled to a camp in nearby Dolina, where they met their death, and another portion was exiled to Kalusz. Rabbi Meczner was among those who were exiled to Kalusz. He died a martyr's death among the members of his community on the 27th of Tishrei, 5703 (October 8, 1942).

May memory be holy and blessed.

{35}

## The House of the Rabbi

### by Moshe Fruchter of New York[26]

The rabbi of the city, Rabbi Yitzchak Tzvi, was pleasant in his interpersonal relationships, and a very modest person. He earned his livelihood with difficulty, and conducted his household as one of the simple folk in the town. Not infrequently, the rebbetzin went on her journey to one of the nearby towns, to visit her relatives or her children, and the rabbi, who remained alone, invited one of the single men of the kloiz to come to his house to sleep over. Not infrequently, I was that young man.

The rabbi would awaken on freezing winter nights, at 3:00 a.m. He would light the stove that warmed up the room, sit next to the simple table that did not have a cloth, remove a book from the bookcase, and begin to study. At 5:00 a.m. he would wake me up to learn a little bit of Torah prior to the prayers. It was difficult for me to get up so early in the morning. However, the rabbi encouraged me with soft words: "Arise, my son, arise to the service of the Creator". He would remove the book "Yoreh Deah"[27] from the shelf and start to read it. I would read after him. He would ask me if I understood the section, and he would repeat it another time, softly and delicately.

Afterward, we would study a page of Talmud. We would discuss the explanation of the topic. We would continue in this manner until the time of the latter minyan (prayer quorum), the "minyan of the rabbi". We would attend the prayers. I would then go about my matters, and the rabbi would continue with his studies. His entire day was filled with Torah.

People would come to inquire about civic matters; or the shochet would come for a light conversation on matters of shechita or the butchers; or a women would come with a question of a chicken that seems to be not kosher – in which case the rabbi would try as hard as he could to declare it kosher[28], for he knew of the poverty and difficulties of the members of his community. If he were to declare the chicken non-kosher, this Jew would have nothing to eat. Therefore he would make every attempt, he would pore over his books, and examine the situation from all angles in order to find a precedent for declaring the chicken kosher, until he found such. When he found room for the leniency, he would say with great joy:

"It is kosher, it is kosher! Dear Jew, go eat and be satiated."

## Members of the Sanctuary

Every one of the Holocaust survivors, regardless of his outlook or relationship to religious matters, when it comes to matters of feelings, each one will give over his entire self to the feelings of the heart, and to the memories of the days that were and are no more, the days of childhood and youth. These feelings raise one up to the highest heavens, the world of piety and Hassidism, the world of quiet, somber tunes that were sung towards the end of the Sabbath, the world of joyous melodies of the festival days, the tunes of Purim and Chanukah; as well as the faces of splendid, dear Jews, with beards as white as snow flowing over their shiny black cloaks with their wide gartels[29] wrapped around their thin waist; Jews with red, black, straight and curly beards; Jews with neat, short, modern style beards; short and fat Jews; those who were occupied and worried; merchants, artisans, wagon drivers, and plain old Jews whose memories bring sadness to the heart. This is the world of dear Jews who once were and are no more. May their memories be blessed.

On Saturday nights towards dusk in the darkened kloiz, the shadows of people going to and fro can be seen. Some of them go to the sink, wash their hands, and dry them on the damp, dirty towel, as they recite with a groan "lift up your holy hands"[30]. They would then sit next to the table, cut open an olive's bulk of challah[31], dip it in salt, and recite the Motzi blessing on bread out loud. A few people would answer Amen after his blessing. They would then pass him a large plate of salted fish. The young man Yankele, the son of the shochet, would sit at the edge of the table, and begin singing Bnei Heichalah (Members of the Sanctuary) and Mizmor Ledavid[32]. A few people would assist him with his tune. The sad, quiet voice would strengthen, getting stronger and stronger, until it stopped.

Suddenly, we would hear the sweet voice of Zeida, the son of Moshele the shochet, singing Yedid Nefesh[33] in a tune that is full of strong longing for "The Merciful Father".

"For so much do I long to see" – cries and supplicates the sweet voice of Zeida, as he repeats the verse over and over again, and then the voice continues pleading: "Please, oh please G-d, heal please, show Yourself please", and he repeats again "show Yourself", and "Spread, oh my dear one upon me Your peace!". The melancholy song, full of longing for "The Merciful Father" continues on until it finishes with the sure, silent promise: "Have mercy upon us as in days of yore". The Jew sitting by the table is comforted, as he awaits the fulfillment of the promises of "The Merciful Father", that he should redeem them and spread His canopy of peace upon them.

Those seated would be silent. Someone would groan loudly, and begin with a quiet, slightly melancholy voice to give a lesson on the weekly Torah portion. On the other side, the voice of another Jew is heard, as he gives over the idea of a certain Tzadik or Rebbe regarding a verse in the weekly Torah portion. Shadows of people skip and dance upon the walls. The room becomes completely dark. The children cling to their parents who are seated around the long table. Someone brings "the concluding waters" to wash hands before the grace after meals[34].

The shamash (sexton) bangs on the table with his hand as a sign that it is time to begin the evening service (Maariv).

Reb Kopel the shamash lights the chandeliers on the ceiling and the walls[35]. The children become happier.

At home, mother recited "G-d of Abraham, Isaac and Jacob"[36]. The holy Sabbath has concluded, and the good week comes upon us that should bring us only good, kindness, mercy, etc.

The additional soul[37] of the Sabbath queen departs, and with it, the serenity of the Jew who is occupied during the six workdays, and awaits the Sabbath that redeems and delivers him from all of his tribulations and worries.

**The Supplication and the Prayer[38]**

There is a well-known adage that in the month of Elul, even the fish in the river tremble. The atmosphere becomes serious and everyone is worried. Everyone is trembling as the Days of Awe approach, may they come upon us for the good. People begin to examine their deeds, and to improve their relationships with their fellowman and with G-d. They become more careful with their prayers. As Rosh Hashanah and Yom Kippur draw nearer, the seriousness and fear increase as the time to welcome "the great and awesome day" approaches. The days of the penitential services (selichot)38 arrive, and people wake up very early in the morning for the recitation of selichot and the shofar blasts that arouse the nation. "Is it possible that a shofar is sounded, and the people do not tremble?[39]"

This month is also the month of the shochet Reb David Roth, who served as our cantor. During the month of Elul, he began to practice the prayers of the High Holidays with the members of his choir. Many people gathered around his house to hear "The Supplication and the Prayer".

Reb David the shochet was a man of pleasant countenance. He had a well-kept black beard, and a strong baritone voice. He enchanted his listeners with his heartfelt prayers.

He composed himself the tunes for his prayers, and practiced them with the members of the choir as the Days of Awe approached. The members of the choir included the brothers Mordechai and Zechariah Rechtschaffen, Yaakov Keller, Yaakov Fruchter, and others.

Along with the internal awakening of the soul, the external feeling was also aroused in us on account of the beautiful landscape and the clear, pleasant air that satisfied the body and soul. The hot days of the fiery summer passed, and the season of some rain and some sun approached. This was the time of the falling of the leaves and beautiful sunsets – the splendid autumn days of Lesser Poland[40].

### The Rebbe of Ulshka

This was Reb Mendele Eichenstein of holy blessed memory who lived in Lvov. My mother was a true Hassid of his. She believed in Rebbes, especially the Rebbe of Ulshka..

Due to her influence, my father also became attached to the Hassidim of Ulshka, and due to the influence of both of them, I also was numbered among the Hassidim of Ulshka. On one occasion, I merited to spend Yom Kippur with him, when I accompanied my father to Lvov to absorb some of the faith of the Tzadikim and Hassidism in me. I was deeply impressed by his pure, holy countenance, for his entire essence was of devotion to G-d. It is told that he sat at the window for days on end, looking and waiting for the footsteps of the Messiah.

Despite the fact that he had a large family, and had a meager income, he distributed all of his donations (pidyon monies[41]) to charity. Not infrequently, the rebbetzin would complain to the gabbaim (the Rebbe's assistants and administrators) that she did not have money to purchase the needs for the Sabbath. When he heard of some special case where it was necessary to support a person, to assist someone in marrying off his daughter, or to stand him upon his feet so that he could continue with his business – he did not hesitate to go himself to the generous people of the community in order to collect money for the special purpose. The Jews already knew that if the Rebbe is going himself to collect money, the reason must be significant, and they would donate generously. The Rebbe perished along with his family during the time of the great Holocaust.

May his memory be blessed.

### TRANSLATOR'S FOOTNOTES

1. Midrash Tanchuma is an ancient homiletical commentary on the Torah.

2. This is not entirely accurate. In Jewish liturgy, there are two hymns based on the theme of the ten martyrs of the Roman government. One is recited on Yom Kippur, and the other in the elegies of the morning service of Tisha Beov. The first half of the quoted segment (first four lines) is the opening

stanza of the Tisha Beov version. The last half of the quoted segment (last four lines) is the closing stanza of the Yom Kippur version.

3. Ketzot Hachoshen literally means "corners of the breastplate", referring to the breastplate of the High Priest. Avnei Milium refers to the precious stones upon the breastplate of the High Priest. Books of Jewish law and rabbinics are often given allegorical titles such as these. Shav Shamata means "seven topics".

4. The most famous of the false messiahs that arose in the Jewish community throughout the middle ages.

5. Kabbalah is the term for the mystical aspects of Torah.

6. Master of the Good Name, referring to his using of the Divine Name to elicit spiritual powers. Besht is the acronym for Baal Shem Tov.

7. Gates of prayer.

8. Most of these appellations are biblical references of some sort or another.

9. Rabbi Yitzchak Luria of Safed, Israel of the 16th century. He was a Kabbalistic master and a precursor of Hassidism.

10. The Tetragrammaton is the four letter, ineffable name of G-d, consisting of the letters Yud and He, followed by the letters Vav and He (pardon my interspersion of words between the first two and last two letters, as I myself will not write out these letters in order, even in their English form).

11. The word Shir means song or poem, and here is an acronym for the name Shlomo Yehuda Rappaport.

12. A verse from the book of Psalms.

13.  A quote from the daily evening (Maariv) service.

14. A quote from the sections of Psalms that form part of the Hallel service on festivals.

15. The Even Haezer is one of the four sections of the Code of Jewish Law, dealing primarily with marital laws.

16. A quote from the end of the book of Deuteronomy, from the blessing of Moses to the Tribe of Levi.

17. I have skipped translating several more adjectival acronyms here, all along the same theme.

18. The word 'Aven' or 'Even' is equivalent in the name Avnei Miluim and Even Haezer. The word 'full' is from the word 'maleh', the root of the word 'miluim'.

19. The booklet of doubts.

20. Literally a 'tent' referring to a booth or canopy over the grave, enabling people to come to the gravesite for prayers and petitions.

21. Another term for Lubavitch.

22. A verse from the book of Numbers, where G-d rebukes Aaron and Miriam for speaking badly about their brother Moses.

23. The hidden Torah refers to Hassidism, mysticism, and Kabbalah; and the revealed Torah refers to the straightforward, legalistic view of Torah.

24. In halachic terms, the 'dust' of something means something that borders on a prohibition, but does not fulfill the actual requirements of the prohibition. The two most common usages are 'the dust of usury' – referring to a transaction that borders upon the taking of interest (the taking of interest from a fellow Jew being prohibited), and the 'dust of the evil tongue' – referring to a statement that borders upon slander or malignment.

25. In several places throughout the text, the name is spelled as Menczer. However, for the most part, it is spelled as Meczner.

26. This section does not have a main title. Each subsection has its own title.

27. One of the four sections of the Code of Jewish Law (Shulchan Aruch).

28. Meat or chicken can be rendered unkosher by various internal blemishes that are not detected until it is cut open, or by inadvertent mixing with milk, or for several other such reasons. If the situation were questionable, a rabbi would be called upon the judge the situation.

29. A gartel is a ritual belt worn primarily by Hassidim.

30. A verse customarily recited upon washing the hands prior to a meal.

31. An olive's bulk "kezayit" is a halachic measurement that defines the minimum amount of food that must be eaten to constitute a formal meal, which would then require the recitation of the Grace after Meals. It is also the minimal amount of matzo that must be eaten on Passover night, and is the quantity of several other halachic definitions. Incidentally, it is far larger than the size of modern day olives. Bread is customarily dipped into salt prior to partaking of it.

32. Bnei Heichalah (Sons of the Sanctuary) and Psalm 23 (Mizmor Ledavid) are two of the custom-

ary hymns of the third Sabbath meal (Shalosh Seudos), that is partaken towards the end of the Sabbath day.

33. Yedid Nefesh (The Friend of my Soul) mentioned in the next paragraph, is another Sabbath hymn. The first line is Yedid Nefesh, Av Harachaman (Friend of my soul, Oh Merciful Father). This explains the meaning behind the sentence above. The next paragraph continues with segments of this song.

34. A meal is started with the ritual washing of the hands. This washing is often known as "the first waters" (Mayim Rishonim). Prior to reciting the grace after meals at the conclusion of the meal, the hands are washed again with "the concluding waters" (Mayim Acharonim).

35. At this point, the Sabbath has concluded.

36. The beginning of a prayer for the conclusion of the Sabbath, generally recited by women at home. The next sentence is a paraphrasing of a part of this prayer.

37. On the Sabbath, it is said that a Jew obtains an additional soul (Neshamah Yeteirah).

38. Harina Vehatefillah (The Supplication and the Prayer) is a quote from the opening penitential service of the days prior to Rosh Hashanah. The penitential services (selichot) are recited before the morning services (and at times in the middle of the night – especially for the first selichot service) starting the first Saturday night prior to Rosh Hashanah, or one week earlier if Rosh Hashanah falls early in the week.

39. A quote from the book of Amos.

40. A term for Galicia.

41. Literally "redemption monies", money that was given to him by his Hassidim who came to visit him, in the hope that the donation would guarantee them success, health, etc.

{38}

# Yisrael Leizer Bencer – One of the Thirty-Six Tzadikim

## by Y. Rechtschaffen

Yisrael Leizer the "Lamed Vov"[1] standing next to the home of Chanina Weisman.

As is known, the world only exists on account of the thirty-six Tzadikim in the world who protect it in every generation. Each generation has its own group of thirty-six. They protect and concern themselves with the peace of the world in every generation. Who would have imagined that we in particular, the people of Rozniatow, would have merited that one of these thirty-six Tzadikim would dwell and spread out his wings with us in particular.

This man was our Reb Yisrael Leizer, and nobody would argue that he was one of the thirty-six. Who was this man; what were the details of his story; from where was he; and to where was he going? Nobody knew of his origins, but there were many rumors about him. They said of him that he came here in his youth, and later left to study the secrets of Torah in a center of Torah.

They said of him that he was a great genius; however in truth, nobody was able to find out by speaking with him, for the man simply did not speak at all. One day, this young man returned from his studies from one of the Yeshivas. Nobody knew which one. All of the people of Rozniatow wished to merit to have this fine young man as a son-in-law. They sent emissaries and marriage brokers, for everyone wished to take him as a husband for their daughter – but everyone returned empty handed. They thought that he was still too young, and that he was not thinking about this seriously. They let him wait for a little while, a year or two.

In the interim, the years went by and the young man did not marry. He was slightly strange. He had a strong and healthy body, but he did not have a beard, only two or three hairs on the left and right side of his face. Furthermore, on one hand he had six fingers instead of five. One looked as an extra one, but who paid attention to such small details? The most important thing was that the young man certainly possessed fine traits, but nobody every saw him in the Beis Midrash or the Kloiz studying a Talmud. He stood by the windowsill during prayers, but he did not move his lips in prayer. Perhaps he worshiped privately, without enunciating the words and without moving his lips, but nobody saw him praying.

The man would disappear on the eves of holidays, and nobody knew where. Later on, when people already gave up on him, they also saw some idiosyncrasies in him. He dressed as a common person, with worn-out and torn clothes. He lived in a small room, four by four, without any furnishings, not even with a table or chair. There was only a large oven in the room, upon which he would ascend to sleep or rest. All sorts of books were scattered on the floor. Did he read them? Nobody knew. How did the man earn a living? Primarily from porting. He was a strong, tall man with muscles of steel. He would unload a transport wagon full of sacks of flour, sugar or some other merchandise in a very short time, without any effort. Early in the morning, one could see him on threshold of Sara Bor's store. She was the daughter of Wolf. There, in the corner, he waited for wagons so that he could be the first to unload them. He made a great deal of money, but what did he do with the money? To where did the great deal of money disappear? They asked him with surprise, until one bright day the mystery was solved, and the secret was exposed.

One day, a merchant from nearby Zolochev arrived in town. After he finished his business and purchases, as he was about to leave, he remembered something and turned to the merchant:

"I am jealous of you, oh people of Rozniatow, you are fortunate and it is good with you!"

"Why are you jealous of us?" asked the man of Rozniatow.

The merchant answered:

"Because you have a very generous and rich man living among you, who gives a great deal of money to the poor, and his charity will stand forever."

"Who is this man?" asked the Jew in surprise.

"He is your great philanthropist who, at the time that Zolochev went up in flames, and our synagogue also burnt down along with all the books in it... After a brief time, we received a gift from this person who is full of mercy, your great benefactor, is he not Reb Yisrael Leizer Bencer, may his honor be raised. He sent us the entire Vilna Shas[2] with fine binding, along with all other books that we require — many copies of the Chumash, Mishna, and Ein Yaakov. All of them were new books."

This news of the unusual deeds of the quiet Yisrael Leizer spread very quickly through the town, and the whole town was astir.

The man disappeared again.

After some time, when the man got older and he was no longer able to work as a porter, he began to sell holy objects – books, machzors[3], tallises, and mezuzas. He was particularly diligent about selling tallises and wearing tzitzit[4]. He requested that the children check if their tzitzit are in order and ritually fit, and if not, he would give new tzitzit to them for free... saying that the mother had already paid.

He would secretly bring in new books that were needed in the Kloiz and the Beis Midrash. He did so in a manner that nobody knew who the donor was.

When he would receive packages of books at the post offices from various book publishers, the tax officials saw fit to check into him and to demand taxes for his wide-branched business. To this end, they sent a special person from the central tax office in Warsaw to investigate the man and his widespread business, and to check out how he avoids paying taxes to the government. One bright day, the tax man appeared and asked all of the passersby where is the store of the bookseller, Mr. Eliezer Bencer in Rozniatow. They showed him the dwelling place of Yisrael Leizer and when he opened the door and saw what was going on there, how Yisrael Leizer was wearing torn and worn out clothing and sleeping on an oven, surrounded by piles of books, newspapers and "sheimos"[5], he shouted out in fear "Boza e Moi" "Oh god", and he quickly closed the door.

He went to one of the neighbors, sat down there, took out a piece of paper, and wrote one word on the entire page: "Zabrak", i.e. "poor and destitute".

Yisrael Leizer concerned himself with children who were reaching the age of Bar Mitzvah. He made sure to bring to their homes a fine pair of tefillin (phylacteries), tzitzit, and other such necessities.

Everyone was convinced that Yisrael Leizer, with his behavior, was none other than one of the thirty-six Tzadikim.

{41}

## Rabbi Hamerling

Rozniatow had great rabbis and scholars. We can read about this from the old monuments in its cemetery. When I was young, my mother once told me that she still remembers that when she was a young girl, they told a story abut a certain rabbi, great in Torah and very intelligent, who served in our city.

Once, a young couple appeared before them, wishing to divorce. It was customary in those days amongst rabbis that if a couple comes before a rabbi for a divorce, the rabbi will start to question them, and to talk to their hearts. He will then send them home, asking them to return after a month or two. In the meantime, the couple would make peace between themselves, and they would not come back to the rabbi. On this occasion, a young couple appeared before the rabbi. When the rabbi invited the husband into his office to hear his complaints, he said to the rabbi: "My father married me off to this woman. We got married only yesterday, but I cannot live with her." "What is the reason?" asked the rabbi. "She is ugly, and I cannot tolerate her". The rabbi sent him out and called the bride into his office. He did not ask anything, but looked very carefully at her face, and afterwards called his assistant and said to him in brief: "Command the scribe to write a bill of divorce (get) in accordance with law and tradition." He arranged for the divorce, and then proposed a proper and fitting match for each of them separately. Thus were the rabbis of Rozniatow.

Rozniatow also had its disputes. After the passing of the previous rabbi, a segment of the community supported the candidacy of a relative of the previous rabbi Reb Itzikel, whereas their opponents wanted specifically Rabbi Hamerling, who was the head of the Yeshiva of Jaroslawow in Eastern Galicia. He was appointed as the local rabbi with great splendor and honor. After his appointment, even his opponents accepted him.

He was of average height with a gray-white beard, and he always wore a black rabbinical hat and cloak. On Sabbaths, he wore a streimel on his head as was customary. He was refined, and beloved by his fellowman. My teacher, Reb Yehudale, or "Yudel Melamed", as he was known in town, would always send me to the home of the rabbi with a "question" that he had regarding the gizzard of a chicken[6], with an enlarged liver, etc. On Sabbaths, the teacher would send his students to the rabbi for a test of their knowledge of Chumash, Rashi, or a page of Gemara. When we appeared at the house of the rabbi on the Sabbath afternoon for our exam, the rabbi would declare in a festive voice to the rebbetzin: "Rebbetzin, the children have arrived. Please prepare a snack for them." The rebbetzin would prepare a snack of dried fruit, sweets, and a cold drink for the students who were being examined. The children always loved the house of the rabbi, whether because of the sweets that they received, or because of the caress that they received from the rabbi accompanied with words of encouragement: "very good, very good", even to those who stumbled a bit and did not succeed at the test. The rabbi caressed everyone on their cheeks, and wished them all that they should occupy themselves with Torah and commandments "mitzvot", and that they should continue to succeed in their studies.

On Shabbat Shuva[7] the rabbi would deliver a lecture to the congregation – as was customary throughout the Jewish world – on issues relating to the holiday. However, he was not blessed with oratory skill. He was not a professional speaker. Nevertheless, scholars and ordinary Jews came from all of the synagogues and kloizes to hear the rabbi's lecture, and they paid attention to his words with awe.

His style was not to look for stringencies in matters of kashruth. He always looked for a way to permit, to make kosher[8]. He knew the members of his community and their level of livelihood. Therefore he worked hard, delved into the books, and searched until he found a reason for a leniency. He would not make the questioner wait a moment. He explained the matter, for the bitter heart of the poor person was beating quickly and impatiently.

When the rabbi died, all of the stores were closed, and all residents of the town, young and old, followed the funeral procession. The town suffered a great loss with the death of its spiritual leader.

{42}

## The Rabbinical Judge Reb Yehuda Tzvi Korn

Until the choosing of a new rabbi, his place was filled by the judge Rabbi Tzvi Korn. He was a great scholar, with a wonderful memory. He would be able to immediately point out the paragraph of Halacha (Jewish law) or the page of Gemara.

He was a living Talmudic encyclopedia. He lived a life of anguish and difficulty, however he never complained, Heaven forbid, about his lot. He was happy with his lot. Since he himself lived in a meager fashion, he understood very well the spirit of those who came to him with questions on kashruth, and he attempted with all his might to find a reason to declare the fowl kosher.

Prior to the outbreak of the First World War, the young rabbi, Rabbi Mecner, the grandson of the rabbinical judge Rabbi Yechiel Nebenzahl of Stanislawow, was accepted as rabbi of Rozniatow.

## Religious Functionaries

Aside from the young rabbi and his rabbinical court, the following types of people were counted among the religious functionaries: shochtim (ritual slaughterers), mohalim (ritual circumcisors), gabbaim (trustees), and shamashim (sextons).

All of these religious functionaries worshiped in the later minyan (prayer group) of the kloiz, that took place at 9:00 a.m. Rozniatow had the good fortune to employ the best shochtim. I will start with them.

## Shochtim

The head of the shochtim and the most honorable of them, as I remember, was Reb Moshele Weiser in his time. He was a Jew with an impressive appearance, of middle height, with a black, trimmed beard and a high forehead. He would size you up immediately with his two shiny eyes, that exuded wisdom and intelligence. You would realize immediately that a Torah scholar and fearer of Heaven is standing before you. He would conduct a regular class in the kloiz for the grown youths, I being among them. He taught us a class in the laws of "Yoreh Deah"[9]. He would explain things in a wonderful fashion, and if he realized that somebody did not understand, he would repeat his words and explain a second time, until the law was clear and understood by everybody. The shochtim did not only engage in their own profession, shechita. They also were involved in teaching, the study of Torah and wisdom, and guiding people on their paths of study – some in Chumash and Rashi, Ohr Hachaim[10], or a page of Gemara. They would study "Yoreh Deah" and other such things with the older boys. Every one of them was fitting to be not only a shochet and bodek[11], but also as an honored rabbi and expert in Torah.

The son of Reb Moshele, Reb Zeida, married Bracha the daughter of Reb Yosef Shimshon Stern when he grew up. He also became a shochet. He was a fine young man, refined, with eyes that exuded love, and good hearted.

There was one other young man in my time, who was a colleague of Reb Zeida Weiser. This was Reb Yankele Hochman. These were children of a Torah imbued generation, whose hearts were captivated by the beauty of truth.

There was also the shochet Bratshpiz. He was a man of impressive appearance, tall with a black beard. He wore splendid clothes, and exuded honor. He left the town during the 1930s to serve as a rabbi and head of a rabbinical court in Czechoslovakia.

Reb David Roth the shochet was also an outstanding person in town.

When Reb Zecharia David Liberman served in town as the head of the community, there was a need for an additional shochet. However, the depleted communal coffers were not sufficient to hire an additional person. However, it became known to Reb Zecharia David that Reb David Roth also had a sweet voice, so he combined the positions of shochet and cantor into one position. When Reb David Roth was accepted as a shochet, the condition was made that as part of his duties, he must serve as the cantor in the large synagogue or the Beis Midrash, that he had to serve in this post for ten years, and that he was forbidden from leaving this post for that duration of time.

For the young man Reb David, this was a splendid opportunity. He jumped upon the opportunity, and signed the agreement with Reb Zecharia David.

Reb David the shochet was from a family of cantors. One of his brothers served as a cantor in the United States, and whenever he composed a tune for a prayer, he would immediately transmit it to his brother Reb David. Reb David also composed several tunes, and he transmitted them to his brother.

Reb David had a very sweet voice, and he was an exceptional prayer leader. He won his acclaim with his sweet prayers that awakened his listeners to great intent in prayer. The melodies that he composed were well known to the townsfolk. He also established a choir of boys, and taught them to read musical notes, and to understand the principals of music and the cantorial arts.

His fame also spread beyond the town. People came to town and took interest in him as a shochet and also as an exceptional prayer leader. He received many fine job offers as a shochet and a cantor. He received an invitation from Stanislawow with a very high salary. However Reb David was bound to his agreement with Reb Zecharia David for the time frame, and he was not able to leave until the ten years expired. At that time, he accepted an honorable position in Przemysl, and signed the contract. Then, he sold his rights as a slaughterer to Reb Yankele Hochman, and left the town.

Reb David was of splendid appearance, tall, handsome, and brave. On one occasion, as he was walking to the kloiz in the evening, four gentile shkotzim[12] started up with him and attempted to beat him. Reb David grabbed one of them, lifted him up, and smote the other three with him. They barely managed to flee.

He perished along with the rest of the community during the days of the Holocaust.

{44}

## Mohalim

Almost all of the shochtim were mohalim. However there were also a few non-clergy who occupied themselves with the holy work of bringing Jewish children into the covenant of Abraham our Father. They did this for the sake of Heaven and not to receive recompense. On the contrary, they would give their own money to poor family who had many children. Yosef Shimon Stern was among these mohalim who did not seek recompense.

He was a wealthy Jew, who had many possessions. He was also a scholar, and had a large family. One daughter married Zeida, the son of Reb Moshele the shochet, who also served as a shochet in the town.

## Rebbes

One of the phenomena that awakened a deep meaning in Jewish life of Poland, was, without doubt, Hassidism, which took its own form in Eastern Galicia. For the most part, the people of Galicia were simple folk, who lived lives of want and poverty. They did not know joy at all, and their entire concern was how to sustain their large families, how to repay debts, and how to pay back what they borrowed from charitable funds. Hassidism was what brought them a new light and hope. It chased away sadness and filled every Jewish heart with joy, as it combined that heart to the community of Hassidim.

If a Rebbe came to town, all of the Jews of the town would stream to him, to pour their heart and agony out to him, and ask for his advice. One would come to the Rebbe to ask about his daughter who had come of age, without him having even one coin for the dowry. The second would come to the Rebbe to consult about an incurable illness. The third would come regarding a domestic dispute. Another would come to ask the Rebbe's advice regarding the leasing of lands from the local earl. Everyone would have his own private issue. When they came to the Rebbe and poured out their hearts to him, the weight on their hearts already was lightened. They already felt some relief of spirit. The Rebbe was the doctor, psychologist and advisor to the simple Jews. As was the custom, the Admors arrived on Thursday, and remained until the following Thursday. There were Rebbes who had faithful Hassidim in town. When they found out that the Rebbe was coming for a specific week, they would go out to greet him at the train station in Krechowice, a distance of seven kilometers from town. They would accompany the Rebbe into town with song.

The Rebbe would stay at the home at one of his Hassidim, and there he would receive his Hassidim "in peace" and hear their requests. On the eve of the Sabbath, they would set up tables in the old kloiz. There, the Hassidim would come after they ate their own Sabbath meal in their home. They would spend time with the Rebbe in song, dance, and great spiritual heights until a late hour of the evening.

Great was the belief of the Hassidim in their Rebbe. His image was always bound before their eyes, and they were bound to him with all the strands of their souls.

The Rebbe of Bolekhov, Rabbi Perlow, always stayed at the home of my revered father, the large house of Reb Hersch Rechtschaffen. The Rebbe of Golina, Reb Betzalel, who was the son-in-law of Reb Chaim of Tzanz (Nowy Sacz), would always stay with Reb Yaakov Shusterman. The Rebbe of Burstyn and others would also come to our town. Each Rebbe had his own Hassidim. These Hassidim believed in their own Rebbe with complete faith, and they would come and go, and conduct their business in accordance with his holy word. They would drink up his words with thirst, and learn from his deeds. They would fine salvation for their stormy souls in the home of the Rebbe, as well as a balm and bandage for all of their woes.

The simple Jew believed that the Rebbe was a holy man of G-d who had the ability to request mercy on the Jewish people; and he also believed that there were other holy Rebbes and great people, so he would also travel to other Rebbes and not just "his" Rebbe in order to pour out his requests and needs. This was not the case with the Hassidim and scholars. Once they had chosen their own Rebbe whom they knew was great in Torah, expert in Talmud and halachic decisors, they cleaved to him and only him. They did not know of and did not travel to a different Rebbe. Often, Hassidim who believed in a certain Rebbe opposed a different Rebbe. From this, all sorts of controversies and disputes broke out. Here is not the place to elaborate upon them. I only wanted to bring here a short list of Admorim who used to visit our town. When a Rebbe arrived to our town, he would often be accompanied with one or two gabbaim (aides).

{45}

### Sofrim (scribes)

Reb Baruch Gelick, who lived outside of the center of the town, in the "Old town", was the Sofer Stam[13] of the town. He provided all holy objects to the population of the town. He wrote Torah scrolls, Mezuzas, and Tefillin. He was thin, with a yellowish small beard. He was always clean and polished, and everyone who saw his externals realized that he was a man who occupied himself with spiritual matters.

**Y. Rechtschaffen**

{46}

## The Old Kloiz and its Worshippers

### by Mordechai Stern

The Old Kloiz, or the "Zhidachevai" as many people called it, was a very old building. The elders who worshipped there would relate that they still remember that their grandparents called it the Old Kloiz.

"Zhidachevai" – since most of the Hassidim of the Admor of Zhidachev worshiped there. Mother Rebbes who visited Rozniatow from time to time also worshipped in the Zhidachevai Kloiz. The main thing was to greet the Sabbath queen in a congregation of Hassidim and men of good deeds. The Hassidim of Zhidachev took pride in the fact that also those who were not members of their own Hassidic group worshipped in their kloiz. Therefore, the worshippers of the kloiz knew how to give honor also to other streams and to Admors from various Hassidic dynasties who came under the shadow of their roof.

I remember how the Rebbe of Bolekhov used to come to Rozniatow annually to visit his Hassidim. As was customary, most of his Hassidim worshipped in the large Beis Midrash, mainly in the first prayer quorum. The Rebbe would lead the Friday night service of Welcoming the Sabbath. Only one solitary Jew objected to this invitation. This was Reb Mordechai Krigel of blessed memory, the grandfather of Mrs. Tzila Fettman, who now lives in the Kibbutz of Ramat Kovesh. Reb Mordechai was a Hassid of Chortkov, and very sharp in Torah. He permitted himself to oppose the Rebbe of Bolekhov publicly, and he demonstrated his opposition by not coming to worship in the kloiz that Sabbath eve.

The place where the Reb Avrahamche Eichenstein of Zhidachev and other members of the Zhidachever dynasty stayed was my father's house, on a street that was later on called Herzl Street, in the house next to the notary. From there he went to the home of Reb Yehuda Weisberg. In the latter years, he would stay with Eli Spigel.

As far as I remember, the Rebbe used to arrive in town on Thursday, and the Hassidim would go out to greet him at the train station of Krechowice. Town notables were among the Hassidim, including Reb Elazar Yitzchak Leib. Despite his extreme old age, he would go out to greet him, and he would invite him to worship the Sabbath Eve service at the great synagogue. The Rebbe answered positively, and on the eve of the Holy Sabbath, the Rebbe would worship in the large synagogue, which was also too small to accommodate the crowd that had come in honor of the Rebbe. Many remained outside and worshipped outside, for the Admor of Zhidachev was famous for being a first class prayer leader. His pleasant voice attracted many from outside the circles of Zhidachev Hassidism. These musically inclined people praised his prayers very greatly.

Hassidim from other Hassidic dynasties, such as Chortkov and others, came to listen to his prayers and words of Torah. They derived great enjoyment from this. The table celebration of the Sabbath Eve was set up in the old kloiz. There, the Rebbe would present to the Hassidim a Hassidic idea or statement, or words of Torah, for there was no shortage of Torah scholars in the old kloiz.

This was an exalted time, and a festive spirit pervaded the kloiz. One Sabbath after another, a different Rebbe would visit Rozniatow, and would feel duty bound, at least on the Sabbath Eve, to worship in the kloiz. The Rebbes of Strettin and Dolina also had the same custom.

The following scholars and Torah giants worshipped in the Kloiz: Rabbi Hamerling, Reb Chanina Weisman, Reb Tzvi Hersch Mendel Artman, Reb Bendet Horowitz, Reb Feivel Reizler, Reb Berish Friedler, Reb Shabtai Spigel, Reb Itzi Krechowicer, Reb Mordechai Krigel, Reb Moshe Weiser the shochet, the rabbinical judge Reb Yehuda Tzvi Korn, and Reb Shmuel Wirt.

Reb Shmuel Wirt was a one of a kind character. He always sat at the back of the kloiz, that is not at the eastern side, not far from the entrance. He did not make himself stand out, and he did not participate in any arguments. There was a candle beside him, and a book of Zohar[14] or Jewish ethics (Mussar) was also always on hand. He was always studying. He did not take any part in communal or public matters. On the other hand, his many sons-in-law were very knowledgeable in communal matters as well as spiritual matters. These were Yosef Shimon Stern, Avraham Zauerberg, Kalman Halpern, Berish Weiss, and Yisrael Kornblitt. They all worshipped in the kloiz.

There was only one occasion during the year that Reb Shmuel made himself stand out, and this was not only in the kloiz. This was every year on the festival of Simchat Torah. On that day, he was glad and he made the congregation joyous. He would dance, and invite everyone around him to join in the dancing. He would go to the outskirts of the town in song, while we boys followed after him. He would call after us:

"Rejoice and Be Glad on Simchat Torah"[15].

We children got tired from all the dancing, while he, despite his advanced age, continued to dance and dance. The voice of his singing filled the entire street.

The following people were numbered among those that worshipped and studied in the kloiz: Reb David Roth, the shochet, who was a proud and fine Jew, a prayer leader who knew music, and a scholar; Reb Lipa Teneh; Reb Meshulam Klinger; Eliezer Ber Klinger; Reb Kalman Frankel; Reb Yisrael Tzvi Londoner the Kohen; and my in-law[16] Reb Leib Falik; Reb Yaakov Hamerman, Mordchai Tisch; the teacher Yehudale Kaufman; Reb Tzvi Akselrad; Reb Yosef Rubinfeld, an upright Jew; and Reb Meshulam Fruchter the Kohen. His place in the kloiz was right next to my father. I always looked at him, with his refined face. He was a pleasant man, with a dear soul. He never reprimanded the children who were creating a disturbance.

The custom was that those who studied Torah in the kloiz would arise early and study to the light of a candle. They would study from a new book. A few of them were careful to worship at sunrise[17], while others continued to study as they were enwrapped in their tallises until later hours of the morning. People studied in the kloiz from the early hours of the morning throughout the day.

I wish to point out a few people here: Reb Itzi Fessberg; Reb Zeida Weiser and his brother Itzi; the brothers Leibish and Yaakov Hochman, the sons of Reb Moshele Eli. Both Reb Zeida and Reb Yaakov inherited the rights of shechita from their fathers, and became shochtim in Rozniatow. There were others, such as Sender Rosenberg; Mordechai Spigel; the brothers David and Monty-Mordechai Stern the sons of Yosef Shimon; Yaakov Keller; Yaakov Fruchter; Shimon Rechtschaffen; Shmuel Leib Rosenbaum (died in Israel); my brother-in-law David Akselrad; Shmuel Londoner. All of them were murdered by the Nazi soldiers. The few who survived included Moshe Fruchter and Yehuda Hamerman-Wiczner (U. S. A.); Mordechai and Yaakov Rechtschaffen (Australia); Reb Tzvi Fessberg;, Avraham Friedler (Saraf), and my brother David (Israel); and David Nussbaum.

There was no need to hire external prayer leaders or cantors in the kloiz, for there were prayer leaders among the worshippers of the kloiz. I remember in my time, when I was still in Rozniatow, that the following people lead services on the High Holy Days: Reb Moshele the shochet, Reb David Roth the shochet, and Reb Reuven Getzel Heisler. On other festivals, the following people led services: Reb Vove Hoffman, Reb Avrahamche Zauerberg, Reb Gedalyahu Weber, and others.

On the High Holidays the services were always commenced by the elder Reb Yaakov Meir Nussbaum, the grandfather of our friend and comrade David Nussbaum-Rubinfeld. After his death, his place as the commencer of services in the kloiz[18] was our rabbinical judge, Reb Yehuda Tzvi Korn. He was an extremely modest man, who behaved discretely towards his fellowman and his G-d. He always distanced himself from communal matters, and he never took interest in anything other than religion and judgement. By chance, I got to know him from up close, for during the time of the First World War, when his home was hit by a shell, he went with his family to live in the home of his brother-in-law Mishel Artman who was our neighbor. However, that home was too small to hold both families, so the family of the judge came to stay with us. The judge sat day and night studying. His mouth literally did not cease from his learning. The reader of the Torah on every Sabbath and festival was Moshe Weiser, who was very active in communal matters.

The old kloiz was badly damaged during one of the many fires that afflicted Rozniatow. It was impossible to continue worshipping and studying there. The community and its activists did not have sufficient financial means to rebuild the kloiz. Therefore, until the kloiz could be rebuilt, all of its worshippers spread out to various other houses of prayer. A few joined the kloiz in the building of Reb Itzikel, and others went to other places of worship. A large number worshipped in the synagogue of Tzvi Rechtschaffen. A Torah class took place regularly in that synagogue. Reb Yisrael Tzvi Londoner the Kohen gave the class. Young and old attended that class on Sabbath eves and on all other days of the year.

During that period, the Gaon Rabbi Hamerling died. This was a great loss. Every Jewish home in Rozniatow was in mourning. During one of the days of shiva[19] Reb Yisrael Tzvi Londoner delivered a eulogy during the class in the Rechtschaffen Synagogue. This was not a prepared eulogy, and many people only found this out afterwards. Shimshon Rechtschaffen was among them. During the time of the second class, Shimshon and David the son of Yosef Shimon Stern approached and asked Reb Yisrael Tzvi Londoner to repeat his eulogy. This was a speech that made great impact, and it included many novel Torah ideas. It also repeated over some of the novel Torah ideas of the late rabbi.

When I was already in Germany, Reb Shlomo Teitelbaum, nicknamed "Shlomo di bard"[20] was sent by the community and the kloiz, equipped with a letter signed by Reb Moshe Weiser the shochet among others, to raise money for the rebuilding of the old kloiz of Rozniatow. Obviously, I acted to the best of my ability among the Roznaitow natives in Germany. When I visited Rozniatow in 1934, the gabbai (administrator) and activists of the kloiz expressed their thanks to me for my help in collecting money for this holy purpose.

The rebuilt old kloiz continued on with its Hassidic tradition. The Hassidim of Zhidachev were centered there, as were other Hassidim and studiers of Torah. Nobody felt themselves disadvantages, Heaven forbid, if they were Hassidim of a different dynasty than Zhidachev.

The gabbaim of the kloiz were good Jews. They were generous people who toiled on behalf of the kloiz for the sake of Heaven, and not for the sake of receiving a reward. The final gabbaim of the kloiz were, as far as I remember: Reb Yisrael Tzvi Londoner, Reb Meir Frankel, and Reb Binyamin Keller.

The square, photographed in 1929. At the right is the home of Kringel, Keller, and Gelobter.

This Reb Binyamin was a straightforward man with a warm Jewish heart. He would run like a deer to a large or small mitzvah. He always knew how to protect from iniquity, and he always would give the benefit of the doubt. He loved the game of chess. Even during a day of the fair, he was able to leave his store to search for someone who would sit and play chess with him.

The father of Reb Binyamin was Reb Baruch of Reb Shmuel Hirsch, as they called him[21]. He was a happy and joyful Jew. Even though he was very poor, he knew how to entertain people at his own expense. It is told that his wife asked him to get some wood to light the oven during the difficult, cold winter. She said to him: "Baruch, go and see wood" (In Yiddish: "Gei ze haltz tzum heitzn")[22]. Reb Baruch went to the marketplace, and returned as he came, without wood. His wife asked him: "So Baruch, what is with the wood? Did you see wood?" Baruch answered her, "I saw wood, for that is what you sent me to do". He knew the yahrzeits[23] of all of the Rebbes and of all of the worshippers in every synagogue. Each morning, he would run from one synagogue to another in order to drink a "lechayim" with the person who had yahrzeit. Apparently, this was also his breakfast.

The shammas (sexton) of the kloiz was Reb Koppel, and someone else by the name of Leib Pares. They called him by his mother's name, Leib Mirches. He had previously been a wagoneer. He drove travelers from Rozniatow to Krechowice and back in his wagon. He was known as a high class wagoneer, since he had a carriage with two strong horses. Leib Mirches would only transport important and well to do people in his fine carriage.

He finally tired of this means of livelihood, and preferred to serve as the shamash in the kloiz. He treated this work as holy work. He concerned himself with the cleanliness and heating of the premises, with the intention that even the poor and the beggars would have a place to warm up on the harsh winter nights. Even the young men who were drafted to the army, and decided to wear themselves down and stay up at night in order to become emaciated, found refuge in the kloiz. Often, they would leave the place in disarray and cause a great deal of work for Leib Mirches. However, Leib Mirches did not chastise them. He did not request that the gabbaim of the kloiz shut the doors of the kloiz to the boys in the days prior to their army interview. On the contrary, he made sure that they had strong drink, and helped them rather than hampering them. The shamash Leib Mirches did not shut the kloiz in the face of Jews, whether they were local poor people, or guests.

Most certainly, many other worshippers of the old kloiz are worthy of mention here, and having a monument erected in their memory, and not just with one word; but who can give due to all of these people after decades? Therefore those whom I skipped over should forgive me. Let this article here serve as a modest memorial to the kloiz and its worshippers who were murdered by the armies of Hitler and his assistants.

## TRANSLATOR'S FOOTNOTES

1. According to tradition, there are 36 special discreet holy, righteous people in the world at any given time. These are called the 'Lamed Vov', the Hebrew numerical value of 36.

2. An edition of the Talmud.

3. A Machzor is a festival prayer book.

4. Tzitzit are the four fringes on the corner of a tallis, and also on the four corners of the 'small tallis' worn inside ones clothing at all times.

5. Worn out holy books that are to be buried in an honorable fashion.

6. This would be a question regarding the kashruth of the chicken. A punctured crop or gizzard would render a chicken non-kosher.

7. The Sabbath of Return, a name given to the Sabbath between Rosh Hashanah and Yom Kippur.

8. This refers to questionable situations regarding punctures in internal organs of slaughtered animals, unintentional minor mixtures of milk and meat, etc. In the case of a poor person who has just submitted the animal to ritual slaughter, such questions can have a major impact on their livelihood.

9. One of the four segments of the Shulchan Aruch (The Code of Jewish Law). Among other things, Yoreh Deah deals with the laws of kashruth and ritual slaughter.

10. Ohr Hachaim is one of the biblical commentators.

11. A bodek is an inspector of the internal organs of a slaughtered animal. The two jobs – shochet and bodek – are often performed by the same person.

12. A derogatory term for gentiles.

13. Stam is the acronym for Sefer Torah, Tefillin, and Mezuzot. A Sofer Stam is a scribe who writes Torah scrolls, Tefillin, and Mezuzas.

14. Zohar is the main Kabbalistic work of Judaism.

15. A quote from the Simchat Torah liturgy.

16. The word here is 'son-in-law' but I suspect that it might have a more generic meaning here.

17. It is considered especially meritorious to recite the morning prayers at the time of sunrise. However, for those who are engaged in serious study, it is considered appropriate to delay the recital of the morning prayers.

18. This most probably refers to the person reciting the Pesukei Dezimra section of the service, which precedes the formal beginning of Shacharit.

19. The seven day mourning period following a death.

20. Shlomo the bearded.

21. This sentence is incorrect in the Hebrew, obviously. I translated it literally.

22. A Yiddish expression for "Go get some wood".

23. The anniversary of death.

{51}

# The Zionist Movement

{52}

## Ch. N. Bialik[1]

Generations will come that will speak of you, and you will be silent. They will sing songs and write dramas of you, without having known you. If there is someone regarding whom it was not known that he spoke in prose all of his life, you will not need to know that you made poems all of your life. But if you think that you have reason to despair, for after decades you accomplished very little – you are making a complete mistake. Your efforts mark the beginning of the healing of our body. The lifeblood stopped flowing through the arteries, which hardened and became blocked. The heart has begun to beat again.

{53}

# Rozniatow During the Days of the Zionist Vision

## by Dr. Chaim Berger

These were the days of the Zionist vision, which filled my entire being so that I saw no other world aside from it. I found my way among the secret activities of the student organization in Stryj. During this fundamental period of my life, I spent my vacations in Rozniatow. There I found young people organized in the Zionist movement. They were of sharp mind, sensitive hearts, alert and active.

The main activities were the setting up of courses in Hebrew, and the nurturing of a strong love of the Land of Israel. In the "Chevrat Zion" hall next to the home of Dr. Wasserman, opposite the "Zrakwa", I organized lectures and discussions on Zionistic topics along with other Rozniatow activists.

The images of the young people of Rozniatow are etched in my mind, as are their desire for action and intense stamina. Far from any abstraction, they saw the realities as they were. Their internal feelings gave them the strength in their actions, and fired their deeds.

I remained in constant contact with the activists of Rozniatow. In 1908, they invited me to lecture on the memorial day of Binyamin Z. Herzl[2] . The hall was full to the brim. The Jews of Rozniatow were anxious to here my lecture in Modern Hebrew, with the Sephardic pronunciation[3]. They enthusiastically accepted the fundamental outlook of Herzl, that the Zionist goal was the normalization of the life of the Jewish people in their national homeland.

My wife Bronya, of the Lifschitz family of Brody, was frequently invited to lecture on the ideal manner of actualizing the goal and attaining personal fulfillment. This was a form of pioneering that not too many people became attached to, for only the choicest of people became chalutzim (Zionist pioneers). These people were special in their strength and bravery, special in their jumping upon the path and continuing along it, special in their ability to overcome and to learn. Such were the youth of Rozniatow.

People such as these are the Rozniatow natives in the land. They are dreamers and people of vision, practical chalutzim and people of deeds, who stood their own during all of the tribulations of the wars, and all the obstacles along the path, covered with blood, sweat and tears. My wife was also active in the organization of Rozniatow natives. She offered assistance to the Holocaust survivors who made aliya, in helping them overcome the difficulties in absorption, and become acclimatized to the Land.

We also implanted in the heart of our son a love for the Rozniatow natives. He succeeded in serving as a professor in the Weitzmann institution. He was awarded the Rothschild prize at a festive gathering of the Knesset for his work in the chemical field. Despite the fact that he is submerged in his professional work, he takes an interest in the activities of the organization of Rozniatow natives, and in the memorial book of that community which was destroyed, and where most of our relatives perished.

**TRANSLATOR'S FOOTNOTES**

1. Chaim Nachman Bialik was a well-known Hebrew author of the 1800s. The paragraph below is a quote from his works.

2. Theodore Herzl's Hebrew name was Binyamin Zeev.

3. There are two main methods of Hebrew pronunciation, the Ashkenazic method prevalent among European Jewry, and the Sephardic method prevalent among North African and Middle Eastern Jewry. Modern Hebrew was revived with the Sephardic pronunciation.

{54}

# The Zionist Organizations

## by Yaakov Rechtschaffen

After the Zionist Congress in Basle, the news of the national revival and the return of children to their borders[1] came also to our town. The first Zionists in our town decided amongst themselves to organize into a Chovevei Zion group, to found a special prayer hall for those of like belief, and to write a Torah scroll in honor of the festive event. As can be understood, opponents to the idea of the return to Zion and also to the writing of the Torah scroll immediately arose in town. They immediately enlisted verses from the Torah to prove their point: "If G-d does not build a house, the builders toil in vain"[2], etc. And whom do you think you are that you should write a Torah scroll? As if the writing of a Torah scroll and bringing it in to a sanctuary of G-d is something only for them, for what connection is there between Zionists and a Torah scroll? This was despite the fact that all of the members of Chovevei Zion were pious and observant Jews, scholars, who behave in all manners like the rest of the residents of the town, except that the concept of the Land of Israel and the return to Zion touched their heart, and, in fulfillment of the verse "on behalf of Zion I shall not be silent"[3], they began to work towards that end with all their enthusiasm.

When they finished writing the Torah scroll, they arranged a Torah dedication celebration with great joy and splendor. They sang and danced in the outskirts of town, and the joy was great.

At first, they all were united in the Chovevei Zion movement. There were no differences of opinion and outlook among them. They all acted according to the same custom. They all were observant of Torah and the commandments, and all of them desired the same, solitary, aim: "Let our eyes behold Your return to Zion with mercy"[4].

After about 20-30 years, the first divisions began to appear. The first ones who began to organize themselves into a separate faction within the Zionist organization were the people of Poale Zion. They separated from the general umbrella as workers, and after the First World War, some of them also began to free themselves from the yoke of Torah and observance, and draw near to the workers' movement. It was natural that they would organize themselves into a workers faction within Chovevei Zion. After them came the people of the "General Zionists", and the "Achva" youth group. Later came the Mizrachi – Bnei Akiva organization, Gordonia, Hashomer Hatzair, and others.

Each of these organizations had hundreds of members and activists, who would come to their headquarters each night to spend their free time in various discussions on Zionist topics. They studied Bible and the Hebrew language, sang Hebrew songs, organized question and answer evenings, debates and lectures, and the youth began to learn the well-known Hora dances.

All of the Zionist organizations worked together to collect money to purchase land in Israel via the Keren Kayemet LeYisrael (Jewish National Fund). Each organization appointed two representatives to the Keren Kayemet. These representatives formed the local Keren Kayemet branch. There was always competition among the various youth groups as to who would collect the most money for the Keren Kayemet, and be registered in the Keren Kayemet annals as "having attained first place".

Only honorable people from among the youth groups were appointed to the directorship of the Keren Kayemet. My brother Shimshon Rechtschaffen was the chairman of the Keren Kayemet for many years. Despite the fact that I am biased, I will permit myself to state that my brother was the epitome of refinement of soul and levelheadedness. He was dedicated to communal work for all of his days. He was also the chairman of the General Zionists for many years. On account of his activism, he neglected his family and also his livelihood. Like all of us, he desired to make aliya to the Land of Israel, but he did not succeed in obtaining the certificate (aliya permit) from the Mandatory government of the time, until the bitter violent day of the total liquidation of the community of Rozniatow came. He perished along with his family.

{55}

## General Zionists

The General Zionists referred to themselves as ordinary Zionists (Stam Tzionim). Members of the establishment and the intelligentsia were generally attracted to them.

The General Zionist organization was the first of all of the political groups to become active in our town.

The chairman was Moshe Rosenberg.

The activists. From right: Shimshon Rechtschaffen, Yeshayahu Lutwak, Shuli Tanne, and Shabtai Falik.

The schism that affected the General Zionist movement in Poland during the 1920s did not affect the local Zionists.

{56}

On the right: Yehuda Tzvi Stern. On the left: Mordechai Hoffman.

The Poale Zion organization had an important past, since it was one of the first to organize in our town. The members related with seriousness and faithfulness to their Zionist activity. Among the most active were Magister Leib Meisels and Moshe Monio Lusthaus, who died in Israel. They conducted intensive activity in a large variety of areas. Its members were for the most part from the working class, workers, foremen and tradesmen. They developed greatly in the cultural realm. They ran a large and orderly library under the direction of Ben Zion Horowitz, and they also established a drama group from amongst their members. This group performed various plays with great success.

It is worthwhile to point out the budgetary problems that made the work of the activists difficult to the point of being almost unbearable. However, the strong will of the activists to fulfill their tasks appropriately, and not to become like the musicians at a wedding[5], caused great power. They knew very well what deeds needed to be done in order to overcome the difficulties. This gave them the confidence to appear before the public and request with a full heart the help needed for their cultural work. The hearts of the youth and the adults were open to greet them.

As has been previously noted, the members of Poale Zion were the first to organize themselves into a separate group within the general umbrella of Chovevei Zion. There were many causes for this. In order to search for sources of income for their organization, they decided to set up a drama group to perform various plays, and the income would be dedicated to the organization.

The troupe developed very well, and they performed many productions of Shalom Aleichem, Peretz, Asch, and Goldfaden in Rozniatow. Students and young men and women participated in the troupe, and their success was exceptional. Of course, they realized a great deal of income from their performances, and all of the income was dedicated to developing a large library, for they strove to widen the perspective and deepen the world of the youth. The success of the library can also be seen from the large number of readers that turned to it to borrow books in a variety of languages. Gentiles, particularly members of the intelligentsia, teachers, and officials, came as well.

The times had their effect. It was after the First World War. Poverty and pressure for a livelihood brought the masses into the ranks of Poale Zion. The vast majority of the youth of the town belonged to that organization. The chairman and life force of the organization was Leib Meisels. Muni Lusthaus, who was the secretary, was very active in the organization. After some years, he also became the chairman of the organization. When I moved over from Hapoel Hamizrachi and turned towards the left, I joined Poale Zion, and took upon myself the role of secretary for a certain period. A few years prior tot he outbreak of the war, I was also appointed as the chairman of that organization.

## Hamizrachi and Tzeirei (Young) Mizrachi

When I desire to write here about the Mizrachi and Young Mizrachi organizations, I must relate it to the splendid personality, the founder and patron of the group, Reb Avraham Zauerberg of blessed memory.

I was still young when Reb Avraham Zauerberg founded the Mizrachi movement in our town. Therefore, I am not able to describe its beginnings and its activities at the time, except by describing the aforementioned Reb Avrahamtze.

I knew the man and his family, for they lived not too far from our house. He had four children, two girls and two boys. The eldest daughter, Miriam, is today in Israel with her family. We were both of the same age, and I always enjoyed talking to her. She was very bright and intelligent, similar in character to her father.

As a youth, I was always used to viewing the elder Jews as strict, prone to anger, scholarly, noisy, always arguing, and always warning us children not to disturb them. However, this was in complete opposition to the character of Reb Avrahamtze Zauerberg, whose personality exuded goodness of heart and love. He always had a light smile on his face. He had a black, well-kept beard. His large forehead, and particularly his eyes, were bright with love and friendship.

He was a scholar, and very particular with his religious observance. Along with this, he was knowledgeable in worldly affairs. He was familiar with modern Hebrew literature, and fluent in the German language. He would read German newspapers. He was pleasant in his dealings with his fellowman. He was beloved by the younger generation, and he made sure to draw them close.

His home was open wide. On Saturday nights after the Sabbath, young adults and even youths would gather in his home to play chess. His wife Tila would offer refreshments, hot tea and delicacies. He was the chairman and life force of the local Mizrachi branch.

After some years, when the branch of this organization developed well, and was recognized in the eyes of the community and its institutions, Reb Avraham founded the Young Mizrachi and Bnei Akiva[6] organizations. Reb Avraham Zauerberg was the honorary chairman of Mizrachi and Young Mizrachi until the outbreak of the final war. He was the patron of the Bnei Akiva religious youth organization. His strong love of Zion influenced all segments of the Orthodox youth.

The young man Eliezer Yitzchak Nussbaum, who was nurtured by him, was appointed by him as secretary. The writer of these lines also served as an activist in Mizrachi and its youth wing for many years. I would travel to national conventions in Lvov, and assist in the organization of hachsharah (aliya preparation) groups for pioneers (chalutzim) in the area. My desire, and the desire of all of the youth in our town, was for aliya. This was not a simple matter in those days, for it was dependent upon the receipt of permits that the Mandatory government would ration to chalutzim. Some chalutzim would wait for their turn for 3-4 years. In the interim, they would spend their time in hachsharah groups, working at all types of difficult labor. Often, the failure to receive a certificate after 4-5 years of hachsharah would cause great frustration and agony. Engaged couples who intended to get married and make aliya together would separate, for they could not wait any longer, since they did not receive their aliya certificate. Anyone who received a certificate was considered fortunate. The entire town would arrange a farewell party, and members from all of the youth groups would come to wish the person well, and accompany him to the train that set out for Stanislawow, and from their to the shores of the Land via Romania. For about an hour prior to the arrival of the train, they would sing Hebrew songs, and dance "We are making aliya to the Land, we are making aliya to the Land". This was the greatest desire of the youth of the town. Fortunate was the person who merited this.

{58}

## Achva

The Achva organization of the General Zionists was one of the most active and well-developed organizations in the town. My brother served as chairman for many years. Dr. David Weisman, Moshe Rosenberg and others played an active role, and took responsibility in various roles.

The life spirit of the Achva youth group was David Weisman.

At first, the General Zionist organization was considered as a non-partisan group, in which both Orthodox and non-Orthodox people would be able to participate together under one roof, with the common goal of Zionism before their eyes.

After the First World War, when the Zionist movement began to develop, and each organization began to work in its own sphere of influence, the General Zionists also took on their own color. They attracted for the most part merchants, officials, and the intelligentsia from among the youth. It was possible to here Polish language spoken among them, but the main language was, of course, Yiddish. Some Hebrew could also be heard.

## Bnei Akiva

The Orthodox youth in Rozniatow had already become attached to a pioneering tradition, bestowed upon them by the personality of Reb Avraham Zauerberg. His influence was recognizable in their behavior and in their studies.

Bnei Akiva conducted many cultural activities, particularly among those people that frequented the Beis Midrash. The Orthodox youth began to become attracted to new paths and principals, with a viewpoint toward the Land of Israel.

{59}

## Gordonia

This organization was founded with the goal of gathering together the youth from all strata of the Jewish community; however, it stumbled upon great difficulties that were impossible to overcome. The youths who were interested in pioneering and work in the Land of Israel streamed towards various movements, and Gordonia remained as a weak movement. In the latter period, it did not even have its own meeting hall. Their influence was not shining among the youths. Its few members participated with great dedication in all communal Zionist activities.

**Hashomer Hatzair**

Youth of Rozniatow on Hachsharah, 1936.

The branch of Hashomer Hatzair in Rozniatow serves as the expression of great hopes and deep waves of awakening amongst the Jewish youth. The vibrancy affected primarily the groups of students among the youth. Nevertheless, the youth from the populist strata of society were also accepted into the ranks of Hashomer Hatzair. The atmosphere in the group was full of longing for actualization and aliya. Its members were very active, and they excelled particularly in their ideological clarity. Political and Zionistic debates, and the ringing Hebrew and Israeli songs left their mark upon the youth. The branch also organized educational activities that educated the youth toward full actualization of the ideological and pioneering tendencies of the movement.

**TRANSLATOR'S FOOTNOTES**

1. A Biblical reference, from Jeremiah 31, to the eventual return of the Jewish people to their land. This prophetic selection is part of the Haftarah reading for the second day of Rosh Hashanah.

2. This verse is from Psalm 127. Of course, this is a manifestation of the classic debate between religious Zionism and religious anti-Zionism, a debate that is still ongoing to this day.

3. Isaiah 62, verse 1.

4. A quote from the daily Shmone Esrei prayer, requesting the return of the Divine presence to Zion.

5. Seemingly an expression for someone who is not in full control of the situation.

6. Bnei Akiva is the name, still used today, for the youth wing of Mizrachi.

{60}

## Beitar – The Revisionists

The Revisionist Movement grew and encompassed wide circles among all of the strata of youth in the town. These youths who were thirsty for new content found their place, and turned toward serious activity. Militaristic ideas and military actualization enchanted these youths. However, it would be incorrect to state that these youths were satisfied with only physical hachsharah and military training. This was a vibrant and alert movement, that attracted to it all of the youths who were not in full agreement with the Zionist establishment, and wished to see drastic changes in it. Many in the Rozniatow branch acted in the spheres of cultural and spiritual hachsharah of the youth, and in instilling Hebrew as a spoken language.

## Stam Chalutz

This was essentially an educational youth movement, connected with the Zionist movement. It educated its members towards the goals of aliya and pioneering actualization. Its goals were: the learning of the Hebrew language, collecting funds for the Zionist funds, and education toward love of the nation and the homeland. With all this, it was a left leaning youth movement, which was not content with the spirit of the ways of Poale Zion or Hitachdut. It did a great deal to raise the level of pioneering, by initiating pioneering education at a particularly young age in order to prepare groups of people whose main motive would be aliya and the building of the Land. Indeed, from among its ranks, many made aliya and became pioneers. Most of their pioneers (chalutzim) were quite capable.

The founders and activists of this pioneering movement were David Rubinfeld Nussbaum, Mordechai Trau, Yehuda Tzvi Stern, Mordechai (Moti) Hoffman, and Izak Barnik.

## "The Casino"

In Rozniatow, there was another "casino" were people would gather to read a book or a newspaper, to play chess, or to converse among friends, without any political motives or Zionistic aims.

There was also a workers' organization where the workers would gather in the evenings to deal with their matters. There was also a merchants' organization and a troupe of actors – a drama group that conducted fine activities and performed various plays.

These were the official organizations of the adults and the youth, whose influence was recognizable, some greater and some less, in the communal life of Rozniatow.

There was one other unofficial youth organization, the Communists. They did not have their own hall, but they conducted a reasonable level of activity underground, as the government persecuted them and made things difficult for them. Many of their members were imprisoned, especially on days that were set aside for demonstrations or strikes.

{61}

The Trumpeldor Covenant Organization. First row, from left: Dvora Hoffnung, Rachel Barnik, Chaim Frisch's daughter, and Beiltsha Kassner

Trumpeldor Covenant in 1933.
First row on left: Yeshayahu Axelrad. Second row on left: Yosef Shapira.

{62}

# The Hebrew Library

## by Avraham Friedler-Scharf

A class in the national school of Rozniatow, 1938.

With the outbreak of the First World War, the Hebrew school that had existed in our town for many years closed down. At the conclusion of the war, when the Polish regime became established in our area, and with the return of life to its normal courses, the Hebrew school reopened. It was Moshe Barnik of blessed memory who took it upon himself to teach. He taught with the Sephardic pronunciation rather than the Ashkenazic pronunciation that had been the norm until that time.

His labors were successful, but he was only there for a short period, since he left our town and moved to Lvov, where he had a wider field of activity.

However, there is always someone available within the Jewish people, and Tzvi Fassberg, who is now with us in Israel, took over the scepter of teaching, and performed his duties faithfully and with great success.

It is my duty to point out with gratitude his dedication and enthusiasm to the imparting of the Hebrew language to all that were in need, even outside the confines of the school. I merited to be among those who had rights of access to his room next to the school hall, in order to read the books that were in his possession, and in order to receive from him explanations and pointers regarding matters of difficulty with the books.

Lag Baomer festivities in the Tarbut school, 1936.

The dearth of books for reading did not give us rest, and we were perplexed as to how to overcome the situation, and to establish a Hebrew library of significant size. We hit upon the idea of a "ribbon day" in the cattle market that took place in the Targowica area; that is to collect money by attaching ribbons to the lapels of the clothes. This task fell upon Yehuda Axelrad (Hamerman), who today lives in the United States, and myself. We went out to our activity with feelings of doubt. With the money we collected, we managed to purchase books that formed the basis of a Hebrew library, and gave us the possibility – albeit restricted – to obtain Hebrew books in return for minimal membership fees.

A lull took place in our efforts to search for ways to expand the library, for Mr. Fassberg left our town in the meantime. We awaited the next person.

Then, a Lithuanian teacher by the name of Reines came to our town, and speedily enriched our lives. When he found out that the existing library did not have the capability of providing for all its needs, he came upon the idea of presenting a Hebrew play, the income of which would be dedicated to the library.

This matter was deliberated upon also by the school committee, which was headed by Mr. Yossi Rosenberg. They decided definitively in favor.

The play that was chosen was "Jacob and Esau". After many rehearsals, the preparations for the performance began. The date was set for a specific day in the winter of 1921-2, in the hall of Sender Friedler. The preparations included the printing of placards, the assignment of places, etc. The sale of tickets also began. The crowd was greater than estimated, and with all of the preparations, one very elementary fact was overlooked: that the number of seats in the hall was limited. Tickets had been sold to anyone who desired.

The Hebrew School, 1922.

When the performance began, the hall was filled to the brim, and the crowding was great. Calls were suddenly heard from the hall: Stop the performance... Danger!"

Without any other choice, the performance was stopped. An announcement was made to the audience that the next day, there would be two performances, the first for the youth and children, and the second for the adults. Of course, some people who had not purchased tickets showed up at the performances.

The success was beyond what we imagined. Numerous books were purchased, and the library grew and expanded.

After a period of time, the school closed due to dearth of means. The library continued to operate; however there were fears for its fate, since we knew that its means were limited, even for the purposes of paying rent. Therefore, we brainstormed for ideas of how to save the library. How? We entered the library, Shimshon Rechtschaffen, Leib Meisels, and myself – and we removed the collection of books by hand, and stored them at Leib Meisels' house.

After some time, when Leib Meisels had to move to Lvov to study in university, it was decided to transfer the books to the general library in the home of Leibchi Yakel. These books became part of that library.

This was the history of the Hebrew library.

{65}

# Reb Bendet Elimelech Halevi Gross –
# "Hamevaser Zion" of Rozniatow

## by Y. Har-Zohar[1]

The first founders and leaders of the Chovevei Zion movement[2] were Russian rabbis and Jewish activists such as Rabbi Sh. Mohilever, Rabbi Alkalai, and Rabbi Kalisher, etc. The masses of people in eastern Galicia were still immersed in their traditional world. Here and there, some enlightened people would appear who were taken by an awakening for a return to Zion. One of these people who forged the path and acted "for the revival of the hearts of the children of Israel, and the awakening of the hearts of the sleepers who are scattered in the four corners of the earth towards settlement in our Holy Land", was the Hassidic Jew, the well-known scholar of Torah and wisdom, Reb Bendet Elimelech Gross of Rozniatow.

Reb Bendet Elimelech received great encouragement from the Chovevei Zion of Galicia, and in response to a special request from the chairman of the central Ahavat Zion organization in Tarnow, Dr. Avraham Zaltz, he authored an explanatory pamphlet about the Chovevei Zion idea, and the idea of physical settlement in the Land of Israel, for in the bible it is first hinted that the land would be settled naturally, and then the Son of David[3] would appear, and the redeemer will come unto Zion.

He wrote a pamphlet entitled "Kol Mevaser VeTorat Emet"[4]. This was published in the year 5658 (1898) in Drohowice (Eastern Galicia). In it, he describes in clear language and ornate Hebrew the idea of the return to Zion, the settlement of the Land, and the working and protecting of the Land. An approbation by Rabbi Feivel Halevi Shreier, the Rabbi of Bohorodczany, is attached to the pamphlet. This work made a great impact on observant Jewry, particularly on the Hassidim of Galicia. This pamphlet reached Dr. Herzl, and when the content and style was explained to him, he praised it greatly, and considered it to be a work of great value on behalf of observant Jewry.

"Ahavat Zion or Chovevei Zion are necessities of life, and everyone in whose heart was implanted the fear of G-d is duty bound to support this holy organization with all his heart and resources – this was the beginning of the raising of the horn of the Children of Israel, and this is the beginning of the redemption." (Kol Mevaser, page 5).

The second edition of this pamphlet appeared one year later, in 5659, in the year "Vehavieini Lezion Bekol Rina"[5].

Reb Elimelech Gross, as a scholarly Jew, used to express his ideas with verses and innuendoes from the Torah and the works of our sages.

Regarding the verse "G-d is the builder of Jerusalem, He will gather together the exiles of the Jewish people, He is the healer of broken hearts, and He bandages their hurts"[6], he would explain in accordance with his manner and his thoughts: "G-d is the builder of Jerusalem" – this is the fundamental Divine promise to physically establish Jerusalem; "He will gather together the exiles of the Jewish people" – this is a sign that when the rebuilding of Jerusalem begins, the exiles will be ingathered; "He is the healer of broken hearts" – he will heal every wound of the Jewish people, and our righteous Messiah will come; "He bandages their hurts" – this is a hint to the resurrection of the dead.[7]

Reb Elimelech did not think at all that his end would come and he would go along the route of all living people. He waited at all moments for the coming of our righteous Messiah, and he was convinced that the resurrection of the dead would immediately follow thereafter, and that those alive at the time would not die. He was convinced that the idea of Chovevei Zion and the physical settlement of the Holy Land to "work it and protect it"[8] was the actual beginning of the redemption.

Despite the fact that he was a scholarly Jew, he kept a distance from the rabbinate, and he earned his livelihood from the tavern that he owned in the center of town. His son inherited it, and it existed until the destruction of the town. His home was known as the "Well Established House of Gross" ("Gross Moier").

A square for the wagon drivers, opposite the house of Chanina Weissman. On the right is Gross' house.

## TRANSLATOR'S FOOTNOTES

1. Hamevaser Zion means the "Herald of Zion", an expression taken from the book of Isaiah.

2. The "Lovers of Zion", a movement of reawakening of Jewish interest in the Land of Israel that predated the formal founding of the Zionist movement.
3. The Messiah.

4. The Voice of the Herald and the True Torah. The "Voice of the Herald" is taken from the liturgy of Hoshanah Rabbah (the seventh day of Sukkot), where there is a liturgical poem "Kol Mevaser" describing events heralding the coming of the Messiah and the deliverance of the Jewish people from exile.

5. The verse quoted here is "And he will bring me to Zion with the sounds of joy". It is the custom in ornate religious literary style to use the numerology of various verses of the bible in reference to a given year to express the theme of a work.

6. From Psalm 147, included in the daily morning service.

7. According to Jewish tradition, the resurrection of the dead is a later stage of the redemption, following the coming of the Messiah and the physical restoration of the Jewish people in the Land of Israel.

8. A reference to the Garden of Eden, in which Adam was placed "To work it and protect it".

{67}

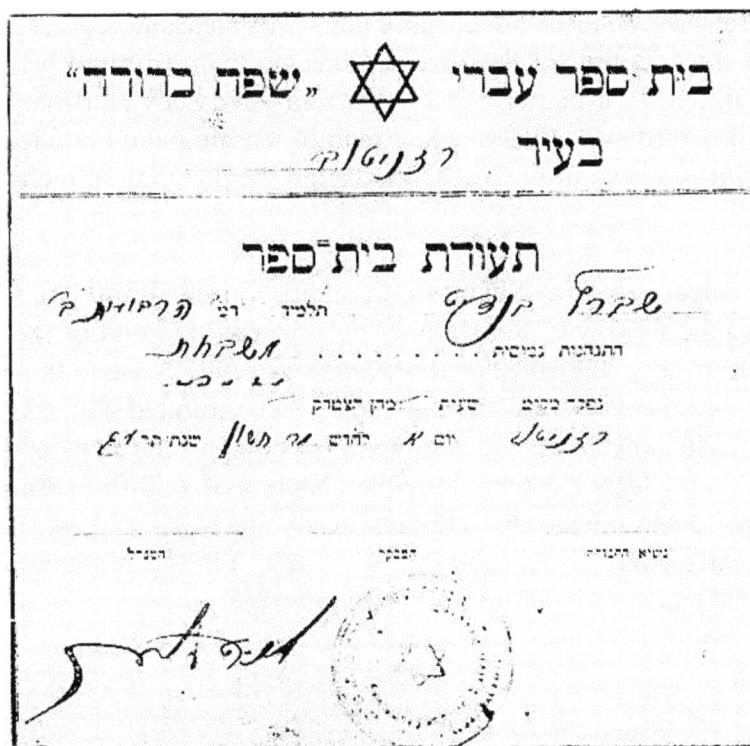

no caption ˆ a report card from the "Safah Berurah" Hebrew school of Rozniatow. The student's name is Bendet Schwarz, a student in the fourth grade in 5673 ˆ 1912). His behavior is excellent, and he was never absent.

{68}

Educate a child in accordance with his way, even when he gets old he will not depart from it (Proverbs)

{69}

# Jewish Education

### And Let Your Eyes Behold Your Teacher[1]
### My Teachers and Educators
### by Ben-David Schwartz

As Rava said: A person does not understand the opinions of his teacher until after forty years... Talmud, Sanhedrin 109.

With reverent trepidation, I lift up the writer's pen to express my feelings of gratitude to Rozniatow in general, and specifically, my feelings of gratitude to all of my teachers and mentors, who influenced me from the wellsprings of their wisdom, thought, and knowledge.

In those days, as Kaiser Franz Josef I sat on the throne of the Hapsburg Monarchy, which was called at that time Austria-Hungary, and ruled over more than ten states and peoples, the Jews of Rozniatow dwelt without fear of the gentiles, for the Kaiser protected them from all bad occurrences. The Jew haters were not so brazen as to lift a head or a hand. Reb Veve Zeev Hoffman, a Jew with a splendid visage, whose beard flowed down to his cloak, a man of learning and knowledge, was chosen or appointed by the authorities as head of the town, and he led the population, including the gentiles, in an agreeable manner.

In those days, Reb Kopel served as Shamash. In addition to his important task as the Shamash of the Kloiz, he was also the "waker of the slumbering". Toward the end of the night, when all of the townsfolk were in a deep sleep, the voice of Reb Kopel rang out "Arise to the worship of the Creator, for it was for that purpose that you were created". In a voice saturated with tragic anguish in the spirit of "the Divine Presence in exile"[2] , he knocked upon the doors of the Jews with his mallet, and woke them up, some for Tikkun Chatzot[3], others to recite chapters of Tehillim (Psalms), and still others to study a page of Talmud. I and a few other children of my age (10 – 12 years old) were accompanied by Reb Kopel in the early hours of the morning (4 – 5 a. m.) in the summer and in the winter to the cheder of my Rebbi and teacher.

## Reb Yitzchak Branik

I attended the cheders of and drunk from the wellsprings of many teachers, such as Reb Yudele, Alter Meir, Reb Eliezer K. Moshes, and others. However the cheder of Reb Yitzchak Branik is guarded in my mind in a positive light until this day, in accordance with the words of Rav Yannai, "Anyone who studies Torah from one Rebbi only will never see a sign of blessing. Rav Chisda states in the name of

Rabba that he responded to him (i.e. Rav Yannai) – those words apply to logic in general, but Talmud is best studied from one Rebbi." (Talmud, Tractate Avoda Zara 19a).

Reb Yitzchak Branik, who was an expert scholar, came to Rozniatow from the city of Kalusz, which was famous for mighty Torah students and scholars. Many Torah giants found it to be a pleasant place to live. When Reb Yitzchak lost his livelihood, he made use of Torah to earn a livelihood.

He had two children[4]. Yehuda, whose son Aryeh Leib lived and worked with us here, and died an untimely death only a few months ago. He had a daughter Matel who is in America, and Dina who died. There was also Moshe who served as a Hebrew teacher in several places around Rozniatow and later was drafted into the army. When he returned home in one piece after the war, he married Sarache, the daughter of Reb Yitzchak Rosenbaum. They then moved to Lvov where they led the Tarbut organization. They made aliya during the 1930s, and he died in 1940 while still in his prime.

Reb Yitzchak Branik opened up the treasuries of Torah for me. He taught me Talmud in depth, as well as the laws of meat and milk and the salting of meat from Yoreh Deah[5]. On Thursday nights, he taught the weekly Torah portion along with the commentary of the Or Hachayim and others. These childhood teachings accompany me to this day. I am deeply grateful that I merited to pour water on his hands[6].

## Reb Yitzchak Hertzberg

I studied not only Hebrew and grammar with the teacher Hertzberg, but also bible and Jewish history. In the higher grades, I studied Ein Yaakov[7]. His biblical lectures on chapters of Isaiah and Jeremiah were quite beloved by the students. All of his commentaries and explanations on various sentences, words or events are still with us to this day.

I merited to receive from him while still in Rozniatow, and later when he visited Pressburg[8] some of his poems upon current events, which were dedicated to me as an excellent student. We renewed our connection in the Land, and he would often visit me in my office for pleasant discussions on various matters regarding the good days in Rozniatow.

His memory and his blessed Torah are kept by me to this day.

May the memory of all of these be guarded by me with blessing and gratitude.

## Reb Yehoshua Reiter

Apparently, he was the first Hebrew teacher who used the "Safa Berurah" (Clear Language) manuals. He died after a drawn out illness (tuberculosis). I studied with him for only a brief period of time when I was eight or nine years old. His image is guarded in my memory. His face resembled that of Eliezer Ben Yehuda[9]. In praise of Rozniatow, let me state here that the mantle of Torah for its own sake, and the spreading of Torah, served as a candle at its feet[10], and that already by the beginning of the current century (20 th century), a Hebrew school existed.

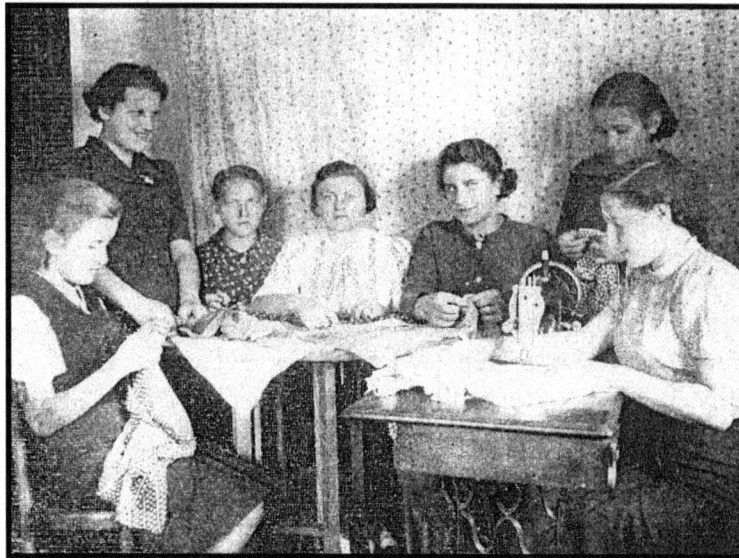

From right to left: Dvora Brand, Miriam Heisler-Yungerman, Rotenberg, Gitla-Tova Friedler, Yehudit Friedman (Heisler-Yungerman).

## Dr. Lipa Leopold Adlersberg

He served in Rozniatow as a teacher of religion in the public school. He was also my teacher for German language and grammar, as well as math, both before he became blind and after. He lived in our neighborhood, and therefore it was easy for me to be assisted by him when I had difficulty in preparing my lessons. I enjoyed his style of teaching very much. From his style I learned that only a superior pedagogue can impart a style of learning to his students that is most important. That style is, reading, being exacting in the reading, for it is Torah and one must study it[11]. This I learned from Dr. Adlersberg. Until this day, when I read a book or article in depth, the image of this person passes before me. With his sharp pencil, as if he was "passing a quill" across the printed lines, he organized the proper divisions and notations, and therefore exposed the secrets inherent in the reading matter. I should mention here that when I was twelve or thirteen years old, I read "Nathan the Wise" by Lessing with his assistance.

{Photo page 72: Exact same photo as page 71, with exact same caption. Must have been duplicated in error.}

{73}

# Reb Yechiel Mechel Faasberg

## by Tzvi Faasberg

If one finds the lost object of his father or that of his teacher
The lost object of his teacher takes precedence,
For his father brings him into this world
While his teacher, who teaches him Torah
Brings him to the life of the world to come.
(Mishna Baba Metzia 33a)

My teacher and Rebbi[12] Reb Yechiel Mechel the son of Reb Yaakov Faasberg of blessed memory was born in the city of Bolekhov in 1876. His grandfather was Reb Shimshon Faasberg, a rabbi in Zworno, and, as I have been told, he was also an Admor. During his youth, he studied Talmud, its commentaries, and Jewish law, and he was also familiar with bible and its commentaries. He was particularly familiar with the commentaries of Rashi, Ibn Ezra, Sforno and Or Hachayim[13]. He also studied works of investigation, and his books included: Moreh Nevuchim, Chovat Halevavot, Ben Hamelech Vehanazir, etc.[14].

My father married my mother Leah Miriam, the daughter of Reb Shimon Fishbein the Cohen, and settled in the village of Holyn near Kalusz. He occupied himself with teaching in Holyn. He excelled in his clear thinking and straightforward logic, and he influenced his students greatly. They honored and loved him deeply. He taught not only holy subjects, but also secular subjects, such as German, Polish, math, as well as German grammar. I learned whatever meager foundations of knowledge I possess from him.

He would arise early in the morning during the winter, and until this day, I can hear the melodic sound of his Talmud studying ringing in my ears. He did not become greatly involved in communal affairs, and he never served as a gabbai. However, on Rosh Hashanah, he did blow the shofar. For him, shofar blowing was an art and a skill, not a labor.

He fled with his family to Rozniatow at the outbreak of the war in 1914. I was not home at that time. I was in Russia, and I spent approximately two years in Tarnopol after that. In the meantime, he was drafted into the army until the end of the First World War. After the war, he settled in Krechowice in the Dolina region.

I parted from him in 1936 and made aliya to the Land. As they tell me, he was murdered on the 22 nd of Elul, 1942.

My parents had two sons and four children until the time that Hitler came and murdered them all. Only I remain alive.

Up until this point were the words of the son Tzvi, who, for obvious reasons, was meager in the praises of his father, following the adage: "teach but leave something over". However, I permit myself to add the feelings of my heart, and I trust that I will not violate the adage "Whomever adds, detracts".

I merited knowing Reb Mechel Faasberg and his family, especially the sons Itzi and Hershel[15], when I was still a lad and I used to visit my grandparents Reb Leib Yosef and Perl Kenigsberg in Holyn. I do not exaggerate when I say that a warm charm and smile always graced the face of Reb Mechel. The pleasantness of his ways and soft words with his fellowman were those of a great man. These attracted me to him the entire time that I was there. He had a splendid visage, which radiated light and goodness of heart. Even though more than fifty years have passed since I have seen him, his appearance and warm eyes are still before my eyes, and I can still feel his loving caresses upon my cheeks.

Woe for those who were lost, and are not forgotten.

**B. D. Schwartz**

{74}

# Youth of Rozniatow

### by Y. Neubauer

The first night of Selichot[16] was, for the children, like the night before army induction for adults. On that night, the children of ages 12-15 exacted their debts from all those who oppressed them throughout the year.

Here are a few of their pranks:

**The Goats of Shlomo Teitelbaum**

In 1934, Reb Shlomo Teitelbaum was chosen as the gabbai in the Kloiz, and he guarded that holy place. The children suffered particularly from him. He did not permit us to speak out loud, even when it was not during the time of prayers. He did not permit us to crack open seeds. He did not permit us to play in the sukka that was build next to the synagogue, etc. All of the children of the town gathered together, including the writer of these lines, and decided to punish him once and for all, and we decided to carry out the punishment. One of the punishment brigade was Shimshon Gross, the son of Mordechai who owned a hotel and a wedding hall. The night of Selichot arrived. We broke into the pen, tied the mouths of the goats so they would not be able to make a sound, brought them up to the third floor, and tied them to the porch.

The next morning when Shlomo went out from the morning prayers to milk the goats, it was as if the earth swallowed them up... Due to his great despair he decided to alert the police. When he left the police station he noticed that there was a crowd of people near Gross' house, who were laughing out loud. He approached, and what did he see? – His goats standing on the porch, tied to the railing.

He immediately realized that the children had a hand in this, and from that time on, there was peace between us.

## The Revenge

When Rabbi Yosef Metzner came to deliver a lecture prior to his being appointed as the rabbi of the city, he had, as is well-known, many opponents who interrupted him during his speech. Reb Zecharia David Liberman attempted to silence the disturbers with all his might, but his efforts were in vain. Due to his great anger, he decided to take revenge on the children whom, for some reason, he saw as disturbers. He approached Yaakov, the son of Reb Yosef Shimon Stern, a lad of fourteen, and gave him a sharp slap on the cheek. Of course, the adults did not accept this silently, and they had a heated argument about the matter. The children also decided to take revenge on the honor of their friend.

On the first night of Selichot, the group purchased a large pail of whitewash from Reb Mordechai Tisch. On the preceding Friday, they had prepared a box of black paint. The son of Leizer Ber Klinger provided two brushes, and everyone got to work. We painted all of the lamps in the synagogue with white plaster, and marked them with a black cross. It is difficult to describe the effect and laughter that this incident had on the town. However Reb Zecharia David learned his lesson, and was very careful never to touch the children.

## The Innuendo

When the children made peace with Reb Shlomo Teitelbaum and thought that they could have a bit of fun, Reb Moshe Friedler suddenly arose to pass judgement upon the children. He warned one of them, pinched another, and even administered a beating with his cane. Once again, the punishment brigade rose to action. Of course, we did not want to inflict great damage, since we knew of his difficult livelihood. We decided to take revenge on him in a different manner. We took three tins of the well-known "Ardal" shoe polish, whose insignia was a frog. One Friday as evening approached, we glued one of them to his seat in the synagogue, and two others to his shtender[17]. When all of the worshippers entered for the welcoming of the Sabbath, they saw the signs, and he also took the innuendo and recognized that the hands of the children were involved.

From that time, peace prevailed on all fronts.

# The Teachers in our City

## by Y. Rechtschaffen

The meaning of the word "melamdim" is teachers who taught children and youth to read the Siddur and Chumash, to understand the meaning of the words, and to study Torah and commentaries. There were several types of these melamdim. There were the teachers of young children, that is to say the teachers who taught the children from the age of three until they began studying Talmud. The second type was the teachers of Talmud. A third type was "the reciters of pages of Talmud), who would explain the specific Talmudic section in depth, turning it upon all its sides, breaking it apart and again reconstructing it. This was called "sharpening the mind". For the most part, none of these teachers had any professional accreditation. They never completed any teaching school. Everything depended on the specific skill of the individual teacher. There were teachers who were naturally blessed with teaching ability.

The cheder was one of the rooms in the home of the melamed. These homes were for the most part either two rooms, or just one room and a kitchen. In that room, there was a long table with one or two freestanding benches. The lessons continued without a break from the morning hours until noon, and from noon until evening.

There were several melamdim of the various types in Rozniatow. I will begin with the teachers of small children, those who taught the reading of the aleph beit. It is told that the Tzadik who was the founder of the Ryzin dynasty, Reb Yisrael, who had many scholars among his Hassidim, used to seat the teachers of young children at the head of the table. He would say: "Indeed, I know that the teachers of Talmud are good scholars and used to teach me the understanding of the page of Talmud and the interpretation of the words, but it was the teacher of young children who taught me the aleph beit who set me on the course to success, with the help of G-d. Therefore, I must honor him first.

Reb David the Melamed

His cheder was in the center of town. He had only two rooms. The large room contained the cheder, and the family lived in the second, smaller room, which included the kitchen. He would warn children who did not want to listen and learn that he would place them in "his nest" in the second room, which was somewhat dark. This was some sort of restraint or other punishment, and nobody understood the meaning of it. Nobody was actually punished with this, for they took heed of the warning about the punishment of being placed in "the nest".

Reb David the Melamed was, in his younger days, a handsome man with an impressive black beard, a straight posture and a pleasant person. Even in his latter years, in his old age, one could still recognize the remnants of his impressiveness. There was always the aura of grace upon his pleasant face. He would explain to young students all sorts of pleasant stories. The students would willingly sit around the table and listen attentively to his words.

## The Melamed Reb Abba

Reb Abba

A sense of duty to his work, and a sense of honor regarding the seriousness of the task – these were the characteristics of the cheder of Reb Abba the Melamed, and these symbolized the stature of Jewish education in our town.

Reb Abba Taneh and his wife Talchi lived close to our house. Reb Abba used to speak to the children in their own language, the language of children. He had a true sense of what it means to be an educator, despite that he was not a trained pedagogue. He would play games with them. He was beloved by the students of the cheder. He had two children, a daughter named Yuta, and a son named Leibish who lives today in Israel.

## Reb Chaim Shimon Lutwak

He was one of the more modern teachers. People would study bible with him, and this was an innovation among the teachers[18]. He was an enlightened teacher, and his students were more familiar with chapters of bible than pages of Talmud. He also educated his own children in this spirit. His children studied in the gymnasia. His oldest son Moshe, who today lives in the United States, studied law and is today a lawyer. His second son Yeshaya is a dentist. He passed through the flames of hell during the Holocaust at the time of Hitler, and after much tribulation, he succeeded in reaching the United States and joining his brother Moshe.

## Reb Yehuda Branik the Melamed

I only knew him after he left the profession of teaching, and only the name stuck with him.

During my time, he served in a sacred role in the Great Synagogue. He was in charge of the charitable coffers for the poor who would gather in Rozniatow to collect donations from generous people. It was a custom in our town that the person appointed over the charity would give a note to the charitable overseer, Reb Yehuda Branik, to give a certain sum of money to so and so. It was forbidden for the poor people to go to the doors of people in town to collect charity. They would receive their allotment, each according to his honor and value, directly from the charitable overseer.

Reb Yehuda Branik lived near the communal building in a small house with his three daughters Matil, Dina and Rachel, and his three sons David, Leib and Izak. I used to visit that house. I was friendly with his children, especially Izak, who was my good friend.

Izak participated in all types of monthly literary journals.

Other friends of mine were Mendel Horowitz and also Pesachia Turteltaub, educated children who knew how to recite entire chapters of bible off by heart. They also read Hebrew newspapers and knew how to use the Hebrew language, both in its written and oral form. They were also knowledgeable in world literature. I was the youngest of this group. I learned a great deal from them, and everything that I know, I learned from them.

### Reb Yehudale Kaufman (Kneiper)[19]

They called him by this nickname "the pincher" for, despite the fact that he was short and thin, and that he had a large class of children in the cheder, both old and young, he knew how to instill his fear upon everyone. Woe to the child who would come late to cheder, or who would not listen to the reading of the Siddur or Chumash. He would immediately approach such a child, give him a pinch, smack him on the face, and shout and scream at him. He would thereby instill his fear upon everyone. His wife would often get involved in order to rescue the child from his beatings.

Even though he was prone to anger and shouting, he was a righteous Jew, ready to give himself over to anyone who had a desire to learn, without concern for time. He would agree to teach anyone Torah.

However, the students would search for means to escape from the studies. One night, someone started to cough suddenly, as a sign for a general coughing attack. Everyone coughed until the lantern on the table went out. Then all of the students rose from their places in the dark and fled from the room.

Echoes of this revolt spread quickly through all of the residents of the town, and it became the talk of the day. The melamed later felt very badly about the situation, and began a new method of teaching. He chose about seven or eight excellent students, with good memories from among all of his students. He would then read them the Torah portion with Rashi's commentary. Then, each student would teach a group of six or seven other students. Thus, by the time the Sabbath came, the student guides knew the weekly portion almost by heart, and the other students also knew the portion, for the learning from the other students without fear was better and more effective. On the Sabbath, there would be an examination.

On Friday, there would only be studies for one half of the day. At that time, the Rebbi would be calmer, quieter, and not as exacting as he was on the other days of the week. We would sit in the cheder and study the "chapter" of the week[20], and the Torah portion of the following week. Once in a while, he would take out a book of moral ethics (Mussar) and read to us about how to conduct ourselves in the world that is full of falsehood and hypocrisy, and how to watch out for the evil inclination that is always trying to remove us from the straight path. He would also read us about the Garden of Eden and Gehinnom (Hell), until he would come to the topic of repentance.

The topic of repentance was the most interesting subject to our teacher. He truly intended everything for the sake of Heaven, and talked from his heart. Despite the fact that all of the students had received at times from him severe beatings, pinches and curses, they never forgot his Torah. What he instilled in us during our youth is still guarded very well in our memory until this day. His hundreds of students still remember the melamed Reb Yudale Kneiper with love and respect all the days of their lives.

He had a son Meir Kaufman who got married and had sons and daughters.

## Reb Moshe Weinrob

He was the Gemara (Talmud) teacher to the more advanced students, over the age of Bar Mitzvah (13), at a time when they were already responsible themselves before G-d and man.

He was a great scholar. His teaching methodologies were completely opposite to those of Reb Yudale. His speech was quiet and calm. His thorough explanations were understood by everyone. Complex Talmudic passages became clearer, as oil spread upon bones...

I never saw him with an angry face. He always explained things to his students in a pleasant manner, and he could take pride in his students: everything that is placed is absorbed in the brain.

His wife Chanchi Perl helped him earn his meager livelihood by selling groceries and bread, as the Rebbi Reb Moshe taught his students in their home.

There were also some external teachers in town, that is to say, who were not local. They came to town to teach, and then returned to their places. It is fitting to make mention of them here, for they also contributed to the raising of the horn of Torah in our town. Everyone taught according to his methodology and ability.

All of them together should be remembered positively, for they came too study and teach the words of His Torah with love and awe.

{80}

# Educational Institutes

### by Y. Friedler

## The Cheder

Rozniatow was blessed with melamdim who came from various circles and walks of life. These included scholars and enlightened people (maskilim), people of fine character and manners, who gained the trust of their students through their pleasant mannerism; as well as others who did not hesitate to punish the "wrongdoers". Each melamed had his own cheder. During the summer, the studies went from 8:00 a.m. until dark, and in the winter until 8:00 p.m. There would be a one-hour break for lunch.

In the cheder, the following subjects were taught: prayer, Chumash and Rashi, bible, rudimentary Gemara, penmanship and arithmetic. The long hours of study did not have a bad influence on the students, and did not make them bored. The cheder was not only a study hall, but also literally an educational institution. The students invented many games and means of having fun. Every student gave of his talents to his friends, whether in jesting, imitating adults, or in other manners. Games that were fitting to the time of year helped lighten up the seriousness, and enriched the lives of the students. These games include buttons, nuts, etc.

## The Talmud Torah

In the year 5680 (1920), the Talmud Torah was founded in Rozniatow. It was overseen by a committee that consisted of important residents of the city, including: Reb Yitzchak Leib, Reb Mordechai Geller, Veve Hoffman, and Reb Yisrael Tzvi Londner. The shochet (ritual slaughterer) Reb Moshe Weiser, a person who inspired honor, would examine the children at the end of the term. Exams in Gemara, Chumash and Rashi would take place semi-annually. The principal and head of the Yeshiva was Rabbi Yisrael Heller of Dolina. Everyone worked diligently to establish and maintain this institution. This labor was carried out without anticipation of a reward.

In general, the students were busy for many consecutive hours with their studies. The students were required to learn entire chapters by heart. They studied Talmud with the commentaries of Tosafot and the Maharshah in the higher grades. The students left the school well fortified with knowledge of Talmud and other holy subjects.

Students learned to read and write in Hebrew in the Safa Berurah School.

## Safa Berurah[21]

The teacher Tzvi Faasberg, who is with us in Israel, taught Hebrew, grammar, and penmanship. His lessons caught the interest of the students, and they listened attentively and quietly. He was beloved by his students, for he knew no anger and bitterness. His words were always issued peacefully. His greatest concern was the progress of his students. This school was unique in the community, and students of the Talmud Torah also studied there.

Prior to Mr. Faasberg, Yitzchak Hertzberg was the teacher, and prior to Yitzchak Hertzberg was Yehoshua Reiter. The latter was a noble person, who knew how to transmit the Hebrew language with love.

A report of promotion from the Talmud Torah of Rozniatow.
The student's name is Yisrael Friedler, the author of the above article

## TRANSLATOR'S FOOTNOTES

1. A quote from the book of Isaiah.

2. It is said that when the Jewish people went into exile, the Divine Presence (Shechina) also went into exile, and suffers along with the Jewish people.

3. Tikkun Chatzot (literally: the midnight rectification), is a series of prayers and elegies recited in the middle of the night lamenting the destruction of the temple, and praying for the restoration of the Jewish people. This set of prayers is not obligatory, and is generally recited only by extraordinarily pious individuals.

4. There are more than two children listed here. It seems as if there are four. This paragraph is quite unclear. It is possible that some are grandchildren.

5. Yoreh Deah is one of the four segments of the Code of Jewish Law. Among other things, it deals with the laws of kashruth, including the prohibition of mixing milk and meat, and the requirement to salt meat after slaughter to insure that the blood is properly drained.

6. An expression meant to indicate closeness between a teacher and disciple.

7. A compilation of the legendary (as opposed to legalistic) segments of the Talmud.

8. Now Bratislava.

9. A famous Hebraist, regarded as the founder of Modern Hebrew.

10. An expression indicating that Torah was disseminated in quite a fine fashion in the city.

11. This is a Talmudic adage indicating the necessity of studying a matter for the sake of the study. It does not refer specifically to Torah.

12. According to this chapter, also his father.

13. These are various well-known bible commentators of the Middle Ages.

14. Moreh Nevuchim is Maimonides' philosophical work – the Guide of the Perplexed. Chovot Ha-levavot is an important medieval work on Jewish thought by Bachia Ibn Paquda.

15. Hershel is the Yiddish form of Tzvi.

16. Selichot is the penitential service that takes place daily starting from one week before Rosh Ha-shanah until Yom Kippur. The first Selichot service takes place around midnight on the Saturday night preceding Rosh Hashanah, or one week earlier if Rosh Hashanah falls early in the week.

17. The bookstand upon which the prayer book rests during services.

18. Generally in a traditional cheder, the study of the prophets and writings (as opposed to the five books of the Torah itself), was down played. There are many historical causes to this, one of them being a reaction to the Haskalah movement, which stressed the study of the bible, as opposed to Jewish law and Talmud.

19. The pincher.

20. Most likely referring to the chapter from "Pirke Avot" (The Chapters of the Fathers – often known as The Ethics of the Fathers). This is a Mishnaic tractate dealing with moral adages. It consists of six chapters, and one chapter is studied each week during the summer months between Passover and Rosh Hashanah. The cycle of six chapters is repeated several times during the summer.

21. Literally "clear language".

{82}

## Events in the Public School of Rozniatow from 1937-1940

### by Sima Letichovski (nee Weissman)

Rozniatow is the name of my small native town. It is located in the eastern Carpathian Mountains, surrounded on two sides by abundantly flowing rivers. On the right flows the Czeczwa River and on the left, the Duba River. The source of their waters is the springs that emerge from the Carpathian Mountains, which are covered with tall evergreen trees. White snow would glisten on them during the winter; and in the spring and summer, everyone could experience their pleasant greenness, their fresh air, and the abundance of mushrooms and red and purple berries that were the source of livelihood for those who gathered them.

There was a pond in the center of town, from which flowed a stream that drove the giant wheel of the flour mill.

The Jews of the city were proud of the beauty of the stream ("teich"), which relieved the heat of the summer air. In the winter, the youths and children would skate upon it with homemade skates. Not infrequently, one would return from this sport with an injured foot or a broken bone. Among those injured was my brother Aharon of blessed memory.

A fence surrounded the pond, and a paved sidewalk went the length of it. During evenings, when the weather was pleasant, many young couples strolled in this area, as did single people who set up a date with their sweethearts.

A hill rose from the pond, which was called the "barg" by the residents of the town. There were groves and rows of trees upon the hill. Benches were laid out along the length of the rows, where hikers could rest. On Sabbaths, people would climb the hill with their families, spread a blanket upon the aromatic grass, and enjoy the sweet air. They would hike among the groves and rest on the benches that were along the walkway. On occasion, the evil jail guard would disturb the rest of the Jews. He would chase them away for having trampled upon the grass that was designated for the grazing of his cows.

There were two large stone buildings at the summit of the hill. There was the jail; atop of which was the courthouse. This was a large, imposing building. To the joy of the Jewish community, Jews were only imprisoned there on very rare occasions.

Not too far from the courthouse was the largest and most splendid building of the town, which served as the public elementary school. All of the children of the town between the ages of seven and fifteen studied there. The students came from all segments of the town's population: Jews, Poles, and Ukrainians.

The language of instruction was Polish. All of the subjects were taught in Polish. The teachers were Christian Poles. Only one teacher was Ukrainian, and one other teacher was a Jewess who taught Judaism in the Polish language. This was the manner in which the Polish authorities expressed their democratic tolerance. The Jewish children were permitted to study books that were translated and anthologized from the bible for one hour a week. This did not enable them to gain an appreciation of bible. This was the only hour when the Jews did not sit together with the Poles and Ukrainians, and when they did not suffer from beatings and insults. In this public school, the Jewish students suffered from overt anti-Semitism at the hands of the teachers. They expressed their live hatred with blows on the back, or slaps with rulers on the tender hands of the Jewish children. The well-to-do people purchased good relationships for their children by means of gifts. The children of the poorer families could not do this, and therefore, the anti-Semitic teachers took out their wrath on the backs and hands of the poorer Jews, despite the fact that they were the most successful students in the school.

To their good fortune, these students were not isolated. Jews made up 50% or more of almost every class. The remainder were Polish and Ukrainian children. The mothers of the Jewish children knew the tribulations that their children were suffering from, and waited on their porches for their return. They greeted their children with a motherly smile and with love. Often, when the Jewish children return home, they would ask about the reason for the beatings and hatred. The parents would often avoid the subject, and would sometimes simply answer: "because you are a Jew".

There were parents who explained to their children the reason behind the Jew hatred, and imparted to them feelings of pride for their people and religion. These children grew up proud, and accepted their beatings with a calm spirit, as if to say: "you are not the beaters but rather the beaten".

I myself learned about and suffered from the poor relations and injustice toward the Jews. Thanks to my Zionist parents who instilled in me feelings of pride toward my nation, I was able to accept all of this with ease.

In the meantime, the years passed. After I finished my studies in the elementary school, I went to continue my studies in a high school and seminary in a large city, and became a teacher. However, a Jew could not find a teaching position in the public schools, and I was forced to subsist by giving private lessons.

Then, the year 1939 came along, which brought the Holocaust upon the Jewish people. Many of the young people, mainly the men, placed a pack over their back and were prepared to flee eastward to the Soviet Union after they heard about the atrocities that were perpetrated in the regions conquered by the Nazis. The desire to remain alive took over any other plan. A miracle occurred. Rather than the Nazis, soldiers of the Soviet Union came to our town and freed us along with the entire Ukraine from the Poles and the Nazi atrocities.

My father of blessed memory was an enthusiastic Zionist. He was a maskil, who was dedicated to Hebrew literature. He taught me to speak Hebrew while I was still of kindergarten age. Even my sister Tsharna, who changed her name to Shechora, spoke a pleasant Hebrew[1]. She founded the Hechalutz organization in Rozniatow, and the young people labored and studied agriculture in the estate of "Shomlo". I spoke Hebrew when I was a girl of five years old. I remember that the older children would mock me, laughing at my desire to speak Hebrew. They would often ask me: "Simale, tell me, is a Susale a ferdele?" Thus did I receive my nickname "Simale Susale a Ferdele"[2].

On the day of the invasion of the Red Army, my father looked out through the cracks in the shutters at the tanks and the Soviet soldiers that were on top of them. Tears of joy welled up in his eyes, and he said that it is good that the Red Communists have arrived, and not the violent Nazis. He was indeed correct. The Soviet soldiers did not kill, murder and oppress the Jews. They only emptied the stores of their merchandise. They were excellent buyers. They bought everything, and paid in rubles without bickering over the price.

Then something strange took place. The Jews of the town, who were for the most part merchants and storekeepers, lost their livelihood. The small amount of merchandise that they had was sold out in the course of a few days, but they were not able to purchase any new merchandise with their earnings. The stores were emptied, and the merchants were left poorer than they were before the arrival of the Red Army.

During the time of Polish rule, there was merchandise, but it was difficult to sell it with enough profit to insure a comfortable livelihood. However, during the time of Soviet rule, there was money, but there were no sources from which to buy new merchandise. Crowds stood in long rows before the stores to buy something – but they left disappointed. There was almost nothing to sell. The stores were locked up after a few hours.

Despite this, the situation of the Jewish children changed. They were hungry, they went about barefoot, but they went to school happy and joyous. They no longer had to fear from the ill-hearted anti-Semitic teachers. Those teachers were removed from the school. Our children were free, loved, and serious.

A new teaching staff arrived at the school. I myself merited being one of the teachers, and I was happy that I was able to teach our children. The children greeted me with heartwarming smiles and pride. In my own youth, I had studied at that school. I implanted feelings of faith and strength into their hearts. The Ukrainian and Polish children were no longer brazen enough to hurt the Jewish children, and if one of them attempted to lay a hand on a Jewish child – he would suffer doubly or more.

Only one teacher remained from among the former Polish teachers. She was the art teacher, Fani Branowa. Here heart was greatly pained when she saw our children raising up their heads with pride. They were able to come to me at any time with any complaint, or simply to chat as they would with a mother or with a sister in the class.

The Jews took advantage of the good opportunity that was given to them by Soviet law, which enabled them to be accepted to secondary and post-secondary institutions of learning. Jews were accepted as officials in various positions. Our youth enjoyed studying, and many streamed to the secondary and post-secondary institutions of learning, where they were accepted for free, without having to pay tuition.

Many started studying productive professions. They did not denigrate any line of work. The professions of the merchant and storekeeper were weakened, and almost disappeared. It was necessary to earn a livelihood for the family, for the older parents and the children. The Jewish young men and women turned to any profession and line of work that was available, so that they could provide sufficient food. Slowly, the longing for the times that passed was assuaged, and the Jews of the town became accustomed to the new lifestyle, to productive professions.

The students of the school had the opportunity to become involve in various sports. They played soccer, basketball, and other games. The sports field, which used to be closed to them during the time of Polish rule, was given over to them, and the anti-Semitic Polish teacher, Mrs. Branowa, was bursting with jealousy. Her heart was pained as she heard the shouts of joy of our youth, and her eyes were darkened as she saw our children happily playing, as if they were freed from a long imprisonment.

She could not tolerate me, and she complained daily to the secretary of the Communist party of Rozniatow: "How can you tolerate this type of Zionist, when it was the fact that during her youth, she went around with the Keren Kayemet box to collect money for Palestine? Do you know that her brother Dr. Weissman is a Zionist leader? He is always speaking and organizing the children into Zionist organizations. He is a Hebrew teacher in the Hebrew gymnasia of Pinsk. How can you tolerate these type of Zionists, and pay them a government salary?"

The tribulations increased – at that time they brainwashed my brother and often summoned him before the KGB (secret police) in Pinsk. They dealt softly with me – I was very young and pretty, and I knew how to dish out smiles. They would often summon me to the party office, and talk to me in order to influence me toward the path of Communism. They even advised me to become a member of the Communist party. I answered politely that I was not yet prepared to do so – it was not yet the right time – I did not know enough about the party doctrine and the works of Lenin in order to free myself from the old ways. I told them that when I would be sure in my heart I would decide. They listened to me with patience, and waited without pressure for me. They permitted me to continue as a teacher of the subjects of history and Soviet citizenship – this was a great honor and unusual level of trust.

I slowly but surely continued in my work. I instilled self-confidence into the souls of our youth, as well as national pride in their Jewishness, and encouraged them to love their fellowman. I developed in them a sense of collective responsibility, among other things.

Our children developed their abilities in all areas. At the end of the school year, we prepared a celebration and put on a play. I will never forget our talented actors and actresses, including Lutzka Kahana, Fintza Rechtschaffen, Tunchia Weizman, Aharon Wasserman, Moshe Diamond, and David Walpress (the son of my sister). These were all children of between the ages of seven and thirteen, who had fine senses of humor, and wonderful voices. They sang, danced, recited, and knew everything.

They were always in my company, and now they live in my memory. I will never forget them, our dear and good children of Rozniatow – it is as if I am the living monument to you all. My love does not diminish, but on the contrary, it grows from year to year. I am aging, and you stand always before my eyes, alive, happy and pure.

Your memories strengthen in me the love for the young people of Israel. I am glad of their accomplishments, and I guard over them, our precious treasures, so that they will not know any agony.

I continue to work as a teacher in the "16 th " public high school in Tel Aviv.

A reception for our fellow townsman Shmuel Rosenbaum of Argentina in 1953

**TRANSLATOR'S FOOTNOTES**

1. Tsharna means 'black' or dark' in Slavic, and Shechora means the same in Hebrew.

2. A Sus is a horse in Hebrew. A Ferd is a horse in Yiddish. The 'le' ending is a Yiddish diminutive, often cute, but at times mildly derogatory.

{87}

# Characters and Personalities

Chanina Weissman

{88}

## Images of Splendor

"And your eyes shall behold your teacher, and your ears will hear something from behind you saying: "this is the matter, go to it!" (Isaiah, 30).

This chapter presents to us incidents and personalities: the scholars and communal activists of Rozniatow; those who lived a life of the spirit in various generations, and those who placed their lot in the ways of the spirit, simple people who laid down deep roots in Jewish tradition, love of fellow Jews and the Land of Israel. The love of the fellow man was particularly deeply ingrained in their hearts. Their manner was modest, with proper behavior between man and G-d, and no less between man and his fellow man. The story of the lives of the wonderful men of spirit is very deep and all encompassing. One can learn a great deal from every detail of their way of life, and even their day-to-day speech, etc. Before us is a rainbow of the many hues of the sublime people of Rozniatow in their community. It is obvious that these personalities were not a separate group from the general Jewish population of the town, however we could not gather material about everybody. We wrote what we could, and eulogize their memories. The holocaust survivors of Rozniatow relate their stories with simplicity and present to us in this chapter that which they guarded in their hearts, including many important details. They were able to merge them together, detail by detail, and to write down their memories and feelings about the community's past, its glory and splendor, images of nobility of the leaders and activists, as well as about the modest, anonymous people, the simple and poor folk. These are people who saw them in their disgrace as well as in their greatness, in their joy and agony, and they knew them well, and were well versed in their ways of life. They know how to tell about them, to describe their wisdom and teaching, the holiness and the fine character traits that they possessed, as well as their splendorous deeds of kindness that are gloriously held in their memories.

**The editor.**

{89}

## Impressions of Happenings

### by Yaakov Rechtschaffen-Ritz, Melbourne, Australia

The town was about six kilometers away from the train station, and nevertheless, it was not just any far off town. Rozniatow was an old Jewish community, and that comes along with all of the treasures that antiquity brings, regarding local happenings, effervescent families, joint memories, which with the passage of time merge into the weight of tradition of the history of the settlement. Rozniatow was the center of a large surrounding area, and people would come to the town from all around the area for various matters. The town itself had a population of about 5,000 residents, about half of them Jews, and the other half Ukrainians with a few Poles.

There was a plaza in the center of town that contained most of the Jewish stores. This central plaza was called "the city", and a route led from it to a quarter that was called "the old town". A narrow path led from the plaza to a sparsely populated area, where the cattle market took place during the fairs that took place at specific times. By the plaza, which was called "Rynek" by the Poles, stood the Great Synagogue, and next to it was the Beis Midrash. The "old Kloiz" (small Hassidic prayer hall) was on the other side entirely.

All of the houses of prayer conducted a set order of study, which was passed along from generation to generation. During the morning and between the Mincha (afternoon) and Maariv (evening) services, they would study a chapter of Mishna or "Ein Yaakov". A "Chevra Shas" also existed for the study of Gemara with Tosafos and other commentaries[1]. A group of young people would study regularly in the Beis Midrash and Kloiz.

Inside the Kloiz, near the entrance, there was a sink with water, and large towels were hanging from the walls. In the middle was the reader's prayer stand. The eastern wall was reserved for the town notables. Next to that wall were shelves that were filled with books, all the way from the ceiling to the wooden floor. Next to the bookshelves there was a large heating stove, which would burn day and night during the winter.

We inherited the love of the book from our parents. Our ancestors knew how to collect hundreds of books in the synagogue, volumes of Talmud, both the Babylonian and Jerusalem version, along with the older and newer commentaries, as well as the four volumes of the Code of Jewish law. The students of Talmud, as well as anyone whose heart desired Torah, would make use of the Talmudic volumes. When a book fell to the ground, we would lift it up, kiss it, and return it to its place. It is no wonder that this love of the book remained well engraved in our memories, and it was not for no reason that our people was nicknamed "the people of the book".

When a young man showed an aspiration for studying Gemara, he would find a place in the old Kloiz. The young men would sit by the long tables, and they would study day and night, all the days of the year. They did not cease from their studies and "the tunes of Abaye and Rabba"[2] were even heard on the street.

Righteous women would stand up and say, "Happy are the children who expend their efforts in Torah, and happy are the fathers who raised such children." Their fathers, storekeepers or artisans, were filled with pride from their children.

Michael the tailor would sit near the stove. He was short, thin, with a scrawny gray-black beard. He was inwardly turned, without paying attention to his surroundings, as he recited chapters of Psalms. He was a quiet Jew, one of the simple Jews, who were calm and unpretentious, filled with worries about their livelihood throughout the weekdays, with the exception of the Sabbath and those evenings when they would be free from the yoke of their livelihood and would spend their time in prayer, and on occasion secular conversation on the porch of the Kloiz.

After the First World War, new winds began to blow in the town, youthful boys and girls began to study and dance modern dances. Among those who frequented the Kloiz, there were those who would clandestinely read secular books. With the passage of time, the number of young men who would make Torah study their occupation dwindled. They cut their peyos (side locks), shaved their beards, and began to visit the theater that had arrived in the town. Slowly, we began to organize cultural and educational activity among the youth.

During hikes that we arranged in the forest, we conducted debates and sang Hebrew songs. The young people who had arrived from the outside world brought with them news of modern culture.

I presented these matters in brief, in black and white, without the different hues, in order that the lives and deeds of those Jews of Rozniatow would be registered in this book. These were Jews with a warm Jewish heart, a hand outstretched to help the needy, working people who owned businesses or were professionals, who were eventually buried by the holocaust. The Nazi devil did not differentiate between the Orthodox and the secular, the young and the old. All of them were pure; all of them holy, and their bright souls shine like the splendor of the firmament[3].

The Czeczwa River below the town

{91}

## Guardians of the City

In the houses of the Jews, there were mezuzos on the door posts of the homes for protection against various evil forces; however, apparently the gentile thieves, as well as the Jewish thieves, paid no attention to them, and there were many thefts in the town. The leaders of the gentiles and the Jews sat down together to determine how to overcome this plague, and they decided that it was necessary to appoint guards in the town to protect against thieves. Since it was a mixed town, it was decided to appoint two guards, one gentile and the other Jewish.

Reb David Wahl was the Jewish appointee. He had a yellowish beard, he was thin, and wore a shiny, torn kapote (Hassidic overcoat), however he was extremely honorable and quiet. His gentile partner was Wiadka the shoemaker. They called him that because he barely knew how to place a patch on a worn out shoe, or to affix a sole to a shoe. His main livelihood was from the Jews, and therefore he was often among the Jews, and knew the Yiddish language as fluently as an actual Jew.

This Wiadka had another source of livelihood. He accompanied and assisted the priest during funerals. He would hold the priest's prayer book in his hand, and carry the cross or the bells at the head of the funeral procession. He had only one eye, and was also knows as "the one eyed shoemaker", and therefore, the guarding of the city was conducted with three eyes.

Since the two guards were already middle aged, they walked through the streets slowly and with difficulty as they conversed with each other. The thieves knew how to get around them, and as the guards reached one end of the town, the thieves would already be able to empty several homes and stores on the other end of the town.

**Wagon Drivers**

Our town was about seven kilometers away from the train station of Krechowice. This was difficult for the merchants who had to waste time in making purchases from distant places. However this was beneficial and was the primary source of livelihood for the wagon drivers who would transport travelers back and forth from the train station. At first, long ago, it is told that there were only two Jewish wagon drivers, Reb Zusia and Reb Pinchas. They had two simple wagons padded with straw and the passengers would sit on the straw in the wagon, with their feet placed on ladders on the sides of the wagon that were tied toward the bottom. Thus did they travel, slowly, at a leisurely pace and they would talk among themselves until they reached the train station.

Later, things changed. In the outskirts of the city, there began to appear wagons with rubber tires, pulled by two black or white horses. The wagon was designed in a comfortable manner, with comfortable sheets and a cover for times of need, whether to protect against rain or the sun. The first who came with a wagon with rubber tires "a splendid carriage" was Aharon Zimmerman. The second was "Melech the carriage driver", and he was no longer called "wagon driver" but rather a "carriage driver". There were also others who transported travelers to the train station, however they had simple carriages with elderly horses that were slightly hungry, as were their owners. These wagon drivers were poor, and they were barely able to feed their families, and therefore it is no wonder that their horses were also hungry.

Later, prior to the outbreak of the war, busses began to appear in the town. They would transport people to the train and also to various towns in the neighborhood. They would even reach Stanislawow. However, the Jews preferred to travel by carriage.

The wagon drivers were for the most part simple and upright people. They would wear a streimel (Hassidic festive fur hat) on their heads on the Sabbath. They would worship in the first Minyan (prayer quorum), and in the afternoons they would come to the synagogue to recite chapters of Psalms or to hear the lecture on the weekly Torah portion. These were precious and straightforward Jews who earned their livelihood with great difficulty. Reb Alter the "deaf" was a pleasant and intelligent Jew, and he was slightly deaf. He would drive his wagon to the train station, one of the neighboring towns, or to Dolina or Kolush. When a traveler would arrive at the field of carriages, Reb Alter would immediately be able to discern to which direction the traveler wished to travel by the expression on his face.

At times, when he was missing one passenger, he would turn half seriously and half jokingly to someone who wished to travel to Dolina and say: "perhaps you will travel to Kolush today?".

When he met a poor Jew who was not able to pay for the trip, he would say to the passengers: "Make room for another Jew, it does not matter".

He would stand in his wagon to make room for the new passenger to sit. He would say to the passengers: "We have to have mercy on a Jew". Despite his difficult circumstances, he would always make sure to invite a guest for the Sabbath.

**Reb Shabtai (Spiegel) the Tavern Keeper**

When he got married to his wife Aidel he merited not only a large cash dowry, but also something more significant than money - a fine and spacious residence with many rooms, and with a "Heavenly window", that is to say a window which faced the road toward the marketplace that was the business center. Without giving much thought, he decided to convert the room that faced the marketplace into a tavern or a small restaurant. For such a business, one does not require much capital outlay. One requires a few bottles of liquor, some herring and bread rolls. The most important requirement was to have many rooms available, where the gentile customers would be able to sit and imbibe their drinks in comfort.

Despite all of his efforts in the tavern, he did not forget that the most important thing was that he was a Jew. He arose early, recited several chapters of Psalms even before he came to his store, and then opened up the blinds wide, and placed an empty liquor bottle with a plate of herring into the window as a sign that liquor and appetizers are being sold here.

The first customer was the Polish shoemaker Krawice. Whenever he finished work on a pair of boots, he would always split the fee between himself and his wife. He would give her half, and with the other half, he would enter into Reb Shabtai's tavern on occasion and request a small cup for 30 groszy. He would leave, and come back some time later and request another serving of liquor, and then leave again. Thus he would come and go all day until he had used up his money.

The second regular customer was "Anna the drunkardess". That is what all of her acquaintances called her. She worked as a washerwoman in the Jewish houses, and she spent her entire earnings on drinks at Reb Shabtai's tavern.

Who was this gentile Anna? Was she single or married? From where was she, and where was she going? Apparently, she was depressed, and she attempted to drown the sorrows of her heart with liquor.

Another regular customer of Reb Shabtai was the shammas (sexton) of the Kloiz. Whenever there was a memorial day (yahrzeit) for a Tzadik or Rebbe, or any private yahrzeit, they would send the shammas of the Kloiz to purchase 96% clear liquor from Reb Shabtai the tavern keeper.

Another regular customer was "Eliahu of the Marketplace". Before he would go very early in the morning to the villages in the neighborhood to purchase a calf or other animal in order to sell it for profit, and thereby to earn his meager livelihood, he would enter into Reb Shabtai's tavern to drink a small glass of liquor. This was his breakfast, for he did not have enough money to purchase breakfast.

In this manner, Reb Shabtai was busy from 5 AM until 8 PM. When his daughters helped him wait on the customers, he would have a chance between customers to "snatch" a chapter of Psalms that he knew off by heart. After 8 PM, he would dedicate the entire time to prayer, charity, and good deeds. He would go out, meet a Jew, and discuss with him the issues of the day. Another Jew would meet up with them, and they would join together.

The final Minyan in the Kloiz was at 9 AM. All of the clergy who were not pressed for time worshiped at that Minyan, where they recited the prayers slowly and with concentration. Those who had arrived from a journey or who had not yet had a chance to pray due to their business, or anyone else who had not yet had a chance to pray, joined in with them. Reb Shabtai felt better about himself there in the Kloiz than at home. At home, all manner of gentiles, drunks, and tipplers would disturb his peace and tranquility. There in the Kloiz he was free, and nobody would disturb him from his prayers and studies.

When his daughters grew up and got married, Reb Shabtai gave up working in the tavern completely. He turned it over to his wife, and dedicated himself completely to prayer and study. He was diligent to pronounce each word of his prayers full of devotion. He would sigh deeply over the tribulations of the exile and over the fact that the young people of the generation were working very hard at the saw-mill or in loading wood onto wagons, preparing themselves to make aliya to the Land of Israel and to rebuild it. "Oh G-d, would that it should be, may it be Your will! All sorts of various evil decrees are afflicting our people, perhaps this is indeed the beginning of the redemption? Perhaps we have to truly wait for the footsteps of the Messiah? Perhaps these are they, the young people who are dedicating themselves to make aliya and rebuild the Land of Israel. Perhaps these are the emissaries of the Holy One Blessed Be He? Who knows?"

He would sit down to study a page of Gemara and to research the sources that this is indeed the correct path to the Days of the Messiah, to the redemption that would be marked by the return to Zion; that the redemption would arrive slowly in a natural manner, and that the resurrection of the dead would take place at the time that the Creator, may He be blessed, desires. Reb Shabtai began to occupy himself with the idea of the redemption, and the birth pangs of the redemption. "We feel the birth pangs of the redemption already very clearly, however who knows when the actual redemption will arrive? Would we merit it?". Would he himself merit it?

The afternoon approached, and Reb Shabtai would still be sitting in the Kloiz. Outside, a light snow was be falling. Suddenly he would hear a sigh, and another sigh. He would look around, and behold the sighs were coming from the broken heart of a Jew who wandered between villages to buy and sell in order to feed his family. The livelihood was as difficult as the splitting of the Red Sea. There is no livelihood in the home, the daughters are growing up and reaching marriageable age, and how would it be possible to arrange matches for them and marry them off. He had no money to pay the tuition fees of the teachers. The Jew sighed deeply and was alone in his hurt in the Kloiz. Here in the Kloiz there is a place also for sighs. Nobody would bother such a person.

The heart of Reb Shabtai broke when he heard the sighs of the unfortunate Jew, whom nobody was assisting. At least he should be offered a comforting word to give him some hope. This Reb Yosef was well known for his pleasant nature, however his lot was very difficult. His entire livelihood was from the village of Strutin. From there he would bring a chicken, some cream, some vegetables, and on occasion a goose or a duck to the town. This would bring him a few coins from which he could support with great difficulty his family. Reb Shabtai approached him and asked him why he was sighing.

"I sighed?" Reb Yosef asked in his innocence. The unfortunate person did not understand how sighs were able to come from his heart. Reb Shabtai encouraged him and said: "Sighs come from the heart of a man, perhaps it is possible to help you a little".

From the facial expression of Reb Yosef, it was possible to discern that there was a storm brewing in his heart, however he controlled himself.

"Behold the winter is approaching and I have no wood to heat the house. The house is full of small children, and I have no money to pay their tuition. I cannot purchase warm clothing for them to warm their bodies. I have a daughter who has reached marriageable age. My livelihood is dwindling..."

"How much do you require for a dowry for your daughter?" Reb Shabtai asked him, "and how much for clothing for the children, firewood, and tuition?" They arrived at a figure of approximately 2,000 guilder.

Reb Shabtai answered him:

"Why do you sigh over every small incident, and over every small amount. Sigh once for a large, fitting sum, and be free of the matter... Don't worry, the Blessed G-d will fulfill you're the requests of your heart for good."

When Reb Shabtai left the Beis Midrash to go home, all of the sighs of Reb Yosef accompanied him and did not bring him any respite. The merciful heart of Reb Shabtai the tavern keeper was filled with the agony of all Jews over the difficulty of their livelihood, and the travails of raising children, and he raised his eyes heavenward with a plea:

"Master of the World, look at the troubles of the Jews, and instill them with the trait of trust, so that they should not have to worry about their livelihood! ..."

## Reb Meshulam Fruchter

We had many neighbors, some closer and some farther. However the Fruchter family is engraved in my memory already from my youth.

I remember the head of the family, Reb Meshulam, and his wife Rivka very well from my youth. I would spend most of my time with their children Yaakov and Moshe.

The head of the family was of average height, and had a pleasant face. Even though he was a Kohen, and for the most part "Kohanim are angry people", he was of pleasant disposition and fine mannerisms. His wife Rivka was also quiet and modest, and she conducted her household as a true woman of valor. She was good and had a pleasant disposition to other people and her own children. They had one daughter named Rosia. Rivka ran their cloth business for the most part, and Reb Meshulam dedicated most of his time to communal affairs.

I remember that when I was young, when Sukkot would arrive and Reb Meshulam was about to build his large Sukka, all of the children of the neighborhood gathered around. One would bring a hammer, another nails, and another a saw. All of them wanted to help him build his Sukka. Obviously, the large numbers of helpers would make the task more difficult, but he never scolded us children. He smiled, and was happy that the children should occupy themselves with fulfilling this commandment. He built a large Sukka in order to make sure that he would be able to accommodate those neighbors who did not have a private Sukka, either because they did not have time to build one, or did not have the wood. He brought planks of different types of wood, large and small. He sawed them and straightened them and finally a beautiful Sukka was constructed. We children began to cover the roof with Sechach and to decorate the interior.

He made sure that his children would be able to study Torah diligently. When he saw the fruits of his labor, his face beamed with happiness. The sons Yaakov and Moshe were sharp in their studies. If they had the possibility to study and pay for higher general studies, they would certainly have become great scientists.

Moshe sat in the old Kloiz and studied Torah, and when the time came for marriage, his parents concerned themselves with marrying him off according to tradition, as do all Jewish people.

I still remember his advice to me that I should attempt to pay for general studies, so that I would be able to leave the town for the larger outside world. To my great distress, I was unable to follow his advice and desires, and I remained planted in the small town until the outbreak of the Great War.

I heard from hearsay that he went through all of the hellish tribulations of the holocaust, and ended up in the United States, where he was able to fulfill the advice that he gave to me in my youth. He began to study secular studies on his own when he was already an adult of forty years old, and he finished his degree. He obtained a position in a certified academy of chemistry. He rebuilt a family again, and lived a peaceful life in the far off United States.

## The Man Who Waited for the Messiah

There was a poor man among us whose entire thoughts were dedicated to waiting for the coming of the Messiah. He never ceased to talk about this, and he never ceased waiting the day of his arrival. Despite his difficult livelihood, despite all of the tribulations that afflicted his poor house, for his wife died while she was young, and his only daughter was sickly, despite all of this he was always content with his lot and was never sad at all. He often would quote the verse that is used to comfort mourners: "Death will be swallowed up for ever, and the L-rd G-d will wipe away tears from all faces"[4].

Due to the fact that he was always immersed in thoughts of the redemption and waiting for the desired time period, he did not see what was going on around him, the difficulties and poverty that afflicted him.

He certainly knew the statement of the Gemara regarding the Messianic era: "There is no difference between the days of the Messiah and the present time except for the affliction of the nations", and since this affliction was difficult and he felt it with his entire body, he dedicated himself to awaiting the Messiah.

Thus was our Reb Yosef Leib.

## The Doer of Charitable Deeds

"Charitable deeds are greater than charity, for charity is for the poor, and charitable deeds are for both the poor and the rich."

I wish to memorialize here and remark on a certain resident of Rozniatow who excelled in his charitable deeds. This was Reb Yosef Kassner. There was not one person in Rozniatow who had need for deeds of charity, old or young, who did not turn to Reb Yosef. Such requests were always answered positively.

This Jew fulfilled the commandment of doing charitable works as if that was the purpose for which he was created, to extend aid and support for the person in need, to be dedicated to this commandment with all of his might and resources. When on occasion it would happen that he did not have the necessary money available for the charitable deeds, he immediately sent his son Sania (Netanel) to see what he could do to find the required money from various people, so that he would not have to turn the requestor away empty handed.

There were other individuals who gave themselves over to charitable deeds, however he in particular watched over this commandment, and fulfilled it in its entirety and with a willing soul.

## The Tailor Yitzchak Meir Hoizler

He was a straightforward, upright, and G-d fearing man who supported himself from his own work. He observed the commandments, both the easy and difficult ones, and he distanced him self from spreading rumors and from any taint of theft. He was a tailor by profession and he was very careful to be exacting in his measurements. He was a charitable person and frequently had guests in his home.

He performed his work quietly and modestly. He worshiped with the artisans "the people of the sunrise"[5], and all that he asked from his fellow man was that when his time came, he would be buried with along with his measuring stick and ironing board, which would testify to his honesty.

Thus was Reb Yitzchak Meir the tailor.

The placid bay in Rozniatow

{98}

## The Jews of my "Old Town"

### by Zechariah Friedler

These memories go back to before the First World War, to my life in Rozniatow, where I was born and raised. I spent my childhood and youth there, and it still lives in my heart. I remember it as it was with longing. I recall everything that happened to me, and that I heard from my father Reb Leibish Friedler, and from the elders of the town.

It stands alive before me, even though more than twenty-five years have passed from the time that I left it and its residents. At that time, I would never have imagined that a time would come when that beautiful corner in the foothills of the Carpathians would be eaten up by fire.

We lived among the gentiles; however the old town had a Jewish character. My town Rozniatow grew from it. Every Jewish holiday left it imprint on it, and on occasion it seemed to me that even the gentiles lived as we did, rejoicing when our holidays came, and experiencing the Jewish holiday with us.

The old town was surrounded by rivers, mountains, and ancient forests. It was uninhabitable until the Jews began to settle there, and they wondrously developed the village until it turned into an urban settlement, built according to plans. The large plaza, which is surrounded by stores, streets and alleys, is testimony to this development.

The first Jews in the old town were brothers-in-law. One of them was named Groner. Here in Israel I met his great-grandson, an elderly man. He provided me with the following details. The two brothers-in-law leased the property from Skarbek along with the liquor stills in order to produce alcohol from potatoes. They built the first three houses in the town for themselves and for the Jews who were employed on their estate. They also built the Kloiz for public prayers.

After the period of the lease expired, they sold the homes and the two brothers-in-laws returned to Stanislawow, from where they had lived prior to coming to Rozniatow.

The home in which I grew up was purchased from them by my grandfather, Reb Sender Friedler. The two other homes were purchased by Reb Leib Berman and Reb Shalom Horowitz. After some time, other homes were added, all the way until the large bridge.

Until this day, I can see before my eyes the Torah scroll that they left as a gift to the Kloiz. It was called "the old scroll".

I remember that when Reb Leib Berman donated a Torah scroll to the Kloiz, many Jews came from the town with Torah scrolls in their arms. The head of the procession was Reb Shmuel Wirt. They sang and danced. It was an exalted scene.

They sang and rejoiced all night until dawn. The honorable men of the town sat on the benches at the eastern wall, and in the surrounding long tables sat the youths and the rest of the worshippers.

This deep experience of my youth remains engraved in my memory. It is a symbol of the love of Torah of the Jews of Rozniatow.

A Jew would suffer many tribulations, and work very hard all the days of the year in the town. He earned his bread at the risk of his life. He worked hard all week, and sufficed himself on crumbs for his existence. All of this sacrifice was in order to prepare the needs of the Sabbath in holiness and honor.

Leibish Friedler of blessed memory

I will not describe the beauty and exaltedness of the Sabbath in the village. How much grace and charm was poured into the day of rest, and how great were the refined feelings that were instilled into us, and the appearance of nobility and pleasantness on every face.

After the period of rest in the afternoon, my grandfather Reb Yitzchak Geller would walk to the Kloiz along with Reb Shlomo Yungerman, Reb Shalom Horowitz, and others. They would go to enjoy their studies of "Ohr Hachayim", "Yoreh Deah", a page of Gemara, or Midrash about the weekly Torah portion or the time of year.

My grandfather was a great Torah scholar, and was well accepted by the people of his community, who revered and respected him. He was pleasant to everyone, old and young. He gave advice, and spiritual support to anyone who would request. The congregation of worshippers would listen attentively to his words, his explanations, and his sharp deductions, which were full of content, meaning, and moral lessons.

After the Mincha service, they partook of the third Sabbath meal together, and then they recited the Maariv prayer and Havdallah.

Thus was conducted the lives of the Jews in the old town until the outbreak of the First World War.

My grandfather died in 1915. Rabbi Hemerling and Reb Chanina Weissman eulogized him beside the Great Synagogue. Many tears were shed that day, and his memory will not be forgotten.

The flood in the old town in 1927

The Kloiz, along with the green plaza and the river were to us children the bosom of the world. There we played, and there Reb Shaul Bunim, the teacher of young children, taught us the aleph beis. The girls also studied with him until they knew how to recite all of the prayers.

When we reached a higher grade, we had to walk the far distance to the town itself, where we studied Chumash and Gemara from various teachers. The class time occupied about 10-12 hours a day. It was already dark when we returned home and we waited for each other, for we were afraid to walk alone, lest the "shkotzim" such as Michen Jagilowice and others attack us.

As an aside, that selfsame Michen Jagilowice was during the period of the holocaust one of the righteous gentiles. He saves sixteen Jewish souls, who remained alive thanks to him.

The Days of Awe are engraved in my memory. Prior to Rosh Hashanah, we would get up early and go to the recital of Selichot (penitential prayers) in the middle of the night, towards to morning of the autumn days, when it was dark and cool. The sound of the Shofar during the month of Elul made the heart tremble.

The Kloiz had a different ambience than usual. Reb Shlomo Yungerman, dressed in his white kittel (prayer cloak), stood in front of the prayer stand and intoned with his enthusiastic voice "The soul is Yours and the body is of Your making..."[6]. His melody was unforgettable, and he had it in his power to arouse the worshippers to tears with his deep feeling and inner longing expressed in his prayers. Trembling and shuddering overtook everyone during that time.

On Rosh Hashanah the Kloiz was packed with people. The melodies of the prayers aroused people to repentance. There were some people who were accustomed to recite various parts of the service, and we listened intently to the melodies of Reb Shmuel Arber during the prayer "G-d who dwells on high". His melody remains in my memory to this day. His son Leib was a strong tenor. During the days of my youth until the First World War I would listen to their prayers each year, and their prayers remain in my heart forever.

The flood of 1927 damaged the home of Mordechai Mark

The public prayer on Rosh Hashanah and Yom Kippur formed a large part of our "Jewish experience". The atmosphere that we absorbed during our youth in the Kloiz accompanies us all the days of our lives, and remains engraved on our souls.

The joy on Simchat Torah was great, when the children, dressed up in their new festive clothes, came with their flags. Everyone was honored with a Hakafah (Torah circuit) and there was no end to the singing and dancing.

My father was very concerned about the prayer books in the Kloiz, about the daily cleanliness and heat during the winter. The key to the Kloiz was always in our house.

On long Sabbath eves all of the Jews of the town sat in the Kloiz as one family and stories were told, by both the young and the old, about the way of life of the Admorim and rabbis. Joy and repose pervaded all around.

Apparently, it seems as if the life in the old town was conducted peacefully, however each family had its own worries, successes, and obstacles. What united everybody was the trust in the living Torah that bestowed an order and spirituality to life, whatever was to come to pass. This way of life accepted as the way things must be, and the faith that the Holy One Blessed Be He, in the Torah, in Israel, in the Land of Israel are one. Along with this, they possessed a great deal of wisdom life, sincerity, a deep love of their fellow man, spiritual peace, diligence, a healthy intellect, pure family life, and spiritual aspirations.

The younger generation honored the elders greatly. Even the "progressive youth" honored their aging parents with respect and politeness, even though they disagreed in their world outlook. The life in the town was a life of togetherness, of good and traditional Jews, and the heart cannot find comfort over their destruction.

This was the image of my old town. There our loved ones lived their lives in the times of happiness and in the times of mourning and agony. There they were murdered along with the six million holy and pure martyrs of our people.

We will never forget them. This book tells about them and about our community, which is engraved in the depths of the heart, our hearts and the hearts of our children after us, until the end of generations.

Yitgadal Veyitkadash.

## TRANSLATOR'S FOOTNOTES

1. Mincha is the daily afternoon service, and Maariv is the daily evening service. For convenience, these services are often conducted at the synagogue in close succession to each other, Mincha shortly before sunset and Maariv shortly thereafter. The time in between is often spent in study. Ein Yaakov is a compendium of the Aggadaic (legendary or story-like) material of the Talmud (the Talmud consists mainly of Halachic - legal - material with the smaller portion being Aggadaic material). Shas is an acronym for the Six Orders, referring to the six main volumes of the Mishna and Talmud. Talmud consists of Mishna (the older succinct legal material - which often forms a volume of its own), and Gemara, which is the verbose commentary on the Mishna. The major commentaries that are printed on the page of a standard Talmudic text include Rashi and Tosafos. Tosafos is considered the more complicated of those two commentaries.

2. Abaye and Rabba are two sages often quoted in the Talmud. The tune here refers to the singsong chant that often accompanies the reading of Talmudic text.

3. This description is based on the well-known 'El Maleh' prayer, which is recited in memory of the deceased at funerals, the Yizkor service, and various other occasions.

4. Isaiah 25:8. This verse is part of the Jewish funeral service.

5. Referring to the early hour of their prayer service.

6. Elul is the month prior to Rosh Hashanah. It is customary to sound the Shofar each morning of Elul during the morning service. On the Saturday night prior to Rosh Hashanah (or one week earlier if Rosh Hashanah falls on Monday or Tuesday), the midnight penitential service (Selichot) takes place. From then on, on each weekday until Yom Kippur, the Selichot service is recited prior to the daily morning service, generally when it is still dark outside. The quote here is from the Selichot service.

{103}

# After the First World War

## by Ben Zion Horowitz

And it came to pass in the year 1918[1]. When I returned to Rozniatow from exile in Russia in September 1918, I found before me a destroyed and pillaged city, as if following a pogrom. There was no steady government, it was a free-for-all, and the young Ukrainians organized groups that fell upon the Jews, and pillaged, robbed and beat everyone who crossed their path. The Jews were not sure of their lives, whether outside on the roads or in their own houses. There was no government to protect their lives. They were abandoned to the evil inclination of the Ukrainian population that hated Jews.

The Ukrainians were pillaging around the entire region, particularly in the villages. There were only five Jewish families in the village of Swaryczow. In Strutyn and other villages close to Rozniatow, the few Jews were completely abandoned and left to the good or bad graces of their Ukrainian neighbors.

Those released from the Russian army, young for the most part, organized themselves in Rozniatow into an independent defense organization in order to protect the Jews of these villages. They armed themselves with all sorts of weapons, including pistols, spears, old guns, even thick sticks, and in particular with a strong will to protect the endangered Jews who lived in the villages that were left abandoned to the Ukrainian hooligans who conducted deeds of terror.

Each evening, groups of the "Jewish militia" were sent out to all of the neighboring villages. The gentiles were already aware that the Jews were sending out and independent defense force that was armed, and slowly they began to cease their attacks on the Jews of those villages.

A further reason for the cessation of the attacks, pillage and plunder was the entry of the soldiers of the Polish army to the region. The Hallerczik army immediately began to take revenge against the Ukrainian leaders and organizers. They acted with a strong hand, took out many to be put to death, and arrested the Ukrainian activists. They also had no mercy upon the Jews. They began to cut off beards and peyos, close down and pillage stores, and enlist the Jews for backbreaking labor either for a useful purpose or for no useful purpose. This was the situation with any change of government in the exile. The Jews were always the first victims, whether of the departing government or the new government that was entering.

{104}

# The First Dramatic Club

In those days, the first days of Polish rule after the First World War, there were no Jewish organizations existing in Rozniatow. The veteran Zionist activists had either died or emigrated. They had departed from the scene. There was no communal activist of any stature. The well-stocked Jewish library had been pillaged and burnt, so that there was no trace of it left. With such a situation, the Jewish community was completely abandoned. There was no person or official organization that was able to represent the Jewish community to the governing authorities.

We attempted to reorganize. We chose the lawyer Dr. Wasserman as the chairman as the "Chovevei Zion" organization. He was elderly and sickly, and was not able to renew communal life in the town. We saw that the Chovevei Zion organization was progressively weakening due to lack of activity. Since we were not satisfied with the lack of activity, a group of young Zionists began to organize into a group that was called "The Poale Zion" organization.

It was not easy to bring this idea to fruition, whether due to the opposition of the elder activists who did not want to give up the reins of authority; or whether due to the government, for it was necessary to obtain a permit in order to be recognized, and this was fraught with various conditions: What was written in the charter of the organization? Who were the leaders and responsible parties for the new organization? What is the organization's political inclination? And other such difficulties. The regional governor in Dolina had to sign the permit, and there too, one had to overcome numerous obstacles.

In addition, we did not have the financial means to support organizational activity, to rent a hall, to pay for lighting, or to conduct any activities that require money. The only means to raise money was to establish a dramatic group that would perform for the community, and then dedicate the income to the organizational activities. However, even for a dramatic club to perform in an official manner, there was a need for a charter and government permits. Therefore we decided to place a request to organize a "Meeting Place for Jewish Culture", which would be non-factional. The activities of the Meeting Place would include performances, a library, and various other cultural activities of which it would be difficult for the authorities to object.

In order to hasten the matter, and ease the obtaining of a permit, we turned to the lawyer Dr. Sapir, and asked that he take on the chairmanship of the organization and present our case to the authorities. Indeed, we received our needed permit from the authorities very quickly.

The following people were chosen to sit on the committee of the cultural meeting place: Dr. Shimon Sapir, chairman; Dr. Edward Sapir; Shalom Rechtschaffen; the lawyer Leon Horowitz; Andza Kanner – all of whom were murdered by the Nazis. Noshe Lutwak of blessed memory; Yitzchak Berman, now living in Haifa; Ben Zion Horowitz who died in Israel; Yeshayahu Lutwak, living in the United States; Sender Friedler, who died in the United States; and Dr. Bendet Berger, who died in Rozniatow.

The following were chosen to the auditing committee: Magister Leon Horowitz, Avraham Hoffman, Ben Zion Horowitz and Meir Taub.

In order to commence activities, we had an immediate need for funds. As had been previously mentioned, our source of funds was to be from the income of various performances. We immediately started to organize a group of actors, to be known as the "Dramatic Club", and was to be affiliated with the Organization of Hebrew Culture. We immediately realized that this was no simple matter. There were many obstacles, differences in outlook, differences in social standing, differences in cultural levels, and differences in sex. All of these matters might today be seen as simple and easy to deal with; however, during the beginning of the 1920s, they were quite significant factors in communal affairs.

We had to overcome all of these obstacles and conduct ourselves with strict discipline, for otherwise we would not have been able to arrange everything. Whomever was unwilling to accept upon themselves the discipline of accepting whatever task was assigned to them was not accepted into the club. We freed ourselves from many of the older ideas regarding personal status, and began to prepare our plays. The first play was "Hasia the Orphan" by Yaakov Gordon.

From upper right: Dr. Nunek Lusthaus, Andzia Kanner, Moshe Lutwak, Dr. Leon Horowitz, Leah Horowitz-Klatsh.

The following were the participants in the Dramatic Club: Women: Freda Nemlich (passed away); Gittel Nemlich, Adela Reis, Anda Kanner, Tuni Laufer, Henia Laufer, Shendel Wiedner, Matilda Prinz (all murdered by the Nazis); Tenci Berger (living in Israel), Sheiche Weinlas, Etka Weinlas (living in Poland); Dora Gelobter (living in the United States).

Men: Avraham Hoffman, Leon Horowitz, Shimon Diamant (Sofler), Shalom Rechtschaffen (all murdered by the Nazis); Philip Perel (passed away); Moshe Lutwak, Yeshaya Lutwak, Yehuda Hammerman (living in the United States); Yehuda Freier, Peretz Sperling, and the director of the group Ben Zion Horowitz who died in Israel.

The first play took place in the Polish Sokol hall with an overflowing audience. Due to the great success and the requests from those members of the community who were not able to obtain tickets for the first performance, we had to put on a repeat performance in short order. This performance was also to an overflowing audience, and was very successful. The income from the performances was divided as follows: 50% for support and other needs of the institution, and 50% for acquiring books. Due to the great success, we planned a new play for two months later. We intended to switch plays every two months, and put on as many performances of each play as was needed by request of the audience.

The success of the Dramatic Club was a thorn in the eyes of the Polish directors of the Sokol. The success was not only to be measured in monetary means, but primarily in communal means. It became known that the young Jews had the ability to prepare a nice cultural event that had an effect on the entire community. The play was the topic of conversation day and night, both in Rozniatow and in the surrounding areas. The anti-Semitic director of the Sokol hall, a pharmacist, requested from us that every second play that we perform be in the Polish language for the benefit of the Polish community who do not understand Yiddish, and are in need of culture as much as the Jews are. When we immediately refused his request categorically, he began to threaten us that he would not permit us to use the Sokol hall for performances. We responded to him that we would then make sure that no Jew enters the Sokol hall for any performance, whether in Polish or Ukrainian. This was a serious threat, since most of the members of the audience of the Polish and Ukrainian performances were Jews. The Ukrainian performing groups were in constant contact with us, for they were very interested in us and in the Jewish audiences. They also attempted to include some plays with Jewish content, written by Jewish playwrights. Jewish theater groups, such as Goldfaden, Zigmund Torkow and others, came from Lvov and Stanislawow. These performances brought in a significant sum of money for the Polish owners of Sokol. The local Ukrainians joined up with us and also opposed the request of the anti-Semitic pharmacist. When the Pole saw the strong front of opposition, and saw that his request had no success of being answered positively, he began to appeal to our patriotic instincts. After all, we were in Poland, and we have to understand him, etc. etc., we should not join up with the Ukrainians who hate the Poles. He also began to make use of the connections he had with the governing authorities, and they began to pressure us in this manner. They summoned the responsible parties and hinted that they heard something regarding the plays, etc., etc., and that we should appease the director of the Sokol in Rozniatow. The pressure caused a division among the members of the troupe. There were those who said that we should maintain our relationship with the Poles, and that the request was valid. However, most opposed this argument, saying: "We are a Jewish troupe, and we should perform only in the Jewish language". In the meantime, we stopped attending performances in the Sokol hall, and the hall became empty. The Poles saw that it was impossible to continue in this manner, and they gave in. We continued to prepare new performances, and the club continued to develop and flourish. We were supported by all of the residents.

The pressure from the Poles forced us to think about finding a new hall for our performances. In the meantime, an event took place that helped us to actualize our idea in a manner that we never even had dreamt of.

The small group of members of the troupe who supported the request of the Poles never came to terms with the majority of the troupe. They secretly decided to put on a performance in the Polish language called "Fat Fish". They made contact with the pharmacist as well as with the Polish priest. They received a great deal of support for their activities. We decided to make it impossible for them to perform. When the day of the performance arrived, the priest made a special journey to Broszniow to issue an invitation to the directors of the well-known Glezinger lumber mill, other senior officials, all of the Christian residents of Broszniow, government representatives from Dolina, as well as heads of the Polish community. They play was supposed to be a demonstration of victory against the Jewish troupe, and a victory for the request of the Poles and the local authorities.

We secretly sent a trustworthy representative to Broszniow, who pretended that he was a representative from the troupe that was supposed to perform that evening in the Sokol hall. He informed the people that the play was postponed for some time due to a sudden illness of one of the actresses.

In the evening, the hall was decorated in a festive manner. The priest, the pharmacist and his entourage were attired in a festive manner, seated in an almost empty hall. The actors were very nervous for they were all prepared, but the audience was not present, neither the local audience nor the audience from the neighboring areas. Finally, the priest realized that the Jews had tricked him, and he decreed in a mournful and almost weepy voice that the play was postponed due to an illness of an actress...

The victory of the Jews made waves throughout the region. The Poles were boiling with rage. We knew that from that time on, the Sokol hall was completely closed to use, and we immediately had to concern ourselves with a new hall.

A few of the heads of the troupe were summoned to the authorities for an interrogation: who arranged this? Who disturbed the performance? Nobody from the troupe... after some time, the matter was slowly forgotten. The chief officials of Glezinger, most of them Jews, were very happy over the embarrassment of the priest and the pharmacist, and they arranged among themselves a donation of wood and lumber for the building of a theater for the Jewish troupe. Influenced by the officials, the firm itself donated a fitting sum for the establishment of a theater for the Jewish troupe. The Jewish director Bauer, as well as Lookstein and the Hausman brothers engaged in significant activity for this cause.

Sender Friedler had a large warehouse, and a house next to it. We decided to merge the house with the large warehouse in order to make a gigantic performance hall, even larger than the Sokol. We decided to quickly renovate and fix up the hall in order to prepare it for the next performance. We received a ready-made wooden stage from the Glezinger firm, as well as benches for the audience. All of the officials of the firm, including gentiles, as well as people from the region came to the first performance in the splendid new hall. After the first festive performance, a large celebration took place with dancing, song and drinks until dawn.

The success of our troupe was complete. The income grew, and with it, our library grew. It slowly became the largest in the area. Most of the Polish intelligentsia, including lawyers, doctors, and officials, were forced to come to us if they wished to read a good book. I was involved as a volunteer with the library from 1920 until 1935.

{108}

## The Jewish Intelligentsia Prior to the Second World War

Despite the small size and poverty of the town of Rozniatow, it had the seeds of a Jewish and Polish intelligentsia, consisting of doctors, lawyers, and later, young students. They were active in communal life and contributed greatly to the cultural and political life of the town. I will try to illustrate a few of them here, as well as I knew them.

## 1) Dr. Sabat

He was born in Prague, Czechoslovakia[2]. He first studied theology and later studied medicine. He arrived in Rozniatow in 1918 with the Czech-Hungarian army. There, he met a young gentile girl, the daughter of an engineer from the city of Dolina. His father-in-law immediately found him a position as the government physician of Rozniatow and environs. He did not distance himself from the Jews, for he had a warm Jewish heart. He was very interested in whatever was taking place in the Jewish community; he donated generously to the Jewish institutions, and greatly assisted anyone who turned to him for any matter.

He was not ashamed of his Judaism in front of his Christian doctor friends. On the contrary, he demonstrated it at any opportunity. He was proud of Jewish nationalism, interested in the Jewish youth, and was their patron. When his Christian wife died in 1942, a Christian funeral was arranged with crosses and a priest, according to their custom. They did not have any children. He then married a Jewish woman. During the time of the German siege, they permitted him to work without any problems, for the Ukrainians spoke well of him and protected him. However when the liquidations and mass murder began, he was not able to sit in peace and watch his people be killed in front of his eyes. He decided to escape across the border to Czechoslovakia. Along the way, he was captured by a band of Ukrainians who murdered him and his wife on the spot, along with his father-in-law and another group of Jews who were on their way to the Czech border. This group included the dentist Bernat Litauer, Lookstein, Shapira, and Director Stein who was a senior official of the Glezinger firm. The wild band left the murdered people on the road and fled. The residents of the area, who recognized Dr. Sabat and Director Stein, both very well known people in the entire region, gathered up the corpses and buried them in a grave approximately sixteen kilometers from Rozniatow. They erected a fence around the grave. When I returned from Russia in 1946, I came to that place, and the gentiles showed me the location of the grave.

The physicians: Dr. Lusthaus, the son of Esther Lusthaus; Dr Adlersberg the son of the teacher of Jewish religion; Dr. Fried the son-in-law of Shmuel Friedler; Dr. Feier the son of the lawyer Isidor Feier; the dentist Bernard Litauer; the dentist Blau the husband of Matilda Prinz.

The lawyers: Dr. Wasserman, Dr. Isidor Feier; Dr. Shimon Sapir; Dr. Kahana; Dr. Minkes; the lawyer Leon Horowitz; Magister Weinfeld; Magister Leib Meisels; the professor of philosophy David Weisman.

{109}

# Where Are You?

## by Reuven Weintraub[3]

Where are you? Oh, where are you Jews
Of "Kol Nidre" and "Unetane Tokef"
Jews of Simchat Torah
Jews of Tikkun Chatzot?
Oh, the community of pure and holy ones
Well acquainted with suffering
Whose bread is the bread of sorrow
And wine of joy is saturated in tears.


{110}

# Notable Communal Activity

## by Pinchas Kanner

### In Memory of Chanina Weisman and his Family

My grandfather Chanina Weisman was born in Rozniatow in 1840 to a merchant of wheat and flour. My grandfather's four older brothers died in their childhood, and therefore, when my grandfather was born, he was taken to the Admor of Vishnitz for a blessing. The Admor changed the name of my grandfather to David and also gave him an amulet for long life, a silver earring that my grandfather fastened to his ear until he reached the age of Bar Mitzvah. At his Bar Mitzvah festivities, the earring was removed and my grandfather's name reverted to his original name Chanina. Indeed, my grandfather reached an old age, had an inspiring visage and an imposing appearance.

His childhood and youth were spent in Yeshiva study. At the conclusion of his studies, he received rabbinic ordination. He also learned the German language. My grandfather married Tzivia Mandelbaum when he was eighteen years old. Her parents lived in the village of Krasna, near the town. After their first son, David, was born, grandfather left his house and spent three years in the courtyards of the Admorim of Belz and Chortkov. There he lived a life of abstinence and studied Kabbalah[4] in depth until it came time to return to his family. My grandfather had three sons and three daughters. His three sons died at young ages. The eldest daughter Esther married Baruch Mintz. They had two sons, Moshe and Yaakov. The second daughter Matilda married Tzvi Angelberg, and they subsequently immigrated to America. The third daughter Rivka married Mordechai Kanner, my father, and I was their only son. Later they had a daughter Chana, who was nicknamed Anzia.

My grandfather made a comfortable living. He owned a hotel, a restaurant, and a business in alcoholic beverages. My grandmother ran these businesses, and my grandfather dedicated all of his time to his holy works. In accordance with the custom of the pious Jews of that time, he would awaken early in the morning to occupy himself with the study of Kabbalah (the book of the Zohar) and Mishnah. After immersing in the Mikva and worshipping in the synagogue, he would come home to eat breakfast. Then he would dedicate several hours to reading the newspaper and rest. In the afternoon, he would receive people in his house, and then return to the synagogue for the Mincha service. He would spend the evening hours in the synagogue, where he would teach Shulchan Aruch (The Code of Jewish Law) and Talmud to select students.

My grandfather served as the mohel (ritual circumcisor) of the town and the environs. He even taught seven mohels, who split the mitzvah of conducting the Bris Milas in the entire region. He himself would perform the Bris Milah for his friends and for poor people. This was done as a gesture of honor or an act of charity. This was the manner of my grandfather, in that he was a faithful servant to his world, and worked at his tasks with all of his glory and all of his energy, honor, and wisdom.

Before the elections took place for the council of the region of Galicia, my grandfather was a member of the council, appointed by the Austrian governor, and he had influence in the circles of the Austrian administration. He would frequently travel to Dolina, Stryj or Lvov to exert his influence for the help of his fellow or for communal matters. After the elections in Galicia took place, he supported the Zionist candidates – something quite unusual for the Orthodox Hassidim. He supported the idea of the study of the Hebrew language, and also intervened for the good of the first Hebrew teacher who arrived in the town from Russia as a refugee. He supported the establishment of a communal meeting place in Rozniatow, an idea that never came to fruition on account of the First World War.

Despite his orthodoxy, he understood the progressiveness and spirit of the times, and did not prevent his grandchildren from studying in the gymnasia. He also did not insist that his daughters cut their hair at the time of their weddings[5]. I remember two events to which my grandfather took me despite my young age. His intention was to instill Jewish customs into my mind. On one occasion, I accompanied him when he went on Simchat Torah eve to drink cups of wine at the home of his friend Leizer Yitzchak Lev, where the honorable people of the town would gather. On the other occasion, on the eve of Passover 1914, my grandfather took me to the place where the matzo shmura was baked, even though I was too young to participate in the singing of the Hallel[6]. One of my childhood memories was with regard to etrogim (citrons), which my grandfather used to receive for each Sukkot from the Holy Land[7]. He would lend them to the rabbi, to my uncle Baruch Mintz, to his cousin Michael Weisman, and to his childhood friend Mendel Artman, the only one of the town who would address him in second person.

My grandfather was known as a learned and righteous Jew. Many people turned to him for advice in personal matters. They requested his advice or his assistance. His manner of speaking was interwoven with parables from the Talmud or Midrash (Jewish books of lore). His solutions to various problems flowed with a very deep-rooted wisdom of life.

When my grandfather reached the age of 78, he took ill with pneumonia, and never recovered. He passed away within a week. He died in the spring of 1918. The people of the town gave him his final honor by closing down all businesses during the time of the funeral. His coffin was prepared from the boards of the table of the synagogue before which he sat and taught Torah for two generations. In his grave, the placed his mohel's knife and a sack of earth from the Holy Land which he used to carry with him at all times. A number of his students recited Kaddish for him[8]. They had taken this obligation upon themselves due to their love and reverence of him. Everyone was connected to him with bands of love. His love of Torah imbued his entire personality, and he loved every student of Torah as his own child.

I wish to point out the connection of the Weisman family to the Holy Land. My grandfather's uncle traveled to the Holy Land in his old age in order to insure that he would be buried there after he died. He lived in Safed, and donated windows to the synagogue of that city, which are still today inscribed with the Weisman name.

On the anniversary of my grandfather's death, after the lighting of the yahrzeit candle, my grandmother Tzivia also took ill, and the physician predicted her imminent demise. My grandmother also died at age 78.

The following members of his families perished in the holocaust: my uncle Baruch Mintz, his wife Esther (nee Weisman) and their children Moshe and Yaakov; my mother and sister perished in Stanislawow; my grandfather's cousin Michael Weisman, his wife, and their very capable son Dr. David Weisman also perished.

{113}

# My Father Moshe Branik,
## one of the most Prominent Sons of Rozniatow

### by Yitzchak Barkai-Branik

Moshe Branik

I remember Rozniatow as if from a gray mist, as a children's story in the past tense... I remember the marketplace in the center of the town, the large schoolhouse on top of the hill, the pond and the small houses of the Jews. I remember the wagons upon which we traveled to the train, as well as the first automobile. I remember the first cheder where I spent a few months. As if from a fog, I remember the large fire, when the windowpanes of the building on the hill became red. I remember some select pictures and remote alleys. This was Rozniatow, where I was born, and where my father Moshe Branik of blessed memory was born. I left the town when I was about three or for, after my mother Sara (nee Rosenbaum) of blessed memory died.

From the stories of my father and his friends, I am able to imagine a portrait of my father's youth. As did most of the youth at the beginning of the 20 th century, Moshe Branik moved to larger cities, Lvov the capital of Galicia, and Vienna the capital of the Austro-

Hungarian Empire to study Torah. These were the spiritual centers for the Jews of eastern and central Europe of that time.

My father was fourteen years old when he left (fled) from his house to the centers of Torah. He completed his studies at the rabbinical seminary in Vienna, however he did not do so to serve as a clergyman, but rather to broaden his knowledge. There he became enthused with Zionism and was drawn to the magic of the Hebrew language, to which he decided to dedicate his life.

In the meantime, the First World War broke out and my father was drafted into the army of His Majesty Kaiser Franz Josef, and send to the Russian front. He returned to Rozniatow at the end of the war and began his Zionist activity by spreading the Hebrew language in Eastern Galicia. My father, Moshe Branik, became the Hebrew teacher of the town and merited to have many admirers. His many students spread all over the world, and the following story will be an example of that:

## A Meeting of Rozniatow Natives in Stockholm

Years ago, on my way from Latin America to Israel, I passed through Stockholm. There, I had to transmit a greeting to a Jew from Tarnopol from his friend in Montevideo. In his time, the man was an active Communist and was sent to Sweden as the business attaché of Communist Poland. After his tour of duty, he decided to request political asylum and not to return to his country.

I visited him, and we chatted about our common origins. A women with a Nordic appearance entered his house and exchanged some words with him in Swedish. In the interim, he told her who I was, and she suddenly started to speak to me in Polish. I then thought that she was not Swedish, but rather a Polish gentile, according to the appearance of her face. However to my surprise, it became clear to me that she was Jewish. As usual, she began to ask me about my origins, and I told her that I was born in the area of Lvov. For some reason, she continued asking: "From Lvov itself?". I answered: "From a small town near Lvov, but you would certainly never have heard of it". After some urging, I told her: "From Rozniatow".

Her face lit up. "You are from Rozniatow? I am also from Rozniatow".

When I saw the look in her face, I told her my name, Barkai. Now she did not let up from me, and asked me for my original name, before I changed it in Israel.

I told her: "Branik".

Then the women became very emotional, and tears welled up in her eyes:

"You are the son of Moshe Branik, my teacher!"

Thus did two Rozniatow natives meet, an Israeli Zionist returning home from a tour of duty in South America, and a Jewish Communist who fled from her "native" Poland to far off Stockholm, and the chain was connected between us – my father Moshe Branik.

However, as I already mentioned, Rozniatow was only the first stop of Moshe Branik. The place was small, and there were few opportunities. My father traveled to Lvov, a major Jewish center. When he arrived, he took on several tasks and he was chosen to lead an educational institution in a village near Lvov.

His personality of an educator inspired him to dedicate himself to the education of Jewish children, mainly orphans, in order to train them professionally and Zionistically to make aliya to Israel. However, during that dark time he was forced to accept upon him the task of general principal of the Tarbut school network of Eastern Galicia.

Moshe Branik had a great deal of gratification from this task. He had the opportunity to develop his pedagogic and organizational abilities. Very quickly, Hebrew courses became part of the curriculum of the schools kindergartens. There were courses for older students in the gymnasia, as well as a teacher's seminary.

Seated: Yitzchak Barkai. Second row from right: Sosha Stern, Matilda Hoffnung, Betty Rosenbaum, Etka Stern, Esther Rosenbaum, Shabtai Rosenberg, Rosie Falik, Ashtzi Trau, Esther Weidman, Avrahamele Hoffman.

The youth was healthy in body and spirit. They desired to make aliya to the Land and to build their future in Israel without thinking about the difficult situation in the Land or the difficult conditions of absorption. They were very interested in lessons on the history and geography of the Land of Israel.

I remember this era very well. I was a young boy watching my father's activities from a distance. Today, with retrospective vision, I remember evenings when my father returned home tired and worn out from his visits to cities and towns in Eastern Galicia. He would tell us with satisfaction about the opening of a school in a certain town, or the expansion of the Hebrew curriculum in another town, etc.

At the end of the 1930s, the network of Tarbut Hebrew schools slowly expanded. Our house turned into a meeting place for dozens of Hebrew teachers. There were meetings of the Hebrew teachers of Galicia during the annual conventions during the summer vacation in the Carpathian Mountains, in

Yaremcha, Mikocin, and other vacation spots along the Prut River. As the years went on, a Tarbut Hebrew gymnasia was founded in Lvov, where they taught various subjects in Hebrew. I myself became a student of that gymnasia and I remember the feeling of being the son of the principal. I had to serve as an example.

{116}

## Bialik and Stavi in Rozniatow

In 1934 I believe, The poet Ch. N. Bialik and later the writer Moshe Stavski (Stavi) visited us. Both of them brought first to our house the blowing breeze of the Land of Israel. Even before that time I had heard and known about the Land of Israel. It was the center of all of our studies. However, until that time, the Land of Israel was an abstract idea. Bialik and later Stavski brought the real land of Israel to our home.

I remember Stavski's visit to the home of the Ukrainian farmer where we lived for the summer. The Hebrew writer stood among the farmers and began to harvest with a sickle, and it was possible to sense what was happening; a Jew knew how to harvest. When Stavski began to place the shoes on the horse with his steady hand, there were no bounds to the respect that he merited among the group of gentiles in the Carpathian Mountains.

These visits of Bialik and Stavski apparently also had an effect on my father. He decided to visit the land of Israel. He could not continue on as previously. Suddenly, he felt as if he must serve as an example for others. How could he continue to educate others when he himself remained there? For my father, the study of the Hebrew language was not just learning for the sake of learning; it was rather a means for attaining an objective. Hebrew for the sake of aliya and life in the Land of Israel.

In 1935, my father went on his first visit to the Land of Israel, in order to decide there about his future. After a few months, he returned home full of enthusiasm and decided definitively to make aliya. The Land enchanted him. People tried to urge him to delay his aliya until they found a replacement for him, however his answer was always the same: "You will not find a replacement for me if I do not make aliya". A year after his visit, in 1936, my father received a valuable "certificate" as a Zionist leader, and made aliya to the Land.

This was the time of the Fifth Aliya. It was the beginning of the "incidents", there were daily casualties; however it was specifically this situation that urged my father to make aliya. His first days in the land were particularly difficult. He had difficulty in adapting, as was the situation with many of the Zionist activists. First of all, he found himself among hundreds of teachers and activists, he came to the land of his dreams... and here "they do not know Joseph"[9].

He overcame his difficulties and began to receive offers. He found a position as the principal of the educational division of the Tel Aviv municipality, at the center for culture of the Histadrut. However he was searching for a position where he could start something from anew, create something out of nothing. That was the reason that he preferred to set up an organization for adults rather than take on more enchanting jobs. The word "etgar" ("challenge") was not yet in use, however my father preferred the task of organizing and strengthening the non-organized public, without fanfare or popularity, such as organizations for householders.

Within a short period of time, Moshe Branik succeeded in turning the individualistic community into an organized center for householders in Israel. He published a monthly economic periodical called "Haboneh" ("The Builder"), and he put all of his energies into this area. However this was not more than he did for his first love, Tarbut.

During the years 1938-1939, my father found a topic that occupied him completely. These were years of siege and incidents, and the organization "Kufar Hayishuv" was set up. My father was one of its directors. He threw himself into this holy work, and found satisfaction when his ideas for public volunteer activities, donations of jewelry, etc. were accepted.

However, his cruel fate caught up with him there. A mosquito bearing malaria bit him, and within a few days he died at the young age of 44. His friends and fans inscribed on his monument: "Here is buried Moshe Branik, the chief of the strugglers for Hebrew culture in Eastern Galicia".

The Hebrew school in 1922.

{118}

# Baruch Keller

### by A. Friedler-Scharf

There was a dear Jewish personality in our town, who was happy with his lot even though he lived in financial distress. He would often tell jokes. He was known to everyone as Reb Baruch Shmuel Hershenes. Here are a few of the jokes he told that I still remember, and I wish to write them down.

When he was once asked: "Reb Baruch, do you yet have anything for Passover?", he innocently answered: "I already have matzos, wine, and meat".

"From where do you have these?"

"Last year, I was left behind a basket of matzos, some flasks of wine, and a pot of meat."

One he happened to be in the railway station of Krechowice, and he was seen feeling his pockets as if he had lost something. When he was asked what he was looking for, he answered: "See, I came here by foot in order to save a few coins, and I lost them in any case."

During a time of difficulty, he asked the Chevra Kadisha (Burial Society) to give him money in order to buy shrouds for his wife. When they came to his house to take away the body, they discovered that his wife was alive and well. They asked him with surprise what happened. He answered them:

"Behold, she will in any case be with you, if not now, then after some time... no matter what she will not escape from you."

Once Reb Baruch asked Tzvi Fesberg to give him a coin, and then he would show him something that he could not wait for!

When he answered, he grabbed the corners of his beard, put them in his mouth and said:

"On the other hand, you do as I am doing..."

{119}

## Avraham Zauerberg – the Man and his Activities

### by Y. Har-Zohar

Among the other cities and small towns in Galicia, famous or less famous, one small town can be found far away from the main communication network, at the outlet of the Bystritsa River into the Dniester. This town is called Jezupol, or in spoken Yiddish, Izipoli, and is near the large regional city of Stanislawow.

Two main Jewish families lived in this town, who were the heads of all of the Jewish families of Jezupol, the Erlich family and the Lublin family. The first supplied all of the families of the fisherman in the town and the area, and the second supplied the other households of the town who worked at various means of livelihood.

The householders, who were scholars, Hassidim of Chortkov and Zidichev, congregated in their kloizes and were like one family. They married off their children to each other, and there was almost nobody who was not connected to the other half of the residents of the town. The entire public and communal life was centered around the kloizes and Beis Midrash. These were places of study, recreation, Hassidic gatherings, weddings, and holy festive occasions.

The rays of the Haskalah and the echoes of the first calls of Chovevei Zion began to break through the openings of the blinds of the Beis Midrash and kloizez. Here and there, one could find under the bench of the Beis Midrash a boy who was hiding with the book "Ahavat Zion" of Mapu or "Chavatzelet", or someone humming "Al Em Derech"[10]. The hearts of the young people beat quicker when they heard the echoes of the footsteps of the first people making aliya to Zion and the echoes of rebelliousness and shooting from far off Russia. These things moved something in the quiet and peaceful atmosphere of the town. Voices of freedom and liberation rose up from afar and made echoes through the iron blinds of the Beis Midrash into the benches of the Beis Midrashes and kloizes of Jezupol. They blew into the heart of the young Avramche new desires, for concealed far off places. The discussions and thoughts that customarily took place regarding difficult segments of Talmud, on the right interpretation of the page, finding an answer to a difficult segment of Maimonides, on the piercing question of Maimonides' Guide For the Perplexed, finding answers for the doubts of the heart, all began to suddenly take on rings that were previously unknown and strange to their surroundings.

Who is the man who understands the great wonder which took root in the hearts and brains of the Yeshiva students, who did not leave the benches of the Beis Midrash, who never set foot in a secular school, and now all of a sudden it was as if a new light was lit in their hearts? Very many abandoned their roots and the rock that forged them, went to drink from foreign cisterns and joined the ranks of those who rebelled against the old world order, forged a new path, and called for freedom and liberty.

The minority who were not swept away by the tempest of the times, who were able to withstand, and who remain strongly attached to the benches of the old Beis Midrash, the warn out folios, were also not passed over by the call for freedom and liberty. Between studying pages of Gemara, between Mincha and Maariv, they found the time to write down on paper the thoughts of their hearts and yearnings of their souls. These were not the voices of the Talmudic sages arguing about an egg that had not yet been born[11], but rather about a poor and downtrodden mother, about a house that was about to collapse, about the high position of the well-to-do and the downtrodden situation of the poor, about the thoughts and aromas of the times. The stanzas almost flowed by the dozen from the pens by themselves, onto the margins of pamphlets and writing paper, onto notes of accounts. However they were almost all lost or destroyed. We will discuss some here and copy the few that survived by chance.

It was hard for father to part from his dear son, his assistant and supporter. However, how can one go against the verse in the Torah: "And therefore a man..."[12]? He joined his blessing with the blessing of the loving mother, and they traveled to Rozniatow to marry off their eldest son at an auspicious occasion, for good luck, to the praiseworthy bride, the daughter of Reb Shmuel Wert. They left behind their child of old age in his cradle.

The boy Avraham became "The Apprentice Reb Avramche of Jezupol", among the rest of the silk apprentices in the town. They set up a place for him in the kloiz, and he continued with regular Torah study as he began his career in his father-in-law's flour business with his young wife helping him at his side.

Their honeymoon period did not last long. The First World War broke out. Avraham the apprentice was drafted to the Austrian Army and was immediately sent to the front. His young wife accompanied him from afar with the fasts of Mondays and Thursdays[13]. She continued her husband's flour business and hid gifts for the poor under her apron. She conducted acts of private charity. She would give out a bit of flour for the Sabbath challas and some hot food for poor women who had just given birth. In one poor house they had to revive her from her swoon. It was Monday, her private fast day for her well being and for the speedy return of her beloved husband. She went on her daily journey to the houses of the poor and forgot to partake of something early in the morning to sustain her for the fast day. Her weakened heart caused her to swoon.

To the thunder of artillery and cannon shells, between hunger pangs and poverty, after a difficult labor and the crying out for mercy in the synagogues and at the graves of ancestors, their firstborn daughter was born. She was small and weak, pale and short of blood. A candle was lit in the home. The father received a brief furlough between the battles to embrace his newborn daughter. When he returned to the front, he dreamt sweet dreams about a warm nest and small nestlings with fragile wings. He sent letters filled with love and longing to his fragile wife and his young nestling who had just recently been born into the air of the world. There was pain and agony in the house of his parents, for his four brothers had been drafted into the army. His parents were exiled to Hungary. They wandered around from place to place, taking with them their young children. They lost contact.

When the storm abated the joy was great, for the children returned to their homes, healthy in body and complete in spirit.

When the apprentice Avramche Zauerberg returned home after the war, he found his niche in communal activity. Here there was a family that was broken due to the war that needed support, there was a need to rebuild the Beis Midrash which had been burnt, and there were storekeepers who were being strangled under the burden of debts which they could not pay. There was a need to set up a charitable foundation to help those who were stumbling, to enable struggling merchants to purchase some merchandise in order to maintain their livelihood.

Avraham left his young wife in the store, and together with Rosenberg or someone else, would make the rounds to people of means in the neighboring villages to collect flour for Passover or for some other mitzvah. In his home, he organized a chess club and a choir for young singers headed by the cantor-shochet Reb David.

Externally Avraham resembled an ardent Hassid, dressed in a kapote cloak, with a streimel on his head, and with a black beard that had never been touched by a pair of scissors. Nevertheless, on Sabbath evenings after the Sabbath meal, one could find him going on a long walk accompanied by his eldest daughter. On his way, he would chat with one youth or another and tell a joke. That youth would tell it over to someone else, and within a few moments, all of young people of Rozniatow suddenly gathered around Reb Avramche, boys and girls, laughing at his stories and jokes.

He was a good conversationalist. He was able to tell stories and gather around him interested people who would drink up his words with thirst, words that were spiced with humor and jokes. Despite his

Hassidic appearance, he did not hesitate at weddings to be at the head of those who entertained and danced in front of the bride and groom. He speedily removed his outer cloak and hat, and with a kippa (skullcap) on his head he began to sing and dance "keitzad merakdim, keitzad merakdim"[14]. Accompanied by the enthusiastic group of singers and dancers, he would speedily arrange the well-known "Kaprosh" dance. He would direct it and issue the orders. Woe to the dancer who was not able to remove his shoe quick enough after been issued the command, or to take out his fringes from the four corners. He would have to pay good money to the band.

He was beloved by his fellowman and he was blessed with great wisdom, and therefore he became 'the' arbitrator of the town. Any difficult dispute between two people was brought before Reb Avramche. With his great intellect and deliberation, he knew how to arrange compromises and prevent strife and bitterness.

If there was a bride who was not able to pay off the little that she promised for her wedding, he would redeem her from her straits. He purchased for a significant sum of money an additional place in the Beis Midrash, in addition to the three that he had inherited. That was his manner, he went about his business discreetly, and therefore everyone loved and revered him. He was a person who exuded both Torah and good character traits, and he was beloved by all who knew him.

At the twilight of the day, when darkness covered the land and the silence of death was not disturbed, not by the victorious sounds of dictators nor by the sounds of the dying, there was only the small sound of flames eating up parchment and the remnants of the martyrs who were being burnt at night. Hear and there, it was possible to see how the earth, which absorbed the bodies of the pure martyrs, trembled and shook from pain and embarrassment. A wounded and tattered person struggled with his last strength after succeeding in coming out of the pit, having been covered by many other bodies. The person was breathing his last breath.

The echoes of the shooting of the martyrs of Rozniatow, who had been shot not far from there, from the prison of Dolina, reached the ears of the six people who were imprisoned. They were waiting for their verdict. These included Zindler, Avramche Zauerberg and his young son Pinieli.

They had finished the others off on Sunday. This day was Wednesday, and Avramche repeated over and over again the Psalm for Wednesday: "G-d is a G-d of vengeance, let the G-d of vengeance appear"[15]. He repeated it over and over again and took comfort. The chain had not yet been broken! There is still reward for his labors! Israel shall not be a widower!!! There, far away in the east, in a place where the heart and thoughts do not stop pining for, there is a survivor! There is a brand plucked from fire[16]. The brand became a fire, and the fire a flame which will burn and light up the darkness of the frightful night.

The next day at sunrise, at the time when you can tell the difference between blue and green[17], the time of reciting the morning Shema, they took the six out from the jail in Dolina and brought them to the nearby forest. Avraham still managed to tie a rope around his waste like a silk waistband[18] in order to read the order of morning sacrifices, and he sanctified the name of Heaven by reciting the Shema as the bullets of the murderers cut down five of the six victims. The only survivor, Zindler, merited to fulfil the will of his friends, to remember and perpetuate them, and to take revenge for them.

Avraham Zauerberg merited to leave behind in Israel a brother Yehuda, who is writing these lines with tears, a daughter Miriam, and two granddaughters, Tamar-Dvora and Esther-Tehila, who remember the memory of this honorable family with trembling.

Yitgadal Veyitkadash Shmei Raba![19]

{123}

# Avraham Zauerberg

### (translated from Yiddish with a non-literal translation)

All of the poets and hymn writers sang of him
With pride, their songs were listened to.
To me, their praises were strange,
My thoughts on him were altogether different.

We waited for you all winter,
At a time when the snow piled up on our roof
The freezing and cold lamented in our house,
They became our constant companions.

At a time when the snow penetrated through the apertures
Inside the house and in all its corners,
The walls cracked from cold and dampness
To you, oh golden sun, is the heart and thoughts of man.

But my disappointment toward you is great.
You behaved like a hypocrite to us! This I will tell you inside.
The faces of the well-to-do and the vain are beaming,
Yet you withhold your rays from the poor and destitute.

Your shine into thousands of palaces
You grace the splendid rugs
Yet you fail the millions of poor
How can you be pleasant in my eyes? How?

Do you expect to receive thanks from the golden calves?
I will explain this to you clearly
They hide from your face in sanatoriums and thick forests
They are afraid of your rays.

I will give you some advice:
Enter our house please,
Please dry our moldy walls,
Please warm the weak back of mother,
Heal her ailing hands and feet.

Rozniatow, May 14, 1939.

{124}

# My Grandfather Avraham

### by Esther Har-Zohar

Avrahamche Zauerberg

The Judaism of the Diaspora, the Jewish town in all of its appearances, splendid looking Hassidim, Beis Midrashes, Kloizes, Rebbes' courtyards, Jews and Jewesses, their deeds and manner of life among themselves and between the gentiles in whose midst they lived – the Judaism of the Diaspora is clearly illustrated before my eyes in the books of Bialik and Agnon. This is especially the case with the books of Agnon, for he was born and grew up in the region where my parents, my grandfather, and all of my family lived. He knew very well how to describe the lives of the Jews there as I heard related on occasion from my parents, who told us girls about the life of our grandfather, uncles and aunts.

"Grandfather" is a foreign concept to us. We never merited to experience the heartwarming gaze of our grandfather, the soft hand of grandfather touching my hand and telling stories to his grandchildren, appeasing his grandchildren during an argument between themselves over a toy or an apple.

A photo of my grandfather Avraham of blessed memory in his prime stands on the bookcase in my parents' house. One day as I was browsing through the bookcase, the picture caught my eye. I stared at it and remembered that this was my grandfather, this was the man who was such a close relative of mine and about whom I had heard so much, and I did not know him. My eyes filled with tears. I looked again at the picture and saw a hearty smile in the eyes of my grandfather as he looked down at me. Thus did I stand for an entire hour, without being able to move from the place. My grandfather was a dear man, a pious man, and a great scholar. He studied Torah and taught Torah to others. He was a loving and dedicated father to his children and his family members. He was beloved by his fellowman. Everyone loved him and everyone revered him. At a wedding, circumcision or other happy event, my grandfather was always at the center of the rejoicing. He also knew how to play a violin without ever having taken lessons. He would play Hassidic melodies and lead the gathering in dance, full of joy of life and happiness. He was a communal activist. He occupied himself with the needs of the community without intending to receive a reward, whether for the benefit of the community in which he played an honorable role or for the benefit of the youth. He concerned himself with the youth. He brought in a Hebrew teacher, organized a choir and introduced the youth to Torah and Zionism.

From the mouths of Rozniatow survivors, I heard that my grandfather went to his death bravely, encouraging the people who were with him so that they would not be distraught. He strengthened their hearts on their journey to sanctify the name of Heaven.

From my mother, we girls have heard a great deal about the refinement and spiritual grace of my grandmother Tila, after whom I am named. Every Thursday as she began to prepare for the Sabbath, she would cook fish and other delicacies for the Sabbath. She prepared everything in honor of the Sabbath queen. My mother told us that on Thursdays, her mother of blessed memory would send her at dusk to bring baked goods and other provisions for the Sabbath to poor people and families who have come upon difficult times, so that they would have something with which to greet the face of the Sabbath.

The following is a story that occurred. One Thursday night, as my grandmother went as was customary to the home of one of the needy people with her gift, she forgot that she herself had not yet eaten anything after her Thursday fast, which she observed to pray that my grandfather would come back healthy and in one piece from the war. She fainted on the street from her weakness.

As our small family sits at the Sabbath table and sings the Sabbath hymns, with the same tunes that my family sung in the exile, tears well up in my parents' eyes. They tell us that when they sing these Sabbath hymns, they can see before their eyes the Sabbath table of their parents, a table filled with children and a grandfather at the head of the table, singing Sabbath hymns, with the house filled with light and joy. The light has been extinguished and the joy snuffed out, and we remain as the only survivors of the conflagration, a small spark from a large flame. I hereby hope that light will shine from this small spark, and a large flame will light up the darkness of our lives.

May their holy memory be blessed.

## TRANSLATOR'S FOOTNOTES

1. The Hebrew form used here is taken from biblical grammatical structure. For example: "And it came to pass in the days of Ahasuerus" (opening line of the book of Esther); "And it came to pass during the time that the judges judged" (opening line of the book of Ruth). There is a Talmudic opinion that any biblical section that opens with 'And it came to pass' denotes a bad event. This certainly applies here, and I suspect that it was the author's intention.

2. Czechoslovakia was only formed in 1918, with the breakup of the Austro-Hungarian empire, so to be more accurate; he was born in the Austro-Hungarian province of Bohemia.

3. This poem appears in a box on the bottom of page 109. Kol Nidre and Unetane Tokef are well-known prayers of the High Holy Days. Tikun Chatzot is a dirge over the destruction of the temple recited by especially pious people at midnight.

4. The works of Jewish mysticism.

5. Orthodox Jewish women generally keep their hair covered after their marriage. This can be accomplished by a hat, beret, snood, wig, or any other type of covering. An orthodox Jewish wig is known as a sheitel. In Hassidic circles it used to be common that women cut of their hair completely prior to their marriage.

6. Matzo Shmura is matzo made with special care for the purpose of fulfilling the commandment of eating matzo at the Seder. Hallel is a selection of Psalms (113-118) recited on various festivals.

7. An etrog (citron), is one of the four species – the others being the lulav (palm frond), hadas (myrtle twigs), and arava (willow twigs) – which are biblically mandated to be used as part of the Sukkot celebration.

8. The Kaddish prayer is generally recited by the surviving sons, but he had only daughters.

9. A reference from the beginning of Exodus, where the new Pharaoh does not remember the deeds of Joseph. Here it means that his uniqueness and qualifications in his hometown were not recognized in his new place.

10. Translates as "Along the Way", seeming a Zionist song of the time.

11. A reference to the opening discussion of Tractate Beitza of the Talmud, which discusses whether an egg born on a festival day can be eaten that day, or on the subsequent festival day.

12. This verse, in the book of Genesis, described the situation of human nature after G-d created the woman from part of the man: "And therefore a man shall leave his mother and father and cleave to his wife, and they shall be one flesh."

13. Monday and Thursdays are traditional days to fast in times of distress.

14. A traditional wedding son: "How does one dance before the bride? A lovely and gracious bride."

15. Each day of the week has a specific Psalm, which is recited as part of the morning service. The Psalm of Wednesday is 94.

16. Several of these phrases are biblical or midrashic in origin. "There is reward for your efforts" is from Jeremiah 31, referring to G-d's promise to Rachel as she was weeping for the loss of her children. "A brand plucked from the fire" is from Zechariah 3.

17. Being able to tell the difference between blue and green refers to a time in the morning, before sunrise, when Jewish law deems it valid to put on the tefillin (phylacteries).

18. The waistband 'avnet' or 'gartel' is worn by Hassidim during prayer.

19. These are the opening words of the Kaddish prayer: Magnified and Sanctified is the Great Name!

{126}

## Righteous Women
### by Miriam Har-Zohar

Due to the fact that, for the most part, the authors of memoirs and lists in the Yizkor book are men; I wish, as a woman, to memorialize and perpetuate the stories of several righteous women. These were mothers, aunts, and good neighbors who did a great deal of work quietly and modestly. I wish to describe here the generous characters and good deeds of several women from our town who did their work unofficially, without being members of a social organization, without telephones, and without meetings and committees. They did their work due to their warm Jewish hearts and their sense of responsibility. They conducted their work quietly and without fanfare; they gathered a bit of flour, a bit of sugar, some foodstuffs from here and there and brought it over to needy families. They did this in a secret fashion, so that nobody would know who the donors were. Thus, the recipients would not be embarrassed by the public knowledge that they were needy. In the darkness of night, covered by a large kerchief, the righteous woman would go around to the homes of the needy, the ill, or other such families who would have preferred to die of hunger rather than having their plight become public knowledge.

A few of these women are engraved very well in my memory. One was Sara, the mother of Avraham Saraf Friedler. On Sabbath eves, immediately after candle lighting, she would put on a large kerchief and take a white bag in her hand. She would begin her holy work, going from house to house to collect challas, cakes and other provisions, and then she would distribute them secretly and quietly to the homes of the needy, in such a way that nobody would recognize her. Certainly, they would impatiently await her arrival.

I remember that when I was still a young girl, the good woman entered our home on the eve of the holy Sabbath, in pouring rain, thoroughly soaked, in order to gather the challas and put them in a bag. I was curious about the woman since I knew her, and I asked my mother if she is indeed so needy that she would have to go out in the pouring rain to gather bread and challas. My mother answered me: "You should know my daughter, the greater the effort, the greater the good deed. She is not gathering the challas for herself, but rather to distribute to the needy who have none of their own. Even on a rainy evening they need to eat, and especially on a rainy day is the good deed so great."

She went about her activities without fanfare or acclaim, without meetings and decisions by noisy activists. I remember one other righteous woman who conducted her activities quietly and modestly in order to fulfill the great mitzvah (good deed) of "giving gifts in secret"[1]. I wish to make mention of her here for good among the other righteous women. This is Ethel Treu.

I remember that once on a Tuesday night Mrs. Treu entered out house and turned to my mother saying:

"Tila, come quickly."

I was frightened by this request, for who knew what had happened, and she told my mother: "Today is the weekly fair, and the Jews have earned some money. I require a sum of money quickly for a great mitzvah, please go and collect money from your sisters and acquaintances, and I will do so also, and we will save a needy family from the disgrace of starvation."

She spoke and she did. Mother did her part and she did her part. After a short while, they had collected the required money and gave it over to the needy family. They did this without turning to the public assistance organizations, without making detailed investigations, and without bloodshed. This was "giving gifts in secret" in the full sense of the word.

It was the warm heart of the righteous woman who felt the necessity, and acted in haste. To the credit of the Jews of Rozniatow, it should be stated that there was practically no Jewish family who, when asked to donate, refused. They would give a little or a lot, everyone according to their means.

I remember one other righteous woman, to whom people would come to her home quietly in order to receive a portion of hot soup, a bit of cholent, or other such foods. This generous woman was Ethel Rechtschaffen. She was very wise, and with her gentle hands she knew how to offer assistance, how to support one who has fallen without the person even realizing. She did it with fineness and modesty. Only very few knew of her activities and deeds. She understood very well how to act out the concept of "giving gifts in secret", without embarrassing people and without causing distress.

## Entertaining Guests (Hachnasat Orchim)

I wish to describe here another sublime and beautiful idea that was in our town, that of "entertaining guests".

I remember one incident, on a rainy Sabbath eve, when my father went to worship at the Kloiz of Reb Hirsch Rechtschaffen due to its proximity to our house - generally, he worshipped at the large Kloiz. He returned from the prayers with a Sabbath guest, as was customary. We had not even gotten around to singing the "Shalom Aleichem" hymn and reciting the Kiddush over wine when the door opened and another guest walked in. He excused himself and said: "I have been invited as a guest by several people, however I prefer to come here even without an invitation. I know from my previous experiences that here in this house, I will not feel myself as a Sabbath guest, but rather as a member of the household, like one of you.

Of course, he was received graciously, and he dined with us.

This era was the time of the well-known "moratorium" whereby the anti-Semitic Polish government decreed that all debts that the farmers owned to their lenders, primarily Jews, would be cancelled. The government decreed an annulment of debts for twenty years. This law affected primarily the Jewish merchants, especially the small-scale merchants who collapsed completely. Bankruptcies became the order of the day in every town. Tribulations increased and livelihood decreased. There were merchants whose economic situation had become so bad that they were down to a morsel of bread, and they did not have anything with which to sustain their family. They were not able to go out and beg for money in a place where people recognized them, so they spread out over the land. Most of them were destitute small-scale merchants, whose staff of bread had been cut off. They restricted their own intake in order to send something to sustain their families.

Some of these arrived in Rozniatow as well, and they had to be treated completely differently from the general beggars and riff-raff. Among these people were scholars and refined people who had come upon difficult times. They sat at the Sabbath table as old friends, sang hymns which they brought with them, and learned new hymns, and they did not see themselves as ordinary "Sabbath guests".

There is much to relate regarding "the entertaining of guests", both regarding the official "Hachnasat Orchim" institution which provided lodging for poor wayfarers who had no place to sleep in the town, and regarding the concept of "Hachnasat Orchim" in the broader sense.

There were Jews in Rozniatow who brought guests into their homes each week on the Sabbath. They would never be seated at a table where there was no guest. On occasion, an argument would break out in the Kloiz or Beis Midrash regarding who would have the honor of bringing home the guest. One would say, "he is my guest", and the other would say, "No he is mine".

There were certain constant guests who would go on the Sabbath to "their own customary home" as a matter of course. These guests did not see themselves as riff-raff, lower in status than those who sit around the table, but rather as members of the household.

Every Wednesday was market day, and Jews came to town from the entire area in order to sell their merchandise and wares. Each Jew had a set place to lodge, where he would store his merchandise and personal belongings. While he would be reciting the morning service (Shacharit), the mistress of the house would prepare a hot drink or a cup of clear liquor. This was the general popular "Hachnasat Orchim" which took place in every home, and nobody minded that on every Wednesday the house turned into a public guesthouse.

## An Event Regarding a Mitzvah (Good Deed) and Transgression

There were difficult times for the small-scale merchants and other artisans. Money was hard to come by. It was becoming more difficult to receive assistance from the average Jew for a few days in a row. This was even the case among the generous hearted Jews, from whom it had always been possible to receive assistance. Now it had become more difficult. One day, the wife of a well-known merchant entered out house and almost burst our crying: "Reb Avrahamche", she said, turning to my father, "You have to help me today, for if I cannot receive any appropriate financial assistance to enable me to pay for the contract, my husband is liable to be imprisoned for non-fulfillment of the conditions of the contract. I have nowhere to turn... Everyone to whom I turned told me that today there is no money, and it impossible to receive any assistance at all. Please try, Reb Avrahamche to visit that specific rich man and ask him for some assistance for this great need."

When my father answered her requests and went to visit that rich man to ask for assistance, he found him leaning against the hot oven. He received my father pleasantly, and asked him about the matter that brought him to visit him.

My father answered him:

"I have come to save a Jew from imprisonment. I require financial assistance."

He answered my father:

"It is a commandment (mitzvah) to lend money to a Jew, but it is a sin to request the money in return. I do not want to perform a mitzvah that will bring me to a sin."

Nevertheless, my father did not leave his presence empty handed.

## Frumtze Brina

From among the "righteous women" whom I am attempting to describe for the young generation "Who do not know Joseph"[2], who did not know their grandmothers and the pure, refined, modest women who did their work modestly and discreetly, there was one who was known as "Frumtze Brina the bagel maker". She was widowed during the First World War and remained alone with her three children. She had to concern herself with providing for her family, educating her children, and selling her handiwork. Therefore she woke up each day at 3:00 AM in order to bake bagels, and later she went out to sell the bagels, to feed her children and take them to school. She did everything in her tiny one-room dwelling, where the kitchen served also as the dining room, the bedroom, and the room where the children did their homework and played. She did everything in that one small room, and she nevertheless kept an immaculately clean house. She was poor, but everything was orderly, and everything was in its place.

She earned her livelihood with great difficulty. Frequently, she had to borrow money for the flour that she needed to bake the bagels, and she was only able to repay the loan after she sold her products.

However, this is not the reason that I am writing about her here. I am memorializing here the poor woman who was alone with her troubles and sorrow, however when she saw a child from a poor home going to cheder or school and she knew that the child had not yet eaten breakfast, she would secretly give him a bagel, so that nobody would see and the child would not be embarrassed.

I myself witnessed this on numerous occasions. She would do it with haste. She would place a bagel in his hand, and disappear quickly so that nobody would notice her.

Our friend Yehuda Axelrad, who today lives in the United States, also related this to me. He told me that often, when he went to school and he was hungry, she gave him bagels that restored his soul.

This is a prime example of giving gifts secretly. May her memory be holy and blessed.

Regarding "righteous women" of Rozniatow, there certainly are many to write about and tell about, especially for members of the younger generation who were born after the holocaust. I myself cannot remember them all, and describe them all for two reasons. First of all, I was a young girl when I left Rozniatow, and I did not have a chance to know them all. Secondly, certainly there were other "righteous women" who did their activities prior to my time. It would certainly be worthwhile for me to write about them. Perhaps others who are older than me, who remember the previous generations, can do so.

## Visiting the Sick (Bikur Cholim)

There was another important social institution in Rozniatow for which Jews worked generously. This was the Bikur Cholim institution. In those days when the penicillin remedy was barely known, and other antibiotics were relatively new, it would happen on occasion that a Jew had a high fever, and it was necessary to lower the fever. They would cover such a person in damp blankets for a period of time until the fever dropped. All the family members of the ill person would busy themselves with his care. They would leave their business and activities and devote their energies would be drained from the effort of caring for the sick person.

A Bikur Cholim society was organized in order to divide up various tasks of caring for sick people among its members. They would primarily make sure to help the sick people during the nights, so that the family members can have some rest from their travails.

I remember Mr. Moshe Rosenberg, Kalman Halpern, Eli-Yonah Koral, my father and other good Jews who would help the sick benevolently and on a constant basis.

### The Financial Assistance (Gemilut Chasadim) Cassa

There was another important voluntary social institution in Rozniatow. This was the Financial Assistance Cassa.

Since those days were difficult for the Jews and there was an economic depression among the merchants, particularly the small-scale merchants; the turnover was very poor and people became worse off. Many people required loans and financial assistance, and therefore it was vital to set up such an institution that would lend money to merchants for a short period without interest.

On several occasions, a woman would enter our house, weeping, and would say:

"Please have mercy upon me, save me from prison and give me financial assistance for a few days so that I can redeem the bill of sale. For if not, they will imprison me, for I was also unable to repay the previous contract."

There were such institutions of charity and kindness in Rozniatow, and good Jews gave of themselves and worked for these institutions with all their soul, and with unbounded dedication.

{131}

## Maskilim and Men of Haskala (Enlightenment)
### by Moshe Fruchter

It is difficult for an outsider to understand how in such a small town as ours, there were a recognizable number of youth and adults who were Torah scholars as well as scholars of secular knowledge and Maskilim. How did it come to pass that physicians, lawyers, students in various institutions in Israel and the Diaspora, youth of the intelligentsia and enlightened people all came from here? How did this come to pass, and who gave them the push and desire for Torah, wisdom, and knowledge?

How is it that the fathers in each generation passed on to their children the desire for Torah and wisdom, for these are our life and the length of our days, and in them we will delve day and night[3].

The youth thirsted for knowledge and study. The Beis Midrashes and Kloizes were full of Torah students. Those that removed the yoke of Torah from themselves accepted willingly upon themselves a different yoke. This was the yoke of socialism, progression and freedom. Those who had the means traveled to institutions of study in various places, where it was still possible for Jews to study. Those who did not possess the means of leaving the boundaries of the town would go to the large library that was run by Ben-Zion Horowitz, and there they acquired wisdom and knowledge.

The desire for Torah and knowledge was the lot of the Jewish children from their childhood. Already in their cradle, the Jewish mothers would sing the following well-known song to their children: "Study Torah - for it is the best merchandise" If one of the children did not wish to study Torah, their father would ask them: "Then what will become of you? You will become a gentile, a boor, and an ignoramus."

There was great respect for the Torah scholars and secular scholars. Everyone honored them, and they were the heads of the organizations. The youth organized themselves into youth groups that dealt with political and Zionist matters. They had question and answer sessions, Chanukah and Purim parties, and they prepared to make aliya to the Land of Israel.

{132}

## Sh. Shalom in Rozniatow
### by Simcha Gross

I wish to relate here in front of the readership how the well-known poet and writer from the Land of Israel, one of the leaders of Hebrew literature, Sh. Shalom, came to visit once in Rozniatow during his childhood.

Once, the Admor of Drohobyczh came to spend the Sabbath in Rozniatow, and he brought with him, among his entourage, a young grandchild who was dressed in traditional garb with a spodek on his head like one of the elder rabbis.

Rabbi Hemerling of blessed memory, the rabbi of Rozniatow also had an orphaned grandchild by the name of Mechli who also wore the traditional garb on the Sabbath with a spodek on his head as was customary among the rabbis.

The two children, dressed in their cloaks and shiny spodeks, held hands and went out to stroll in the streets of the town.

The entire town went out to see this splendorous site of the two young "Rebbes" with spodeks on their heads strolling through the town and talking among themselves.

What was the fate of these children? Mechli, the grandson of Rabbi Hemerling of blessed memory is still alive, but I do not know exactly where. However the second child is very well known to me. He is our great, famous nationalistic poet Sh. Shalom, who lives with us here in Israel, may he live to 120 years.

{133}

## The Beloved and Pleasant ones
### by Mordechai Stern

Godel Schwalb and Godel Yampel were the grandchildren of our neighbor Reb Meshulam Kliger, who was a short person, with a quick gait, and very diligent. He was affluent, for he owned a large store that sold household equipment and other such items. His only son, Eliezer-Bar-Dov, a refined young man, assisted him in his business and his communal work. He came early to the Kloiz every day, and he would study a page of Gemara daily prior to the prayers. Eliezer his son, as commanded by his father, would inquire regarding the neighbors who requires financial assistance. He would also concern himself with setting the prices of the merchandise appropriately so that it would not cause difficulty for the other merchants who were struggling with difficulty for their livelihood.

Godel Schwalb's father was Reb Yisrael Schwalb, a resident of Rozniatow. The parents of Godel Yampel resided in the village of Spas.

Reb Meshulam concerned himself not only about his children, but also made sure that his grandchildren would study Torah. The two grandchildren lived with their grandfather so that he could supervise their education. They were the same age. I studied together with them under the teacher Reb Yehudale Kaufman, as well as in the same class at the public school. The two Godels slept in one bed, and together they shared the sweets of their grandmother Rosia. They celebrated their Bar Mitzvas at the same time. The two of them studied with great diligence. They progressed greatly and attained a high level. They also became proficient in the Hebrew language though self-study. Both of them aspired to make aliya to the Land of Israel. The influence of Moshe Rosenberg, the Zionist leader, was significant upon them.

I met Godel Schwalb in 1934 in Rozniatow during the winter months prior to my aliya. This was at an evening celebration in Sokol. The performance was for the benefit of "the organization which supports travel to the Land of Israel for needy pioneers under the auspices of the Labor Zionists". A bespectacled youth, with a pleasant demeanor, stood in front of me, and I did not recognize him. Later it became known to me that Godel was the chief speaker of the Revisionist Movement. I was surprised, and apparently he realized that, however it would not be like Godel to disrupt the performance of a rival group. He was not willing to give up his ideas, however on the other hand, he was prepared to help pioneers who wished to make aliya, for there is no greater merit than that. This was a very interesting meeting, and we exchanged memories of the past. This was the final encounter I had with my childhood school buddy, my playmate with whom on occasion I had slept in the same bed. He told me that his cousin Godel Yampel returned to his parents in the village of Spas to assist them with their agricultural work.

Both of them desired to make aliya even in an illegal fashion, however their parents forbade this. Both of them honored their parents, and did not leave their parental home. In any case, "from where would it be possible to obtain an aliya certificate?", he concluded.

In the summer of 1936, Mr. Lieberman, an aliya representative from the Jewish Agency arrived. He was given the authority by the Mandate government to bring young Jews, who were experts in agriculture, to the Land of Israel. Godel Yampel had the opportunity to make aliya as an agricultural expert. He registered and received a permit. Prior to his departure, Godel Yampel married his beloved, his cousin the sister of Godel Schwalb.

Godel made aliya himself and settled in Petach Tikva. Godel acquired strong horses, and after a few days, he was employed as a ploughman by the orchard owner and poet Streit. The overseer of the orchard was a native of our town and my good friend, Shimon Lustig of blessed memory. To their merit it should be pointed out that in the Streit's orchard, only Jewish workers were employed.

## A Purim ball for the benefit of the Keren Kayemet Leyisrael 1935

A Purim ball for the benefit of the Keren Kayemet Leyisrael 1935.
(note, Yiddish text says 1936)

Seated from the right: Bronka Berger, Dvortza Gelobter, Roza Mintz, Matilda Prinz, Salka Horowitz and her sister, Reizsha Rechtschaffen, Matilda Hofnung, Dr. Minkes and his wife, Etka Adlerstein, Blumtza Rechtschaffen. Behind them: Shabtai Falik, Estzi Treu, Marek Roter, Rozia Falik, Yehuda Hirsch Stern.

Second row from upper right: Dr. Leon Meiseles, Max Adelstein. Above them: Philip Fuerst.

In the center holding the scroll: Shabtai Rosenberg, Godel Schwalb

There were difficulties of absorption, challenges of language, and work shortages - for him and others, but his dedication to work was boundless. He was very successful. In his small notebook, he recorded the names of the farmers who waited for his work. Now that he was sure of his success, Godel wished to bring his wife to the Land, and he presented an immigration request to the Mandatory authorities. He rented a dwelling in the center of the Moshava and waited for his wife. However the government was not of the same mind. He was imprisoned while he was sleeping in his bed. I immediately decided to work for his freedom, and I began to intercede with the national authorities. He was freed from prison on the eve of Yom Kippur after I made the matter known to Mr. Moshe Chaim Shapira, who served later as the interior minister of the government of Israel. Our fellow native Yisraelke Horowitz the son of Shlomo Shmerel of blessed memory and the Zionist fighter Dr. Ramon Yaval of Petach Tikva, may he live long, both paid a monetary pledge.

About three days later, he was re-imprisoned. The Mandatory authorities wished to imprison him, claiming that he gave incorrect information to the aliya department of the British government, since on his certificate, he indicated that he was a bachelor. They pushed aside all requests for a proper trial that is even granted to confessed criminals. The Hebrew newspapers did not fill their mouths with water, and did mention this strange and unusual occurrence.

Godel Yampel was an enthusiastic Chalutz. He dreamed of settling in one of the Moshavs in the Galilee. He was a member of the "Working Zionists", and his objective was to make aliya with his wife, and later to bring his parents. However, he was forcibly expelled from the land, and against his will, he was forced to return to Rozniatow, to his wife, parents, extended family, and his cousin-brother-in-law Godel Schwalb. Neither of them merited to make aliya to the Land and to see the establishment of the State of Israel.

This entire large, dear family fell prey to the Nazi claw. Godel Schwalb and Godel Yampel were not separated in life and in death.

### Shaya Parish and his Grandson

I knew this family, who lived a few houses away from our house, in the "Rynek" plaza. Reb Shaya had a large cloth store, from which he earned an honorable and substantial livelihood. He was a well-to-do large-scale merchant. He was one of the prime supporters of Reb Itzikel and he fought his battles enthusiastically. Along with his brothers-in-law Reb Tzvi Rechtschaffen and Reb Chaim Schwartz, he made it his business to ensure that Reb Itzikel would be accepted as the rabbi of the city, despite the fierce opposition from a majority of the residents.

During the time of the First World War, Reb Shaya and all of his family, including his daughter Chana and her husband Melech Lustig along with their children, moved to Vienna. Shimshon my friend came to bid farewell along with his parents and his grandparents. They went from house to house, until the home of his brother-in-law Rechtschaffen. Parish's large house remained desolate and empty; however, we, the friends of Shimshon, went to play beside this house specifically. It was as if we were keeping guard, and fulfilling a covenant of friendship.

At the conclusion of the war, Shaya Parish and his wife returned to Rozniatow. Chana and the children, however, remained in Vienna. How happy we were when our friend Shimshon came to visit his grandfather. On that very day, he was sent to the teacher Yehuda Kaufman. The relationship between the grandson Shimshon and the grandfather was particularly close.

{136}

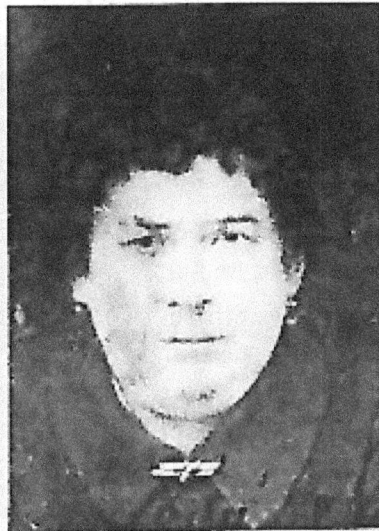

שאיע פריש

וונצ'י פריש

מלך לוסטיג

הנה לוסטיג (פריש)

   Upper left - Shaya Parish; Upper right - Henche Parish; Lower left - Melech Lustig; Lower right - Chana (Parish) Lustig

## Shimon Lustig

Shimon Lustig (note - in the text, this name appears as Shimshon)

There was no shortage of fires in Rozniatow. The Ukrainian residents wished to take revenge on the Jews, and they would ignite fires in the middle of the night. There was very little fire-fighting equipment, and most of the houses were built of wood. When a fire would break out, it would destroy a portion of the town. The store and home of Parish in the Rynek, the business center where the weekly fair would take place, was on several occasions a victim of fire.

That year, all of the residents of the town celebrated the holiday of Simchat Torah in the home of Parish. They moved aside the merchandise and furniture, and let the entire house and store be used by the celebrants. Tables laden with delicacies were set up. How great was the joy in the home of Shaya Parish.

About a year later, he sold the white house to Ben Zion Yekel. He left Rozniatow and made aliya to the Land of Israel. He requested that his beloved grandson Shimshon join him.

The Parish and Rechtschaffen families had relatives in Petach Tikva, the Streit brothers of blessed memories. They were communal activists, directors and founders of the agricultural bank, owners of an orchard, and the founders of the Achad Haam High School. One of them was a well-known Hebrew writer. The Streit brothers willfully employed Hebrew workers on their farm. This was the era of "cheap labor", and the Jewish settlement was suffering from work shortages. The Streit brothers advised Shaya parish to settle in the young town of Herzlia. There, Shimshon would certainly find work, and there were good opportunities to purchase a home and a plot of land. Shimshon worked with all his energy in the blossoming orchard. The grandparents looked upon this with mixed feelings. The absorption was difficult. The climate was difficult for the older people. Shaya Parish was a well-known and respected rich man in Rozniatow, and his decision to make aliya to the Land of Israel created waves in town. However here in Herzlia, the young village, he was lonely and less powerful. He had no regrets, G-d forbid, and was happy with his lot. The most important thing was that he merited to make aliya to the Land of Israel with his beloved grandson Shimshon.

At the time of the writing of these lines, the terrible news of the passing of his only brother Reb Zechariah of blessed memory reached us. He lived in Ramat Gan, and was beloved by all who knew him. He would meet with Rozniatow natives with great joy, even though he did not remember anything of Rozniatow. He was meticulous in observing the commandments. He left a wife and two children.

May their memory be blessed.

{138}

## Shimshon Lustig by Yona Lustig

When he was young, his family moved to Vienna, and there he received his education. His grandparents returned to their hometown after the war, however after their store burnt down three times, they decided to leave the exile and settle in the Land.

Shimshon, who at that time was on an agricultural hachshara (aliya preparation) program in Austria, joined them, and in 1925, they all made aliya to the Land.

At first, they joined their relatives, the brothers Yeshayahu and Shalom Streit in Petach Tikva. In accordance with the advice of the Streit brothers, the grandparents and their grandson settled in Herzlia. There, there was no problem with Jewish labor, as there was in most of the settlements at that time. The grandparents' money was sufficient to purchase only a house and small yard, and Shimshon worried about earning a livelihood.

After the death of his grandparents, Shimshon married Yona (nee Kinor) may she live long. He met her at the home of the Streits, their mutual relatives. The couple lived for a few years in Herzlia, and later they moved to the Kfar Ganim neighborhood of Petach Tikva. There they built their home and established their family.

It is important to point out the activities of Shimshon to bring his parents to the Land at the time of the outbreak of the Second World War. His father was imprisoned by the Gestapo, and the certificates that were distributed here in the Land were very few. Shimshon did not spare any effort, and for an entire week, day and night, he kept guard at the doors of the agency offices, until he finally received the requested aliya certificates. Thus, he rescued his parents from the teeth of the Nazi beast. His sister managed to escape to England. However, he never merited to see her again.

He worked in agriculture for all his time in the Land. He rose in rank until he became an overseer of orchards.

He lived a working life, quiet and straightforward. Because of the goodness of his heart and the joy of life that he had in his heart, he was beloved by all who knew him.

His final year, the year that he suffered from his dreadful illness, was difficult to bear, however Shimshon did not worry about himself even at that time. He concerned himself with his family members and tried to hide his pain in order to ease the suffering of his loved ones.

He was one of those to whom our national poet must have surely been referring in his poem:

"May my lot be with you, oh the suffering people of the world..."

{139}

### Dr. Sabat by Mordechai Stern

Dr. Sabat was born in Czechoslovakia, which at that time was part of Austria. He fulfilled his duty as an army doctor during the First World War. With the retreat of the Russian occupiers, the Austrian authorities returned to our area, and Dr. Sabat arrived with them. This was the first time that Dr. Sabat met with the "Ostyuda"[4], which left a strong impression on him. Despite his strange clothing and his strange behavior, he did not distance himself from us. On the contrary, he attempted to set up connections with these Jews.

He discovered quickly that these people had fine souls and healthy intellects. He was astounded by the mutual aid that people would extend to one another despite their difficult circumstances during the war.

In 1917, a typhus epidemic broke out in Rozniatow and surroundings, and Dr. Sabat, as a military doctor, dedicated himself to fighting the epidemic. The home of Yehuda Weissberg, which belonged to the notary, was set up as a hospital. Due to a shortage of space, some of the sick were transferred to the hospital in Dolina. Healthy people who had not been affected were transferred to quarantine camps in Krechowice. The epidemic affected most of the families in Rozniatow. The town suffered greatly, and mourning hit many homes.

In our family, four people, myself included, were stricken, and taken to the hospital in Dolina.

Dr. Sabat worked day and night in order to save people, and his name was mentioned by everybody with the additional praise: "an angel from heaven". He spent a long time in front of each bed, and despite his difficult work he was always full of good humor. Everyone spoke of his wonderful manners, his courtesy, and his joy when he spoke to anybody.

After the conclusion of the war, Dr. Sabat did not return to Czechoslovakia. He remained in Poland and settled in Rozniatow.

His house was next to the house of the Falik and Kaufman families. His ties of friendship with the Jews of the town were strengthened. Since he was a famous doctor, he took a central place in the societal life of the town. He knew how to encourage and support people, to strengthen tired hands from morning until the darkness of night.

With his great patience, he knew how to relate seriously to anyone, especially to those who required medical assistance. Many of those who required his services were poor, and he supported them with his money.

He attended the Great Synagogue on festivals, and he took his natural place amongst the large crowd. He extended his hand to everyone, as if this was the place where he received his life force.

{140}

## Vove Hoffman, Mayor of Rozniatow (Bergenmeister)

Vove Hoffman

Vove Hoffman was one of those who attained leadership due to their many actions; actions that are considered together, however each one was important in its own right, and the doer of such deeds would perform them with devotion due to his own enthusiasm and a recognition of the importance of the action at that time. Vove Hoffman attained his position of mayor through a long route, due to many deeds that were necessary in their right time. His deeds were manifold and beneficial to the public with regard to the development and flourishing of the town.

Vove Hoffman was born in Kolusz, and he married Paula the daughter of Meir Teneh of Rozniatow. At that time, Meir Teneh was the mayor. After his death, Walszinowice was elected as mayor of Rozniatow. The Jews of the town thought that, in the interests of peace with the gentiles, it would be preferable to elect a gentile. However it did not take a long time for people to realize about Walszinowice, that even though he was not an anti-Semite, he was incapable of running the civic matters, of protecting the interests of the residents, and of acting for the enhancement and development of the standard of living.

This was the era of modernization and technological progress. The people of Rozniatow had contact with the outside world. They would travel to Lvov, Vienna, Germany and America; they would read newspapers and books, and were very interested in the news and innovations of civilization. In addition, Rozniatow was in the center of many villages, and was fourteen kilometers from Dolina, and therefore it had the conditions necessary to develop as a business and manufacturing center. However, in the district offices of Dolina, the Jews of Rozniatow met with trumped up difficulties that made all efforts difficult. The struggle was very difficult, and when the chance came to choose a mayor, the Jews of Rozniatow preferred a Jewish candidate. They chose Vove Hoffman, who was very intelligent, had a vast knowledge, and was fluent in Polish and German. This honorable candidacy came to him on account of an activity undertaken not to receive a reward, but rather due to the circumstances of communal life. Once he was elected mayor, he acted as a father and a faithful problem solver. He concerned himself with all the needs of the town, however most of his efforts were directed toward the Jews of his town, toward their physical well-being and the maintenance of sanitary conditions. He bore the weight of the public. He took all matters seriously and excelled in his activity and counsel. He insured that roads were paved, that there was adequate lighting, and that the schools were in good shape. He played a major role in the building of the post office, and he took particular pride in the building of the Great synagogue, for which he dedicated supreme activity.

Vove Hoffman, the noble and aristocratic man, was exacting and pedantic. Even though he stood his ground with vigor and was not frightened of anyone, he was loved by all. His uncommon appearance, with his vigor, his long beard like a lion's mane, instilled respect upon everyone with whom he came in contact. However, after a short time, any person would see the gentleness and pleasantness that flowed from him. He left a pleasant impression upon anyone who came in contact with him, and everyone greeted him with obvious reverence.

His orthodoxy did not impact his understanding of the younger generation. Even though he himself was not a Zionist, he taught all of his grandchildren Hebrew. When his grandson Motek Treu left for the Land of Israel at age fifteen in an illegal fashion, the grandfather gave him his blessings and assistance.

On the High Holidays, Vove Hoffman conducted the services in the Great Synagogue. On other holidays, he led the services in the Kloiz. He was an enthusiastic prayer leader. Through his sweet, powerful voice, he was able through his prayers and melodies to arouse the congregants to tears of great joy and celebration.

In 1914, when the First World War broke out and the Austrian army retreated from the town, the Ukrainians prepared to cause trouble for the Jews, who were deathly frightened and confounded. Vove Hoffman attempted with all his might to combat the fear and confusion. He went out with a white flag to meet the Russian army, he found housing for the captains, and he promised that any Russian soldier would be able to take from the stores whatever he wanted, provided that he register his name. Thus, he prevented them from engaging in pillage and murder. He received permission from the authorities to conscript young Jews to the civic militia, so that they would be able to protect the town from any attempt of pillage.

The nationalist Ukrainians hated him and pursued him. When the army garrison changed, they immediately began to contrive against him. The new authorities did not hesitate to demonstrate their strength against the Jews, and they imprisoned him with the intention of exiling him to Siberia.

However, he managed to escape by travelling on foot to Kolusz. He was forced to live in hiding until the Austrian army returned to Rozniatow. Then he resumed his public activities.

His civic duties caused him to neglect his private business, and he often tried to free himself from his job of mayor, however he was unsuccessful in doing so. His honesty and uprightness won the hearts of the residents and officials. He was also revered by his few opponents. When they pleaded with him to stay on, he did not have the strength to refuse, so he answered positively.

Vove Hoffman was an outstanding personality who demonstrated the ability to overcome his private interests. He was characterized by a combination of wisdom and goodwill, benevolence and purity, moral uprightness and responsibility.

{142}

# Our Family - From Generation to Generation
## by David Stern

Our family, the Stern family, resided in Galicia for many generations, and included praiseworthy and precious people who set up deep roots in Jewish tradition; in whose hearts there were very deep feelings of love of Israel and love of one's fellowman; who inspired with their spirit and their being their entire surroundings; people of fine character, full of reverence for Torah and general knowledge, These larger than life ancestors of ours were our roots.

Our family tree reaches back to Rabbi David the son of Shmuel Halevi Segal (1586-1667), who served with glory as the rabbi of the community of Lvov. He spread the fame of that community widely, for he was well known as mighty in Torah and a great arbiter of Jewish law. He would enlighten the eyes of his students with his methodology of learning. He was the author of the work "Turei Zahav" which explained the Code of Jewish Law and had a comprehensive list of sources. He was full of depth, sharpness, as he cut down to the truth of Torah. His lofty spirit was made known also in his book "Divrei David", which is an explanation of Rashi's commentary on the five books of the Torah, in which he opens up the gates of light of understanding with his wondrous depth.

In the year 5424 (1664), on the 8th of Iyar, there were attacks on the community of Lvov, and his the two children of the author of the Turei Zahav, Reb Mordechai and Reb Shlomo, may G-d avenge their blood, were murdered.

This era was one of many in the family tree of our family as it spanned the generations. Many fine traits shone out also from my grandfather, Reb Mordechai Stern, the great-grandson of the murdered Reb David Shmuel Halevi. His renown spread out due to his personal charms. His work as the owner of flour mills and fields did not distract him from his labor in Torah.

Even during his youth, all of his acquaintances recognized that he had an open and merciful heart, caring about every soul. He was born in 1809 in Mizon that is near Dolina. According to the request of the elder Admor of Zydaczow, Reb Hirsch of holy blessed memory, he went to live in a village near Rozniatow. Through his generous character, he served as a sign and example to all, and when he died at age 95, in 1904, all of the Jews of the town participated in his funeral. On that day, all of the stores and workshops in the town were closed.

His six sons: Tzvi Yaakov, Zelig, Avraham, Chaim, Moshe and Shlomo, and his three daughters: Chana, Altza, and Feiga, all excelled in their nobility and refined personalities. My father Shlomo Stern owned a store that sold a variety of flour products as well as a general store. Even with all of his work for a livelihood, he found the time and great interest to concern himself with the problems of the public. My mother as well, the daughter of Reb Meir Fruchter, followed the path of my father and dedicated herself to her fellow man - to everyone. Our house was always open, and anyone who entered was accepted pleasantly.

We were several brothers and sisters. Of them, the three brothers Moshe, David and Mordechai survived. They immigrated to the Land of Israel in the 1930s, and live there to this day. Also surviving are the children of our sister Leah, Baruch Tor and his sister Rachel, who immigrated to the United States.

Our father Shlomo and mother Esther, our brothers Yehuda Tzvi and Hirsch, our sisters Leah and Miriam were all killed in the terrible holocaust in 1942.

{143}

## Moshe Rosenberg

Moshe Rosenberg

His name preceded him. All of the townsfolk, both young and old, knew him. He was the solid pillar, dedicated and faithful to Zion, active in doing sublime good deeds. Is there anyone from among us, Rozniatow natives, who is able to describe Jewish communal and Zionist activism without mentioned Moshe Rosenberg? He was the son-in-law of Reb Feivel Reisler. His major occupation, which he fulfilled with dedication, willingness and without tiring, was for the sake of the community, especially for the sake of Zionism. He was the inspirer of the public, the volunteer, who worried about culture and publicity. Great was his joy when somebody was sent off to the Land. Joy would beam from his face.

Before his eyes was the realization of the dream of the return to Zion. He dedicated himself with love to the upbuilding of the nation and the Land, to changing our lives and setting them onto healthy foundations.

## TRANSLATOR'S FOOTNOTES

1. Giving gifts in secret to the needy (matan beseter), entertaining guests (hachnasat orchim) particularly those in need, and visiting the sick (bikur cholim), are several of many practical manifestations of the commandment of "Love your neighbor as yourself" that are noted in Jewish law.

2. "Who did not know Joseph", refers to Exodus 1, where a new Pharaoh arose who did not remember the kindness of Joseph, and therefore began oppressing the children of Israel.

3. The last part of this sentence is a quote from the daily Maariv (evening) service.

4. This refers to "Ostjuden", the Eastern Jews who were more traditional in garb and behavior than the Jews of central Europe.

{144}

# Those Were the Days
## by Yehuda Har-Zohar

I wish to relate to you, children and grandchildren, the "generation that did not know Joseph"[1], a small bit of the customs, events and behaviors on Sabbaths and weekdays, on days of joy and mourning; how the Jews went about life and how they danced, how they toiled under the yoke of Torah and the yoke of earning a livelihood. In short, I wish to relate a bit regarding Jewish life in Rozniatow.

I am writing for you, children and grandchildren, despite the fact that I know that you have studied or are still studying in Hebrew schools, studying Jewish literature including the works of Shalom Aleichem, Mendele, Peretz and Agnon, each one of whom tried to the best of his ability to describe Jewish life in the towns of Russia, Ukraine, Poland or Lithuania. Agnon, as a native of eastern Galicia, attempted to portray in his books Jewish life in Galicia as we still well remember it. I do not wish to compete with his ability, only to perpetuate the memory of the martyrs of our town. These are chapters of life of our parents, grandparents, uncles and aunts, in order to memorialize them.

Day of Consciousness and Celebration with our Grandfathers

In those days, when communication was not like it was today, the age of jet planes and Boeings, when if you wish you visit the Lubavitcher Rebbe you can fly from here to there quickly and comfortably in twelve hours and behold you are in New York with your Rebbe. In those days, if your parents or grandfather wished to travel for a Sabbath or a festival to the rabbi of Bolekhow, Oleska or Zidichov, a few Hassidim would together take a wagon with two horses, spread the floor of the wagon with straw, put a cover on top of it, load the wagon with food and a few bottles of liquor, sit on it and travel to the Rebbe.

When they reached their destination, the Rebbe's court, on the eve of the Sabbath or festival, they would be greeted by the crowding and pressure of throngs of Hassidim who also came there to spend the Sabbath with the holy Rebbe or to worship with the Rebbe on the festival. At home, he left his wife and family members, who would spend the Sabbath or festival without the head of the family. On occasion, the father would take with him his eldest son, who would reach the age of Bar Mitzvah in a few more years and would have to become a man. Therefore, the father was obligated to introduce him to the ways of Hassidism, despite the fact that this was accompanied by the difficulties and many trials of a long journey.

On the eve of the holy Sabbath, after each of the visiting Hassidim finished his Sabbath meal at the home of his respective host, they would all gather together around the Rebbe's table. Very late in the evening, the Rebbe would begin the recital of "Shalom Aleichem", and would enunciate the "Ribbon Kol Haolamim"[2] word by word. Hundreds of Hassidim were gathered around the table, listening intently to every word uttered by the Rebbe. Silence pervaded in the large hall where the Rabbi partook of his Sabbath or festival meal.

Reb Tzvi Hirsch Rechtschaffen, a Hassid of the Rebbe of Glinna

The Rebbe was enwrapped in his tallit (prayer shawl), burning from an internal flame and from the enthusiasm of the Sabbath, recited the Kiddush[3] , enunciating each word. He would sip from this large silver cup and pass it around to his family members. His wife the Rebbetzin and his daughters would hear the Kiddush from the women's gallery. The Rebbe's assistant (shamash) would then pass them the Rebbe's cup of benediction. A bowl for hand washing would be brought before the Rebbe, and he would lave his hands, raising them up and reciting "Lift up your hands in holiness, and bless the L-rd". He would then recite the blessing over the bread (challah), and the Rebbe's Sabbath meal would commence.

Until the food was served, the Rebbe or one of the Hassidim would quietly hum a melody, without words. Those close with the Rebbe, his confidants, would then begin to sit down at the table. The gabbai (manager of the proceedings) would invite them to the table, each person according to his importance and rank.

There were Rebbes who were great in Torah and thought, whose entire contact with the people was through Torah philosophy, through words of teaching, Torah novellae, and lessons in the ways of Hassidism. Their entire desire would be to grow in Torah, to study Torah, and to spread Torah.

In Rozniatow, there were Hassidim who were Torah scholars and lofty people, and there were Hassidim of Strolisk, Burstyn, Czortkow, and Sasow, populist Hassidim of the simple folk. Both types observed the days of Hassidic consciousness. On the memorial days (yahrzeit) of various Tzadikim, they would make a small celebration, drink a toast, wish each other well, and break out in a Hassidic dance, filled with enthusiasm.[4]

At the Hassidic gatherings with the Rebbe, when throngs of Hassidim from all areas of the land gathered together, people became friendly with each other. They would make business deals with each other, and on occasion they would "shake hands" between themselves in agreement to marry their children to each other. There were occasions when the Hassidim became so friendly with each other, that if news arrived from home that the wife of one of the Hassidim gave birth at a propitious time, many of his Hassidic friends would hurry toward him to make an arrangement for an agreement to marry off their own recently born child with the newborn.

In order to cement the connection between the Rebbe and the people, the Rebbes would "go down to the people", that is to say, they would visit the towns of their followers once or twice a year. The Rebbe would stay with one of the influential local Hassidim for approximately a week, and he would receive the local Hassidim each evening until a late hour of the evening. The Rebbe's Sabbath table would take place in the kloiz. If the Rebbe were accustomed to leading prayers with a nice voice, he himself would lead the prayers that Sabbath. If not, one of the experienced Hassidim who knew how to sing would lead the prayers. Anyone interested in song and music, either alone or with a choir, would be present, and thus did the melodies of the Rebbe's table pass along from mouth to mouth, so that they would be able to be sung by the people throughout the year, until the Rebbe appeared again and taught a new melody.

**In the Cheder**

I wish to tell you, oh youth who did not know the life in exile, something about the life of the Jews at that time. You have certainly read about and heard about the schools that were called "cheders", where the children of the "house of the rabbi"[5] were taught. When a child reached the age of three, he was already "big", for he already had another younger brother or two. In order to enter him into the yoke of Torah, his parents would decide to give him over to the teacher of young children (Rebbi). During the course of the year, the child would learn the aleph beit, and begin to read the Siddur (prayer book). The children had an extra measure of joy on the day that the teacher would take the young children, aged between three and five, to the house where a young baby boy was born, and they were placing the infant in the cradle.[6] Before they placed the child in his cradle, the young children of the nearby cheder gathered at the home, recited "Shema Yisrael", and threw candies and nuts into the cradle. The joy of the children was very great.

It was a great day for the parents, family members, and certainly for the young child, when he would start the study of Chumash[7] at a propitious time. They would dress the child in his Sabbath clothes. The child's father or a good uncle would tie a large gold chain around his neck, to which was affixed a large watch that could be opened by pushing its two sides. All of the family members gathered together, the grandmothers and grandfathers from both the father's and mother's side, uncles, aunts, brothers and sisters, and the house would be full of people. On account of the festive occasion, they would light the Sabbath candelabrum; they would have the young child stand on the table that was full of delicacies and presents for the children. The Rebbi would stand next to the child, holding him with his hand so that he would not fall off the table, and so that he would not become confused due to anxiety, and cause anguish to the Rebbi for not teaching properly. The Rebbi would then begin to ask him, "What are you learning, oh young child?". The child would answer with a festive voice, "Chumash, to my good fortune". "What is the meaning of Chumash?" the Rebbi asked, "Chumash means five", answered the child.

"Why five?", asked the Rebbi, "Perhaps it is five coins for a bagel?". "No", answered the child with laughter and self-assurance, "Chumash refers to the five holy books". "Perhaps you know their names?", asked the Rebbi. "Certainly!", answered the child, "The first is Breishit, the second Shmot, the third Vayikra, the fourth Bamidbar, and the last one is Devorim".

This continued with a special festive chant, and all those gathered around were melting with laughter and enjoyment. The mother discreetly wiped away a tear, due to her great pride in her progeny.

The Rebbi continued with is questions:

"What book are you going to study?". The child answered, "The third one, Vayikra". "Why Vayikra?", asked the Rebbi. "Because the book of Vayikra deals with holy things, and I, a Jewish boy, who is starting to learn Torah at a propitious occasion, am also holy. Therefore, I will start with the book of Vayikra."

### Days of Vacation

There were very few vacation days for the students of the cheder, for it is written explicitly: "You shall toil in them day and night"[8], so how would it be possible to gave vacation days and desist from the study of Torah. Nevertheless, we cheder students remember a few days of vacation and joy. First of all there were the days of "krishma leinen", the recital of the Shema that I have already described to you, when we went all together along with the Rebbi to the house where there was a newborn child, and we received candy and sweets. There was also Lag BaOmer[9], when we went out, along with the Rebbi, with bows and arrows made from reeds or small sticks. We would go to the edge of the forest where we would play, shoot arrows, and jump on the trees. It would be very joyous.

There was another day when we were quite happy and playful. This was when we all went to the river or the pond for Tashlich.[10] The adults went on Rosh Hashana and recited their prayers from the Machzor[11], and we children concerned ourselves with casting "ships" into the river, with candles burning on them. Despite the fact that it was forbidden to light a candle on the festival, someone made sure to provide us with candles[12]. We made "boats" out of all sorts of boards, planks and other floating material. We chased after them along the river, and it was very joyous.

We would play with cards or dreidels (tops) on Chanuka. On Purim, we would play "even or odd" with nuts. There was no shortage of nuts, and sometimes, children would wander around with pockets full of nuts. The game was very popular and beloved by the children.

During the winter, when the studies commenced immediately after the festivals, and the days became shorter, we would continue to study at the cheder until night, and we would return home late, when it was dark. The children were frightened. There were parents who equipped their children with all sorts of lanterns to light up the way home. Once, as I was going home with a lit lantern in my hand, two gentiles fell upon me, removed the lantern, and fled. I arrived home trembling in fear. My parents comforted me. After that time, we went home in groups. In order to calm our fear, we sang the entire way until we reached home in peace.

We Remember.

At a Chanuka party in 1958 in Tel Aviv. From left: Yechezkel Neubauer, Zecharia Friedler, Nechemia Tanne, Mordechai Trau, the widow of Archie Berger. Mrs. Tanne, Mrs. Trau, Lischi Trau, Mrs. Weissman, Rosie Stern-Falik, Mordechai Stern

{149}

# A Candle in their Memory
## by Mordechai Stern

### My Parents Shlomo and Esther Stern

The man was very humble as I remember him. He was modest, and went about discreetly. He never aspired to be a communal activist, and he never agreed to be even the gabbai (trustee) in the kloiz. He was a Hassid of Zidichov and he was also faithful to Rabbi Betzalel, the Rebbe of Glinna. He honored him greatly when he came to Rozniatow. Once the Rebbe of Glinna left Rozniatow and arrived in Bolekhov. As the Sabbath holiness was commencing, his soul departed as he as saying the words: "Light is sown for the righteous". The following week, my father was sent by the community to be present at the coronation of his son Reb Chaim as Admor.

In accordance with the advice of the Admor, my father left the village Zinowa in 1907 and moved to live in Rozniatow, where he continued conducting himself as a G-d fearing Jew. He was discreet. He did not flee from small things, and did not aspire to greatness. He shared his heartwarming smile with anyone who he met on the street. In conducting his business, he never agreed to take anyone to court or to a rabbinical adjudication, so as not to cause an oath[13]. At one time the son of his brother, David the son of Moshe of the village of Sliwka, left an inheritance to the community, which became the cause of controversy between the notables of the city. When the matter came to litigation, my father was summoned to court. He refused strongly to present himself and to give testimony under oath.

The farmers called him Szlomko Zytlani Zhid. That means: righteous Jew. He was brimming with love of his fellow and friendship.

Our mother Esther was known as a refined and noble hearted woman. She was fluent in the German language, and even with all of her education, she kept the commandments. She went to worship in the synagogue every Sabbath and she remained faithful to her path for all of her days.

Their fate was the same as the fate of all of the Jews. They were exiled to Dolina and perished in the Holocaust.

## Moshe the son of Meir Fruchter the Cohen

My uncle Moshe Fruchter was the only brother of my mother. They were born to their father Meir of Zinowa, a village infamous for its Jew hatred. The priest Swyka, who was a delegate to the Austrian parliament in Vienna, hailed from there. The intelligentsia and Ukrainian leaders of Lvov, known for their hatred of Jews, hailed from there.

My grandfather Meir was one of those who fought on behalf of Reb Itzikel, that he should be accepted as the rabbi in Rozniatow. This was the factor that decided the matter in his favor. That is what the elders of Rozniatow relate.

Grandfather hired the best teachers for his children. Among other subjects, they studied German and Polish; however his main desire was the spreading of Torah and the study of Torah.

During the time of the occupation, when the Czarist Russian army occupied the area, my grandfather and my Uncle Moshe were expelled from the town. Their property – two flour mills, a tavern and a store – was confiscated. The Russians made a libel against my grandfather, and took my Uncle Moshe as "surety". He was freed after a time due to the intercession of Baron Walysz, who was one of my grandfather's friends.

My Uncle Moshe became ill as a result of the libel. At that time, he began to take on students, whom he taught Torah and the vernacular written language. He was an erudite and scholarly man, who loved simplicity. He was modest. His greatness was his modesty.

His wife Chaya Eti was the daughter of his sister Nessi[14]. They all perished in the Holocaust.

May their memory be a blessing.

## Leib and Chaitzi Falik

Leib Falik, the son of Shabtai, was born in a village near Chorodow. He married Chaitzi the daughter of Veve Hoffman. They moved to the village of Strutin, where their sawmill and store was located.

They moved to the city in 1908 or 1909. Their large and spacious home was built near Baron Walysz.

He would go to his work early each day. He employed Jews and gentiles, and he maintained cordial relations with them all. He came to worship in the kloiz each Sabbath.

He was a modest man who distanced himself from all communal activity, and never became involved in any controversy in town. They both maintained good and proper relations with their neighbors, and all residents of the city respected them. He excelled in his patience, and nobody ever saw him angry. He would attempt to convince the opposing party quietly and calmly.

His wife Chaitzi was an exemplary housewife. She conducted the household with a good spirit. She raised her family, blessed with many children, in the spirit of grandfather. She knew how to instill good manners into her children, and taught them first and foremost to honor their fellowman.

They were known in the entire area for gracefully receiving anyone who entered their home.

After a tiring and busy day at work, she found time to read books and the newspaper. Over and above anything else, she thirsted to hear news and words about the Land of Israel.

The Nazi claw did not pass over their home.

May their memories be a blessing!

## Ethel and Yisrael Trau

Ethel, the second daughter of Veve Hoffman, was the husband of Yisrael Trau, one of the regular attendees at the "parliament" of Yosef Kanser. He expressed his words with reason and order. His reasoning was convincing. He did not have to be given permission to speak. Everyone listened to him with attention and interest.

Reb Yisrael excelled in sublime character traits. He was always an optimist, and always in a good mood. He was a scholar, and rooted in communal affairs. However, he distanced himself from communal activity, and did not agree to become one of the community's chief spokesmen, despite the numerous requests that came his way.

Ethel and Yisrael Trau owned the largest grain store in the city and the area. Many purchasers from the entire area came to them. The good service, friendliness, and business honesty were taken for granted by everyone.

Ethel Trau faithfully assisted the needy with love and dedication.

## Perl and Chana

The two youngest daughters of Veve were Perl and Chana. Perl married Eli Yona Koral, who was born in Bolekhow. Chana married Shmuel, the oldest son of the respected Berish Friedler. The two of them, Eli Yona and Shmuel, were respected by the residents of the town. Both of them were well-known donors to the funds for the Land of Israel and for all the needs of the community. People would first turn to Eli Yona Koral and Shmuel Friedler for needs of "Hachnasat Kalah"[15]. They were both known as scholars and educated people, attached to tradition. They educated their children to the Zionist idea. Eli Yona went around with a wonderful smile, and he was at ease with people. Shmuel Friedler was blessed with purity of thought, and therefore many turned to him for advice. They had great faith and love for him.

Perl and Chana were known for conducting their households in a good, orderly, and traditional fashion.

Eli Yona was a flour merchant and wholesaler. Shmuel Friedler acquired the daughter of Chanina Weissman, and transferred his large and spacious store to that home[16].

## The Brothers Shalom and Leibele Aryeh

Shalom was a son of Veve Hoffman. He was a diligent, orderly and efficient person. He owned a large, well-organized grocery store. His wife Leah was pleasant to both the old and the young. The second son Leibele continued on in his father's business. Shalom was active in communal affairs. He did not take things for granted, and did not hesitate from entering into an investigation. Everyone valued his uprightness and honesty in communal affairs, for he was known as a person who spoke the truth from his heart.

Leibele was known as an educated person. He studied during his youth with Reb Yehudale Kaufman, who developed Leibele's knowledge and diligence to exemplary levels.

They were both righteous and dedicated to tradition. The Zionist movement and its factions were close to their heart. However, they did not want to join any one of them, in order not to reject the others. They were among the worshipers of the Great Synagogue, and on occasion, they also worshiped in the kloiz with their father.

## Reb Efraim and Perl Rechtschaffen

Reb Efraim owned a flour mill in the city next to the large pond (the teich). He was a man of deeds, and of fine character. Many called him "Uncle Efraim", for Reb Efraim was a friend and comrade to everyone. He was known by this name to relatives and strangers, to the young and old.

There were many reasons to visit the flour mill and to observe it and the deeds of the owner of the flour mill Reb Efraim. Nearby were the cheder of Reb Yehudale; the river, which was worthwhile to visit in the summer and the winter; the route to the old city; the bathing place at the Rynika or the river, etc. We were always received graciously and with a smile. Uncle Efraim was never angry at the children who disturbed him. He received our inquiries patiently, and he willingly answered the questions of everyone.

I had many opportunities to be in the company of Reb Efraim and his wife Perl when I was sent to the mill by my father for various matters. I also used to visit their house to visit my school chum, their son Kasriel Serel, may he live long. He lives in Antwerp. His sister Reizel also lives there. Their home is open to guests.

Perl and Efraim Rechtschaffen offered faithful assistance, discreetly and quietly, to all in need. Efraim Rechtschaffen worshipped in the Great Synagogue. I often saw him among the worshippers of the kloiz. He was received there with the honor and graciousness that was befitting for him.

### Leitzi Lea the daughter of Leib Falik

She was married to the honorable and well-known Leizer the son of Baruch Geller. Leizer had a large textile store, and his customers had faith in him, for he served them faithfully and honestly. He made a comfortable living. He was considered to be among the firmly based young householders. He took interest in all communal matters, and he was active in various organizations.

He had studied with Reb Yitzchak Branik. Leizer was though of at the time as a scholar in Jewish studies. General studies were also not strange to him.

Leitzi and Eliezer[17] Geller found a broad range field of activity with the Hebrew school. They supported its activities with dedication. They distanced themselves from all controversies, and he only saw the good and his own obligation in everything.

All of these families were destroyed by the Nazi enemy.

May their memories be blessed!

{153}

## Yaakov the Lame
### by Zeev Weinfeld of Hadera

I wish to recall to the natives of Rozniatow one Jew who faithfully served them all the days of his life, and provided them with various items of food, such as chickens, eggs, fish, and on occasion even kosher butter from our farm in Swaryczow. This was none other than Yaakov the Lame, or as he was known to all in Yiddish, "Yankele der Krumer".

This Jew lived alone and lonely amongst the gentiles in the village of Swaryczow, far from the farm of the Weinfelds who lived in that same village. He would purchase several eggs, chickens, fish, potatoes and apples from the gentiles of his village. He would load the merchandise into baskets and sacks. Despite his severe disability, he would travel by foot on unpaved roads a distance of ten kilometers until he arrived in Rozniatow. There they took pity on him, gave him something to eat and drink, and purchased his meager merchandise from him. Thus did Yankel the Lame, who lived a life of agony and poverty, earn his livelihood. He was the only Jew among many gentile villagers. He lived with his wife and two children.

He suffered from many trials and tribulations; however in his dealings with the Jews of Rozniatow, everyone showed him feelings of love and brotherhood. They all opened their hearts and homes to take him in as a guest. This had its influence on him, and his face glowed from good-heartedness and good hope.

{154}

## In Memory of Those that have Passed
### by Y. Neubauer of Petach Tikva

There is no speech in my mouth, or word from my tongue
Regarding the tragedy of the daughter of my people, which is as large as the sea[18]
For the pure Jews, members of the community
The community of Rozniatow, who once were and are no longer.

During the day and during the night, awake or in a dream
I remember them as if it was yesterday.
I lived with them in the peace and friendship
That accompanied all of them on all paths and routes.

In the present reality – all that remains is pain and agony
That eat at my heart without respite
For the young children who were torn by the wolf
That fed our nation a full cup of poison.

For the elders of the city, people of Torah
How can I forget you for even a small moment
You who were erased from the face of the earth with a swipe from the back of the hand
During the days of the camps and the terrible Holocaust.

These do I remember

Reb Yehuda Hirsch the old judge
Reb Menachem Yosef the young rabbi
Reb Moshele Weiser, the elder of the shochtim (ritual slaughterers)
And Reb Zecharia David Liberman, the vice mayor of the city

## TRANSLATOR'S FOOTNOTES

1. A reference to the book of Exodus, where a new Pharaoh arose who did not remember the good deeds of Joseph to the Egyptians, and therefore initiated the slavery. The colloquial expression here means that the new generation does not remember the details of the previous life.

2. Shalom Aleichem is the hymn recited at the beginning of the Sabbath eve welcoming the angels into the house. These angels are said to accompany a man home from the synagogue on Friday evening. Ribon Kol Haolamim (literally: Master of all the worlds), is a prayer often said before the Sabbath meal, welcoming the Sabbath.

3. Kiddush (literally: sanctification), is a prayer over a cup of wine recited at the beginning of the Sabbath or festival meal.

4. In Hassidic circles, yahrzeits are not looked upon as sad occasions, but rather as days to celebrate, reminisce, and learn from the life of the departed Rebbe.

5. A term used to describe young students immersed in Torah studies at a cheder. The Hebrew term is "tinokot shel beit rabban". This teacher is often known as a Rebbi. I spelled it differently in order to differentiate it from the Rebbe, who is the Hassidic leader.

6. There is a custom that young children come to recite the Shema (the main Jewish prayer and confession of faith) at the crib or cradle of a young child on the night before his circumcision.

7. The five books of Moses, or Pentateuch.

8. A verse from the book of Joshua, referring to the need to toil in the study of the commandments day and night.

9. A minor festival occurring on the 18 th day of the month of Iyar, usually in May.

10. A ceremony that takes place on Rosh Hashanah by a riverbank. It is a symbolic casting away of sins into the water.

11. Holiday prayer book.

12. On the Sabbath, it is forbidden to kindle or make use of a flame. On a festival occurring on a weekday it is forbidden to kindle a flame from scratch, but it is permitted to transfer a fire from one flame to another. Thus, it would be permitted to light a candle from a pre-existing flame. Someone must have brought a pilot light to use to ignite the other candles.

13. According to Jewish law, it is a very serious matter to take an oath or to cause someone to take an oath, and it is considered praiseworthy to avoid such situations wherever possible.

14. According to Jewish law, it is permissible for a man to marry his niece, although it is forbidden for a woman to marry her nephew.

15. Hachnasat Kalah is the giving of assistance to a needy bride.

16. The meaning of this sentence is unclear.

17. Leizer is a diminutive for Eliezer.

18. The first two lines of this poem are taken from liturgical sources. The first line is from the opening petition of the reader's repetition of the morning prayer (shmone esrei) of the second day of Rosh Hashanah. The first half of the second line is from the book of Lamentations.

{157}

## During the Years of the Holocaust
### by Yeshaya Lutwak

"So that the latest generation shall know, children shall be borne who will then relate to their children."
(Psalms 78, 6)

In earlier times – in a place that once was called Eastern Galicia, in the Stanislawow region, near the city of Dolina, in the Carpathian Mountains, between the two rivers Czeczwa and Danuba, there was a small town called Rozniatow. It had a population of 500 Jewish families, consisting of about 1,800 souls amidst a large population of various gentiles, some bad and some good.

Twenty some villages surrounded this town. They were populated by members of the Ukrainian minority of the Polish nation. These are the selfsame Ukrainians who are remembered in disgrace from the days of pogroms and slaughter perpetrated by their hero-murderer Petliora, may his name be blotted out. These villages had several dozen Jewish families, spread out and isolated among the gentile community of the region.

Rozniatow was small in area. One of the boundaries was between the houses of Bendet and Moshe Yampel and Zusia Aryeh Kuperberg, behind the town. The other boundary was near the houses of Alte Kassner and Yisrael Hirsch Londoner, opposite the house of Meshulam Fruchter. A third boundary was near the house of Chaya Adler, opposite Mordechai Deutscher in the "Old Town".

Most of the Jewish residents were concentrated in the center of the town. They were small-scale merchants, artisans, members of the intelligentsia, and low-level officials. As in other towns of Galicia, there was no shortage of desperately poor people, whether known or "secret". The secret ones tried to hide their economic straits by wearing fine clothing that they still had from the "good" days that they had enjoyed in the distant or not too distant past.

The market day, the only day when most of the population earned their livelihood, took place on Wednesday. On that day, gentiles from the entire region came to Rozniatow with their wares on their heads or on their wagons. One would bring a cow for sale, another a horse, and someone else some potatoes, wheat or barley, grown on his own land with his own labor. The Jews would buy them, or serve as a broker between the buyer and seller, in order to earn a few coins to sustain themselves and their households.

All of them waited for the longed for day, the market day, which would save them from their dire situation and enable them to redeem a contract whose payment day had already passed. On more than one occasion, it happened that a certain merchant would be in dire straits due to the fact that this awaited redemptive day, the market day, did not stand at his side and did not fulfill the desires that he had placed in it, so he was not able to pay his debts to his many debtors from whom he borrowed money with the intention of repaying it after the market day. There were great tragedies among the small-scale merchants, whose world dried up for them in one day. Their staff of bread dissipated and they became impoverished, having to go begging from door to door.

Thus was conducted the cultural and economic life in a peaceful fashion, some with better luck and some with less luck, until the frightful days of the holocaust arrived.

I will begin to relate in a chronological fashion the events of my town Rozniatow during this frightful period, as best as I can, as well as my memory serves me correctly, and as well as I am able to overcome my personal feelings. May it be the will of the Creator of the World that appropriate words flow from my pen, and that I not stumble, that I not mislead, and that nobody Heaven forbid stumble because of me; that I publish the truth for the sake of history and so that future generation can learn from here.

## 1938

When the Polish Jews of Germany were expelled at the German-Polish border at Zbaszyn in the middle of the night, after they had been awakened from their sleep without even having being given the chance to get dressed, the towns of Galicia and Poland awaited the exiled Jews who were wearing only their pajamas and slippers. These Jews were downtrodden and dumbfounded. Their world had been destroyed in one night. In many towns, committees and soup kitchens were set up to take care of the stream of refugees, which increased daily. These refugees had previously been respected householders, owners of large-scale businesses in Germany, members of the free professions, who had been suddenly turned into paupers who receive their paltry sustenance from communal kitchens, due to their forceful expulsion.

Many took their own lives, since they could not tolerate this great disgrace. Confusion and perplexity pervaded the towns of Galicia, and each town attempted to help the refugees to the best of its ability. The organizations attempted to help them with loans to support them, so that they might be able to stand on their own two feet, and not fall as a burden upon the impoverished community. As far as I can remember, there were a few Rozniatow natives among the stream of refugees who were expelled across the border that night.

Meir Ungar – the son-in-law of Moshe and his wife, Menashe Yampel and his wife, Bendet Kassner the son of Alti Benzi Kassner, the son of Yossel Kassner, Zalcha Wasserman with her son and daughter, Avraham Kahn, the son-in-law of Hirsch Rechtschaffen and his entire family, Aharon Weissman and his family, Avraham Korenblau, the son of Mechel, David Wernick the son-in-law of Berel Berger and his family, Chaya the daughter of Menashe Rosenberg with her husband and children, Shlomo Gross, Benzi Klinger, Chaim Walgschaffen, Sender Rosenberg, Yossel Laufer and his family, Kalman Laufer and his family, Kalman Horowitz the son of Sara Esther, Leika Horowitz and her husband.[1]

All of us attempted to help these poor people.

### The Invasion of 1939

Friday, September 1, 1939, the bitter and violent day that is etched in the world's memory, was the day that Hitler's army invaded Poland. The confusion among the population was great. Nobody knew what to do. The young people in our midst understood that they must immediately present themselves at the army enlistment centers, and they indeed did so. A few waited for the draft orders, however no draft orders appeared. Even those who went to enlist returned, since there was nobody before whom to present oneself. Chaos reigned in the army ranks. Only a few of those who enlisted received their fatigues. Some received weapons without fatigues.

On Sunday, September 3, a few of the "smart" merchants tried their luck and attempted to travel to Stanislawow to acquire merchandise; however, when they arrived in Stanislawow, they found the city half destroyed. There were dead and wounded people in the streets. The Germans bombarded the city during Friday and Saturday, and caused great damage in the city. When they returned home, they experienced an air raid. A German airplane pursued their bus and bombed it. They were saved by a miracle.

The fear and trepidation became worse. The nights were dark, and nobody was brazen enough to leave his home. Whoever owned a radio listened to the news with a pounding heart. The first of the refugees who escaped from the cities that already had fallen to the Germans on September 1st began to arrive in the town. The following people returned to the town: Dr. Wilek Adlersberg, his two brothers Zigo and Lanek, Dr. Leon Horowitz and his wife Jadwiga Sapir, Dr. Nunek Lusthaus and his wife Irina Feier, Dr. Avraham Fried, the son-in-law of Shmuel Friedler, Sara Geller, and others.

On Friday September 15th, the following people attempted to cross the border into Romania: the head of the community Reb Zecharia Lieberman, Rabbi Yosef Metzner, Shabtai Rosenberg and his brother-in-law Bernard Metzner. When they arrived at the foot of the Mountain of Krasna on the wagon of Meilech Landsman, the horses refused to go further. The travelers decided that this was a sign from Heaven that they should not leave the town without leaders, and they returned to their homes along the same path that they had gone. On Sunday, September 17th, early in the morning, the speech of the Soviet Foreign Minister Molotov was heard on the radio. He announced that the Red Army was poised to enter Western Ukraine at any moment.

The next day, on September 18th, anarchy pervaded. There was no government. The police had fled across the Hungarian border, and we, the young people, feared that at any moment pogroms would begin against us. Therefore we decided to secretly organize a self-defense unit, with all kinds of defensive weapons that anyone was able to obtain, so that we would be able to defend ourselves.

The population was in dire straits. We did not know whether to be happy or fearful about the entry of the Red Army into our midst. The German murderers were in the city of Stryj the Red Army was in Stanislawow. We did not know who would save us. From where would our salvation arise?

When they heard the rumor that the Red Army was poised to enter the town at any moment, the local Ukrainian population rejoiced as if their messiah had arrived. They had reason to rejoice. How do they rejoice? Of course, through the Jews. They immediately began to pillage. The first victim that fell to their murderous hands was Reuven Diamand, the son of Bini Anshel.

On Wednesday morning, September 20th, Doni the son of Hirsch Landsman succeeded in escaping from the city with two friends. They ran to the village of Holyn and from there they returned victorious, riding on a Russian tank, the head of the brigade of the Soviet army that was entering the town.

Immediately a period of the restoration of law and order began at the hands of the Red Army.

At first, they began to nationalize property: houses, stores, and factories. Who were the first victims? Of course, the Jews, the "bourgeois". They confiscated the homes of the following people: Yisraelche Rosenman, Mordechai Gross, Yaakov Lew, Shmuel Leib, Izi Friedler, Izi Rosenberg, Meir Frankel, Shalom Frankel, Shalom Hoffman, Ethel Rechtschaffen, Leizer Geller, Yisrael Leib Artman, Yosef Kurtz, Mattes Wilner, the brothers Shlomo and Yosef Berger, Pini Berger, Sasi Heller, Leib Falik, and Wiczi Teneh.

The sources of livelihood were shut, and everyone attempted to find whatever employment they could. Without a work permit, it was not possible to subsist. The slogan was "No work – no food". People were afraid to go outside without their work permits, for they were liable to be deported to Siberia as non-productive members of society. Most people began to work. A few, who still had some money and were able to get by without working, equipped themselves with work permits, which turned into a commodity that was passed from person to person. A few began to conduct business in secret with various types of merchandise that they succeeded in hiding from the watchful eyes of the Russians.

Immediately with the declaration of war between Russia and Germany, there was great chaos among the residents of the town. We felt as if we were standing between great events. The Russian captains with their families left the city, and the regular army followed them. As far as my memory serves me correctly, this was on June 30th 1941. About 150-200 Jews left along with the Russian army, some by vehicle, some by foot, and some with any means of transport. They fled in order to catch at the last minute the train that was leaving for Stanislawow. There was no other route by which to flee. However, the lot of those that succeeded in boarding the train was very bad and bitter. The Germans detected the train that was fleeing through the forests, and bombed it ceaselessly. By the time it reached Husyatin, not one person remained alive.

I will never forget how Shalom Rechtschaffen, as he fled with his family through the town, shouted loudly: "Jews, why do you wait? Leave your property and follow me."

In this chaos, I had the opportunity to bid farewell to my relative and friend Baruch Horowitz. His last words still ring in my ears: "Why do you remain here? Why do you not leave your property and flee? Are you concerned about your property?"

When the last of the Russian soldiers left the town, disorder and great chaos prevailed. Everything was a free-for-all. In the meantime, the non-Jews, as they did when the Russians entered, began to pillage and plunder the homes of the Jews who had fled, as well as the official stores of the Russians and the cooperatives that they had set up while they were in the town.

The last troops of the retreating Red Army were attacked during their flight by one of the groups of pillagers next to one of the official stores that was being pillaged. In anger, one of the soldiers lowered his gun and shot at the group of youths who were laughing at the retreating army. He injured the son of Wasyl Slapak. This shot served as the pretext to begin a pogrom in a serious manner against the Jews. Moshe, the son of Yaakov Strassman was a victim of this pogrom. He innocently passed by the street at that time, and suffered severe beatings at the hands of the murderers.

On Friday, the 4th of July, 1941, the first members of the Hungarian Army entered the town, but in fact as soon as the Red Army left, the Ukrainians took over the administration of the town, under the leadership of Dr. Korbas, Dr. Shlapkas the priest, Kostiok Lupinski, Kowel and others. That same day, in the afternoon, the provisional committee of the Ukrainians issued an edict to the Jews stating that they must come immediately and destroy the statue of Lenin that the Red Army had erected in the middle of the city.

Late on Friday night, one of the righteous gentiles, the farmer Ivan Wishinski, appeared at the door of Mordechai Gross, and secretly told him that he had just heard about the decision of the Ukrainian committee: the next day, on the Sabbath morning, as the Jews would leave the synagogue wearing their prayer shawls, the Ukrainian militia would stop them all in the square next to the broken statue of Lenin, and would force them to bring a coffin from the cemetery, to put the broken pieces of the statue inside it, and arrange a grandiose funeral procession with the Jews wrapped in their prayer shawls and the non-Jews drumming behind them.

This righteous gentile who revealed the evil ones' conspiracy to Mordechai Gross told him that if he wanted to avert this embarrassment to the Jews, he should clear away the pieces of the broken statue by morning.

Reb Mordechai Gross did not vacillate even for a moment about whether to profane the Sabbath.[2] After midnight he went to awaken the son of Chaim Riwali the guard and together they quietly gathered the pieces of the broken statue into a wagon. They brought the broken pieces to a place near the slaughterhouse outside the city as quickly as possible, and threw them into the sewage conduits.

All of the friendliness that existed, so to speak, between the Jews and the Ukrainians dissipated overnight. The Ukrainian militia, under the pretext of searching for Communist and illegal merchandise, entered Jewish homes and pillaged everything that came into their hands.

Between the hours of seven in the evening until daybreak, despite the oppressive heat of the summer months, the Jews stayed inside their homes in fear of the Ukrainian pillagers that were out of control and did whatever they wished to the Jews. The Jews were gripped with fear, and waited for what was to come. One night, a group of Ukrainians burst into the home of the elderly Doctor Isadore Feier and searched his son-in-law Dr. Nunek Lusthaus, with whom they had a private account, and at this moment they wanted to take their revenge. Since they did not find him at home, they took out the elderly Dr. Feier and beat him with murderous blows. They took a sack of flour from his house and commanded him to carry it on his back to one of the homes of the perpetrators. For no reason they stopped Itzi Reis, the grandson of Kalman Frankel, Azriel Wasserman, and several other Jews. They beat them and sent them home.

Twice a week, on Mondays and Thursdays, the Jews were forced to appear in the Market Square to sell their wares and to obtain food that they needed for sustenance. On rare occasions someone would buy or exchange merchandise or an expensive object for food. The non-Jews did not bring any food to sell.

When I lived in the central square, I often witnessed in the home of Mordechai Gross all kinds of accusations and cruel deeds from the non-Jewish neighbors. On one day I saw with my own eyes how Pintzi Berger, an elderly Jew, broken and crushed, was leaning against the wall of the house of Mottel Friedler. A young gentile named Janek Shajok – the bastard of the Anke – approached him and without any explanation dealt him cruel blows, threw him to the ground, and trampled upon him.

He left Pintzi Berger lying on the ground and came to the house of David Reiner. There the bastard met Leib Weitzner and attacked him, but Weitzner was young and full of energy, so he was able to escape and flee for his life.

Avraham Hirsch, the son of Miriam Bines, was lame. One day he came to Dr. Korbas to request something of him. The evil man did not even want to hear his request. He removed the canes that Avraham used to support himself, and as he fell to the ground, the murderer trampled him with his feet.

Every day, the Jews had to fill the quota of workers for communal work, so to speak. All sorts of trivial and unnecessary tasks were devised in order to torment the Jews.

Once, I, along with Yisrael the son of Pini Berger and Magister Marek Rotter[3] had the job of cleaning the stables of the police, which was located on a hill next to the courthouse.

The work was difficult and smelly, and in order to sustain our souls, Yisrael took out a piece of dry sausage that he had obtained somehow, and divided it among us. By chance, Atamnaczok, the head of the militia, passed by and saw us chewing something. He fell upon us like a wild animal and beat us with his gun.

I wondered why Yisraelik, who was mighty and never tolerated any injustice, controlled himself and did not give the swine back his due. However, I will never forget the question that he asked me once: "Shaike, shall we sometime take our revenge?"

Even worse off were the Jewish workers who were sent to work at the Krechowice train station. Once, a group of 25 Jews were sent their to remove the thorns, thistles, and gravel stones from the area of the train tracks with their own hands – without any utensils. This group included Dr. Leon Horowitz, Magister Leon Meiseles, Shimshon Rechtschaffen, Shabtai Falik, Shabtai Rosenberg, his brother-in-law Bernard Menczer, Shalom Deutscher, and several others whose names I do not remember at this time. This work had to be done while they were bent over, and crawling step by step. Woe to any Jew who attempted to straighten out or rest for even a small moment. The German guard would immediately fall upon him and deal him murderous blows.

One day, Leib Meiseles weakened from the work and slunk to the ground. Shalom Deutscher hid him with his body so that the Gestapo man would not see him. Nevertheless, The Gestapo man detected that something happened with regard to the work. When he asked who was sitting, immediately and without hesitation Shalom Deutscher answered: "I". Immediately, he received a beating from the German.

Shalom never mentioned this to his own glory. When he was once asked, incidentally, why he did this, he answered with simplicity: "I did this because I knew that Leib would no longer be able to continue on after the beatings that he would receive, and this would have been his end."

Once I had to work alongside him in dismantling the statue that the Russians had erected. We were told that woe would be upon us if we were to damage even one board, or if we were not to remove a nail in the same straight fashion in which it was placed. The men worked with all their might to fulfill the desire of the Gestapo. Shalom ran from one to the other in order to help. When I asked him again: "Shalom, why do you not watch out for yourself? Why do you run from one to the other to help?" He answered me: "I do not wish to see the Germans standing from afar, screaming at and mocking the Jews, with the Ukrainians standing to the side, laughing and jesting as we receive beatings from the Germans." This was the character of the man Shalom. This was the greatness of Rozniatow.

The high council of the Ukrainians, who worked hand in hand with the Germans, issued a decree to the Jewish residents, that starting from August 5th, 1941, they must wear a yellow band on their right arms in order to be recognized. Since the day of Tisha Beov[4] fell exactly two days prior to the set date, that is on August 3rd, Rabbi Metzner, Zecharia Lieberman the head of the community, and Dr. Feier began to wear the yellow ribbons two days earlier than the set date. When the gentiles saw this, they joked and called them "the Jewish militia".

Until the outbreak of the war, I had excellent friendly relations with Dr. Katz and his Christian wife, who was the widow of the judge Luzinski. At the time that they were under financial pressure, I lent them money on several occasions. I would enter their home as a true friend, and they would always treat me pleasantly and with respect. At the time that chaos and disorder prevailed in the town, when there was no governing authority, and it was literally dangerous to walk on the streets, I entered on one occasion to the home of Dr. Katz and requested if I could stay with him for a day until the anger passes. Dr. Katz agreed immediately, however his evil wife immediately answered: "In my home, there is no room even for our own Jew." I left the home and the accursed mistress immediately, and my heart was filled with pity for the poor Dr. Katz, who suffered in silence from his gentile wife. Of course, he was the first victim from among all the Jews.

I wish to relate another incident.

A young gentile official named Melnikowicz worked for the notary. We were always buddies, good friends. During the time of the Russian rule, I literally saved him from imprisonment for many years, when he was once late for work and was brought to court for disparaging his work. He was liable to receive a prison sentence of six years. I obtained for him a medical certificate stating that he had been ill for three days, and I came to testify on his behalf in court. He was completely exonerated. Now, with the evacuation of the Russians and the arrival of the Germans, he became filled with self-importance. Under his supervision, food was distributed to the workers. I once came to him with a small request, that the paltry portion of bread, 100 grams daily, that was distributed to the Jewish workers should be distributed through the medical clinic in which I work so that we could distribute it to the workers prior to their going out to work. This was opposed to how it was done previously, when it was distributed during the course of the day, while the workers had already commenced their work without food.

I greeted him, and he did not answer me. He only shouted in anger: "Our dear nation is still young, and we cannot fulfill the needs of everyone. We have to worry first of all about ourselves."

New decrees were issued daily. The situation worsened daily, especially when the Jews who had been expelled from the neighboring villages arrived in town. They filled up the houses and placed an additional burden upon the economic situation. The food rations were only distributed to the workers, and the entire population, including those people who did not work, had to subsist on the rations that were distributed to the workers.

Despite the bribes with items of great value, and despite the negotiations with the governing authorities by people such as Dr. Sabat, Dr. Sapir and Lieberman, the Ukrainian authorities decided to free themselves from all the Jews, and to expel them completely within a short period of time.

## The Expulsion

On Tuesday, August 27 toward evening, Dr. Sabat was told by the Ukrainian Security Council that he must inform the Jews that as of September 1st, 1941, it would be forbidden for any Jews to remain in Rozniatow. They were given the choice of four places of refuge: Halicz, Dolina, Krechowice, and Kalush.

Rumors spread in the street that the non-Jews were intending to expel all the Jews so that they can pillage their property in an unhindered manner, and then they would return them home. "For Jews that are poor and destitute do not bother them" – this is how the Jews comforted themselves. They began to bury their money, and gold and silver valuables. The Jewish medical workers, who had a special permit to go on the streets at night, were told the sad news that they had to inform the Jews that they should prepare to leave the town. We went from house to house with these tidings of Job, and warned all the residents.

Early the next morning, we saw that we were surrounded by thousands of non-Jews with wagons, carriages, and all sorts of containers for transport. They came, so to speak, to bid farewell to their Jewish "friends" and to receive "parting gifts". It was impossible to hire a wagon or any other vehicle for any money. It was only possible to do so with silver, gold, furs, valuable articles of clothing, sewing machines, etc. Many gentiles came to the town in order to witness the scene of the expulsion of the Jews from their town where they had lived for generation upon generation. Since it was difficult to acquire wagons for transport, several families had to hire a wagon together, upon which they loaded the children and the most important belongings that they were able to take with them. When a family mounted a wagon, the gentiles did not even wait until they had left the place in order to begin pillaging the home. They placed everything that came to their hands upon the wagons that they had brought. Everyone made haste, lest someone else precede him. The pillaging took place before the eyes of the Jews. The Jews were still standing with their belongings on the street, and behold, their houses and properties were being plundered before their eyes by their friends of yesterday. The best of the gentiles approached the Jews and promised them foodstuffs in return for their belongings, only that "it will come later", since "we also do not have anything to eat at this time". The Jews pretended that they did not see, for they were afraid of death, and they were thankful that they were not murdered on the spot.

The Market Square was crowded with wagons, bundles of belongings, and Jews who were trying to leave as quickly as possible, since they were afraid that those who would leave late would not find anywhere to go.

On the main street, which was full of wagons, the Ukrainians cruelly stopped the wagons, beat the travelers, and insisted that the people throw down all their belongings. The families that had already passed the Ukrainian guards and were able to continue on with their flight were fortunate.

The final days of August were very hot. The sun was shining in full force, as if with its heat it was adding to the suffering of the refugees. There was not a drop of water or drink. The children were shouting "Water! Water!" Not even one gentile who lived along the route that the caravans were travelling had mercy on them, to give them even a drop of water.

Usually, on a hot summer day, the dams of the rivers that flowed through the towns would be opened in order to make the atmosphere more pleasant. Today, they purposefully did not open the dams, and the entire landscape was dry, without even a drop of water. Many of the refugees fainted from the stifling heat and weariness. The first to faint was Feiga, the wife of the ritual slaughterer (shochet), after her Sara Lindenbaum, and several other people whose names I do not remember now.

The Jews did not forget to take their most precious belongings on their flight from town: the kosher Torah scrolls.[5] The non-kosher Torah scrolls, as well as other holy books, prayer books, festival prayer books, and other holy objects that were located in the synagogue and Beis Midrash were placed in closets in an orderly fashion. They hoped that when they would return home, everything would be renewed, and everything would be in its appropriate place.

After a few weeks, it became known to us that Dr. Korbas had taken out all of the holy books that were in the closets and transferred them to Kalush. The rest of the books and holy objects were pillaged by the non-Jews who used them for their own private purposes.

Those who thought that after the searches and beatings of the Ukrainian militia they would be already free from further torture and searches were completely wrong.

The Ukrainians informed the Gestapo in Kalush that the convoy of expelled Jews was ready to leave. They came to see with their own eyes the wondrous thing that their own work was done by others. The Gestapo men arrived, looked at the Jews and ordered to turn over to them four blankets and two sacks of flour. Leizer Geller and his partner Yisrael Leib Hartman provided them the blankets. Drs. Nunek and Dolek Lusthaus, Dr. Leon Horowitz, Shimshon Rechtschaffen and others took it upon themselves to gather the flour.

It is hard to describe the heartbreaking scene that took place at the moment permission was given for the caravan to travel and leave town. The Jews hugged and kissed each other, and broke out in communal weeping. A sea of tears came from their eyes, and it was only with difficulty that they were able to move their legs from their place and walk behind the wagons that carried their children and family members who were not able to walk on foot.

Most of the Jews went to Dolina and Bolekhov. They were afraid to go to Kalush, since they had already known that a week previously, the Gestapo, with the assistance of the Ukrainians, gathered all of the intelligentsia of the city – doctors, engineers, pharmacists, and teachers – according to a list, and took them out to a nearby forest to be shot. By chance, Bendet Spiegel had traveled to Kalush from Rozniatow that week in order to rent a dwelling while there was still time, for the Jews of Rozniatow had to leave shortly. He was caught with the rest of the intelligentsia and shot along with them in the forest.

Along the way, when they passed the neighboring villages such as Swaryczow, Strusyn, and Spas, the gentiles fell upon them. These were "neighborly" gentiles, who were known by name to the Jews of Rozniatow. They were considered friends for generations, and now, at the time of despair "they attacked all the weak ones" [6]. They attacked the Jews, and pillaged from them the remainder of their belongings that had remained after the previous episodes of plunder and pillage. Those who already succeeded in arriving in Dolina or Bolekhov were fortunate. We arrived in Dolina. The local Jews displayed a glorious scene of brotherhood, love, and participation in our tribulations.

## Exile In Dolina

It is impossible to describe the cramped living conditions. Families took up residence in any hole or corner where it was possible to place a bed. Two families would live in one room. Many who did not succeed in acquiring a dwelling place for money or even the equivalent of money literally lived on the streets. It was fortunate that it was summertime, and therefore it was possible to sleep outside. Refugees from other nearby places, such as Mizon, Vygoda, Veldisz also arrived in Dolina. Those that were able to take care of themselves, who had hid away some money, searched for dwellings with the gentiles in the suburbs of the city. For good money, it was possible to rent out the barn or one of the silos or empty storehouses as living quarters. Of course, all of the houses of prayers, Shtibels, and Beis Midrashes were immediately taken over by the large stream of refugees. The terrible tragedy began with the arrival of the cold, rainy autumn days, with cold nights.

According to the command of the S.S. Commissar Bebel, a Judenrat had to be set up within 24 hours. The Judenrat had the job of fulfilling the commands of the S.S. and providing all of their needs at the expense of the Jewish community. At first, every Jew had to pay a "ransom money" tax, to give over all silver and gold objects. The exact accounting was the responsibility of the Judenrat. After a few days, the Jews were commanded to supply them with new furniture. From where could the poor Jews obtain furniture, and certainly how could they provide new furniture, since they all lived as several families in one room, and the entire furnishings consisted of several beds and rotting mattresses?

It was forbidden to own horses and cows. Any furs, including streimels (Hassidic fur hats), which were made out of tails and remnants of furs, were forbidden to the Jews. Everyone had to provide for the Germany army, which was expending its entire energy at this point on cold, distant Russia.

Every morning, the "Jewish Committee" had to supply several men for various jobs, and several more workers had to be available if needed. One cannot envy the position of the members of the Jewish council. Their task was difficult, and a particularly heavy responsibility fell upon the chairman of the committee, Dr. Julius Weinreb. By nature, he was a quiet man, a man of scruples, and he possessed an excellent personality. On numerous occasions, he stood before a difficult crisis and deliberated about how to act, about whether to fulfill the command of the S.S. or not, and about what would be the effect on the community if he refused. A heavy responsibility fell upon his shoulders, and he would have gladly left his position if it had been possible.

On occasion, Krieger or Mueller visited suddenly from Stanislawow. Schultz came from Kalush on occasion, and he did not speak to the local commanders Bebel and others. The murderers conducted a discipline of iron. Every command had to be fulfilled with immediacy. When a fur was not provided at the requested time, Dovchi and Yanliz were taken to Stanislawow, and they never returned from there. The same cold fate occurred to Miriam Deutscher, the widow of Mordechai Deutscher and the daughter of Shmuel Schwindler, on account of the fact that she did not tie her yellow band in the correct place.

Not infrequently, we met our dear, honorable vice-chairman of the Jewish committee, Efraim Weingarten who was beloved to the Jews, as he was going from house to house with a basket in his hands, pleading: "Give us at least one egg, one egg for the Germans, for our lives depend on it."

The first Jew who had his beard and peyos cut off by the Germans was Leibish Kluger of Dolina. From that time, Jews began to fear incidents such as the cutting off of their beard publicly with a knife in the road, so they decided to remove their own beards. A few who were not able to bear the thought of shaving off their own beards would walk around even in their own houses with their faces covered with kerchiefs.

Once, when I took a turn acting as an orderly in the Jewish hospital, someone came inside and asked me: "My dear Lutwak, I wish to ask a small favor from you." I looked at him and saw a shriveled Jew whom I did not recognize. "Who are you, Mr. Jew, I do not recognize you", I answered him. The Jew burst out crying bitterly, and through his groans and sobs I heard, "It is the time of the Messiah, it is the time of the Messiah", that is to say, the Messianic era has arrived since a brother does not recognize his fellow. "Behold, I am Yosef Shimon Stern".[7]

I want to make sure that those readers who still remember the face of Reb Yosef Shimon Stern, who had a long beard and a glorious visage, should know that he now appeared before my eyes as a shrunken, clean-shaven Jew, shriveled, broken, and crushed.

Immediately after the expulsion from my town of Rozniatow, when we had begun to get ourselves set up in Dolina, torrential rains began to fall, which destroyed all of the produce in the fields. The gentiles said that this was a punishment from the Heavens, a punishment from the G-d of Israel for the expulsion. Indeed, all of their harvest, all of their work, had been destroyed; however they still had freedom of movement. They began to import wheat and foodstuffs from far away places. They were able to pay for them with the valuables that they had pillaged from the Jews. The situation of the Jewish refugees was not that fortunate. The extreme shortage of food began to leave its mark on the Jews. Nobody even dreamed of acquiring flour, for the Ukrainians were also forbidden from importing flour. We were required to supply the German army with specific rations of flour and other foodstuffs. They did not go to the mills to grind wheat, for they feared that a portion would be confiscated for the German army, in accordance with the law. Even potatoes turned into a rare and desirable commodity. It was possible to obtain them only in exchange for objects of value. For example, 1 kilogram of potatoes cost a suit, and 1 kilogram of corn cost a pillow or a fine woolen blanket. Famine and hunger began to show its signs outside. The refugees who were not local suffered in particular. The hunger did not have mercy, and did not pass over anyone. Everyone came to know it. Hundreds of people who were starving for a loaf of bread roamed about the outskirts of Dolina, wearing fine clothing and remembering the better times that they once had. The cold winter approached, and along with it, the hunger grew. People stopped going out onto the streets, either because of lack of energy, or because of the embarrassment of being seen in their dire straits. Those who still succeeded in obtaining a few grains of barley, grits, or corn ground them in their coffee grinders that they still had in their houses, which the gentiles had not yet succeeded in pillaging. Alternatively, they ground them with grinders and graters, and made from the corn or barley flour a dish that was known as Tsher. When spring arrived, even the corn and barley flour disappeared. The gentiles completely stopped bringing foodstuffs into the town. Without any other options, the Jews began to search in the fields, yards, and any other possible place for something that was possible to put in the mouth and chew. They would eat all kinds of plants, good and bad. The important thing was to satisfy the hunger and stomach pangs. Daily, the number of dead increased. The work of the Chevra Kadisha (burial society) under the supervision of the Judenrat was extensive. People stopped being embarrassed, and begged mercy from one to the other: "A spoonful of food for the mouth", "Give me a crumb of bread, and I will give you everything that I have."

Regarding the severity of the hunger, I will relate a story that I heard from Mrs. Henchie Shapira, the daughter of my uncle Reichels Horowitz.

One young gentile by the name of Stash Jurzki, the young son of Herin Heiduk, gave to her in return for a new suit a sack that was supposed to contain 20 kilograms of potatoes, and a small sack of wheat that was supposed to contain 8 kilograms. When she weighed it after he left, she found that instead of 20 kilograms of potatoes, there were 30, and instead of 8 kilograms of wheat, there were 12. When they met again, she told him that she found the error, and she wanted to know what she could give him further on account of the error. He answered her in an embarrassed fashion: "It does not matter, next time add something on to what you give me. I really know that what I gave you is worth far less than a suit, and when I have another chance, I will give you additional food."

Every morning, I met Shalom Hoffman, the son of Vove Hoffman, as he was walking with his basket that contained a little food. He was going from house to house, in particular to the houses where he knew there were Jews who simply did not have the energy to go outside to search for food, or who were embarrassed to do so, and were dying silently from hunger and shame. He distributed food to them, to one a spoonful of food, to another a crumb of bread, in order to keep them alive. He also collected money in order to purchase boards for coffins, and cloth for shrouds. The corpses of those that died of hunger began to pile up outside, with nobody to collect them.

Slowly, we became accustomed even to the corpses that were strewn on the streets.

**TRANSLATOR'S FOOTNOTES**

1. This list, in paragraph form, is not clear. Commas are not used consistently, and it is not often clear if a succeeding name is a qualifier to a previous name, or a name in and of itself (i.e. Bendet Kassner the son of Alti Benzi Kassner – not clear if both are intended to be part of the list, or if only the son is, and the name is being qualified with the father's name.)

2. Collecting and transporting building material and debris are among the types of work forbidden on the Sabbath day. However, all forbidden labor on the Sabbath is permitted in a case when life is at stake, which would have been the case here.

3. Magister is a Polish academic title that is equivalent with a Master's Degree.

4. A stringent summertime fast day commemorating, among other things, the destruction of both temples.

5. A Torah scroll with an error or other defect is considered not kosher, i.e. not fit for synagogue ritual use. This situation is generally rectifiable by a Torah scribe. The kosher Torah scrolls are considered to have a higher degree of sanctity than the non-kosher ones.

6. A quote from the Book of Exodus, describing the tribe of Amalek attacking the weakest of the Jews from behind as they were traveling through the desert after leaving Egypt.

7. A reference to various Talmudic statements indicating that prior to the advent of the Messiah, there will be great social upheaval in the world.

{170}

## Hirsch Gelobter

I hereby wish to fulfill an obligation of conscience toward a man of great spirit and strength. At a time when the refugees were weak and oppressed, a man from among the simple folk of the nation raised himself up to the great heights and selflessly helped any Jew, simply because he was a Jew.

There was a Jew by the name of Hirsch Gelobter, the son of Susi-Feiga Gelobter of Rozniatow who lived in the nearby village of Krechowice, near the train station. At the time of the expulsion, he was exiled along with his wife and daughters to Bolekhov and went to live with his married daughter Genia Salitir.

At the time of the first German aktion in Bolekhov, he lost his wife and two of his daughters. Afterward, he went to live in Dolina and settled in the place where his sons worked, in Roshkov at the Pfeffer sawmill. For entire days, he would walk among the homes of the Jews to see how he could help the weak and poor in their straits. Since he was a known cattle merchant, he knew many of the gentiles in the area. Despite the danger to life that existed in searching for merchandise, he began to conduct business with the neighboring gentiles in all types of foodstuffs in order to supply them to the local Jews at cost price. He attempted to purchase calves or larger animals. He secretly slaughtered them in accordance with Jewish law and distributed the meat in small portions, without differentiating between rich and poor. At night he would stealthily bring the animal to the barn of my brother-in-law Mordechai Kornblit who lived outside the city. Every Wednesday, the shochet (ritual slaughterer) knew that he had to go there secretly in order to slaughter and make the meat kosher.[1] The meat would then be distributed to all the needy in accordance with a list that had been drawn up previously. He would take no profit for himself. This enterprise was fraught with mortal danger, for if he would have been G-d forbid caught, he would have been shot on the spot. He placed the innards, bones, and leftover meat into bags in his pockets and gave them to my sister to divide up among the poor of the city, most of whom were Rozniatow natives. This took place each week. My sister Mantzi did great deeds. She cooked the bones and leftovers in a large pot into a meat soup, and went from house to house on Thursdays to distribute portions of soup with small pieces of meat.

I remember that once, Kasrielchi Koflis, who used to frequent our home, came to our house and received some cooked victual on occasion to restore his soul. Once he turned to my sister Mantzi and told her: "Listen, Mantzi, perhaps you can give my Thursday portion today, for I am afraid that I will not merit to receive my portion on Thursday."

Hirsch Gelobter acted in this fashion for several months. There was no home, no Jew, who did not know him and the good deeds that he did for them. It once happened that he met a group of weak and feeble Jews who were being beaten by the butt of the gun of a German oppressor. Gelobter approached the S.S. man and pleaded to him: "Please have mercy upon these weak, elderly Jews. Leave them and do not beat them."

The German left the elderly Jews and began to beat Gelobter with his gun. Despite his advanced

Hirsch Gelobter and his wife.

age – he had already reached the age of 60, -- he was strong and muscular. He grabbed the German with his two hands, quickly took the gun from his hand, and began to beat him and bite him with his teeth. He pushed him to the ground and beat him with all his might. The German fell to the ground, wallowing in his blood like a slaughtered swine. The Jews who stood around and witnessed this frightening scene were trembling from fear.

Gelobter fled and hid in one of the hiding places in the city. His hiding place was known to almost all of the Jews; however they all kept the secret and nobody turned him in or slandered him, for everyone loved him and revered him for his selfless dedication and strength of heart.

The Jews lived in constant fear, trembling, without knowing what to do.

The Judenrat – the Jewish Council – turned their eyes away from him even though they were responsible for him. Even the members of the local Ukrainian militia who knew him, and would have been able to search for him and find him, did not get involved in the matter, for they feared that if it became known to the oppressor Krieger in Stanislawow what a Jew did to an S.S. man, they would be punished severely.

The members of the Gestapo in Dolina also did not want to do anything, out of embarrassment that a Jew was brazen enough to beat an S.S. man. They also suspected that the matter was known to their superiors.

Hirsch Gelobter always told people that he prayed to G-d that he would not fall alive into the hands of the Germans. His request was fulfilled in a dramatic and heroic manner.

After the liquidation of Dolina-Broshnev, they found him lying in his dwelling riddled with bullets, with an axe in his frozen, bloody hand.

When the S.S. men entered his home on the day of the liquidation of the ghetto and wanted to take him out to be murdered, he greeted them with an axe and killed several S.S. members. He held his stand and fought like a lion with the axe that was in his hand until he fell in sanctification of G-d and the nation.

May the holy memory of this righteous, brave person be remembered for a blessing forever.

"For these do I weep, my eyes, my eyes drop with water, because the comforter who should restore my soul is far from me; my children are desolate, for the enemy has prevailed". (Lamentations I, 16)

"My eyes fail with tears, my innards burn, my liver is poured upon the ground on account of the breach of the daughter of my people; because the young children and nursing babies faint in the open areas of the city." (Lamentations II, 11)

The famine worsened. Every day became more and more difficult. People spread out in the fields, and attempted to find something to eat in any nook and cranny, without success.

People endangered their lives and went to the neighboring villages with all sorts of items of value in order to swap them for food. Yosef Halpern was walking along the paths of the villages in the area of Rozniatow where he had previously done business. The villagers found him on the path and murdered him on the spot. The daughter of Itzi Rothbaum of Krechowice went along with her husband Tishenkel to the villages in order to swap items for food. The enemy Krieger found them on the route. He beat them and tortured them, and finally shot them and murdered them on the road.

The enemy Mueller built a death camp in Vishkuv. On occasion he would appear in the city, capture a few Jews from the street, and beat them and then shoot them in the street. His first victim was the young son-in-law of Yosef Kassner, the husband of Baltzi Kassner – Meir Nestel. A few days later, that selfsame despicable person met a young handsome Jew, Shaya Stern of Mizon, among a group of working Jews. He invited him to his office, quietly took out his revolver, and without saying a word, as if he was going about his daily affairs, shot him in his handsome face and murdered him. He immediately enlisted several Jews to clean the floor well "from the blood of this swine", so that there would remain no trace or memory of him.

Every two weeks, the Jewish Council had to supply 25 or 30 Jews to Mueller to work in the death camp of Vishkuv. It is hard today to understand the reasons why there were many volunteers to go work there, even though it was known that nobody returned from there.

The Germans established with the Jewish Council that the workers be changed monthly. To the credit of the members of the Jewish Council, I wish to point out, that despite their hard work and the tremendous responsibility which was placed on them to fulfill all of the request of their Germans, they did not lose their Divine image[2] and did not turn into oppressors of the Jews, as the Germans had intended of them. Since it was not clear what the situation was with the Jews in Vishkuv, a delegation consisting of the director of the council and the chief of the Jewish militia Edzi Pfeffer traveled there on a mission of the council, along with a new group of Jewish workers, in order to see what was transpiring there. Of course, they also never returned to Dolina.

The council attempted to maintain contact with friends and acquaintances from all the neighboring towns in order to find out what the situation was in those towns, so that they could be prepared for the same fate when such a day arrived.

I maintained a constant connection with my relatives and friends in the area in order to find out what was happening with them; what was going on in Stryj, Stanislawow, Bolekhov, and Kalush. I maintained very frequent contact with a few friends in Kalush. My friend Shabtai Rosenberg visited me for a week, as well as Lunek the son of Vevzi Teneh. When Shimshon Rechtschaffen and his daughter Fantzi came to me, they urged me to visit my friends, the Rozniatow natives who were in exile in Kalush. They had some sort of premonition that perhaps this may be the last time that inspired them to urge me to visit my friends.

The time that I spent in Kalush was a time of frightening chaos. I did not succeed in visiting many of my acquaintances, for they hid in their houses and were afraid to go outdoors. There was great crowding in the rooms, with fifteen or twenty people in one small room. Since the residents of Kalush had already tasted the bitter taste of an "aktion", and saw with their own eyes what was being done with the refugees, they were extremely frightened about what was to come. They felt that something ominous was approaching. It was hard to recognize the Jews. They had simply lost their human visage – they walked around outside like as shadows. The despair and devastation could be seen in their eyes without even a sound being uttered from their lips. They looked at one another with their despairing eyes as if they were taking leave of each other. Their eyes, so to speak, uttered eternal words of parting.

I will never forget the heartrending scene in which the children approached me with screams and bitter weeping. These children included Shimshon's Fantzi, and Tenchi and Izo of Rivka. They simply were not willing to permit me to return "home" to Dolina. Despair and agony enveloped the ghetto. Everyone was trembling and frightened. Those who did not want to sit with their hands folded in despair searched for means of escaping this valley of the shadow of death, this cemetery. They made various plans. Dr. Nunek Lusthaus and his wife Irina the daughter of Dr. Feier, as well as their daughter and mother Mrs. Esther Feier, went to live in the village of Vytoicha where he worked as a physician. Dr. Hilman went to the village of Spas. Dr. Fried and his wife Loti Friedler went to the village of Yasenovetz. Dr. Fold-Karp and his wife Eva went to the village of Lipovetcha. They all worked as physicians in those places, and were completely isolated. They left behind relatives and friends without knowing their fates. Four Jewish families continued to live in Rozniatow. These were Dr. Sabat and his wife (nee Weinreb), Litower, Dr. Mina Froiman, her husband Fishel and daughter Aviva, and the pharmacist Margolis. Weekly, one of them came in stealth to Dolina to find out what was happening with their friends and relatives, and to draw some support and Jewish spirit so that they would be able to continue living amongst the gentiles. Those who were sitting, so to speak, on the "fleshpots" were jealous of us Jews who were starving and perishing of hunger, tribulations, and fear. At that time, they understood the meaning of the adage: "shared troubles are half a comfort".

Along with the refugees from Rozniatow, Krechowice, and other such places, several hundred refugees from Hungary also arrived in Dolina.

At the end of April 1941, The German commander issued an edict that all the Jews of Hungary were permitted to return to their homes until the 1st of May. After that time, the border would be sealed. The Hungarian Jews literally ran to the border in confusion. Many Jews of Galicia joined them, hoping that they would be able to save themselves together with the Hungarian Jews.

The Germans gathered together all the Jews at the border. On May 1st, Commander Krieger along with several S.S. men arrived on two automobiles and murdered all those gathered at the border, more than 500 Jews, the elderly, children, and women. Not one of them survived.

When the Jews of Dolina found out about the terrible massacre at the border, they began to tremble in fear, and the town was ill at ease. The Germans immediately figured out what was bothering them, and began to calm the Jews. They said that no harm would befall the Jews of Dolina. On the contrary, they were quite needed, so they have nothing to fear. The Jewish Council had only to pay for the bullets that were used during the aktion. An accounting is an accounting. They must maintain their order.

I wish to relate here an incident that took place, and illustrates how cheap were the lives of the Jews.

Schultz, the Gestapo chief of Dolina, used to practice his shooting skills by shooting at birds in the garden of his home. Once, when he was practicing his shooting in his garden, Yankel Leib passed by along the old road that was next to the courthouse, with two buckets of water in his hands. Without thinking, Schultz pointed his pistol directly at him and shot him on the spot.

The lawless situation, the hunger and despair, took their toll. The Jews became indifferent about their lives. They no longer hid in their homes, and no longer were afraid of the Gestapo on the streets. It did not matter to them if they would receive a bullet in the head. They no longer were afraid of death, which could only save them from the pangs of hunger. Daily, some Jew was found dead on the street, or someone was taken to Stanislawow, never to return.

{174}

### In the Valley of Murder

On the Sabbath of August 29th, 1942, the eve of "the day of murder", I met by chance Rudek Karp, the brother of Dr. Leopold Karp, who had returned from his work in the nearby village of Sukhodol from the Sabbath. I also met Dolek Lusthaus and Boral. They were among those who worked outside of the city, and were free to go home. The reason for their being freed for the Sabbath was strange to others and myself. The Germans do not free people from work without a reason. When I said this to Rudek, he tapped me on my shoulder and said with a bitter smile: "What can still come? They will kill me, so what? Today it will be me, tomorrow it will be you."

Late Saturday night, my neighbor Shaya Teichman brought me the news that in the town from which he had just arrived there was great chaos. Several busses filled with soldiers and Gestapo agents, headed by the enemy Krieger, had arrived and surrounded the town. Krieger and Mueller sat down for a meeting with the Jewish Council and were engaged in a discussion with Dr. Julius Weinreb. We immediately warned our neighbors what was about to happen in the city. However, to my great surprise, the matter made no impact, and did not frighten anyone. "They will kill us? So what? It is better to die quickly than to die slowly from hunger."

The victims of the sword are better off than the victims of hunger.[3]

The first of those who left Berlin for the United States after the War.
Standing is Shaya Lutwak, Sashi Gelobter-Weidman, and Meir Ungar.

Sunday, August 30th, 1942, the 17th of Elul 5702, was the day of murder. At 4:00 a.m. I heard shots. I had enough time to place a large lock on the outer door of the barn that was filled with rows of wooden planks. We arranged a place of refuge, where myself, my sister Mantzi, Mordechai[4], and their children Saraleh and Devora hid. I quickly ran to the house of the parents of my brother-in-law where my other sister Hentzi was, and I told them to flee quickly to us. However my sister did not want to leave her home under any circumstance, since she felt that nothing serious would happen. On the contrary, she requested that I remain with them.

Suddenly, we saw throngs of Ukrainians with axes and other weapons of destruction in their hands. They broke down the door with their axes and shouted like beasts of prey: "Jews, get outside!" They attacked us and everyone else in the vicinity with their axes and guns. The screams of the smitten Jews reached the heavens. The Ukrainians removed anyone who was in the room. I myself do not recall how this took place. At that time, I happened to be in the dark room, and I instinctively slunk under the bed to hide.

Hirsch Ratenbach and Yeshayahu Lutwak at the entrance to the Berlin D.P. Camp in 1946.

To this day, I do not know how I was able to overcome my fear during those few moments. I heard clearly one murderer say to another in Polish: "It is too bad that I did not bring my electric flashlight". They passed by me without noticing me. After a few moments, silence pervaded the house. I heard the murderers close up the house with boards at the front and back doors. I crawled out of my hiding place on my belly and saw there were signs pasted on the windows, which said: "Whomever pillages this house will be shot by the Gestapo."

My brain worked as fast as lightning. I realize that at this moment, I was out of danger. In the meantime, due to the harsh warning on the sign, nobody would be so brazen as to break into this house to pillage it. I quietly went up to the attic, beneath the shingles, and from the cracks in the boards I was able to see everything that was taking place outside. My eyes saw how the S.S. men and their Ukrainian assistants, armed with all kinds of destructive weapons, dragged out any person who was found in the Jewish homes. The S.S. along with the Ukrainians lined up the large crowd of prisoners into five lines and began to bring them to the central square of the town. S.S. men, with their guns aimed, lined both sides of the route. After them a large crowd of Ukrainians followed, happy and rejoicing over the spectacle. They followed after the Jews, who were their former neighbors and friends.

From my house, I could not see the frightening scene of the screaming and wailing Jews gathered in the central square. However, I heard a detailed report of the events from Sani Kassner, who was an eyewitness. I met him a few months later in the Stryj ghetto. He related to me what happened. After the murder of his brother-in-law Meir Nastel in the Dolina ghetto, he left the Bolekhov ghetto and arrived at the home on Friday, exactly two days prior to the mass murder. He was not able to leave there, for the entire town was surrounded by S.S. men, and nobody could come and go. His parents lived in the town square. A portion of their house had been confiscated by the Germans for use as an office, and his parents lived in cramped conditions in one small room in the back.

Since the windows of the front of the house belonged to the Germans, and there were all sorts of German notices and placards on them, the Germans passed over this home and did not damage it. From that house, which was in the center of town, they were able to witness with their own eyes what was taking place in the square.

"In the center of the square, the Jews were ordered to kneel down with their hands over their heads. Woe unto anyone who took a stand and lowered his hands. Immediately, such a person was attacked by the Ukrainian militia and S.S. men, and was dealt deathblows with their guns and sticks. Several people were shot on the spot. When the Germans saw children in the arms of their parents, they removed them by force from their parents' arms and beat them on their heads with stones from the heap that was at the side of the road. Then they would toss the dead children down before their parents' eyes. The shrieks and wailing were beyond description. With my own eyes, I saw one of the murderers approach Moshe Shulman, the son-in-law of Avraham Strumwasser and husband of Chaya, and attempt to remove by force the young child that was in his arms. Shulman fell upon him and began to wrestle and strangle him. Immediately, some S.S. men approached and killed him on the spot. We saw Aharon and his sister Mintzi Enis struggling with the Germans, refusing to be brought alive to the valley of murder. The murderers shot them on the spot. Enis was still able to throw his homemade hand grenade, and he killed several of the murderers.

The Jews, half naked and flowing with blood, some of them not recognizable, without any desire for life, were then brought straight to the Jewish cemetery, where previously the Jews had dug three giant pits.

After a few days, Dr. Washkowitz, the son-in-law of Kardash, told me details of what took place to the Jews in the cemetery. He had heard these details from one of the members of the Ukrainian militia who participated in the mass murder.[5]

In the Jewish cemetery, the Jews were commanded to strip naked. To the melodious tunes of records of joyous German marching music, the Jews were brought, strapped together in a row, to the edge of one of the pits. There was a wooden plank going across the pit, and the Jews were ordered to cross. The Germans stood with machine guns next to the pits, and shot incessantly at the Jews who were walking across the plank. Some were immediately killed by the bullets, and others were merely injured or were not hit at all. However, all of them fell into the pit one after another. The pit filled up with dead, half dead, and living people who were not able to climb out of the pit due to the heap of corpses that were on top of them.

The German machine guns operated until 1:00 p.m., and cut off all remnants of the Jews, men, women, and children, brothers and sisters, bridegrooms and brides, old men and women, young cheder students, Hassidim and people of worthy deeds along with Maskilim and working people. The blood of all of them mixed together into a mighty stream that covered the entire Jewish settlement in which generation of dear Jews had lived, worked, and dreamed about a joint life with their neighbors, about a life of Torah and work, a life of righteousness and happiness.

Throughout Monday, the day following the slaughter of the Jews, the Germans enlisted throngs of gentiles to clean up the streets from the blood of the Jews, to remove the corpses from the houses and yards, and to bring them to an additional pit that had been dug for this purpose. I saw how they succeeded in capturing Leizer Geller and his young son Bodzo, Hirsch Mordechai Schwalb along with his wife and children, his son-in-law Mordechai Leib Bunim, the dentist Yosef Blau the husband of Matilda Prinz, his brother Salek Blau, Avraham Ratenbach, and Yankel Yampel the son of Moshe.

Those who were captured from their hiding places were gathered into one place and murdered together with machine guns.

On Monday evening, when everything was quiet and no people were about, I decided that it was time for me to come down from the attic where I had lain for two days without moving. Quietly, crawling on my belly, and looking around with every move I made, I arrived at the storehouse of wood and hay. From there, through a break in the wooden plank, I went at the barn where the rest of my family members who remained alive were hiding: my sister Mantzi, her husband and their children Sarache and Devora. There, hidden in the heap of ruins, I saw my dear friends Yasi Lindenbaum and Chaim the son of Wolf Wigdorowitz, who escaped during the time of the slaughter and came to that place by chance, and thus survived. From my friend Lindenbaum I found out that we had no hope of remaining alive there, since Dolina had been declared Judenrein (free of Jews), and since all the members of the Jewish Council had been slaughtered as well on the day of the great slaughter.

{178}

## A Monument to a Dear Soul

My friend Yosef Lindenbaum told me some details about the last days and bitter end of the holy martyr Dr. Weinreb, the head of the Jewish Council. I wish to dedicate a few lines in his memory.

He was a native of Dolina. He was a Jew with a warm and sensitive heart. He was an enthusiastic Zionist, quiet and modest, not striving for high position. When the heavy burden was placed upon him, he did not lose for one instant his Divine image. He understood his position, and the bitter lot that was imposed upon him due to Divine providence, and he attempted with all his power to help the members of the community over which he had been appointed by the governing authorities. He posted notices and announcements in fulfillment of his duties, in order to requisition the good requested by the Germans. He supplied workers, made sure order was kept, and supervised the Chevra Kadisha (burial society), which was very busy. He did his duty, and no more. When the Germans arrived in Dolina at the conclusion of the Sabbath, headed by Krieger and Mueller, and requested that he supply 1,200 Jews to be murdered, Dr. Weinreb answered them with honor and pride: "I am responsible for the Jewish property and for the work force, however I am not the master of their bodies. This is only dependent on G-d who is the ruler and judge over all."

The proud answer of Weinreb aroused the wrath of the murderers Krieger and Mueller. The end of Dr. Weinreb was evil and bitter. First, he was taken to the S.S. headquarters in Dolina, where he was tortured and beaten severely. Finally, Mueller asked that he be given into his custody and taken to Stanislawow. Nobody can imagine the forms of torture that the Nazis inflicted upon their victims, in particular when they wished to take revenge or punish somebody. Mueller had a special torture house in Stanislawow, in the Rudolf depot[6], where he had a staff who was expert in sadistic torture. Dr. Weinreb was brought there, and there he gave up his holy and pure soul.

May his memory remain holy and blessed forever.

{179}

## My Wanderings

I noticed that it was no longer possible to remain at home, since the Ukrainians laid a siege around every home, as perhaps there might be a Jew hiding who should be murdered or turned over to the Gestapo to be taken care of.

On Tuesday night, we left the home and went out to the forests near Odenitza. We met some gentiles along the route who beat us, but they allowed us to continue along our journey. In the forests, we met several Jews who had survived and fled to there. We continued to travel through the forests at night, and rested during the day. We had not eaten for four days.

Weak, tired, and filled with bitterness and despair, on Thursday, we arrived to an area of the forest where there lived a gentile whom we knew. He was Stefan Kardash, the son-in-law of Dr. Ibshkovitz. He received us with love and compassion, gave us some water to wash ourselves, and permitted us to hide on his property, under the floor of the barn, for several days. We rested under the floor of the barn all day, and at night we came out to take in some cool air and straighten out our bodies, which were almost frozen from lack of movement.

Dr. Ibshkovitz and his wife Olga gave us some warm food, and also prepared some food for us for the days, when we would be resting beneath the barn.

Sunday arrived. Gentile friends of Dr. Ibshkovitz arrived in his yard, and the entire conversation revolved around the slaughter of the Jews. We who were hiding in our hiding place heard one of them relate that immediately after the Gestapo and the Ukrainian militia sealed up the pits of corpses, they all swarmed like locusts upon the clothing of the victims. They searched for items of value such as silver ornaments and rings. The pit was pulsating, and voices of weeping and bitter screams pierced the heavens. The murderers were terrified and fled from the cemetery. A few days after the slaughter they still saw that the earth was pulsating up and down. There were still Jews buried alive and wounded in the pits who were attempting without success to escape from the pit of death.

We heard stories such as this from the people that were seated in the yard. Everyone added details about what they had seen without expressing remorse or pain, as if they were simply relating an interesting story. We realized that the place was not safe for us, and we decided to leave immediately. We also thought that if we were to remain hidden, our hosts would also be punished with death by the Gestapo.

The Gestapo put up large posters in the Ukrainian language stating that anyone who turned in a Jew, alive or dead, would receive as a reward a half kilo of sugar, and some boxes of tobacco or a bottle of liquor. The gentiles could not stand up to such an enticement. They spread out in the fields, forests, and houses and searched for living Jews.

Meir Ungar, the husband of Dora Gelobter (who lives today in the United States) related to me the following story.

Near Bolekhov, a gentile captured a young Jewish girl in the forest, and immediately brought her to the Gestapo in order to be eligible for the great reward of a half kilo of sugar and some boxes of tobacco. However before turning her over to the Gestapo, he told them that he wishes to request something else in addition to the customary prize which is due to him. He wished that they would remove the girl's dress and give it to him before she was to be murdered by a bullet. "Why?" asked the Gestapo man. "Simply, I want a dress without a bullet hole in it." This price was too high even for the Gestapo man, and without saying a word, he took out his revolver and killed the gentile with the first bullet, and the Jewish girl with the second bullet.

Dr. Ibshkovitz knew that in Bolekhov, in a place where there previous had lived farmers of German extraction, several Jews were hidden. He made contact with them and told them about me. My cousin Ethel and her husband Shmuel Gelobter were there. They told me how to get there, and at night, having traveled through fields, forests, and all types of hiding places, I arrived to near Bordishkov. There in the nearby forest, I met people who were wasting away from hunger. They were very weak, and they were afraid of any shadow, sound, or rustling leaf. There I met, among the others, Miriam Kirshenbaum, who was the wife of Leib Kunis and the daughter of Yitzchak Schwindler from the village; and Chantzi Strassman who was the wife of Moshe Strassman and the daughter of Chaya Adler. I could not stay in that place for more than three days. During the days, when the Jews worked as agricultural laborers in the fields, I hid in the roof of the home of my friend Shalom Deutscher. During the evenings, I would steal away to the home of Mordechai Gross and Zisha Aryeh Kuperberg who lived together in one dwelling. There in the small house we were able to discuss our deep crisis and everything that took place with us during these terrible days. We wished one another that we should be able to meet under better circumstances.

We left Broshkov to go to Bolekhov.[7] I stayed there only for a short period of time, for I was greatly afraid to stay there. From there, we went to Stryj. There, Yaakov Leib helped me to find a place to put down my head and to rest a bit from all my wanderings. He was already there with his family. However my period of rest there was not to be for long. I remained there for three or four weeks.

In November, another large aktion took place "to empty the city from Jews". They transported the Jews of Stryj to the Belzec death camp. More than 2,000 Jews perished in that aktion, including my friend and benefactor Yaakov Leib and his entire family, Gittel Adler, Stultzi Rosman, and Avraham Fogel and his entire family who were at that time in Stryj.

The Gestapo men captured me and beat me with deathblows until I fainted and fell among the dead. I lay there in pools of blood and mud on Lvovska Street until night fell. Then I began to move until I arrived to the edge of a house that had been completely destroyed by bombs. There amidst the ruins I lay down and fell asleep.

When I awoke three days later it was dark. I left the ruins, and saw nothing other than rubble and destruction. In the meantime, the Germans gathered the corpses from the streets. The Jews who survived the aktion walked around like sleepwalkers. I began to wander around the ruins. The period of reprieve did not last long. After a few days, they gathered up all the Jews into the synagogue. They stuffed 1,500 people into the synagogue, which was barely able to hold 500 people. People who had to attend to their bodily needs did so in the place where they stood, since it was simply impossible to walk forward even one step. Many died from weakness or hunger, and the dead lay there among the living. We were not even given a drop of water. The women shouted: "Water, give us a drop of water to restore our souls". Many went crazy from the tribulations, the hunger, and the thirst. The Germans, who still required workers, in particular the intellectuals, decided that it would be a waste to kill all the people who were still needed. When they found out that I was a dentist and a licensed mail nurse, they immediately took me to the Jewish Council to be registered as a necessary worker.

After a few days, I met by chance someone else who had survived from Rozniatow. This was Susi Weitzman (who today lives in the United States), the daughter of Yosef Gelobter. She endangered her life and went by foot from Bolekhov to Stryj in order to try to save her father and other family members from the Stryj ghetto, or at least to meet them and see them while they were alive.

I was together with Drezel Parish, the daughter of Meir Parish, as well as her husband for a few days. He was rescued from the concentration site in the synagogue at the last minute prior to the Jews being sent to the gas chambers of Belzec. However, due to the extremely cramped and unhygienic conditions in the synagogue, they caught typhus, which was epidemic among the Jews, and died with great suffering.

I now remained alone, forlorn, and weak. Like a wandering dog, I went from one ruin to another, without food and without a place to sleep for even one night, until Susi Weitzman-Gelobter had mercy upon me and brought me to the house of her aunt Chantzi Sobel, the daughter of Pini Berger, who lived in the Stryj ghetto. There, for a short period, I found a place to rest my head and to eat what was still available to eat.

Several Jews who remained alive from the neighboring villages succeeded in stealing into the half empty ghetto at night. Among those who found there way in was Dr. Leon Horowitz, the son of Shmuel Benzis, Mottel Hoffman the son of Shalom Hoffman and the cousin of Marek Rotter, Yaakov Yampel the son of Bendet Yampel, their cousins Buni and Tzippy Angelman, Chaya Stern the daughter of Golda and her five year old daughter Edzi. Dr. Leon Horowitz did not wish to remain in the Stryj ghetto and desired to leave there with his sister Klara Beigeleizen to go to the Lvov ghetto.

After a few days, I found out that members of the Ukrainian militia captured Dr. Horowitz and brought him directly to the Gestapo headquarters where he was shot on the spot. Mottel Hoffman and his cousin Magister Marek Rotter, accompanied by Dudo Blaustein of Stryj arrived at Skole and hid there with a gentile that they knew, who gave them an underground hiding spot. A few months later, it became known to me that that hiding place, where there were some thirty Jews, was found out or reported, and all of the Jews who were there were shot on the spot.

From Bolekhov, where there was still some form of work camp where Jews hoped to be able to continue living until the day of redemption would come, a few Jews began to steal into the Stryj ghetto. Sani Kassner and his wife, his sister Beltzi and her child, Rivka Fruchter the wife of Meshulam, and her cousin Tzipa Kreiter the daughter of Tzipi Kreiter, the son of Meir Zimmerman, Avraham Yechez-kel, Meir Laufer, Herman Laufer the grandson of Efraim Rechtschaffen, Moshe Milstein the husband of Bluma, the son-in-law of Chaya Gittel Strassman, Shaya Strassman, Getzel and Yisraelki Frankel the sons of Meir Frankel, and the children of the tailor Yaakov Yehuda – Yenti, Chaim, Wolf, and Shimshon – managed to arrive there, among others. Dolina natives who had survived to this point and arrived there included Mordechai Teicher, his wife and their daughter Beila, along with her husband and children; Moshe Landis the husband of Gittel Enis; Dr. Herman Neuhauser; Shlomo Rotenbach and his wife; Itzik Heker; Yosi Landenbaum and his sister Maltzi; Yaakov Klieresfeld and his young brother; Motka Leiter and his brother; and Moshe Geller with his wife and their children.

## TRANSLATOR'S FOOTNOTES

1. After ritual slaughter (shechita), which is accomplished by a cut at the neck with a sharp knife, meat must have its blood removed by salting, and certain other thick veins and arteries must be removed in order to render the meat kosher.

2. According to Jewish tradition, every human being is created in the Divine image, which figuratively means that all humans have a divine spark in their soul, which accounts for their spiritual tendencies.

3. A verse from the Book of Lamentations.

4. Presumably, Mantzi's husband.

5. The following description is a classic description of an 'Einsatzgruppen aktion', which was one of the most prominent methods of murder used during the holocaust in the Soviet occupied territories. There were four roving groups of Einsatzgruppen militias. They made their rounds to the cities and towns, rounded up the Jews, and gunned them down, often into a ravine or a pit dug in the cemetery. In this area of Ukraine, it would have been the Einsatzgruppen C that was active. The most famous Einsatzgruppen aktion took place in Kiev, where over 33,000 Jews were gunned down in a three-day period at a ravine known as Babi Yar. It is estimated that the Einsatzgruppen aktions caused the death of at least 1.2 million Jews, a full 1/5 of the Jews murdered during the holocaust.

6. See the Stanislawow translation from the Pinkas Hakehillot, which was translated by myself (Jerrold Landau) and is published on the JewishGen website http://www.jewishgen.org/yizkor/pinkas_poland/pol2_00359.html

7. The subjects of the sentences in this paragraph seem to interchange from singular to plural.

{182}

## Reb Moshele the Shochet – Weiser

It is hard for me to describe in words the great tragedy that occurred to the family of Reb Moshele the shochet (ritual slaughterer) Weiser, may G-d avenge his blood. I do not have sufficient words to describe the pain, agony, and tribulations that came upon this fine family.

I was able to obtain details of this story from his grandson, Yankele Weiser, a boy of 16 or 17. He was the son of Zida and Bracha Weiser, and lived in the Stryj ghetto.

About ten days after the great slaughter in Dolina, his good friend and my friend Lusi Zitzer snuck out of the bunker one night. A large number of Jews were hiding in this bunker, who were standing at the threshold of death due to hunger and thirst, since they spent all their time in the large, dark bunker without any food and drink. Lusi decided on his own to go out in the darkness of night to search for any type of food that he would be able to chew and hold in his mouth, or to find a source of water so that he could show it to those who were thirsty. The bunker, in the basement of Dr. Redish, was quite well fortified. Aside from his parents, the following people were there: Lipa Teneh and his wife, Reb Moshele the shochet and his wife Feiga, their son Zida and his wife Bracha who was the daughter of Yosef and Shimon Stern, as well as their own two daughters Chitza and Reizele and their son Yankele, who told me the story. The other young shochet was there, the son of Moshe Eli, as well as Yaakov Hochman, his wife, and his two children, and some other people.

Lusi went around and looked for anything that he could carry. He did not find anything that he could bring back to the bunker in order to sustain the souls who were dying there of hunger and thirst. He estimated the situation with astute eyes. In Dolina there were already no Jews, and he saw no means of escape for those who were hidden. Even though it was possible for him to escape and not to return to the bunker, he did not do so. He decided that if he were to die, it would be best to do so along with everyone who was gathered in the bunker. Due to his great despair, he decided to put an end to the great suffering and the slow death in the bunker.

There were several dear families there, and he was no longer able to tolerate watching their slow demise and great suffering. He did what he did. The Germans came there, discovered the bunker, took out all the half-dead Jews who were there, who could barely even see daylight anymore, and brought them straight to the cemetery to be slaughtered.

Reb Moshe the shochet, as long as his soul was still with him, did not walk but rather ran to greet death. His eyes glowed with happiness. He raised his eyes towards heaven and began to sing the Psalm of David: "Even though I walk through the valley of the shadow of death – I fear no evil since You are with me"[1]. Singing and reciting Psalms, he was brought straight to the open grave, where the S.S. men were standing at the edge with their machine guns. The S.S. men began to shoot the people with machine guns as they were being brought one by one to the pit.

The bullets injured Yankele in his hand, and he jumped into the pit, keeping near to the edge of it, near the wall. In the meantime, other people fell on top of him. The murderers finished their job and began to cover the pit. Yaakov was able to make a small opening for air. At nightfall, he was able to free himself from the corpses that were on top of him and beside him, and through quick movements, he was able to free himself from the pit. No dog barked and no bird chirped. Here, death reigned.

Yankele, who was lightly injured on his hand, overcame his pain, and by means of an unknown source of strength, he was able to flee quickly from the place and escape to the neighboring forests. He arrived in the Stryj ghetto and told us his sad story. However even here, death pursued him. On one of the days toward the end of October 1942, he was killed in an aktion.

I thought for a great deal of time, over and over again, about the story of the youth Yankele Weiser and what happened to his holy grandfather Reb Moshe Weiser, how he went to greet his death with enthusiasm. Only believers who are descended from believers are able to die in such a holy and pure manner, and to display such deep feelings of belief. This was not the frightened death of sheep brought to slaughter. This was the death of holy people, angels the son of angels, literally.

I heard various other stories that other survivors told me, describing how Jews went to meet their deaths. I heard the story how the Germans discovered a bunker in which the Meir family was hiding. The young daughter of Kutzi Meir mocked and scored the Germans as she walked with strength and honor to meet her death. She laughed at the Germans to their eyes until they began to scream from anger and shame.

The daughter of Moshe Sanes, Mrs. Klara Patrich, hurried to be the first. Holding her husband's arm, she jumped together with him into the open pit before they had been shot. This was not the death of the fearful, but rather the death of mighty people, mighty people who raised themselves above the armed murderers and greeted death with honor and valor. Even though they could kill our bodies, they could not kill our souls. We are spiritually greater than you are, oh you nation of Goethe and Schiller, you nation of murderers.

Every Jew who lived in the ghetto felt that death stood before him, and that any moment he might meet it. In the meantime, he must take advantage of the time and the day while still alive. "Blessed is G-d day by day"[2] was the slogan of everybody.

Until death would arrive, one had to eat, drink, and somehow sustain the body. One had to live, work, possess a work permit. How could one obtain a work permit? Regarding the obtaining of work permits, and entire industry arose, with connections, favoritism, and payments. The "work permit" became somewhat of a purpose of life for the residents of the ghetto. I was fortunate to be a licensed nurse, and I owned a card permitting me free movement. I could wander around freely everywhere. I worked for some time as a male nurse in the Jewish hospital, as well as a janitor. In these positions, I had some connection with the civic prison. I was able to have constant contact with the poor Jewish prisoners who were imprisoned there, and was able to bring them news about what was taking place in the city, and what was going on with their relatives who were still alive. I was able to find out why they were imprisoned, and what might be done to free them. In the prison, I met Esther Lusthaus and her daughter-in-law Orna Feier with her daughter Ana Maria. We both wept over our bitter fate. I requested that we remain in contact, so that I could know who was imprisoned, and what was going on with the people who were imprisoned. I knew that Dr. Nunek Lusthaus, who worked as a doctor in the village of Vytoicha near Bolekhov was searching for a way to escape from there and go to the Stryj ghetto. He preferred to be among his suffering brethren rather than in the gentile "Garden of Eden". However, as he was on the route from Bolekhov, before he arrived in Stryj, the German murderers captured him. They brought him to Stanislawow, and he was murdered there by Mueller. His mother, wife, and children were transferred to a prison in Stryj. Yaakov, the son of Bendet Yampel, worked hard to obtain freedom for the Lusthaus family. He succeeded in collecting all sorts of items of value to be used to redeem the prisoners – to free the family. However in the meantime, the notice came of the liquidation of a certain number of Jews from the ghetto, and the first were to be those in the prison.

In order to extricate themselves from the tribulations of hell that awaited everyone imprisoned in the ghetto, each person tried to obtain a few cyanide capsules. People would spend their last coin and exchange foodstuffs needed for the sustaining of life in order to obtain a small portion of that fatal poison, which would "rescue and save" from the physical and spiritual torture and put and end to the tribulation.

Jews who obtained that potent poison tied it around their necks as an amulet, and did not let it off of their bodies even for a moment. There was a great demand for this commodity, and there was even a "black market". There were forgeries as well. On numerous occasions, someone would give all of his money and property in order to obtain a tablet, and at the end all they would have would be a small forged tablet, a simple saccharin tablet.

In order to find refuge from the constant searches before and after each episode of extermination, the Jews invented all sorts of gadgets and devices to help them build hiding places, and in particular to camouflage them. Some people became expert in this area. Everyone put forth his best effort in order to secure the hiding place, and in particular to hide from an evil eye. A few of these Jews who became expert at the building of hiding places became well known to the residents of the ghetto. People would pay good money in order to have a hiding place built for themselves and their families. According to my memory, the following people were expert in the building of such bunkers: Yankel the son of Bendet Yampel, Buni Angelman the husband of Tziso, Herman Laufer the grandson of Efraim Rechtschaffen, Meir Laufer the son of Yaakov Laufer, and Avraham Yechezkel Zimmerman the grandson of Sashi Feiga. It is worthwhile to describe one such bunker in order to illustrate the devices used for camouflage and in order to give the readers and idea of what was such a bunker.

In the Stryj Ghetto, on 14 Lvovska Street, in the home of Welian-Milsteon, the following families lived at the side of the lot where there was once a shoe store: Leibush Feldman and his two daughters Tzili and Minka; Buni Angelman and his wife and four year old daughter Edzia; Buni Milstein; and myself. We all "lived" in one small room. The following people were cramped into the small kitchen: a relative of the Milstein family Mrs. Sara, her daughter Chana and son Moshe who jumped off a moving train on its way to the crematoria, and as he fell he broke a leg and remained alive. There was also a young and pleasant boy with us, Moshele Hauser.

In the room that faced the yard, Magister Hesi Hoffman lived with his elderly, ill mother and sister

Libchia. Once in a while another guest came to us to spend the night, Yaakov Yampel.

In the large, enclosed yard there was also a lavatory, which was next to a small shed. A deep pit was dug underneath it, and we placed thick wood shavings and boards over it. We covered them with the earth that was dug from the pit and made a strong ceiling. Next to the wall we left a small hole for air. The entry into this bunker of refuge was through the lavatory. We would lift a wooden plank from the floor and enter the bunker via a narrow wooden staircase. In the shed there was all kinds of junk, broken vessels and chairs. It was in disarray. There was a large, strong lock on the door of the shed, and it was kept lock. We conducted a practice session for entry and exit to the pit, and we calculated that it would take five minutes for all residents of this house to enter the bunker.

This was the appearance of a typical refuge bunker, in which many Jews would live and hide. Some would live there for months at a time, and their eyes would become dim, for they were not accustomed to daylight and sunlight. There were those whose backs became stooped since they were required to live in their bunker with bent backs at all times, due to the low height of the bunker. Those who lived in bunkers for long period of time would go out at night to attend to their bodily needs, and in particular to search for a small amount of food and water to sustain themselves, and the souls of those who lived with them in the bunker.

The residents of a bunker were like one family. The tribulations united them, and they all supported each other and attempted to help each other in a brotherly fashion.

{186}

## In the Stryj Ghetto

At the end of December or the beginning of January 1943, the Germans in Bolekhov began to gather together the men who were fit to work into various camps. The old people and children were either already killed, or were hidden. The most important thing was that we did not expose before their eyes any young person, child, or old person. At around the same time, the Rabbi of Bolekhov, Rabbi Shlomo Perlow, and his entire family were brought into the Stryj ghetto. The residents of the ghetto, including the Judenrat, treated the Rabbi of Bolekhov with exceptional reverence and respect. All of them took comfort in their hearts, and hoped that in the merit of this holy, righteous person that was now with them in the camp they would merit life. However, the situation immediately turned against them bitterly. The situation worsened daily, and every movement was at the risk of one's life. We discussed among ourselves that all of the curses of the reprimand[3] fell upon our heads, and even more so. Nevertheless, people did not lose their Divine image and attempted to help each other, and especially to help the stumbling and weak.

One day, a ray of light shone in the camp in the form of a young woman by the name of Blumka Horowitz-Laufer. After the terrible slaughter in Dolina, she succeeded in saving herself and returning to Rozniatow. There she lived for six months in a haystack that was owned by Stash Jurzko, who saved Jews. This was at the edge of the forest near Rozniatow. Twice a week, Stash would bring food up to her by a ladder in order to sustain her, so that she would not perish of hunger. On one occasion, children were playing near the hiding places, and they entered into the haystack to hide, and noticed the form of a person there. They immediately told this to Stash, who understood the situation, and speedily transferred her, with the assistance of her friend Duzia Dodenko, to the Stryj ghetto. It his hard to describe in words what happened to those gathered around when they heard her name from the non-Jew. I don't have the ability to describe the shock to you. Before us there stood a skeleton of a person, and it was difficult to figure out if she was alive or dead. She lost the power of speech during the six months when she did not utter a word from her mouth. She was not able to look into the light of the world, and she always kept her eyes closed. Her words could barely be heard due to her great weakness. A few weeks passed until she was able to utter a comprehensible sentence from her mouth, and until she began to eat her food with zest. Slowly she returned to her strength, and turned into one of G-d's creatures.

Stash and Duzia were indeed among the righteous gentiles. They advised us to organize ourselves into partisan groups, to hide in the forests and to fight against the Germans with weapons. Stash advised me to choose a group of 10-15 people who would be willing to hide on his property and to fight against the Germans when the time came. He was prepared to set up a bunker for refuge not far from his house – at the edge of the forest, and to provide food and any other requirements of such a group. When I came with their advice to Dr. Kahana and two other friends, who still had some financial means for such an endeavor, they told me that it was forbidden to believe such a person, to place oneself in his care and to pay cash. I defended him, for I was convinced that one could trust this good man who wanted sincerely and honorably to help us. However, nothing came of the meeting. His last words to me are etched in my memory: "When you find yourself in a bad situation, turn to me and I will help you!"[4]

At the same time, Hirsch Ratenbach, the son of David and Mamtzi Ratenbach of Dolina, arrived in the ghetto. I was a friend of his from my youth. We studied together at the Dolina gymnasia. I found out from him that in Dolina there were Jews from various different places of the region, who were hiding there with the help of the brothers Stach[5] and Heryn Babi. On several occasions Hirsch Ratenbach endangered his life by going to remove Jews from the ghettos of Stryj and Bolekhov and bringing them to the forest. Hirsch made a plan to remove the rabbi of Bolekhov from the ghetto, but in the meantime someone reported him, and he barely escaped with his own life. Thus ended the attempts to save the rabbi from the ghetto.

{187}

## Rabbi Shlomo Perlow, the Rabbi of Bolekhov
## may G-d avenge his blood

I had the special merit to spend time with him every Friday afternoon at a time when the ghetto was quiet. I had the honor of being his assistant, bringing him to the bathhouse that was next to the Jewish hospital. During the evenings, I searched for opportunities to enter his residence and spend time with him. There I was able to meet people who brought with them news about what was taking place in other ghettos. The days of Passover were approaching and many began to worry about how they would observe a Seder and fulfill the commandment of eating of matzo. The Rabbi gathered nearly 100 people in his house, and each one received a half of a piece of matzo, which was completely kosher. I to this day wonder about from where he was able to obtain the matzos.

It is difficult to describe the emotions of those who were gathered at the Seder. Sighs and weeping were heard. A sea of tears were shed and filled the cups of agony. Everyone recalled his relatives who were no longer alive, and did not even merit burial. The fear was great that the Germans might fall upon them, since they knew that it was a Jewish holiday, and might wish to take revenge on the Jews in their manner. Watchers were set up in the corners and streets so that word would travel fast if any-one strange was approaching the ghetto, and those present at the Seder might be alerted. The guards stood at every street corner: Lvovska, Batorgo, Luna-Perk, Koshnievsla, and Berko Joselvitza. Just as those who reclined in Bnei Brak[6], we sat all night, observed our meager Seder, and planned about how to escape from the ghetto. A few advised to go out to those who were already in the forests. Others advised crossing the Hungarian border, for they had heard that the situation there was still not as bad as here. The brother of the son-in-law of Rabbi Hersheli, an intelligent and astute young man, brought with him detailed plans about how to cross the Hungarian border. Some people attempted to follow this plan. The first group of twenty people who set out, including Dr. Schiff, were captured and shot on the spot.

I approached the rabbi and told him about my friend Hirsch Ratenbach, who was hiding in the forests of Dolina, and I asked him as to whether I should follow in his path. The rabbi took my hand into his, and with great warmth squeezed my hand and said: "The accursed enemy will not succeed in killing everybody. Go my son, go and succeed in your path..."

Aside from my work in the hospital as a male nurse and disinfector, I also worked twice a week at laying the tracks at the Stryj railway station. My work there included a half a day of working with mortar and bricks, and a half a day as a nurse administering first aid to those who were injured from the work. My infirmary was in a hut made of wooden planks and worn out sheets of metal. It had a sign saying "First Aid". When I worked on the railway tracks, I often had opportunity to walk through the "Aryan" streets, and how painful was it to my heart to see how life went on quietly and with secu-rity, as if nothing was taking place. The children were frolicking, with laughter in their mouths. Girls would walk slowly through the streets wearing splendid dresses. I remembered what they were doing to our own infants and children, what they did to the Jewish youth, the types of strange deaths that they inflicted upon them. My heartache was often more severe than my physical suffering which I suffered every day.

Once, as I was crossing an Aryan street, I ran into a group of children who were playing the game "botzea aktia", that is to say, a game about the killing of Jews. They held small wooden swords in their hands, and with laughter, they would capture a child and shout at him "Juda raus!" As we passed by, they mocked us, laughed at us, and pelted us with stones. The parents who witnessed the "might" of their children beamed with pride. When I returned to the camp, I said in my heart: "I am no longer going to perform this work."

{188}

## The Escape from the Camp

At exactly this time, an order arrived at the heads of the camps to provide 100 Jewish slaves to work at the pottery factory in Bolekhov. A competition arose amongst the Jews, for everyone wanted to be among the 100 "fortunate" people who would leave here, and the price reached 20 dollars a person. I did not have that sum and I could not hope to be among the fortunate ones. Dr. Kahana, who was responsible for the workforce in the camp, did not want to send me. This was not due to my lack of money. He saw me as an important worker in the ghetto, and attempted to convince me as much as possible to continue my work in the ghetto, and not to be in a hurry to leave it.

Everyone knew that I had no desire to continue with my work, and that I was looking for a way to leave the ghetto. Dr. Allerhand, the vice director of the Stryj camp who was responsible for fulfilling the quota of 100 workers for the Bolekhov camp, hinted to me to be ready and to present myself at the gathering place of those who were going. Prior to my going, I went to the home of the rabbi in order to receive a parting blessing from him. He took my hand and whispered quietly. I understood that this was a prayer and a blessing for my journey. He patted my shoulder and said: "Go in peace, and may you merit salvation." I barely refrained from weeping. Many of my friends in the camp accompanied me to the gathering place.

Two trucks covered with tarpaulin were waiting for us at the gathering place. One of the drivers was a good acquaintance of mine. He was the driver of Archie Berger Bil, an intelligent gentile. After a few words that I exchanged with him, he immediately understood my intention. He took my personal belongings, placed me in the spare tire compartment, and covered me with sheets and his raincoat. Thus did I arrive at the camp without being enumerated, and without them knowing about my existence. Shoka Weidman helped me greatly there. He introduced me to the Jewish director of the camp, Rumek Samual, the son-in-law of Leizer Sheinfeld. He alerted a few of my friends about my arrival. Magister Zalman Shuster, the grandson of Mishel Artman, as well as the dentist Bomek Hamburger of Voynilov came to me. They concerned themselves with obtaining a work permit for me.

I went out daily with the people who were going to work, and returned with them. Many friends and acquaintances met me at work, including Sasha Gelobter, Yenti Freudenberg, Kalman Sastritan, Shlomole Spiegel, and others. Mrs. Riva Weidman brought me something to eat almost every evening. She worked in a different camp and went out from there via all sorts of cracks and breaches in order to provide me with a bit of food.

On Sunday morning, July 6, 1943, they woke me up from my sleep and told me in great confusion that the entire camp was surrounded by Gestapo men and Ukrainians. I did not even realize what was happing when they hauled me out in my leather coat to the courtyard. I was informed that the Germans were gathering up the workers who arrived there from the Stryj ghetto, apparently to murder them.

To my good fortune, at that moment the Jewish commander of the camp, Rumek Samual, arrived and told the Ukrainian militia man who hauled me out to allow me to return to my dwelling to get dressed.

He winked to me with his eyes, so that I should know to what he was referring. Instead of returning to my dwelling, I hid under the planks of the roof. I had a chance to tell Blumka Kalman of Stratyn to remove the ladder and place it in another place. Within a moment, I was caught in a small, narrow place under the boards and the planks, and there I rested. I heard people entering the house and searching, and they began to ascend the roof. A shiver passed over my body, but I rested silently, and in the dark they did not see me, and descended.

The Germans gathered that day all of the 100 men who were transferred from the Stryj ghetto. They added to the group all the members of the local Judenrat and other "extraneous" workers. There were 300 people in total. They were brought to the Jewish cemetery and shot there into a pit that had been prepared the previous day.

After dark, the Germans and their Ukrainian accomplices left, and those that remained alive continued in their normal work.

I descended from my hiding place, and along the way, I met Shlomole, who brought me some sort of coat. Susi Gelobter brought me some bread, a bit of sugar, and shoes. The brought me through a tortuous route to the edge of the forest, to a place where there were already some Jews. These included Yechezkel Zimmerman the son of Meir Zimmerman, Meir the son of Yaakov Laufer, Hesio Rosenman, and Barron and his sister from Kalush. I wish to make note of the parting words that Rivtzi Nussbaum, Yaakov Meir, and others said to me: "Go Shaika, and be saved. Then there will be an extra bullet for us"...

{190}

## In the Forests of Dolina

Those that fled had the intention of hiding in the forests of Dolina and remaining there until the redemption would arrive. However, who would show them the way, and who knows the paths through the thick and dangerous forests? I was given the task, and it was up to me to be the guide for a group of people who had escaped from the camp into the thickness of the forests. I had to make plans for living, how to go on, and how to exist. Every one of us and some implement, one had a knife and another had a thick stick. Someone had a gun with bullets. We decided among ourselves that we would be a united group. We would go together, die together, and fight together.

At sundown we went on our way. We walked for about an hour and a half, and then suddenly, from a side road, a young, armed gentile met us, and told us, getting to the point directly: "I know who you are and to where you are going, and I wish to save you. Don't go further along this route, go along this other route, so that you will not meet up with the bands of Germans and Ukrainians who are swarming through the paths and ambushing Jews..."

I thanked the young Pole, and told him that I had a clear plan, and we know the route that we are taking. The meeting between the young Pole and us was exactly at the crossroads, and, despite the danger that might be, I decided to go along the path which he pointed us to. We continued along the paths until we reached a railway crossing, when we suddenly noticed by the light of the moon that a shadow of a man was accompanying us the entire way. Since we were six in the group, and the shadow was of a single person, we quickly overcame our fear. We stood and called for him to approach us. It became clear to us that this was a Ukrainian worker who was on vacation from his work. He was one of the local residents, and he knew the routes very well. He told us that a few days previously, on June 6, 1943, a terrible aktion took place in the Stryj ghetto and very many people were killed there. We asked him to guide us. This was too far a deviation from his route home, but with a bit of urging, and a small "gift" he was convinced, and began to run with us along the path until we reached the banks of the Bistritza River, where there was a large bridge. Then he left for his home.

As we walked quietly across the bridge, a man armed with a gun approached us. When he saw that we were a large group, he was afraid and positioned himself at the edge of the bridge. We continued on our path across the bridge to the other shore, and reached the main road that leads to Dolina.

We were tired from all the exertion of that night. We turned off the road and entered an open field, where we all fell down into the haystacks and fell into a deep sleep.

Some sort of unknown internal power awakened me from my deep sleep, and I began to awaken the rest of the group. We continued along the main road to Dolina when it was still quite dark.

We already arrived at the edge of Brodotzkov, a neighboring village of Dolina, when suddenly a pocket flashlight shone in our eyes. Shivers passed through us all, for we had fallen into a trap, directly into the arms of the Germans. After a few moments of confusion, we saw a form hiding in the bushes. The man was holding a flashlight in one hand, and in the other hand an automatic rifle pointed directly at us, and he began to speak to us in Ukrainian: "Myself Stas and my brother Heryn Babi help Jews who are escaping from the Germans. I have just come from the Stryj ghetto. There I was on a special mission from Regina Pilzen of Kalush, to bring her brother and two others from the Stryj ghetto. One of them is Shaika Lutwak."

From his words, we could see that the person was speaking the truth, and was sincere. He certainly was looking for monetary reward – but he was true to his task. To convince us further he said: "I am waiting here for a man by the name of Leizerke Schiffman who went to the village to prepare food for us, and afterward, we will return to the forest."

I was a friend of Leizerke Schiffman from the time that we were in Dolina, and I knew him well. We were still talking, when he appeared before us with a full pack on his back. When he saw me, he fell upon me, hugged and kissed me, and sighed loudly.

We all joined them and entered the thick forest with them. They led us until we arrived to a valley filled with pine trees, which at one time was the summer retreat of Yaakov Laufer. In that wonderful place, filled with trees and small creeks flowing among the rocks of the forest, Yaakov Laufer (the husband of Blumka Horowitz), as well as his sister and brother Leibele Linek had a wonderful summer resort. Leizer and Heryn gave us instructions about how to conduct ourselves in the forest. They informed us of the secret password of the group, and told us how to make arrangements for ourselves in that place. Along with this, he alerted the other residents of the forests who were scattered around in all sorts of secret places that a new group of Jewish refugees had arrived, with Shaika Lutwak among them.

Who has the ability, who has the pen to be able to describe to you our feelings as we rested in the thick forest, in the splendid grass between the pine trees, with the wonderful mountain air blowing, as if indeed we were here on vacation rather than being refugees from the sword who were fleeing from the fear of death? I had the feeling that the blessing of the rabbi of Bolekhov was accompanying us. As we were getting our bearings in our new place, various residents of the forest came to us. The first to come to us was the head of the group, Heryn Babi, who spoke to us pleasantly, as a father would speak to his son. Regina Pilzen arrived with him. She brought us bread and potatoes. After them came Moshe Klein (who today lives in the United States), Avraham Haber, Srulka Helfer, and various other people who I did not know. One of them brought a pot of soup with him. Is it possible to describe what it was like to eat some cooked food after we had not eaten for two days? This was a hot cooked dish that was brought by comrades in the midst of the thick forests surrounding Dolina.

The next day, after the customary payment of "kashim"[7], that is to say dollars of pure gold, Heryn began to guide Hesio and the two Barrons to the forests of Perehinsko, where Hesio's brother-in-law and other relatives were. They wanted to be together in the forest. Yechezkel Zimmerman and Meir Laufer returned to the camp in Bolekhov to fetch from there some necessary items and perhaps to bring as well some friends to the forest. However, their luck did not hold out. They were captured and murdered on the spot.

Heavy rain began to fall in the forest, accompanied by thunder and lightning. The pouring rain soaked our already damp clothes, and penetrated to the marrow of our bones. Here we were, with our teeth chattering, shivering from the cold, with nowhere to flee and nowhere to hide. From every branch, raindrops were falling onto us, which penetrated the soul and made us feel like pieces of rags. However, our friends did not allow us to remain out in the torrential rain without protection for too long. A few of them came to us to bring us to their "den". It was deep in the ground, with broken pieces of wood and branches as a roof. This roof frame was covered with earth and many branches, which prevented the rain from penetrating. There were wooden couches which served as sleeping accommodations. One could also sit comfortably on them. We had all our necessities taken care of at this time.

Another group of Jews lived not far from us. This group included Yosef Frischer of Dolina, Chana Deutscher, and a few other people from various places. They already had a connection with a certain gentile from the area, who brought them food in return for a good sum of money. Moshe Klein was the "expert" in finding sources of food in a variety of manners. On occasion, he would bring a live calf or twenty heads of poultry in his sack, which he succeeded in obtaining in a variety of manners.

I attempted to help out in all sorts of ways, including the maintenance of cleanliness, cooking, and serving. I became like one of the family to the residents of the forest.

At that time, expulsions and massacres were taking place in all the cities of Galicia, and Jews who were fleeing for their lives came to the forest from all sorts of places. With such a situation, Heryn began to become jealous of his brother Stas, who also had some Jews under his care. He decided to enlarge his "kingdom" and his areas of shelter, and he began to gather any Jew who came by, of course in return for money, silver, copper, diamonds, or any other objects of value. Generally, anyone who would flee to the forest would bring with him all sorts of necessities and items of value in order to be able to meet any circumstance that arose. He would gather these items for "safekeeping". There were those who did not desire his protection in the forest, and went out into independent groups. These included the Pilzens, Helfer, Haber, Izi Lindenbaum, Velvel Kofalis-Kuperschmid, Yeshua Teichman of Dolina, Zelig Eber and his sister from the village of Rybno, the two Feier brothers of Stryj, Shlomo and Zani Ratenbach with their two nephews, Sobel of Stryj, and Chanale the daughter of Abramche Zilberberg.

In Heryn's group there were a few other people who I still recall: Shaika and Yanka Shrager, Muni and his sister Fanka Kandler, Mondik Zahen and Rita, Karel Ister, Fitzer, Leib and Dvora Schvitzer of Stanislawow, Wilekkowel of Nadworna, Wilech Yasiunech Garfinkel of Stryj, Fred Kowaler, his sister Lotti, and their mother, Desio Zilberman-Landsman and his grandchild of Kalush, Aharon and his wife Regina Walkentreiber, Hirsch Katzman, Dontzi Hochpelzen of Zawirona, Dr. Neuhauser of Dolina, Dr. Stern and his wife and daughter, Pinio Stern of Mizon, the dentist Schindler and his wife of Bolekhov, Max and Sabina Katz of Stryj, Shmuel Shlakes, and Shmuelko Teitelbaum the son of the rabbi of Neisands. I got to know the latter at the rabbi's house during the time of the occupation of Dolina. Afterwards, I met him many times at the home of the rabbi of Bolekhov in the Stryj ghetto. He was also a participant in the Passover Seder at the home of the rabbi of Bolekhov.

Now I met him again in the forest. He told me that, when he was still in the Stryj ghetto, his job in the workgroup was to bury in a large communal grave anyone who was killed, or who died via any other means of death. Once, when he was busying himself with burial, he suddenly came across the body of the rabbi of Bolekhov, Rabbi Shlomole Perlow, may G-d avenge his blood. He endangered his life and secretly removed the body. When he finished burying the rest of the dead, he began with holy solemnity to take care of the body of the rabbi. He washed the body, changed it into new clothes, dug a separate grave, buried the rabbi in that grave, and recited Kaddish afterwards, quietly and with holiness.[8]

When the liquidations of the ghettos and camps became more frequent, as has been noted, the number of refugees who fled for their lives into the forest increased. Meirka Turteltaub and his son Itzil Leizer were among those who arrived. I will later tell about his might and the beneficial service that he provided. Slowly the life in the forest began to take a regular pattern. The residents began to acclimatize to the life of quiet and fear in the forest. There was enough food, for some people were dedicated to this task and insured that there would be a sufficient supply of food. These were strong young men who were prepared to go out for any need. These people included our own Wilosh Weinfeld, Meir Turteltaub, and others. Hershka Ratenbach maintained a list of gentiles who had on occasion caused trouble for the Jews of the area. These people were the targets of the group of people who concerned themselves with the food supply. They would fall upon them at nights, and forcibly obtain food from them. The gentiles of the area were afraid of the Jewish "partisans" who lived under the protection of the brothers Stas and Heryn Babi. All types of legends developed about the deeds, caprices, and bravery of these partisans. It was told that their number was 10,000, perhaps even more.

{193}

## High Holy Day Prayers in the Forest of Dolina

The summer passed, and autumn arrived, with its days of rain, cold, and dampness. We were before the High Holy Days of the Jewish people. The two days of Rosh Hashanah passed by with sighing and weeping. Everyone made his own accounting before the Holy One Blessed Be He silently, with stifled weeping. However, when the great and holy day, Yom Kippur, arrived, all the people of the forest gathered together, without exception, both the observant and secular. All of them felt the need to appear before their Creator together.

Our prayer leader was David Lieberman. The efforts of Reb Moshe Kalman should be remembered for good, for he found one Machzor (holiday prayer book) which the cantor used. The entire congregation listened and repeated the words after him, word for word. The prayers took place in Stas' yard. The women somehow found some candles, and lit them carefully so that there would not be, Heaven forbid, a fire.

It is difficult to describe that Kol Nidre[9] night in the forest, the great weeping of the pitiful congregation of Jews who were being pursued up to their necks. Everyone remembered their relatives, parents, children, or family members who were slaughtered, murdered, or killed by all sorts of unusual forms of death by the Germans or their Ukrainian neighbors. The prayer leader Reb David attempted to pray slowly, so that we all could follow along and pray with him. However often, his prayers were interrupted by the great weeping of the congregation who could not hold back the tears, which were choking their throats.

We did not all understand the meaning of the prayers; however, it was not necessary to understand the words or to translate them. Reb David, with his prayers, screams, sighs, and gestures of his hands toward the heavens, expressed exactly the meaning of the words, and we all felt as if we were saying the words ourselves. We felt at this time as if our prayers were certainly ascending and penetrating the Heavens, and He Who Dwells in the Heaven should hear our prayers, save us, and open up for us the gates of mercy.

The Yom Kippur prayers in the forests of Dolina penetrated far beyond the forests, all the way up to the Throne of Glory, and even perhaps beyond.

## TRANSLATOR'S FOOTNOTES

1. From Psalm 23.

2. From Psalms 68:20.

3. The 'tochacha', reproof or reprimand, refers to two chapters of the Torah which outline the punishments awaiting the Jewish people if they do not follow the word of G-d. The two chapters of tochacha are in Leviticus 26, starting from verse 14 (Bechukotai Torah portion), and Deuteronomy 28, starting

from verse 15 (Ki Tavoh Torah portion).

4. It is not clear to who this is referring, but it seems to be the words of Stash.

5. Here, the name is Stach, but in all subsequent references, it is Stas. The first occurrence may have been a typo, or alternatively, the two versions may be alternative nicknames for the same person. Other names in this section are also presented with inconsistent spelling in the Hebrew text.

6. A reference from the Passover Haggadah (liturgy book for the Seder), which described how five great sages of old reclined at a Seder all night in the city of Bnei Brak.

7. I am not sure of the meaning of this word here. Kash in Hebrew is straw or hay – kashim would be the plural. More likely, the word has some Polish or Ukrainian significance.

8. There are various regulations that are followed in preparing a body for burial in Jewish law. These include washing the body, dressing it in shrouds, and placing it in a coffin for burial. The Kaddish is the prayer recited after burial, as well as at various places in a religious service. It has taken on the connotation of being a prayer for the dead.

9. Kol Nidre is the opening prayer of Yom Kippur.

{193}

## The Battle and Murder in the Forests of Dolina

On the day of Simchat Torah, towards evening, we suddenly heard the sound of heavy truck wheels and columns of battle tanks approaching us. An alarm went out, and all of us fled for our lives. We spread out and only very few remained in the camp.

The tanks appeared in the forest. They were driven by the Vlosoviches – the rebel battalion of the Russian general Vlosov under German command. They opened fire and spread out quickly throughout the camp. They destroyed the camp almost instantaneously, so that no remnant remained. The following people were killed during the attack: Chana the sister of Hershko Ratenbach, Dania Schwartz, and Emil Beril of Krakow the son-in-law of Hugo Fisher.

After a few days we began to reorganize ourselves, this time with greater seriousness and caution. We set up watches at the edges of the forest. We moved deeper into the forest and arrived at the place that was known as "the place of the cross".

Rumors circulated that the Germans had begun to attack the partisans in the forests, for a command was issued from the higher authorities to clear the forests of partisans along the path of retreat of the army that was defeated at the gates of Stalingrad. We agreed together that in the event of a new attack upon our section of the forest, we would retreat toward the direction of the forests of Vygoda, Vorokov and Krechowice.

On the following Sabbath, we all began to pack the movable objects and move toward the new location. In the evening, we began to walk through the forest to the new place, and toward morning on Sunday, we arrived at "Babiovka", where there was a young sparse grove which had only recently been planted. Suddenly Stas Babi arrived, running frantically and all covered in sweat. He informed us of the bitter news that we had fallen into a German trap. We had entered directly into the snapdragon. The entire forest was surrounded by troops of the German army who were waiting to storm in and clear the area of partisans.

As we were discussing among ourselves and debating about where to flee, a frightful orchestra of all types of guns began to be heard in all areas of the forest. Not one meter was free from bombardment. Automatic weapons, guns, cannons and tanks all participated in this orchestra. The earth under us shook from the bombardment. There was no hiding place around us. The trees were low, almost bushes, and everything was open and exposed.

Suddenly everything became silent and the Germans began to storm in. They advanced in rows, armed with guns and bayonets. They searched under every bush. Under one bush, not far from the bush beneath which Meirke and myself hid, they discovered two people and commanded them to stand up. These were Gartenberg the son of the shochet of Bolekhov and a girl from Kalush. Machinegun fire was heard, and both of them were killed on the spot. We were not more than three or five meters away from them, and we witnessed this. Until today I ask myself: What is the supreme power and secret of life that enables one to witness death before one's very eyes yet have no fear at all? On the contrary, some sort of feeling of peace passed over all my limbs. I wish upon myself that when my time comes to depart from the world, I should feel the same feeling of tranquility that I felt when I saw the Germans approaching us, step by step. I prayed in my heart without uttering any words and strongly embraced Meirke who was lying next to me trembling. I drew near to him, kissed him, and whispered in his ears: "Meirke, in another moment it will be better for us".

Behold, rather than continuing along their steps directly toward us, they suddenly changed their direction. What happened there? As they slowly walked, they found a radio and electric wires next to the previous bush. They lifted it up and examined it, and immediately changed their direction to follow the electric wires that they had just discovered. An overt miracle happened to us, and I believe with complete belief that the hand of G-d was involved in this. The Holy One Blessed Be He wanted us to remain alive so that we could relate to the next generation what the gentiles, may their names be obliterated, did to us.

On that day, more than sixty Jews were murdered in the forest. In order to instill fear among the gentiles of the area so that they would not assist Jews in any way, they captured twenty gentiles randomly and hung them in the village square, so that everyone would see and take heed. This matter left a deep impression upon the gentiles, and they began to tremble with fear. From that time, a terrible period of tribulations, hunger and hell began for us. We were pursued like dogs up to our necks. We were warned that the Germans had captured several Jews, and by means of torture, they forced them to inform them about the hiding places of the partisans. Therefore, we were forced to leave all of our hiding places, and move on. Despair and depression overtook our ranks.

For the entire time, I was in the company of Meirke. Now another pair joined us. Meir had always been quite resourceful, and dared to perform brazen and dangerous deeds. Even at this moment, when hunger, pain, and oppression overtook everyone, Meir was brazen enough to enter a nearby village in order to visit a gentile who he had known for some time, despite the fact that this endangered the life of both of them, both the gentile who would offer assistance, as well as the person who would receive the assistance. One Saturday night, he stealthily entered into the village of Krive to visit a farmer whom he knew. He knocked quietly at the window. The farmer opened the door and served him a plate of potato soup, a few hard-boiled eggs and a cornmeal roll, and requested that he quickly leave.

It is impossible to describe the joy and brave deeds that Meir performed. I wish to describe his re-fined and noble manner. He never ate alone. He always shared his morsels of food with others. He joy-fully extended help to his fellow, even though this was fraught with mortal danger. The two of us lived like one family. We shared our food, and took counsel together regarding our future, our situation, our various plans for escape, etc. Nothing could come between us. The two of us desired and hoped to survive through the difficult times together, and to arrive at better days together.

The situation became more desperate and sad day by day. The security situation and means of find-ing food particularly worsened. The farmers stopped completely assisting us with food, even in return for large sums of money. They were fearful for their lives. No underground existence could continue without external help. In a place that we spent the day we could not spend the night. We wandered from place to place. The German attacks became more frequent. The number of victims increased. Daily we were informed of a friend who was captured and murdered on the spot. We were like animals seeking refuge.

My strength dwindled and I could no longer maintain my stand. I realized that I was beginning to slow down the movements of Meirke. He was armed with a gun and belonged to the group of armed fighters of the forest dwellers. I was not similarly armed. Therefore I requested of him that we separate for a while, and I would find a shelter in the forest. He did not leave me completely. He would visit me on occasion, and bring me food. We took counsel together and he promised me that under no cir-cumstance would he leave me alone in the forest. Wherever he would go, I would also go. The group of fighters made plans to cross the Hungarian border.

Due to my strong connection with Meir, they wished to take me with them to cross the Hungarian border. However, I knew from the outset that my strength was minimal, and I would not be able to withstand such a difficult effort, crossing mountains and valleys on the route to the border. I would only be a burden to them. Therefore I requested of them that they leave me here, and I would join up with the other wanderers of the forest, including the Babi brothers.

Aside from the hunger, cold, dampness, and lack of a roof over our heads, another terrible affliction came upon us, the plague of lice. The rivers and ponds had frozen due to the cold, and we had no op-portunity to wash our bodies and our clothes. Since we had nothing to change into, we did not take off our clothes for weeks and months. It is small wonder that lice came upon us and devoured our flesh ravenously.

People gathered together in the ruins without a roof and without foods. They simply sat or lay down on account of the great weakness, and awaited a miracle. Whoever had any strength rose up and scavenged through the fields for some plant, potato, or vegetable that had by chance been left in the fields. They would light a few branches, roast them in fire and eat them. They would share this food with others. A few literally died of hunger on the ground. There was a problem as to how to bury the dead. We did not have any implements with which to dig a grave. The ground was frozen, and we did not have the energy to dig with our hands. Without having any other choice, we would carry the corpse deep into the forest and cover it with branches and wood. That was all. I said in my heart that it would not be long until the same thing happens to me, and perhaps there would no longer be any branches left with which to cover my corpse. A shiver passed through my body. No, at least I should be buried. I decided to leave the forest and to try my luck in some other place, where I would merit to be buried like all other dead people, and would not simply be placed on top of the ground.

When I left the Bolekhov ghetto, the news came to me that a certain gentile from Rozniatow was searching for me. He told people that if they were by chance to come across me, they should inform me that he was searching for me and wished to assist me.

I knew that Aharon Weidman had heard about this story. He was far from me, in a different group. I received an answer from him regarding my question that Mosko Jagelavitz is searching for me. Of course, I took counsel in this matter with Meirke. He had just decided to leave the forest; however he promised me that if I finally decide to leave, he would accompany me the entire route until Rozniatow, and would not let me travel alone.

At that time, a strange event happened to me that sealed my fate. One day, on a Sunday morning, Pinieli Stern of Mizin saw me, attired in tefillin (phylacteries), leaning against a tree and praying with devotion. He was talking to himself out loud saying: "Why should I remain here dying of hunger. I will go to the village of Stratin-Vizna, where a calf of mine is with a certain gentile. I will take it from him by force and we will be able to live... I will take with me Hesio and Muni Pecker..." I told him "I will join you..."

I informed Meirke of my decision, and I felt that my strength returned to me.

We began to travel at evening. Meir joined us.

Snow fell. We were frozen and damp to the marrow of our bones. There was no place to seek shelter. We reached a pond. On the other side of the pond, through a large garden, we arrived next to a house with two residents. Meirke said to me: "See Sheike, on one side of this house Mosko lives, but I do not know on which side." He stood at a distance with his gun, ready for any eventuality. I approached the window and knocked on it very carefully. A clean curtain was pushed aside, and a young girl appeared in the window. She looked at me and immediately came to open the large gate of the courtyard for me. With great caution I asked who lives here. She answered me: "Here lives my uncle Mosko Jagelavitz." Even though I was quite unkempt and would instill fear into anyone who saw me, he recognized me immediately. A stone was removed from my heart. Indeed, this was the house in which I had hoped that I could find some shelter and rest from my pursuers. I uttered our password from the forest, and

Meirke immediately came into the house. She, Stefka, recognized him immediately. She brought us into the house. Without saying a word, she went into the kitchen and brought out two bowls of potato soup, a piece of meat and a whole loaf of bread.

With a smile on her face she said: "Please, eat to your hearts content."

I restrained myself and also insisted that Meirke not make haste to eat, lest the food harm us after such a long period of hunger. Eating fast could injure us. We ate slowly, drop by drop.

After the meal, she spread a clean white sheet on the carpet that was on the floor, she wished us "good night", and left the room.

Who would have imagined that after years of hunger and troubles, without a roof on our heads, pursued as leprous dogs from place to place, we would receive such a fine and tasty meal, and be able to sleep on a white sheet in a warm room.

Early the next morning, Stefka came in and wished us a hearty "good morning". She brought us to the second part of the house. When we entered, we were surprised to see Idzi in front of us, the daughter of the well-known Rozniatow resident Hersch Landsman. She fell upon us, kissed us, and broke out in great weeping. We did not realize at all that Mosko had mounted the wagon that was about to transport her to a work camp in Germany, removed her, and brought her to his house.

We then received a good breakfast, and in the meantime Stefka prepared a warm bath for us. It had been years since we had tasted such a thing. After a haircut and a shave, we changed out of our filthy, tattered clothes.

Mosko was not yet in the house at this time. He was in Stanislawow to conduct his various business affairs. Stefka was afraid of the tax collectors who might enter at any moment. Therefore she advised us to leave the house for a short period, until the tax collectors had finished their investigations and leave. They would be searching for tobacco and liquor that was being held without a permit. Earlier, we had thought we would hide in the nearby forest, however due to the great cold and dampness, we had dire thoughts about this. Meirke, with his great resourcefulness, found a hiding place for us. Pinkovski lived not far from the house, and there in his yard we found a large haystack that protected us from the rain and dampness. We jumped on top, lifted several bundles of hay from the large stack, and thereby made a large hole in the stack so that we would be able to lie and sit there. Thus did we set up for ourselves a "house" where we would be able to live for a few days.

On Friday night, we again entered Mosko's house. Meirke decided to return to the forest on Saturday night to bring back a doctor. He wanted to save him from a certain death in the forest.

Dozia brought me to a certain farmer, Stas, who brought us directly to the grain shed. There, he removed several bundles of hay and showed us a door that led underground.

I crawled into the dark bunker, and with the light of a small torch I saw in front of me Aharon Weidman and Meir Ungar, the husband of Dortzi Gelobter. I cannot describe to you my feelings upon this sudden meeting in the bunker, after what each of us had experienced until this time.

I joined this group, and due to the great weariness and travails that I had experienced over the preceding days, I fell asleep on the spot. They let me sleep for 24 straight hours, for they said that the sleep would strengthen me.

When I woke up, I experienced a great hunger. I had nothing to satisfy my hunger. Simply, there was nothing to eat there.

Stas brought into the bunker a spoon, and a cup, as well as a bottle for my physiological needs.

I do not want to discuss at length the ideological ideas and moral state of the people who were pursued and were hiding in the forests and bunkers. This I will leave to sociologists or other researchers. I simply want to point out how people are capable of raising themselves to great heights.

At first, when Stas would bring the plate of food to us in the bunker, the order of eating would be as follows: Meir Ungar would take the first spoonful, then Aharon Weidman, and I was next in line. I suddenly realized that the food in the plate was beginning to be finished. Meir dried the spoon and made a face as if he was becoming tired of the food. Aharon did the same thing, he made an expression with his lips as if to say "enough, I am not eating any more. Perhaps you will finish the bit of soup." After a few days I realized what was transpiring there. They withheld food from their mouths, even though the food was never sufficient, so that I would be able to regain my health a bit and return to my strength.

After some time, Meir Ungar moved to the bunker of Mosko, in the place where Harold was. From time to time the Ungars, who were with Mosko, would send Dozia, who was in the house, to our bunker with some food that they had obtained for a great deal of money. Once they sent to us an entire loaf of bread, some onions, garlic, and a bottle of liquor. Mendel Landerman and his wife Chana were also in Mosko's bunker.

Deeds such as this strengthened our spirit and will to continue to bear our burdens. Perhaps, even with all this, we would merit salvation, and go out from darkness to great light.

However, the situation in the underground became more difficult and serious daily. For months we did not go out in daylight, and we did not wash, or change our clothes. Inside, it was stifling and smelly. People began to lose their strength. Aharon Weidman stopped eating completely, and slowly began to waste away in the bunker. Stas advised us about where we could dig a secret grave for him, so that it will not become known to others.

## The Budding of Freedom

Immediately after Passover, in April and May 1944, we began to hear good news from the fronts. However our own situation was quite bad. We did not have enough food, or any fresh air and light. However the hope and desire for freedom and liberation gave us the strength to maintain our stand.

In the beginning of August, we had already begun to hear in the bunker the echoes of the Russian artillery. We would rejoice at the sound of every explosion of a bomb, for we knew that it would be falling on the German positions nearby, and that their end was coming quickly. The echo of the bombing was so loud that we had to close off the hole that let fresh air into the bunker.

After about half an hour, we heard that the Russians were already next to us. On Friday might, our Meirke appeared with a Russian soldier. He brought out Harold and took him to Mosko. On the Sabbath, we heard that there was a heavy battle in the area of Dolina and Rozniatow. We left our bunker and sat in the grain shed. On Sunday we saw through the cracks the throngs of gentiles with their wives, children, and cattle leaving the villages and going out in the direction of the forest. All of them were collaborators with the Germans, and all of them played a significant role in the murder of the Jews. They knew that the Russian army would take revenge against the Germans and their assistants.

Stas also took his family and cattle and went along with those that were leaving, so as not to arouse suspicion. When we saw our savior and protector leaving, and that all of those who were hiding with Mosko got into a transport truck to escape to Stanislawow which had already been liberated, myself and Aharon Weidman – who in the meantime had regained his strength – decided to go out in the daylight and walk along the paths that lead to Rivnia and from there to Stanislawow. When we reached the mountain at Krasna, we met other Jews who had left the forests and bunkers, and were walking in the direction of Stanislawow. Among them we met Hirsch Ratenbach, David and Tzili Keish, Hesio and Munio Pecker, Klara Segal, and Wilech Kanohal. We all walked together in a group, until we arrived at the home of Wilech in Nadworna. There I stayed for two or three weeks, for I was not able to continue along the route. After a few weeks, when the Russians had already set themselves up in the area, I decided to return to my home in Rozniatow. I went to Stanislawow and then to Kalush for a few days to see who had remained alive.

I arrived in Rozniatow at dusk. I slept in an abandoned house, and the next morning I went to see my parents' home and my birthplace, where I had spent the best of my years and days.

I arrived to the synagogue and looked from afar upon the lane where I had lived together with my family, and my eyes became dark. I saw nothing at all. I could not believe what I was seeing – from all of the houses that were on that lane, starting from the house of Yitzchak Shaya Katzman, afterward Avraham Hoffman, Hindi, Zishia Ziring and the children of Rikel Schwalb – Chaya and Esther and their families, Kuni and Leib Kertshman, Chaim Shimon Lutwak, and behind us – Avramtzia, Marek, Yosel Robinfeld, Avraham Itzik and Mindel Lenderman, Somi Zimmerman and Shmuel Hirsch Wechter – there was not even one remnant of all these houses. The ploughed earth was divided up into lots and planted with potatoes. On the opposite side, only the house of Shmuel Rosenberg (Shmukel) and the bathhouse stood. It was only because of these houses that I was able to get my bearings and realize where I was.

With great heartbreak, devastated by what my eyes were seeing, I leaned on the side of the fence that overlooked the place of my house, and I let out a great and bitter scream from my throat:

May G-d avenge the blood of the pure and holy martyrs. Remember what the Nazis did to us.

Yitgadal Veyitkadash Shmei Raba[1].

{201}

## Our Mighty Ones

With the conclusion of the writing of my memoirs from the time of the holocaust, and what happened to us at that time, I now want to strongly push aside all allegations that people went to their deaths without any opposition, as if they were animals going to the slaughter. Certainly, nobody who makes such an allegation can even imagine what he would have done had he been in their place, at a time when the Germans did everything possible to take away the desire to live, at a time when the entire thought of a Jew was for a slice of bread in order to sustain his soul. The Jew was downtrodden and persecuted, all of his friends and admirers had abandoned him.

There was no place to flee or to hide. The Jew was conspired against even in the forests and meadows. The murderers pursued him in the treetops and in the depths of the earth. In all of these dire straits, he did not lose his hope. The desire for life and the will to live gave him the strength to help those who were downtrodden in the camps. We could see how people of other nations who were sent to the camps very quickly lost their Divine image; they gave up upon life and could not even maintain themselves for several months. The situation was different with the Jews. In all difficult situations, without bread, without air to breath, persecuted up to the neck, they fought for their lives and their existence with the hope that they would still merit to overcome the difficult time, and that better and more pleasant days would arrive.

It is strictly forbidden for anyone who has not been tried with this situation to pass judgement on the oversights and negligence of those who were persecuted, claiming that they did not do enough to overcome the enemy and to die the death of the mighty, taking a stand and without giving in. There indeed were such people, however most of the people were elderly or young, who did not have the physical strength to struggle. Even they assisted and took pride on any occasion where they saw Jews openly struggling against the murderers. There was one instance of many of which I was an eyewitness, which I now wish to relate, in particular to the young readers, so that they would not think that there were not any incidents of supreme power. There were mighty people whose stories will yet be written about in the annals of the world.

There were two youths with us in the forests of Dolina. One was Meir Turteltaub of Rozniatow, the son of Itzi Leizer Turteltaub. The second was Hersch Ratenbach, the son of David and Mamtzi Ratenbach of Dolina.

Meir – or as we called him "Meirke" – and Hersh – "Hershke" – will both undoubtedly be recorded in Jewish history as mighty men of Israel. It is obligatory to tell of them and their might. It is good that I have the opportunity in the Rozniatow Yizkor book to perpetuate and honor their activities and their might. This is my modest contribution to their honor.

At the outbreak of the war in 1939, Meirke served in the Polish army in an artillery unit. He was wounded in the foot, and he returned home when the Soviets were still ruling the town. As a person who was wounded in battle, he became involved in the life of the youth that still existed in the town, and he began to become interested in sports. He quickly became the organizer and chief activist in the sports club. With the outbreak of the war between Germany and Russia, Meirke volunteered for the Russian army and was immediately sent to the front. After a very short time, he was again injured, and he returned back home, where now the Germans were in charge. His parents were exiled to Dolina, and he joined them.

The life of the exiles who were sent to the Dolina ghetto from the entire region became more difficult by the day. The hunger was increasing. Jews were perishing in the outskirts of the city from hunger. New decrees were issued daily, each one harsher than the preceding one. Meir, with his active temperament, was not able to tolerate the situation, sitting and doing nothing, and waiting for what was going to happen.

Then something took place. One day, some Gestapo men came from Kalush in order to teach the members of the Dolina militia how to behave with the Jews, and how to make their lives more difficult. On the road, they met a young boy who wore the shameful Juda insignia on his arm slightly lower than was required by law. This happened to be Meirke. They took him to the Judenrat office to teach him a lesson about how things should be, so that people should take heed and be afraid.

A few days later I met by chance Moshe Ziring, who happened to be present at the time when they were teaching Meirke his "lesson". They began to shout and beat him. They took a chair from the office and began to beat him angrily from the right and left. Nobody could stop them, until he finally succeeded in escaping and fleeing from there.

He did not hold his peace. He made plans as to how to escape from this hell, how to cross the Hungarian border, and from there he would figure out where to go and what to do.

In Vishkuv at the Hungarian border he was captured, put into chains, and brought to the prison in Dolina. It was decided to give him over to Kriger, to send him to his famous place in Stanislawow, Rudolf's depot. Meirke was brought to the transport truck with his hands bound in chains, and that began his time of inhuman torture and backbreaking work without food. He again began to think about how to extricate himself from this hell. He succeeded in a manner that we cannot figure out even today to jump over the high wire fence, to escape between the nearby houses and to return to Kalush. However, the Jews were afraid to let him into their houses. With an empty sack and a pack over his shoulders, as a gentile going about his work, he continued on his journey. After much wandering, he arrived at the town of Rohatyn, where his relative, the grandson of Mendel-Nechis lived.

At the beginning of June 1943, when they began to liquidate all of the ghettos and concentration camps of eastern Galicia and bring the Jews to extermination, Meirke escaped over the fence of the ghetto and went to the Stryj ghetto. However he arrived there just at the time of the large aktion when hundreds of Jews were brought to be slaughtered. They attempted to capture him but he escaped from their hands. He fled to the bridge. They shot at him, however he jumped with a jump of Nachshon[2] into the depths of the Dniester.

He hid in the riverbanks until it became dark. In the darkness of the night he again began his wandering. He hid at night and traveled during the night until he reached the gates of the Bolekhov ghetto. He remained there in order to regain his strength, and then he continued his wandering until he reached the border again. As he fled from Bolekhov, he on occasion ran into some Ukrainians who were attacking the Jewish passers by. Shimshon Katzman the son of Shaya Katzman and Herman Laufer the grandson of Efraim Rechtschaffen of Rozniatow were killed near him by the Ukrainian bandits who collaborated with the Germans.

All of his wanderings were accompanied by a long string of miracles. On more than one occasion, it seemed as if he was about to fall directly into the impure hands of the Germans or their Ukrainian helpers. Finally he succeeded in reaching the forests of Dolina, and there he met up with those of us who had been hiding there from the murderers already for some time. He became part of the group, and was loved and appreciated by all of those who were in the forest.

Given that the main problem of the fighters in the forests was the obtaining of weapons and various other fighting implements, he was given this responsibility. His duty was to search out connections with gentiles and obtain weapons, explosives, and bullets from them. He decided to set out in the direction of Rozniatow, where he hoped that he would be able to obtain weapons and assistance from his former friends and acquaintances. According to the plan, he was to return to the camp whether or not he managed to obtain weapons. Two weeks passed, and there was no word from Meirke, as if he was swallowed by the earth.

One bright day, Stach Babi, one of the righteous gentiles, appeared. He had helped us greatly and he served as our contact with the outside world. He did not do this for free, for he received a fitting payment for this; however at that time it was a brave deed to endanger oneself and assist the Jews, even for money. No gentile wished to give us any help. Stach Babi brought us the news that some young Jewish man killed a Gestapo man and fled for his life, and all of Dolina was in turmoil.

After a few hours, Stach appeared with a form that looked like a human being. He was wounded, his face was swollen and blue, and his clothes were tattered and torn. He bore no resemblance to a living soul, for he was like a blue piece of flesh. It was hard to recognize who he was, whether he was young or old. Was this the man who killed the Gestapo man and fled? All of us residents of the forests gathered together quickly to lay eyes on this anonymous hero who fought with a Gestapo man and defeated him. Everyone looked at him and did not recognize him until he, with great difficulty, began to utter words from his throat. Then we realized that he was none other than Meirke.

After some time, when he returned to his strength after the meager medical care that we could offer in the forest without medicine and without a physician, we learned of the details of his adventures when he went out in search of weapons.

When he arrived in Rozniatow, he met up with a few of his school chums, friends from days gone by. He revealed to them his request, and his reason for his presence there. They brought him to his former friend, the bastard Vasyl, who worked for Baron Walisz. Vasyl advised Meirke to hide in one of the storehouses in the outer houses. There, he would bring him a bit of food and drink, and later he would advise him as to what to do about these matters.

Meir Turteltaub

Meirke entered the courtyard of the postman Jagelavitz, and there, in one of the storehouses, he waited for his friend Vasyl to bring him food. Instead of bringing food to him, Vasyl went to alert all of the neighbors and the Ukrainian militia, headed by the German Jarasch. The militia surrounded like a chain all of the homes that were near the storehouse where Meirke was hidden, and they began to close in on him.

Meirke saw all of this activity which was brought on him by his friend, and he understood what had happened. Having no other option, he surrendered. After a few days of physical and spiritual torture by the local militia, they decided to transfer him to a prison in Dolina.

In the prison, he succeeded by means of a nail which he had hidden in his pants to make a hole in the wall, and to remove the first brick from its place. He continued with this activity until he made a hole that was large enough for him to escape from the prison. However, his efforts were noticed by the prison guards. He was captured as he was carrying out this activity, and he was tied with fetters and placed on a pillory. There in the dark he conducted all sorts of experiments as to how to free himself from the fetters. By means of a metal wire which he had succeeded in bringing with him, he was able to open the lock of the fetters. He repeated his experiment several times and made plans as to how to escape.

A few days later, they took him out with the fetters on his hands, and loaded him onto a transport car to take him to an unknown place. A guard armed with automatic weapons boarded the driver's cabin, and another German Gestapo guard was right next to him. As the car neared the Jewish cemetery of Dolina, a hilly area, and the car slowed down, Meirke decided that the time for freedom had arrived. He placed the wire into the lock and unlocked the fetters. By the time the guard realized what had happened, Meirke had already jumped out of the car and began his desperate run for life or death.

The car stopped. Meir ran to one of the gates and attempted to jump over it, however the guard opened fire upon him and injured him in the thigh. As Meirke was holding on with all of his strength to the wire fence in order to climb over the gate, the armed guard approached him, hit him over the head with his gun so that he fell to the ground. Meirke, who was wounded badly and was bleeding, began to struggle with the guard. He hit the Gestapo man directly in the face with the metal wires that were still upon his hand that he had freed. The man fell to the ground, with his face bleeding profusely. Meirke removed his gun and attempted to shoot him, but there were no bullets left so he hit the dying guard as hard as he could until he had finished him off. He hung him on the gate and began his desperate flight. In the meantime, the second guard had gathered some militiamen from the area, and they began to search for the Jew who had killed the Gestapo man. They spread out among all of the monuments in the cemetery, and began to fruitlessly search for him. Meirke had founded a place to hide until the evening. In the evening he began to walk toward the forest until Stach Babi met him and brought him back here, wounded but still alive.

After a few months of recuperation and primitive treatment for his wounds, and after the siege that the Germans had laid against the dwellers of the forest, and having been saved with great miracles, I am able to relate all this from my memory of the days of the Holocaust. We returned to Rozniatow...

I hid with the fine gentile Mosko Jagelavitz and Meirke hid with Stash Jurezko.

After the Soviet army had liberated Rozniatow, Meirke approached the army and requested that they enlist him immediately so that he could take revenge for the murder of his parents and the members of his nation. He was immediately sent to the front, and fought his battle until victory.

Today, he, may he live until 120[3], lives with his family here in New York. He lives a calm and peaceful life.

{206}

## About Another Brave Person

As I begin to turn the pages of my memory, page after page, remembering all that had taken place to me during my wandering, from my time in the Stryj ghetto until my escape to the forests of Dolina, remembering everything that had happened to me and how I reached this point, I cannot conclude without relating a few words about Hirsch Ratenbach. I must tell about his deeds and bravery in saving his fellow Jews.

Hershko risked his life by entering the ghettos of Stryj and Bolekhov in order to take Jews out into the forests. It is only thanks to him that those who were transferred to the forest were saved. He also attempted to take the rabbi of Bolekhov, Rabbi Shlomo Perlow, out from the ghetto, but he did not succeed.

He himself was a quiet Jew, calm, and greeting everyone pleasantly. He was always willing to help. However, when it came to taking revenge against the non-Jews and fighting against them, he knew no mercy, and pursued them unto death. After an area was liberated from the Germans, when the survivors who had remained alive in the forests and bunkers gathered together and began to reestablish their lives anew, Hirsch Ratenbach being among them, a gentile girl approached the Jews. She was one of the few who helped the Jews during their time of difficulty in the holocaust. Later on, when the Jews decided to leave Dolina out of fear of Ukrainian oppression, it was Hirsch Ratenbach who decided to take the girl with them wherever they might go, in order to save her from the revenge of the gentiles who would certainly wish to take revenge upon her for the help she offered the Jews, and her approach to the Jews. Thus, she joined up with the group of Jews who went from place to place searching for a resting place.

Hershko found out that there was a Jewish child who had been given over to be guarded in a Catholic monastery in Lvov. He succeeded in bringing the child out from their hands, and he made the child part of his family.

During his return wandering he discovered a Torah scroll with a gentile. He redeemed it for a large sum of money, and arrived in the displaced person's camp in Berlin with a gentile woman, a Jewish child who had been rescued, and a Torah scroll that had been redeemed. The woman converted to Judaism, they married, and she conducts a kosher Jewish home. They had a child of their own, and they live a peaceful and modest Jewish life.

May their be honor and praise for the mighty people of Israel.

**TRANSLATOR'S FOOTNOTES**

1. The opening phrase of the Kaddish prayer.

2. A reference to the crossing of the Red Sea, when by legend the Children of Israel were afraid to enter into the sea, until Nachshon the son of Amminadab, the leader of the tribe of Judah, jumped into the sea first. When Nachshon jumped in, the sea parted.

3. A traditional Jewish blessing for a long life.

{207}

## What Happened to Me During the Holocaust
### by Ben Zion Horowitz of Holon

Gloomy days began to appear and heavy clouds covered the skies even though it was the middle of the summer. I left Rozniatow in 1939 and moved to Borislaw, which was not far away. I spent about ten days under German government. The day after Yom Kippur it was made known to the Jews that the Russian army had placed a siege around Borislaw and surrounded it with tanks and other armored vehicles. In the meantime, the Germans took out their wrath against the Jews with everything that came to their hands. Cries of oppression and screams of agony were heard, but nobody answered.

Two of my friends decided to leave the place and to walk toward the border along unknown paths in order to join the Russian army. I immediately joined them. Along the way, we passed the post office, and we noticed that the Germans were pillaging the mail, removing all equipment including telephones and machinery, as they prepared to leave.

When we met the Russian guard along the way, I asked them to take me to their commander. My two friends remained there under military guard, and the Russian guards brought me directly to the commander of the unit. The commander put me aboard a covered transport truck. There were three commanders on the truck, one of them a colonel. When I told him that I was a Jew in response to his query, I saw a light smile on his face.

Hi listened to my story about what took place in Borislaw. When I told him that we saw Germans removing all the electronic and telephone equipment from the post office as well as beds from the hospital, the colonel became red with anger. He immediately issued an order to bring him an armed vehicle and two tanks, and he told me to enter the vehicle.

I requested that he give order to the guards to free my two friends who were under guard. He issued an appropriate order, and said that it would be best that they wait there until we return. One tank went in front of us, we were in the middle, and another tank followed us. We approached the main post office. The colonel descended from the vehicle and met a German captain of the Hauptman rank at the entrance to the post office. The German saluted, and the colonel became furious, pointed to his watch, and shouted: "Where is your German punctuality? At 11:00 there should have no longer been a trace of you here, yet you are still swarming around like lice... You had better return all of the telephone equipment that you stole from here within 20 minutes, otherwise I will issue and order to open fire upon you, and you will find no place of refuge".

When we returned, a command was issued to prepare for battle. The tanks fanned out and the Russian army unit took up battle position. The heavy movement of the Russian army machine began, and by 3:00 p.m. Borislaw was in Russian hands. However, the Germans did not fulfil the request of the colonel. They did not return the telephones and other equipment, and therefore an order was given to pursue the German army and to force them to return all of the pillaged equipment. The Russians caught up with them on the route to the Sambor and, under the threat of fire, took back all of the pillaged equipment and returned it to Borislaw.

The conquering colonel was appointed as the governor of Borislaw. He later invited me to his office, and when we were alone, he revealed to me his secret that he was also Jewish, and wished to help the Jews. I told him that I was from Rozniatow, and I wished to return to my home. He provided me with appropriate papers, and I arrived in Rozniatow in peace. I immediately found work.

At the outset of Russian occupation of eastern Galicia, they behaved according to all of their policies of "freedom and equality". They began to remove all of the merchandise from the Jewish stores. They also imprisoned the Zionist activists and exiled them to Siberia. They issued orders to turn over to them all fruit, silver, gold, and radios. The people began to be a "free people" – free from worries of livelihood, since they had no livelihood at all.

When the Germans opened their attack upon the Russians without declaration of war on June 28, 1941, we left Rozniatow. The Hungarian army entered from one side and the German army from the other side. The Russian army conducted a disorderly retreat.

All routes led to Stanislawow, where the Russian control was still intact, and from where it was still possible to escape onward. However Stanislawow was also severely attacked. The route from Rozniatow to Stanislawow was approximately 50 kilometers, and it took us 20 hours to make the journey on that occasion, since the entire road had been bombed, and it was impossible to progress.

When we finally arrived in Stanislawow, the city was burning with fire due to the heavy bombardment. Several officials and party men fled together with us. They managed to find a side train station with a few open platforms and wagons for animals. Despite the heavy rain that fell, we decided, to our great joy, to leave the place. However, the German airplanes pursued us and bombarded us every few minutes. They were the only ones who had control over the area. It was not sufficient that we were attacked from the air, for we were also attacked on the ground by bands of ruffians who roved around the roads and made trouble for the retreating Russians as well as the Jewish population who still remained in one depot. In Przeworsk, they attacked us from the village, however at that time, some army vehicles joined us, consisting of tanks and heavy artillery machines that began to shoot at the village. They scored a direct hit on the church, and then the shots were silenced.

The train upon which we had originally left Stanislawow continued to grow as we traveled onward. At every station, crowds of people escaping and full wagons joined us. During our long period of travel, German warplanes attacked us. Several wagons were bombarded, and many people were killed and injured. There was nobody to attend to the injured, nobody to administer first aid. A few of my acquaintances were killed during that bombardment: Chaitza Laufer the wife of Yaakov Laufer, Mordechai Segal the husband of Beila, the son-in-law of Shmuel "Shmukel" Rosenberg, Shaya Zamel the son of Aharon Zamel, his brother Shmuel, Rosa Kalman the wife of Edelsberg, her brother Meshulam Kalman, Baruch Zimmerman, Chana Pares the daughter of Moshe Pares, Hirsch Friedenberg the son of Leibche and Halchi, Meir Rabinowicz from Perehinsko, and Bronia Brand the daughter of Chanina Brand. The following people were injured badly: my sister Perel Horowitz, Bida Zimmerman, Yechezkel the son of Meir Zimmerman, Leib Laufer the son of Yankel Laufer, and Chana Rabinowicz from Perehinsko. I was lightly injured in my left knee. I was busy helping my sister who had been badly wounded. I held her bleeding hand the entire time. I was afraid that she would die from loss of blood, and therefore I held her from above as the blood dripped upon my own body. Anyone who saw me was terrified, since it seemed like all the blood was coming from me.

After the frightening attack, there were those who were afraid to continue on that train without any protection or refuge, given over completely to the mercies of the German bombers, so they decided to return home. Shalom Rechtschaffen along with his wife and two children, Yechezkel Zimmerman, Leib Zimmerman, Yaakov Zimmerman, Chaya Zimmerman and Chaya Rivka Zimmerman, the children of Meir and Marchi.

This train with those that had survived the bombardment moved onward and continued along its journey until it reached Husyatin. We were again bombed along the route by German airplanes, and many of the travelers were hit. After some time I found out that among those who had been killed in a different wagon were my brother Baruch, as well as Hirsch Frost and his wife.

After the second bombardment, as we calmed down a bit, some members of the N. K. V. D. and the police came aboard the train and began to sort out the dead and those who were lightly and seriously wounded. The dead were taken out to a special place, the seriously wounded to another place. Later on, the injured were taken to a special sick-train with orderlies and doctors. Two graves were dug for the dead, one for members of the army and others for civilians. The order of boarding the train was as follows: first the army men, and after them, if there was any room left on the floor or in the halls of the train, the civilians boarded. The army men each had private bandages, and each one bandaged himself or was bandaged by others. This was not the case for the wounded civilians, they had no bandages, and they traveled with their wounds still open and dripping with blood.

Before the journey started, some slices of bread and drinks were brought aboard the train. My sister Perel was not able to eat, and she was only able to drink with difficulty. She had a high fever, and the situation of her wound worsened.

The train started to travel, but we did not know to where. The situation on the front worsened. The power of both the fighters and the citizens began to dwindle both in Kiev and Kharkov. There was another retreat. There was no place that was an appropriate destination for the train with the wounded, so that they could be taken to hospitals or at least to houses, where they could rest in beds rather than on the floors and hallways of the train.

At one of the stops, a doctor boarded the wagon that carried the wounded, and immediately began to take care of the wounded. When he examined my sister Perel, he saw that her injured hand had become gangrenous. It was all green and black. He decided to amputate her hand immediately. My sister refused, for she preferred death to living without a hand.

After wandering from stop to stop and station to station, after eleven days of travel, the train reached Karmonchik, and all of those who were seriously wounded were taken to the local hospital for treatment. They released me from the hospital after three days, for my injury was healing. That was not the situation with my sister. She had to remain in the hospital, but she refused to remain without me. Despite the opposition of the doctors to release her, she forced the management to release her. The management made arrangements to transfer us to a remote village, where the heads of the village were given instructions to allow the sick person to receive daily treatment from the regional physician.

I worked in an office that distributed food to the workers. However, we were not able to find peace even there. The German army began to approach, and was already sixty kilometers from the village. We began to think of wandering again. The doctor opposed this strongly. He promised that even if the Germans were to arrive, he would protect my sister and tell them that she was his own sister. I approached those who were in charge of the village, and told them everything that took place to us, and the bombardments that we had experienced. I requested that they send us deeper into Russia, where we would be able to relax a bit after everything that had taken place to us up to this point.

They joined us up with a convoy that was setting out in the direction of Stalingrad. They sent us to the village of Lipoka, to be put up by a poor farmer who set up a bed for us on the floor. Work began at 6:00 a.m. and concluded at nightfall. We did not starve there, and it was quiet. However, after a period of time, I received a notice to present myself to the draft office. I was immediately enlisted to the army and sent to the Volga to guard the Stalin army warehouses. In November, I was sent to Saratov, where there was a gathering depot. From Staratov, I was sent to some kolkhoz (collective farm). I was transferred from place to place until I was finally sent to Stalingrad as a Russian soldier on the front. There, we began to feel the war in all its fury. I was injured during one of the heavy bombardments. I was discovered unconscious, and brought to the hospital. There, they discovered that I had no wounds at all, for I was only in shock due to the shock of the bombardment. I returned and remained on the front. I advanced forward with the Red Army all the way to Berlin.

## In Rozniatow after the War

I returned to Rozniatow on July 21, 1945.

These days left me with many memories. Perhaps I can describe part of what I saw after I returned there following the terrible destruction. All of the Jewish homes that had been built out of wood or other similar material were burned or destroyed without even leaving a remnant. Of the houses that were built of stone or brick, half of them were destroyed, and those that were still intact were inhabited by Russian gentiles. The Germans sold all of the storehouses that were covered with tin sheets to the gentile villagers in the area. The Ukrainians, who transported every usable item that still remained to their homes in the villages, finished off the rest of the property.

In the meantime, I saw horrors, graves and destruction. In the town, I found the following Jews who survived the holocaust: Dr. Karpf and his wife, Meir Ungar and his wife, Dora Gelobter and her two children, Sosia Gelobter, Shayka Lutwak and Meir Turteltaub. All of them registered with the government offices to transfer to Poland, for from Poland, there was a chance to emigrate to another land, either Israel or the United States[1]. I could not accustom myself to the appearance of the destroyed town. The Beis Midrash was still standing, but it was without windows or doors. The Great Synagogue had been turned into a storehouse. In the empty and half destroyed Beis Midrash, the beautiful pictures of "running like a deer" and "strong as a lion" were still on the walls[2]; however it had now become a public washroom. I requested from the governing authorities that they take down the walls of the building completely. They acceded to my request, and thus did I save the Beis Midrash from serving as a public lavatory. The Kloiz now served as the office of the local newspaper.

In 1945, all of those who registered to transfer to Poland left the town, and I remained the only Jew in Rozniatow. My sister was still in far off Kazakhstan, and did not know anything regarding me. I worked in the "Glezinger" factory as I had done previously, and the gentiles liked me and protected me from the riots of the Bandrobches[3] who pillaged the area at that time. There was a Jew by the name of Lehrfeld in Brosznow. The Bandrobches fell upon him and murdered him. In the meantime, my sister returned home after her injuries had healed somewhat. A few other Jews returned, including Nechemia Shapira and Chaim Goldschmid.

We all worked together in the Glezinger factory without problem until 1953. That year, a group of Russian prospectors came to check out the possibility of drilling for oil in the region. On one occasion, one of them stood in the middle of the plaza and began to speak against the Jewish doctors in front of the farmers. This was the era of the Doctors Trials[4] under Stalin. The prospector concluded with the well-known statement: "beat the Jews and save Mother Russia". I discussed the matter with those who were appointed over the public safety of the Jewish workers, and I received the following response: "We in Russia have complete freedom of speech and thought. Everyone is allowed to say what he wishes. We cannot disturb anyone from speaking what he wishes." When I heard this, I began to search for ways of making aliya to the Land.

I found out that Jews were making aliya from Chernovitz, and that it was possible to hear the "Kol Yisrael" broadcast in Yiddish at a certain time each evening[5]. It was dangerous to listen to a foreign radio station, and therefore I always placed my sister outside the door to be on the lookout for any problems as I tuned in to Kol Yisrael from Jerusalem. I found out that many Jews were leaving from Poland and Romania. I made a request to the authorities, and after ten months of trials and tribulations, I received a notice that I must present myself in Stanislawow. There they told me that my request had been accepted and they told me very politely that I should visit the Russian ambassador in Tel Aviv in order to request any help that I might need. They further told me that I would be allowed to return "home" any time that I wanted.

One month later, we received the notice that we must pay the "Yas"[6] of 1,600 rubles as the fee for travel, and then proceed with the receipt to the captain of the Stanislawow region in order to receive the permit to travel abroad. In September 1956, we left Rozniatow to make aliya to the new Land with new hopes, and to begin a new chapter in our lives.

On Hoshanah Rabba[7], September 29, we arrived in Haifa, and from there we went directly to Ramat Gan, where our relatives were waiting for us.

Thus ended our wanderings in a world that was completely false and artificial.

Here, we hope to live a proper life.

{212}

## Our Saviors (Righteous Gentiles)[8]

During the time of the German reign of terror in Eastern Galicia, when any Ukrainian or Pole who did not harm a Jew was already considered as a good gentile, how can we describe and what words of praise can we use for a man who literally endangered his life in order to save Jews from a certain death, and to help a Jew as much as possible with out expecting any benefit in return.

One of the righteous gentiles was Misko Jagelavitz. I do not have sufficient words to praise, laud and extol this man and his deeds, and how he endangered his life in order to save and hide Jews from their persecutors. He was good hearted and did all of this solely due to his conscience.

I will describe one event to you that characterizes the man and his outlook upon life. At the beginning of 1943, when the Germans began to liquidate the ghettos and concentration camps, Misko Jagelavitz immediately approached Dr. Sabat and offered his assistance to transfer him to a safe and secure place. In the meantime, Dr. Sabat and his wife Gizo (nee Weinreb), the dentist Mausmaloda, Berka Litower, the director Faher, Shapira and Maulik Diamond made plans to cross the Hungarian border, and they declined the offer of Misko. When they arrive there, along with a gentile who was a friend and close associate of Dr. Sabat, the gentile fell upon the entire group that he was leading with his weapons near the Sochodola Forest, and murdered them all.

After the liberation, at the conclusion of the war, when I met Dr. Karpf, he told me that, at the time, when he was the doctor of the local committee that conducted an inquiry into the deaths of the cara-van in the Socholoda Forest, they all decided that this was premeditated, cold-blooded murder. The gentiles came to the place and identified the victims, in particular Dr. Sabat, who was well known in the entire area. They buried the victims and surrounded the grave with a wire fence to mark the burial place. Years later, my friend and relative Ben Zion Horowitz, who is now in Israel, told me that when he was still in Rozniatow after the liberation, he met on the streets of Rozniatow a deranged person who wandered around the outskirts of the town, deranged and confused. People told him that before the death of this deranged fool, he confessed to the priest of Rozniatow that he murdered the entire caravan of Dr. Sabat in the forest.

Misko hid eighteen Jews, and concerned himself with their safety and sustenance. Among others, the following Jews were hidden by him: Mendel Landsman and his wife Chana who were miraculously saved from the Kalush ghetto during the time of its liquidation; Shalom Shapira, his wife and child; as well as another child from Kalush. Misko sent Stas Jurczko and Dozi Didoko to the Bolekhov ghetto in order to rescue a few Jews. They came back with Dora Gelobter, her husband Max Ungar, their son Herman, daughter Fridi, her sister Sosia Gelobter, and Aharon Widman. Misko understood that such a large group, with their unstable health situation after the period of hunger that they suffered from in the ghettos of Kalush and Bolekhov, would require a doctor to visit them on occasion and administer assistance when they needed. Therefore he made contact with Dr. Avraham Fried, the son-in-law of Shmuel Friedler of Rozniatow, who still worked as a doctor in the nearby village of Soritshov. On several occasions, he summoned the doctor for us due to some urgent need.

When he recognized that our situation became more serious, he sent his wife to Dr. Fried and re-quested that he come and hide along with his group of hidden people. However Dr. Fried first wanted to make arrangements for his children to be looked after by gentiles, and he said that he would come in a day or two. He never succeeded in arriving. The Germans captured him and murdered him that day.

Misko was very generous. He never refused to do a good deed or to fulfil the request of one of the group of hidden people. He cared for them as a faithful father with great dedication, even if he did not receive money from them. His biggest problem was how to feed such a large group in a manner that his neighbors and fellow villagers would not recognize what was going on. He enlisted the assistance of the following gentiles to provide food for the group in a hidden manner: Stas Jurczko may he be remembered for his good deeds and Dozia Didoko. They also concerned themselves with the personal care and guarding of Aharon Ungar and Widman. I was also brought to them. They took care of us faithfully, and provided for our sustenance. This Stas employed his niece Stefka as an assistant in his house. To his neighbors, it appeared as if she was his housekeeper and cook, however her main job was to cook and provide food for the Jews. She also had a baby, and it is told that Misko cursed her baby so that she would not be able to speak. Indeed, this child did not begin to talk until he was about three or four. He did this all for our security, so that the child, in his innocence, would not Heaven forbid disclose our hiding place or our existence.

Misko believed that G-d would help him in his great task of saving Jews.

At the beginning of 1944, when there were already no more Jews in the forests, and there was nobody to pursue and murder, the Ukrainians began to fall upon each other. They organized various terror groups and began to pursue the Poles, as well as some of their fellow Ukrainians who did not share their outlook. They fell upon, murdered, and pillaged each other, and the situation became very dangerous.

On one Saturday evening, they invaded Misko's home, overturned everything in his yard, and searched for Misko in order to murder him. He immediately understood that it was not only he that was in danger, but all of the hidden people as well. He jumped out from his hiding place under the roof, and went via a circuitous route to the river when he hid until night. When the hooligans left his house after they finished pillaging it, he returned home and told us that it was only thanks to the fact that he helped Jews that he was saved from a sure death, and he gave thanks to G-d for saving him. However, he realized that the place was no longer secure for him. He moved to Stryj and from there he directed his associates as to how to conduct his business. He once undertook a very brazen deed. He dressed up as a Hungarian captain, showed up at his house and gave all sorts of instructions. He commanded his assistants to watch over the hiding place of the Jews in order to insure that no harm should befall them.

The gentiles Stach and Heryn Babi, Salsko Kozaik, Dr. Washkovitz, Stash Jurczko, Dozia Didoko, and Stefka all assisted him. In the forests of Lipowa, the following people helped the Jews: Kirila Lutak, Henet Herblinski, and Irina and Rozman Paripa.

After the liberation, the Bandrobches fell upon Stash Jurczko and injured him severely. Dr Karpf made every effort to save him. With great difficulty, he was able to summon a transport truck to transfer him to Stanislawow. His wife Ava, the wife of Dr. Karpf, and myself also traveled with him. He passed away en route.

The saviors Kirila, Kenet[9] and Irina died in 1945. Misko Jaglovitz died in 1962 in Poroshkov.

May their memories be blessed, and may they be remembered for good as righteous gentiles.

{215}

## In the Place of Murder
## in the Dolina Cemetery after the Liberation
### by Zeev (Wilush) Weinfeld

When the Red Army entered to our area in the forests of Dolina on August 8, 1944, all of those who remained alive in the forests came out of their hiding places and began searching for a place to go and restart their lives. I decided to go to Rozniatow to find some sort of work there. I found only two Jews in Rozniatow, a couple who had survived in the forests.

Not one of the wooden houses was still standing. All were burnt and destroyed. All sorts of vegetables grew in the fields. The gentiles of the area divided up the fields among themselves and worked them. A few houses that were built from stone remained standing. Gentiles took them over to live in them. They did not touch the Jewish cemetery of Rozniatow. I found the monuments intact there.

Not so in Dolina.

A few Jews who remained alive in the area banded together and decided to go to the place of murder in the Dolina cemetery. I was the only one there from Swariczow. There was nobody there from Rozniatow. Hesiu Peker, his wife Klara and brother Munio Peker were there from Dolina. Yaakov Adelstein was there from the village of Spas. One young man by the name of Pinile who had previously worked as a wagon driver, and another by the name of Leizerke were there from Dolina.

We went together to investigate the state of the cemetery where Jews from all around the region had been slaughtered on the terrible day of slaughter. All of the monuments from the cemetery, without exception, had been removed from their places. The Ukrainians used them as building material for their houses. There was no remnant of the fence that had surrounded the cemetery. The graves were no longer there and the ground had been flattened. Everything was as smooth as a field, however nothing grew there, for the Germans had poured plaster over all the bodies and the ground that covered the gigantic pits, and this prevented anything from growing from the ground. In one place I saw horse legs sticking out from the ground, and I understood that the gentiles had used the place as a burial ground for their animals.

Forty Ukrainian men, women and children who were murdered by the Germans on account of their hiding Jews in their homes were also buried in that cemetery in 1943. At the time, this had a great impact upon the residents, and from that time, no gentile was brazen enough to give any help to the Jews. Those murdered were relatives of three Ukrainian men who protected Jews, gave them a place of refuge, and later fought alongside them against the German army in the forests of Dolina. These men were: Stach Babi, his brother Hernio Babi and Slovko Kosczki.

Eight Russian captains who had fought along with the partisans against the German army were also buried there. These eight Russian captains fell in the aktion that cleared out the forest, when almost all of the people who were in the forest were killed. These eight Russian captains were also captured.

They were hung in the outskirts of Dolina and later buried in the Jewish cemetery as a sign of disgrace and shame.

After the liberation of Dolina by the Russians, when they found out that eight captains were buried in the Jewish cemetery along with the Ukrainian partisans and their families, they removed all of these bodies and arranged an official government funeral. These bodies were buried in a Christian cemetery with much fanfare. Only the carcasses of the horses remained in the Jewish cemetery.

Munio Peker wished to take revenge against the German murderers and their assistants. Therefore, he enlisted in the Russian army and immediately joined the secret police. After some time, he was murdered in the vicinity of Stryj by the Ukrainian Bandrobches, who swarmed in the forests of the regions and took action against the Russian army.

Pinele the wagon driver enlisted in the Polish army, and was killed on the way to Berlin.

Leizerke of Dolina once went to the village of Strutyn after the liberation with a Russian guard. There, he had left a gold watch and other articles of value with a Ukrainian friend. The Bandrobches fell upon him and murdered him on the spot. The guard disappeared.

Yaakov Adelstein is alive. He is living in Haifa. Myself, who writes these lines with tears, lives in Hadera...

{217}

# Righteous Gentiles
## by Wilush Weinfeld

### Stach Babi – A Savior of Jews

In the winter of 1942-43, when I was hiding in the forests of Dolina from my S.S. pursuers and their assistants from the Ukrainian militia, I would sleep in a pit that I prepared for myself in a secret place in the forest, or in a haystack in one of the huts of the neighboring gentiles in which I would steel a night or two of sleep, making sure that they would not notice me. In the day, I would wander around the fields and gather leftover vegetables or potatoes. I would gather some dry branches in the forest, light a small fire and bake the potatoes or boil the vegetables that I had gathered from the fields in a small plate. On occasion, I had the opportunity to sneak into one of the barns in the region and milk a bit of milk into a bottle, or I would drink my fill right there. I would also sleep in one of the corners of the barn until morning. In this manner, I lived and sustained myself in the forest through the entire winter until the beginning of 1943. Around March of 1943, I met in the forest Yaakov Adelstein, from Spas, a village close to Rozniatow. He and another Jew from the same village by the name of Bitkover hid in the forests that surrounded Dolina. The three of us stayed together as a group and our worries were common, whether they were worries about food or sustenance, or personal safety. Finally we met a gentile, an acquaintance of Adelstein, and with whom he had left all of his clothes and valuables for safekeeping. Due to the goodness of his heart, this gentile agreed to let us spend the night in a straw hut on his property. The fodder provided us with some warmth on cold nights. On occasion, he would leave us some potatoes or a piece of bread, as well as a bit of milk.

One morning as we set out for the forest, we found out that there were two women in the forests, who were certainly also Jews hiding as we were. After some time, we heard the rustle of burning branches. When we approached, we saw two forlorn women sitting and warming themselves over the fire that they had lit from dry leaves. We recognized them immediately. They were the wife of Philip Fuerst of Rozniatow and the widow Golda who was the cousin of Yutzi Farosh or Fisher of Dolina (living today in the United States with his wife Chantzi Laufer of Rozniatow). These women had been imprisoned in the Dolina jail. On of the invasion of the jail by a group of partisans lead by Stach Babi, many of the prisoners escaped, including these two poor women. They succeeded in reaching the forests close to Dolina.

These women were ill, covered with wounds on their faces and hands, short on sustenance, and almost falling of their feet. They requested that we not leave them alone in the forest. They had a bit of wheat and corn flour, and they also gathered potatoes in the fields from one of the gentiles, with whom Mrs. Fuerst had left her valuables including a valuable fur coat. They would go to this gentile's property secretly in order to sleep there, without them knowing, for they knew that if he found out, he would expel them from his property despite the valuables that she had left there.

During the era of evil caused by the Nazi occupation of Poland, when most of the Polish nation was influenced by the virulent anti-Semitism, and many of them assisted the Nazis in the work of exterminating the Jewish nation, it is befitting to mention to those who risked their own lives to save Jews. One of these was Stash Babi, a refined person and a faithful fighter against the Germans.

Stash Babi, who saved Jews, in front of his house.

Once when I was in the forest, I heard the rustle of wood and fire, and I realized that certainly someone else was hiding in the forest, warming himself by the fire. This was a Jew from Dolina by the name of Terpner, an acquaintance of mine from the time of the liquidations in Dolina. After the liquidation of the ghetto, Terpner along with his eighty-year-old father fled into the forest. His father, however, preferred to die in his home. He returned home and died there. Terpner was also among those who escaped from the jail when it was broken into by Stash Babi and his group. He was about forty years old, healthy, brave, and strong, and very diligent in the gathering of food. He equipped himself with a large pail, an ax and a sack, and went from village to village, stealing from the farmers' chickens, ducks, eggs and any thing else that was possible to obtain by physical force. His unkempt appearance instilled fear and trepidation.

The number of people in our group became unmanageable, so the group split into two: the first group consisting of Adelstein and Bitkover, and the second group consisting of the two women, Terpner, and myself. Despite the constant fear, life became more meaningful, for we had people to talk to, people to concern ourselves with, people to take counsel with. We all hoped together for liberty and freedom.

In April 1943, two other men who had been hiding appeared in the forest. These were the Peker brothers. I knew their entire family. They used to live in the village of Adnitza, close to Dolina. I knew their father, their sister and her husband, and their younger brother Jozek. They owned a small estate in that village. This family was well respected and beloved by all of the Ukrainian residents of the town, as well as by all the residents of the surrounding area. This was a very fine and upright family. During the time of the liquidation of Dolina, I fled to them and was put up as a guest in their home.

After some time, Yosef Lindenbaum appeared in the forest. In his time, he had made a great trip around all of Europe. He had also been in the land of Israel. The Pekers brought another youth by the name of Bronislaw Kremer to the forest. He was a Christian. His mother was a Pole and his father a German. They lived in Galicia, and the youth, due to his great refinement, could not tolerate seeing the suffering of his school friends. Despite the fact that he was a German, he gave up everything and joined in the suffering of his friends, to the point of going out with them to the forest. The Peker brothers had previously worked the Bolekhov work camp as "required workers". They were diligent and good workers.

Stash (Stanislav) Babi, one of the righteous gentiles.

In May 1943, we found out that in the forest next to the city of Veldzizh, there were groups of Jews headed by an influential Christian by the name of Stefan Babi, the brother of Stach Babi. Stach Babi was also a well-known influential person. He fought faithfully on the Russian side against the Germans and against the Ukrainian bands. Many legends circulated about his bands of fighters and his brave deeds. The Peker brothers and Adelstein decided to join up with the bands of fighters.

There is a great deal to tell about Stach Babi. Others who have written about this period of time in the forests of Dolina have also done so. He lives today in Poland, and I am in touch with him by letter. One of the Peker brothers lives here in Israel in one of the Kibbutzim near Netanya. Adelstein lives in Haifa. Trepner, Bitkover, Mrs. Fuerst, and Golda died in the Carpathian forests in 1943 as they were fighting against the Germans. Lindenbaum and his wife were killed at the Hungarian border as they were attempting to cross. Muni Peker died at the conclusion of the war when he was in the service of the Russian N. K. V. D. in an action against the Ukrainian Bandrobches in the area of Stryj.

{220}

## A Jewish Boy in the Cave of Dogs

After I came out of my hiding place in the forests around Dolina and entered one of the fields of the local farmers, to my great surprise I saw in one corner of the yard a young child wandering around in the dog cave along with a large purebred dog. When I approached the owner of the yard for an explanation, he broke out in laughter about his mighty deed, and told the following: "This is a Jewish child that I found abandoned one of the roads. I had mercy on him and brought him into my yard, and behold, he lives and is fed along with the other animals in my yard. See how beautiful he is."

I looked at him, and saw the face of a boy aged between 5-7 sitting under the hut that he made for his dog, and being fed from the same plate from which the dog receives his food. He was fed the same food and the same water as the dog. The dog and the child became very good friends, and lived their dog-lives together. When I asked the boy to come out to me, he refused, for he was happy there with the dog. He knew only that they called him Eli.

The child got older and became very attached to the house and the householder. The householder placed him in one of the warm stables where the larger animals live. He took him out to work at guarding the ducks in the marsh. The child learned from the children of the neighboring farmers how to make the sign of a cross before the crosses on the roads, how to bow down to the crosses, to recite some of their prayers, and how to be like one of the local gentile children.

On one occasion, the Russians surrounded the village, entered into the room of the owner of the purebred dog, shot the dog and killed it on the spot. When the child saw what happened to the dog, he kneeled down, kissed it, patted it, and attempted to revive it. When he saw that it was not working, he broke out in terrible screams, as if he himself had been shot and injured.

I attempted by various means to convince him to come with me, that I wanted to save him from the hands of the gentiles, but I was not successful. I began to interrogate the gentile – incidentally, since he thought that I was also a Russian – and I found out that during one of the expulsions of Jews from Stryj, some Jews left the child in the fields, and he brought him into his house. He was afraid that his neighbors would reveal to the Germans that the child was a Jew.

## TRANSLATOR'S FOOTNOTES

1. Rozniatow, which had been part of Poland prior to the war, became part of the U.S.S.R. following the war.

2. These pictures were a reference to the rabbinic adage that one must "run like a deer" and be "as strong as a lion" with regard to the service of G-d.

3. Seemingly, some sort of Ukrainian militia.

4. This was a period of time when Stalinist Russia was purging the Jewish intelligentsia. This was known as the Doctors Trials.

5. Kol Yisrael (literally "Voice of Israel") is the Israeli Broadcasting Corporation.

6. Presumably an exit tax.

7. The 7th day of the Sukkot festival.

8. This section does not have an entry in the table of contents, so my assumption is that it is by the same author as the previous section.

9. Here it is spelled as Kenet and previously as Henet. There are several other spelling variations in this section.

{221}

# Perehinsko

Youth of Perehinsko in 5688 (1931)
Translator's note: The Jewish and secular years do not correspond here. The Jewish year 5688 would correspond to
1927-1928, not 1931.)

{222}

## The Town of Perehinsko
### by Avraham Winkler (Bobchio)

It was a settlement in the region of Stanislawow. The Carpathian Mountains were to the south and southwest, and there was a chain of mountains to the East from the Lomnica River. Until the year 1929, when it attained the status of a town, it was considered to be a particularly large village.

In the years 1929/1930 it attained the status of a town so that it would be able to collect more taxes (obviously from Jews) in Eastern Galicia. It had more than 13,000 residents, including 12,000 Ukrainians, a few Polish families, and 1,000 Jewish souls.

In addition to three houses of worship, the Old Beis Midrash, the New Beis Midrash, and the kloiz, there was a charitable fund and a guesthouse.

The Zionist movement arose to life in 1919, in the midst of the First World War[2]. I remember, and I was ten years old at the time, that my older brothers came home and began to dress up in festive clothes. They told me to do the same. This was November 2nd, the day of the Balfour Declaration. We went out of the house and arrived in the center of town, next to the public school. There, I found all of the Jewish youth. Everyone had a blue and white flag in his hand. I also received a flag. We began to march along the main street. I thought that this was the end of the war, but then they explained to me that this was in honor of the Balfour Declaration that enabled the establishment of a national homeland. This was on November 2nd. The organizers were three youths who had returned from their studies in Vienna. These were as follows:

Alter Hilman, Fishel Mintz, and Yehoshua Yosef Lauber. The latter has two sons who are living in Israel. The youngest is Pinchas Eliav, a senior official in the Foreign Ministry. The elder is Mordechai Eliav, a professor of Jewish History at Bar Ilan University.

Local branches of "Herzlia", "Hatikva", and "Shachar" were opened. The Zionist movement found enthusiastic supporters, and the echoes of the ideological excitement in the Zionist organizations of Eastern Galicia reached also to Perehinsko. Every faction set up its local branch, including "Hitachdut", "Gordonia", "Beitar", and "Noar Hatzioni".

There was one area where there were no factions. This was the dramatic club that put on the plays: "Chasia Hayetoma" ("Chasia the Orphan"), "Yaakov Hanafach" ("Yaakov the Smith"), "Kalandri", "Kashe Lihiyot Yehudi" ("It is Hard to be a Jew"), "Hazar" ("The Stranger"), "Hakamtzan" ("The Miser"), "Mirele Efrat", "Hashodadim" ("The Robbers"), and others.

On every holiday, traditional or nationalistic, a celebration was arranged and the money collected went to purchase books for the library, which contained 3,000 books. A Hebrew school was also opened.

On Chanuka of 1932, the "Beit Am" ("House of the Nation") was dedicated. This building served as a center for all cultural and other activities. It also had a large hall for performances and celebrations.

All of the Jews of the town, with the exception of those who served in ritual positions, such as the rabbi, the shochtim, and the teachers, donated money for nationalistic funds when they had an aliya to the Torah[3]. Once, a particular merchant refused to donate to the Keren Kayemet Leyisrael (Jewish National Fund). When he wished to lead the services[4] one day, the youth protested publicly and did not allow him to do so until he promised to make such donations in the future, and pay a fine.

There were also functioning "Chevra Linat Tzedek" and "Bikur Cholim" organizations, whose job it was to visit the sick and stay with them during the nights, and to provide food if the sick person was alone and had no means.

In 1929-1930, the Pacificzia[5] began, and the Ukrainians began to organize themselves to commit destructive acts. They would set fire to the wheat in the fields and in farms. Obviously, they did not neglect the Jewish houses, and every night, a Jewish house was ignited. A self-defense organization was established, whose task it was to guard and protect Jewish property in the event of a fire. Each night, a different group of individuals was on duty. Those who were not on duty slept in their clothing, in order to be prepared if they were called upon.

It happened that they set fire to the house of David Rosenbaum the shochet, a pious, upright, G-d fearing man. We tried to save the most that we could. We removed all of the furniture, and took down the doors and windows. When the insurance adjuster came to estimate the damage, the shochet did not allow his son Shmuel Leib to conduct the business, lest he not tell the truth, and hide from the adjuster the fact that some things were saved. He himself told the truth, even though he did not know Polish. The adjuster said in his own words that he was surprised that a Jew was telling the truth.

A horse dealer named Weisman traveled to the city of Stryj on the day before the market day. He stayed in a hotel next to the train station. In the evening, he left his room, and in the hallway ran into men and woman dressed in festive clothing, whispering and milling about. They told him that a wedding of an orphan girl was bout to take place; however since a dowry of 500 Crown had been promised but there was only 300, the groom did not wish to go to the wedding ceremony. Weisman went to talk to the adoptive father of the orphan girl, and told him that he would be willing to add the 200 on the condition that he be allowed to dance the first dance with the bride (known as the Mitzvah Dance). Obviously, they agreed, and the joy was great.

Nachum Weisman's father was known as a fine man, and he was ready to help his fellowman day or night. Once he saw a Ukrainian beating a Jew, so he approached the gentile and gave him a slap. The gentile fainted, and they carried him unconscious to the hospital. He died a few days later. The police came and arrested Weisman. My grandfather Yitzchak Kanol (the gentiles called him Itzko Holoboti) traveled to Vienna and returned with a pardon for Weisman from Kaiser Franz Josef.

I cannot fail to mention the person of Motka Sharanzal the shoemaker, who excelled in his entertaining of guests. Each day, there were as many as eight or ten guests in his home.

These people that I mentioned here were just a very few, and each one is a world unto himself. It is not possible for me to mention everybody. Each one of us can bring them to our memories even more so, for they are all rooted in the depths of our souls, and will not ever be forgotten, as long as the breath is within us.

{224}

### Rabbi David Rosenbaum of holy blessed memory
### Shochet and teacher of the community of Perehinsko, Galicia
### By A. Brandwein

Reb David the son of the Gaon, Tzadik, and Kabbalist Reb Shmuel Aryeh, a teacher and judge, was of the well-bred stock of the great maggid of Nadworna, and the grandson of the pious rabbi Rabbi David Zlatis. He was known as great in Torah and a great expert in Talmud and rabbinic adjudicators. He would issue judgements on practical Jewish law. He was a very honorable person who was beloved by his fellowman. He would greet every person in a friendly manner. The people of his community liked him very much and revered him. They would go to him to be blessed by him and receive advice, whether in personal matters or communal matters.

He was a man of truth, with generous character traits. He would go himself every Friday to check if the eruv was in order[6]. He was very diligent regarding any mitzvah (commandment). He would give a class daily in the Beis Midrash to the residents of the town, and also to the young men who came to his house. He was very generous with distributing charity, and he would especially collect money to send to the Land of Israel. He was a warm and feeling Jew. When he led services on the High Holy days, he would pour out his soul, and recite the prayers with great sweetness.

He was close to the Admor of Belz, and he married off his daughter Sara to the Admor Reb Yechiel Michel, the Rabbi of Turka-Strettin.

He died there on the New Moon (Rosh Chodesh) of Shvat, 5696 (1936).

His wife was the Rebbetzin Shifra, the daughter of the rabbi and Tzadik Reb Yehoshuale Langnauer of Zhidachev. She was a modest and pious woman, and was renowned for her good deeds. She died on Rosh Chodesh Tammuz in her prime, and left five young children.

Reb David's second wife was Rebbetzin Feiga. She did not merit having children of her own, and therefore dedicated herself wholeheartedly to the raising and education of the children who were in the home. She cared for the children with extra special love, and they reciprocated with honor and reverence, as she deserved.

Her lot was the same as the lot of the rest of the holy community, who perished by fire and water, and by all sorts of unusual deaths, may G-d avenge their deaths. Reb David had one son and four daughters.

His son Reb Shmuel Aryeh was a scholar, who taught Torah in public, both to young and old.

One daughter, Chana (Chantsha) died before the war. Another daughter Rachle was married to Rabbi Yisrael Lipiowker, a Boyaner Hassid and a shochet in his place of residence. They had a daughter and son, Shifra and David. The destruction reached them as well, and they perished along with the community. His youngest daughter Chayale perished in the Holocaust along with the rest of the community. One daughter, Sara, lives in Israel, may she live long and well. She is married to Rabbi Nachum Brandwein7 of Bnei Brak. They have a large, multi-branched family in the Land, who try to continue the dynasty of their holy ancestors. It was from them that we obtained the details about the shochet of Perehinsko.

{225}

## Fathers of the Settlement

This was a typical town in Eastern Galicia, with a splendid landscape that overlooked the foothills of the beautiful Carpathian Mountains. It had about 10,000 residents, including several hundred Jews who lived there in relative tranquility. They were merchants, officials, artisans, homeowners, clergy, and simple folk, who lived by the toil of their hands and distributed charity to their fellowman.

During the time of the Holocaust, the cup of agony passed over them as well, and they perished in the furious storm at the hands of the Nazi troops and their assistants, may G-d avenge their deaths. There were only a few isolated survivors who escape due to the grace of G-d, and who have the duty of guarding the coals of memory of these holy martyrs.

The Jews of Perehinsko were dear and pleasant during their life, and in their death they were not separated[8]. The vast majority of them were murdered in sanctification of the Divine name, may G-d avenge their blood.

{225}

### Our Grandfather Rabbi Yitzchak Juner of holy blessed memory, may G-d avenge his blood.

He was an upright Jew, modest, discreet, righteous in all of his deeds, a scholar and a fearer of Heaven. He recited the midnight service[9], and he woke up again early in the morning to study Torah and worship.

To hear his recital of "Modeh Ani Lefanecha"[10] each morning and his melody when he was studying Torah – these were special experiences that caused the heart to tremble. He was revered and beloved by everyone, especially by his children and grandchildren. The home of their noble grandfather bestowed some of its glory upon them, and set them upon the correct path.

He was very conscientious in receiving guests. He built a special room for guests, and any visitor who passed through the town knew the address of this renowned benefactor. Any poor person who came by received food, drink and lodging, as well as some charity.

Father treated important guests with wisdom and understanding. If a certain Rebbe, or descendent of a Rebbe came to town, as was customary in those days, grandfather would take the guest to his room, and grandmother Chana of blessed memory, his partner, would sleep in a different room. The entire house was turned over to the important guest, who would conduct his Friday evening and Sabbath day table gatherings there in the presence of Jews of the town.

Grandfather was a faithful, well-to-do merchant. He had a good name, was generous, and never hurt or embarrassed anyone. In addition, he was a pleasant prayer leader, and he would lead the prayers on the High Holy Days. The walls of the Beis Midrash would quake when he mentioned the name of G-d during his prayers. On the day that our grandfather of blessed memory donated a Torah Scroll to the synagogue of the town, there was a great celebration in town.

{226}

## Grandmother Chana of blessed memory

Grandmother Chana was known as a "woman of valor", whether in business, or in the entertaining of guests. She worked hard in her preparations, and received every guest and poor person who came to the home in a friendly manner. She assisted grandfather in fulfilling his sublime objectives with diligence and holy awe. Any utterance of his mouth was holy to her.

Our Father and Teacher Reb Yeshayahu Juner of holy blessed memory
He was splendid in appearance and pleasant in his mannerisms. He always had a good-hearted smile on his lips, and there was never a stain on his clothes. He inherited the trait of entertaining guests from his father, and he was well known for distributing charity to anybody in need, and any forlorn soul.

Our father served as the head of the community and a gabbai (administrator) of the kloiz. There were many charity boxes in our home, and he gave to the poor beyond his means. On Sabbaths, wayfarers ate at his table. He gathered them from all synagogues, as he was concerned that nobody should be left without a Sabbath meal.

He did many charitable works throughout his life. He made sure that the poor of the town would receive sufficient wood for fuel. He tried to bring peace between people, and he made sure that the needs of the scholars were met. He gave money for the Land of Israel. On Tu Bishvat, he brought fruit of the Land of Israel to our home, and he instilled a love of Zion in our hearts. He paid for a special tutor to teach the Hebrew language and bible to the local children.

He inherited his pleasant voice from his father as well. He led services with great emotion and feeling, and he served as a prayer leader on festivals and the High Holy Days.

He was beloved and revered by everyone, including the gentiles. He was upright, spoke the truth in his heart, set times for the study of Torah, possessed wonderful character traits, and always acted beyond the letter of the law. He was a Hassid of Belz. He loved his fellow Jew with his whole heart, and gave everyone the benefit of the doubt.

He merited visiting the Land of Israel as a tourist in 1937, and he spent about three months there. He returned home to liquidate his property in the exile, and to make aliya with his entire family to the Land of Israel.

"Many are the thoughts in the heart of man, but the will of G-d prevails". The war broke out, and he did not merit to fulfil his dream.

**TRANSLATOR'S FOOTNOTES**

1. The Jewish and secular years do not correspond here. The Jewish year 5688 would correspond to 1927-1928, not 1931. Back

2. There is obviously a contradiction of dates here as well. From the context, it is apparent that the year 1917 is meant, the year of the Balfour Declaration. Back

3. During the reading of the Torah in the synagogue, various people are called up to take part. The honor of being called up to the Torah is referred to as an "aliya". The number of people receiving an aliya on a particular day varies with the occasion (weekday, Sabbath, festival, New Moon, etc.) In many synagogues, a pledge to charity is made upon receiving an aliya. Back

4. Weekday synagogue services are often led by a person observing yahrzeit (an anniversary of death of parents) on a particular day. Back

5. Evidently, some form of nationalistic uprising. Back

6. On the Sabbath, it is forbidden to carry from a public domain to a private domain, or approximately six feet within a public domain. It is possible to construct an enclosure around a public domain (not a Torah defined public domain but rather a rabinically defined public domain) in order to convert it into a private domain, and thereby allow carrying on the Sabbath therein. Such an enclosure is called an 'eruv'. Often, an eruv is constructed around entire towns. Back

7. A different husband was mentioned above. This one must have been a second marriage, as presumably her first husband perished in the Holocaust. Back

8. This is a paraphrasing of the eulogy that David composed for Saul and his sons, recorded in the first chapter of Samuel II. Back

9. Tikkun Chatzot is a lament over the destruction of the temple that is recited at midnight. It is not an obligatory service, and is generally only recited by exceptionally pious people. Back

10. The first statement to be made upon awakening in the morning, thanking G-d for returning the soul after the night of sleep. Back

{227}

Sara Itta Juner.
"The wisdom of women
builds the home",
(Proverbs 14, 1)

Rivka Ettinger the daughter of Reb
Yitzchak Juner

Reb Yeshayahu Juner

Whoever knew them and their conduct understood the words of King Solomon that it is the wisdom of special women who build the home. Theirs was not an ordinary home, but a home filled with nobility and warmth, open broadly for all charitable matters.

{228}

Chana Juner was an extremely pious woman, sincere, and not knowing and not tolerating facades. She raised her daughters in an exemplary fashion and attempted as best possible to raise them in an honorable and glorious fashion both for this world and for the next world.[1]

In the center is Chana Juner, to her right is her daughter Tzila Finter, and to her left Batya Kertenstein.

Tzipa Rotenberg, daughter of Reb Yitzchak Juner

A new branch arose of noble stock, who continued in the good deeds that she inherited from her forbears. The daughters of the Juner family were full of love and kindness to their fellow man, splendor and fineness. They did kind deeds at all times, they entertained guests, concerned themselves with helping the downtrodden and poor, and extended their arms to embrace anyone who was suffering.

{229}

## Our Mother Sara Itta Juner, may G-d avenge her blood

She was the daughter of Chava and Reb Baruch Teomim – the great-grandchild of Reb Baruch Frankel Teomim (the author of the book "Baruch Taam") and the son-in-law of the Gaon Rabbi Chaim Halberstam of Tzanz.

The majority of the rabbis of Galicia, such as Horowitz, Babad, etc. were related to her illustrious family. The regal splendor of holiness was poured over her noble face. She helped her husband in fulfilling his spiritual and public roles, and in educating the children in Torah and good deeds. She served as an example for her children with her charity, her pleasant ways, and her wisdom.

Our mother founded a charitable fund whose purpose was to give money for the needs of the Sabbath on a weekly basis to the poor of the town. She would give charity discreetly. She would send her children at night with provisions of food to the outskirts of the town – to a woman who had just given birth or a childless woman.

The children of Reb Yeshayahu Juner: Rivka, Batya, Baruch

Our mother made sure that we would also study sciences. However, as a daughter of a rabbinical dynasty, she stood her guard lest we should, Heaven forbid, forget the source from which we were hewn, and our Torah. Her words were engraved very well in our hearts, and serve as our guiding light until this day.

At the time of the outbreak of the war, rabbis from her family were serving in the towns of Jaworow,

Przeworsk, Stanislawow, Jaroslaw, Halicz, and others.

We, her children, pray to G-d that we can emulate our parents – in their generous characters and their personal sacrifice for their fellow man.

{230}

## Our Brothers and Sisters

We were nine brothers and sisters, of which only three survive. The profane hand did not touch us, for we made aliya to the Land prior to the outbreak of the war.

Our eldest sister Bayla was good hearted and righteous. Her husband was Reb Yitzchak Bretler, an intelligent and handsome man. He was the son of the Hassid Rabbi Rafael Bretler. They had two darling children, Yenta and Tzvi. The destruction reached them as well. We will never forget their words of farewell and their efforts on our behalf when we made aliya to the Land.

From right: Reb Yitzchak Bretler, his wife Bayla and father Reb Rafael Bretler of Dolina. Bayla was the daughter of Reb Yeshayahu Juner

From right: Reb Yitzchak Bretler, his wife Bayla and father Reb Rafael Bretler of Dolina.
Bayla was the daughter of Reb Yeshayahu Juner.

The rest of our siblings – their good name preceded them, both regarding the honor of parents as well as their love of their fellowman – were cut off at a young age.

Chava the beautiful, Rivka the intelligent, Baruch the charming, Batya the philosopher, and Yaakov, the youngest.

## Uncles and Aunts

Aunt Rivka was the eldest sister of our father. She was a noble and refined woman. Her husband was Reb Tzvi Ettinger of Kolomea. He was an ordained rabbi, and toiled in Torah day and night. They had three sons: Nota, Moshe and Zelig.

Aunt Tzippy was the second sister of our father. She was a woman of valor. Her husband was Reb Yehuda Tzvi Rotenberg, the son of the rabbi of Skula. He was a very intelligent, learned scholar. He served as an adjudicator of various disputes on a voluntary basis. They had three children, refined and very bright: Rivka, Yosef, and Tova. They all wished to make aliya to the Land of Israel, but they did not merit to fulfill their desire.

Aunt Rachel was the third sister of our father. She was a refined woman. Her husband was Reb Eizik Kertenstein of Stanislawow. They had two children, Yonah and Tzvi.

Aunt Tzila was the fourth sister of our father. Her husband was Reb Mendel Finter of the Rokach family of Borislaw, who were related to the Belzer Rebbe. He was a well known cantor, and during the last period served as the cantor in the city of Rotterdam, Holland. They were killed in sanctification of G-d's name with their four children.

Yenta and Tzvi Bretler, the grandchildren of Reb Yeshayahu and Sara Itta Juner

It is difficult to make peace with the fact that only so very few remain from such a splendid and illustrious family. We, the children who survived in Israel due to the grace of G-d try to bring forth the memories of the past with honor, to learn from our forbears, and to teach our children to follow in their path.

May the souls of all of the holy martyrs be bound in the bonds of life.

Moshe Frankel (Juner)
Malka Bretler (Juner)
Esther Borenstein (Juner)[2]

## TRANSLATOR'S FOOTNOTES

1. Referring to ensuring both their physical and spiritual growth.

2. There is no indication in the text as when the previous section by A. Brandwein ends, and when this section by the Juner family starts. The author name of the Brandwein section is listed at the beginning, and the three authors of the Juner section are listed at the end. It would seem that the Juner section begins on page 225, with the discussion of the Juner grandfather.

{232}

## Yehuda Berelfein
### by Yonah Yungerman of Sderot Dvora

In the pages of this Yizkor book, in the memorial candles for the martyrs of Broszniow, I have come to light a memorial candle for my grandfather Yehuda Ber Berelfein.

My mother told me a great deal about her father, and she portrayed the sublime image of my grand-father to my eyes. His story is certainly not different than that of many others in that era: he was a well to do Jew who returned from America to Poland, to his wide-branched family. He rejected life in the city and turned to Broszniow – a town at the beginning of its development. There he built his house. At first, he worked in agriculture, and later he opened a store.

Everyone knew that his home was open to every needy wayfarer. When he saw that there was not sufficient room in his house for all of those in need, he built a special room in his yard for these un-fortunate beggars who wandered along the roads. He set up beds, bedding, mattresses, etc. with his own hands. Everyone who wanted was able to find a warm bed and a roof over their heads during the summer or the winter.

He cared for those needy people with his own hands. He gave them of his own bread, and on occa-sion he even loaned them money, knowing full well that the loan would not be repaid, for those un-fortunates would be leaving the town in the morning and would not be returning. Others would arrive and take their places. There was never an empty bed, and the family never sat down to eat at their table with themselves alone.

Do not think that only Jews ate at my grandfather's table. His home was also open to gentiles – Ukrainians whose reverence for him knew no bounds. He did all of this discreetly, and did not publi-cize his generosity and his good deeds. However, finally such good became revealed. Everyone knew that his heart would not permit him to see a person stumbling in the world of the Holy One Blessed Be He. The scoffers would say: "Again there is a minyan[1] of 'tourists' at Berelfein's". Indeed, on occasion there was more than a minyan.

The local police also knew about this situation. When someone would come to the police at night requesting a place to sleep, they would send him to Berelfein. There, without a doubt, they would find a place for him.

I can see him, my grandfather, waking up in the middle of the night during the difficult days of win-ter when there was a knock on the door, a voice asking for help, a person who could not find a place to warm his bones, and was freezing outside... My grandfather went out, despite the cold outside, to the person who was wasting away from hunger and cold, make for him a bed, and give him some hot food to restore his spirit.

I have attempted with my poor words to describe his greatness, however the words do not have the power to describe what all of us, his grandchildren and his entire world, knew.

There is no doubt that it is only in the merit of Tzadikim (righteous people) such as he that the world exists, and may his soul be comforted by that.

{233}

## In Memory of the Martyrs of Perehinsko

Here are a few words from the sole survivor of the family of Reb Shalom and Freida Rachel Rosenbaum, may G-d avenge their deaths.

Perehinsko is a small town at the foothills of the Carpathians in the area of Rozniatow. It's Jewish community was not large, approximately 150 families, most of whom were murdered by the wild Nazi beast.

The Jewish community consisted of people of all strata: rabbis, merchants, artisans, intelligentsia, and ordinary Jews.

The youth were exemplary. The youth had a pioneering spirit. The youth worked and studied. Most of them participated in Hachsharah (preparations) for aliya to the Land. Some of them even succeeded in making aliya and escaping the Holocaust.

These are the martyrs of Perehinsko, whose entire lives were dedicated to G-d.

For example, there was the rabbi and Gaon Rabbi Avraham Mordechai Babad of holy blessed memory, who served as the rabbi of Perehinsko until the destruction came. He was a modest and quiet Jew, happy with his lot, G-d fearing, and content. Rabbi Avraham Mordechai Babad was a great Torah scholar, and was also blessed with sublime character traits. He dedicated himself to the properness and purity of the town. He did not concern himself at all with himself and his family. He was an exemplary spiritual leader.

Who does not remember the prominent family of Reb Yitzchak Juner of holy blessed memory. This family included his son Reb Yeshayahu, his son-in-law Rabbi Tzvi Ettinger of holy blessed memory, his son-in-law Reb Yehuda Tzvi Rotenberg, grandchildren and great-grandchildren. This family had Torah and greatness in one package. They were upright merchants, and first class observers of Torah. They were fitting prayer leaders, and charitable people.

Caring for guests and tending to poor brides were their lot.

Whoever came in hungry to the home of Reb Yitzchak Juner of holy blessed memory left satiated. Whoever came in downtrodden left happy. One could find a solution to every problem with his advice.

In his old age, when Reb Yitzchak Juner built a house, he also built a private synagogue. At the time of the dedication of the Torah scroll his synagogue, it was said that: whoever did not participate in this joyous event had never witnessed joy in his life.[2]

### "Torah and Greatness in One Place"[3]

My father Reb Shalom the son of Reb Shimshon Rosenbaum of holy blessed memory was a scholar and an observer of the commandments who lived all of his days in holiness and purity. He would get up in the middle of the night for the Tikkun Chatzot service.[4] My mother Freida Rachel the daughter of Reb Shmuel Lustig was a paragon of courtesy and uprightness. She was a woman of valor who concerned herself at all times and in all conditions to the giving of a good education to her children. Her whole desire was to inculcate faith and belief in G-d in her children. She taught us to not despair during the worst moments, to go with full faith to meet all life events, and to accept everything with love.

To the end of my days, I will never forget the final moment when I separated from my mother and the entire family. This was on the first intermediate day of Sukkot in the year 5700 / 1940. I left the home and the town in which I was born and grew up. I was taken to serve in the Red Army at the Japanese border.

The parting was very difficult. The weeping of my father, my brothers and sisters and all around was heartbreaking. I was the first young Jew to leave the town. Only my intelligent mother parted from me with a kiss and a blessing of peace, without shedding a tear, in order not to cause me agony. In the merit of the faith that she instilled in me, I was able to traverse all of the setbacks that came my way from the day I left my home until today. I was the only survivor of the large and illustrious family of Reb Shalom and Freida Rachel Rosenbaum, who ascended on High along with their sons, daughters and grandchildren during the time of the Holocaust.

May their memory be blessed forever.

{234}

### Another Example of a Wonderful Jew

My uncle Reb David the son of Reb Shmuel Leib Rosenbaum 5 of holy blessed memory, the ritual slaughterer of Perehinsko, was a complete Tzadik, who never hurt his fellow. He came to live with us after his house burnt down. I was then about ten years old, and my uncle invited me to sleep with him. I was very happy. At midnight, my uncle would arise to recite the Tikkun Chatzot service. I awoke in bed and paid attention to him. He came over, caressed my head and said: "Sleep, my child", and then he sat down to immerse himself in the service of the Creator until daybreak.

Every Jew of Perehinsko was a world unto himself, and I am not able to put all of their merits onto paper, for they are many.

It was possible to find a place to sleep in every home, and even more so, some food and drink.

## Institutions of Perehinsko

The following were the synagogues: The old synagogue (The old Beis Midrash), the new one (the new Beis Midrash), the kloiz, the private synagogue of Reb Yitzchak Juner, and other private minyanim.

There was a special house for guests next to the kloiz. There was a Talmud Torah. The most senior of the teachers was Reb Feivel Friedman. We studied with him, beginning from the aleph beit. I remember the happiest Sabbath in my life when I was five years old, and I began to study Chumash. On the Sabbath, they arranged a lovely celebration, and the teacher came to examine me, with the wondrous set of questions: "What are you learning, my child?"[6]. The entire family was happy that I knew how to answer well all of the questions of Reb Feivel Friedman. Then, I went to learn with Reb Yosef Zisser, and later, at the age of nine, with Reb Moshe Walder of Tarnopol. We studied Rashi's commentary and Talmud with him.

In Perehinsko, there was also a government school in the center of the city, where we studied from noon. In the afternoon until the evening hours we learned again in cheder. The school day was very full. In the winter, we would return from cheder with a lantern "a product of Perehinsko", made of cardboard. Inside the lantern was a potato with a hole, and in it, there was a candle to light the way.

There was a wonderful institution in Perehinsko. It was called "The House of Jewish Culture", where all of the Zionist factions were housed. On occasion, we would organize performances there, whose proceeds were dedicated to the assistance of the needy. Speakers from various factions would often come to Perehinsko. They would say their words in the house of culture. Aside from this, the culture house served as a center for evenings of entertainment.

## The Days of the Week in Perehinsko

Sunday! Life returned to its normal daily routine, however the merchants did not open their stores, for on the other side, the church bells rang, for it was the holy day of rest of the Christians.

Almost no movement was perceived in the town until the afternoon hours. Trade was forbidden. Only in the afternoon did people make discrete[7] purchases despite the watchful eyes of the police.

Monday was the market day. The town was bustling with life from the early hours of the morning. The stores were wide open, and wagons with all types of merchandise streamed in from the area. Buyers and sellers bargained and debated the quality of the merchandise and the price. People went from one stall to the next. Despite the hustle and bustle, no man of Perehinsko forgot to go the synagogue morning and evening.

Tuesday was a relatively quiet day. It was peaceful after the tumult of the previous day. It was an ordinary and routine day.

Wednesday was a day of preparation for the market day that was to take place the next day. It was the day that the poor came from afar in order to seek out donations, or to remain in Perehinsko for the

Sabbath.

Thursday was very similar in its essence to Monday, since it was a market day. It was even noisier due to the advent of the Sabbath.

Here, the housewife played an honorable role, for she was toiling and working to prepare the traditional Sabbath delicacies.

Friday: the movement was restricted to local purchases, and the interior of the house. The housewife attempted to speedily complete her daily work and her preparations for the Sabbath. The house was cleaned, and the aroma of fish, hot dishes and baked goods intermingled with each other and filled the air. The children were already wearing their festive clothing. When the sun went down and the candles were lit, the men and children went to the synagogue to welcome the Sabbath with the "Lecha Dodi" prayer. At the conclusion of the service, everyone would return to his home and family to recite the Kiddush over wine and to sing the hymns at the meal with an exalted spirit of a sublime soul that rises above the difficulties of the day. The Sabbath hymns that were heard from every home merged together into one ancient chorus. An atmosphere of rest descended upon the town, the atmosphere of the Sabbath Queen. This is the Perehinsko of the days of the week, the Perehinsko that was known to everyone, with its simplicity and its upright people who walked with pleasantness.

Many days have passed since then, however the taste of that existence will never melt away. It is alive and existing in the hearts of all of those who remember it, and thus shall it remain forever.

Certainly, much more than what can be read in this book should have been written about the lives of the giants of spirit and deed. However, who am I to be able to actualize the debt to the martyrs of Perehinsko?!

May their merit stand for us and all of Israel. Amen

From right: Reb Yeshaya Juner and his father Reb Yitzchak, with the Admor of Bolekhov and his gabbai (assistant)

{237}

# Father's House
## by Yehuda Langnauer

My father Yisrael Langnauer of blessed memory was a religious, G-d fearing and scholarly Jew. He knew how to entertain guests. Our house was always filled to the brim with guests. On Sabbath eves, father would have over rabbis from various cities. Rabbis enjoyed spending the Sabbath with father. Father was not only a scholar, but also high spirited. This high spirit gave him the power of his belief in G-d.

On the last day of Passover of 1931 a large fire broke out in the synagogue. Father was concerned about the place. He entered the burning synagogue to salvage a number of Torah scrolls. Father was involved in the communal life of the town. Father was always honored with the reading of the Megillat Esther (Scroll of Esther) in the synagogue on Purim, and the blowing of the shofar on the High Holy Days. Father also played an active role on Simchat Torah.

My mother Freida of blessed memory was also well liked in town. She was a righteous woman. Even though she had eight children and was an exemplary housewife, she made a point of helping the needy and the sick.

My eldest brother Yehoshua was a member of the intelligentsia and an enthusiastic Zionist. He was a member of the Zionist organization of the town. He headed the Zionist organization along with Bendet Spiegel, Moshe Spiegel and Mordechai Hausman.

The rest of my brothers, of blessed memory, Shlomo, David, Gadi, Tzvi, and the youngest Yitzchak-le, as well as my sister Feiga, were each involved with their own activities.

I took leave of them in 1941, three months prior to the outbreak of the Second World War between

Russia and Germany. I served in the Red Army. I never saw them again after that.

Uncaptioned. A group photo of the family of Yehuda Langnauer

{238}

We will remember our communities: Rozniatow, Perehinsko, Broszniow, and Swaryczow that were destroyed and wiped out; their children who were murdered; who were brought to slaughter in the wagons of death; whose honor was violated and whose blood was spilled by impure hands – in sanctification of the Divine Name.

We will remember the children, pure ones the son of pure ones, who were stolen from the bosom of their parents, who were broken and murdered by strange deaths; children and infants who were shattered on stone walls and cut off from life with the hatred of cruel hands – in sanctification of the Divine name.

## TRANSLATOR'S FOOTNOTES

1. A minyan is a quorum of ten adult males needed to conduct a prayer service.

2. This is a mishnaic quote, referring to the joy of the water drawing ceremony on the Festival of Sukkot in the Temple.

3. A Talmudic quote referring to a person who possesses both great Torah scholarship and material means.

4. A private midnight service that consists of lamentations over the destruction of the Temple. It is not obligatory, and only recited by particularly pious people. It is very rarely observed today.

5. If this uncle is his father's brother, there is a confusion of names between the name of the uncle's

father and the father's father (in the previous section) which should be equivalent. Alternatively, perhaps his mother had the same surname as his father (i.e. cousins married – a common occurrence in that era), or the uncle was really some other relative.

6. A traditional, canned, set of questions and answers recited at the occasion of a child beginning to learn Chumash (the books of the Torah).

7. Literally "back door".

## YIDDISH PART OF THE YIZKOR BOOK

{239}

# Yizkor Book
## To perpetuate the remembrance of the destroyed Jewish Communities

### Rozniatow, Perehinsko, Broszniow, and Neighboring Communities

{241}

## Our Yizkor Book
### by Zecharia Friedler

### Translated by Jerrold Landau from a draft by Isak Shteyn

Our Yizkor Book in remembrance of the destroyed Jewish community of Rozniatow needs no prefaces and clarifications. It is the only monument that we can erect for the martyrs of our shtetl, which drank of the cup of poison in its entirety. As long as there are still living witnesses, it is our sacred duty to gather all kinds of materials, our remembrances, knowledge, and feelings about our shtetl.

I want to relate here how our society, the Organization of Rozniatow Natives, came into being, and how the idea to edit this memorial book, dedicated to the memory of our community, arose. This happened in the years following World War Two, when there was a mass Aliyah[1] from Poland and the first immigrants from Rozniatow arrived. Among these immigrants was a friend of mine, whom I last saw thirty years ago. He came to see me from the immigration center in Haifa. There was great joy mingled with deep sorrow. Old reminiscences were awakened of the personalities of our dear relatives who perished so brutally.

Just a few years previously, we still received greetings from them, full of warm love and concerns, and today all are speechless ... all dead.

Our parents, sisters, brothers, friends and colleagues perished terribly. The Nazis and their Ukrainian helpers did not spare young children, not even babies. All of a sudden our shtetl became a dreadful slaughterhouse from where it was impossible to emerge alive.

An important duty became apparent to me. All of us who were originally from Rozniatow, and now living in Israel and other countries, had a sacred duty to immortalize our martyrs, all those Rozniatower Jews who hoped to live a better, quieter and nicer life, but did not live to see it.

The next day, I met our fellow natives of the same town, Samuel Spiegel and Izak Rotenberg. I told them about the first immigrants and their poor material circumstances. We were convinced that our first task was to secure material help for them and to set them on a firm footing. Two days later in my apartment, the first gathering of a larger group of Rozniatower natives took place, and in this way, the organization of Rozniatowers in Israel came into existence.

We sent out invitations to all our countrymen from Rozniatow, Perehinsko, Broszniow and Szwary-czow. Simultaneously we announced the place and the date of the first general meeting in the press.

The meeting passed very solemnly. All former citizens of Rozniatow and surrounding communities living in Israel, the old people and the new immigrants, people who went through different infernos during their lives, and now who live in the State of Israel, met for the first time.

People became closer to each other and tight relations were formed amongst our fellow natives. People who had not seen each other for decades fell upon each other, embraced, kissed, and wept.

These were cries of joy and of grief.

A committee was elected to lead the new organization with Bendet Schwartz as its head. The committee undertook the task to collect money to help our brethren with their first requests. We clung to the hope that some of those rescued from the valley of fire, ashes, and death would still appear.

We organized a free-loan institution, which appeared to be very useful. Our society was helpful to newcomers with such matters as getting an apartment, finding work, etc.

With the help of our countrymen living abroad, we increased the funds in our account. The members of the committee were always ready to help everyone who needed it.

We honor the memory of our martyrs, coming together every year on a fixed day for an "Azkara"[2] for our saintly departed.

A very important deed was accomplished when we erected a monument for the martyrs of our shtetl in the Martyr's Forest in Jerusalem. Simultaneously, we understood the huge importance of compiling a Yizkor Book, this holy work, to which each Jew originally from Rozniatow should contribute by writing down his own or somebody else's reminiscences, facts, events, episodes, legends — all that is related to Rozniatow, to Rozniatower Jews, and to Jewish life in Rozniatow.

We felt that an important and holy duty was incumbent upon us, a duty that we are obliged to pay back to the tragically slaughtered Rozniatower community, with whom we lived and suffered together, dreamed, fought, and strove for better times, for a better life.

We accomplished this. First of all we strained all our resources to procure the material basis for editing and printing this book, which we are now presenting to you. The assistance that we received from our natives in America, Belgium and Australia was great.

We did all that we could to make this Rozniatower Yizkor Book look richer, more valuable in its content, better and more aesthetic in its exterior form.

Our shtetl was small and poor. But it had a rich way of living well established in Judaism and Jewish traditions. Jews lived in Rozniatow for centuries, and they endured misfortunes, torture, evil decrees, and persecution. Nevertheless, they laid down deep roots there.

All that characterizes Jewish life was present in Rozniatow. Our shtetl had interesting types of healthy common folk and fine scholars[3], Hassidim[4], and enlightened people (Maskilim)[5]. There is plenty to tell about them and we tried to immortalize them, to erect a monument for all those people, whom we will never forget.

We are doing this for our exterminated shtetl Rozniatow.

With bowed heads and wrung hands, we stand before the modest monument to our vanished Jewish community. We unite with the holy memory of the killed martyrs.

We feel bad about those who were annihilated and will never be forgotten!

May this Yizkor Book serve as a permanent reminder to the future generations, who will see in it a document and a mirror of a rich way of life, which is no longer here.

May the scream that emanates from this book never be silenced, and never cease to be heard by people, until the end of time.

**Zecharia Friedler**

The committee at a memorial service in 1971 From left: Dr. Alter Berger of blessed memory and his wife, Bendet Schwartz, the Cantor Binyamin Unger, Zecharia Friedler, Yehuda Har Zohar-Zauerberg and Mordechai Stern

## TRANSLATOR'S FOOTNOTES

1. "Aliyah" means immigration to Israel.

2. "Azkara" is a memorial gathering.

3. "Scholars" is to be understood as scholars of Judaism.

4. "Hassidim" are adherents of a Hassidic sect, who are faithful to their Hassidic Rabbis.

5. "Enlightened" are adherents of the Haskala enlightenment which introduced secular wisdom into Judaism.

{245}

# The History of Our Shtetl
## by Moshe David Lutwak

### Translated by Jerrold Landau from a draft by Isak Shteyn

Elementary school and the post office on the left.

{246}

**The End Came**

The life of the shtetl is gone. The noise of the weekly bazaars, the tumult of the buying and selling in Rozniatow, the hubbub of the street vendors and peddlers near their stands with different merchandise has ceased forever. The roads and lanes are wasted and voided.

Kith and kin went their last way together.

Never again will the voices of the prayers from the Rozniatow synagogues rise to the heavens. The chant of the youngest students from the Cheders[1] and the tunes of the Yeshiva students will never be heard again. No one will tell of it until the era of the Messiah and the redemption.

Our shtetl is empty, vacant of its Jews, deprived of its Jewish character.

Only the silent walls of the houses lament the orphaned and bereaved cry of a well-rooted Jewish shtetl that lost its children and builders[2].

All were strangled and immersed in blood.

The blood is still seething.

**The Editors**

{247}

## My Years in Rozniatow

I, a modest Rozniatower native close to seventy years old, will try to relate my recollections as a contribution to the Yizkor Book to be assembled in honor of our shtetl martyrs, those good and precious Jews who perished for the sanctification of G-d's name. Those memories will cover the time from my earliest childhood, since my senses started to function and I understood that I also belong to G-d's creation and can also have a say or simply talk at random; until August 1932, when I left Rozniatow on the way to the golden land of America. My brother Yeshaya and other natives, men who themselves experienced and miraculously outlived those difficult years, will report the subsequent events that occurred until the Hitlerian Holocaust.

The Beginning

Rozniatow is situated in Eastern Galicia not far from the Eastern Carpathian Mountains. It is a small remote town that is not even on the map, 7.5 km from the railroad station Rozniatow-Krechowice on the Stryj-Stanislawow[3] line. Two rivulets, the Czeczwa and the Duba, flow through the region.

There are two versions of the origin of the name "Rozniatow."

One version asserts that many centuries ago, a huge massacre of the inhabitants of the town occurred. Why? Perhaps the enslaved peasants stirred up a rebellion against their oppressors – the magnates, knights, counts, etc., and therefore a massacre was perpetrated upon them. In Ukrainian the term for massacre is "resnya" which led to naming the town Rozniatow.

The second version also originates from the time when noblemen, who enslaved the peasants, reigned over the town and its environs. One of those noblemen was Count Rozniatow, and the town took the aristocrat's name, Rozniatow.

There is evidence that the rulers of Rozniatow and its environs waged war with their neighbors. The rivulet served as a defense line against an attack from other noblemen. The courthouse was constructed as a stronghold with a tower as an observation point. The hill upon which the court stands and the hill that leads to the forest demonstrate the same fortifications.

Austria-Hungary ruled over all of Galicia, which was given to her during the 1772-1793 partition of Poland among the great powers — Russia, Prussia and Austria. This partition is known in history as "Rozbior Polski". In 1772 Austria obtained Western Galicia and in 1793 it also obtained Eastern Galicia. Contrary to the expansionist external policies of the Hapsburgs, which consisted of seizing and annexing foreign territories, their internal policy was liberal. The citizens enjoyed all the freedoms, with no differences between different races or nationalities. These liberal policies started in 1848 with the reign of Kaiser Franz Josef I, whom the Jews considered as a benevolent emperor and who was revered by all the citizens of the country.

The political status of the population of Eastern Galicia under Austria, the Jews included, experienced several metamorphoses. Under the reign of Kaiser Franz Josef I, the Jews enjoyed all civil rights and freedoms on an equal footing with all other citizens. Jews worked as government officials, and in all branches of commerce and industry. There were Jewish judges, teachers in elementary and middle schools as well as university professors. There were even Jewish officers of all ranks in the army. The Jews elected their own deputies to the parliament in Vienna.

The Jews of Eastern Galicia lived among Poles, Ukrainians and Germans. In Galicia there also lived Karaites[4] near Halicz, Armenians, Gypsies and Nomads. The Poles were in the majority in Galicia. The legal status of Galicia was autonomous self-administration under the control of the Austrian crown. Actually the Poles, who were notorious Jew haters, ruled in Galicia. The language of the country, mandatory in all government offices, was Polish. In the schools, Polish and Ukrainian were taught but German was also mandatory. The official language of the government was German. Government buildings carried Polish inscriptions as well. Nevertheless, the Jews carried on their daily life undisturbed. If an injustice were committed against a citizen, he could turn to a court with a complaint and have it adjudicated.

{249}

### The courthouse

Aside from the fact that it excelled in its architectural beauty and surrounding landscape, the courthouse building was of enormous importance to the town and made for closer relations with the surrounding community. Rozniatow had excellent Jewish attorneys who enjoyed solid respect in the court. Relations with the Christian population were proper.

The courthouse

## The Great Fire

I remember when the great fire broke out in Rozniatow and half of the town burned down. I was a little child then, not yet attending school. I saw people with their meager belongings standing near the Polish monastery below the hill. It looked very strange to me. I ran around and could not understand what was going on. Years later, when I spoke to older Rozniatower Jews about that event, they told me that it was really a huge fire and almost half the shtetl burned down.

The fire broke out outside of the town at Bendet Yampel (Herzl's son) and proceeded along all the houses of that same side to the Ringplatz, where Yossel Berger erected his brick house years later. Further, the fire consumed the whole row of houses belonging to Klein and Frenkel and all the way to the corner of Nissen Shindler's house. Years later, the victims of the fire reconstructed their homes.

At that time, the general population of Rozniatow constituted about three thousand people including 180-200 Jewish families. Ukrainians were the majority. A few tens of Ukrainians were rich landowners with houses and huge herds of livestock. The others were poor landowners with small houses that had thatched roofs plus a cow and a pair of piglets. Some Ukrainians were government officers and craftsmen.

{250}

## Jewish Livelihood

Most Jews were merchants, government officials, craftsmen, animal traders, brokers, peddlers, coachmen, teachers, private tutors, lawyers, writers, solicitors, match-makers (Reuven Getzl), members of the burial society, a few grave diggers, stall keepers, tavern keepers (Chanina Weissmans).

Four Rozniatower Jews possessed fields, Leizer Turteltaub (who also managed the birth registry), his sons Itzi and Motty and Lipa Taneh. Only Itzi Turteltaub cultivated his fields by himself. He was the only real Jewish peasant. The other three hired people to work their fields.

In addition, there were attorneys, physicians, barber-surgeons (feldschers), cupping glass[5] and leech[6] placers, female charmers and wax founders (Sosye-Feyge Gelobter), clergymen, beadles, women prompters of prayers for female worshippers (Sara-Malka Wechter), women administering ablutions to women, midwives (Zlate Bera Zimmermann).

Most of the Poles, who were new arrivals, were Austrian government officials, and a few peasants and craftsmen.

Rozniatow itself was never an industrial city, but in the neighboring town of Broszniow, some 8 kilometers from the city, there was a huge steam sawmill (tartak paravy) under the name "Firm F. Glezinger", whose center was located in Czyeszyn. This firm employed Jews as well as others both as officers and workers. In 1910 the firm built a narrow-gauge railway. Every day it drove from Broszniow through Rozniatow, Perehinsko and other villages deep into the forests to Osmoloda, which is near the Hungarian border. From there, it brought cut logs to the sawmill for further processing. On its way there and back, it transported passengers free of charge.

In Rozniatow the firm had a farm near Nachman Sheiner, the bookbinder. The manager of that farm was a Hungarian man named Shamlo who was fat and had long hair. He was very talented in breeding pigs. Weinless was his housekeeper. Shimke Hillmann from Perehinsko was also employed there.

There were naphtha pits not far away from Rozniatow. There was a refinery in Ripne where the naphtha was filtered. In that old village and located on the river Fyszarka there was a water sawmill and a water mill belonging to Vovtche Taneh.

About 2 kilometers from the city, on the way to Swaryczow, there was an oil refinery owned by Hersh Rechtschaffen. The refinery worked only with cheap oil called "Lachting" that was used only by the gentiles.

In all, there were three water mills. One was at the monastery below the hill belonging to Yaakov Meir Lehrer, where the manager was Yossel Helfman who had a son in America who was a garment manufacturer. Our father taught the miller's son, Eli. The second water mill was across the river. From all the millers of that mill I remember only Efraim Rechtschaffen. In that mill there was a worker called Chaim Kasner whom people called "Chaim from the mill" and who lived near the Beis Midrash[7].

The landowner Lipa Weinfeld, a rich Jew who possessed many fields, lived in the village of Szwaryczow, about 3 kilometers from the city. His son Moynik was also our father's student. One of his grandchildren, Sanye Freier, is a real estate broker in New Jersey and is very wealthy.

{251}

### Communal Relations between the Jewish and Christian Communities

What were the communal relations between the Jews and the Christians in Rozniatow like? The Jews carried on no conflicts with Christians, besides those arising in trade exchange when one bought something from the other and at similar situations. Rozniatow was no exception to other cities when it came to anti-Semitism. The Ukrainians and the Poles were anti-Semites. The slogans for both of them were "Bij Zyda"[8] or "Zyd Zlodzej"[9], "Parch"[10] and other expressions such as "Zyd z nieba to wiezyc mu nie trzeba" [11]. This proverb speaks for itself. Besides that, the clergymen used to preach hatred and enmity to Jews from their pulpits. There were exceptions to this in Rozniatow — Malinowski, Jaczkowski, and others.

The majority of the Ukrainian peasants were small landowners and their harvests were sometimes insufficient to feed even their own families. They used to walk barefoot all summer and until late autumn. They envied the Jews who lived and dressed better, and they were convinced that all the money that the Jews realized from sales they kept. They didn't trust Jews, thinking that they were charged high prices and were obliged to sell their produce almost gratis. Besides that, among the peasants were many illiterates.

The Poles, most of them governmental officials with good salaries, were materially better off than the Jews and the peasants. The trouble with them was that they preferred to enjoy life and to squander almost their whole salary in a few days on drink. When the bartender refused to sell beverages on credit, they vented their anger on the Jews.

We can divide the Rozniatower Jews in several economic groups. There were people with well-established businesses who owned their own houses, earned their livelihood with surplus, and lived comfortably according to the standard of living of that time. In Rozniatow there were no very wealthy people, possessing huge capital, houses, fields and forests. Another group was composed of the small storekeepers. They earned their livelihood through toil, but they possessed their own little houses. Among the craftsmen were some who could hardly procure all that was needed for the Sabbath, and there were even some very poor people.

About 90% of the Jews owned their own little houses — some were bigger, others smaller. The house and land taxes were very low because the government wanted to stimulate the building of industries and agriculture.

All of the stores were concentrated around the "Ringplatz" and along the city in a dense configuration — one shop next to another — and sometimes one shop was divided into two separated by a little wall. The inscriptions on the stores' signboards announced what was for sale. There were haberdashery stores with articles for peasant women like corals, ribbons in all kinds of colors, beads, mirrors, combs, needles, thread, yarn, earthenware pots, glassware, plus more trifles and embellishments.

A piece of leather on a stick announced that leather was sold there. Meat or bone-markets didn't need signboards because the meat could be smelled outside.

{253}

**Fairs**

The fairs and the weekly market days held on Wednesdays played a very important and large role in the amount of money realized by sales. Every city from the Dolina District had its fairs on different weekdays several times a year. They were called Michaela, Ivana, Yakova, Yuria, etc. The fairs were looked at as a Messiah, because the money realized from the sales meant a great deal to Rozniatower merchants. Good sales helped to pay the bills of promissory notes and debts in a timely fashion and helped with the purchase of new merchandise. Therefore the preparations for the fairs started weeks earlier.

The fair in Rozniatow began at daybreak. Out-of-town merchants were already there laying out their goods on stands. Peasants with their cattle and horses for sale as well as cattle and horse merchants came to the animal bazaar. Every empty corner of the market place and its side lanes was occupied by peasant wagons loaded with agricultural products for sale.

Then the taverns filled with peasants with drunken voices even though the fair was still in full and fervent swing. People bought and sold, comic actors showed their acrobatic tricks, fire-eaters appeared as did burglars and stilt walkers. Poor people played on their street organs and sold cards that were pulled out by a parrot beak and that predicted everyone's future. All kinds of beggars and cripples were begging with their traditional tunes. An old beggar with a white beard and big spectacles on his nose was seated and read monotonously from a big book written with an evangelical handwriting; nobody understood him. Not far away from him, seated on a bundle of straw, was a blind beggar with a "shire"[12] singing and playing melancholy songs that tugged at the heart. A huge crowd of peasants surrounded him. The peasant women cried bitterly and threw coins.

Violent cries of drunkards were heard from the tavern of Melech Gross. They fought with each other and started to riot in the tavern. Mordechai Gross seized a bench and hit the peasants over their heads. Several of them were lying already quietly on the floor and in this way he mollified the drunken crowd.

In the late evening the crowd scattered and gradually drove off and with this the fair ended.

The whole family — the wife and the children who have finished school and the Cheder — had to help provide for the family's livelihood. In Rozniatow there were women who did better in business than their husbands; they had "business heads". These included Adela Leizer's[13] Geller, Feyge Beyle Shlomo Foygel's, Mamze Yosef Shimon's, Gittel Chaye Adler's, etc.

This was the way life went on in Rozniatow day by day. The yoke of sustenance was heavy. Only with trouble and pain could you gain your daily bread plus something to put on the bread. The small merchant, the craftsman, the village teacher and the impoverished man fared the worst. During the week they used to survive on anything — black bread, coffee with chicory sweetened with saccharine. The main concern of the poor man was how to provide for the Sabbath! They were glad to have a little animal head, a leg with a marrowbone, tripe, lungs, liver, other giblets, and a potato pudding (kugel). For the third Sabbath Meal there was available drelia.[14] At times there was also calves foot jelly (pt-cha), and sometimes even a spicy dish, but no frozen goods.

Every Jew, rich or poor, used to discard his weekly crudeness, feeling a kind of spiritual elevation until the end of the Sabbath. With the arrival of the new week, there was a return of the yoke of sustenance, a burden more difficult than the parting of the Red Sea.[15]

The most popular food in Rozniatow was potatoes. There were houses where potatoes were eaten thrice a day — the whole week, the whole year. As the little song asserts "Sunday potatoes, Monday potatoes..." They were eaten in different ways: not peeled, "in their shirts," with herring, fried, cooked with soup, with fat, and with grieven[16]. Even a pudding (kugel) for Sabbath was made from potatoes, as well as pancakes for Chanukah (latkes), and drop scones for Passover. There were also muffins stuffed with potatoes (knishes), and dumplings fried with onions (kluskes).

{255}

## Hassidim and Maskilim

Hassidim[17] and Maskilim[18] lived in Rozniatow. Leftist elements first appeared after the First World War. The enlightenment was unavoidable. Young Hassidic men used to devour enlightenment books. Differences in their mode of dress also became apparent. They started to wear short jackets, long pants, whole shoes, hard hats like the Germans, and hard stiffened collars with neckties. They cut their sidelocks (peyos) and beards. In winter they wore a jacket or a short or long pelisse[19]. Women had more difficulty changing their appearance. They wore their own hair instead of a wig, and a cap over the head.

The Hassidic dress was traditional: a large cloth or velvet hat, a large cap, a coat, a ritual four-cornered garment, short pants, white socks, and half shoes. On the Sabbath they wore a streimel[20] with lace, a silk gabardine; in summer a light jacket and in winter an overcoat or a sheepskin coat. On Saturday, unmarried young men used to wear a kind of a fur cap called a "spodek."

1) Dr.Sapir, 2) Dr.Feuer, 3) Dr.Sabat, 4) Dr.Diamand, 5) Dr.Redisch, 6) Director Blaustein, 7) Dr.Kahane, 8) Dr. Katz, 9) Dr. Menkes, 10) Magister Leib Meizeles, 11) Magister Leib Horowitz, 12) Prinz, 13) Director Rosenberg

During the whole week Hassidic women wore floor length dresses. In summer, the dresses swept away the dust. On rainy days, the dress had to be lifted up with one hand while the other hand held an open umbrella. A blouse with long sleeves closed up at the neck was worn over the dress. On the Sabbath, they wore the same clothes, adorned with a little bit of jewelry, as well as a jacket called a "yupke".

The enlightenment movement brought Zionism in its wake. Among the first enlightened and Zionist pioneers in Rozniatow were: our father Chaim Shimon Lutwak; the brothers Leibtshe, Meir and Abraham Yankel; Meir Kaufman; Yudele Melamed's son; Bendet Spiegel; Mendel Horowitz; Yisrael Leib Ortmann; Meir Ortmann; Hersch Mendel; Shalom Rechtschaffen; Aharon Weissmann; the brothers Shlomo and Itzi Gross; Vove Chaye Adlers from the old village; Hermann Horowitz; Moshe

Barnik; David Barnik; Yissachar Stern; Leizer Tepper; the brothers Bonye and Azriel Reizler; Yechezkel Nussbaum; Yomtzi Frisch; Binem Geller; Dr. Alter Berger; and may he live long Dr. Yaakov Yankel; Yehoshua Ortmann, a son of Mishel Ortmann; Dulik and Nunek Lusthaus. Leizer Tepper was from Rozniatow, his former wife was Gustava and her father was Pinchas Reiter. He used to worship in the Beis Midrash. He was an intelligent man. He wore a "Kaiser beard" like Franz Joseph and a pincenez. He lived a short time in Rozniatow in the house of Meir Taub and Blume Ayngemachts from Stryj where I attended the gymnasium.

At that time, almost a century ago (in the 1870s), our father was already openly reading enlightenment books and the Hebrew weekly "Hamitzpeh", which he read for many years." He did not hide this from anyone. For him it was quite natural and he saw nothing bad or heretical in his readings. But Jews of his age and environment could not understand how a Jew who teaches Torah to Jewish children could read newspapers and seemingly heretical books. They felt that such a person departs — G-d forbid — from the right path. Our father knew how to learn well, like every other Rozniatower Jewish citizen of his age and environment. He served as the Torah reader in the Beis Midrash. He had nice handwriting, which was an important trait in those days, and was able to compose a good Hebrew letter written in flowery language.

We lived in our own house near the synagogue. We purchased it from Yitzchak Schwalb. He manned the tollgate in Stryten Nizjtne in his earlier years. This was a city gate that charged a toll for wagons that entered or left the town.

{257}

A group of communal activists. From right: Shlomo Widmann, Peretz Sperling, Feivel Weber, Sender Friedler, Shalom Rechtschaffen, Herman Rubin, Avraham Groll, Zishe Aryeh Kuperberg, Leizer Deutscher, Shalom Hoffmann.

When I was born, our father was already a teacher and did not take part in local politics. The enlightenment movement broke the ice in Rozniatow. People started to study secular subjects in addition to the Torah. They dressed in a German style with short jackets. They wore white hats with a crease in the middle as well as hard hats.

At that time the first worldwide Zionist Congress took place in Basle under the chairmanship of Dr. Theodore Herzl of blessed memory. The enlightened in Rozniatow were also the pioneers and first members of the Zionist association "Chovevei Zion"[21]. It was located in the house of Moshe David Yekeles where Esther Lusthaus used to live. Later on, the association was in Sosye Heller's brick house. Other members of the Chovevei Zion were the baker Wolkentreiber who did not return home from World War I, Dr. Alter Chaim Berger, Meir Taub, Shaul Schwalb, the son of Avraham Schuster, and our brother Hersch Mordechai Lutwak. Dr. Alter Berger and his sister Tinka now live in Israel. Artzi Berger died in Israel. Our brother was an Austrian officer, fell into Russian captivity, came to America in 1921, died young, and left a wife with two children. His son is a doctor and conducts scientific research for the American Government. He is a lecturer at Cornell University.

{258}

**First Drama Circle**

The association did good work for the Zionist idea, collected money for the "Keren Kayemet Leyisrael"[22] and for the first time in the history of Rozniatow performed the play "The Jewish King Lear" By Jacob Gordon. Thanks to my brother, I had the privilege to assist at the general rehearsal and the performance itself. It was performed in a hall in Moses Rosenman's brick house, where the Poles previously had their sports club called "Sokol." It was performed to a packed hall with great success.

The members of the drama circle included Shalom Rechtschaffen in the main role, David Mosheles as the Jewish King Lear, Aharon Weissmann as Shamai the servant, a certain person who was a writer for Dr. Sapir, Meir Taub, and others. Shaul Schwalb was the prompter. The performance was unusual because men — Yissachar Stern and David Barnik — dressed in women's clothes and played women's roles. It is necessary to take into account the circumstances of that time, in that a Rozniatower girl would not dare even to look at a boy never mind to perform with him in the theatre. This would have been rakishness; may the merciful G-d save us. The boys would do it willingly. They would like to have romances with the girls, but a girl of a good family was permitted to be friendly only with girls of her class.

{258}

**A Torah Scroll is Carried to the Synagogue**

It happened during the intermediate days of Sukkot[23] 1909. A huge Sukka was erected near Melech Gross. Late in the night, the Torah Scroll was brought into the synagogue where a huge crowd was assembled. Some people stayed outside. Hersch Rechtschaffen sang "LeDavid Mizmor"[24].

From there people went to Itzi Eli Rosenbaum's house where a banquet in honor of the delegate of the Central Zionist Organization took place. Music played and people amused themselves until late in the night.

The preparations for the celebration at the conclusion of the writing of the Torah Scroll went on for a long time. Money was collected in and around Rozniatow at every possible opportunity. The Torah Scroll was written by Lipa Sofer[25] from Rozniatow, the father of Shmuelzi Sofer and the uncle of Moshe Fruchter.

The first Hebrew school was in the house of Eli Mordechai Brodfeld. Most of the students were boys. The older girls were seated at separate desks. I was also a student at that Hebrew school. The Hebrew teacher was Yehoshua Reiter, who was the first Hebrew teacher in Rozniatow. We had other teachers after he left.

Of the Hebrew girl students, I remember Esther Haftel the daughter of Hersch Rechtschaffen, who died young.

This was the blossoming period of the Zionist movement in Rozniatow. Later on the activity waned because some members left — some for Germany, some for other places — where they remained and got married. No new members came. This situation lasted until the outbreak of the First World War.

{259}

### The Activity of the Jewish Community and its Head Vove Hoffmann

Like all other shtetls in Galicia, Rozniatow was a typical Jewish shtetl with all its virtues and defects, with its solemnity and humor, and with a traditional Jewish lifestyle that was organized by an entity called "die Judische Kultusgemeinde"[26]. The Jewish Community had its legal status as an autonomous body under the supervision of the "starostowa"[27]] of Dolina. The functions of the Jewish Community were to provide for the religious needs of the city's Jews including: support for the synagogues, the rabbi, the judge, the ritual slaughterers (shochtim); the appointment of the trustees of the synagogues (gabbaim) and the beadles (shamashim); support for the city bathhouse, the "Hekdesch"[28] where they brought the dead corpses from the region to be prepared for burial; and support for the cemetery. The Head of the congregation was Wolf (Vove) Hoffmann, who represented the Jewish Community before the Dolina starostowa. He was a rich, respected citizen, always serious, energetic, a traditional Jew, neatly dressed, tall with a nice beard, whose business involved naphtha and heating wood. He worshipped the whole year in the Kloiz[29] and led the services one day of Rosh Hashanah in the synagogue and Simchat Torah[30] in the Beis Midrash. From there faithful congregants used to go to his house; my father used to take me with him. After "Musaf"[31] there was served "Kiddush"[32].

Vove Hoffmann was the president of the Rozniatow Community until the First World War. I do not remember elections on democratic principles. He was appointed by the starosta[33] of Dolina as president of the Jewish Community and was simultaneously the Bürgermeister[34] (burmistrz) of the city itself. He was also appointed to this office by the starosta. Elections were first held for the presidency of the Jewish Community and for the mayoralty only during the 1920s, under Polish rule.

Hoffmann's children earned their livelihoods honorably. From the family there survived his daughters Taube, and Eszye and Motek Weissmann. They all live in New Jersey. Rozie Falik, Eszye Treu and Leib Hoffmann's two sons live in Israel.

Zecharya David Liebermann played a very important role in the community and in the city. For many years he was active in the administration of the community. For a time he was its president and a member of the City Council. He concerned himself with Jewish interests, was esteemed by the starosta in Dolina, and his views were respected. Together with Vove Hoffmann, he belonged, to the elite of the city. He was an intelligent person who was fluent in Polish, German, and Ukrainian. He possessed great life wisdom, was modern, dressed neatly, wore a patriarchal white beard, and was well groomed. He lived on the way to the Church. Earlier his house was at the "Ringplatz," but he sold it to Yosef Shimon Stern. He presided over an aristocratic, traditional Jewish home, where Yiddish and Polish were spoken. If a Jew entered his house, he felt comfortable and wasn't compelled to hold his hat in his hands. He was popular in the whole region.

Leizer Itzik Lew, Liebermann's father-in-law, lived in the same building. He was a Jew with a delicate face, a silvery beard, neatly dressed in a Jewish style, held in his hand a stick with a silver handle. He used to greet everybody, bidding his "good morning" before his acquaintance could do so. He sold brandy many years ago in the old house where Vove Hoffmann also lived.

I used to go there every Friday to buy brandy for Sabbath for 1.5 "kreuzer." There stood huge barrels filled with brandy. A Jewish bookkeeper worked there, who sold the drink, pouring it into small or large bottles. When I came there for the first time, I was astonished that the salesman was measuring the brandy so stingily. When I said to him: "Give me a bit more brandy. Why are you so sparing?" he became angry with me.

Yankel, the son of Leizer Itzik, lived not far away, on the way to the river near Yosef Yehuda Gedalya's Rotenberg. He married Zecharya David Liebermann's daughter.

Yankel's brother, Mottel Lew died as a young man.

Leizer Itzik Lew, together with his son and son-in-law, continued in partnership to trade in beer, brandy, and other alcoholic beverages. Leizer Itzik Lew and Vove Hoffmann were in-laws.

From these two large families only a few survivors remained: Klara Diamand who is the widow of the Dr. Morris Diamand, Simon (Shimke) Liebermann, and Anda (Chanele) Sternglass. All of them are living in New York.

The rabbi of the city, Rabbi Hemerling of holy blessed memory, was the spiritual leader of the Rozniatower Jews. He was an honest and refined person, a scholar and a G-d fearing man of stately appearance. He was involved night and day with the study of Torah and the service of G-d. He used to pray in the Kloiz and was very modest. He lived in his own house near Meir Taub. The community paid him a weekly salary. He also performed marriage ceremonies for which he was compensated. The rabbi was also the judge at religious lawsuits, for which he was paid by the litigants. However, very few religious lawsuits were adjudicated in Rozniatow, for most Jews preferred the courts.

The Rozniatower Rabbi passed away in the 1920s. They did not hire a new Rabbi until the 1930s. The "dayan"[35] Reb Yehuda Hersch Korn of blessed memory substituted for the deceased Rabbi. Although he did not have the title "Rabbi," he took over and accomplished all the Rabbi's functions.

The sources income of the community were from: the fee for slaughtering, the sale of the "Aliyot"[36] on holidays, the use of the bathhouse, the fees paid for the burial of the deceased people which the heirs had to pay from their inheritance. No fees were charged from poor deceased people.

The community also had the right to impose a tax on the local Jewish population. However this was not practiced to avoid shaming[37] poor people who could not pay the tax.

{262}

### The Synagogue, the Kloiz, and the Beis Midrash

There were three large places of worship in Rozniatow: a synagogue, a Kloiz, and a Beis Midrash. They were located in one area of the town on the way to the bazaar. This street was called "Ulica Boznica"[38] during Polish rule. There was also a "Minyan"[39] in the old town where those that lived there worshiped, because it was too far for them to come to worship in the city.

In the synagogue there was a special room called "Shulchel"[40] where services were conducted as well. The Hassidim and the rabbi worshipped in the Kloiz. The elite, the aristocrats, and on the High Holy Days also the intelligentsia, worshipped in the synagogue.

The general public as well as important citizens — such as the brothers Pinye and Yossel Berger, Shmuel Schwindler, Chaim Rotenberg, Meir Taneh, etc. — used to worship in the Beis Midrash. The congregants elected the "Gabaim"[41] but anybody could become a shamash (beadle) if he wanted. The community did not pay the shamashim. They were paid for lighting lamps at the anniversaries of the congregants' ancestors' deaths (yahrzeits) and from participating at weddings, circumcisions, and funeral ceremonies. They could not earn their livelihood from their roles as shamashim alone. They needed some supplementary occupation.

Before "Mincha"[42] on the eve of Yom Kippur, the shamash put a plate on a table in the antechamber of the Synagogue where the worshippers used to leave some money. The shamash also received a few groszy[43] for beating "Malkot"[44].

The Gabaim received no monetary reward. Their work was a matter of honor.

For many years, the shamash in the house of Worship was Kopel, an elderly Jew with a white beard and joined eyebrows who loved the bitter drop,[45] which was never too small. Every day one person or another observed "yahrzeit" to celebrate an ancestor's death, or a circumcision, a wedding or other joyous occasion. He never got drunk, even on Purim and Simchat Torah when it is a "Mitzvah"[46] to be drunk.

He was typical of Jewish shamashim from the old days. He considered his work as a shamash to be sacred task and performed his duties faithfully. The Kloiz was cleaned regularly with the help of his wife.

Kopel awakened summer and winter at daybreak and knocked at Jewish houses with his hammer and sang his call: "Arise to the service of G-d!" He also used to announce the midnight services[47]. He was a quiet man and lived near the teacher David Rotenbach.

On a night of Rosh Hashanah during the 1920s, a fire broke out, and the old Kloiz burnt down along with many other Jewish homes. The House was later rebuilt as a brick house.

## Katriel the son of Kopel, the shamash of the Kloiz

Katriel the son of Kopel, the shamash
of the Kloiz

The shamash was a central figure in the Kloiz, where the worshippers felt as if they were at home. People from all of the strata in town would come in — rich and poor, scholars and simple Jews. It was the task of the shamash to satisfy all groups. He created a good atmosphere in the Kloiz.}

All the Torah Scrolls were rescued from that fire.

The shamash of the synagogue at that time was Moshe Kaywisz. He lived near Yankel Lew. After reading the "Ketuba"[48] under the "Chupa"[49] during wedding ceremonies in front of the synagogue, he used to fold the Ketuba and to present it to the bride with the following wishes in Polish "here is your contract for 120 years." Although he was not very healthy — he used to cough — he was also devoted to his duties as a shamash.

I remember the old Beis Midrash and the initiative of Shmuel Schwindler and Chaim Yisrael Yaakov's Rotenberg to build a new Beis Midrash. These two people worked indefatigably until late at night. Shmuel Schwindler even kneaded the clay, plastered the walls, and doing other work for the new House of Study.

Shmuel Schwindler lived near the bazaar on the way to the "Zarynok" where people used to bathe. He used to export calves to Vienna in his younger years. He was an honest pious Jew and of good character. He asked for no honors and was far from mingling in community affairs. He was an adherent of the enlightened people, meaning the Zionists, worked assiduously his whole life, went to the House of Study twice a day to pray, and studied the Torah as well.

During the winter, he used to come at daybreak into the House of Study and heated the stove to warm up the room before people assembled to pray with the first minyan. The words that the cantor recites before the Musaf prayer on Sabbaths can be applied to him: "and all those who occupy themselves with communal affairs in faithfulness". He did everything that he did faithfully, with all his heart, while not seeking recognition. On Rosh Hashanah and on Yom Kippur he used to conduct the Shacharit[50] service.

I was still too young to know from where the money came for building the new Beis Midrash. Of course, the community gave its contribution. Some money was collected and, I am sure, that Jews helped as much as they could with their own means. All the seats for the High Holy Days were sold, and this money also went toward the new Beis Midrash.

Considering all of the virtues of Shmuel Schwindler, the following question arises: how did it happen that such an honest Jew bears the name "Schwindler"[51]? The story is as follows. When Austria gave the Jews surnames, every Jew could select for himself a name of his desire; otherwise an official gave him a name. An official came to Reb Shmuel's great-great grandfather, who gave evasive answers to all the official's questions. He even mocked the official a little bit. The unsatisfied and angry official then said to the stubborn Jew in German: "You are a schwindler and that will be your name."

Herman Lutwak

Our name Lutwak originates as well from that era. However, the story is slightly different. Our great-great grandfather fled the Russian pogroms from Lithuania and crossed the Austrian border bleeding from his wounds. After he received medical help, the officials asked him where he was from. He said he was from Lithuania, and this is the origin of the family name Lutwak.

In Rozniatow the services were conducted in all prayer houses according to Nusach Sephard prayer rite[52]. In other communities, the services were conducted according to the Ashkenazic prayer rites.

The Lutwak family. Reb Chaim Shimon and his daughter. David Moshe and Shaya.

{265}

## Shamashim (Beadles)

The shamash of the old Beis Midrash was old Meir, an old Jew with a big white beard stained brown from tobacco. Every Chanukah he was the one who lit the candles in the Beis Midrash. He sweated with his two besoms[53] while sitting on the highest bench in the bathhouse.

After him, the shamash was Baruch Leib Milrad, the father-in-law of Pintzi Schwalb. He was a tall man with a gray beard, and he smelled of tobacco. In the intermediate weekdays of Sukkot, he used to carry to the Jewish homes the "Etrog"[54], so that the women and the children could fulfill as well the commandment of blessing the Etrog. He was rewarded for that with a few coins.

Pintzi Schwalb became the shamash after Baruch Leib. In his younger years, he was a cobbler. Of short stature, he had a blond beard, cocked his head a little bit to one side, and his health was weak. He owned a little shop with different used articles located on the Ringplatz corner near the store of Meir Frenkel. He was intelligent, and he was very familiar with the ways of serving as a shamash. He directed and managed the House of Study independently; nobody could dictate anything. He used to divide the "Aliyot" to the general satisfaction of all and was friendly with all of the worshippers. He had an admirable memory and remembered by heart everybody's Yahrzeit[55]. If somebody forgot a yahrzeit, they could get the correct information from Pintzi. He could read and write in Yiddish only. He could have been a minister had he also known Polish and German.

Michael Weissmann, the manufacturer of soda water, had a good memory as well. On Sabbaths the siphon bottles were taken on credit because it was prohibited to write, and Michael had them all in his memory. He used to collect the empty bottles on Sunday and he was never mistaken regarding the money. He used to worship in the Beis Midrash and his factory was on the Ringplatz.

Pintzi Schwalb was also the communal shamash. Friday evening he used to call out in the center of the market place "Go to the synagogue" which was a signal that the stores should be closed and people must attend the synagogues for the welcoming of the Sabbath. Later on this function was taken over by Leib Press, the shamash of the Kloiz.

{265}

## The Maskil[56] Chaim Yoel Taneh

The prayer houses were not only places to worship, but also places where local news was aired and local and world politics discussed. A big expert in world news was Chaim Yoel Taneh, a Maskil, who dressed in a modern style and conducted a lottery. From time to time he used to go to Vienna where he worked on licenses and tarried pretty long. When he came home for the Sabbath, people surrounded him in the Beis Midrash and he told them world news in detail until the candles in the chandeliers burned out.

He was a well-educated and intelligent man, as were his children. Years later he moved near Lipa Taneh, and after World War I, he lived with his family in Vienna. The further fate of Chaim Yoel Taneh and his family is unknown to me.

{266}

## The Parliament of Yossel Kasner

There was another place where there was a source for domestic and foreign news. In the front room at Yossel Kasner's home, everybody had free admission from the morning until the night each day of the week except on Sabbaths and festivals. It was a kind of a casino, if not a small parliament. Order reigned there automatically. Everybody could speak undisturbed when he wanted to and about what he wanted. The meetings (one in, the second out) and the members were permanent.

Sometimes, serious moments predominated there as well — people poured out their hearts. The spokesman was Vovtshe Taneh, a humorous man who was experienced in community affairs and who owned a sawmill on the river Fyszarka near the hill. Unfortunately, nobody from his family survived.

Yossel Kasner was by nature a good and friendly man. One of his biggest virtues was his fulfilling the commandment of benevolence[57]. Every shopkeeper, small or large, could get a loan any time from Yossel Kasner; nobody was refused. For a businessman this was like a breath of fresh air. He even helped out some merchants with larger sums of money. He held the "trafik", that is the monopoly for tobacco in Rozniatow, as well as the sale of postcards, postmarks, and stamps. (A monopoly was a government concession given out to certain people in a city for the sale of certain types of merchandise – tobacco, alcohol, etc.) Estzye Walter from New York and Dwossye Orthmann from Vienna were the only survivors from this family.

From his earliest youth, he was distinguished by his delicate ambitions and his enterprising initiative. He was an officer in the Austrian army. He was imbued with the love of Zion and he was the founder of the Chovevei Zion organization in Rozniatow.}

{267}

## Chanina Weissmann

Chanina Weissmann was an important person and respectable citizen in Rozniatow. He ran a strictly orthodox house, was a smart man, had a say in the Kloiz, and his views were considered in the city. He managed a hotel and a restaurant in the center of the Ringplatz together with his two sons-in-law — Kanner who was a Zionist and Baruch Mintz. Tzvia, his wife used to receive guests with a very friendly greeting and to serve them tasty meals. The hotel was famous far and wide, as far as Vienna.

Chanina Weissmann was a scholar and a Hassid of the Gliener Rabbi, Reb Betzalel of holy blessed memory, who used to come every year to Rozniatow, where he worshipped in the Beis Midrash on the Sabbath. For that Sabbath, Hassidim from far away places used to congregate in Rozniatow. On one Sabbath, I saw in the Beis Midrash his substitute, the young Gliener Rabbi. I still remember the Bolekhower Rabbi Perlow of holy blessed memory, who perished in the Hitlerian Holocaust. I knew other Rebbes as well, who used to come to visit their Hassidim in Rozniatow.

Years later Rivkale Kahner's House was sold to the Friedler brothers, who owned dry goods stores in Rozniatow. Their father Berish Friedler has a brother, Nachum. A son of Leib Friedler, Berish, lives in Israel.

Pinye Kanner, a very well educated man and a descendant of the Weissmann family, lives in Israel.

{268}

### Feivel Reisler

The Jew Feivel Reisler, a Hassid who was a big scholar with a long white beard, lived in Rozniatow, and was a leather merchant on the Ringplatz. Every dawn, he used to perform the midnight service in the Kloiz. In summer and winter, even during the severest frosts, he used to take a bath before the morning service in the cold ritual pool. Then, he worshipped by heart counting every word loudly like pearls. It would already be ten o'clock in the morning when he came home.

{268}

### Mordechai Kriegel

Mordechai Meir Ber's Kriegel distinguished himself with his wisdom. A scholar, he used to worship in the Kloiz and to study there in the winter nights. Before Passover, he was one of the inspectors in the matzo bakeries. He owned a tavern on the Ringplatz. His wife, Sosye Meir Ber's, was a pious God-fearing woman and was very devoted to her husband and her children.

Itzi Gross was one of the Rozniatower Zionists. He loved Yiddish literature. He simply devoured the books of Shalom Aleichem and knew them almost by heart. He carried them about and many of his Yiddish books ultimately became part to the library in Rozniatow. As a boy, he studied in my father's school. He died as a young man.

I want to mention here the teachers as well: Yudale Kaufman, Itzik Barnik, Zeinwill David Roten-bach, Abba Taneh, and Yossel Avraham who became blind in his older years. Years later, there were also other teachers.

{269}

## Hersch Rechtschaffen

Hersch Rechtschaffen was a respected citizen of the city. He conducted himself and his family along traditional lines, attended the daily prayer services, studied, and conducted his affairs. His children behaved like their father, wore coats and side-locks and were his choir singers when he conducted the services. He had no influence only on Shlomo, because he was already suspected of heresy, i.e., in the enlightenment.

Hirsch Rechtschaffen was one of the best prayer leaders in the Beis Midrash on the High Holy Days. He worshipped with great fervor and heart, and the services extended until three o'clock in the afternoon.

Three of his sons survived, Yankel in Australia, and Mordechai and Zecharya in Israel.

When Hersch Rechtschaffen called out on Yom Kippur during Neila[58] "Open for us the gate," it seemed that the Heavens opened.

Due to a quarrel, he left the Beis Midrash and his place as cantor was taken over by Gedalya Weber, a leather merchant in the market center. He was a Kohen and he conducted services nicely. Years ago I met his brother and daughter.

{269}

## Reb Itzikel's Kloiz

There was another prayer house, called Reb Itzikel's Worship House, near Itzik Barnik. Reb Itzikl was not an official Rabbi. He did not lead Hassidic gatherings on Sabbaths and did not accept "kvitlech"[59] During my childhood I passed the old Kloiz almost every day on my way to school. It was located where the Jewish Community was located later.

This house was later rebuilt in a modern fashion, with a bathroom and mikva[60]. It became a big house. Still later it was sold to Leib Bermann. The niece of Rabbi Itzikl, Malkale, was married to Lipa Weinfeld's son from Szwariczow.

Elkone (Konye) Kortschmann led the first Minyan in the Beis Midrash on the Sabbath. He was a tailor and the head of the burial society (Chevra Kadisha); he busied himself with dead bodies. He was a firm person with a white beard and wore bifocal glasses. When he came to the cemetery, he brought a thick prayer book with all the prayers for the deceased. He lived near us in the closest house on the Schulgasse. He died in his great old age.

He has children and grandchildren who live here. One of them is Shmuel Kortschmann, the son of Leib Konye, who attends our meetings from time to time.

Chaim Landsmann lived near to us. One of his nephews, Max Strommwasser, lives in New York. His father, called Yankel Strommwasser, was our neighbor. He was a scholar and a cantor in the Beis Midrash. In his early years, he immigrated with his family to Germany, after having sold their house to Sosye Reiss, a sister of Meir Frenkel. Sosye's daughter Henye lives in New York. Finally, Avrumtzi Mark, the son-in-law of Melech Gross, bought the house.

Melech Gross, a pious, honest Jew, used to worship in the Beis Midrash. His seat was at the Eastern wall. He possessed a tavern on the Ringplatz and he sat in his office with an open book ready to study. His wife, Freyde, a clever and active woman, helped to manage the tavern. Survivors from this family were Shlomo Gross in Vienna or Israel, and two grandchildren Simcha and Moshe Gross in Israel. Years later Mordechai[61] Gross built a one-story brick house, where he managed a hotel, a tavern, and a restaurant.

There was another Jewish cartwright in Rozniatow, a brother of Avrumtchi Mark, an experienced workman. He lived in the old town and was sometimes engaged as a cartwright in the workshops of the Joint[62] in Stryj.

At the first Minyan on Sabbaths, Hersch Leizer Wechter distinguished himself knowing by heart all the special prayers for the Sabbath. He held his hands in the sleeves of his gabardine, walked over to the Beis Midrash and worshipped. He was a grave digger and a coachman; he lived near the market on the shore of the rivulet Mlienowka. He participated in Purim in the performance "The Sale of Joseph," had a sense for humor, told Jewish bon mots, twisted rhymes, sang Purim songs, and could mimic all the women. His brother, Ruvale the coachman, used to play the role of King Achashverosh[63].

The reader of the Torah at the first Minyan on the Sabbath was Yankele Moshe Eli's Hochmann. He finally became the main cantor at this first Minyan on the Sabbath and conducted services with a nice melody.

Itzik Meir Wechter wore a white beard, was honest and pious, and used to worship in the synagogue. He was one of the Psalm Society. He has a son, Samuel Wechter Kanye's son-in-law, living here.

{271}

## Advocates

The first Jewish advocate in Rozniatow was Dr. Shlomo Wassermann. He lived and had his office across from the Russian Church. He was an ardent Zionist and had a huge clientele.

To represent the opposite side in Rozniatow there was a notary public, Locaczewski by name, who was a decent man and a fine gentile. He lived in Yudel Weissberg's house and had his office there. It was a time of prosperity and lawsuits. The Jews of Perehinsko bought and sold fields, did businesses with wood and forests, were at law with every trifle, wrote contracts, and Dr. Wassermann was always busy.

Aharon Meir Lusthaus worked with him as a solicitor. He was a very intelligent and capable person. Leizer Schindler was engaged as his secretary. Under the Ukrainians, he was the president of the Zion Society and the Jewish National Council, and led the aid program for needy Jews in Rozniatow. His son Karl (Lolyek) lives in New York and a married daughter, Halya, lives in Israel.

Dr. Isidor Feuer came to Rozniatow. He lived and had his advocate's office on the first floor of Sosye Heller's brick house. He was the general representative of the Schlesinger firm in Broszniow. For a brief time during the period of Polish rule, he was the head of the Jewish Community, then councilman in the city administration and even mayor. In his later years, he started to attend the club of Yossel Kasner, returned to religious observance, used to go to the prayer services and even conducted the service when he observed yahrzeit.

Dr. Simon Sapir was a solicitor at the advocate Wassermann and opened his own office in the first floor of Yossel Berger's house. He was witty and dropped bon mots and was considered a good lawyer. During the Polish reign, he was a councilman in the city administration and head of the Jewish Community. His children, a son Karl (Lolek) who is a veterinarian and a daughter Jadzia, live in Poland.

Later on new advocates appeared in Rozniatow, such as Dr. Korbas, a national Ukrainian chauvinist and anti-Semite. He had his office where the girls school was once located near the Russian Church. Other advocates were Dr. Menkes; Dr. Katz; Dr. Redisz Mattel, the son of Redisz from Dolina; Dr. Leo Horowitz, the son of Shmuel Bendzis Horowitz and a cousin of Simon Liebermann from New York; and a son-in-law of Dr. Sapir. There was Magister Leo Meizels, Chaim Shlomo Meizels' son Leo, a cousin of Dr. Leo Horowitz. Dr. Kahane lived and had his office in the house of Dr. Wassermann. Eli Mordechai Bradfeld, a hedge lawyer[64], tried jurisprudence and made his living that way. I knew Eli Mordechai very well. He used to react loudly to wrongs and people thought that he was ready to administer bodily harm, but in reality he did not harm anybody.

Chaim Schnaper (on his mother's name) was a Jew who longed for advocacy.

{272}

## Physicians

From the first physicians, I remember Dr. Berwid who lived at Walisz's. Later there was Dr. Sekanine, called "regiment agent", who lived where Dr Sabbat later lived. There was Dr. Aharon Bart who did not accept money from poor people and who fell victim of his occupation; he died of typhus during the epidemic in the city. There were Dr.Yanek Yekl and Dr. M. Diamant, the son-in-law of Zecharya Liebermann. They were known in the whole region.

In Rozniatow, there were good barber-surgeons, called "feldschers," like Motye Berya who used to recommend medicines, pull out teeth, and set leeches and cupping-glasses. He was friendly, and honest. He did not accept money for haircuts from poor people and cured them for free.

He had his barber shop on the Ringplatz. His wife Zlate, called "the Babbe"[65], was a midwife and accoucheuse[66]. She was a clever and active woman was by nature a good and compassionate person and did not take money from poor women in labor. When she passed away, she was accompanied to her eternal rest by the whole shtetl. Her son Moshe Berya, who was a barber, died here.

Hersch Frost, besides being a good barber-surgeon, was a girdle manufacturer as well. He lived in the lower apartment in our house. Wagons would be brought from the villages to carry him to sick peasants to whom he recommended medicines. In addition to that, he was a big joker. Some of his children and grandchildren are living here. I encountered his son Mishel Frost here. His son, Shlomo, was a good tinsmith, a big joker as well like his father. For a certain time, he was a member of the Community Council. Philip Frost was the president of the Jewish workmen association "Yad Charutzim"[67] in Rozniatow. He was active in the drama circle and he used to make up the actors for their performances out of his love for the theatre. He shed tears during dramatic scenes.

Later on he drove a bus for his brother-in-law Aharon Zimmermann.

Azriel Wassermann, a barber as well, used to set up leeches and cupping-glasses.

Samuel Wirth (Unktom), a Hassid, used to celebrate with huge ardor, dancing in the streets of the shtetl with an oven fork held high in his hands wishing the Jews all the best[68]. Mockers, whom he called "sacred sheep," used to follow him and to say "Amen" after every congratulation. He had very educated sons-in-law — Binyamin Spiegel, Kalman Halpern, and Srulke Moshe Mechels Kornbluth.

Avrahamtsche Zauerberg, an intelligent and modern person, had musical abilities. His daughter Miriam Zohar lives in Israel and Miriam's daughter is studying Hebrew here temporarily. Meir Frenkel used to worship with great ardor, as is said "all my bones plea."

Yitzchak, the son of Shlomo Fogel, had a store where he sold flour and herring. He died at a young age. Rivka, the daughter of Shlomo Fogel is living here. Hitler killed some of his other children. There was only one pharmacy in the city. It was near Shmuel Nussbaum's home, whose two sons, Mordechai and Leibtsche, live in Israel. The owner of the pharmacy was an old Pole called Skalka who had a white beard. Yisrael Schwalb, a relative of the shamash Pintzi Schwalb, was a well-educated man, neatly dressed, with a nice beard, and wore glasses. He was the intellectual in the family and many years the reader of the Torah in the Beis Midrash.

The trustees in the Beis Midrash were: Abraham Groll, who ordered new benches for the Beis Midrash; Chaim Shlomo Meizels and Yossel Chaskel's Gelobter, the son-in-law of Pinye Berger. Two daughters of Yossel Gelobter, Dora Ungar and Sophia Widmann, live in the Bronx.

{273}

Shmuel Rosenberg, who lived across from the bathhouse, used to work in Yossel Gelobter's butcher's shop. His daughter Beila lives in Israel.

Yehuda Barnick, a very educated man, was a shamash in the synagogue and a teacher. His daughter

Mattl lives in New Jersey. His son Isak, of blessed memory, was active in the Zionist movement and another son, Leib Barnik, died in Israel.

A third son, David, was killed by the Nazis.

Moshe Barnick, an intelligent man and one of the leaders of the Zionists in Rozniatow, was a Hebrew teacher in Zharovna and for a brief time in Rozniatow during the Ukrainian rule. He died in Israel.

Mendel Horowitz was a walking encyclopedia; he knew everything. Being an autodidact, he could have further developed his intellect if he had had better circumstances and conditions. Veritable pearls of wisdom came forth from his mouth, but he remained a practical person. His words and advice were worthy to be heard and followed. His father, Chaim, was a peddler and the children managed a store for pottery and other articles. At one of our meetings here, I saw a brother of Mendel's, Hersch Horowitz.

{275}

Sitting from left: Yulek Turteltaub, Moshe Lutwak, and Dr. Nunek Lusthaus. Standing: Pinchas Kanner, Lulek Adelsberg, Lefel, and Dr. Dolek Lusthaus.

Avrahamtsche Hauptmann, the son-in-law of Eli Mordechai, came from Bolekhow and was a well-educated young man who was self-taught.

Yossel Rubinfeld lived in the lower apartment of our house. He was devoted to the yoke of livelihood the whole week. On the Sabbath, he sung hymns with ardor and heart that was unequaled by anybody.

A respectable and honest Jew was Wolf Zisye Rosenmann, a peddler who lived on the Ringplatz. He was a Cohen and prayed in the House of Study. His two grandchildren, the children of Moshe Leib Rosenmann, are Shimon, who lives in a Kibbutz, and Yisraelke, who died in Israel. A daughter of Wolf Zisye, Chane Kornbluth, lives in New Jersey and a granddaughter lives in New York. She is also the granddaughter of Mendel Wechter who lived near the hill.

The traditional Sabbath pleasure was strictly observed at Hersch Landsmann's home. His Sabbath hymns, so enthusiastically sung by the whole family on Friday nights and the Sabbath day, resounded over the lane.

Hersch Landsmann was very devoted to his household. He was by nature a good character and supported poor people.

A tragic event occurred in his family. When his son David was a child, he drowned in the cold mikva of the bathhouse on a Friday. His daughter Danye lives in the Soviet Union. His son Mendel lives in the Bronx and another daughter Ida in Proszkow, Poland. Her husband, Mishka Yagelawitch, was one of the pious among the gentiles. He rescued many Rozniatower Jews, now living here in America, from death and hid them in his house at the risk of his own life.

I remember when Yossel and Pinye Berger's brick house was built at the beginning of the 1910s. Both brothers were respected citizens of Rozniatow. Yossel Berger used to export calves to Vienna and Pinye Berger owned a butcher shop. Yossel's children — Dr. Alter Berger (together with our brother Hersch-Mordechai they were among the first gymnasium students), Tuntzia Berger, and Pinye Berger's grandchildren from Stryj — live in Israel. Artzye Yossel Berger died in Israel.

Binyamin Stern was a rich citizen and a fine specialist in the horse trade. His daughter Chane Yampel lives in London and another daughter Ettl Mannheim lives in Brooklyn. Binyamin's brother, Shlomo Stern, a well-educated man, was a merchant. Shlomo's son Yehoshua lives in London. His son, Yissachar, died not long ago in London. He was married to Sheyntshe, the daughter of Chaim Schwartz. Chaim Schwartz, a short man with a black beard, a Hassid and well educated, a good merchant, and managed a bank in Rozniatow in partnership with Pinchas Rechtschaffen and Leib Bermann. Chaim Schwartz's daughter, Chana Pantzer, and his son, Shmueltzi, live in New York. Another son, Bendet, lives in Israel. Baruch Keller Shmuel Herschin was a Jew who used to say bon mots; he was always good-humored. He was a pious Jew, negligently dressed, with a white beard, his nose always clogged up with snuff. He lived across from the Kloiz. Uri Ashkenaz lived in another apartment in the same house. I encountered his son at a meeting here. Binyamin Keller lived and had a store on the Ringplatz for articles of peasant garment. His beard and side-locks were always disheveled. He had the voice of a lion, which was heard outside even when he conducted the service with closed doors. Yankel Hammermann was a hide merchant. Yudele Hammermann (Akselrod) was his relative and lived in New York. His mother, called Devora the widow, lived near Binyamin Stern. Shlomo with the beard (Teitelbaum) wore a thick, blond beard, lived near Berl Yoel Rosenmann. He traded in refuse from sawmills. Nachumtzi Laufer, the son-in-law of Berl Yoel Rosenmann, lived and had his store at his father-in-law house. He traded first in sugar and sweets then in wooden instruments. Itzik Rosenmann was very observant of the commandment of Simchat Torah and every year he was tipsy on this festival. He lived in the second apartment of Baruch Shmuel Hersch's house and had a fruit trade. Friday evening and on Sabbath young people used to purchase Sabbath fruits from him. Prior to my emigration to America in 1932, he was an assistant in Philip Fuerst's bus company. He had a hard but honest life all his years. His son Yechezkel lives in Holland and his son Levi lives in Israel. His brother, Max (Mechel) Rosenmann, lives in New York and is the president of the Rozniatower Society.

Their brother, Nachman, was tragically killed in the 1920s by the murderer Stefan Lapianecki, their neighbor.

It happened when Nachman passed over the "perelez", which is the lowest point of a common fence between two properties. When the gentile saw that, he hit Nachman over his head with a metal object. Nachman was brought to the hospital in Dolina where he died from his wounds. I visited him in the hospital a week before his death. The gentile was convicted for the killing by the Stryj Court and sentenced to one-year imprisonment.

Nachman's son Shalom lives in Pittsburgh, Pennsylvania.

Shaul Miriam Binyes Bleicher used to administer the symbolic flogging on the eve of Yom Kippur, for which people paid him with a few coins. I am sure that many people still remember when the floors in all prayer houses were spread with hay for Yom Kippur[69]. Abraham Hersch, the son of Shaul Bleicher, loved to lead services, and almost every Sabbath he conducted service at the first minyan.

{277}

Abraham Hoffmann

Abraham Hoffmann was an interesting figure in the shtetl, especially for his dynamism and unique abilities. In addition, he had an extraordinary thirst to learn and to know. He learned, read, simply devoured books, and elaborated for himself a very serious look at life, the world, and people.

Wolf Landsmann was a peddler in his younger years, always somber, and not satisfied. Sitting Saturday evening at twilight in the House of Study, he used to complain of a headache. When it became intense he called out, "may an apoplexy hit such a head."

Sosye Feige Gelobter used to conjure an evil eye, melt wax, bake bagels, and made her living from that. Her house was across from the Russian Church, where later on lived Chaim Leizer Turteltaub, a leather merchant. His wife was a pious person, and during the good times a poor man could eat there to satiety.

Sosye Feige's husband, Meir Avraham, was a butcher. He was a mighty Jew who could stop a running wagon hitched up and pulled by two horses with his two hands at the hind wheels. This is not an exaggeration; it is a fact.

His son, Hersch Gelobter, resembled his father. He was tall, broad-shouldered, strong, and an artilleryman in the army. He lived in Krechowice. His grandchildren Jack, Sam, Aharon, Sidney and David Zemel live here.

Avraham Hoffmann was an autodidact. He knew a little bit of Hebrew, stenography, accounting, chemistry, and photography. He was tolerant of everybody. He loved to do favors and he gave practical advice. He had good humor, sympathetic to people, said bon mots, and was active in the Jewish drama circle. He lived across from the synagogue. His father was Yehoshua Hoffmann, a pious Jew and a peddler who traded in dry mushrooms. His mother Sosye used to sell grease for wagon wheels.

Shaya (Shayenyu) Katzmann was a man of principles and a cobbler. Later, he made embankments for bridges, managed affairs for the Baron Walysz, and delivered gravel to pave streets for the baron.

Avrahamele Shaya's former spouse, Gitzye, lives in America.

Yisraeltshe Rosenmann was eager to occupy himself with civic politics, but he did not take part in the social life. He managed a tavern in his brick house on the Ringplatz. His regular guests were Polish "Pany"[70] a joyful fellowship. Yisraeltshe Rosenmann's daughter, Lotke Sapier, lives in Poland. Two of his three nephews from Dolina, Pitzye and Monik Enis, live in New York, while Solek Enis lives in New Jersey.

The second half of the brick house belonged to Yissachar Friedler, the son-in-law of Moshe Rosenmann and a brother of Leibish Friedler from the old town. Yissachar Friedler was an egg merchant and exporter.

It is normal and natural for parents to be devoted to their children. But such devotion as Yissachar and Hentshe Friedler showed to their only son Sender is worthy of admiration. His father never took his eyes off of him. Sender Friedler enjoyed a good childhood, but his father died prematurely in 1915, at the age of 56 years.

Sender owned in Rozniatow a good conditorium that sold confectionery, cigarettes, soda water, and other good edibles. But the times went from bad to worse, and some people became unemployed and ill humored. Sender and his family succeeded. A few months before the outbreak of World War II, Sender Friedler, his mother, his wife, and two children went to America. In this way they escaped the catastrophe.

Sender began here like every one of us — with a heavy gait, as one says. Then he settled satisfactorily in Brooklyn.

Even in his early years, Sender Friedler showed some talent as an actor, possessed a good sense of humor, and could play the fiddle. On Saturday afternoons he performed in the attic of their house. Young folks came running to the performances. Admission was three buttons. The kids tore off the buttons from their pants and tied them with the suspenders of their coats just to see the comedy. I came on trust, because I was not willing to tear buttons on Sabbath.

Old benches and patched up chairs were used as the seats. The scenery was placed in front on propped up boards. Somebody was the comedian. He performed dressed in a long skirt, his head wrapped in a shawl, and his face smeared with soot. He made faces, jumped, sang and did somersaults. People watched with pleasure.

Sender was active in the amateur's club and distinguished himself in comical roles. He was the initiator and the leader of many performances played in Yiddish. He was the president of the Rozniatower Society in America.

Sender died as a young man, he was just 59 years old. His mother died a few years earlier at the age of 80. He left his wife and two married daughters.

Hersch Mendel Orthmann was a respectable grain merchant in the city. His grandchildren Leo and Butzi Tepper, the sons of Sarahtshe Tepper; Butzi Widmann, Shlomo Widmann, a grain merchant lives in New York. Dr. Orthmann, Isak Orthmann's son, lives in Poland.

Orthmann lived in Broszniow, had affairs with the Glesinger firm in Broszniow and was in partnership with Yankel Rosenthal from Perehinsko for a little sawmill in Sliwka. I was employed by them for a few years in Perehinsko, since I was a partner in the mill and sawmill in Sliwka as was his brother-in-law Shmuel Rechtschaffen.

Shlomo Widmann has two brothers who live here. Not long ago Yosef Orthmann, a son of Hersch Mendel, died here. He was a pious Jew who was in the shoe business in Vienna for many years. The son of Pinchas Rechtschaffen, Yechezkel, owned a boarding school in Haifa and died in Israel. His daughter Chana Gelber lives in Haifa.

Yosef Shimon Stern was a non-commissioned officer in the Austrian army. He was a Hassidic Jew. He did business with flour, tobacco, and other merchandise. He lived and conducted his business in the Ringplatz. He had a thick blond beard. He was the gabbai in the Kloiz. His wife Mamtzia helped him in business, and his children were also good merchants.

# Sprawozdanie
## KOMERCYALNEGO TOWARZYSTWA KREDYTOWEGO
### (przedtem Komercyalny Bank kredytowy)
stowarzyszenia zarejestrowanego z ograniczoną poręką

### w Rożniatowie
# Dyrekcya:

Leib Bermann
dyrektor

Chaim Schwarz                    Pinkas Rechtschaffen
kasyer.                          kontrolor.

## Komisya rewizyjna:

Wolf Hoffmann                    Berisch Friedler

Feiwel Rosenberg                 Leiser Geller

Sacharias Dawid Liebermann

The seal of the firm of Bermann & Co.

Y. Sh. Stern's son-in-law was Zeyde, the son of the slaughterer Moshele Weiser, a slaughterer himself and a reader of the law in the Kloiz. His wife Broche, the daughter of Yosef Shimon, managed a food store on the Ringplatz.

Yankel Diamond was an intelligent, smart craftsman. He was the president of the "Poalei Zion"[71] association during the Ukrainian reign. Besides carpentry, he dealt with patents his whole life. However, both these professions could not provide him with a good livelihood, and he died at a young age as a poor man. His faithful wife, a clever and active woman, took over the livelihood yoke. She did hard labor, baked, and carried heavy baskets with baker's wares to sell in the old town. Their children were very successful. Shimon Diamond used to erect tombstones, made signboards, ran a matzo bakery for Passover, and was a prompter during the rehearsals of the Yiddish theater performances in Rozniatow. His brother Ruvale was a good tinsmith and a strong man. The youngest, Anshel, was successful as well. Manye Diamond lives in Israel and has a responsible job.

Baruch Diamond, a tall and broad-shouldered man, sometimes managed the bathhouse. Then he became the community shamash. During Purim he used to go around with the Purim players. He had a brother-in-law, the brother of his wife, who died here.

Bunim Geller was a prodigious scholar and distinguished himself with special sagacity and understanding for the idea of the return to Zion. He was one of the founders of the local Zionist association and inspired the younger generation to Zionism. During World War II, he fled as a refugee to the Soviet Union, but could not endure the bad conditions and died there. His son Yitzchak lives in Israel. Two other sons and a daughter, Sarah, live in Sweden. Another daughter lives in Belgium.

Dr. Leopold (Lipa) Adlersberg, a religion teacher for Jewish students in the government "Folks Schule"[72] was a pious man and a good teacher. He went blind in both eyes and had to be carried to the school to teach Jewish religion to the Jewish students. He was also a tutor and gave private lessons and specialized in preparing students for the entrance examinations to the Gymnasium. I was also one of his students and I learned my lessons by heart. His sons Wilek, Sigo and Lonek were very intelligent people. Wilek was a good Medical Doctor.

Hertz Shapira was a cattle merchant who lived in the same house as Rachel Widmann, who managed a bakery. On the same street lived Leibish Frisch, who owned a shoe store and was Hersch Mendel Orthmann's son-in-law. Scheintzie Kasner, the widow of Leib whom people called Aybie Kasner and who fell in World War I managed a bakery in her house near the Beis Midrash and provided in this way for her and the children's livelihood.

Avraham, called Amie Kasner, was a cobbler. He was Aybie's brother. He married Samuel Rosenberg's daughter, Bina. He returned from Russian captivity, lived near the rivulet, and died at a young age. Their sister lives in New York. Before the war, Wolkentreiber possessed a regular bakery. He did not return home from the war. Having no choice, his wife managed the bakery. Her father was Berl Berger, who lived on the Ringplatz and worked in the slaughterhouse. Years ago, I encountered one of his brothers here. One of his sons, Getzl, died here. Eli lives in California. Note possesses a grocery in Brooklyn. A married daughter, Esther, lives in Georgia. A married grandson, the son of his daughter Chaya, lives in New York.

Munye Mintz managed a regular bakery in the school director Korecky's house, across from Binyamin Stern. Baruch Mintz, his father, worked for him.

Munye Mintz got his bachelor degree in Stryj and was authorized by the Zionist Organization to collect money for the "Keren Kayemet" in Rozniatow and the surrounding region.

Lipa Sofer wrote the Torah Scroll that the Zionists donated to the Rozniatower Synagogue before the war. His wife Tehilla was in America, died several years ago, and according to her will and wishes was buried in Israel. His children Bracha and Shmueltshe live in New York.

Zisye Arye Kupferberg, a merchant of agricultural products, lived on the way to Szwariczow. He was deported to Russia during World War I, and returned safely home after the war. His daughter Adela Tepper lives in Bridgeport, Connecticut.

The Russians also deported Yaakov Yehuda Leinbrat, a handsome man. He hid in the trenches, dug out in the village of Rakowy, and came home safely as well. He enjoyed conducting the services. I still remember his father, Shimshon, who lived across from the Beis Midrash.

Lipa Taneh was a good merchant, ran a middle-class household, and did many favors for Jews. He was a strong man and a good swimmer. One of his sons lives in New Jersey and two daughters, Shlomtzi and Merke, live in Israel. Another son, Yisrael, lives in Argentina.

Yisrael Hersch Landner, a brother of Berl Landner, was a renowned charitable man and died at an early age. Yisrael Hersch was a Hassid and used to worship in the Kloiz. He managed a grocery and was one of the few Jews in the city who still wore the Streimel on Sabbaths and festivals. Their father, Reb Aharon Meir the Kohen, departed for Israel by the end of the 19th century, where he became the head of a kollel[73]. His grandson, Reb Yehoshua Spiegel, lives in Israel. Another grandson, Yehoshua Landner lived in Antwerp and distinguished himself with his generosity for Israel as well as some charitable institutions.

Leib Falik, Eli Yona Koral, Israel Treu, and Shmuel Friedlender were respectable merchants who were sons-in-law of Vove Hoffmann. Leib Schnitzer, a peddler, and his son were house painters. Shimshon Strassmann, an exporter, was once our neighbor and used to conduct the "Ata Hareita"[74] prayer on Simchat Torah in the Beis Midrash.

Shalom Laufer was a merchant, a quiet Jew, and a decent man. After his second marriage, he used to sell newspapers, magazines, periodicals by order, writing implements, and other small items. His daughter, who was very beautiful, used to perform in the Yiddish theatre and was one of the prima donnas. Her older sister, Rivtshe, was married to Chaim Zeinfeld, a rich wood industrialist in Perehinsko. A younger brother Yoska left Rozniatow years ago. Her stepsister Regina Hochdorf was active in social enterprises.

Shmuel Horowitz, the son-in-law of Leizer Itzik Lew, was an intelligent man who managed a grocery in the brick house of Sosye Heller. Near him was the dry-goods store of Mates Willner, a son-in-law of Leizer Itzik Lew another quiet person. Dr. Leo Horowitz, the son of Samuel Horowitz, was an advocate who directed the city library for a certain time and played in the Yiddish theatre.

Moshe Yaakov Lustig, a cattle-merchant, was for many years Gabbai in the synagogue and conducted the services as well. He had a seat near the eastern wall.

Moshe Mechel Kornbluth lived in Germany for many years. His son Srulke studied to be a cantor but did not finish the course. Although he had a nice strong voice, he could not make his career with it. He married the daughter of Samuel Wirth and had a little store on the Ringplatz where he sold various merchandise.

Aharon Weissmann married the daughter of Moses Mechel and lived for a long time in Germany. Dr. David Weissmann, a brother of Aharon Weissmann, was my colleague in the Gymnasium and one of the best students. Then he was a teacher in a private Jewish Gymnasium in a shtetl in Eastern Galicia.

The daughter of Mechel Weissmann, Sime, lives in Israel.

Mendel Nemlich, a brother-in-law of Ben Zion Yankel, lived many years in Germany then in America, came home and managed a hardware store. His two daughters Freida and Gittel played Yiddish theatre in Rozniatow.

Sara Samuels Erdmann and her husband sold flour, salt, petroleum, and other good things. Years ago, I encountered a member of their family, Anshel Efraim Michel, at a meeting of our club. Allegedly, he was a clergyman, a reverend, or a rabbi.

Yankel Spiegel traded in petroleum and food articles. He lived and had his store on the Ringplatz. He immigrated to Israel after World War I. Shalom Hoffmann, a son of Vove Hoffmann, bought the house and continued the same trade.

For many years David Wohl was a civic night watchman who slept in the daytime. His wife managed a little tavern. David Wohl boasted that he was a descendant of the renowned Wohls, one of who was once a Polish King according to Polish legend.

Hersch Tzales Wechter was a Jew with disheveled red hair and a beard and side locks. Malka, his wife, was a trustee, a prompter at the cemetery[75] and a kneader at the matzo bakery. Their son Leib was for many years a cook at Vove Hoffmann's house. He cooked, baked, did the dishes, cleared off and cleaned the house. He was very reliable and responsible in his job, the only man in the city to do women's work. His brother, Yisrael Yankel, toiled as a porter. His brother-in-law, called Biegem was a porter as well and another brother-in-law, Chaim Reuvel, was a coachman.

I remember his youngest brother as a boy, he was called Eli Pogodes. Why? Pogoda in Polish means good weather. Eli always used to wear his hat on his head twisted, sometimes upwards, other times on a side, never in the right place. If Eli appeared to the morning service with his cap upwards over his forehead, the Jews said that today will be "pogoda" — good weather. Proof? Eli wore his cap upwards! If the cap was under his forehead this was a hint the weather was bad. Actually, there was no prophecy in his behavior, it was simply his habit to wear his cap up on a nice day and down on a rainy day.

There were good dentists in Rozniatow including: Berko Litauer; Bekesz; Blau, the son-in-law of Printz; Shaya Lutwak; and Wilek Turteltaub, who died in Poland. Yankel Scharf, a brother-in-law of Leibish and Yissachar Friedler, was a merchant and lived near Dr. Wassermann. His sons Sender and Avraham live in Israel. Yossel Kreiter, a Jew with a white beard who lived near the Kloiz, had a son who was a captain in the Austrian army. Nobody of my age has ever seen him in Rozniatow since he left the city for his army service. His brother Yankel, whom I remember very well, left Rozniatow as a young man and never returned.

A son of the old Meir, called "the red teacher," was a good service conductor and was attracted to the cantor's desk like a magnet. One of his sons, called "Chaim the Rabbi-le" with long side locks (later cut short), was musically talented and died at a young age.

Yisrael Yakum Wassermann was a tailor. I remember him as an old man with a white beard. A physically strong Jew with a high resounding voice, he was the head of the Psalm Society. Every Sabbath after the siesta he used to chant at the cantor's desk almost all 150 psalms with his resounding, hearty voice and in clear words. He had three sons, all of them were tailors.

Itzik Aharon Wassermann, a brother-in-law of Pintzi the shamash, enjoyed conducting the services and he did that very well. He was a tailor, then he managed a store for used articles, and finally he was a tailor again.

The second one, Yehuda Wassermann, a former tailor, was in America and came home. He helped his wife Chana Grunim's, a stall-keeper in the market.

The third was Simcha Wassermann, worked formerly at Konye Kortschmann's, and married in the village of Jassin where he was a tailor.

The female stall-keepers, Leitzonye, Devora-Henye, Yutele Pinchas Leib's Neiman, Polye Landmann's sister and Chana Grunim's Wassermann, had bad fortune for earning a livelihood. Their stalls were near the well (the meeting point of all maid servants). They used to sit at their stalls until the deep autumn, in heat and rain, selling cherries, berries, sour cherries, apples, pears and plums. They had a difficult life with their meager earnings.

Mechel Fessberg, a scholar and an enlightened smart Jew, was a teacher in Rozniatow during the war, and then moved to Broszniow.

{286}

## Folks-Schulen[76]

For six years when I was a child, I attended the elementary school that was located where the City Council is now. Besides this, some classes were held in three different places: one in the reading room near the Russian Church, another at the cobbler Dombrowicz's over the rivulet Malinowka, and the third at Wolf Horowitz's where Strauchler the watchmaker lived later on.

The school for girls was where Dr. Korbas later had his advocate office.

For us boys, the school was a punishment not because we were not willing to study but because of the beatings. All teachers, without exception, beat us. The beating was such a natural, accepted phenomenon that it was usual in all schools and for all kinds of transgressions: for not learning well, jumping over the benches, etc. The procedure itself was a simple one. The guilty person was taken out of his place, laid down on a bench, his pants lowered, and hit with a stick over his rear end. The conviction of the fathers and teachers was that if you hit the bottom the effect rises upwards, i.e., into the head. The mothers, thanks to their gentle hearts, did not believe in that theory.

There were some guys who refused to be dragged away from their seats to be beaten. In such cases the school guard Andras Szpycak Grabowski, a brutal gentile, was called in. This happened frequently to Avrahamele Hoffmann. The class went awry. Afterwards, his mother Sasil used to come crying to the school director, while Avrahamele did not attend school for a week. During such a struggle, he once used a pin and tore open the hand of the teacher Korecki or Kowalski.

Some students were beaten right in their seats. There was a gentile student whose name was Szliachetka, who was sitting near the window. When he got beaten, he used to jump out through the window and run home. I cannot remember a case when Jewish or Christian parents had brought a complaint over that brutal educational method either to the court or to higher school authorities.

The girls were not beaten so brutally. Their teachers just beat their hands with a ruler; this punishment was called "patza."

My teachers in Rozniatow included a wicked woman who was an old unmarried spinster. She was always angry and somber and an experienced beater who beat us successfully. She was our teacher for a short time only. Our second teacher was Wladyslaw Heinrich, who was blind in one eye, a good teacher but an intractable alcoholic. Sometimes he did not attend school because he could not get sober. Other teachers substituted for him. He loved gymnastics and used to exercise with us outside. He was the head of the Polish sports club "Sokol." He was an excellent dancer and used to organize the summer festivals in the open air on the hill.

Our next teacher was Michael Korecki, a Ukrainian, a liberal person and good teacher, a solid and true family man. He had a son who was a captain in the Austrian army and a wife who was friendly with Jewish women. He was our teacher until I entered the Gymnasium in Stryj. While Heinrich was our teacher, Pyotr Rozwany, a son-in-law of Korecki, taught us only Polish for a short period. He used to send us to learn different craft specialties like glazing, carving, etc. During the Russian invasion he was a teacher in a village near Rozniatow and did other work as well. Later on Rozwany became the director of the boys' elementary school in Rozniatow and the president of "Sokol." Before him as school director there was the Pole Kowalski who was an old bachelor. Teachers of other classes were: Titus Karbanowitcz, Wladyslawa Kiernicka, whose husband was a tax officer and an alcoholic; Miss Mondszein, a pretty person, who lived at Chaim Yoel Taneh's, where Abraham Groll later lived. She quickly abandoned her career as a teacher.

Korecki was the school director when I was a student. Later on Heinrich became the school director, but I was no longer there.

A few years before the war, a new brick house was built on the hill to serve as the elementary school for boys and girls. The old premises became the residence of the city council. I still remember when the city council was in the old house, where later on the new pharmacy of Macyadzinski was located. Petro Woloszynowicz, a rich landlord, was mayor at that time. He was hardly able to sign his name but he was a descendant of the well-known and aristocratic Woloszynowicz clan. His son Wasyl was my classmate.

My Jewish classmates were: Abraham Hoffmann; Chaim Schwalb, who was the son of Pintshe

Schwalb and who passed away while young; both Yissachar Bergers, the sons of Pinye and Yossel; Shlomele Rosenbaum, a brother of Blumke, and who died at an early age; Moshe Berei, who died as a young man in America; Leonik Erber; Itzye Reiss a nephew of Meir Frenkel; Schitzye Korn the son of the judge; David Reiner who managed a flour store on the Ringplatz and was well educated in Torah; Azye Friedler; Yankel Rubinstein; Anshel and Avraham who were brothers; Moshe Leib's Leizer whose sister Rikl was married to Meir Schoel's Kornbluth from Dolina; Herschele Sarah Mamtzi's; Yankel Kreiter and a son of Baruch Shimshon Chaim's Klinger. I am not familiar with the later structure of the schoolteacher's staff in Rozniatow.

{288}

## The Mobilization

The Jews carried on their life in Rozniatow quietly and peacefully and were concerned only to provide for their livelihood. No new rich men appear, the poor did not get poorer, and sensational events did not occur. All of a sudden, the peacefulness of the city and of the whole world was disturbed and destroyed. This happened in the summer of 1914 on Saturday, August 1st which was Tisha B'Av[77]. On that day, a general mobilization was officially proclaimed through posters and personal summonses to reservists. That Sabbath the Jews worshipped with half a mouth, for it was really Tisha B'Av. The whole city was on alert; people walked around as if in a dream. After almost fifty years of peace, why was there such a misfortune? It is impossible! The Jews were Austrian patriots and many predicted that the war would not last long. We will participate in a just war and victory will, with G-d's help, be ours. Nobody thought to take the Sabbath siesta. Groups of people started to assemble in the city — a group here, another there. Some individuals ran from one group to a second in search for some news. Maybe there will be some good news. But, as zealous as the patriotism of the Jews of that time may have been, nobody was eager to jump into the fire.

On that Saturday a delegation of Rozniatower people, with Dr. Feuer as its leader, departed for the Starosta in Dolina. They came back the same day with precise information about everything. Those who will not be inducted now will be required to go later. Gentiles drank. The gendarmes were on alert to maintain order in the city, which looked unusual, like neither a Sabbath nor a weekday. But the war was already ongoing. Czarist Russia declared war on Austria-Hungary and Germany. The countries allied with Austria declared war on Russia, Britain, and France. After small patrol battles, the Austrian Army retired to the Eastern and Western Carpathian Mountains. How did Rozniatow look and how did it live before the Russian invasion?

Whereas Rozniatow was a remote town a distance of 7.5 kilometers from the railroad station at Krechowice, almost no military movements occurred there. Army units were transported by railroad to the eastern front. Various military formations marched along the major roads to carry provisions and war materials for the army.

People were tense and they talked and debated. They were eager to hear good news from the front. It was rumored that Russian soldiers rob, kill, and rape young girls— one rumor more horrible than the prior one. Local older gendarmes-reservists, summoned by the gendarme's commander Furmankewicz, guarded the bridges and roads. The courts, the schools, the tax offices, and the post offices closed. For the present, there was enough food. Only later on, when the refugees from the eastern border cities arrived, did it became obvious that the front was approaching.

The railroads were only transporting military units, and railroad commerce stopped. Meanwhile the families of those summoned to military service had enough food because they bought sacks of flour and other products for the monthly stipend that they received from the government, some more and some less depending on the military rank of the mobilized family member. Besides that, everybody stocked up with unlimited free potatoes from fields outside the town. The flour merchants and grocers restrained themselves from selling food because no produce came in, even with simple wagons. Therefore, the prices became sky high.

The question "what to eat?" hit heavily on the remaining older governmental officials who were left without salaries and on the poorer inhabitants as well. With enough time on their hands, they strolled through the city and complained about the high prices. Worse yet was the plight of the tobacco smokers. Tobacco prices were sky high and it was difficult, almost impossible, to buy tobacco. Many people smoked dry leaves that were rubbed into small pieces.

Hungarian Hussar units appeared in the city on patrol service in Rozniatow and environs. A larger military unit with many wagons of provisions rested several days on the Moczar hill outside the city. Then they left. The Hussars left Rozniatow as well. It was a question of just counting the days until the Russians would occupy Rozniatow. The Jews hid their meager assets in cellars out of fear of Russian burglary, being convinced that cellars were the best places to avoid robbery.

Thanks to the horrible rumors about the Russian atrocities, the fright grew from day to day. The city looked empty without people, for people stayed indoors.

Finally, the uninvited guests appeared in Rozniatow on a weekday. It was already autumn, just before the High Holy Days. Thus started a new chapter in the life of the Rozniatower Jews.

A patrol consisting of two Cossacks on horseback came into town. The Mayor Vove Hoffmann, accompanied by the policeman Majewski, went out to meet them with palpitation of the heart. The encounter ended with a little bit of fear. When the Cossack patrol left the city, other Russian military formations appeared. The girls hidden in the cellars started to come out, because the rumors of the abuses perpetrated by the Russian soldiers appeared to be exaggerated. Indeed, some burglaries occurred here and there and there were other acts of violence. But by using bribes — and this means was always helpful — one could always avoid trouble.

To the credit of all inhabitants of Rozniatow, it needs to be emphasized that in the time between the withdrawal of the Austrians and the Russian invasion, when the city was actually left as a free-for-all without any administration, no robberies or other bad incidents happened.

The following people left the city before the Russian invasion: Dr. Wassermann; Dr. Feuer; Dr. Sapier; Dr. Barth; Michel Orthmann who left two administrators in charge of his house and flour store,

Aharon Wolf Press the son of the rabbi and his brother-in-law Yankel Rubinstein. Shaya Frisch left the administration of his house and the dry goods store to Itzik Aharon Wassermann, the brother-in-law of Pintzye the shamash.

All other inhabitants remained in Rozniatow. The city became the main road that led to the Eastern Carpathian Mountains and the front between the Austrians and the Russians developed along the Carpathians.

The front stabilized itself around the mountains. For weeks and weeks, different Russian military formations passed through Rozniatow in the direction of the Carpathians. Many Russian soldiers fell, because the Austrians had the better position, shooting down from the mountains. The Russian military commander and his staff occupied the mansion of the Baron Wyszla. The soldiers were ordered strictly to not harass the civilian population. Some merchants began to do business. Special permission was needed to ride from one place to another. Civilians could ride only on horse drawn wagons, the railroad being reserved for the military. Obviously, products became more expensive, but there was not any shortage. Russian tobacco was sufficient as well. There was a cheap tobacco, which looked like small splinters, called "machorka." Its price was affordable for the poor smoker as well. It was possible to buy a good black bread from the Russian soldiers. The situation was more complicated with garments, but people were not overly concerned about that, because everybody still had clothes from the good times and wore them now. Some people purchased military clothes, dyed them over, and had them refurbished by a tailor to fit them properly. Others wore them as is, if they fit. The same situation applied to shoes. Some people put patches upon patches and waited for the end of the war.

The Jews learned Russian relatively quickly. That is, they could not really speak Russian, but they could understand what the soldiers wanted from them and what the question was. When the Russian soldier said to the Jew "davay chasy" or "davay diengi," the Jew understood immediately that he must give away his watch or empty all his pockets and give up all his money...

A stable Russian garrison was quartered in the city in both public buildings and in private homes. A military hospital was established in the school building. Military units that marched to the front rested on the Ringplatz with their convoy and field kitchens, the soldiers being quartered in private apartments where they slept on straw on the floor. Soldiers came and went. It was permanent motion.

Camping in the city, the soldiers first set about to light fires to boil tea. Meanwhile they broke fences to obtain combustible material. Tea was their national beverage and they used to drink 4-5 seething glasses of tea while biting sugar candy. To avoid burglaries and other acts of violence, it was strictly forbidden under threat of the harshest punishments to buy and sell alcoholic beverages in the bars, taverns and restaurants. The soldiers were good sources for realizing appreciable money from sales, especially in the tearooms, where white bread, white loaves, baker's wares, potatoes, sweets, tobacco, and other tidbits were for sale. Every front room in the city became a tearoom. Besides this, stands with various food items were erected in the market. The whole trade was concentrated on food and useful articles like petroleum, candles, and others. Elderly people and ordinary Jews who were temporarily without occupation spent their next winter in the Kloiz where it was warm, discussing the general political situation. There were pessimists and optimists and everybody tried to prove his point of view. All agreed that the war was going to last.

What little news there was from the battlefield was brought in by strangers and merchants who "have heard from others this and that". No official war reports were publicized and the data from the Russian soldiers were absolutely unreliable because according to their stories they had reached Vienna already.

Some incidents occurred in Rozniatow, but they ended smoothly and peacefully. Thanks to the intervention of the Baron Walysz with the military commander of the city, Vove Hoffmann and Chaim Schwartz were exempted from being deported to Russia. The interventions were also helpful in other cases. Naturally, it cost money.

Late in the winter, the Austrians started an offensive from the Carpathian Mountains and advanced up to Rozniatow, where a battle lasting seven days took place. The Russians dug trenches on the hill and shells flew over the city. The civilian population remained indoors. As soon as the shooting ceased, people went out to breathe fresh air and some even dared to venture into the city.

The Russians pushed back the Austrians, who withdraw to their prior positions in the Carpathian Mountains. The fallen soldiers were buried at the edge of the woods and some Russians were buried in the fenced garden of the Russian Church, right at the entrance near the bell tower.

The shells damaged the school on the hill. The Austrians knew that the Russian general staff were there and they aimed towards it, killing several officers. There were no civilians among the victims. Small pieces of shrapnel damaged some roofs but only insignificantly.

During the battle, some families stayed in the Kloiz and in the small synagogue. They thought that there they will be better protected from the bullets.

After the eight days of depressed mood and fear, people recovered their breath and normal life — as normal as it could have been in those circumstances — was restored. As time passed, the problem "what to eat" became more acute. All other needs could be neglected. If there was a shortage in many provisions, e.g., in coffee, the women fried barley and this replaced coffee. Instead of sugar, saccharin or candies were used and so on. Potatoes became the main product, which was served three times per day, and even the Sabbath pudding was made of potatoes.

After a siege of more than six months, the stronghold of Przemysl fell, which was a bad event that caused much depression. The Jews cherished the hope that Przemysl would hold out and that the Russians would be defeated there, but the opposite occurred.

{294}

## Surprising Events

It was after Purim and the Jews prepared themselves for the traditional Passover holiday. All went smoothly without any disturbances. Matzos were baked, and wine was made from raisins, because real wine was impossible to obtain on account of the strict ban on sale of alcoholic beverages. Various vegetables needed for Passover were also procured. The Jewish soldiers stationed in the city were quartered in Jewish homes and supplied with matzos and vegetables.

Thus, the Passover holiday was celebrated in 1915 in Rozniatow.

With the arrival of the summer, the mood of the Jews became more hopeful thanks to some good news from the front lines. It was not long before the Austrian-German offensive began. The front was broken through at Gorlica in the Western Carpathian Mountains, compelling the Russians to withdraw almost without any resistance from Western and Eastern Galicia and from the Eastern Carpathians as well. The Russians, laden with their battle gear, retreated from the Carpathians through Rozniatow and other ways, back toward the east from where they came.

In June 1915, on a Friday morning, an Austrian patrol of five or six soldiers arrived and, after a short encounter, chased a Russian patrol from the Motszar hill. Shortly afterwards the city was full of different Austrian military formations. People greeted the soldiers and some cried out of joy and were in high spirits. Every soldier was a hero in everybody's eyes. The soldiers were well outfitted and well armed and the wagons were fully loaded with provisions for them. Russian prisoners were carried off. The honey weeks passed quickly and the usual weekdays started again. All became normal again. The government services opened and were functioning again except for the school, which began in September after the summer vacations. The government officials and the families of the mobilized reservists received their pay for the whole time of the Russian invasion until the return of the Austrian army. Civilian passengers were accepted by the railroad, if places were available, for they were always full of military servicemen and businessmen, who began again to travel out of the city. People who fled Rozniatow came back — Dr. Wassermann, Dr. Feuer, Dr. Sapier, Dr. Barth, Mishel Orthmann, Shaya Frisch — all returned to their former occupations. Even those deported to Russia — Yaakov Yehuda Kleinbrod and Zusye Arye Kupferberg. Tzvi Fassberg — returned just after the war.

Surprises now came one after another. The first one was the conscription of all men from 18-50 years to military service, after they were checked by a medical commission in Dolina and classified as serviceable.

Ration cards were introduced for bread, flour, sugar, salt, petroleum, and other necessities of life. These articles were not available on the free market. These cards were called "maximal cards" because every family had a limit on what it could buy determined by the number of family members; so much and no more. Soon the maximum cards became minimum cards and since this was not enough to live on, people were compelled to turn to the black market where everything was available at inflated prices.

Whereas the majority of the husbands were in the military service, the women and the girls set about to trade with fervor. They used to go by train and to transport little sacks with flour and tobacco in their girdles under their skirts. It is easy to imagine how the tobacco burned their skin like mustard did on hot summer days. In this way, merchandise was smuggled in and — in difficult cases — the guards were bribed. Besides that, some articles were brought in with horse drawn wagons via roundabout ways to avoid military controls. The prices rose from day to day. The appetites also rose and the black market blossomed. A barter market evolved as well. The peasants exchanged their produce for sugar, salt, petroleum, and other articles.

The longer the war lasted, the worse was the supply of goods for the civilian population in the country. In addition to that the quality of the necessities of life worsened as well. Bread, which was baked with cornmeal, ground small beans, oatmeal, and sweet beet roots, was impossible to eat. There was even bread mingled with straw. I saw such bread with my own eyes. I personally tasted it, but I could not eat it under any circumstances.

The shortages of the necessities of life became more acute day by day. Traveling people carried bread with them because restaurants did not serve it. There were tearooms that opened, which served sweet baker's wares made from yellow cornmeal. The yellow loaves were called "ersatz broyt"[78]. The gentiles began to plant tobacco. The green tobacco leaves were cut and dried out and became a kind of "ersatz tobacco." Certainly, real tobacco could not be obtained. The critical economic situation in the country strengthened the hand of the anti-Semites who accused Jews of increasing the prices, speculating, profiteering, and other such things.

In 1917, the Russian army undertook an offensive on the eastern front under general Brosilov, which pushed the Austrians back to Stanislawow where they stopped. In this way, the entire Rozniatow region became included in the theater of war.

The events of November 1918 were unexpected in Rozniatow. After the revolution and civil war broke out in Russia, rumors were heard that something unusual was occurring at the front. On a Saturday morning in November 1918, an elderly Austrian soldier, belonging to the unit stationed near the Russian Church, loaded wagon provisions and other military objects, hitched two oxen to the wagon, left the city via the old town on the way to Hungary. Several hours later, some Rozniatower non-Jews who had dodged military service captured him. They brought him back to Rozniatow with the wagon, the oxen, and all the goodies.

The next day, on Sunday, it became noisy in the city. Other hidden soldiers crept out from their holes and a lively movement began. Stefan Lapianecki, the murderer of the coachman Nachman Rosenmann, commit robberies and acts of violence with his younger brother Jerzy and other helpers. Every soldier on his way home to his village, was stopped, his bag taken away, and if he struggled he was beaten severely. The cries and calls for help resounded over the whole city. This situation lasted almost a whole week. Terror broke out the same day the gendarme patrol was disarmed and the troublemakers patrolled the city.

Everything was in confusion. The Jews were afraid to travel in order obtain in the necessities of life, because no city was willing to permit the export of provisions.

The wheel of history turned farther and a new era began. The political status changed. The entire area of eastern Galicia became Ukrainian and together with the Ukraine on the Dniester, which earlier belonged to Russia. A new state was born — Ukraine — which became a socialist republic.

All the Ukrainians, from large to small, with the exception of some intelligentsia, were inveterate anti-Semites breathing hatred and enmity for Jews. The city administration of Rozniatow came into Ukrainian hands without any difficulties. Fedorenko, who lived on the other side of the river, near Moczar, was appointed mayor. He was the son of Michany Borodaty Fedorenko, a man with a long white beard, who was respected as an honest person. He was a specialist of letting blood from animals who got inflated after grazing green oats. He was called in on such cases and he rescued many animals from sure death.

{298}

**The Jewish National Council**

The administration of the "Judische Kultusgemeinde" in Rozniatow passed to the Zionists. The elections to the community, which was called "The Jewish National Council", took place during the intermediate days of Passover 1919. Dr. Wassermann was elected its president. The Zionist Association revived as well and its office was in the old house of Mordechai Gross.

Shalom Rechtschaffen, inspired by the "Poalei Zion" movement, was one of the founders of the "Poalei Zion" association in Rozniatow. Its president was Yankel Diamond, a craftsman like most of the members. There was not much unity in the association. It did not last a long time and soon dissolved. But, during its existence, the association managed to perform the drama of Jacob Gordon "Chassya the Orphan Girl". The following members took part in the performance: Shalom Rechtschaffen in the main role, Motye Streichel, Tintzye Berger, Chantshe Turteltaub, her brother Miliasi, Yaakov Erber, Chatzye Diamond, who later married Yitzchak Schuster Katzmann, a brother of Yankel Laufer. My modest contribution was as the prompter.

Disturbances occurred in different cities and villages where single Jews lived. It was quiet in Rozniatow. One incident happened when a group of young Ukrainian tricky fellows beat up the policeman with the sideburns, Wojtko, first when he was dry. Then they threw him in the river Mlinowka, took him out from the water, and beat him up when he was wet. I do not know for what "good deeds" they did this.

The Jews of Eastern Galicia were neutral in the Ukrainian-Polish struggle. Eastern Galicia was isolated with no ties to foreign countries. Trade with the outside world ceased. The economic situation in Rozniatow worsened from day to day. The supply for the city was very insufficient. There was a great shortage in food and in articles of prime necessity. The ration cards for food and other articles were insufficient to satisfy the needs of the inhabitants and people were compelled to turn to the black market, where the prices got higher from day to day. There was no way to earn a cent.

In those days a committee was created, led by Dr. Wassermann, which distributed the necessities of life to poor Jewish families. Jewish merchants were threatened with expulsion for price gouging. To avoid this, they refused to sell provisions, maintaining that they had none and that they had to import flour, etc. Only those who voluntarily paid prices higher than the maximal could buy some food clandestinely.

The situation with garments and shoes was very bad. People who came home from the military service wore pieces of their uniform and military shoes that they brought home, although it was prohibited and should have been returned for the needs of the new army.

In May 1919, the Polish Army began its offensive. Ukrainian military formations passed through Rozniatow on their withdrawal march and several days later a Polish military unit went through the city singing anti-Semitic songs.

The third stage of the metamorphosis began: the Rozniatower inhabitants became Polish citizens with fresh troubles and new calamities. Nevertheless the merchants dared to leave the city to buy and bring in merchandise, despite the danger of harassment and of having their beards cut off by the hooligan soldiers.

The police arrested the leaders of the Ukrainian civic administration. They were let go after an inquiry. The brothers Lapianecki hid themselves. Jerzy, the youngest was shot to death, when he was discovered and tried to escape. After that, the older brother Stefan (the murderer of the coachman Nachman Rosenmann) who was hiding in the cemetery, surrendered voluntarily to the Polish government which released him several days after his inquiry.

In those days the gendarme commander Braianowski, a Rozniatower Pole, became notorious by ordering his policemen hooligans to bring in Jewish girls to wash the floors and to do other kinds of housework in their office. This was strictly accomplished.

The government offices started to function again, and the former officials got back their positions, without any national discrimination. The tax office was moved to Dolina and the post office settled down in the vacated tax office premises. The administration of the city passed into Christian hands. Zecharya David Liebermann took over the functions of the president of the Jewish Community.

It was still difficult to earn a livelihood. Help came in from America in the form of food packages for the population. In the middle schools, the students got a warm meal, a soup or hot chocolate, and a piece of bread. The help of some American Jews to their relatives in terms of money and even used garments was significant.

Only a few Communist adherents or sympathizers have been in Rozniatow, but no Communist propaganda was propagated.

The first bus transportation company in Rozniatow was Maciazinski & Co. run by the postmaster Denenfeld and the judge Dr. Maiakowsky and called in short "Maciazinski." After its collapse, Melech

Landmann and Aharon Zimmermann, both former coachmen, took over but they were unable to pay off their debts. Then Philip Fuerst took over the bus company, because he guaranteed to pay his dues regularly to the bus owners. In this way Philip Fuerst remained a "coachman" for his whole life.

This same destiny befell Mane Nadlers' bus from Perehinsko, which shuttled between Perehinsko and Stanislawow. There were different reasons for the bad business environment for the transportation companies. First of all, the Polish roads were unfit for motorized travel; they were muddy and contained potholes after a rain. To maintain the roads in good shape some kind of sandy soil was spread out, but it contained small pointed stones, which made holes in the tires of the vehicles. Repairs were necessary after almost every trip and sometimes a tire burst on the road and it had to be replaced immediately. If the auto owners were themselves the drivers and had some mechanical experience, they could avoid significant expenses. Drivers were paid 100 zlotys a week; their expenses exceeded their incomes.

Meanwhile, life was going on as usual. The political parties, left and right, carried on their activities. The Zionist organization expanded its activity creating the "Chalutzim" (Pioneering) movement, which prepared the Jewish young boys and girls for the "Aliya" emigration to Eretz Israel (then Palestine).

In the twenties there came a lull in the Zionist movement of Rozniatow. The only activity was to collect money for the National Fund and Manye Mintz occupied himself with that for a long time. The grown-up young people were passive. Even the progressive Jewish scholars in the Kloiz, who studied secular disciplines as well, although they felt themselves as national Jews, did nothing for the Zionist movement. Part of the fault for this situation is ascribed to the Zionist Center in Lemberg as well, because they rarely sent their delegates to Rozniatow to revive the Zionist movement. They were satisfied with the money collected for "Keren Hayesod"[79] that was sent to them.

The Communist propaganda began to penetrate into Rozniatow as well. Several Rozniatower young intellectuals became persuaded by Communist ideas and clandestinely promoted Communist propaganda. Punye Kanner was convicted for Communism.

Through a denouncement, Philip Fuerst was arrested by the district Court of Stryj for alleged Communism. He had an inquiry and, because of lack of evidence, he was released. It was a real mockery; Philip Fuerst was as much a Communist as the Rabbi of the city.

No progress occurred in the field of culture in Rozniatow. The "fathers" of the Rozniatower Community were not at all concerned about Jewish education. For a long time there was no "Talmud Torah"[80] in Rozniatow. It was not even possible to discuss the acquisition of a modest subsidy to maintain the Hebrew School, which survived on a very weak support. Nevertheless, the Hebrew School existed in Rozniatow for many years with serious difficulties. After a short interruption, a committee of interested parents led by Dr. Diamond was created and provided for the further maintenance of the Hebrew School and hired a Hebrew teacher, whose name was Kamarowski.

At the beginning all went smoothly, later on the School began to limp. Then they played Yiddish theater and the income was given to the Hebrew School. In this way several pieces were played and the income was dedicated to the School. Every semester the salary of the Hebrew teacher was reduced. Having no choice, the teacher led the school for some time on his own. After a while he packed his belongings and left Rozniatow.

The city was without a Hebrew School for a long time. It coincided with a period of general bad economic times for the Polish Jews. Middle class Jews, craftsmen, peddlers and other Jews with small income simply could not pay for their children's tuition in the Hebrew School.

## TRANSLATOR'S FOOTNOTES

1. Cheders were private Jewish traditional elementary schools.

2. The Hebrew words used here for children (baneyha) and builders (boneyha) form a play on words.

3. Stanislawow is today called Ivano-Frankivsk.

4. The Karaites are a sect of Jews who do not accept the oral Torah rabbinic tradition but strive to live their lives according to the Hebrew Bible alone.

5. A cupping glass is a glass cup placed on the skin. A vacuum applied to the cup raises the underlying tissue. This therapeutic technique was thought to be efficacious for a variety of ailments.

6. Until the late 19th century, leeches were used for medicinal purposes. The leeches were placed on the skin where they would suck blood from the patient.

7. "House of Study". It is a place whose primary function is for the study of Torah, but also serves as a synagogue – generally more informal than a regular synagogue.

8. For this and the following expressions, I have used the Polish version of spelling. The phrase "Bij Zyda" is repeated twice in the text, once with the pronunciation "Bei Zhida", and the second time with the pronunciation "Bei Zheda". I suspect that this is the difference between the Polish and Ukrainian pronunciation. I only included one version in the translation, as the Polish rendition is equivalent. This expression means "hit the Jew".

9. Jew thief.

10. A person who is an outcast and does not belong to the community. It could describe someone of bad appearance.

11. "A Jew comes from heaven so he does not need to pray." The two phrases of this adage, divided before 'to', rhyme with each other.

12. A "shire" is a "song" in Hebrew, but it is not clear if that is the origin of this word.

13. When a possessive name is added to a name, it would mean the name of the father – i.e. this name is Adela Geller, Leizer's daughter (This type of name structure is frequently used in this article, and will not be footnoted each time).

14. I could not find the meaning of this term.

15. This is a reference to miracle of the Red Sea following Exodus from Egypt.

16. Goose skin fried in fat.

17. The Hassidic movement was founded in the 18th century in present day Ukraine by Rabbi Israel ben Eliezer, who became known as the Ba'al Shem Tov. His teachings emphasized bringing G-d into all aspects of one's life, particularly through intense prayer and joyous singing.

18. The maskilim were proponents of modern, secular education for Jews.

19. A pelisse is a sleeveless cape that is lined or trimmed with fur.

20. A streimel is a cap edged with fur.

21. "Chovevei Zion" means "Lovers of Zion." This movement predated the formal Zionist movement.

22. "Keren Kayemet LeYisrael" is the "Jewish National Fund."

23. Sukkot is the 9 day major festival that occurs five days after Yom Kippur. The five middle days are not full fledged festival days, and are known as the Intermediate Days, or Chol Hamoed. During the days of Sukkot, one eats meals in the Sukka (Tabernacle) in accordance with the biblical command. Passover also has Chol Hamoed days between the first two and last two full festival days.

24. "LeDavid Mizmor" means "A song of David". It is the first words of several of the Psalms.

25. A Sofer is a scribe who writes Torah scrolls. Thus, 'Sofer' here is not the surname, but rather the title.

26. "Die Judische Kultusgemeinde" means "the Jewish Community Organization."

27. "Starostowa" was the government of a province.

28. "Hekdesch" means "the filthy place". It literally means "the holy place", but it is a negative euphemism.

29. A Kloiz is a small, informal, Hassidic prayer hall.

30. The last day of Sukkot.

31. This refers to the latter portion of the Sabbath and Festival Morning Prayer.

32. Kiddush is the blessing recited prior to the night and day meals of Sabbaths and festivals. Here it refers to the refreshments served in the morning after reciting the Kiddush blessing.

33. The head of the province – i.e., the head of the starostowa.

34. Bürgermeister " means "mayor." Burmistrz is the Polish term for mayor.

35. "Dayan" means "judge".

36. "Aliya" (plural "Aliyot") is the honor of being called to the reading of the Torah during a service. Various numbers of people are called up for an Aliya when the Torah is read. The person called to the Torah is often expected to make a monetary contribution, especially on the High Holy Days.

37. The literal term here is the "killing" – probably referring to people who would be left bereft of their livelihood due to poverty, after paying such a tax.

38. "Ulica Boznica" means "G-d's street."

39. "Minyan" refers to a quorum of at least ten men required for public worship.

40. A "Shulchel" is the diminutive of "shul" and is a small synagogue used for services on weekdays.

41. "Gabaim" are the "trustees."

42. "Mincha" is the afternoon service.

43. Groszy are coins of small denominations. It is the Polish equivalent of 'cent'.

44. "Malkot" or "malkes" refers to the punishment of 39 lashes for some sins during the time of the Temple. Here it refers to a symbolic enactment of this beating that is administered on the eve of Yom Kippur in order to inspire repentance.

45. A reference to brandy.

46. "Mitzvah" is a religious commandment. On Purim, it is a mitzvah to get drunk, but this is generally not observed literally. Here the term is used rather loosely – i.e., where it is 'traditional' to drink a great deal.

47. A reference to "Tikkun Chatzot", an optional midnight service, generally recited only by the most pious.

48. "Ketuba" is a marriage contract.

49. "Chupa" is canopy used in a wedding ceremony.

50. "Shacharit" is the morning service.

51. "Schwindler" means "swindler" in German.

52. There are two main prayer rites in Judaism: the Sephardic prayer rite of the Spanish, North African, and Middle Eastern communities, and the Ashkenazic prayer rite of the European communities. When the Hassidic movement arose, the prayer rite of Rabbi Yosef Luria, a precursor of Hassidism, was adopted. Given that Rabbi Luria was from Safed in Israel, this prayer rite was similar to the Sephardic prayer rite. It later became adopted in many communities that were heavily influenced by Hassidism, and is known as 'Nusach Sephard', i.e. the Sephardic rite, as opposed to true Sephard. In reality, it is a blend between the Ashkenazic and Sephardic rites.

53. In the traditional Jewish bathhouse, water was poured on burning hot stones to produce steam. People sweated in the steam and fanned themselves with bundles of oak or willow leaves called "besoms." Some enthusiasts used two besoms.

54. Etrog is a citron. On Sukkot, it is a biblical commandment to take the 'four species' in the hand, consisting of a palm frond (lulav), Etrog, myrtle branches (hadas), and willow branches (arava).

55. Yahrzeit is the anniversary of a relative's death.

56. Enlightened.

57. Giving loans without interest.

58. Neila is the closing service of Yom Kippur.

59. "Kvitlech" are notes with requests, where Hassidim ask their rebbe to intercede with G-d on their behalf. These notes are often accompanied by a monetary donation.

60. A mikva is a ritual bath.

61. The change in name from Melech to Mordechai here may be a textual error.

62. "Joint" refers to the Joint Distribution Committee, which collected donations from American Jews and distributed them to the needy Jews in other countries.

63. Achashverosh is the silly King of Persia, one of the main characters in the Book of Esther, which is the story of the holiday of Purim.

64. A "hedge lawyer" is a person without legal education who would write applications, affidavits, and other documents for modest remuneration.

65. The grandmother.

66. An "accoucheuse" is an educated midwife.

67. "Yad Charutzim" means "organization of the diligent."

68. Presumably this occurred on Purim and Simchat Torah, or perhaps at weddings and other festive occasions.

69. They prayed in their socks, as it is forbidden to wear leather footwear on Yom Kippur.

70. "Pany" means "Lords."

71. "Poalei Zion" means "Zionist workers."

72. "Folks Schule" means "elementary school."

73. A kollel is an advanced Talmudic seminary.

74. "Ata Hareita" refers to the prayer recited responsively prior to the seven processions with the Torah Scrolls on Simchat Torah.

75. Leading the women in elegies and lamentation.

76. "Folks-Schulen" are elementary schools.

77. "Tisha B'Av" occurs on the 9th of Av and is the anniversary of the destruction of both temples and is a day of mourning. If the 8th of Av occurs on the Sabbath, the observance itself is postponed until Saturday night and Sunday, the 10th of Av.

78. "Ersatz broyt" is "substitute bread."

79. "Keren Hayesod" refers to a "National Fund."

80. "Talmud Torah " is a Jewish elementary school.

{302}

## Sport Clubs

There were sport clubs in Rozniatow, a Polish one - "Pogon" and a Jewish one - "Chashmonaim". They used to play football on the Moczar on the other side of the river, near the small railroad of the Glesinger firm. These were local sports clubs with no official status. They did not belong to and had no relations with the Polish Sport Association, and therefore they did not have sport competitions with other football clubs. They played in competition with each other, and sometimes with the Broszniow football club, which did already belong to the Polish Sport Association. Ripne also had a strong football club with good players and their own sports field. They called themselves "Czarny"[1], on account of their black uniforms. They also belonged to the Polish Sport Association, competed in competitions and had victories. The leader of the Rozniatower Jewish sport club was Itzye Reiss.

For various reasons, there was no friendship between the Polish and Jewish sports clubs in Rozniatow. Each club was for itself.

We used to get the "Czwylia", "Der Morgen", etc. Jewish newspapers from Lemberg (Lvov), which published the most current reports from the country and the entire world. They had good Jewish writers. Some people ordered other newspapers through Shalom Laufer or directly from the editors. Often three subscribers banded together to purchase one newspaper.

A group of Jewish sportsmen from Chashmonaim in Rozniatow, where our youth practiced physical culture through a variety of sporting activities, from gymnastics to serious competitions with other groups.

A group of sportsmen

{303}

## Yad Charutzim[2]

There was a worker's society in Rozniatow called "Yad Charutzim", whose president was Philip Fuerst. According to its charter, the society was to serve the interests of the Jewish craftsmen. It did not have its own premises, and used to meet in Philip Fuerst's barbershop. Some members paid their fees, but the huge majority did not, therefore they had no money to rent a room. They even managed to perform a Yiddish theatrical performance and to organize a dance evening. Philip Fuerst was a member of the Rozniatow Community Council for a certain time.

The Rozniatower Yad Charutzim organization dissolved by itself, because the Jewish craftsmen were already struggling to provide livelihood for their families, and did not have the means to pay membership dues. As well, the central Yad Charutzim organization in Lemberg did not care about the destiny of its branch in Rozniatow and did not send a delegate to try at least to reorganize the organization in Rozniatow. The same fate overtook the cattle merchants' society. That organization began with the founding meeting in Yossel Gelobter's house and concluded at the same moment. Nothing was heard of it since.

The Yiddish Society under the nice sounding name "Casino Mieczanske", located at first at Rivka Kanner's on the first floor and then in two big rooms in Sosye Heller's basement, had more luck and a better destiny. According to the name of the society, one could think that its members were simply Mieczanes, i.e. significant, honorable, serious citizens, smart people with significant life experience, well placed and on a solid material foundation, regarding whom one should look from the bottom upwards. Indeed such people like you and I and many others, mostly unmarried, with few worries, cheerful fellows belonged there.

It was a real social club, where people gathered, mainly in the evenings, for entertainment, some with a game at cards, surrounded by banterers, some conducting interesting conversations about local and general questions. Ideologically the casino was neutral, leaning neither to the right or the left. No Christian members belonged to this society.

The Casino Mieczanske was many years attached to the City Library, whose development began from the Jewish books that remained from the Chovevei Zion Society, which dissolved before World War I. The books were lent out for a certain fee, and more books were bought. New bookcases were ordered from the carpenter and put in the first room of the Casino. With the growing number of books, the number of readers from the city and surrounding villages increased. Most of the readers from the villages were schoolteachers. The new books were almost exclusively in Polish. The president of the Casino Mieczanske was Dr. Sapir, who added to it prestige and authority. I[3] was the secretary. At first there were enough members and the Casino was able to sustain itself. Later on, the number of members declined, and many of those remaining ceased to pay their dues. Sosye Heller[4] lived in Germany and the rent was rarely paid to her in-laws, the Schnitzers from the old town, or to Yossel Kasner, a relative of Sosye Heller. The only support of the Casino was the library, which paid the rent, its only expenditure. Later on the library totally ceased to pay rent, because Yossel Kasner, who was the administrator of the house where besides of the Casino there were three more tenants, was so amiable and did not demand the rent.

{305}

## Yiddish Theater

The elementary school to the right, and the post office to the left.

A very important cultural phenomenon in Rozniatow was the practice of playing Yiddish Theater. During the summer vacations during the time of the war, we used to play Yiddish theater under the direction and supervision of Dr. M. Diamond. The performers at that time were Dora Liebermann, Grynberg and the author of these memoirs. Chanale Liebermann used to recite Polish and Yiddish. I performed a monologue by Shalom Aleichem. Hershele Fassberg took part in the performance of "Agents" by Shalom Aleichem. Dr. B. Berger was one of the stage-managers of the Yiddish Theater in Rozniatow. Later on during the Polish government, Yiddish plays, dramas, operettas, comedies by Yiddish and non-Yiddish writers, like Yaakov Gordon, L. Kobrin, Shalom Aleichem, Moliere, etc. were performed. We performed: "God, Man and Devil" by Yaakov Gordon, "The Wild Man", "The Niggard" by Moliere, etc.

Yiddish amateurs performed Yiddish theater in Rozniatow until the outbreak of World War II. The greatest merit for the development and successes of the amateur Yiddish theater in Rozniatow belongs to Sender Friedler for his intensive collaboration and personally played roles. He used to play comic character roles with great success. Besides those already mentioned, the following people performed in the Yiddish theater in Rozniatow: the sisters Freida and Gittel Nemlich, Tanya Laufer-Orthmann, Andzia Kanner (prima dona), Hanya and Leika Horowitz, Mathilda Prinz Blau, Sapir, Mathilda Hoffnung, Esther Widmann, Sindler, Same Hoffmann, Alte Landner, Estsche Treu, and others. The following performed in a Hebrew performance: Regina Birenholtz, Adela Kupferberg-Tepper, Lotke Rosenmann, Brantsche Berger and Janina Brand. The Yad Charutzim Society performed a play, composed by a relative of Zelikl Elye Mordechai Bradfeld, where he personally and Eltsche Schwindler played roles.

The following males played roles as well: Shimke Liebermann in a Polish performance, Yudele Hammermann-Axelrad, Shaya Lutwak, Avraham Hoffmann; Yadke and Sanye Freier, the grandchildren of Yisrael Winnfeld from Swaryczow; Meir Taub, Itzye Fassberg; the brothers Dr. Dan (Doliek), Dr. Naftali (Nanyek) and Moshe (Manye) Lusthaus; Dr. Leo Horowitz, Godel Schwalb, Radek Loefel, Lanner, Adelsberg, Dr.Wilek (Wolf) Adelsberg, the Hebrew teacher Komarowsky (a Lithuanian), and the dentist. Ben-Zion Horowitz was the stage-manager and Shimon Diamond was the prompter at every performance. Very little Polish and Ukrainian theater was performed in Rozniatow and never with the success of the Yiddish theater. Professional Yiddish theatrical troupes would come to Rozniatow as well.

Simultaneous with the renaissance of Polish statehood, persecutions of the Jews began. They were discriminated against in employment in government officers. I had a colleague in Gymnasium named Efraim, who was a Jewish student, a descendant of authentic Jewish parents. He spoke Polish with a Jewish accent. He was compelled to change his name into Friedrich, and only in this manner could he get a teacher job in a Polish governmental Gymnasium. There were many other such cases.

The tax informers were a real plague for the Jewish merchants. They were official governmental officers who concerned themselves with every taxpayer. They calculated the amount of the taxes owing on the basis of the copies of the invoices that they received which accompanied the merchandise that was transported by railroad, post or other means. Whereas this information was often not correct and very exaggerated, it drove many Jewish merchants to ruin.

There have been cases where a merchant received a package of books or other merchandise for his own use and study, but the informers registered these as wares for sale. Poor storekeepers who would come to the tax office to clear up some misunderstandings encountered hearts of stone.

The economic situation worsened from year to year. A tax executor from Dolina would periodically visit Rozniatow. The Jews called him "Konye with the Maavar Yabok[5]" on account of his long overcoat , which looked from afar like Konye's frock. He was an elderly man like Konye, he wore the same kind of eyeglasses which he used to prop up on his forehead and then shove back, and he carried a thick tax register under his arm. The first Jew who noticed him in the city immediately announced it to the first merchant whom he encountered. One person told the next, and every merchant who owed taxes could hide himself, but only for a short while and not more.

The Jewish storekeepers, small-scale merchants and the craftsmen suffered the most from the economic crisis in Rozniatow. The peasants were in a better shape, despite the fact that their position was also not enviable. Thanks to the general poor economy in the country, it was difficult for them to sell their produce, and if they found the buyer, the prices were low. During the winter, they were unable to find work to earn some money for garment or a pair of shoes for themselves and their families.

The Jewish merchants, upon whom the heaviest burden of government taxes fell, struggled with the poverty. They looked out for a purchaser as if for Messiah and they did not know from where their help will come. The only hope was to G-d for better times.

During these times, the Ukrainian cooperatives were created. To become a member, people had to first pay the established fees, and then they could buy some food and household articles – however not in sufficient quantities. They did not have great success in Rozniatow and were not serious competitors, since the Christian population did not have money to become members of the cooperatives.

{308}

## Jewish Victims of World War I

Rozniatow lost the following Jewish inhabitants on the battlefields of the First World War: Leib Aibye, the son of Chaim Kasner from the mill; Elye Fogel; two Benczer brothers, the sons of Azriel Fishel, and son-in-law of Wolf Horowitz[6]; Shmuel Rosenbaum; Shmuel Yankel, the son of Hersh Baruch Yankel; and Shlomo Feyge-Beyle's son. Aharon Meir Lustig died in the hospital.

The following were missing in action: Wolkentreiber, the husband of Brontzye the baker; and Leo Bloch, the son-in-law of Konye Kortszmann.

The following were prisoners: Avraham (called Ameye) Kasner, the son of Chaim from the mill and son-in-law of Shmuel Rosenberg; Abraham Groll; Leibtzye Friedenberg, a son in law of Nissan Schindler, killed in a village near Rozniatow.

A huge fire broke out in Rozniatow on the night of Rosh Hashanah night during the 1920s. It started from Mechel Weissmann and went until Yehuda Berger, and then from David the Melamed (teacher) until Yossel Kreiter. It engulfed the old Kloiz, later restored in brick; and from Yitzchak Katzmann until Zusye Zuring, the father of Moshe Laches.

All who had suffered from the fire rebuilt their houses.

{308}

## In Perehinsko

During my childhood and later on as a student I used to spend part of my summer vacations in Perehinsko at my father's relatives. I am very familiar the Jewish life of that shtetl of those times and I remember almost all its inhabitants, so that it is possible for me to share my Perehinsko memoirs as well. Perehinsko, which Jews called Prensk in short and jokers called little Paris, was officially registered as a city like Rozniatow and other small cities of Eastern Galicia shortly before World War I. Until then it was one of the biggest towns in Galicia. It is situated in a valley, 3 miles (22.5 kilometers)[7] from the railroad station Rozniatow-Krechowice and 2 miles (15 kilometers) from Rozniatow, on the main highway that leads to the eastern Carpathian Mountains, called Eastern Besides, and reaches the Hungarian border at approximately 10-12 miles (81.5 kilometers).

People used to ride from Perehinsko with horse drawn wagons or walk to the railroad station. From there, they continued on by railroad. Later on, in 1910, the wood firm Glesinger built a narrow railroad, which shuttled every day from Broszniow until high in the mountains. From there it carried timber to the sawmill in Broszniow. On its way, at certain stations where it used to stop, passengers were admitted and carried for free.

According to the oral tradition transmitted from generation to generation, generations back Perehinsko was a wild spot, an unpopulated area of just grass and trees. Gradually, Ukrainian peasants began to settle there and cultivate the soil. Jews also settled there and conducted business with the gentiles. Nearer to the Carpathians there were huge meadows, overgrown with dense grass, which were excellent for pasture and nutritious for domestic animals. Those meadows are called "polonyny" in Ukrainian.

This was a good, fat pasture for cattle and sheep. The inhabitants of Perehinsko and environs as well as the cattle merchants used to hire shepherds to drive their herds for the entire summer to the polonyny. In autumn, the herds of cattle, sheep, oxen, horses were driven back from the polonyny, some to the stables of their owners, and others to the merchants in the cities to be sold on the markets. All of those herds passed through Perehinsko day in day out. In Ukrainian "perehonye" means a location through which one "drives" living creatures. The name Perehinsko came from the Ukrainian "perehonye".

A swift flowing mountain river, Lamnica, flows through Perehinsko. The Jews used to call it "Lavnitza". It is a tributary of the Dneister. During the summer the river was used to transport timber from the Carpathian Mountains to Halicz. The logs were tied to each other, according to the width of the water, forming what was called "tratwes" or "splawes" in Polish. Rudders were affixed to the sides of the splawes, and the men who drove the splawes were called "splawniki" or "flyaskes". It is self evident that the water could not be used for transportation during rainy or stormy weather because it would present a serious danger to the life of the splawniki.

Perehinsko was much larger than Rozniatow in area. The general population of Perehinsko was over 9,000 souls. The Jewish inhabitants lived mainly in the center of town, and were occupied primarily in commerce. There were also craftsmen, such as cobblers, tailors, carpenters, barbers, etc. There were only 55 Polish inhabitants, so that Jews and Poles were in the minority. The peasants lived compactly, in small houses. They used to have a garden around the house, some fields, a cow for milk, a pair of horses or oxen to cultivate the fields, which guaranteed their livelihood. They were called Chalupniki. There were very few wealthy peasants. In their free time during the winter, the peasants carried wood or timber from the forest to the railroad station in Krechowice to earn a few Zloty. Very few non-Jews were craftsmen. Many gentiles were employed at the Glesinger firm to work in the forests with the manipulation of lumber. They worked in the woods for the entire week, coming home Saturday after noon, staying at home all Sunday, and returning to work in the forests on Monday morning.

The gentiles were culturally backward, and many of them were illiterate. About sixty years ago[8] they still wore their national garments. Men and women alike, both sexes, wore short, sleeveless pelisses in the summer, and ones long sleeved ones in the winter. Men used to wear their shirts over their pants, and they proudly marched on Sundays through the center of town in their national clothes. On their feet they used to wear chodoki shoes made from one piece of leather, tied to the feet with leather-straps.

There were two Greek Catholic churches in town and two Greek Catholic priests.[9]

Gradually the national garments were abandoned and the peasants started to dress in a more modern fashion, but still poorly. They walked barefoot the entire summer in order to spare their shoes, boots or chodoki for the winter. In the region the Perehinsko peasants were called Biakes.

The local peasants were slightly less anti-Semitic than the people of Rozniatow. They were occupied for the entire week with the exception of Sunday and their holidays with manual labor, and they did not have any time to concern themselves with local politics.

The town hall was in an old building in the center of town. I saw it in 1930 in the same shape. The mayor was Mikhail Kropovitch, a rich citizen, a drunkard, who could barely sign his name.

A Pole, Michael Tisowski, academically educated, the son of the wealthy citizen Frank Tisowski, a building contractor, was active in the municipality. I do not know whether or not the Starosta officially appointed him. He had no occupation and was supported by his rich father. The town council was not concerned about the well-being of the town. There were no sidewalks, as there were in Rozniatow, until the 1930s, and the local residents did not care. There were no street lamps. The Ringplatz was not paved, so there was no shortage of deep mud there.

The following government institutions functioned in Perehinsko: a general elementary school for boys and girls, located in a pretty brick building; a post office and a police station. For judicial questions it was necessary to turn to the district Court in Rozniatow, and for tax matters, to the tax office in Dolina.

The Jews of Perehinsko lived almost the same lifestyle as their brethren in Rozniatow and other small Galician towns. There were Jewish wood and forestry merchants, wealthy businessmen, store-keepers, craftsmen, cattle merchants, peddlers, brokers, teachers, and ritual slaughterers in Perehinsko. There were fewer poor Jews than in Rozniatow, and, in general, the Jews here made a better living than did those of Rozniatow. 95% of the Jews lived in their own houses, in accordance with the living standards of those times. There was no Jewish community institution in Perehinsko, its Jews being affiliated with the Rozniatow community. However, this was nothing more than a formality, because the only liaison between the two communities was the burial of the Perehinsko deceased Jews in the Rozniatow Jewish cemetery, with payment for the graves according to the financial situation of the deceased. The Jews of Perehinsko by themselves supported the two Beis Midrashes, a Kloiz, the rabbi and the ritual slaughterers. They obviously supported these institution from the slaughtering and the bath house income. If this was not sufficient, they collected money from the Jews of the town.

There were three rabbis in Perehinsko during a period of sixty years. The old rabbi took for his son-in-law Yudl Rechtschaffen. He was a merchant, the son of Meir Rechtschaffen and the brother of Hersh Rechtschaffen. Shlomo Rechtschaffen, a third brother, was for many years the gabbai (trustee) of the Perehinsko Beis Midrash.

The bathhouse was directly adjacent to the Beis Midrash, and could not be compared to the Rozniatow bathhouse, which was bigger, more comfortable and better furnished. The Russian soldiers, great experts in saunas, highly praised the Rozniatow bathhouse. The second rabbi was brought in from a Galician shtetl, and after his death, his son, still a very young man, took over the rabbinical post in Perehinsko.

The prayer houses conducted themselves according to the orthodox manner as in Rozniatow. The form of the prayers was Nusach Sephard.

There were no Zionist movements and societies, no culture house, and no library in Perehinsko. Just after World War I, in the 1920s, things began to move, and young people started to collect money for the Jewish National Fund.

In those days, it was stylish to dance, and there was a dance teacher. They used to dance until late in the night in the hall at Isak Rabbiner's. There was a youth society without any program. It was allegedly intended to be a Poalei Zion organization, but it was more of a gathering place for young boys and girls, with dancing, singing and entertainment. They knew almost nothing about the Poalei Zion movement.

Periodically there was a theater group playing on a stage improvised from boards at Isak and Sosye Rabbiner's hall. There was even a permanent Ukrainian hall with a stage that could be rented. However, since it was in the gentile area of town, and the accessibility was inconvenient especially during inclement and rainy weather, it was rarely used.

There were pious Jews and Hassidim, who went to the synagogues or worshipped in their homes on weekdays. On Sabbaths, all Jews went to the Beis Midrash or the Kloiz to attend the services. The following were Hassidim: the Rabbi; Itzik Juner, a rich dry-goods-merchant; Michael Lauber, who managed a small grocery store; Hershele Ettinger, a modest dry goods merchant, the son-in-law of Itzik Juner, a very honest and pious Jew; the old slaughterer Hochmann; the slaughterer David Rosenbaum; the slaughterer Shalom Hochmann, a son of the old slaughterer; Moshe Hersh Reinhartz; Meir Rechtschaffen and his brother Shlomo.

There were no tycoons, even much smaller than Rothschild, in Perehinsko. There were some wealthy, well-situated Jews, such as: Chaim Seinfeld, who was a wood-merchant, and owned his own sawmill outside of town. He had a large house and a large home economy. He was always a busy man except on the Sabbath. Because of that, he showed very little interest in local affairs. He was during the days of Dr Sapir the representative of the Perehinsko Jews before the Jewish community in Rozniatow. His father Zeinwill was already retired from his businesses. In his young years, he was a successful merchant, who thought highly of himself, and a respected citizen, from the elite of the city. His seat in the Beis Midrash was on the eastern wall. If Perehinsko were an independent community, Zeinwill Seinfeld would certainly have been its president; Shalom Orthmann and his two sons Lozer and David, were wood and forest merchants. They had a house like a villa; Shmuel Abraham Landmann, a Jewish tiller of soil, who personally worked on his fields and behaved himself according to the established order of tillers of soil; Shamei Gottlieb managed a tavern and possessed some fields; Moshe Hersh Ungar owned many fields and his own pretty house; Isak Rabbiner, the brother-in-law of Chaim Seinfeld, was the only hotel and restaurant owner. His wife Sosye was a Jewess with an earring, who was very capable in their business and used to cook and serve tasty meals. Her husband Isak played the role of a politician and was a community man; Itzik Juner, a rich dry-goods-merchant, was well known in the Hassidic world; Buchtzye Drimer owned a grocery store, where better food products were available. He was a respected person in the city, very devoted to his wife and children, and used to invite a guest for a Sabbath meal; Nachum Buchhaber, was impoverished , then worked his way up, and owned a leather store; Alter Hillmann, was a rich dry goods merchant, and a modern and intelligent person; his uncle Shmuel and aunt Sara Hillmann, an elderly childless couple, owned in their younger years a mill, and in their older years a little tavern, which sold tobacco, cigarettes and stamps.

These people were the elite of the city, used to embellish Jewish celebrations with their presence.

Uncle Shmuel used to sit on his place on the eastern side of the Beis Midrash, as befits a well-placed Jew. Pinye Hillmann, a tall man with a nice beard, was well-placed. His son, Manye, an old bachelor, had a store with different articles.

The local Jews lived with calculation, striving always towards a higher material position. They collected and saved one groszy (cent) after another, as they lived economically. There were even Jews who wore chodoki on their feet during their younger years, until they worked their way up.

Aside from the fairs, the Sundays were days of active trading (the Police looked away[10]). The gentiles, free of their domestic and agricultural worries and wearing their festive garments, came to the streets of the business center, the taverns and the stores, which they entered through a back entrance, buying food, clothing and household articles.

The middle-class consisted of merchants with mediocre earnings, small-scale cattle merchants; and finally, peddlers, brokers, craftsmen and teachers with even more modest incomes. Socially, all Perehinsko Jews were equal, as it is said "all Jews are comrades". They would enter each other's house without knocking on the door. There were no aristocrats there, as there were in Rozniatow. In comparison to Rozniatow there was a very small Jewish intelligentsia in Perehinsko, and even smaller Ukrainian one. Jewish intellectuals in Perehinsko included: Shmuel Leib Rosenbaum; David the son of the slaughterer, Alter Hillmann, Manye and Elye Hillmann, Malkele Hochmann the daughter of the old slaughterer, Itta Ludmir, Yankel Rosenthal and his brothers Dodl and Itz, plus a few Jewish students who studied privately in their homes with private tutors.

Dovtzye Seinfeld finished a Gymnasium and worked at his fathers businesses; Lolly Haber studied medicine and Fantzye Drimer Rosenthal completed a women's seminary with matriculation. Perehinsko did not produce any Jewish or gentile intellectual professionals such as a doctor, a lawyer or other diploma holders. Fishel Mintz and Yosef Yehoshua Lauber must also be included among the local intellectuals.

Yosef Czaly was an itinerant teacher. He used to teach the children Hebrew in their homes and, to make a living, he traded at the same time with hens, eggs and other little things. He carried these around in his basket, along with his siddur[11], from which he taught the children. He accompanied his lessons with the traditional melody in order to impart to the children a desire to learn.

He also was a waiter at weddings, and he earned his livelihood from all these occupations. His brother Feivel with a red beard was also a teacher of small children. He had a cheder and served as the shamash in the Kloiz.

There was another teacher of young children, David, who had a cheder. Kamul was a teacher of older children. He also had a cheder. Two other itinerant teachers were Shlomo Rechtschaffen and Shalom, the son of the slaughterer, a bachelor, who used to hide his peyos (side locks) under his ears. Another itinerant teacher who came from another city, taught older children in the guesthouse where itinerant poor people could sleep over during the night. Michael Lauber, a Hassid, occupied himself with that matter. He used to collect a few zloty for the poor. No Hebrew school lasted very long. After one Hebrew teacher left, another came, and then a third, etc., until nobody came anymore and there was no more Hebrew school in Perehinsko. The reason was that the teacher could not earn a livelihood and the local Jews also could not or could just very barely provide for their livelihoods on account of the general bad economic situation in the country, which did not pass over Perehinsko.

Until after the First World War, there was no physician in Perehinsko. The doctor at that time was Dr. Antler, a women's physician. At the same time, a pharmacy opened. Dr. Witlin, a relative of Dr. Sapir was there for a short time. After him, Dr. Weissbraun came, and, years later, Dr. W. Adlersberg, the son of the religion teacher from Rozniatow. Thus, Perehinsko had two medical doctors and both made a living.

There was a coachman in the city, Zelig Leib Fishbein. He shared the destiny of all martyrs of the European Holocaust.

Two brothers Moshe Konye and Yossye Wolf Kleinbrot were partners in a butcher shop. Moshe Konye was also a prayer leader in the Kloiz during the whole year and also on the High Holy Days. He possessed fine musical abilities. His Sabbath meals were conducted there with great pomp. The hymns that were sung could be heard in the street. The third Sabbath meal was conducted in the same manner. Much later, in the 1920s, the tinsmith Yaakov Hermann with his son Mottel founded a soda water factory in Perehinsko. Since the townspeople did not need enough of this refreshing beverage, Mottel Hermann loaded up a large wagon with soda water and sold it in the markets of the neighboring cities.

There were a few Zirler families who were called Brettler. Moshe Nussbaum was a successful merchant, and Pinchas Knoll was formerly a wood merchant. Most family names were: Haber, Hillmann, Nussbaum and Drimer. There were also other Jewish family names. Hersh the Rabbi's son was a Torah reader in the Beis Midrash for many years. There were no places of entertainment there. The youth played from time to time in the Yiddish theater.

In the winter of 1928 there was a strike of the wood workers of the Glesinger firm. They worked in the forest for the whole week, coming home from the mountains Saturday evening. Most of them were Perehinsko gentile workers. They lived in poorly heated barracks, blackened with smoke from the iron stoves. This was the only strike that I experienced in Poland. The town looked as it would before an invasion. Patrolmen with armbands on their sleeves, representing the striking workers, walked on the streets. The strike was lost already before he began. The Glesinger firm brought in to Perehinsko a powerful police detachment to help break the strike. As soon as the police appeared, the patrolmen vanished, hiding in manholes. A curfew was proclaimed and nobody could be on the streets after seven o'clock in the evening. Some workers were arrested. Despite the supervision of a strengthened police force, a group of workers succeeded in stopping the narrow railroad that carried strikebreakers into the forest to work instead of the strikers. The railroad was compelled to return from where it came. The police came a little too late and they could only drive away the strikers, who were assembled near the railroad station.

The next day the Starosta personally came to Perehinsko and, under the pretext that the stopping of the railroad that carried the strikebreakers was an act of violence, put an end to the strike with the assistance of the police. There were several telephones in the city and also several radios. Manye Nadler's (now living in Israel) bus shuttled daily, except on the Sabbath. It departed from Perehinsko very early in the morning, and set out for Rozniatow, Broszniow, Kalish, etc. until Stanislawow. It followed the same route back, returning to town in the evening.

Another innovation was the practice of the Rozniatow court to hold some of its sessions on a monthly basis in Perehinsko, called in Polish "Roki Sondawe". The economic crisis did not pass over the local Jews. No rich people appeared, on the contrary, poor people did appear. It became difficult to earn a living. Parallel with their struggle for existence, the Jews of Perehinsko did not forget their old dream to create their own Jewish community structure, and thereby become independent from Rozniatow. Preparations to build a "Beit Am", a National House, and later to work out the statute for the future community, were in full swing. After I left Poland in 1932, I do not know of further developments. In any case, World War II destroyed everything. According to some information, the Jews lived undisturbed for some time by bribing the German Gestapo, until they exhausted their means. They then had nothing more to live on, and nobody would help them. In the best case, they could only postpone their inevitable end for a short time.

The evacuation of the Jews of Perehinsko occurred unexpectedly, so the German murderers could accomplish their aktion easily. They were driven into the Bolekhov ghetto, where the remaining Jews of Rozniatow, Dolina and other cities of the region were already located. From there they were transported to the extermination camps.

Almost none of the Perehinsko Jews survived this aktion. They went on their final journey together with the Jews of Rozniatow.

These are my memoirs about Rozniatow and Perehinsko until August 1932, written down objectively according to my best knowledge. I described in these memoirs their daily life, on weekdays as well as on Sabbaths and festivals; the characters of the Jews with their virtues and defects, and their manner of life. I have spoken to and socialized with these Jews, and I grew up together with many of them. I saw them in their homes and on the street. I hope that other townsmen will be in position to relate their memoirs and impressions from Rozniatow. Rozniatower eyewitnesses who survived and now live in America or Israel will most certainly provide accurate information about the martyrdom and destruction of the Jewry of Rozniatow and the surrounding region. The annihilated Jews of Rozniatow and region are a part of the six millions martyrs in the Holocaust.

Moshe David, the son of Chaim Shimon Lutwak, 20 Sivan 5724, April 1, 1967[12]

**Jsak Mayer, Rabbiner**
MAGDEBURG
Rotekrebsstr. 22-23, Tel. 6542. Montag 2 0. VIII. 1928

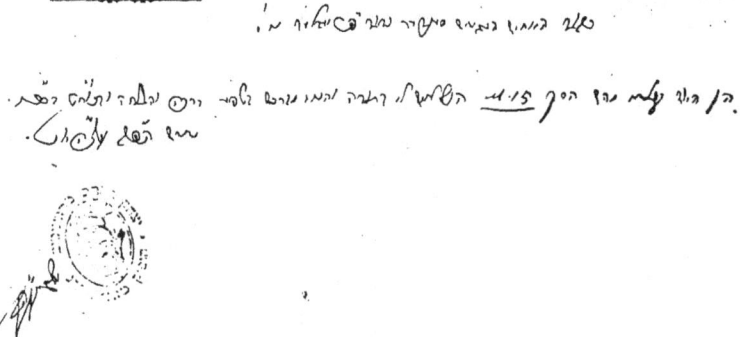

*[Hebrew handwritten text]*

{Photocopy page 318: Jsak Mayer Rabbiner Magdeburg, Rotekrebsstr. 22-23 Tel 6542. Montag 20 VIII, 1928. 13}

{319}

# Through the Changing of Times and Years
## by B. Z. Horowitz

### Translated by Jerrold Landau from a draft by Isak Shteyn

It was a small shtetl, with lowly Jewish houses. People wandered about on the narrow and crowded lanes, each of them representing a world unto himself. The Jewish manner of life was so diverse, that it is not easy to describe it in a proper fashion.

Imbued with deep nostalgia, I see the river in the city whose waters drove the mill that was leased by Efraim Rechtschaffen. Near the river is the hill with the old branching linden trees, the benches to sit on, and the path that led to the nearby woods.

On the Sabbaths and festivals of the summer, almost all city inhabitants, young and old, spent time on the hill or in the forest. The songs of the youth could be heard in the whole shtetl.

Rozniatow belonged to the powiat (district) of Dolina, Stanislawow Wojewostwo (region). The railroad station was in Krechowice, 7 kilometers from Rozniatow. Six Jewish families lived eve there. The connection between Rozniatow and the railroad station in Krechowice was with horse drawn wagons and busses to every train. In latter times, the station was called Rozniatow-Krechowice.

Rozniatow was divided into following parts: Podmonastyr, where the most inhabitants were gentiles; beneath the city, where gentiles and Jews both lived; the Rynek, inhabited by Jews and two gentile butchers; Targowice, inhabited by Jews and gentiles; the Moczor, where only gentiles lived, and where the city cattle grazed; and the old town, inhabited by Jews and gentiles.

Fires broke out very often in Rozniatow because all of the houses were made of wood. After every fire, single brick houses appeared. Huge floods took place in Rozniatow. After every torrential rain the two mountain rivers, Duba and Czeczwa, used to inundate houses and gardens, and cause great damages to fields. They tore away the two important bridges: one, located in Podmonastyr, that connected Rozniatow with the railroad station at Krechowice; and the second, in the old town, that connected Rozniatow with Perehinsko and environs.

The Ukrainian Church stood in the center of town.

The Polish Church stood on the hill. The "Sokol" Polish hall and the sports field are nearby. Across the church are the post office, the two-story school building, the court, and an historical building with a tower, dating from the "Panczyzna" (peasant-slavery) times, the apartment of the court president, the prison and the police station.

There was no industry in Rozniatow, and no shortage of poor people. There were cobblers, tailors, carpenters, tinsmiths, house painters, dyers, coachmen, horse wagon drivers, barbers, cupping-glass specialists, teeth-pullers, butchers, skinners, chickens and egg merchants, peddlers, bagel bakers, bakeries – open and hidden, small stores, big and modern shoe factories, manufacturers, confectioneries, haberdasheries, and food and grains businesses.

There were large-scale cattle merchants who exported to Vienna and Prague, and egg exporters – all Jewish. There was no shortage of thieves, card-players and idlers, of all kinds of types from all strata of society. There were brokers, matchmakers and other professionals.

The first hotel in Rozniatow was "Hotel Weissmann", belonging to Chanina Weissmann, a respected Jew.

The restaurant with a hotel belonged to Srultzi Rosenmann.

The third hotel with a restaurant belonged to Mordecai Gross.

During the era of Franz Josef (Austro-Hungarian Emperor) a "Profanatzia", that is a monopoly for the sale of brandy, existed in Rozniatow and environs. Leizer Itzik Lew was the owner. His son, Yankel Lew was the exclusive representative of Kalisher beer. The representation of Ukazhamer beer was Srultzi Rosenmann.

There were more than enough taverns and bars. The oldest tavern belonged to Melech Gross.

Wolf and Leahche Landsmann had an import house, where various merchants who came to weekly Wednesday fairs, used to stop. Many families earned their living from this enterprise.

{321}

## Outbreak of World War I

Until 1914 our shtetl belonged to the Austro-Hungarian Empire under the rule of Kaiser Franz Josef, who was a benevolent ruler. In his times, the Jewish population enjoyed peaceful and good years. The Poles had autonomy, but they were not autocrats, and the Jews occupied high positions. In our shtetl there was a Jewish judge, Hoffnung, a Jewish mayor, Vove Hoffmann and a Jewish criminal supervisor, Prinz. The Jews felt that they had a protector looking out for them. This was one of the golden eras of the Diaspora. Generally, those years were without any wars or revolutions.

The First World War brought plenty of misfortune and pain to our shtetl. The Russians entered during the same week that the war broke out. They invaded like wild hordes, robbing and pillaging Jewish belongings, and beating and raping Jewish women and girls. True, in comparison to the Nazis, they were saints, but it is a fact that the Jews suffered greatly from these saints. The Cossacks murderously beat Hersh Rechtschaffen. He remained alive only through a miracle. My father, sitting at the third Sabbath meal, was threatened to be killed by a Cossack with his sword. My father lost many years from that. They opened all stores and cellars, throwing the merchandises into the street. Our dear neighbors stole everything that they wished. There was no limit to the Jewish anguish caused by these evil beasts.

Thus, life continued on quietly and modestly, with the rhythm established generations ago. There was no big city wealth, but rather a well-to-do middle-class. Some merchants carried large-scale business, including with other cities. There were also storekeepers, who hardly could make a living. There were craftsmen, everybody with his own ideas, philosophy of life, worries and occupation.[14]

{322}

## A Foreign Culture
### by Avraham Zauerberg

Only a wicked hand
Could dare
On the water's edge
To make you suffer.
Duck eggs were smuggled to you
You must sit on them for three weeks
You are inclined
. To do this for your own children.
When they hatched
You made no distinction,
With pure wings you protected them and delighted in them
And they sang your own song.
And when they grew up
They did not understand your language,

And they left you swimming in the river.
You fled to shore full of terror,
Lest they drown.
They thought you were a fool
And they did not wish to hear your fearful call.
You oh man! With your corrupt ideas,
With your sin did you exhibit wonders?
You stood there willingly with your hands
And forgot that you also have children.

**(Rozniatow, August 5, 1939)**

**TRANSLATOR'S FOOTNOTES**

1. "Black" in Polish.

2. The organization of the diligent.

3. Literally "my humbleness" or "my littleness".

4. The landlady.

5. Maavar Yabok refers to the forefather Yaakov crossing the Yabok River on his flight from Laban. In Jewish lore, it also refers to the passage of the soul over the threshold of death. A book called "Maavar Yabok" outlines the rituals of death in Judaism. Konye is apparently a local personality who resembled this tax executor.

6. Evidently referring to one of the two.

7. The term 'miles' here obviously does not have the modern meaning.

8. This book was dated in 1967, so this refers to the early years of the 1900s.

9. In the text, this sentence appears in the previous paragraph prior to the last sentence – obviously out of place.

10. Officially, stores had to be closed on Sundays.

11. Prayer book

12. There is an error in the dates here, as 20 Sivan 5724 corresponds to May 31 (and the evening of May 30), 1967.

13. Isak Mayer Rabbiner is mentioned earlier in the text as a resident of Rozniatow. This is a note

in Hebrew script from him, written in Magdeburg. The Hebrew script is small, and cannot be readily made out.

14. This final paragraph seems to be a summary of the entire article rather than the current section.

{323}

## Parties and Organizations

The photo is uncaptioned.  The banner in the photo reads:  A Hachsharah group of Kibbutz Hamiflas

{324}

## Parties and Organizations
### by Y. Rechtschaffen

After the first Zionist congresses, when more Zionist parties began to rise, Rozniatow still only had one party, the Chovevei Zion organization.  Right after the First World War, various parties began to arise, including the general Zionists under the name Achva, Hitachdut Poale Zion, Mizrachi and Bnai Akiva, Gordonia, Hashomer Hatzair, Beitar, General Chalutz – the left arm of Poale Zion, and A.Y.A.P.(The General Jewish Workers' Party) which was completely to the left.  Since Communism was illegal, they disguised themselves under various names.  When the A.Y.A.P was closed, it appeared under a second name.

The only ones missing from this mix were the Aguda on the right and the Bund on the left, but those two organizations did not yet exist in town. There was also always a Jewish merchants' union, a tradesmen's union, a union of voluntary amateur artisans, and also a non-partisan organization called "Casino" where one could play chess, dominos, cards, and read newspapers and books. Even more important, the Casino hosted various performances in conjunction with the artisan's union, and all of the income went to purchase books.

Indeed, through the years, thousands of books in Yiddish, Polish, German were collected, originals and copies from famous writers. The Jewish library immediately obtained any Yiddish book that appeared on the book market. For a small fee, one could take out books two times a week. For a larger amount one could take out four books a week. Others would take out three or two books a week.

The libraries were always run by volunteers. I, the writer of these lines, was also the issuer of books[1] for a period of time. The only privilege of the book issuer was that he could be the first to read a new book that came to the library.

All of the listed organizations were active, and played an important role in the life of the residents of our town. Each organization could write its page of history in life, creating and forming the characters of its members. Each organization had its specific roles.

## Achva

The general Zionist called Achva played a very important role among the Zionist parties. Their chairman for many years before the war was Shimshon Rechtschaffen. He was also the chairman of the Keren Kayemet Society for the entire time.

The Keren Kayemet Society was composed of members sent from all of the various parties. Dr. David Weisman, Moshe Rosenberg and others played very important roles in the early years of the general Zionists. They played the role of non-partisan Zionists when the party spirit had not yet warmed up.

Achva Group. First row, from right: 1) Soshia Stern, 2) Tusia Fendel, 3) Esther Trau, 4) Tinchia Koral, 5) Yehuda Teffer (Lerer), 6) his wife Yutka Teffer, 7) Yaakov Taneh, 8) Malka Trau. Second row: Itka Lerer and her brother Yisrael Lerer, Miriam Zauerberg, Salka Lerer, Soshia Gelobter, Sholo Taneh, Mania Fendel, unknown, Chana and Shimshon Rechtschaffen, Ester Adlerstein, Rozia Weinfeld, Vove Strassman.

This helped them to stay on guard for the collected banners of Israel and also in all matters relating to Zionist society. However, in the last years before the outbreak of the war, the general Zionists became involved in the party camps exactly as the other parties.

In Achva, one could hear boys and girls speaking to each other also in Polish. For the most part, the youth of Achva were children of merchants, or as they were called, children of householders. However, the Yiddish language was dominant in Achva, and a large portion of the members also studied Hebrew.

## Hitachdut – Poale Zion

Hitachdut – Poale Zion had a very early beginning, and developed into one of the largest or the largest parties. The following people played important roles in that organization and served as its leaders: Leib Meizels who was killed in sanctification of the Divine Name, Moshe Lusthaus who is today in Israel, and others. For the most part, the members came from the handworkers. This organization conducted widespread cultural work, and gave no small number of representatives to the Zionist Movement.

## Mizrachi

Mizrachi had a good beginning. As it grew, a Young Mizrachi sprung up from the older Mizrachists, consisting of several dozen youths. Bnei Akiva[2] started a bit later. All of them together played an important role in the story of general Zionist life.

Reb Avraham Zauerberg was the first president of Mizrachi. He took interest in all of its numerous activities until the later years, and he remained as the honorary president of Mizrachi and Young Mizrachi until his murder in sanctification of the Divine Name.

The male youth of Mizrachi were composed for the most part of children who had studied in cheder and later studied Gemara and other holy subjects in the Kloiz; who then became more modern and their ways led to Mizrachi. The girls had very Orthodox parents, and their ways also led to Mizrachi.

## Gordonia

Gordonia existed as a small organization, whose members were committed to the idea of Socialist Zionism. They took part in various Zionist undertakings including collection campaigns, conducted cultural activity, but in the last years did not have their own permanent headquarters.

## Hashomer Hatzair

Hashomer Hatzair was indeed a lively organization, despite the fact that it did not have a large membership. However, those who belonged to the organization were dedicated to it. They often held performances, and ideological, organized Shomer evenings, that made a strong impression. They would go out to the forest, which would have a great reverberation among the youth.

## Beitar

Beitar was a dynamic organization, full of life. The spirit of revisionism, to struggle against the conventional forms of Zionist organizations, led that movement to attract a following of youth who were dissatisfied with the milder leadership of political Zionism. These people found their way to the revisionist Beitar.

## Stam (General) Chalutz

Stam Chalutz was a young organization, founded only a few years before the Second World War. Its members were not sufficiently satisfied with Hitachdut Poale Zion. It was primarily a pioneering organization. More members went on various Hachsharah events of Stam Chalutz than on other organizations.

All of the listed Zionist organizations were active. They all, some more and some less, conducted a broad set of cultural and Zionist activities. Lectures, speeches, and gala evenings were always the order of the day. As was the case with youth, they never missed an opportunity to dance horas. From time to time, they arranged dance evenings and various performances.

## Communists

The Jewish Communists conducted cultural activities. There was a time when they conducted religious debates. Later, they stopped this. They distributed Communist propaganda, primarily for

Russia. At that time, working youth who were official members were quite sympathetic to the studying youth. Polish anti-Semitism, the unstable situation, and mainly the economic difficulties without prospects for a better future drove a large number to radical activities and to the belief that justice and equity comes from Russia. The active work of the youth included the printing and posting of placards at various points in town with Communist mottoes around the time of May 1, as well as hanging a red banner on a telephone pole or other such place. Generally, the police kept a sharp eye out and tracked them. Not infrequently, there were arrests on May 1. There were those who spent months or on occasion years in jail.

From among the girls of the townsfolk, Sara Geller was at the summit of the Communist leadership. She was imprisoned more than once. She was dainty, pretty, and slim, with a fine head of hair. She conducted herself proudly.

After the war, I saw her in Lower Silesia. We were happy to see one another alive. Her father was a learned man, a first class Torah reader, and an Orthodox Jew. She also had a sister and two brothers. One of her brothers requested from me a permit to Australia via Sweden. I sent it to him, but it seems that he remained living in Sweden.

The handworkers' union had its own Minyan. There were Jewish furriers, tailors, shoemakers, and other tradesmen, generally married men. Shimon Diamand was their secretary. In the last years before the war, the movement only existed on paper. On the other hand, the merchants' union always existed. This was an organization where one could play chess, read a newspaper, spent time, talk, and sometimes conduct business.

When one reads through such a long list of modern organizations, one can come to the conclusion that Jews, Heaven forbid, left their Judaism. One must quickly admit the Jewish adage, "What is to G-d is to G-d, and what is to man is to man." The great majority of the town, more than 90%, conducted Jewish lives, and worshipped at least once a week, on the Sabbath. Jewish businesses were all closed on the Sabbath. The sound of Torah never ceased to reverberate from the various cheders and Beis Midrashes. The daily page of Gemara was studied every day in the former Old Kloiz. Not one Jewish youth did not go to cheder for several years. The respect for Torah was strong. Children from the cheders went each Sabbath to be examined by specific notables. Jewish wives and girls conducted themselves with modesty, and all together conducted a genuine traditional Jewish life.

On an excursion in 1934.

{329}

## Activists

In the various organizations, there were always some people who carried the burden of their specific organization more than others. For example, the youth Eliezer Nussbaum (Wolf Horowitz' grandson) was such in Bnei Akiva. His father, a teacher, was killed when serving as a soldier in the First World War. He left behind a widow Esther with two children, Eliezer Yitzchak and his brother Leib. They were all murdered in sanctification of the Divine Name.

E. Y. Nussbaum was a fine, well-read youth. He was scholarly, with a strong Zionist enthusiasm, along with being observant. He was given over to the idea of Torah and work[3]. He was among the founders of the Bnei Akiva organization. That organization later grew, and there were always several of its members on Hachsharah in the various locations in eastern Galicia.

Izak Barnik, the son of Yehuda Barnik, a member of Stam Chalutz, played an important role in the aforementioned organization. Izak was on various Hachsharah locations for many years. The war overtook him, and he was murdered in Sanctification of the Divine Name.

Chaim Ekstein was for many years the leading power of Hashomer Hatzair. He himself spent several years in various Kibbutzim.

Hashomer and Stam Chalutz always had members on Hachsharah locations in Easter Galicia. However, these organizations did not have great luck in obtaining certificates. Unfortunately, those who prepared to go to the Land of Israel were murdered in sanctification of the Divine Name along with their families.

Godel Schwalb played an important role in the leadership of Beitar

Uncaptioned. An Achva group with 8 men.

{331}

## The Zionist Movement
### by B. Z. Horowitz

I remember as a child the first Zionist organization in Rozniatow. In the year 1900-1901, the Zionists donated a Torah Scroll in the synagogue. This was a great festivity with the participation of the Kaluszer Music. People went through the city, carrying the Torah scroll under a canopy, accompanied by music, dancing and singing, until it reached the synagogue. Youths, children and adults, observant and non-observant, all participated.

At that time, the leaders of the Zionist organization were: Meir Yankel (chairman), Bunim Geller, Buni Reizler, Leib Yankel, Mendel Horowitz, Hersch Horowitz, Shlomo Gross, Chaim Asher Yankel, Psachya Turteltaub, Velvel Adler, Y. L. Ortman, Herman Horowitz, and many others whose names I cannot recall.

This was the only Zionist organization for the entire time until the First World War. It conducted large scale cultural activity in Rozniatow, and had a large library. It was liquidated during the war years.

A Jewish people's kitchen for the poor was established in Rozniatow in 1936. The head of the people's kitchen was the physician Dr. Moritz Diamand. A women's committee participated.

### Leaders

The Magister Leib Meizels was the chairman of Hitachdut. Shimon Rechtschaffen was the chairman of Achva. In Beitar – Sh. Zindler, in Mizrachi – Sh. L. Rosenbaum. The Hechalutz and Hashomer youth organizations were also active, however I do not recall the names of their leaders. Shmuel Lew was the chairman of A.Y.A. P – The General Jewish Workers' Party (Communists). Philip Feurst (Parizer) was the chairman of Yad Charutzim. Muni Lusthaus was the chairman of the Maccabee Jewish sports club.

Moshe Rosenberg was the chairman of the Keren Kayemet. There were Hebrew courses that took place in the home of Avraham and Pesia Groll.

I recall the following Hebrew teachers: Moshe Barnik and Z. Fasberg (living in Israel). There were others whose names I do not remember.

**The Drama Circle**

In that time in Rozniatow, there was no organization. The old leaders of the Zionist organization disappeared. Some died during the war, and others died in epidemics that spread in those days. The well-stocked library was pillaged. The final attempt was made to renew the life of the Zionist organization. The lawyer Dr Wasserman, a sick man, was selected as chairman. The organization flickered away. The newly founded organization did not conduct any activity, for it did not have the needed powers.

Seeing that the Chovevei Zion had no chance of continuing to exist, several young men decided to found a Poale Zion organization. It was difficult, both because of the hostile opinion of the Polish authorities of the time toward the Jews, as well as the lack of money. The only way to raise money was through a drama club.

Hechalutz in Rozniatow. Seated: Mordechai Trau, Yehuda Hirsch Stern, Levi Rosenman. Second row: David Nussbaum. Third row: 4th Izak Barnik, 7th Mordechai Hoffman.

A drama club also had to be legalized by the Polish administration, and had to have an official name. We requested a grant to open a culture club, without party affiliation, which would also serve as the drama club. In order to expedite the permit, the committee asked the lawyer Dr. Sh. Sapir to be our honorary president. Thus was our organization created.

The committee consisted of Dr. Shimon Sapir, Shalom Rechtschaffen, Leon Horowitz – a jurist who was murdered by the Nazis, Moshe Lutwak (in America) Yitzchak Berman (in Haifa) and Ben-Zion Horowitz (in Holon).

The most active young people in the town, bright and with sparkling temperaments, belonged to the drama club. Although it was officially not aligned with a party, most of the members were Zionistically inclined. The Zionist ideal ignited and swayed the hearts of the Jewish youth and the middle aged intelligentsia. Everyone felt an initial sensation of ascent and renewal. We conducted debates, and hastily realized the dream of a Jewish nationalist restoration. The nationalist awakening, which stormed through the mind and instilled hope for a blessed, fortunate tomorrow for the redemption of the long victimized Jewish people, progressed in parallel with the cultural life

People who were dedicated with heart and soul gathered around the drama club. Among them were those who felt that this work was like a holy mission. They threw themselves into the activity with sincere enthusiasm. At that time our town went through an era of social and nationalist ascent. The spirits were warmed both by the bustling activism and the orderliness and calmness of the revelation of people in their spiritual manifestations.

{334}

## Planting in the Land of Israel
### by Avraham Zauerberg

I intended to have seven cups
Of the six, only one unfortunately remained
However, misfortune gestured to me from the ground,
That I have, blessed is G-d, two full ones there.

As I wished, so it was
I have, blessed is G-d, one more cup
However since I cannot see it
A tear often falls from me.

I am going to plant the first twigs in the land of Israel
With tears of joy I water the saplings.
Tilla! We will, G-d willing dance there
When we make use of the lovely fruit

…. Your parents

Rozniatow January 16, 1939

{335}

## Personalities and Ways of Life

Reb Zecharia David Lieberman, the head of the community of Rozniatow.

{336}

## Jews of my Old Town
### by Zecharia Friedler

I was born and raised in Rozniatow. There, I spent my childhood and my youth, until I left the town. However that which I will relate here stems not only from what I experienced, but also from what I heard from my father Reb Leibish Friedler of blessed memory and from other Jews.

The Old Town was the earliest root of the city of Rozniatow. The town was surrounded by water, green mountains and forests. With the first Jewish settlement in the town, Rozniatow became a community, and was built up in accordance with a plan. One could see the large central square, with the surrounding business enterprises in nearby streets.

The first Jews in the Old Town were two brothers-in-law. One of them was called Gerner. (I met a great-grandson of Gerner here in Israel, already an old man. He confirmed this.) They, the two brothers-in-law leased the entire Skorbek farm with the still that produced alcohol from potatoes. They built the first three houses in the Old Town for themselves and their Jewish employees. They also built the Kloiz, so that there would be a minyan.

After that, the contract between the Possessors (as they called the two brothers-in-law) in Skorbek ended. The Possessors went back to Stanislawow, from whence they originated.

They sold the houses. The house in which I was born was purchased by my grandfather Reb Sender Friedler from the Possessors.

The houses of Reb Leib Berman and Reb Shalom Horowitz also used to belong to the Possessors. Further on, there were other Jewish houses, until the large bridge.

Before my eyes, until this day, I see the Torah Scroll that the Possessors left behind in the Kloiz as a gift to the householders in the Old Town. It was called "the old scroll".

I still remember when Reb Leib Berman donated the second scroll to the Kloiz. Reb Shmuel Wirt came from the city at the head of a large crowd with scrolls being carried under a canopy, with music, singing and dancing. We celebrated until the early hours, and ate and drank as if at a wedding. I still see to this day the honorable householders in the Kloiz, sitting at the eastern wall. The young people and other worshippers sat along two long tables.

Several Jewish families lived in rented dwellings.

On Sabbath afternoons, my grandfather Reb Yitzchak Geller, along with Reb Shlomo Yungerman, Reb Shalom Horowitz and others, would study Or Hachayim and Yoreh Deah. My grandfather's vision was quite poor. However, he was a great scholar, and he knew everything by heart. He could intelligently explain a difficult matter.

After the studying, they worshipped Mincha and Maariv, and then continued learning.

Thus did the Jews in the Old Town conduct themselves until the First World War. My grandfather died in 1915. Rabbi Hemerling of blessed memory and Reb Chanina Weissman of blessed memory eulogized him in the great synagogue.

The Kloiz with the green yard, trees and water was the center of the world for us children. There we played. There Reb Shaul Miriam-Bunam, our teacher, taught us the aleph beit. The girls studied with him until they were able to recite their prayers well.

To study Chumash, Gemara, Bible and other such subjects, we children had to walk a kilometer into the city in order to study with various teachers. As we returned home at night, we waited for each other for each of us alone were afraid to go the far way on the road, where shkotzim[4] such as Michan Jagelowicz and others lay in wait for us. That selfsame Michan Jagelowicz showed himself to be one of the righteous gentiles during the Second World War. He risked his life and hid sixteen Jews, who survived.

The High Holy Days are still etched in my mind until this day. It was already 3:00 a.m. when we went to Slichot. It was already quite cold outside, even frosty. Reb Shlomo Yungerman dressed up in a white Kittel, as he said with great enthusiasm: "The soul is yours and the body is your handiwork", and literally wept.

The Kloiz was filled with worshippers on Rosh Hashanah. Everyone listened to the prayer leader. A large proportion of the householders had certain customary portions of the service that came to them as an inheritance. Reb Shmuel Erber would sing the hymn "Kel Dar Bamarom". I recall his tune to this day. His son Leib had a strong tenor voice.

My pen will now try to bring to you the mood and feeling of fear that pervaded on the eve of Yom Kippur. At dawn, the kapparos ceremony began. Then there was the hataras nedarim (release of vows), the giving of lashes, and the giving of charity each in accordance to his means[5]. I can see before my eyes the faces of the worshippers filled with fear of the Day of Judgement.

The joy of Simchas Torah was wonderful. All of the chandeliers were fully lit, and all of the families came for the hakafot (processions around the synagogue with the Torah scrolls). Each child had a torch in his hand. Reb Yaakov Strassman called each person up for the hakafot (he had the custom of doing this). Each child would receive a hakafah, and then would get a candy. He called people up with the statement, "I honor you with a Torah honor". We children then waited until the singing and dancing began.

At that time there were two camps with regard to selecting a new gabbai (trustee). My father Reb Leibish Friedler was selected as gabbai, and a new gabbai must give a kiddush. Mother was already prepared, and we had drinks, cabbage rolls, egg kichels, chickpeas, etc. in the Kloiz. Afterward, we had a little dance.

With joyous, radiant faces, everyone went home and wished each other a good holiday.

My father of blessed memory was always concerned that the Kloiz should be clean and warm, even when he was not the gabbai. We lived in two houses away from the Kloiz, and the key to the Kloiz was always with us.

On winter Friday nights after services – it was warm – and all of the worshippers sat down as one family and talked about Rebbes and rabbis, experiences and various stories I was always interested in hearing these discussions, and I sat down together with the older men until the lights went out.

Everyone wished each other a good Sabbath, and went home.

This is the way things went until the First World War in 1914.

After the world war, in 1918, everything changed. Some of the people were no longer alive, and others were away from the city. I myself moved to Germany in 1921.

The Jews of the Old Town had a livelihood. Every house had a store, and every store had its customers. Chaya Adler had the official tavern. I still remember her husband Michael Adler. She remained a young widow with ten children. My father offered the widow assistance, since Michael Adler was a cattle merchant and a partner of my father. The tavern in the Old Town was run by us. My father gave it over to Chaya Adler, and with the intermediation of Chanina Weissman, it was signed over to Adler's name. She was required to enlarge it by one room.

Chaya Adler had an open hand, and they had an open door for the receiving of guests. A poor person would go out satiated, and with a coin in his pocket. She also provided for the needs of poor brides.

I visited my hometown in 1932. During the 12 years of my absence, our town changed greatly for the better, especially in the area of cultural activity. Organizations, unions, well-stocked libraries in Hebrew and other languages had all sprung up. An honorable young intelligentsia had arisen. I did not know any of them, and I had to ask them who they were. The same can be asserted for the Old Town. Now, none of them are alive any more.

For them, the martyrs, I bow my head in honor.

Yisgadal Veyiskadash

{339}

### Sara Esther Horowitz

I have a duty to write a few words about our neighbor, the pious Sara Esther Horowitz, who had a good heart and a source of trust, always with a smiling face.

With all of her deeds and her large business, she always found time to help someone in need. When there was someone in need, she would close her business in the middle of the day, and go out to do what was needed for an ill person or someone suffering from a tribulation.

Her husband Reb Shalom of blessed memory, a scholar, was our Torah Reader and prayer leader for Mussaf on the High Holy Days. He died on the eve of Tisha BeAv of 1914, the day of mobilization for the First World War.

Sara Ester had a business in the Ringplatz. She conducted the business in a fine house industriously and conscientiously. This took a great deal of time and energy. However, when it came to offer assistance, or to do another mitzvah, she always went immediately.

She new about and concerned herself with every poor person.

She was the only woman in the Old Town who came to worship every Sabbath.  No type of weather or frost could keep her from hearing Kedusha or Barchu[6].

She died at an old age.

Two daughters, Feiga Shnitzer and Zlata Sheiner, live in Israel.

{341}

## There Once Was a Town
### by Avraham Friedler-Scharf

Coming from the Old Town, I first met up with the river.  Aside from the fact that it provided fine scenery, it also served the heavy industry of Rozniatow, for it drove the mill.  In the winter, ice was chopped from it, which brought great profits to the economy.

The river was also our sporting place, in the summer for bathing and in the winter for skating.

From the river, one could also catch fish in honor of the Sabbath.

On the other side there was a mountain, through which there was a path to the meadows and the forests, where one could pick berries, raspberries and other fruits.

The square in the middle of the city was the business center of Rozniatow.  A fair took place there every week.  A little father was the Torgowicza, where the cattle fair took place.

The building style was not uniform. There were roofs made of tin, shingles and straw.  Without paying attention to this, a warm, Jewish life was conducted there, with every economic strata [does this sound better] having its representatives.  The communication by Alter the deaf;  the lighting by Motshe Tisch;  water from Juzi Chozek and later from Yossele the water carrier, who used to deliver a fiery speech on May 1;  health – Motshe Beri who would perform cuppings, leechings[7] and tooth extractions; justice – Eli Mordechai Bratfeld;  literature – Yisrael Leizer who would go with a sack on his shoulders, and with a certain pride on his face, always made sure that the Jews of the town had siddurs, machzors, tzitzit, tefillin, and storybooks.

Hersch Mordechai Fintshes maintained the statistics, and from him, one could  obtain information about every resident.  Avrahamele Hoffman was the address for documentation and passports.  For the civic lottery one went to Chaim Yoel Taneh.

It is no wonder that the youth saw no future for themselves there, and they traveled to all corners of the world.

Thanks to that dispersion, there are remnants here and there of our dear town, that was so cruelly cut down. There once was a shtetl, and it is no longer.

{342}

**Rozniatow My Shtetl**  by Yechezkel Neubauer

Two peaceful flowing rivers,
Like two silver serpents.
Singer birds in the morning,
Only my heart is captive.
Every minute I remember,
That there was a small shtetl there,
Dear Jews, women and children,
Who were murdered with torture and pain,
On occasion I weep in the quiet,
My hot tears in the eyes,
Each house, the synagogue, the Kloiz.
Each child who grew up there.
There is no corner there that I can forget.
I always have them in my mind.
Despite how far I am from them,
I often remember them.
Rivers still flow there,
However, it pains me deeply,
Empty is the soul,
The heart weeps and cannot be comforted…

{343}

## Times and Surroundings
### by Simcha Gross

Geographically, Rozniatow was located somewhere in the corner of the world.  The telegraph poles ended in Perehinsko, and the highway ended.  One could only see mountains, sky and water.

Rozniatow had two rivers, the Lomnica in the east and the Czeczwa in the west.  If one wants, one can count a third river, the Rika.  The water from the rivers falls down  to the mill, and from there makes a turn behind Reb Itzikel's house, until the homes of the gentiles. Then first at Wisotzky's house behind the bath, it turns once again into a Jewish river. Women wash clothes and dishes in it. The Rika flows into the Lomnica at Zarinik.

Rozniatow had no railway station, and one had to go seven and a half kilometers to Krechowice. Despite this, one could enter the city from two directions, from Stryj and from Stanislawow.

On the Sabbath, people went to walk in the forest, on the meadows atop the mountain. There we children used to follow the girls. When they came down the other side, we went together. We were embarrassed to meet, and we also did not want people to talk about us in the town.

The surrounding villages were poor. Swaryczow was always anti-Semitic. The best relations were with Strutyn Nizhny, whose residents brought onions and garlic into the city. Wood was imported to the city from other villages.

Once, a Jew from Perehinsko had to appear in court and needed to engage a wagon driver, but someone forgot. The Jew was worried, and began to run on foot from the village to Rozniatow. Along the way, he encountered a peasant carrying wood to the city, and asked him how much he wants for the wood. He answered that the cost was 50 Greitzer. The Jew said that he would pay the price, on the condition that he put down the wood and immediately transport him to the court. The peasant began to cross himself, being certain that the Jew had gone crazy, and did not want to leave his toil for naught.

Many Jews went to the villages. They got up at dawn and set out the villages on foot, taking with them a jar of petroleum, sacks of kindling, salt, thread, buttons and other such things. Back from the village they brought a few dozen eggs, a hen, a duck, and a... secret. The secret was that the cow of some farmer in the village was about to have a calf, and one could purchase the calf from him. One could pay the farmer and leave the calf with him until it was weaned. If the Jew wanted to earn two Reinish, he would have to wait an entire month.

Those who were in the egg business, and who were storekeepers, factory workers, and various wholesalers earned a better livelihood. There were also brokers who would make the rounds in town. If one wanted to purchase a wagon load of wood, a hen, a quantity of mushrooms, one would go to the broker, tell him what to bring to the house, and pay him 10 or 15 Greitzer for his service.

Marriage brokering was also an honorable profession. I recall that a mother once came with her son from a village to arrange a marriage for him. She went to Chaya Adler, who suggested a nice girl who would be able to pay 1,000 Reinish as a dowry. However, the mother negotiated, as she wanted more.

Observant Jews in Rozniatow woke up very early. It was still dark outside when Koppel Feiger, the shamash (sexton) of the Kloiz, went around to knock on the doors with his wooden hammer. He would knock seven times on each door and say, "Jews, holy nation, arise to the service of the Creator."

Every Thursday, Koppel was paid for his effort. Dr. Wasserman the lawyer, from whom he requested 10 Greitzer, once asked him how much it would cost for him not to knock.

The Sabbath had a unique charm in Rozniatow. The house was bedecked with good things. On Friday, people prepared a pipek (chicken gizzard), a chicken neck, a liver, stuffed knishes, onion crackers, poppy seed cookies, rogelach with raisins and cinnamon, and other tasty things.

The craftsmen had their own minyan. They conducted the first service in the Beis Midrash. By 8:00 a.m. they had already completed their services and made kiddush. However, they still had to wait for the cholent, which was taken out of the oven at 11:00 a.m., when everyone left the Beis Midrash or synagogue. My grandmother Freda's kugels were famous. She made a different kugel every week, a noodle (lockshin) kugel with salt and pepper, a sweet rice kugel with chopped liver, a carrot kugel with kishka, and various others. After the meat, there were large, black beans.

After such a meal, the parents went to take a nap, while the youth got dressed up and went outside to stroll.

At 3:00 p.m., the craftsmen once again gathered in the synagogue to recite Psalms. The sounds broke through the heavens. Yisrael Yukum Beila Gitze's, the tailor of the gentiles, conducted this service. Afterward, Michael the women's tailor led the Mincha service.

Michael would make new, white wedding dresses, costumes and coats. People went hungry at his home, for he would remain in the Kloiz until 11:00 p.m., come home tired, and not have energy to work. He would make a weekday bekishe (Hassidic cloak) for my grandfather every year. He would come to our house during Chanukah and say, "Melech, we are going to get merchandise." They went to Shaya Frisch's workplace and, each year, Michael asked him to give more linen. When Grandfather asked him, "Michael, am I still growing?", he answered him, "You not, but my son is growing, may their be no evil eye..." He would save over a shirt for his son.

On Saturday night after Havdalah, Adela Geller would come to us to make the accounts for the flour. Shortly after, various guests would come over for a chat. The main topic was the Messiah. They talked about world politics. They talked with Grandfather about verses of the Zohar, and various numerological exegeses (gematria) that demonstrated that we were approaching the Messianic era. They also told stories about the Baal Shem Tov, about the Rizhiner and Zidichever[8].

In the year 5651 (1911) my grandfather published a brochure called Kol Mevaser. It was published by the A. H. Zupnik publishing house. The brochure appeared in two editions. The first one had 4,000 copies, and the second one had 40,000 copies. All were sold. The main idea of the brochure was that the miracle of the coming of the Messiah would happen in a natural fashion, that is through travelling to Israel and settling there. Dr. Herzl later received an edition, and wrote a letter to Grandfather. Among other things, he wrote:, "When in later times, one will write the history of Zionism, your name will also be mentioned".

Dr. Herzl's prophecy was fulfilled. In the "Encyclopedia of Religious Zionism", there is an entry on my grandfather, Reb Bendet Elimelech Halevi Gross, a native of Rozniatow.

Grandfather's best friend was Reb Mordechai Krigel, who was called Mordechai-Meir Ber's. His house was between those of Yoel Reiner and Binyamin Katarina. Reb Mordechai was the greatest scholar in the city after Chanina. He excelled with his multi-faceted mastery of Gemara, Bible, Kabbala, books on morality, and Jewish history. He also knew how to read and write German. Throughout his life, Reb Mordechai always had more books than livelihood.

Reb Chaim Yoel Taneh is a person about whom something should be written in our book. He conducted the lottery. He owned the group of houses from Shmuel Wirt's until Chaim Asher Yankel's. He slowly sold them and lost the money. However, even in the most difficult of times, he would give the best donations. He was a maskil, and in later years he even studied chemistry.

It was told in our home that when I was one year old and sick with diphtheria, Reb Chaim Yoel found my father weeping, and asked him to visit the rabbi so that he would give him permission to travel on Sabbath to a gentile physician. Shortly thereafter, he gave my father money, so that my father would have money for the expenses. That event was later followed by further experiences, when the conductor took me for dead and did not want to put me on the wagon. My mother claimed to him that I was still alive, and the conductor should let us board. There was a professor with six assistants in the children's hospital, and I, the year old child, was immediately given artificial respiration. I was brought back to Rozniatow six weeks years later, having recovered and regained my health.

Reb Chaim Yoel came to look at me and said:

"The child will yet throw stones."

Thus it was, during the first elections to the Austrian parliament, I went as a young child to collect money for the election fund. Reb Chaim Yoel asked: "What do you want to buy with the money? Candies?"

I was insulted and answered him that for such words, I would break the glass and take away the lottery. Reb Chaim Yoel told me with a smile:

"That is what I knew already when you were one year old."

Jews often traveled from Rozniatow to Germany. They were concentrated in specific cities such as Magdeburg, Dasburg, Bockum, Cologne, etc. In Magdeburg, there was a minyan of Rozniatow Jews at the home of Buni Reizler. That minyan even had its own rabbi. At Passover, the Rozniatow youngsters in Germany would travel to their old home, where everyone had a mother, a grandmother, and where one would seek a marriage partner.

There were also those who were never heard from after they left. They were missing. It would sometimes happen that such a person would suddenly be seen in the town after ten or fifteen years. He would make an impression. Everyone would talk about him, and then he would once again disappear.

There was a Jew by the name of Aharon Hirsch in town, who lived in the intersection across from Yossel Kastner. He was in the honey business. He was a partner Ben-Zion Yankel from the metal shop. Both would set out on a journey in late summer with a wagon filled with empty barrels. A few weeks later, they would return from the journey with the honey that they purchased. A portion of that honey was manufactured into mead in the Stanislawow brewery. This was the mead upon which the Jews of Rozniatow became tipsy on Simchas Torah.

## TRANSLATOR'S FOOTNOTES

1. I assume that this means that he served as the librarian.

2. The youth movement of Mizrachi, still in existence today.

3. "Torah and Work" (Torah Vaavoda) is the motto of religious Zionism.

4. A derogatory term for gentiles.

5. Various ceremonies on the eve of Yom Kippur include kapparos (the ritual slaughter of a chicken, which is then swung around the head, and donated to the poor), a formal declaration of a release of vows, and the giving of lashes as a form of penitence.

6. Various parts of the morning service.

7. The medicinal drawing of blood using leeches.

8. The latter two are various Hassidic dynasties.

{348}

## The Rabbi's Son in Vienna
### by Simcha Gross of Hadera

Not everyone knows that our town often had great rabbis during specific periods, despite the fact that the Jewish community never excelled with great wealth. Permit me to relate an episode that took place when I was once doing business in Vienna with a dress manufacturer. As I was sitting with him, he told me that he was the son of a rabbi, and that his father had authored an important book. He remarked that I seemed a bit skeptical. He took out a book from the bookshelf, and to my great surprise, under the name of the author was written the words "Head of the Rabbinical Court of Rozniatow". This was a great experience for me but unfortunately, I have forgotten the name of the book and its author.

**Rabbi Avraham Blank**

The rabbi Rabbi Avraham Blank was greatly beloved. He was a people's rabbi. All matters regarding the community went by him. His greatest accomplishment was that the building of the synagogue, and effort that had lasted for 30 years, concluded during his tenure. The city erected a canopy over his grave in the cemetery after he died. When faced with difficulties, people would go to his grave to request that he be a righteous intercessor.

**My Teachers**

At that time, there were three children's teachers in Rozniatow. Two of them had large playgrounds, and the children were able to spend a long time in the fresh air. When they were called in to learn, they were happy and cheerful. One of the teachers was Reb David. He began to study aleph beit with the children, and then taught them Hebrew and Chumash. The second teacher was Reb Yosef Avraham. He taught approximately 100 children in his cheder, which was a difficult job for him. It was particularly difficult for him when his wife Frady died, and he was left alone. He had nobody to cook or provide food for him. He was in despair for quite a while, until the misfortune of the fire came, which to him turned into good fortune. At the beginning, he indeed did not have a place upon which to lay his head. However, when he sold the place in which he had his dwelling, he purchased a smaller place, built a house with a shop, and had money left over.

He was able to start a new life. He went around well-dressed, with a fine walking stick. Very soon, someone suggested a match for him with the lessee of the bathhouse, whose daughter was a beautiful and intelligent girl. They got married, and within a year, she bore him a son. This son was the recently deceased, able merchant in Hadera, who also served as the fire chief. It seems as if he as well was involved with fire, thanks to which his father had been helped.

The third teacher, Reb Abba, was more modern. When one would begin to study Chumash with him, he would hang six broken watches on the child, and conduct a Torah celebration on the Sabbath, along with all of the child's friends. One of the children, with a functioning watch, was designated as "the asker". My asker was Davidel Frisch, who today lives in Mexico. After the good wishes on the Sabbath, the following dialog began: "What Torah portion is conducted today?", "My rebbe does not conduct Torah portion". "What does that mean? Does your rebbe not conduct a Torah portion?" "No my rebbe teaches me a Torah portion". "What Torah portion do you study with your rebbe?" "Vayikra". "What does Vayikra mean?" "He called." "Who called?" The shamash in the synagogue?" "No, G-d called to Moses...".

Later, I transferred over to a Gemara teacher, in the cheder of Reb Chaim Shimon Lutwak. With him, broad horizons were opened for the children. He also taught Yiddish writing. He took his calling very seriously. He was also a maskil, the only one in the city who subscribed to a Hebrew newspaper.

Every Sunday, the mailman brought the "Hamitzpe" to the cheder. This paper was published in Krakow. This was a solemn moment for Reb Chaim Shimon, and the class was automatically recessed for a half an hour. The Rebbe glanced through the newspaper, and we behaved with great respect.

We did not disturb the peace. After he finished reading, the Rebbe related to us some news from the newspaper, which we repeated over at our homes.

Once, while he was looking through the newspaper the Rebbe told about a great philosopher who lived in Dolina and published many books. His name was Dr. Shlomo Rubin. He died at the age of 80 years. Hamitzpeh published an article written by a friend of Dr. Rubin's in Dolina on the occasion of his 25th yahrzeit.

### An Encounter with the Centenarian Jew from Rozniatow

35 years ago, I had a business in Vienna. An old woman was among my regular customers. One day I saw her, and then I saw her a year later. She introduced me to her father, a very old, shriveled Jew. At the beginning of our conversation, it became clear that he was from Dolina. As soon as he mentioned his name to me, my memory went back 35 years to the cheder of Reb Chaim Shimon, and I recalled the story with Dr. Shlomo Rubin. I quickly made the association. I reacted and asked him, "Did you not write an article in Hamitzpeh about Dr. Shlomo Rubin about 35 years ago?[5]" Rather than answering, he began to cite the article by heart. He indicated that he was the author, and that he used to come to Rozniatow, but this was 50 years earlier.

I asked him if he knew Elimelech Gross. He stood still, deep in thought. With a gaze into the distance, and with a thoughtful voice, he said, "Yes, I taught him how to write". When I told him that I was a grandson of Elimelech Gross, he looked at me silently, continued to stare at me, and then recited the Shehechayanu blessing, invoking G-d's name[1].

That day, I traveled to father, who was already and old man, and I told him whom I had met. Then I found out that he had been married to my great-grandfather's sister. Once, he was caught smoking a cigarette in the bathroom on the Sabbath, and he had to get a divorce. On the day that I met him, he was over 100 years old.

### A Rozniatow Jewish Girl – the Wife of the Anglican Archbishop

One day, as I was leaving the public school, the children ran after an old man. He was tall with a long, white beard, dressed in tattered clothes, and he carried a cane in his hand. He was mumbling, "Where are my daughters?" Later I found out that he had suffered a terrible tragedy. He used to have a wheat business in Rozniatow. He had a large house, and when a Rebbe would come, he would stay at his house. He had married off a son, and he still had two fine daughters. However, when somebody opened up a shop in the neighborhood with the same merchandise, a bitter competition ensued. A terrible tragedy overtook him, and after his wife's death, he left town. His two daughters went to look for him. They went to Lemberg, and never came back. Nobody knew what happened to them. Twenty years passed, and the Jew was once again seen in the town, and began to search for his children. He went through the streets without his full wits, and asked every passerby, "Where are my daughters?"

Another 35 years passed, and the Second World War broke out. A young American appeared in Rozniatow, who inquired about his family. He was the son of one of the two lost daughters. He said that his father was an Anglican Archbishop in Boston, who had published several theological works. When news of the danger that was threatening the Jews in Europe became known, his old mother asked him to travel immediately to Rozniatow and save her brother and his family.

He told us further that his mother had another sister whose husband was a well-known lawyer, and she was seeking a match for her daughter with a Jewish young man from Rozniatow. We never heard anything more about them after the Second World War. Nobody survived of the family in Rozniatow.

## A Lost Talent

My father had three brothers: Mordechai, Shlomo and Itche. Itche was a wild youth, physically strong. He did not go to the synagogue or the cheder, and did not submit himself to any authority. He spent the entire day in the forest, raising pigeons and catching fish. I was his closest friend. When he was twelve years old, something overtook him. He sat down at the table and began to write something in a notebook. He used to write until late at night.

After a time, a Yiddish translation of an English book came to his hands. This made a great impression upon him. He began to read it. He became a member of the Lemberg library. After a few years, without taking lessons, he read through books of world literature, and began to write novels and stories, which were published in a Lemberg daily.

When the First World War broke out, he left Rozniatow and reached Vienna, where he was mobilized and sent to the front. He was wounded. While in the hospital, he began to help in the hospital kitchen. However, after a brief period, he became ill with dysentery and died. It is clear that Jewish literature lost a great talent with his death.

{353}

## Prayer Houses
### by Ben Zion Horowitz

Ben Zion Horowitz.

The largest synagogue was near a small synagogue. Moshe Keves was the long serving shamash. He was followed by Yehuda Barnik. The so-called "fine Jews" and the intelligentsia worshipped in the synagogue. The craftsmen worshipped in the small synagogue.

A large Beis Midrash was opposite the synagogue. It was built in the years 1902-1905 under the supervision of Shmuel Szwindler. The local householders worshipped in the Beis Midrash. The gabbai was Avraham Groll and the shamash was Pinchas Schwalb.

The large brick Kloiz was in the same neighborhood. The local Hassidim worshipped there.

There was a small Kloiz on Herzl Street that Hersch Rechtschaffen set up when he became angry with the Beis Midrash.

There was a Beis Midrash in the Old town where the Jews from that neighborhood worshipped. Leibish Friedler was the gabbai.

Below the city, in the home of Taube Lerer, there was a small synagogue where the Jews of that neighborhood worshipped.

Not far from the synagogues was the steam bath, the mikva (ritual bath), and a poorhouse where the poor people who came to Rozniatow from other places could spend the night.

In 1936, the community set up electric lights to light up the large synagogue, the Beis Midrash and the Kloiz. They purchased a diesel motor that ran during the times of services. At that time, lighting was also set up in the bathhouse.

Until the time of the Second World War, there were no electric lights in Rozniatow. The Russian liberators provided us with electric lights. The electrical station was set up in the city mill, where there was a turbine whose blades were driven by the water from the river. Thus, the mill was converted in to an electrical station that operated only in the summer. When the river began to freeze over, there was no light.

Until the outbreak of the Second World War, the rabbi, Rabbi Yosef Menachem Maczner, led services in the large synagogue. People hastened to hear the rabbi worship and sing over all other prayer leaders.

Yaakov Hochman, Hersch Rechtschaffen, Reuven Getzel Heizler, Shmuel Nussbaum (in Rechtschaffen's small Kloiz), Gedalya Weber, Shlomo Yungerman, Reb David Glass, Shmuel Szwindler and Avrahamcha Zauerberg[2].

The ritual slaughterers were Reb David Glass, Reb Moshe Weizer, his son Reb Zeida, Reb Yaakov Hochman and Reb David Roth.

We Remember

A group of Rozniatow natives at the dedication of a monument in the forest of the martyrs. Photographed by Mordechai Stern.

{355}

## Mordechai Strassman

The head of the family, Mordechai Strassman, was called Motialon. He was an athletically built man, not tall, and in his forties. He went around to the villages, and also conducted business. He earned his livelihood. The gentiles of Rozniatow and the surrounding villages were afraid of Motialon's strength. When drunken gentiles would become wild in a Jewish tavern and they could not be calmed, people would run to Motialon for help. Motialon would calm the wild gentiles with his fists. Similarly, during the fires that often broke out in Rozniatow, Motialon would be one of the first to come to the rescue, when it was possible. Motialon would gladly help anyone in need.

His wife Rivka, a peaceful homemaker, was occupied with raising their four children. There were three girls, Neshi, Esther Rachel, and one son Avraham. They lived on Herzl Street, opposite Rechtschaffen's small Kloiz. For a certain time after a fire, we rented a dwelling from the Strassman's. Their children were calm and well raised.

In 1941, when Hitler's hordes entered our town, Jews began to flee in a great panic. We wanted the Strassmans to go with us. They categorically refused, but they allowed their only son, Avraham, to travel with us. Thus did we travel, and Avrahamche always came with us.

We often had to flee, whenever possible, on account of the frequent bombardments by the German airplanes. Avrahamche Strassman once disappeared from us. We searched for him for a long time but could not find him. Thus we arrived in Russia without Avrahamche.

Mordechai, Rivka, Neshi, Esther and Rachel were all killed.

I again took interest in Avrahamche when I returned to Rozniatow from the Russian army in 1945. The Russian military commandant (Voyenkom) named Samolov told me the following:

"Avraham Markovitch Strassman was mobilized in Russia in 1942. He joined a Cossack unit. He was greatly loved in his unit. He was promoted to sergeant and took part in all the battles of his unit.

In May 1945, he fell in battle near Koenigsberg, a few days before Hitler's downfall[3]. Taking revenge for the murder of his father, mothers and sisters, he gave up his young life. Honor to his memory."

He was decorated with a high medal. Since he had been killed, the medal was sent to the military commandant in Rozniatow, with the hope that someone from his family would be alive to receive the documents and the accompanying documents.

A person came to the city commandant, presenting himself as a relative of the Strassman family. He received the medal and accompanying documents. I was unable to ascertain where these ended up.

Thus was a family wiped out, without leaving any memory.

{356}

### Reb Shmuel Wirt (Ingtom)

It was told that he was a cattle merchant in his younger days, making the rounds to the fairs, buying and selling. He was very successful, thanks to his honesty and intelligence. People proposed the best matches to him.

After his marriage, he had a business with meal, bran, and seeds. G-d blessed him with seven daughters, a son, and great wealth. For his daughters, he searched only for scholars as matches. G-d indeed helped him, and sent him one by one sons-in-law who were scholars. He used to always say:

"With sons, one must always have Divine help, for they might either be good or bad. However, with daughters one only needs a large pocket of money, and then you can purchase for them whomever you want."

Indeed, he did not spare any money. He paid for and purchased the best sons-in-laws for his daughter. From his daughters and son-in-law he had a very large family with children and grandchildren.

All of the seats in the marketplace and half the Rynek (town square) were for his sons-in-law and grandchildren.

Reb Shmuel Wirt merited to have contentment from his grandchildren as well. They also married scholars.

His funeral, already during the Hitler times, took place with the participation of the entire town. It is fitting for his honor to mention his sons-in-law by their names:

Reb Shmuel Wirt.

Reb Yosef Shimon Stern, Reb Binyamin Spiegel, Reb Kalman Halperin, Reb Avrahamche Zauerberg, Reb Yisrael Karnobli, Reb Dov-Berish Weiss, Reb Ben-Zion Strassfield, and his only son.

It would be appropriate to fully describe each of these young men. Each was a world unto himself, a scholar, a merchant, a communal activist, intermingling Torah with business. However we cannot describe each one separately in such a restricted place.

Why was he called by the nickname "Ingtom"? I asked that question to many Rozniatowers, and almost nobody could answer, until I came a cross and old time native who now lives in Hadera, Mrs. Gross, the grandson of Melech Gross. He told me the following story:

Reb Shmuel Wirt was a wealthy man, content with his lot, and a great prankster. Among all else, he was known in the town for his deeds on Simchat Torah, when he moved worlds to ensure that everyone was happy, both young and old. He used to gather together children from all of the Kloizes and synagogues, give them candies, act silly with them, and present himself as an officer. Why this? It was very simple. He took his silk kapote, and stuck its corners into his belt. He took hold of his gray beard and divided it into two parts, took a hoe and spade and arranged them with his arms on his shoulder, and issues a command to the children: "Hop, follow me!" He walked with the hoe and spade through the streets, and the children followed him with shouts and laughter. Then he began to issue orders like a veritable officer: "Right, left, right". Adding "Uhm" in the Austrian language. An old man, without teeth, the, "Links-uhm" sounded like "Ing-tom", and thus did he get the nickname "Ingtom". Nobody knew him as Shmuel Wirt, but rather Shmuel Ingtom.

### Binyamin Keller

He was another Jew with a known nickname, "Katarina". Why was he called thus? Reb Simcha Gross from Hadera continued on with the following story:

Binyamin, the son of Baruchl, had the habit of shouting out with great ecstasy "Viktirna Ktores" during the recital of "Pitum Haktoret" at the Mincha service. "Viktirna Ktores" – and he continued on silently "Tamid Lifney Hashem Ledoroteichem"[4]. Thus came the nickname "Katarina".

### The Spiegel Family

In the region of Rozniatow, there were larger and smaller villages in which Jewish families had lived for many years. They lived well-organized lives with their own businesses. There were also poor families who barely eked out their living from various sources. The children studied in the surrounding towns. Most of the Jews spent the festivals in the nearby towns.

The communal life of Jews in Ukraine was for the most part peaceful. Every gentile had his own Jew. When the gentile was in need of help, he turned to his Jew, and always found good neighborly assistance.

After the first World War, unfriendly winds began to blow toward the Jews in the villages. Ukrainian agitators began to stream into the villages and conduct incendiary agitation against the village Jews. Ukrainian national cooperatives, Ukrainian shops and stores, and cooperative purchasing agencies were set up in the villages so that they could purchase all of their agricultural needs from the peasants. The gentiles were compelled to sell all of their agricultural products at cheap prices. The Jews had formally paid them higher prices. Thus were the Jews in the villages squeezed out of their livelihoods. The anti-Semitism strengthened materially and physically.

Thus was the Jewish-Ukrainian ideal destroyed.

Without any option, the Jews began to leave their well-established homes in the villages, and began to reorganize their lives in the towns.

The Spiegel family was one of the Jewish families who left the villages and settled in Rozniatow. They were a large family. The head of the family was Eli Spiegel, a middle aged man, industrious, with a good character, and beloved by all of his neighbors. His wife Chaya was a good, industrious homemaker, who helped people in need.

They lived in their own house, worked their own field, and had cows. During those times, Jews would say, "It is nice when a person has a sufficient supply of his own potatoes, and a cow in the barn that gives milk. He is protected from hunger." The Spiegel family were such people. They married off their children and helped them to establish themselves. Grandchildren were born. They were content.

However, the "Nazi plague" broke out, to the misfortune of mankind, which put an end to the hopes, fine dreams, and plans.

Disturbances, terror and despair pervaded in the Spiegel family. The parents did not know what had happened with their children in Germany. When the "Ost-Juden" were driven out by the Nazis from Germany back to Poland, and were left helpless at the border at Zbaszyn, Moshe Spiegel, his wife and three children were among those unfortunate, helpless Jews. The first victim there was Moshe Spiegel's daughter, who was unfortunately shot before the eyes of her parents. We know nothing about the fate of the remaining children of our neighbors who were in Germany.

Eli and Chaya Spiegel and their children who lived in Rozniatow were driven to the ghetto in Dolina.

Two children were left of that large family. Yitzchak Spiegel left Germany in 1933, made aliya to the Land of Israel, got married and lived in Haifa. He died recently. Chana Spiegel made aliya to the Land of Israel from Rozniatow in 1937. She got married to Philip Hirsch, and they established themselves well. They have a married daughter and three picture beautiful grandchildren. May they be well.

## The Zimmerman family

The head of the family was Meir Zimmerman, and was known by the nickname Meir Kozeh. He was a shoemaker by trade. He was a widower, for his wife Mirchi the daughter of Sashi Feiga died in 1933. Meir Zimmerman was a quiet, sincere person. He was a father of five children. It was not easy to raise five children under those circumstances, with only the help of the hammer and the shoemaker's thread, and without any outside help. The children were raised well.

Dvorah's husband was Nachum Leib Zimmerman, the son of Moshe and Keila Zimmerman, a tailor by profession. Their son was Mottel. They lived with her father. There was also Avraham Yechezkel, a hair stylist. Leib worked for Shmuel Friedler in his manufacturing enterprise. There were also Chaya Rivka and Yankel.

When the children grew up and began to work and earn income, they helped their sick father. Thereby, they lightened the difficult life of the family. This continued until the catastrophe that came in June 1941, which put an end to everything.

When the murderous hordes began to enter the town, and the danger was very great, the Jews began to gather on the roads, seeking out hiding places. Two groups formed. A smaller group decided to leave immediately, and set out on their way. The larger group decided to remain in their homes at Hitler's mercy. Horses and buggies were provided for Communist functionaries. The only available route was to Stanislawow, 49 kilometers away.

With great fear of being shot, we set out to Stanislawow. Meir Zimmerman's four children, Avraham-Yechezkel, Chaya-Rivka, Leib and Yankel also went with us.

It was not easy to continue on with the train from Stanislawow. The city was already evacuated. Therefore, we had to gather in the train and travel further. The train was often bombarded.

Thus did we travel on to Husiatyn, where our train was once again bombarded strongly. There were many dead and wounded, and there was no assistance of any kind. A great panic ensued. People ran around shouted, and did not understand each other. People began to run home on foot.

We used all means to calm our people and convince them that for us, there was no other way but to travel on, despite the many different dangers. There, there would be many chances to save ourselves. No means of argument helped. A significant number of our people left us with the aim of returning home, without paying attention to the fact that the way itself was a great danger.

Among those who returned from Husiatyn were also the four children of Meir Zimmerman: Avraham-Yechezkel, Leib, Yankel and Chaya Rivka. Back home, they suffered the same fate as millions of martyrs.

This was the tragic end of the family of Meir Zimmerman, which was erased from the earth.

The same fate suffered by the family of Meir Zimmerman was also suffered by Moshe Zimmerman, his wife Keila, two sons and two daughters.

May G-d avenge their souls.

## TRANSLATOR'S FOOTNOTES

1. The Shehecheyanu blessing is made on joyous occasions (Jewish holidays, as well as personal occasions of joy such as moving into a new house, wearing new clothes for the first time, etc.). If there is a doubt whether a blessing needs to be recited, it is recited without using G-d's name. The inclusion of G-d's name indicates that there was no doubt about the requirement of reciting the blessing.

2. This list of names has no description, but I believe from the context of the previous paragraph that it is referring to prayer leaders.

3. Hitler actually committed suicide on April 30, 1945, but the war lasted for another several days.
4. These are quotations from the daily recital of the incense ceremony of the Holy Temple. This is re-

cited at the daily morning services, and also in some customs at the daily afternoon (Mincha) service.

5. The article states '15' years ago. I suspect that this is a typo, and 35 was intended.

{362}

## The Third Sabbath Meal in the Old Kloiz[1]
### by Moshe Fruchter

You feel a holy shudder when you recall a world that once existed, isn't there anymore, and will never be again.

It is dark in the Kloiz. People wash their hands for the third Sabbath meal (shalosh Seudos).[2] Sabbath loaves (challas) and herring are on the tables. People recite the blessing over the bread, dip a slice of bread into salt, and eat challa with herring. The slaughterer's son Yankele sings "Bnei Haycholo"[3], and everyone else joins in. Shadows move over the walls, and we children cling to our fathers. All is so secret, so mysterious. From time to time there is a sigh "O Father in Heaven, have pity on us." Zayde, the slaughterer's son, sings "Vetzivo"[4]. Someone repeats a nice saying heard from the Bolekhower or Belzer Rebbes.

Finally following the meal, recitation of grace begins in the darkness -- loudly, calmly, and gloomily. It's a pity that the Sabbath is ending.

"Vehu rachum yechaper"[5] is heard at the beginning of the evening service. The beadle (shammash) Kopel lights a candle. The mystery vanishes for us children. It becomes less happy, but the sadness doesn't vanish. We do not wish to take leave of the holy Sabbath, which is passing, and we feel that a part of our soul is being torn away. It is the "additional soul"[6] of the holy Sabbath that is departing.

The month Elul[7] in the Shtetl

Who does not know that when Rosh Chodesh[8] of Elul arrives, even the fish in the water tremble. The Jews start to make a personal inventory of the soul comprising their sinful deeds during the year. They try to improve the situation – which is still possible this last month of the year – through prayers, charity, and good deeds. During the whole month of Elul, the shofar[9] is blown every weekday after the morning prayers. The Rozniatower Jews crowd the synagogues for the morning and evening prayers, more than they had done during the rest of the year, and collect donations for local people as well as strangers, wishing each other at every opportunity a good "kvittel"[10], and a "Ksiva vachasima tova"[11]. At every "lechayim"[12] during Elul, the main wishes were to obtain by prayer a "Ksiva vachasima tova" for the next year.

A very important place for prayers for Jews is the cemetery, also known as the "house of eternity," or, as they called it usually "the holy place". From the first day of Elul until the eve of Rosh Hashanah[13] the holy place is full of living people. Old and young visit the holy place. With a little book in their hands, a special book containing prayers recited at graves, a prayer book or a book of psalms, they come to the graves of dead parents, aunts, uncles, grandparents, and other relatives. They come to ask them to be defenders[14] for them, to pray for a good year for their relatives and to obtain salvation for the New Year.

The noise of the assembled crowd can be heard before entering the holy place. On the other side of the gates, the poverty stricken Rozniatowers – women, men, and even children of different ages – sit in a row waiting for donations. The Rozniatower Jews give these donations; some give more, others less. There is never a lack of beggars in the shtetl. Worse is the lot of the secret poor, who are ashamed to take donations. Some even give a donation out of shame.

The cries by the entreating Jews at the tombstones can be heard from afar. After calling out to dead relatives and strangers, people go to the "shtiblech"[15], where "tsaddikim"[16] are buried. Many candles are lit. Who can understand the soul and feelings of a Rozniatower Jew who cries his eyes and bitter heart out at the tombstone of a relative?

If someone finishes prayers at the tombstone, the "tuckern"[17] Sarah-Malka comes by to speak to the dead with a touching but firm voice. She knew everybody's "tzores"[18], i.e., where one's shoes pinched. This one has to marry off a daughter, a second needs "parnosse"[19], a third one a male child, etc. With her voice she could touch a stone[20], thus people near the tombstone started to weep and to sob even more. Everybody was convinced that Sarah-Malka is an honest and "kosher"[21] Jewish daughter and that she is begging mercy and spilling tears for the troubles of a whole shtetl of Jews.

**TRANSLATOR'S FOOTNOTES**

1.   A Kloiz is a Hassidic prayer hall.

2. Three meals are mandatory on the Sabbath. The third meal, late in the day, is often eaten in the synagogue.

3. "Bnei Haycholo," which means "Sons of the Temple," is hymn sung at the third Sabbath meal.

4. "Vetzivo," which means "He commanded," is another Sabbath song.

5. Vehu rachum yechaper" means "Let the Merciful One forgive." It is the opening verse of the weekday evening service, which would immediately follow the Sabbath.

6. It is thought that Jews are imbued with a supplemental soul on the Sabbath.

7. The Jewish month of Elul commences in August or early September. It precedes Rosh Hashanah, and is a month of penitence.

8. Rosh Chodesh is the first day of every month.

9. A "shofar" is a ram's horn, blown on Rosh Hashanah, and also on each weekday morning during the month of Elul.

10. A "kvittel" is a note, referring to the divine decree on a person for the upcoming year.

11. "Ksiva vachasima tova" means "a good entry in the book of life." It is a popular belief that in heaven a ledger is maintained (in a figurative sense) where the verdict of each person for the coming year is stored. On Rosh Hashanah, this verdict is determined.

12. "Lechayim" means "to life" and is the traditional Jewish toast over a drink.

13. "Rosh Hashanah" is the Jewish New Year.

14. "Defenders" are advocates, persons or angels, who put in "a good word" for you when needed.

15. Shtiblech are modest memorial rooms built of brick or stone over the graves of tsaddikim.
16. "Tsaddikim" are especially pious Hassidic rabbis.

17. A "tuckern" is an attendant in a mikveh (ritual bathhouse).

18. "Tzores" means "troubles."

19. "Parnosse" means "livelihood."

20. An idiomatic expression similar to "her voice could shatter glass."

21. In this context "kosher" means "just."

{364}

# A Winter Sabbath
## by Shmuel Kirshenbaum of New York

It was cold. The frost was especially strong in the back alleys at the water near the Torgowica. There were large, thick forests around our town, but there was not enough wood for heating in many houses on my alley. On such a cold Sabbath early morning, the Sabbath Goy[1] would come, extinguish the lamp and put on the heat. Through the snow and frost covered windows, one could see smoke coming out of the chimneys here and there, leaping skyward like a spring.

The alleys come to life. The Jews go toward our shtibel to the right of the Beis Midrash. I can see Hirsch Lozer Wechter with his old, faded streimel and long kapote crossing the small bridge near the bath.

My father Leibele is already dressed in his American suit, and is ready to go to the first minyan. I get dressed in the Sabbath cap that my mother bought for me for Passover and a white shirt, and I am also ready. We hear a knock on the window, "Leibel, Shmuel, come". Through the ice-covered window, one can only see the gray beard of my grandfather Kuni.

My father and I are already on the street. We exchange the greetings, "Good Sabbath Father! Good Sabbath Grandfather! Good Sabbath children!". We go to worship in the first minyan. We throw off our weekday worries. It is the Sabbath. One jump and we are in the Beis Midrash. Grandfather is already at the reader's podium. That was his place, and it had already been his custom for many years to call up the wagon drivers, tailors and shoemakers to the Torah. A feeling of exultation sparkles in his heart. The old but healthy tailor stands at the reader's podium, his entire height covered with his tallis, enveloped in sanctity. We are reciting Shacharis (the morning service). I stand with my father Leibel near the podium, but my glance is fixed upon the tall Jew at the podium, my grandfather Kuni.

We take out the Torah scroll. I am already next to Grandfather. The scroll is unwrapped – and my grandfather's time arrives:

"May he arise!"[2]

{365}

# Fires in the Town
## by Y. Rechtschaffen

Fires always broke out at night, mainly among poor Jews. The fire would completely ruin them, and the community had to help them get back on their feet. Intelligent people would solve the riddle: since there were several dozen gentiles whose job it was to build houses, in the event that there would be a period without work, starting a fire would be their only way not to go through the entire summer without work.

All of the writing cannot portray the experience to someone who has not experienced a fire in a small town. A fire is a bizarre experience, one of those that provokes and terrifies moods. A portion of the Jews went around in a panic, and others did not come for a while, until they heard the shout, "Emergency, emergency, a fire!" A panic ensued. One asked the other, "Where is it burning?", and then they themselves began shouting, "It's burning!".

It took a bit of time until people realized what was happening. At first they began to ask: "Where? Whose house is on fire?" Everyone got dressed, and people prepared themselves. They ran outside, and saw the large fire. The sky was red, the fire got larger and larger. The houses were all built of wood, and they dried out with age. It would only take a small incident for such houses to catch on fire. The residents were greatly afraid of such. The nearby neighbors already had already dragged out all of their belongings in sacks and handbags. Even those far away were already prepared, packed up, sitting outside with their belongings.

Those at the other side of town would also not go to sleep until they saw with their own eyes

When one recalls a fire in the town, one remembers the dedication and devotion of the large number of Jews who always excelled with their restraint and calm at the fires as they went about their work: some of them saved the neighbors' belongings, others put out the fire. Even in the modern times when there were professional firefighters, our Jewish brethren worked quickly and effectively at fires in town. There were those who were always active and had sufficient experience. I recall that Shalom Hoffman, Vove's son, used to be one of the first to come to the rescue. He specialized in extinguishing. My older brother Shalom was also one of those who ran to extinguish a fire. There were many others like them.

At the beginning of the 1920s, a fire broke out in the middle of the Rynek. The house of Mendel Nemlich, who had returned from America a week before the fire, had now gone up in flames. Terrified and panicked, he ran out onto the street half-naked and began to shout frightfully.

A large portion of Rynek burnt down in that fire. The home of my uncle Yeshaya Frisch, whose wife Henche was my mother's sister, was also burnt down. They sold the place, took their grandchild Shimshon with them, and traveled to the Land of Israel. A fire was a terrible experience, and those that lived through it suffered materially for many years thereafter.

## Mendel Horowitz

Mendel Horowitz and his wife lived not far from the communal buildings, in a house that used to belong to the rabbi Reb Itzikel. They had no children. They had a business in the market that sold earthenware pots, cutlery, lamps and other similar merchandise. As a youth, Mendel was already one of the first Maskilim, and later one of the first of Chovevei Zion. He was deeply immersed in Bible. In those days, if anyone stepped away from the path trodden by their fathers, such as for example by reading books, studying Bible and not only Gemara, studying Hebrew, shaving – such a person would be known by the term "Germanized". With time, the numbers of such people increased, as one became accustomed to the new winds. There were already youth who shaved, but not all were as intelligent as they once were.

Every day, Mendel would read every daily publication, Hatzefira, and other weekly and periodical publications. He would constantly analyze political situations, and arrive at certain conclusions. In general, his political diagnoses were valid from an intellectual standpoint. Intelligent people always wanted to know the opinion of Mendel Horowitz. Dr. Sapir, the former communal leader, an active lawyer, would always visit the store of Mendel Horowitz if new political news from the world came.

Mendel was always immersed in world problems. He had innumerable friends and acquaintances. Psachya Turteltaub was his close friend. He was a bookseller by trade. He was also proficient in Bible, and he read world literature. David Barnik was cut from the same cloth. Moshe Krencler was a recently arrived Hebrew teacher, and a contributor to Hatzefira. If I ran into them hashing out an issue, it would be a truly uplifting experience to listen in on the debate.

All the aforementioned, and tens of others of their friends died in sanctification of the Divine Name along with their families.

### Reb Lipa Taneh

Reb Lipa Taneh and his family lived below the town. He was a neighbor of Baron Waljusz. He had a large house, a yard with pens and stalls, cattle, fowl and horses. He had a large, long garden and an orchard, whose trees were bedecked with various fruits, such as apples, pears, and plums, at the time of ripening.

With his fine black beard and fine appearance, Lipa looked like someone from the old world, as described in books. However, our Lipa stood in the new world with both feet. At a time when Jews had no future in business, he himself had fields, cattle, and a pair of horses upon which he could ride through his fields. His son Yisrael worked together with him. He obtained experience in agriculture, and at the first opportunity; Yisrael went away to Argentina, where I believe he lives with his family.

I cannot believe that the fine and sturdy Lipa, who had a pair of strong working hands, ever hurt someone with his hands. To this day, I cannot believe the goodness of the man, for he would open up his orchard to the entire town for the entire summer, and let people pass through his property so that they could have a shortcut to the large body of water, as we called it. So that Jews would not have to go out of their way by several hundred meters, he opened up his own property, even though the Jewish pranksters often played tricks while walking through the garden.

The large body of water, as we called it, was very popular in the summer. Lipa Taneh's garden turned into a public domain on the hot days. After bathing, some people even went into Lipa's house to eat a meal. People were always greeted pleasantly in that house.

His young daughters were already modernized, but they carried with them the goodness of their parents. Only their daughter Mirchi was fortunate to come to the Land of Israel. Shlomtzi and Mirchi Taneh got married and built up a fine family in Israel.

Lipa Taneh upheld the customs and traits of the old generation. He recited his prayers three times a day. He bore the yoke of Judaism and demonstrated that one could be a Jewish farmer while serving the Creator and remaining true to one's people.

## Yossele Wassertreger (Yossele the Water Carrier)

Yossele, or as he was called "Yossele Biegem" came from Bolechow with his older brother. His brother got married, became a porter, and lived on the Torgowica. He worked from morning to night at carrying sacks of grain, and brought home the few zlotys that he had earned for the day to his wife. He was a slender young man of average height and with a long face. He was young, but with a forehead full of wrinkles like an old man. By looking at the young man, one could not believe that during the course of a day, he would move entire wagon loads of grain and flour from place to place.

Why did he leave his birthplace of Bolechow? Whose concern is this? He brought his young brother Yossele with him. He was short, wide boned, flesh and bones, smooth faced, and his eyes were always blinking. He always had a childlike smile on his face, and he attracted everybody with that smile.

He was tattered, always with old clothes, and a torn cap on his head. He carried his water pole on his shoulders, with two buckets of water. He charged 5 groszy for each time he carried water.

In his childhood, Yossele studied in cheder. He had heard all of the stories from the Chumash, and he absorbed them. His imagination worked hard. When he got a bit older, together with the young workers, he heard about a Communist Party and about Lenin, Trotsky and others who will help humanity. They influenced him. Everything got mixed up in his head. His greatest ambition was to hold speeches. He only had to have one or two listeners, and he launched into a speech. Moses and the righteous Joseph were entangled with the names of Marx and Trotsky. Miriam and her drum[3] were never lacking from his speeches. When he went forth in ecstasy, he shouted out, "And a time will come when one carrying of water will cost 10 groszy, and not the 5 groszy of today. This will be when the revolution is victorious…"

He was an idealistic, refined soul, and one says, the world gave him something. His brother became very ill and died. Yossele continued to carry water from morning until night and became somber and gloomy. His thoughts concentrated on his late brother whom he loved. He wished to carry on the revolution for him, so that he would get 10 groszy for two cans of water rather than 5.

{370}

# Vove Hoffman
## by Tauba Weissman-Hoffman
## Obtained by Mordechai Stern

Vove Hoffman was born in Kalusz to his parents Leib and Lea. He married Meir Taneh's daughter Paula in Rozniatow. Meir Taneh had several children. From among them, I would like to mention Vovche Taneh, whom everybody knew. Meir Taneh was the mayor in those days. Later, after he died, I recall only Wlaszanowicz, a gentile, as mayor. The Jewish Jews of Rozniatow felt that it was worthwhile to elect a Christian as mayor for the purposes of maintaining peaceful relations. However, this turned out to be a mistake. In truth Wlaszanowicz was not an anti-Semite. However, he did not defend the interests of the civic population, and he did not have the power to impart a civic character to Rozniatow.

This was at the time of modernization, when the train, telegraph and other services started. The Jews of Rozniatow came in contact with the modern world, and traveled to Lemberg, Vienna, Germany and America. They became familiar with world news, and read newspapers and books. Furthermore, there was the geographical situation. Rozniatow lay between towns. It was 14 kilometers from Dolina, and had the best possibilities for development as a center of business and crafts. However, the Jews had difficulties. If a Jew wished to build a house, a room or a roof, he would have to obtain a permit from Dolina. That city was the center of all offices. Therefore, it was natural that the Jews of Rozniatow selected a Jew as mayor. This was Vove Hoffman.

He excelled with his initiative and energy. He had command of German and Polish, both orally and in written form. He was tall, with a fine, long beard. He was Hassidic, but he dressed neatly. He was not fanatical. In his heart, he wished to understand the younger generation. It was not easy for him to become accustomed to the new times, but he had no toleration for those people who said on every occasion that it was impossible.

Despite the fact that he was not a Zionist, all of his grandchildren studied Hebrew with his permission. When his grandson Matek Trau was 15 years old, he traveled to the land of Israel illegally; however there is no doubt that he was given his grandfather's blessing.

He would lead the services at the Great Synagogue on the High Holy Days. On other festivals, he would lead services in the old Kloiz. He had a pleasant voice. He interceded for Rabbi Hamerling together with Chanina Weisman and Feivel Reisler. This was a battle for the sake of Heaven.

Reb Naftali was a rabbinical judge in the city. Later, when he died, Reb Yehuda Hirsch Korl was appointed as judge. My father was known as a scholar. On Fridays, he studied Gemara and other holy books at home. He was a relative to the Sambor Rabbi, Reb Uri.

His business was salt, kerosene, and wood. In the afternoon, when he was finished his work, he read

Yiddish, German and Polish newspapers. He read them all very quickly. He had a sharp and quick comprehension. The opinion of everyone of today's generation is that Vove Hoffman was a strong personality.

When new laws were decreed, he always attempted to ease them for Jews. He wished to improve the sanitary conditions. He concerned himself with sidewalks, highways, and lighting. He worked particularly hard for the local schools. In those days, people did not send their children to the public schools together with the Christian children.

He put efforts into building the post office in Rozniatow. They built the large bathhouse, and, saving the best for the last, the large, fine synagogue. He put his energy into all of these.

I recall that, prior to the First World War, we almost had to pay no taxes to the city hall. The Austrian regime did not concern itself with small towns. Small towns did not receive financial assistance, and also did not have the rights to levy taxes. Later, the majority of Rozniatow residents paid taxes. Michael Weissman's soda factory was often closed. My father always searched for ways of opening it.

Lehtcha Falik and husband Leizer Geller.

Vove and Paula Hoffman.

Their children Adela and Baruch Bodzhi.

The daughter Chayacha and her husband Leib Falik.

The First World War broke out in 1914.  Jews fled to Vienna.  People were afraid of the Ukrainians. My father did not want to leave the city.  The entire family also remained.  Warnings or entreaties did not help.  His strong character was able to withstand fear.  Various families left Rozniatow.  This was justified, if one knew about the Ukrainian peasants.  When the first military patrol appeared, the peasants of the area arrived with sacks, baskets, horses and wagons to rob the Jewish businesses.  He was greatly worried and tired because of the robbers and other tribulations.

As soon as the Russian military began to arrive, he went out with a white flag.  He arranged dwellings for the Russian officers, and requested that the Russian soldiers desist from stealing.  He guaranteed that every Russian soldier would be able to obtain anything he wanted from the businesses without paying. He only had to write it down.  At the same time, he requested that the youth with stripes on their arms be permitted to stand watch at night to protect against assailants.

The Russian military continued to grow.  New troops came.  He was then arrested, and they intended to send him to Siberia.  When he arrived on foot to Kalusz, he succeeded in getting freed.  The Ukrainians were not satisfied, however.  They continued to incite against him, and he succeeded in hiding. Only when the Austrian military returned to the city, was he able to appear in open.

Despite his usual manner, particularly with Jews, he was also a struggler.  Everyone held his honest and open character in esteem.  His opinion was often sought, even if he was one against everyone.  For example, when he engaged the new shochet David Roth, he realized that the shochet was also a good prayer leader.  However the city could not afford another shochet, and if one must absolutely have one more, there were the two sons of Reb Moshe Eli Hochman – Leibish and Yaakov Hochman.  Fifteen years later, Yankel Hochman received the rights from David Roth, and it was once again shown that Vove Hoffman had been correct at that time.

Until his last days, he was consulted on all important or less important questions, on educational problems or business matters.  He neglected his private affairs on account of the mayorship and the communal leadership.  There was always a feeling of discontent in the family.   He often went to the leadership council and asked that he be freed from this.  However, nobody wanted to free him from this pleasure.

My mother endured all this with great amazement, good judgement and difficulties.  We all knew the difficulties that were part of the day to day life, but we had great understanding for his important work in dealing with the difficult problems of that time, until the First World War, with tact and good judgment.

He was a fascinating type of person, who unified his wisdom and good will with a large measure of moral fineness.  He lived with the problems of the town, and in the event that something was not proper, he strongly objected.  Similarly, he rejoiced at every achievement.

Honor to his memory!

{375}

## Homesickness and Duty
### by Salo Enis of New York

Rozniatow was my second home.  My relatives lived there.  I spent my vacations in Rozniatow, and therefore, I fell in love with the town, its people, and the lovely landscape.

It was a typical Galician town, with its unique houses, yards and alleyways;  with the castle on the hill upon which the courthouse stood; with the underground tunnels that were connected with the courthouse building; the river;  the farm with the meadows that belonged to Chrabia Skabek.  The large wall in the middle of the city testifies to the fact that once, Ukrainian and Tatar invaders once came, and there were battles.

Jews in Rozniatow were employed in business and crafts.  In the beginning, some Jewish families lived in the Old Town and near the convent.

In Rozniatow there was:  a farm, 3 mills, 3 breweries, and two soda water factories.  Every Wednesday was market day, which brought in merchants and farmers from the entire region.

The Jewish youth were organized into various Zionist organizations.  Many of them wandered through the wide world.  After the great destruction, a small cluster of Jews remained, spread out over various lands, primarily in Israel and America.

Very few Jews from Rozniatow remain.  Therefore it is the duty of each of us who is able to hold a feather in the hand to write, tell and lament the horrible destruction of those who were dear and close to us, the martyrs of our town…

How much tenderness, love, longing and homesickness do we express to the personalities of our dear, good Jews – how can we forget them?

Who can forget you, my dear town of Rozniatow?!

{376}

## The Lamed Vovnik[4]
### by Yehuda Akselrad of New York

It is said that the world exists in the merit of the 36 righteous people, who are found in every generation.  If this is true, I am convinced that one such Lamed Vovnik of our generation lived in Rozniatow. I want to recall him.

Among the residents of Rozniatow, Jews and gentiles, there were two brothers who were mailmen. One was called Wojciech Burak and the other Pawela Burak. Pawela spoke Jewish as if he was a convert, and he knew every Jew, even children, by name.

When I was ten years old, I was looking as Pawela was carried the mail at the end of the street where we lived. He asked me, "Do you know how to write?" I told him aloud, "Yes, yes". "Come", he said to me, "summon Yisrael Leizer for me".

Yisrael Leizer lived not far from us on an alley near Moshele Shochet. I brought Yisrael Leizer to him. Pawela had a package for him. The fee was 1 crown and 15 heller. Yisrael Leizer took out the money from a pocketbook and gave him the money. The mailman told me: "Yisrael Leizer will make an X and you will write: Yisrael Leizer Benczer in Latin script." Thus did I find out that Yisrael Leizer's surname was Benczer.

I am certain that few people in Rozniatow knew the surname of that wonderful man. It is possible that I am the only one who remembers it.

Who indeed was Yisrael Leizer, whom the entire shtetl knew? He was a tall, large, wide-boned Jew, with large hands. Each hand had six fingers. He had a white face with 8-9 hairs on his beard. He had large feet. He went around barefoot. He wore a white, clean shirt. His pants were tied with a rope. He wore an unfashionable cap. A sack adorned his shoulders. He was unmarried. He had a sister. He earned his livelihood from selling prayer books (siddurs), supplication sheets, tzitzit, benchers (booklets containing the grace after meals), and other holy books. He barely spoke – only what he had to. Nobody called him by his name. Rather, they would make requests of him thus: "Hey sheketz, a bencher? Perhaps tzitzit?[5]" With a cold smile, he continued along his way.

He lived with his sister in a small, clean, sparse room in which was found a table, and a bench. The windows were always covered with curtains. He slept on sacks, or he simply lay there and thought. Nobody ever saw him at prayers, either in a Beis Midrash or Kloiz, not on the Sabbath and not on festivals.

Those people who new him a bit better related to him with honor, and considered him to be one of the hidden righteous persons who marked the exile. Others called him crazy on account of his abnormal conduct.

In truth, his conduct was strange, and he differed from all the people in town. Various personality traits and mysteries radiated from him which cause the most pious Jews in the town to forgive these things, which they would not have done had others behaved in such a manner. It seemed as if everyone wanted to admit in their hearts that one is unable to understand his ways, the ways of a concealed righteous person, of which ordinary people are not able to comprehend.

More than once he surprised the town with his deeds. It would take many words to describe everything. Here, I wish to only mention one event that in its time astonished the people in our town:

One fine morning, they found an exquisite, golden bound, new Vilna edition of the Talmud, books of Midrash, and other books in the bookshelf in the Kloiz in which the scholars, the Talmud studiers and general dignified people of our town worshipped. Nobody knew who had brought them to the shelves, and who had donated the set of Talmuds and other books. However, everyone surmised that this was Yisrael Leizer's work – the hidden Lamed Vovnik of the town.

{378}

## To Our Land
### by Meir Hauptman

Outside it is quiet, the sun is setting.
A peaceful, lovely night spreads out.
The songbird in the forest cheerfully ends its song,
Other birds also sing with joy.

In a small house, not far from the forest,
A gray-white old man lives.
From his face and from his entire personality
One can see that he is in great need.

Tear after tear falls from his face
Silent and like hot fire are his tears.
His mouth is contorted from great agony,
He scarcely breathes, it is harder and harder.
This is the wandering Jew.
How many tribulations has he already endured,
Sent into exile for thousands of years,
On all the willows hangs his weeping.

Jew, where does your honor lie?
The pride of your people, the prophets,
Always beaten and downtrodden.
You silently suffer another blow, you are constantly driven –
Locked into a ghetto, surrounded by iron gates,
Did you lose your vigor and strength.
Believing that books are stronger than chains,
That they will avert the enemy's rod.

The inquisition came, the powers
That brought you burning and hatred,
The books – your sword and your splendor
Did not save you from your cruel enemy.

Where were your Torah scrolls?
The lamps, menoras and candelabra!!
The air, which breathed throughout generations?
Sinks further into tears and blood.

G-d will protect me, you said.
Where was He, when they murdered your child,
When they tormented and plagued you
And you were in agony and woe?

You wished to die like a hero,
As you have done many times.
You did not go out with a sword in your hand,
You only battle alone.

Already at the height of times, you nation, once so honorable
Throw off from yourself the bonds of exile,
It is time to come to your own soil,
Under blue skies, sunny and happy.

The holy earth, our fatherland,
Which always belonged to us,
Known by the name of the Land of Israel
And desires that name again.

We, builders of the great ideal,
When our small and young Land,
Will once again be esteemed over everything,
We will jubilate with joyful song.

Stand up, you new Jew,
Go and fight together with your tribe,
Refine yourself with great ardor,
Already blessed with the flame of the prophets.

(Written in Rozniatow, 1936, when he was 12 years old.}


## TRANSLATOR'S FOOTNOTES

1. Literally, Sabbath Gentile. The Shabbat Goy would perform various necessary work (such as putting on the lights and the heat) that are forbidden for a Jew to do on the Sabbath.

2. The beginning of the statement that is used to call people up to the reading of the Torah.

3. A reference to the drum that Miriam played at the song of the sea.

4. A term for a hidden, righteous person – based on the rabbinical legend that there are always 36 (lamed vov) hidden righteous people in the world at any time.

5. Sheketz is a derogatory term for a gentile. Here it is simply used as an insulting appellation.

{381}

# Broszniow

## My Shtetl by Meir Auslender

Broszniow was a small town, with only 200 Jewish families. However the communal life of the families was close and heartfelt.

As in all other towns, people earned their livelihoods in different manners:  small business, and crafts.  However, there were also two lumber factories – one Y. F. H. Glezinger was Jewish owned, and the second was government owned as well as a refinery.  Most of the Jewish families were employed in the Jewish factory.  The factory was the entire future of the Broszniow youth.  Thanks to this enterprise, the town developed economically and culturally.

A fine Zionist organization called Herzliya was established. It had a large library in three languages: Yiddish, Hebrew and Polish.  The youth would gather there.  Bendet Szpiegel was the president. He did a great deal to develop the organization.

A fine Tarbut Hebrew school existed, with the energetic president Presser.  He was a postmaster, but he had a great deal of free time to give to the development of the school.  Young children as well as older ones studied there.

Both institutions worked together.  They would organize various cultural events, lectures, readings, etc.

They also organized a dramatic ensemble that used to conduct various plays, of which all of Broszniow was proud.

The kibbutzim were a very important contributor to the cultural development.

{Photo page 382: Hechalutz in Broszniow, 1934}

It is appropriate to mention that the Jewish factory employed several hundred chalutzim on their hachsharah. Many of them played a large role in our cultural development. The ensemble was at a fine level. A dramatic director came from the kibbutzim in order to direct and often to take part in the performances. The entire income would go to purchase new books and to develop the school.

Others were involved with charitable works, the distribution of charity through the charitable and sick visiting organization. Chaim Logstejn was the creator of this organization. There, they concerned themselves with visiting the sick, sitting with them through the entire night and providing financial stipends to those in need.

They also did not forget the families who were in need of Sabbath food or who had to marry off an orphan. Chana Liberman occupied herself with that. She had a special room in her house for poor wayfarers who would come to request donations. There, one could eat, spend the night, and continue on. Yudel Berlfajn maintained a similar home in the other end of town.

Broszniower Jews also concerned themselves with setting up a fine synagogue. A new synagogue was built in 1936. The plan was sent from the Land of Israel. Julius Szapiro, the director of the factory, took care of the finances. Thanks to his prestige, the needed capital was raised – although he himself was a non-observant man.

Broszniow was not derelict in sending pioneers to the Land of Israel. The first family, Kimmel, already set out in 1920. They settled at the baths of Kfar Saba. We also had business connections with the Land of Israel. The Jewish factory was the chief provider of citrus crates for the orchards.

We, the few survivors here in the Land of Israel, take accounting of our soul and recall our native town, where the bestial Nazi hand with the assistance of the Ukrainian neighbors destroyed all the Jews in such a cold blooded fashion, along with everything that had been created throughout so many years.

Today, our town is no longer for us. The factory is no longer there, the creative work is no longer there, and our dear mothers, fathers, brothers, sisters and children are no longer there. They are no more!

All the fine people who toiled hard throughout all the years are no more. Even more than their material wealth, they aspired to spiritual matters. Their greatest desire was to live as Jews, and to educate their children in the Jewish spirit, in love for the Jewish people.

Each of us carries that love in our hearts together with the memory of the martyrs, the beloved, dear Jews.

They all live in our memories.

We will never forget them. We will never neglect to recite Kaddish in memory of their souls every year. We will perpetuate all of their names, both in Yizkor books as well as in other undertakings which might possibly be created, so that the future generations will know about the high morality and culture of our forbears, and that they also played a great role in the building of the Land of Israel.

{384}

## The First Jews in the Town
### by Berl Nirenberg

I wish to perpetuate the small Jewish settlement of Broszniow with my memories. These are memories from my childhood and youth that I experienced, and from what I have heard from my parents and other veteran Jewish families. The memories are from the end of the 18th century until the end of the First World War in 1918.

Speaking about the history of the Jewish settlement, the question arises: What inspired the first young couples to settle in Broszniow? They arrived with young children and came with the intention of building their futures there. It is clear that the source of their livelihood was in the large wood factory. It was known that the Jews were fine professionals in the wood factory. The owners of the wood factory were Jews. The firm was Schreier from Vienna. They were also interested in Jewish professionals. The refinery was also located in Broszniow, and one could also obtain work from it.

The following are the names of the first families that settled in Broszniow:

Yosef Segal, Leibish Zimmerman, Wolf Tiger, Izak Mendel Hausman, Yisrael Gelobter, Wolf Kimmel, Hersh Leib Weinreb, Herzl Nirenberg, Michael Kleinfeld, Peretz Liberman, Avraham Ost, Aharon Neiman, Berl Sprauch, Wolf Lichtman, Avraham Finkelsztejn, David Szmerzler, Fishel Scharfer, Yisrael Langnauer, Zigmund Lerfeld, Yisrael Fishbein. There were also others whose names I am not able to recall.

Jews lived in peace there, not taking part in any politics.  Apparently, they did not even read any newspapers, and the radio had not yet been invented.  They were busy with their work, earned their livelihoods, and conducted a Jewish life.  In the latter years, I would often hear stories about that early period of their settlement in Broszniow.  Their first concern was a synagogue.  They indeed collected money and built a synagogue.

The years passed and the children grew up.  The issue of hiring a teacher came to the fore and my father Herzl Nirenberg then brought Mitlfink from his hometown of Nizniow.  He set up the cheder and served as the melamed of the town.

Some of the families settled in Krechowice, two kilometers from Broszniow.

Nathan Lastner, Itzik Rothbaum, Hersh Gelobter, Shlomo Zim, Weingarten and Stern all lived in Krechowice.

Itzik Szpiegel, David Eksztejn, Eliahu Horowitz and Heisler came to Broszniow.

Eliahu Horowitz later left the town and settled in Rozniatow.

From both towns, Jews came to the synagogue in Broszniow and sent their children to cheder.

It must be noted that all of the aforementioned families did not come together at once, but rather gradually.

Of course, Polish families as well as ethnic Germans (Volksdeutschen) also came to live there during that time.  Just like the Jews, they also looked for work and livelihood.

At that time, no Ukrainians lived with us.   However, with time, Ukrainian families also arrived.

The settlements developed.  There was already a post office, a police station, and a public school.  There was a train station in Krechowice.

Thus did life in both towns slowly develop, until the First World War broke out in 1914.

Several Jews were already drafted into the army at the first mobilization.  There was unrest in the town, and the Jewish residents began to think about what to do and where to flee.  There were several suggestions.  Some felt that they should travel to Vienna.  Others rejected every suggestion to flee, and believed that one should remain in the place.  Others felt that they should go to Rozniatow.  They believed that Rozniatow lay a distance from the main highway, which was called the Kaiser Strasse.  They believed that the Russians would not come there.

Several families, including my parents, indeed set out for Rozniatow.  We went to the family of

Mendel Gans. My aunt Irka Finkelsztein and her children also went to Rozniatow. Her husband was in the army.

When Rozniatow was attacked, we went to the Rozenberg family, where we remained in the cellar for several days until the shooting stopped, and the Russians arrived.

A new life began. We worked and conducted business. The children were sent to cheder with the melamed Listinger. The girls helped their fathers with their livelihoods.

My father went to Broszniow from time to time to find out what was happening there and to visit with acquaintances. The Jews who remained there did not live badly.

After remaining in Rozniatow for approximately 10 months, we returned to the town. My aunt and her children also returned.

Michael Kleinfeld died in our town during the winter of 1915. There was no cemetery in the town, and the dead had to be brought to Rozniatow. The route was difficult. After great trouble, they obtained a horse and wagon from a farmer, but it was dangerous to go along the way due to the frequent attacks. My father also became involved in the problem, and traveled with the widow and her 14-year-old son Menashe to accompany the dead to his final resting place.

As they were en route to Rozniatow, Cossacks arrived, stopped the wagon and searched the bier to ensure that they were not smuggling contraband or conducting espionage.

The son, Menashe, who was then 14 years old, lives in America today. He came to Israel in 1971 to visit his daughter who lives in Haifa. We visited together and reminisced about the experiences of that time, and recalled the day when the Austrian army repelled the Russians. Then, it was still somewhat lively in the town and the surrounding villages. In our town they built a railway station, a military hospital and large military storehouses.

During the wartime, the large lumber factory was completely destroyed, and a second one was erected, which was always managed by a military committee.

This continued until the Austrian Empire fell. Then, we lived in the town for a short time together with the Ukrainians, who were later driven out by the Poles when they obtained their independence and took over parts of Ukraine.

When the war ended in 1918, all those who were in the army as well as all those who fled returned to the town. Life returned to normal. Some worked in the factory, and others opened shops.

At that time, the melamed Michael Fesberg lived in our town. He was called a teacher (Lehrer) as he also taught German.

The first chalutz (Zionist pioneering) organization was established in 1922. The organizer was Shmuel Kimmel. The following people belonged to the organization: Moshe Kleinfeld, Yosef Lichtman,

Moshe Szpiegel, Mordechai Hausman, Getzel Szprauch, Reuven Freulich, and others. Of them, only one, Shmuel Kimmel, made aliya to Israel. Two others left for America.

The organization disbanded, but a short time later the Herzliya organization was set up. The members consisted of the youth of the town. The first chairman was Mordechai Hausman, and his deputy was Moshe Szpiegel.

Organized cultural activity began. A dramatic club and a library were established. The library had many books in Yiddish, Hebrew, Polish and German.

At the same time, work was conducted for the Jewish National Fund (Keren Kayemet), led by Bendet Szpiegel.

We had a good Tarbut School in which children aged 7 and older studied. There were also courses for adults. Every child of ours was able to read Hebrew.

The organizers of the Tarbut School were: Shlomo Liberman, Yehoshua Litwak and Dov Nirenberg.

The organizers of Hechalutz were: Wolf Finkelsztejn, Yehoshua Litwak, and others.

A chapter of Hashomer Hatzair was also created, as well as a Gordonia chapter, organized by Pinchas Yungerman.

The synagogue burnt down in 1931, and with time, a barracks was built for worshipping. Obviously, this did not satisfy people, and thoughts were given to build a new, larger and finer synagogue. The initiative was taken by the administration of the Glezinger firm.

Quickly, a plan was created. An architect in Tel Aviv was contacted, who drew up a plan for us for a new synagogue in Israeli style.

The chief participants in the planning of the building of the synagogue were: the Glezinger firm, the director Karl Far, Yehuda Szapiro, Chaim Loksztejn, Engineer Lichtenfeld, Yaakov Izak Artman, and others. The synagogue was indeed a superb building, which would not have been put to shame by today's fine synagogues.

The gabbaim (synagogue trustees) were: Wolf Kimmel, Aharon Neiman, Herzl Nirenberg, and Fishel Szarper. They rotated every year.

The Torah reader was Avraham Ast.

We had a Gemilut Chasadim (charitable) fund, an organization for visiting the sick, and a WIZO (Woman's International Zionist Organization) organization.

The children of the Tarbut School put on their final performance in 1939. They had a specially organized Chanuka evening.

On Purim, the Herzliya organization together with the representatives of WIZO organized a Purim ball, which was unfortunately the final one in our community.

On the first day of the war in 1941[1], I left home, was drafted into the army, and never again saw my hometown.

**TRANSLATOR'S FOOTNOTES**

1. The Russian – German War.

{389)

# Swaryczow

### Jews in the Town
### by Zeev Weinfeld

This was the town were I was educated, grew up and lived through the terrible catastrophe that overtook the Jews of Europe and annihilated the Jewish communities in our region.

The town of Swaryczow, three kilometers from the city of Rozniatow, had a population of approximately 3,000 residents. They were mainly Ukrainians, with a large number of Poles, and only a few Jews, five families in total. The Weinfeld family of which I was a member was among these 5 families. The Fink family, who ran an inn, also lived there. The Hochman family dealt in fowl, eggs and fish. There were two Taneh families who were merchants.

The Weinfeld family was large and wide-branched, consisting of a grandfather and grandmother, five sons, five daughters and grandchildren. Our family had a farm, a large field and a water mill. The sons worked the farm and the mill with the assistance of the hired Ukrainians.

We belonged to the community of Rozniatow. We went to worship in Rozniatow on all festivals. In cases of need, a minyan (prayer quorum) was gathered in town so that we could worship and recite Kaddish. The Jewish children of the town would study in the Rozniatow school. We had a governess to teach the children and a melamed to teach the children Yiddish. My grandfather and grandmother were pious people who upheld Judaism. The children studied Hebrew in the Rozniatow Hebrew school. Their teacher was Fasberg. The school was in the home of Avraham Groll of blessed memory.

After the First World War, various nationalist organizations arose in our area. Among them was Gordonia in Rozniatow, in which I actively took part. Various cultural activities, publicity work, excursions into the mountains with music, and sports matches took place. A Jewish Delegation from

YK"A, Baron Hirsch's colonization organization, came to Swaryczow in order to organize hachsharah for Jewish youth so that they could learn agriculture. In our estate, preparations were made to accept chalutzim to study agriculture, gardening and other aspects of farming and necessary work.

In the summer season of 1923, young men came to our farm to work in our fields. Among them were the following students from Rozniatow, Dolek Lusthaus, Nunik Lusthaus, Liberman, Tintcze Berge, Anda Kanner, Wolf (Wilush) Turteltaub, Lutwak and others. They participated in harvesting hay and other field work.

Each year, our close relatives from Vienna, Drohobycz, Kolomyja and other places came to Swaryczow in order to spend their vacation in the bosom of nature. Young people were among the guests who came. The young guests created a sports club in Swaryczow, and took part in various sporting activities. The chief instructor was my cousin Buni Kleiner from Drohobycz, an academic, hypnotist and telepathist. I was a fan of all types of sports. Training took place every day. Matches with sportsmen from Rozniatow, Broszniow, and Perehinsko took place. There were also excursions with the small train of the Glezinger firm of Broszniow to the Carpathian forests and Osmolodo.

Buni Weinfeld, the organizer of the Swaryczow sport club, perished in Russia apparently from starvation.

{391}

### A Tear for the Beautiful Murdered People
### by Yehudit Heisler-Friedman

Already 23 years have passed since I was torn away from my family, but their images are always ingrained in my thoughts and heart.  I could never imagine that a human heart could hold so much longing and sorrow.

Sorrowful tragedies began for me already in 1936, at the time of the death of my father Moshe Heisler.  I, the eldest daughter, who was still then a child, wanted to lighten the load of my unfortunate mother and help her raise my sisters and only brother.  Bearing such a great yoke, I lived with the hope that I would fulfill my purpose.  However, in the middle of the summer of 1941, a dark cloud suddenly fell over the Jews of Rozniatow.  I was torn away from my family.  I left the town with the hope of reuniting with them shortly, but the hope was never realized.  The Nazi German murderers who wiped out European Jewry, also murdered the Jews of Rozniatow.

The murder of my family in Rozniatow were as follows:

{Photo page 392: Uncaptioned group photo.  The sign in the photo reads "The Hebrew School in Perehinsko", and a small second sign to the left reads "grade 1".}

My mother Roza Heisler the daughter of Shlomo Yungerman, my sisters Miriam, Perl and Sara, my brother Hersch, my aunt Gittel Meisels and her children, my cousin Moshe Brenfeld, my aunt Perel Roth with her husband and children.

## Destruction and Murder

{Photo page 393: Zecharia Friedler, Bendet Schwartz and Mordechai Stern-Nussbaum light the candle at the memorial in Tel Aviv, 1971.}

## In the Vale of Lament and Anguish
### by Yeshayahu Lutwak of New York

Great is the sorrow and greater is the pain. The heart weeps and asks with despair: "How doth sit in loneliness" [1], my town of Rozniatow? How have you become devastated, a cemetery of devastation? I bend my head and weep for the pure martyrs, for our tragedy, and the great disaster.

Who can forget and how can he who has the talent to do so not write? I wish to tell so much, to remember so much, and to once again relive the days in our town, with close and dear people. I wish to proceed chronologically, to the extent that my memory can help me, and concentrate on those stories that have a connection to Rozniatow. I will relate a portion of them that describe the experiences that our martyrs endured during the last days of the destruction in Rozniatow, in order to help erect a symbolic monument for our holy and pure martyrs, who we will never forget.

\*

In the former area of East Galicia in Lesser Poland, Stanislawow Wojewoda, Dolina Powiat, in the Carpathian Mountains with two rivers, the Czeczwa and Duba – there was the small charming town of Rozniatow, a settlement of approximately 500 Jewish families, number approximately 1,800 souls, excluding the Jews from the twenty-something villages around Rozniatow. It was small in area, with a kilometer marker between the home of Bendet and Moshe Yampel and Zisia Aryeh Kupferberg below the city. The second one was near the old Kassner, Yisrael Hirsch Landner, opposite Meshulam Fruchter. The third was before Chaya Adler, opposite Mordechai Deutscher in the old city. Our town was indeed small, with its nickname being "nebech" (unfortunate). However, it was clean, modest, and full of life.

The Jewish population, which lived for the most part in the center of the town, consisted of merchants, tradesman, a few professional intelligentsia, officials, and of course it was not lacking in poor people. The central economic event took place every Wednesday, when the market day took place.

Jewish life literally flourished with us. All parties from the extreme left to the extreme right were organized. They regulated the social, cultural, religious and communal life, and influenced our youth. We should mention here a few people who led these efforts, as follows: Shimshon Rechtschaffen, Moshe Rosenberg – Pesi Reisler's husband, Binyamin Adler, Shabtai Falik, Shule Teneh, Max Edelstein, Avraham Zauerberg, Moshe and Yankel Fruchter, Munti Stern, Yehuda Hersch Stern, Shmuel-Leib Rosenbaum, Getzel Frenkel, Agronomist Leib Meiseles, Muni Lusthaus, Izi Berman, Dr. David Weisman, Izak Barnik, Shabtai Rosenberg, Baruch Horowitz, Wilusz Turtelbaum, Dini Landsman, Philip Ferst, the Brand brothers, and others.

The amateur theatrical club at the "Casino Meczszanski" was led by Shalom Rechtschaffen and Ben-Zion Horowitz, with the participation of people from all parties. Every winter, they livened up the town with performances and balls. They contributed greatly to our communal and cultural life.

Thus did life go on peacefully until Hitler may his name and memory be blotted out began to attack, torture, and drive out our brethren from Germany.

In 1938, when the Jews who were deported from Germany arrived in our town from Zbaszyn, we immediately realized that terrible times were approaching. With feelings of compassion and warmheartedness, we took in the people who were deported from Germany. Downtrodden, robbed of their belongings, set out to wander, they were a bit happy at that time – for they were simply fortunate to be together with their families and friends.

As far as I remember, the following were among the first of the refugees: Meir Ungar – the son-in-law of Moshe Gelobter, and his wife Dora and two young children; Shmuel Friedler the son of Moshe, and his wife; Menashe Yampel and his wife; Bendet Kassner the son of Alte; Benzi Kassner, the son of Yossel; Zelda Wasserman with her son and daughter; Avrahamche Kahn, the son-in-law of Hirsch Rechtschaffen and his family; Aharon Weisman and his family; Avraham Korenblau, the son of Moshe Mechel; Eli Spiegel's son with two daughters; David Wernick the son-in-law of Berel Berger and his family; Chaya the daughter of Menashe Rosenberg with her husband and children; Shlomo Gross; Benzi Klinger; Chaim Walgschaffen; Sender Rosenberg, Yossel Laufer and his family; Kalman Horowitz the son of Sara Esther; Leika Horowitz and her husband (Kielce). They lived where they could, and they wished to forget about the difficult mood and the tense political situation.

On Friday, September 1, 1939, Hitler's army crossed the Polish border. A panic ensued. Many of our young people who had mobilization cards hurried to their designated military points. Others wanted to be called up. Order did not prevail during the first moments, and few of the mobilized soldiers received their fatigues and weapons.

On Sunday, September 3, a few of our merchants traveled by bus to Stanislawow to acquire a bit of merchandise; however, they returned empty handed and described the terrible scenes of murder and destruction that was inflicted upon the city by the Nazi airplanes. They were also bombarded at as they traveled home. The fear and panic worsened day by day. The nights were dark, and nobody ventured out onto the streets. Whoever owned a radio listened with a pounding heart to the speeches and proclamations that incited anti-Semitism.

The first of the refugees came to town from western Poland. The following people came home: Dr. Wilek Adelsberg, his two brothers Zigo and Lagek, Dr. Leon Horowitz and his wife Jadwiga Sapier and child, Dr. Nunek Lusthaus and his wife Irina Feier, Dr. Avraham Fried, the son-in-law of Shmuel Friedler, Sara Geller, and others.

On Friday September 15th, the following people set out for the Romanian border: the head of the community Zechariah Lieberman, Rabbi Yosef Matzner, Shabtai Rosenberg and his brother-in-law Bernard Menczner. When they arrived at the foot of the Mountain of Krasna on the wagon of Melech Landsman, the horses refused to go further. They returned home and believed that this is probably the will of G-d.

On Sunday morning, September 17th, Molotov delivered his speech, saying that the Soviets would liberate eastern Galicia from Polish domination.

On Monday, anarchy pervaded. Even the police left for Hungary. We, the young people, secretly organized and armed ourselves to protect ourselves from potential ambushes. We lived in great tension, not knowing if we should be happy or fearful. The German murderers were already in Stryj. The Soviets were in Stanislawow. We asked: From where would our salvation arise?

When the local Ukrainians heard Molotov's speech, they were certain that their messiah was arriving, and they began to revolt. The first to be beaten was Reuvele Diamand, the son of Bini Anshel.

On Wednesday morning, September 20th, bright and bold Doni the son of Hirsch Landsman succeeded in escaping from the city with two friends. They ran to the village of Holyn and returned to town on a tank with a Soviet military unit.

Immediately a period of the restoration of law and order began at the hands of the Red Army. The Jews had mixed feelings. Some were happy and some sighed and wept secretly. They began to nationalize property, that means simply confiscating the hard-worked-for businesses and homes of our very wealthy people: bourgeois such as: Yisrael Rosenman, Mordechai Gross, Yaakov Lew, Shmuel, Leib, and Izak Friedler, Meir Frankel, Shalom Hoffman, Ethel Rechtschaffen, Leizer Geller and his partner Yisrael Leib Artman, Yosef Kurtz – Suchi Hersh-Mendel's son-in-law, Mattes Wilner, Shlomo, Shaya and Aharon Weidman, Shaya Sternbach the son-in-law of Mendel Menlich, Leib Eizner, Yossel  Berger, Pini Berger, Sasi Heller, Leib Falik, and Wiczi Teneh.  In one word, private enterprise and ownership ceased to exist.

It was not so easy for our brethren to get used to the new social and economic structure, along with the removal of class structure.  Each of them attempted to obtain whatever work or employment was available, for the motto of the Russians was, "He who does not work does not eat".  Furthermore everyone was afraid, for some families were threatened with deportation to Siberia.  Despite the difficulties, Jews managed. Most of us worked and a few of us conducted a bit of business.

It was June 22, 1942.

Already on the first day of the war, everyone was nervous.  We felt as if we were standing on the threshold of significant events.  All of the Soviet officers and their families hastened to leave the city. The Red Army followed them.  If I am not mistaken, this was on Monday, June 30th.  About 150-200 Jews left on foot to catch a train to Stanislawow.  There was no other means of transport in our region. Unfortunately, their lot was fatal.  A Hitlerist airplane attacked the moving train, and almost all of them were killed at Husyatin.  I will never forget how Shalom Rechtschaffen, as he fled with his family through the town, shouted loudly: "Jews, why do you wait? Leave your property and follow me."  In this chaos, I had the opportunity to bid farewell to my relative and friend Baruch Horowitz. His last words still ring in my ears: "What are you waiting for? Are you afraid to leave your property?"

These were people with clear intellect and foresight.  Unfortunately, not all of the Jews made an accounting about the magnitude of the danger.  Just the opposite, there were Jews who thought that it would be possible to live with the Germans.

The city was in chaos.  Nobody dared to venture on to the streets. They remained locked up in their houses in great fear.  The Ukrainians, waiting with great joy for their Hitler messiah, began to organize and rampage through the city.  No Jew wished to look, even from afar, as they pillaged and emptied the remaining Soviet businesses.  As the last few soldiers could be seen leaving the city, they were accosted by brazen gentiles who mocked the soldiers at one such store near the Ukrainian church.  One of them injured Wasyl Slapak's son with a bullet.  This was sufficient pretext for our gentile citizens to begin a pogrom against the Jews.  Until today, I do not know who was able to prevent us from being victims of the events.  During the ceremonial parade, the gentiles caught Moshe Strassman, the son of Yankel, who was innocently passing by, and beat him severely.

On Friday morning, the 14th of July, 1941, the Hungarian Army arrived.  But in fact, the Ukrainians took over the police supervision and administration of the town, under the leadership of Dr. Korbas, Dr. Shlapkas, the priest Kostak, Lupinski, Kowel and others, may their names be  blotted out. On Friday afternoon, the Ukrainian militia captured some Jews and ordered them to destroy the statue of Lenin that the Soviets had erected in the Ringplatz, opposite Mechale Weisman. On Friday night, one of those whom we termed a righteous gentile, Ivan Wishinski, came to Mordechai Gross, and secretly told him that the Ukrainian committee had decided that the next day, on the Sabbath morning, as the Jews would leave the synagogue, the Ukrainian militia would gather them all in the Ringplatz, force them to put on their tallises, bring a coffin from the cemetery, put the broken pieces of Lenin's monument inside it, and arrange a grandiose procession to the Jewish cemetery to bury it. Wishinski advised Mordechai that in order to avert the scandal, he should clear it out during the night. Mordechai risked his live, and at 3:00 a.m. on the Sabbath morning, he woke up the son of the guard Chaim Reubele's, and both of them placed the broken pieces into a hand wagon, dragged them to a place behind our slaughterhouse, and buried them in the filth.

From 6:00 or 7:00 p.m., despite the heat (it was July and August), no Jew would appear on the street. The nights were more terrifying than the days. With palpitating hearts, everyone awaited an attack on his house. On one such night, while they were searching for Dr. Nunek Lusthaus (a few gentiles who had a personal accounting), dragged out his father-in-law, the elderly Dr. Isadore Feier, who lived at the time with Yossel Kassner. They beat him and ordered him to carry a sack of flour, which they stole from him. For no reason they arrested Itzi Reis who was Meir Frankel's relative, Azriel Wasserman, and many others. They beat them fiercely. Twice a week, on Mondays and Thursdays from 10:00 to 12:00, the Jews were permitted to come to the Market Square to purchase food provisions for an inflated price.

As I lived in the home of Mordechai Gross in Ringplatz, I often witnessed the Jewish trials and tribulations from a distance. On one market day, Pintzi Berger, an elderly, broken Jew, was leaning against the house of Mottel Friedler. Janek Shajok – the bastard of the Anke, may their names be blotted out – approached him and beat him for no reason, threw him to the sidewalk, and trampled upon him. He left Pintzi Berger lying there and came to David Reiner. There the bastard met Leib Weitzner and attacked him, but Leib was young and full of energy, so he was able to escape and flee.

Avraham Hirsch, the son of Shaul Miriam Bine's, was lame. One day he came to Dr. Korbas may his name be blotted out to request a favor. Not even hearing the request, he gave him a push, and removed the cane that the lame man used to support himself. He fell to the ground, and the murderer trampled him with his feet.

Every morning, the Jews had to fill the quota of workers for the filthy, hard and awkward work, that only the devil himself could conceive of. All sorts of trivial and unnecessary tasks were devised in order to torment the Jews. Voluntarily, without being called up, men and women organized themselves and provide the required number of workers at any order.

Once, I, along with Sacherl the son of Pini Berger and Magister Marek Rotter (Shalom Hoffman's nephew) had the job of cleaning the manure from the police stables, which were located on a hill next to the courthouse. The work was very difficult and the stench almost caused us to faint. In order to sustain ourselves, Sacherl took out from his sack a piece of dry, kosher sausage, which at that time was like a treasure, and divided it among us. Exactly at that moment, Atamnaczok, the head of the militia, passed by and saw us chewing something. He fell upon Sacherl like a wild animal and beat him with his gun. I wondered why Sacherl, who was mighty in strength and character and never tolerated any injustice, controlled himself and refrained from expressing his anger. However, I will never forget, how he once asked me with teas in his eyes and a broken voice: "Shaike, will we survive and take our revenge?"

Even worse off were the Jewish workers who were sent to work at the Krechowice train station. Once, a group of 25 Jews were sent there to remove the thorns, gravel and other refuse from the area with bare hands. This group included Dr. Leon Horowitz, Magister Leon Meiseles, Shimshon Rechtschaffen, Shabtai Falik, Shabtai Rosenberg, his brother-in-law Bernard Menczer, Shalom Deutscher, and several others whose names I unfortunately do not remember at this time. This work had to be done while they were bent over on their knees and crawling step by step. When the Gestapo noticed from afar a Jew who attempted to straighten out or rest for a small moment – there would be nothing more to be jealous about.

When Leib Meiseles weakened from the great heat work and slunk to the ground, Shalom Deutscher inconspicuously went over to him and hid him with his body. The Gestapo man noticed this, and came over to ask who is resting. Shalom answered that it was he, and he immediately received his punishment – beatings with a gun.  Shalom did not boast about his deed.  The others and Leib related this to me.  When I later had the opportunity to ask Shalom about this, he answered me: "I had to do this, because I knew that Leib could no longer withstand beatings."

Once I worked alongside Shalom and others in dismantling the statue that the Soviets had erected in the Ringplatz. We were warned about damaging even one board, and even damaging any nail. Poor Shalom did the work of everybody.  He ran from person to person to help. When I asked him: "Shalom, why do you not watch out for yourself? Let us also sweat a little." he answered me: "You see that they are not all capable, I do not wish to see the gentiles rejoicing as we get beaten."

These were the characters of the Jews that our Rozniatow produced.

The Ukrainian committee, issued a decree that starting from August 5th, 1941, all Jews must wear a yellow band on their right arms.  Since Tisha Beov  fell exactly two days prior to the set date, that is on August 3rd, our Rabbi Yosef Metzner,  Zechariah Lieberman the head of the community, and Dr. Feier began to wear the yellow ribbons then to mark the double tragedy. When the gentiles saw this, they joked and called them "the Jewish militia".

It is indeed difficult to understand and believe how the Ukrainians, with whom the Jews had conducted business, had been good neighbors and lived with closed friendship – were able to turn over night into the bitterest of enemies, and relate to us in such a cruel fashion without shame and without mercy.

I wish to relate a small incident.  Until the outbreak of the war, I had a friendship of long duration with Dr. Katz and his wife at the time, who was the widow of the judge Luzinski. At the time that they were under financial pressure, I lent them money on several occasions. At the time that chaos and disorder prevailed in the town, and one could not remain in one place, I came to them and requested if I could stay over for a day. Dr. Katz agreed immediately, however the witch immediately answered: "In my home, there is no longer any room even for my own Jew." As I left the home my heart was filled with great sorrow for the poor Dr. Katz, who later became the first victim.

For all the years that I knew Melnikowicz, who worked for the notary, I was, as is said, a very good brother. During the time of the Russian rule, he was threatened with a jail term for coming late to work or for not showing up at all to work. I obtained for him a medical certificate, stating that he had been ill for three days. I testified on his behalf in court. He was exonerated. When the Ukrainians took power, he became one of the most important rulers. Among other roles, under his supervision, food was distributed to the workers. I once sent a request to him, that a small portion of bread be set aside each day for the Jewish workers. It would be placed in the medical clinic, and would be distributed to each worker as he went out to work. I greeted him, and he did not answer me. He only shouted in anger: "We are a young nation, and we cannot fulfill the needs of everyone. We have to worry first of all about our own."

New decrees were issued daily. Life became more difficult each day, especially when the Jews who had been expelled from the neighboring villages arrived in town. At the same time, our Ukrainian supervisors were looking for ways to free themselves of us and make Rozniatow Judenrein. Despite the bribes with items of great value, and despite the negotiations with the governing authorities by people such as Dr. Sapier and Zechariah Lieberman, the Ukrainian authorities secretly decided to round us up and drive us out.

On Tuesday, August 27, 1941 toward evening, Dr. Sabat was issued an order that as of Sunday September 1, no Jew could remain in town. Dr. Sabat immediately informed all of the Jewish medical workers, who were permitted to go out on the streets during the evenings. We knocked on the door of every Jewish home and informed everyone of the tragic, black news, so that everyone could have the chance to prepare to go into exile. We were given a choice of four towns where we could go: Halicz, Kalush Dolina, and Bolechow. Later, rumors spread in town that the non-Jews were intending to expel all the Jews for an extended period so that they can pillage their property in an unhindered manner, and then they would return us home. Therefore many Jews buried their possessions such as gold, silver, dollars and other valuables. On Wednesday morning, the town was teaming with gentiles, as a fair in the good times. They came from almost all the neighboring villages with carts, sacks, axes and hand wagons. They came with the intention of helping and bidding farewell, but the real truth is that they rejoiced over our troubles and tribulations. One had to give over ones most precious and finest belongings, whatever the gentile wished, in order to hire a cart, for they did not want to drive for merely money. Thus did two or three families go together on one cart, taking only their most necessary and important belongings, and set off for exile. The gentiles grabbed items as if from a fire: linens, dresses, bedding, sewing machines, furniture and other household objects. Naturally, the gentile, in order to express sympathy, promised to return them or to exchange them for food products. Jews let themselves be deceived – did they have a choice? They were thankful to have less to take with them, and wanted to flee from the city as quickly as possible.

The Ringplatz and all surrounding lanes were filled with loaded carts. The upper street leading to Dr. Sabat's house was filled with three carts in a row. There, the local gentiles (Ukrainian militia) showed their true murderous evil face. They threw off all the things from every cart, and took whatever they wanted. Fortunate were the families who passed the inspection and were off on their journey. The sun beat down mercilessly, and the heat was stifling to the point that it was impossible to catch one's breath.

ЧЧЧЧЧЧЧЧЧЧЧЧЧЧЧЧЧЧЧЧЧЧЧЧЧЧЧЧЧЧЧЧ

---

In normal times, on such hot days, the dams of the rivers would be opened so that water could flow through the entire town. However, today, they ensured that we would not have even the minutest comfort. Many people fainted from the stifling heat, weariness, and lack of food and drink as they were standing by their group: including Feiga, the wife of the ritual slaughterer (shochet), Sara Lindenbaum – Yossi Rosenberg's daughter, and others. We did not forget to take the kosher Torah scrolls. The non-kosher chumashim, prayer books, Gemaras and other books were packed away and left in the Beis Midrashes with the hope that we would soon return and everything would be in its appropriate place.

We heard that after a few weeks Dr. Korbas, may his name be blotted out, had taken out all of the remaining Torah scrolls and holy books, and transferred them to Kalush. The rest of the books and prayer books were pillaged by the non-Jews who used them for their own private purposes.

After the search of the loaded carts, we were not able to leave the city until an automobile with Gestapo men came from Kalush to take a look at our bad situation. They immediately ordered that we provide four blankets and four sacks of flour. Leizer Geller and his partner Yisrael Leib Artman provided the blankets. Drs. Nunek and Dolek Lusthaus, Dr. Leon Horowitz, Shimshon Rechtschaffen and others ran among the carts, and anyone who had even a bit of flour gave it over in order to be freed from the murderers, and to be able to leave the city quicker. The heartrending scenes among the Jews were indescribable. Without words, the Jews fell into each others arms, hugged, kissed, and shed bloody tears.

Most of the Jews went to Dolina and Bolekhov, for they were very afraid of Kalush. One week previously, the Gestapo, with the assistance of the Ukrainians, went around with a list and gathered all of the professionals of Kalush, such as doctors, engineers, teachers and engineers. Exactly at that time, our Bendet Spiegel, Nachum Artman's son-in-law had traveled from Broszniow to Kalush to rent a dwelling, for the Jews of Broszniow had to leave. The murderers included Bendet among the 300 Kalush Jews who were taken out to the forest and shot.

The pained, suffering, brokenhearted Jews who set out on their journey to the designated cities with their few belongings were attacked and robbed of what they had by the gentiles of Szwaryczow, Krechowice, Vishna Strutyn, and Spas. Those who already succeeded in arriving in the city were fortunate. We arrived in Dolina. They found a place to rest the head and relax their broken bones. The Jews of Dolina displayed great sympathy for the wandering Jews, and helped them with what they could. It is impossible to describe the cramped living conditions. People were literally lying around on the streets. We must not forget that it was not only Rozniatow Jews, but also Jews from Broszniow, Krechowice, Mizon, Vygoda, Beldisz and other nearby towns streamed into Dolina. Those Jews with the greatest means rented dwellings from Christians in the neighborhoods outside the city, and paid with valuable objects or foreign currency – dollars. A large number were put up with relatives or other Jews who wished to help Jews in this type of tribulation. 10-15 people were crowded into small rooms like herring. Dwellings were made out of former shops, stalls, stables, rooms, anywhere where one could have a bit of room for one's head. The deportees also lived in the synagogue, Beis Midrash and kloizes.

At the beginning, the situation was still bearable. However, already in November 1941, when the cold, snow, and blizzards began, the true tribulations began. According to the command of the Dolina S.S. Land Commissar Bebel, may his name be blotted out, a Judenrat had to be set up within 24 hours. The Judenrat had the job of fulfilling the commands of the S.S. and providing all of their needs at the expense of the Jews of Dolina. At first, every Jew had to pay a certain amount as a contribution, each according to his means. Soon after that, they had to give over all valuables of gold or silver. After a few days, the Jews were commanded to supply them with new furniture. A Jew was forbidden from owning cows and horses. Any furs, including streimels (Hassidic fur hats), had to be given to the murderous army, which was already crawling into Russia, so that they would not freeze there. Every morning, the Judenrat had to supply the requested number of Jewish workers. Over and above this, a reserve of several more workers had to be available if needed, so that any request throughout the day could be immediately fulfilled.

The Judenrat of Dolina did not have an easy job. The task of the Judenrat chairman, Dr. Julius Weinreb, was particularly unenviable. By nature, he was a quiet man, a man of scruples, and he possessed an ideal personality. He had a warm, Jewish heart. On many occasions, he was put to a test and had to endure great tribulations and pain. Almost every second day, Krieger and Mueller, may their names be blotted out, visited from Stanislawow; Freitag may his name be blotted from Kalush; and Schultz and Mueller may their names be blotted out from Vyshkov in order to confer with our local Dolina commissar Bebel, may his name be blotted out, and others. Every command had to be fulfilled with immediacy. When a fur was not provided at the requested time, Dovchi Weinless was taken to Stanislawow, from where he never returned.

The same cold fate occurred to Miriamche the widow of Mordechai Deutscher and the daughter of Shmuel Schwindler, on account of the fact that she did not tie her badge of shame, the Magen David, in the correct place on her arm in accordance with the orders.

I often recall how we yearned for proper bread or potatoes, and it is difficult to comprehend our Judenrat was able to provide items that had not been available for a long time, such as fabric, shoes, various expensive drinks, hens, eggs, butter, and even chocolate. Not infrequently, we met our dear, honorable vice-chairman of the Judenrat, Efraim Weingarten who was beloved to the Jews, as he was going from house to house with a basket, pleading with weeping eyes for one egg from every person.

The first Jew who had his beard and peyos cut off with a knife by the Shupo (Shutz Policei) was Leibish Kluger of Dolina. Jews who had to go out on the streets and to work would cut off their own beard and peyos out of fear of enduring this torture and embarrassment. Even those who were able to remain in their houses would cover their faces covered with kerchiefs out of fear.

Once, when I took my turn in the Jewish hospital, a Jew entered and said: "Lutwak, I beg a favor from you!." I saw before me a broken and worn our Jew, without a beard and peyos, whom I could not recognize at all. I asked, "Who are you?" The Jew burst out weeping bitterly and said, "It is the Messianic era, since one brother does not recognize the other. I am Yosef Shimon Stern."

I want to make sure that those reading these lines will think for a minute about such an image, how our dear and close Jews looked without a beard and peyos.

Immediately after we were expelled from Rozniatow, torrential rains fell endlessly for two weeks and destroyed the wheat and all other produce in our region. The gentiles said that the Jewish G-d was taking revenge upon them for the persecutions that they had perpetrated upon the Jews. Despite the fact that the farmers had to give over to the Germans all sorts of produce necessary for life, they still had a way out. They had freedom of movement and were able to travel to Podolia to purchase and barter the pillaged Jewish belongings. The life of we Jews was bitter and difficult, especially those who had been driven out of their homes. Hunger did not pass over anyone, and everyone was worn out and plagued, and nobody was satiated. It was not possible to obtain milled flour. The gentiles did not bring their wheat to the mill, for they would have had to give a portion to the German regime. Life was even more difficult for the Jews. For a few measures of wheat, rye, barley and even grits, oats or a few potatoes, one had to give over such articles as pillow, bedding, suits, dresses, and other household objects. A price in monetary terms almost did not exist.

We still had a bit of grits in the house, which we ground in a coffee grinder. Others took a piece of metal, made holes in it as in a meat grinder with notches, and turned it day and night so that they would be able to have something to put in a pot with boiling water and produce a dish which we would call "Tsher".

Shortly after Passover, the Tsher already became scarce. The gentiles brought fewer products into town. The hunger grew from day to day. Jews barely dragged themselves on their feet, searching in the streets, the gentile yards and the fields. Any blade of grass that remotely resembled food was quickly devoured. The number of those how died from hunger grew day by day. The Chevra Kadisha (burial society) under the auspices of the Judenrat ran about all day with hand wagons to bring the dead to a Jewish burial.

Henchie Shapira, the daughter of Dudi Reichels, told me at that time that Stas Jurezko, Heryn Heiduk's youngest son, about whom we only have good things to say, came to Henchie Shapira and purchased a new suit for 8 kilograms of rye and 20 kilograms of potatoes. When he brought the products, it became obvious that instead of 8 kilograms, there were 12 kilograms of rye, and instead of 20 there were 30 kilograms of potatoes. When she next saw Stas and asked him why he gave her the extra kilos, he lowered his head in embarrassment and said: "Don't worry! I know that this is less than a suit is worth, and when I have another chance, I will give you additional food."

Almost every day, I met Shalom Hoffman, Vove's son, going around with a basket and a few pots to distribute a bit of food to home bound families who were suffering from hunger. He also collected money to purchase boards, and cloth for shrouds for the dead.

I feel a moral duty to give honor and make mention of a Jew of great character, who assisted many hungry Jews during that terrible and difficult time. Hirsch Gelobter, the son of Sasi-Feiga Gelobter of Rozniatow, who lived near the train station in Krechowice, and settled in Bolekhov with his wife and three daughters after the expulsion. They went to live with their eldest daughter Genia Salitir. At the time of the first aktion in Bolekhov, he lost his wife Shendel and two daughters. Afterward, he went to live in Dolina and settled in the place where his sons worked, in Broshkov. For entire days, he would go among the homes of the deportees from Rozniatow to help them with what he could.

As a former merchant, he made contact with gentiles with whom he had formerly conducted business. Despite the fact that conducting business carried the punishment of death, almost every week he succeeded in bartering a calf or a large animal in exchange for various items. He did this alone or with the help of his son. At night, he would stealthily bring the animal to my brother-in-law Mordechai Kornblau, who lived outside the city and had stalls and barns. The shochet would come every Wednesday night to slaughter and render the animal kosher. He would sell portions of meat to his customers who had the means for a preset price, without Heaven forbid taking any profit. He only took the amount that he would need to purchase a second animal.

I remember that Kasrielchi Koflis, who used to come to our house almost every day to get something to eat, once said: "Mantzi, give me Thursday's portion today, for who knows if I will still be alive then."

Hirsch Gelobter continued with his work for several months with self sacrifice. He was known, loved and esteemed by all the Jews of Dolina.

Once, as he was walking through the city, Hirsch found a group of Jews chopping stones on the street. An S.S. man was behind them, beating them over the head with the butt of a gun. He sat there like a hardened stone, no longer being able to watch the murder. He asked the German to have mercy on the weak, hungry Jews. The murderer threw himself upon Hirsch and began to beat him. Hirsch was a healthy, tall and well-built Jew, despite already being 60 years old at the time. He broke out in a wild fury, took the gun from the hand of the murderer, beat and bit him with his teeth, left him lying there wallowing in his blood, and fled into the fields that surround the city.

Everyone knew where Hirsch was hiding, for nobody wished to do harm to him on account of his good deeds. Even the Judenrat did everything possible to ignore and downplay the event.

{410}

## He Fell as a Hero

Hirsch always wished that the murderers would not take him alive to slaughter. His wish was fulfilled. After the liquidation of Dolina, they found him lying in his dwelling riddled with bullets, with a bloody axe in his stiff hand. The Christian neighbors told about his heroism. Every S.S. man who entered the threshold of his dwelling was honored with his axe. They saw themselves how several dead, bloodied murderers were taken out. The battle continued for a long time, until the hero Hirsch Gelobter, may G-d avenge his blood, gave up his soul in sanctification of the Divine Name.

The famine worsened to the point that people risked their lives to get something to eat. For example, Yosef Halpern went to Rozniatow with items that he exchanged for food. On the way back, several gentiles murdered him near the non-Jewish cemetery. The daughter of Itzi Rothbaum of Krechowice went along with her husband Tishenkel to Odenica-Dolina to exchange something with the gentiles. They encountered Krieger in his car on the route. He beat them murderously and then shot them.

Mueller built a death camp in Vishkuv. He would appear in the city a few times a week, capture a few Jews and murder them. One of the first victims was the young son-in-law of Yosef Kassner, the husband of Baltzi – Meir Nestel. A few days later, that selfsame murderer Mueller noticed from the yard of the "Kripa" amongst the forced laborers, the fine handsome youth Shaya Stern of Mizon. He summoned him to his office and shot him in the head without reason. He then ordered Zafart to clean up and leave no trace of the Jewish blood.

Every two weeks, the Judenrat had to supply 25 or 30 Jews to Mueller for Vishkuv. It is impossible to believe how Jews volunteered to go there with the hope that they would at least receive food for the work. The agreement with the Judenrat was that the workers would be exchanged after a month of work in Vishkuv. In praise of the Dolina Judenrat and the Jewish militia, I must mention that despite their tragically difficult work, they did not lose their Divine image, and always treated the Jews of Dolina in a humane fashion. When it seemed that nobody was returning from Vishkuv, and in order to find out what was taking place there, the chief of the Jewish militia, Edzi Poper, went to Vishkuv with a group of Jewish workers, and never returned from there.

{411}

**In Constant Fear**

By remaining in contact with relatives and acquaintances in other cities, through messengers or via those who escaped, we found out what was going on in Lemberg, Stryj, Bolekhov, Kalush and Stanislawow. Incidentally, I wish to mention that a few friends visited me for a week, and Lunik the son of Vovche Teneh also came for a few days. When Shimshon Rechtschaffen and his daughter Fanchi came to Dolina, they urged me to visit my friends in Kalush for a few days. He had the premonition that perhaps this might be the last time to visit with friends.

During the two days that I was in Kalush, I did not have the chance to see even a portion of our Rozniatowers. A great panic pervaded there. People were afraid to stick their heads out of their houses both during the day and the night. There was great crowding, with 14-20 people in one room.

The residents of Kalush had already tasted the bitter taste of a bestial "aktion" several times. Therefore, they lived in constant fear of the inevitable end. It was hard to recognize the people. They were weary and downtrodden, having lost the spark of desire and hope of living. They did not talk and converse, despite the fact that there was a great deal to talk about. They only looked at each other, etching the image in our memories, feeling that this might be the last time. The scene at my visit with the children was heartrending: Fanchi Shimshon's, Rivcha's Tenchi and Izi. Their weeping and begging of me to remain with them will never cease to resonate in my ears.

People searched for ways and made plans about how to escape. Dr. Nunek Lusthaus and his wife Irina the daughter of Dr. Feier, as well as their young child and mother Mrs. Esther Lusthaus, went to live in the village of Vytoicha where he worked as a physician. Dr. Fried and his wife Loti the daughter of Shmuel Friedler went to Swaryczow to work as doctors. Dr. Hilman of Dolina went to Spas, and

Dr. Leopold Karp and his wife Eva went to Lipovetcha.

Jews felt somewhat safer in those places – either as physicians or as other workers, and did not suffer from hunger in those places, as did the Jews in the city or the ghetto. On the other hand, they did suffer from isolation and longing. The following Jews remained in Rozniatow: Dr. Sabat and his wife (nee Weinreb from Asmalada), Litower, Dr. Mina Froiman, her husband Fishel and daughter Aviva, and the pharmacist Margolis. One of them came to Dolina every week and stayed for a day or two to be together with Jews, and draw some moral support. They were very jealous of us, for we were among Jews: shared troubles are half a comfort.

Several hundred exiled Hungarian Jews also lived in Dolina. At the end of April 1942, the German commander issued an edict that, until May 1st, the border at Vishkuv would be open, and they could return home. Aside from the Hungarians, many other Jews set out with sacks on their shoulders and hurried so as not to be late. They fled to the border with a slight hope that they might save their lives. When they were already all at their place in this trap, Krieger arrived with 2 busses of murderers. They murdered all 500 Jews. Later, the Judenrat had to pay for the bullets, and all other costs associated with the slaughter. Thereby, we were assured that there would be no more actions in Dolina, for the 500 martyrs were reckoned on the Dolina quota.

I wish to relate here an incident that illustrates how cheap the lives of the Jews had become. Schultz practiced shooting in the garden of the Gestapo building by shooting at flying birds. Directly on the other side of Altastrasse, near the Dolina courthouse, Yankel Lew was walking home with a pail of water. The accursed man saw the badge of shame upon his arm, recognized him as a Jew, and shot him in the back.

The lawless situation, the hunger the constant fear about tomorrow created such a feeling of apathy within us. The arrival of the murderers at the Judenrat no longer created a panic, and people no longer ran to hide as in the beginning. Not one day passed in which a Jew was not murdered or sent off to Stanislawow.

A day before the bloody slaughter, on the Sabbath of August 29, 1942 I met Rodek Karp, Dr. Leopold Karp's brother, who came home from Waradol for the Sabbath.; Dolek Lusthaus and Baral. They were astonished; not being able to understand what was coming. However each of us was certain that there must be some reason why particularly on that Saturday and Sunday, all of the Jewish workers who were employed in the surrounding villages were sent home to their families.

Knocking his hand on his shoulder, Rodek said: "What can happen hear? Death? Nobody is afraid of that anymore. Today me, tomorrow you."

That same Sabbath, late at night, my neighbor Yehoshua Teichman brought the bitter tidings that a panic is pervading in the city from where he just came, and everyone is frightened about the next day. Several busses with Gestapo men arrived, and Krieger and Mueller are in the Judenrat conducting discussions with the president Dr. Julius Weinreb. We both immediately went to inform all the neighbors.

I heard shots on Sunday, August 30th, 1942, the 17th of Elul 5702, at 4:00 a.m. I had enough time to place a lock on the door of the barn that was filled with wooden planks. My sister Mantzi, brother-in-law Mordechai, and their children Saralche and Devora and I hid there. I quickly ran to the house of the parents of my brother-in-law where my other sister Hentchi was. Under no circumstances did they want to hide, for she had great faith. They even tried to convince me that nothing serious would happen.

Suddenly, the wild beasts broke down the front door with their axes and shouted: "Get outside!"
They began to beat people with their clubs. There were laments and cries, but the murderers mercilessly dragged out the remaining victims from the beds and couches. At that time, I happened to be in the dark kitchen, and I hid behind the bed. To this day, I do not know how I was able to overcome my fear and maintain control of my senses. I heard clearly one murderer say to another in Polish: "It is too bad that I did not bring my electric flashlight".

After a few moments, silence pervaded the house. I heard the murderers close up the house with boards at the front and back doors. I crawled out of my hiding place on my belly and saw that there were signs pasted on the windows, which said: "Whoever pillages this house will be shot by the Gestapo."

I immediately realized that I was safe for the moment, for nobody would break into the house on account of the warning on the windows. I went up to the attic, and from the cracks I was able to see everything that was taking place outside. I saw the S.S. murderers and the Ukrainian militia, armed with machine guns, dragging out the victims from the Jewish homes. There were civilian gentiles with axes and boards, and one with a list to note which Jewish homes were already clear of Jews. They lined up the Jews five in a row, with their hands in the air. The sadistic murderers, pointing their guns from both sides, gathered the Jews into gathering point at the Ringplatz in town.

A few months later, I heard a detailed report of the dreadful scene that took place in the Ringplatz from Sani Kassner, with whom I was in the Stryj Ghetto. After they shot his brother-in-law Meir Nastel, Baltche's husband in Dolina, he came on the Friday before the slaughter to take his father Yossel and his son from Bolekhov. In the meantime the wild action broke out on Sunday morning. They lived in a back room at the home of Meir Nastel's older brother in the Ringplatz. There was a German office in the front room, and the windows facing the Ringplatz were covered with placards and notices, so that the murderers did not attack the house and especially this room. Everyone packed in there, and they were able to hear and see what was taking place in the Ringplatz.

The Jewish victims who had been forced there, half naked and in pajamas, had to sit in a kneeling position. Anyone who moved from his place was fiercely beaten by the wild S.S. men and the Ukrainian murderers. Many were shot there. Without mercy, the murderers grabbed young children from their parents, and, holding them by the feet, beat their heads over a heap of stones until they died.

When one of the murderers snatched a child from Moshe Schulman, the son-in-law of Avraham Strumwasser and husband of Chaya, Schulman fell upon the murderer and began to choke him. Immediately, other murderers came to help him, and beat the unfortunate, anguished father to death with they bayonets. Aharon and Mintche Enis and their children Fanche, Tantche and Kuba struggled like lions, and did not let the murderers take them live to the slaughter. They gave up their souls in Sanctification of the Divine name by throwing hand grenades at the murderers from their own home.

After a few days, Dr. Iwashkewitz, later the son-in-law of Kardash, told me about the terrible scene that was told to him by a Ukrainian militiaman who had been present at the slaughter in the cemetery. At 1:00 p.m., the beaten, tortured Jews were placed in front of the three large graves. They were ordered to strip naked and march in a row over a plank that was laid over the pit from one side to the other. Accompanied by loud music, the machine guns sprayed a volley of bullets and mowed down the lives of our fathers, mothers, sisters, brothers, and unfortunate children.

Rivers of Jewish blood flowed through all of the streets where Jews had lived. Throughout Monday, following an order of the Gestapo, the gentiles collected the Jewish corpses and cleaned the thick blood from the streets, in order to obliterate all traces of the murderous crime.

At the same time, the Dolina Shupo group, the Ukrainian militia with the assistance of local gentiles, ran through the fields and forests like poisoned mice to drag out the surviving Jews. Among others they captures Leizer Geller and his young son Zundele Bodzi, Hirsch Mordechai Schwalb along with his wife and children, his father-in-law Mordechai Leib, the dentist Yosef Blau the husband of Matilda Prinz, his brother Salek Blau, Avrahamel Ratenbach, and Yankel Yampel the son of Moshe.

Late Monday evening, I came down from the attic and crawled on all fours like a bloodhound so that I would not fall down and hurt myself. I removed a board from the ceiling so that I could enter the barn where my sister Mantzi with her husband and children Sarache and Dvora were hiding. To my fortune, I found in the ruins my two friends Yossi Lindenbaum and Chaim Wolf Wigdorowicz' son, who had remained here for a while while fleeing from the city. From Yossi I found out that there was no more hope of remaining alive in the city, for Dolina had been designated as Judenrein, and all of the members of the Judenrat had been murdered.

Yossi told me that nobody could forget the heroic behavior of our president, Dr. Julius Weinreb. With a feeling of awe and honor, and a duty to perpetuate the name of this martyr, I wish to relate to you the following:

Our Judenrat president, Dr. Julius Weinreb, was a native of Dolina. He was a lawyer and a Zionist with a warm Jewish heart. He never lost himself in the darkest moments, and never harmed anyone. When the murderers Krieger and Mueller asked Weinreb on the Saturday night of the eve of the bloody slaughter to provide 1,200 Jews with the help of the Jewish Ordnunsdienst (militia), he immediately answered categorically that he is the director of Jewish affairs, and he can fulfill any of their desires on the moment but G-d is the master over Jewish lives.

That answer made the murderers so angry that they immediately decided to liquidate all the Jews and declare the city Judenrein.

The end of Dr. Weinreb was evil and bitter. First, he was held in Dolina, where he was tortured and beaten severely. Then he was taken to Stanislawow. The human imagination cannot conceive of the forms of torture that the sadist Krieger inflicted upon his Jewish victims in his own famous, terrible slaughter house known as Rudolf's mill. There, our president Dr. Weinreb gave up his holy soul in sanctification of the Divine Name.

It was no longer possible to remain in the city and hide at home. The local gentiles would hang out near the Jewish homes and check to see if they heard a sound in the house. Then they would inform the Gestapo. On Wednesday night, we went out to the fields and forests on the Odenitza. On several occasions, we met some gentiles along the route who beat us, but they allowed us to continue along our journey.

We met several Jews in the small forests.

On Thursday night, we arrived hungry, tired, broken and desperate at the home of Stefan Kardash, who lived in a small forest. His son-in-law Dr. Iwashkewitz received us in a very friendly manner. He displayed sincere great sympathy with us, and allowed us to hide in the "fadeni", that is under the floor of the barn, where we had to remain in a lying position. We crawled out every night to straighten out our stooped bodies.

The doctor and his wife Olga gave us some warm food, and also prepared some food for us for the coming days. They told us news about what was taking place.

On Sunday afternoon, when the gentile neighbors sat in Kardash's yard, the sole topic of conversation was about the bloody slaughter of the Jews. One person said that his father-in-law, who lives in the Harisha opposite the cemetery, told him how the Ukrainian militia with the help of the neighboring gentiles quickly covered the graves and fell like locusts upon the heaps of clothing, searching for valuables.

They also told how the heap of fresh earth over the graves began to pulsate like waves on the water. Sounds of bitter weeping and sighing could be heard from under the ground, where the half living people struggled with the angel of death. This cast a pall even upon the gentiles, and drove them out of the cemetery. The weeping and sighing of those who were not shot did not cease for several days and nights.

It was impossible to remain hiding with Dr. Iwashkewitz. He was indeed a good man, and often helped the Jews. However the Gestapo posted notices that anyone who hid or assisted a Jew would receive the death penalty. We had to find a way to continue on as quickly as possible.

A the same time, the Gestapo put up notices promising that anyone who would turn in a Jewish victim would receive a reward of a pound of sugar, a box of tobacco or a bottle of liquor. The gentiles could not stand up to such an enticement. There were many volunteers.

Meir Ungar, the husband of Dora Gelobter (who lives today in the United States) related to me the following story.

In a village near Bolekhov, a Ukrainian captured a Jewish girl, and asked the Gestapo that, aside from the designated reward, he should first be allowed to take the girl's dress before they shot her. The Gestapo asked him, "Why?" He answered that he wanted an intact dress without a bullet hole in it. This price was too high even for the Gestapo man. He shot the gentile with one bullet and the unfortunate Jewish girl with the second.

Dr. Iwashkewitz knew that in Bordishkov (a village near Dolina in which only Germans lived in the time before the war) there were Jews in the farm area. He made a special trip there, and sought out my cousin Ethel and her husband Shmuel Gelobter. They got in contact with us.

At night, having traveled in a roundabout way through fields, and forests, we succeeded in arriving in Bordishkov. In a forest in front of the city, we met among others, some people who were hungry without energy, and without the will to live: Miriam Kirshenbaum, the wife of Leib Kunis, the daughter of Yitzchak Schwindler from the old village with one child, and Chantzi Strassman who was the wife of Moshe the youngest daughter of Chaya Adler.

We could not remain in Bordishkov for more than three days. During the days, when the Jews worked in the fields, I hid in the Shalom Deutscher's attic. During the evenings, I would steal away to the home of Mordechai Gross and Zisha Aryeh Kupferberg who lived together in one dwelling. There I always met close friends. We talked from our broken hearts, and wished each other that we would meet again while alive.

We left Broshkov to go to Bolekhov, where we remained for only a brief time, for the fear of illegally hiding Jews was great.

We went to Stryj. There, Yaakov Lew, who had already been there for a while with his family, helped us to find a place to lie down and rest after having tired ourselves out and depleting our strength.

We were unable to remain there for long. A wild action broke out there 3 or 4 weeks later, in which they sent 2,000 Jews to the gas chambers of Belzec. This was at the end of November of 1942.

The following people perished in that bloody action: Yankel Lew and his family, Gittel Adler, Srultche Rozman, and Avraham Fogel and my entire family. At that time, I was beaten by the Gestapo and left lying among the corpses in the yard of 21 Lvovska Street. After a few hours of lying there, I regained consciousness somewhat and realized the situation I was in. I crawled into a mikva (ritual bath) that was located behind a bombarded, ruined building in the same yard that was covered with garbage. I lay there for 3 days.

The scene that took place in the synagogue for those three days that I was there is impossible to describe. More than 1,500 Jews were packed into a synagogue that could possibly hold 500 people. Many people suffocated, and the dead lay one atop the other. People attended to their needs on the floor. People were not lying, not sitting, but were simply hanging in the air without even a glass of water. The physical and moral suffering torments me until now.

At that time, they still respected and required professional craftsmen and tradesmen. I was taken out during the selection and taken to the Judenrat.

After a few days, I met Sasi Weidman (today in New York), Yossel Gelobter's youngest daughter who risked her life by coming from Bolekhov to Stryj with the hope of saving or at least seeing for the last time her parents, Yossel and Batya Malka, for the last time. Yossel Kassner was killed in that same action. I was together with Drezel Frisch (Meir's daughter) and her husband, for a few days. He was taken out of the synagogue at the last minute. Later, they both died in Bolekhov of typhus, which they had caught in the synagogue.

I now remained alone, like a lost dog, without a home, and without a family. Sasi brought me to the house of her aunt Chantche Sobel, the daughter of Pini Berger, who lived in Stryj. She took me in and treated me like an only child. Almost every night, surviving Jews from various towns and villages that had become Judenrein snuck into the ghetto. The following people arrived with one such group: Dr. Leon Horowitz the son of Shmuel Benzi, Mottel Hoffman the son of Shalom, his cousin Magister Ratner, Yankel Yampel the son of Bendet, his cousins Buni and Tzippe Angelman, Chaya Stern the daughter of Golda and her five year old daughter Edzi.

Dr. Leon Horowitz did not remain in the ghetto for long. He felt unfortunate and alone, and wished to go to his sister Klara Beigeleizen in Lemberg. Two days later I found out that members of the Ukrainian militia captured Dr. Leon Horowitz in Mikolaev on his way to Lemberg, took him to the Gestapo and shot him.

Mottel Hoffman and his cousin Magister Marek Ratner, accompanied by their uncle from Stryj, Blaustein, went to Skole and hid there with a gentile in a bunker. Two months later, at the beginning of March 1943, we were informed in the ghetto that the bunker was revealed, and the approximately 30 Jews who were hiding there were shot.

In Bolekhov there were still some work camps where Jews worked hard with the hope of surviving until the liberation. They slowly began to come to the Stryj Ghetto. Among others there were: Sani Kassner and his wife, his sister Balcha and her child, Rivka Fruchter the wife of Meshulam, and her cousin Tzipora Kreiter the daughter of Moshe Tzipa's, Avraham Yechezkel Zimmerman the son of Meir, Meir Laufer the son of Yankel, Herman Laufer the grandson of Efraim Rechtschaffen, Moshe Milstein the husband of Bluma, the son-in-law of Chaya Gittel Strassman, Yehoshua Strassman, Getzel and Yisraelka Frankel the sons of Meir, and the children of the tailor Yaakov Yehuda – Yenta, Chaim, Wolf, and Shimon.

Dolina Jews who were saved included: Mordechai Teicher and his wife, their daughter Beila with her husband and children, Moshe Landis the husband of Gittel Enis, Dr. Herman Neuhauser, Shlomo Ratenbach and his wife, Itzik Peker; Yosi Lindenbaum and his sister Maltzi, Yankel Klieresfeld and his younger brother, Yutka Leiter and his brother, and Moshe Geller with his wife – the daughter of Leib Hermans of Perehinsko – and their children.

{420}

## Piniele

Piniele was a 14 or 15 year old child with the nickname "Simchat Torah" for he was always a happy, joyous child with laughing, intelligent eyes. Now he was like a broken, weary old man. He came almost every evening to see me in the ghetto. He talked about his home, and his terrifying experiences. He had great faith, and like an experienced adult, he hatched bold plans about how to survive the terrible time. He remained in constant contact with his cousin Shlomole Spiegel, the son of Sara Rivka, who in that time was in the Bolekhov camp, and had reserved places in a bunker for both of them. Unfortunately, the Stryj Ghetto was blocked off, and the liquidation began on June 6, 1943.

It is hard for me to describe in words the horrifying, heartrending scene of the death of Moshele the shochet (ritual slaughterer) Weiser, along with his family and others. His grandson, Yankele the son of Zida and Bracha, a firmly built lad of age 16 or 17, brought the following news to me in the Stryj Ghetto. About ten days after the great slaughter in Dolina, Lusi Zitzer snuck out of the bunker one night to find something to eat for his parents and the rest of the people who were languishing in the same bunker, which was located in the cellar of the house of Dr. Redish. Unfortunately, he was unable to do anything. He realized that there was no salvation for them, for Dolina had been declared Judenrein. Lusi was able to do what many others had done – to try and save himself by fleeing into the forests. However, he gave himself over to the murderers like a hero, and informed them of the bunker in order to put an end to the hellish tribulations and anguish of the unfortunate people. From there, they were transported to the Dolina cemetery. Aside from the Zitzer family, there was Lipa Teneh (the son of Hersh) and his wife, Moshele the shochet and his wife Feiga, their son Zida the shochet and his wife Bracha who was the daughter of Yosef and Shimon Stern, as well as their two daughters Chatzi and Reizel and their son Yankel, There was also Moshe Eli's son Yankele the shochet Hochman, with his wife and two children, as well as others..

Moshe the shochet, did not walk to the grave that was dug, but rather danced as if at a celebration in the former good times. With a radiant face, eyes lifted toward heaven, he recited the confessional with great enthusiasm, and recited David's Psalm with a raised voice: "Even though I walk through the valley of the shadow of death – I fear no evil since You are with me" [2] as he lead the group toward the open grave. With the murderers began to shoot, a bullet hit Zida's son Yankele in the hand. He jumped in to the grave and remained near the edge. After the communal grave was covered with earth, he began to move, and was able to crawl out of the grave at night. After wandering for a long time, he arrived in the Stryj Ghetto. But unfortunately this was not for long. He was murdered in sanctification of the Divine Name during a wild action at the end of October, 1942.

For a long time thereafter, I could not at all understand how one could greet the Angel of Death with such joy. I had earlier heard about how Klara Patrich, the youngest daughter of Moshe Sanes of Dolina, jumped from the death board into the grave holding the hand of her husband Donek Shechter on the bloody Sunday. Among the Jews who were lead to death from an exposed bunker in Bolekhov was Gitzi, the young daughter of Meir Frisch, who marched on her last way with a raised head and a smile on her face as she mocked the murderers.

I thought that I would have the energy to explain in order everything that I had seen, heard, experienced and absorbed. However, I have now realized that a person is too weak to digest all this. I often have the feeling that I will be suspected of exaggerating the horror, therefore, I make an effort to tell only the main points. You, my dear readers, should forgive me when I mention or discuss martyrs who are not actually from Rozniatow or its areas. I do this with the intention of fulfilling my own and our collective moral duty to friends with whom we endured the hell, and who unfortunately have nobody living to remember them.

Every Jew who lived in the ghetto felt that death stood before him, and that it might come at any minute of day or night.

When fear and terror are a daily occurrence, when the impossible and the unbelievable become an actual phenomenon, all that one can do is to adapt to the prevailing situation. Simply, one accepts the uncanny reality.

The main thing was to obtain a work certificate – a legitimization that gave one "the right to live". One could deceive oneself that one might be saved. I worked for a time in the Jewish hospital as a disinfector, and I often had to go to the Aryan street outside the ghetto to the jail ostensibly to obtain disinfectant. When Jews were imprisoned, I was able to find out the reason for the arrest, to assist them, and free them. In this way, I met Esther Lusthaus in prison, with her daughter-in-law Irena Feier and child. Together, we bemoaned and wept over our common fate. We remained in contact and found out that Dr. Nunek Lusthaus, who worked temporarily as a doctor in the village of Vytoicha near Bolekhov, was searching for a way to escape from there and go to the Stryj ghetto. The murderers captured him as he was already far from Bolekhov on the way to Stryj. They brought Dr. Nunek Lusthaus to Stanislawow, and his mother, wife, and children were brought to a prison in Stryj. Yankel Yampel, the son of Bendet, worked hard to obtain the valuables and funds which were needed within 3 days to free the Lusthaus family. Unfortunately, a contingent action took place in the meantime, and they were the first victims from the prison.

\*\*\*

There are moments in the life of an individual that are etched in the memory and remain there in perpetuity. For I, who lived through the hell, every event, episode and shock that we endured each day is a frequent guest, and often comes to me in nightmares. I recall that almost every night, the doctors came to a room in the hospital and conducted spiritual séances. They sat around with their hands resting on the table, spoke about death, asked questions and came up with answers to explain the tragic situation. When I once was shaking, not agreeing with Dr. Herman Neuhauser's opinions and belief in the séances, he simply got angry at me. A few months later, when I was living together with him in the forests, he mentioned that it is the psychological nature of humans to believe in good news and keep away from evil prophecies. Often, we would deliberately interpret and put a positive spin on the apparent good news from the front that we heard on the underground radios, and spread it among the Jews in the ghetto to sweeten their bitter lives.

There was an adage in the ghetto, "the salvation under the shoulders and the angel of death before the eyes". The greatest acquisition for Jews in the ghetto was when one could obtain a portion of "cyankali", that is capsules of strong poison that look like saccharin crystals. People would wear it as a pouch around the neck like an amulet from a holy rabbi. They would guard it carefully and be prepared to use it at the last moment, in order not to fall in the hands of the murderers. Many Jews gave away their last belongings to the gentiles for fake poison, which was nothing more than saccharin.

{424}

## Bunkers

The Jews displayed a great deal of initiative, original ideas and inventiveness in constructing and building the various bunkers and hiding places. Ensuring a place in a bunker during the time of an action was a great worry and problem.

Many Jews earned their livelihood by digging and building the bunkers. The following people were experts in camouflaging such bunkers: Yankel Yampel the son of Bendet, Buni Engelman the husband of Leache Chaya Golda's, Tzipa's husband Herman Laufer the grandson of Efraim Rechtschaffen, Meir Laufer the son of Yankel, Avraham Yechezkel Zimmerman the son of Meir, and grandson of Sashi Feiga's.

It is literally something to marvel at and something unbelievable how Jewish minds created such brilliant concepts in the building these bunkers. I will attempt to describe one of the several bunkers in which I hid myself during the actions in the Stryj Ghetto.

In the Stryj Ghetto, on 14 Lvovska Street, in the front room home of Wolman-Milstein where there had been a shoe workshop, the following people lived: Leibush Feldman and his two daughters Tzila and Minka; Buni Engelman and his wife Tzipa and four year old daughter Edzia; Buni Milstein; and I. Milstein's relative Sara, her daughter Chana and son Moshe who jumped off a moving train during an action and broke his leg, all lived in the kitchen. Another relative of theirs, the young, fine boy with us, Moshele Hauser, was also with us. The agronomist Hesi Hoffman lived with his elderly, ill mother and sister Libchia in the lower room. Yankel Yampel was often with us.

In the closed yard there was a well and a shed that had a common wall with a lavatory. A pit was dug in the entire area of the shed, covered with beams and boards, and then covered over with earth. At the end of the wall, parallel to the lavatory, there was a small opening with a striped cover. Various utensils and broken furniture filled the entire room. A lock hung on the outside of the door. By removing a board from the roof of the lavatory, one could descend through a corner of the shed straight into the pit with the assistance of a small ladder. The last one in had to fold up the ladder, replace the board on the lavatory, and also close the opening of the pit. It took no more than five minutes to arrange ourselves completely in the hole. In order to mislead the murderers, we would always throw articles of clothing near the well and on top of the ladder that hung folded up atop a high fence.

At the end of December 1942 or January 1943, all of the working Jews were concentrated in Bolekhov. The old people and children were either hidden somewhere or already killed. At that time, the

Rabbi of Bolekhov, Rabbi Shlomo Perlow, and his entire family were brought into the Stryj Ghetto. Yechezkel Reder of Lvovska 16 took the rabbi and his family into his house. All Jews, including the Judenrat, treated the Rabbi of Bolekhov with exceptional reverence and respect. They comforted themselves and hoped that in the merit of this holy man that was now with them, their agonized lives would become easier. Unfortunately, the situation worsened, and every movement in daily life was fraught with great mortal danger. People would say that all of the curses of the reprimand[3] fell upon our heads. Despite all this, people did not lose their Divine image and they helped each other in any way possible.

{425}

## Righteous Gentiles

I saw a ray of hope through contacts outside the ghetto walls, when Blumka Horowitz-Laufer was suddenly brought into the ghetto. After the bloody aktion in Dolina, she succeeded in coming to Rozniatow after difficult wanderings. She lived for six months in a haystack that was owned by Stas Jurezko, at the edge of the forest. She was brought something to eat once or twice a week.

On one occasion, children were playing in the yard, they noticed Blumka. That night, Stas and his friend Duzia Dodenko brought her to the Stryj Ghetto.

I would have to have a writer's talent and be able to write books in order to describe her experiences. To this day, I cannot forget the terrible situation she portrayed. She lost her power of speech from her six months of not talking. She simply could not express a word. She could only whisper. She was terrified of everything, including the light. It took a few weeks until she was able to regain her human form, and then they took her back to Rozniatow.

Both gentiles were among the righteous gentiles who helped and saved Jews. Stas advised me to organize a group of 10-15 Jews with financial means. He would dig a bunker in the Rozniatow forest not far from his house, provide food and all necessary supplies, and thereby help us survive the difficult time. When I took this plan to Dr. Kahana and two other of his friends who were able to provide the finances, he laughed at me and wondered why I wanted to place myself into the hands of such a person as Stas Heidok. My arguments and convincing did not help. Stas' words to me are etched in my memory: "When you find yourself not far from me, I will help you!"

At almost the same time, Hirsch the son of David and Vovche Ratenbach of Dolina, arrived in the Stryj Ghetto. I was a friend of Hirsch from my youth in the Dolina gymnasium. I found out from him that in Dolina there were Jews from various different places of the region, who were under the supervision of the brothers Stach and Heryn Babi. On several occasions Hirsch endangered his life by going to remove Jews from the Stryj Ghetto and Bolekhov camp and bringing them to the forest.

His plan to bring the Bolekhov Rebbe to the forest unfortunately did not work out. When he was in the ghetto for the last time, someone reported him, and he barely managed to escape from the ghetto.

{426}

## A Seder Night in the Bolekhov Ghetto

Every Friday afternoon, in quiet times when there was no panic in the ghetto, I had the privilege of taking the Rebbe to the mikva which was at the Jewish hospital. At that time, I spent almost every evening with the Rebbe's family, hearing stories from the past and news that was brought to him during the day by messengers from other places.

We were close to 100 Jews at the Passover Seder of the Rebbe. Each person received a half a piece of matzo, which was very rare in the ghetto. To this day, I do not know from where he obtained the matzos and wine for the four cups. The Seder proceedings, with biter weeping and sighs, cannot be described. We were afraid of a sudden attack. Therefore, we strengthened our guard throughout the entire night, and checked the entrances to the ghetto every hour: Lvovska, Batarego, Luna-Park, Koshniersla, and Berko Joselevitza.

After the Seder, we discussed the tragic situation and discussed how to save ourselves from the ghetto. Should one go to hide with gentiles, or go out to the forests? The brother of the Rebbe's son-in-law, Hershele, a very intelligent man, had come from Hungary and brought with him plans to transfer Jews across the border. Unfortunately, already at the outset, this did not succeed, and the first group of 20 Jews, mainly doctors including Dr. Schiff at the head, were shot at the border. When I told them about Hirsch Ratenbach in the Dolina forests and about Stas in Rozniatow, the Rebbe said, "The accursed enemy will not succeed in killing everybody. Go in good health and be successful."

Aside from my work as a janitor at the Jewish hospital in the ghetto, I also worked two days a week at building a new train station in Stryj. I worked a half a day with mortar and bricks, followed by 2-3 hours in a wooden hut that carried the name: "Medical Center for Jews". My work was to administer first aid, bandage wounds, etc.

When I worked at the train station, I had the opportunity to walk through the Aryan streets and see the normal life of the gentiles, with children playing happily in the streets. I painfully recalled what they were doing to our Jewish children. My spiritual suffering was often worse than my physical anguish.

Once, when I was walking to work with a group through the Aryan street, I ran into a group of children with woolen sweaters who were imitating an aktion, running and grabbing each other with wild childish shouts: "Juda! Laus!", exactly as the Gestapo men. They did not neglect to mock us as we passed by. The parents who stood by the houses beamed with pride.

When I returned to the ghetto broken in spirit more than in body, I stated with resolution, "I am no longer going to work."

At exactly this time, an order arrived at the Judenrat to provide 100 Jewish workers for the barrel factory in Bolekhov. A price of 20 Harta, that is golden dollars, was the price set to become one of the workers. I did not have this. Therefore, Dr. Kahana did not have any desire to send me. He tried to convince me that we could still live long enough in the ghetto. I did not have that sum and I could not hope to be among the fortunate ones. Dr. Kahana, who was responsible for the workforce in the camp, did not want to send me. They all knew that I did not aspire to go to work for Hitler in Bolekhov, but rather that my objective was the Dolina forest.

Dr. Allerhand, Kahana's deputy, who was responsible for providing the 100 workers, told me to be ready and to present myself at the gathering place of those who were going, and he would sneak me out.

Prior to my going, I went to the home of the Rebbe to bid farewell. He took my hand and whispered quietly. I did not understand that this was a blessing. He patted my shoulder and said: "Go in peace, and may you merit salvation."

Many of my friends in the camp accompanied me to the ramp, where two trucks were waiting for the workers. One of the drivers was Bil, the former driver of Archie Berger, whom I knew well. He was a sophisticated gentile. After a few words, he understood my situation and my wish. He took my sack, placed me in a corner near the tire that was close to him, and covered me with his raincoat. Thus did I arrive illegally at the barrel factory camp.

Shika Weidman helped me greatly there. He introduced me to the camp director, Rumek Samuel, the son-in-law of Leizer Schindler. He treated me as one of his own. He alerted a few of my friends about my arrival. Magister Zalman Shuster the grandson of Mishel Artman, as well as the dentist Bomek Hamburger of Voynilov came to me. They concerned themselves with obtaining a work permit for me.

I mixed in and went out daily with the people who were going to work. After work, I went to see Sasi Gelobter, Yenti Freudenberg, the children of Striten Kalman's, Shlomole Spiegel, and others.

Riva Weidman, Hersch Mendel Artman's daughter, brought me something to eat almost every evening. In order to get from her waterworks camp to my camp, she had to pass through an opening in a board. I often asked her how this was possible. If one has the intention to do good, one can even cross an iron wall.

On Sunday morning, July 6, 1943, they woke me up from my sleep and told me that the camp was surrounded by German police and Ukrainian militia. Somehow, I was hauled out to the yard, still in my night shirt and pants. There I was informed that they were gathering up the 100 workers who were provided by the Stryj Ghetto.

To my good fortune, at that moment Rumek Samuel, removed from the hands of the militia, to allow me to get dressed. From his wink, I understood what he meant. Instead of returning to the camp, I entered the attic. I had a chance to tell Blumka Kalman to remove the ladder and place it on the other wall. Within a moment, I was caught like a mouse in a small place under the planks. They searched everywhere, including the attic. The bandits then included the Bolekhov Judenrat and Jewish police, and took all 300 Jews to the cemetery, where they shot them.

When I later descended from the attic, I saw that they had removed all items from my camp. Shlomole brought me a jacket and shoes. Sasi brought me some bread and sugar, and Yenti brought me some tobacco. They brought me through a tortuous route to the refinery that was not far from the barrel factory, where the following people were gathered and waiting: Yechezkel Zimmerman the son of Meir, Meir the son of Yankel, Hesi Rosenman, and Barron and his sister from Kalush. As I bade farewell to those who were remaining in the camp, I wish to mention the words of Rivtza Nussbaum, the granddaughter of Yaakov Meir of Rozniatow: "Go and save yourself. Then there will be an extra bullet for us."

The decision was to set out toward the forests of Dolina. The question arose as to who would show the way. The Kalushers did not realize that the way was completely unknown to them. We became confused and had not yet decided to leave Bolekhov. The lot fell upon me. Each of as had some utensil – a knife, an iron bar, and Hesia had a revolver.

At sundown we went on our way. We walked for a while through the fields and were almost out of the city when suddenly, from a side road, a young Pole came to us and said to us in Polish: "I know you are Jews who wish to save yourselves. Take my advice and go along this way (he pointed with his hands), and you will avoid the police and the militia who are now on all the ways searching for Jews who are fleeing from Stryj, where the liquidation of the ghetto has begun."

I thanked him and told him that we already have a plan and know what to do.

The meeting between the young Pole and us was exactly at the intersection of three roads. As if by magic, I pushed on and set out along the road which he had shown us. Suddenly, we noticed a shadow parallel to us. We were six people and felt strong enough, so we called him over. It became clear to us that this was a Ukrainian worker who was returning home for a two day vacation from the Budinst work camp in Stryj. He told us that the liquidation began during the day of June 6, 1943. We asked him to guide us along a way that would avoid the murderous militia in Hashuv. This was far out of his way, but with some urging and a high price, he was convinced. He began to run with us and led us along a path with thorns and stones that ended up at the banks of the Hashever water, that is the Bistritza it seems, where there was a large bridge. Then the sheketz returned to his home in his village.

As we were on the bridge, an armed man met us. Seeing that we were a large group, he positioned himself near the railing on one side of the bridge. We were on the other side, and we did not encounter each other.

We were ten on the main road that led toward Dolina. We were very tired from the strenuous day with so many events. We turned off and entered a field, where we all fell down into the haystacks and lay down for a bit of rest.

I do not know for how long we slept. I suddenly awakened, and awakened the rest of the group. Everyone got up and set out on the main road to Dolina.

It was still very dark when we arrived at the edge of the village of Brodotzkov. Suddenly, someone shone a flashlight into our faces. He lay on the grass in the Kolodzin yard which led to the highway.

He was holding a flashlight in one hand, and in the other hand an automatic revolver. Without ceremonials, he began to speak to us openly: He knew from where we were coming and to where we were going. He is Stach Babi's brother Heryn. He helps Jews to save themselves from the Hitlerist murderers. He was coming now from Stryj, where he was on a mission from Regina Pilzen of Kalush (who was already in the forests for two months), to bring her brother Feivish, his wife and others from the Stryj ghetto. He mentioned my name as well.

From his words, we could see that we had met an honorable man, for he was capable of killing all of us with a series of bullets. To convince us further he said that he was waiting for Lozerke Schiffman who went to Kolodzin to get food, and then we would return to the forest."

I was a personal friend of Lozerke for many years. We were last together in Dolina. A few minutes later, he arrived with a backpack full of food. He was accompanied by Plovka Kozak, who was Stach's right hand man in the forest. When Lozer saw me, he embraced me, kissed me, and wept. Then we all set out for the forest.

When day broke, we were already in the forest. They led us to a valley filled with trees, which at one time was the summer residence of Janek Laufer. In that place Yankel Laufer (the husband of Blumka Horowitz), as well as his sister had their retreat. Lozer and Heryn gave us instructions about how to conduct ourselves clandestinely in the forest. They would alert the people in the forest about us.

{431}

## In the Forest

Who has the ability to describe our feelings that we all felt as we rested in the grass of the forest, enjoyed the crisp, fresh air, and completely forgot about our situation? I reckoned that it was not my wisdom and daring, but rather providence alone that had dictated to me how to conduct myself and what to do. How can one interpret otherwise the march from the Bolekhov camp to the forests of Dolina, which should have taken two nights, and only took one night? The exit from the camp, the meeting of our two specially sent guides, and the arrival to the right place in the forest. I had the feeling and strong belief that the blessing of the Bolekhov Rebbe accompanied me above all removed my terror, and strengthened my faith that I would survive.

The first to come to us was Stach Babi. He spoke to us pleasantly, about how he would help us. The following distinguished guests came to us at midday: Moshe Klein (who today lives in America), Avraham Haber, Srulka Helfer, and Regina Pelzen. They brought us bread with a full pot of cooked potato soup. It is impossible to describe in words what this was like for us.

The next day, after the customary payment, Heryn began to guide Hesio and the two Barrons to the forests of Perehinsko, where Hesio's brother-in-law Kupferberg and other relatives were hiding.

Yechezkel Zimmerman and Meir Laufer returned to the camp in Bolekhov to fetch from there some necessary items and perhaps to bring as well some friends to the forest. Unfortunately, they were captured and murdered. At that time, it began to rain and the wind began to blow to such a degree that it penetrated the entire body, and it was very difficult on the heart.

Not far from us, in another group, lived Yosef Frischer of Dolina, and Chana Deutscher. All of these Jews had lived in the forest for about a year already. Every one of them had already made contacts with gentiles, who provided food in return for valuables. The best expert whom I found in finding sources of food was Moshe Klein. He would bring a live calf or 10-20 hens into the forest on his shoulders. I attempted to help out in all sorts of ways, including cooking, the maintenance of cleanliness, and keeping the home in order. I became one of the family.

At that time, liquidations of the ghettos and camps were taking place in almost all the cities of Galicia, and those who succeeded in escaping came to the forest from all sorts of places. Heryn became jealous of his brother Stach, who also had some Jews under his care. He decided to take Jews in to his so called "kolkhoz". In order to get into a camp, one had to pay money and valuable objects, such as gold watches, rings, and jewels. Generally, any Jew who fled to the forest would bring valuables with him. There were also Jews who formed their own groups, such as: the Pilzens, Helfer, Haber, Yosi Lindenbaum, Velvel (Kopel's) Kuperschmid, Shea Teichman of Dolina, Zelig Eber and his sister from the village of Rybno, the two Feier brothers of Stryj, Shlomo and Zani Ratenbach with their two Sobel nephews from Stryj.

The following were in Heryn's group: From Stanislawow – Shaika and Yanka Shrager, Muni and Fanka Kandler, Mondik Zahen and Rita, Karel Ister, Fitzer, Leib and Dvora Schvitzer, Wilek Knoll of Nadworna, Wilech and Siunek Garfinkel of Stryj, Fred Kowaler, his sister Lotti, and their mother, Czesia Zilberman the granddaughter of Landsman from Kalush. Aharon and his wife Regina Walkentreiber, Hirsch Katzman, Dontzi Hochpelzen of Zawirona. Dr. Neuhauser of Dolina, Dr. Stern and his wife and daughter from Mizon, Piniele Stern of Mizon, the dentist Schindler and his wife of Bolekhov, Max and Sabina Katz of Stryj, Shmuel Shlakes, and Shmuelke Teitelbaum the son of the rabbi of Neisands. I got to know the latter at the house of the rabbi of Dolina. Afterwards, I met him many times at the home of the rabbi of Bolekhov in the Stryj ghetto, including at the Passover Seder, and now I met him in the forest. He told me that he worked as an undertaker in the Stryj Ghetto until the last minute. He risked his life by washing and dressing the body of the Bolekhov Rebbe with clean linens as shrouds, and burying him alone in a separate grave at the time when everyone else was buried in a mass grave.

At that time, when Jews were streaming into forests trying to save themselves from the ghettoes, Meirka Turteltaub the son of Itzi Leizer came to us. I will write about his heroism separately.

I slowly became accustomed to life in the forest. It seemed that the danger had passed, and that we might witness the salvation. The main thing was that there was sufficient food. When there was a lack, Hershke Ratenbach gathered together a group of his youths for a "skak", that is an ambush. He maintained a list of gentiles who had stolen from or caused trouble to Jews. In all of the operations in Dolina, Bolekhov, Rozniatow, Swaryczow, Krechowice, Hershke had at his side our best experienced and heroic Jews: Wilus Weinfeld and Meirke Turteltaub. They brought entire herds of livestock and clothing. They would destroy the property of anyone who did not let them. I remember on one occasion, when they took linens and dresses from a gentile from Dolina. They broke into the house, broke open a crate of eggs, and mixed it with a sack of flour.

At that time, almost everyone had a roof over their heads, that is an attic covered with tree bark, which served as a place to sleep and take refuge on rainy days. Thus we lived with tension and awaited the true liberation.

{434}

## High Holy Days in the Forest

In the meantime, the High Holy Days approached. The two days of Rosh Hashanah passed by with groaning, sighing and memories of past holidays. For Kol Nidre, all the Jews in Stas' camp gathered together. Everyone was in a sublime mood. The candles were lit. Our prayer leader, David Lieberman, made an effort to recite the prayers out loud so that everyone could repeat silently after him. It was impossible to control ourselves. The sobbing and weeping drowned out the voice of the cantor, and not everyone could follow what he was reciting.

Slowly, we calmed down, and only occasionally did one let out a deep sigh and a tear. David led the services with a broken heart and great emotion. The Yom Kippur melodies accompanied by tears rang through the forest like heavenly music, and the each of us trembled with our whole hearts and with tears in our eyes.

How could Jews who left the inferno and arrived in the forest worship with more devotion to the Master of the Universe? Even if someone did not understand the meaning of the prayers completely – our prayer leader David with his weeping and shouting brought us to such a state of ecstasy that all of our limbs trembled and we had the feeling that this time, our prayers would open up the Gate of Mercy and arrive before the Seat of Honor.

{435}

## The Battles

Toward dusk on Simchat Torah, we suddenly heard the zooming of engines approaching us. An alarm went out and we fled. Twenty tanks with Vlosoviches driven by German officers first fired shots and then entered the camp. Everything, including the kitchen and all the bunks, was destroyed. The first victims were: Chana the sister of Hershko Ratenbach, Dania Schwartz, and Emil Beril of Krakow the son-in-law of Hugo Fisher. It took us a few days to reorganize and move ourselves deeper into the forest under the "Viesza".

Rumors circulated that there would be more raids on the partisans in the forests. From that time we began to take more precautions. We stood guard and we left the camp less frequently. From that time, there was more fear in our life in the forest.

In October 1943, we received news that a special army unit came to Dolina to battle he partisans in the forests, clear them out, and make way for the German army which was forced into retreat. This was after the defeat of Stalingrad. It was decided that during the time of the raids, we would move from the Viesza which was in the region of Vygoda, in the forests of Rokov and Krechowice. We packed up on Saturday, and set out on our journey at night.

On Sunday we arrived at the Babiovka, a small young grove near the suburbs of Dolina. According to our plan, we had to wait there for the entire day and move on to other forests at night. Suddenly Stach Babi ran in and brought us the bitter news that we had fallen into a trap. We were surrounded. We should search for places to hide.

The machine gun fire began a few minutes later, and the bullets passed over our heads. Everyone had to lie down under the low, young trees. At first, they shot toward a certain area of the forest. After that, the murderers formed a swarm line of commandoes, which we heard and saw. They spread out into different directions, and searched section by section under the trees. From one place under a shrub near the place where Meirke and I were lying, the murderers discovered the son of Gartenberg the shochet of Bolekhov and a girl from Kalush, and made them stand up. Both fell dead with one machine gun volley.

Until today I often ask myself: How is it that one can see the Angel of Death before one's eyes and have no sign of fear? I spontaneously embraced Meirke and held on to him as if we were one body. I kissed him and said the tender words: "Meirche, in another moment we will already be in the place of eternal goodness".

A few meters from the place where we were lying, the murderers found Stach's radio equipment. They immediately became occupied in searching that area, and left the area where we were lying. There, I witnessed a miracle with my own eyes, for it was impossible to believe that we were able to escape from the hand of the Angel of Death at that time.

On that day, more than 60 people were killed. In order to frighten the gentile population from helping or hiding Jews, the murderers took 20 gentiles from around the Babiovka and hung them in the Dolina town center. Stach's mother and sister were among the victims.

Earlier, during our good times in the forests, the rumor spread throughout the entire Dolia area that the Babi brothers have an army of partisans numbering 10,000. Therefore, nobody dared enter the forest. However, after the slaughter, the truth became known. We were warned that the murderers, accompanied by a pair of captured Jews such as Dr. Monek Lubliner and David Lieberman, would come to search through the places in the forests where Jews were recently hiding. This caused a great panic. I hid together with Meir, and another pair joined us.

After the raid, it was impossible to find a gentile who would even want to talk to a Jew, let alone help, for a great terror had fallen upon them. Meir was always a risk taker. When the need was great, he entered the village of Krive one Saturday night, where he formerly had an acquaintance. It is impossible to believe that he succeeded in bringing to us a full pot of hot soup, baked potatoes, and rye meal crackers. Our situation at that time cannot be described in words. I want to make note of Meir's ideal character here. He never ate a morsel of bread alone. His greatest joy was when he could help someone. Not everyone was like Meirke! We lived like one family, took council together, and constructed joint plans about how to protect ourselves and how to survive the terrible situation.

However, as became obvious, not everyone could be strong enough to survive the tests of trying times.

The will to live among Jewish people is stronger than anything, especially when one finds oneself in a state of hardship and sees certain death before ones eyes. The situation became more desperate day by day – it simply became unbearable. One could no longer find a place to rest. We wandered from one place to another for the entire day to protect ourselves from attack. At night, we would catch some slumber under a tree. Almost every day, there were victims from a bullet, or cold and hunger.

In November, the cold and wet snow began. Without a warm dwelling, covered with moss, it was impossible to survive in the forest. I could not longer keep up with Meirke – I simply had no more strength. Meirke had weapons, and as a brave youth, he belonged to the group of heroes in the forest. He remained in contact with me, and came to me as often as possible to see me. If it was possible, he would bring me something to eat, and he assured me that he would not leave me alone in the forest. His group planned to wander into Hungary. According to Meirke, they wished to take me with them. However, I reckoned that I was not able to withstand such a journey. I would only be a burden for them, and create problems for them. I absolutely wanted to avoid this.

Aside from the hunger and cold, we suffered with the serious problem of scabies and lice, which ceaselessly made our lives miserable. We all felt a sense of indifference and despair. On account of the frozen earth and lack of implements, we did not even bury the dead. Every evening, we would gather together from all corners of the forest to Slavka Kazak's destroyed house in the Babiovka. We would ignite the oven, and whoever had a potato would roast it and cover it in straw until the morning. Those who still had strength and a strand of hope to survive the present desperate situation would return together to the forest. However, many starving, desperate people would remain lying with closed eyes and wait until dawn, when a pair of Gestapo men on motorcycles would come by in the darkness, and kill the already half dead people with a volley from machine guns or a hand grenade.

As we wandered through the forests from one place to the next, we would encounter dead bodies of relatives and friends. It was completely impossible to bury them. As I came across such scenes, I imagined myself in such a situation. After a long deliberation, I decided conclusively to leave the forest and try to go to Rozniatow.

I wish to mention: After a week or two of living in the forest, a Jew from Bolekhov told me that after my escape from Bolekhov, a Pole from Rozniatow inquired and requested that if anyone come in contact with me they should tell me that someone in Rozniatow wishes to help me. I found out that Aharon Weidman knew about this. Through a messenger, he told me that the person was Mishka Jagelavitz. Aside from Viska, Stas and Dozio, I also had trust and relied on help from Ivan Vishinski, Jorka Jaczkov (a policeman) and Jazia Fisher. They came to me in Dolina on more than one occasion and assured me that in a time of need, they would help me. However, now, after the punishments and the hanging of the innocent people in Dolina, a pall fell upon everyone who even thought about helping a Jew.

I had never felt myself in such a desperate situation. After thinking it through, I realized that remaining in the forest is a certain death. There were gentiles that I knew in almost all the villages of the region, and if they did not want to or were not able to help me, they would at least bury me after shooting me. That thought strengthened my resolve to leave the forest.

I took counsel in this matter with Meirke. He was not yet prepared to leave the forest, but he told me that when it was time to part from me he would accompany me to Rozniatow in order to find out my later fate. This was how it happened: On Sunday at dawn, Piniele Stern of Mizin was standing there, attired in tefillin (phylacteries), leaning against a tree and worshipping. Suddenly, I heard him talking to himself: "When one prays, G-d helps and gives good advice. Why should I die here of hunger? It is better for me to go to Stratin-Vizna and take the heifer that I left with a gentile... I will take with me Hesio, Muni Pecker, and Wilek Knoll, and go there at night..."

When Pinie had time to talk, I was already next to them, and I asked them to take me along with them to the crossroads, from where I could go myself to Rozniatow.

I awakened Meirke and told him the news. Suddenly, I felt renewed strength, like a newborn.

We left that place in the evening. Along the way in the forest, we noticed that during the last few days, they killed many of our friends in various places in the forest. I shuddered in terror, and my heart raced.

We were already out of the forest at the crossroads, when Meirke told the group: "I will take Shaika to a gentile and will catch up with you on the return journey.

As they were crossing the long Statin bridge, we snuck along the edge until the Malinuvka next to the Stratin-Vizna gentile cemetery. From there we went through the meadows, and then we were already in the Rozniatow territory. After a few minutes, we were at the house of Jakob Broszka the mailman, close to the Rozniatow forest.

Meirke stood guard with his pointed gun and I knocked on the window. Instead of Jakob, out came an anti-Semite, whose name I no longer remember, who was a coachman in the yard. I did not say a word. The gentile saw before him a personage with a long beard, a tall hat on his head, and a sack over his shoulders held by a pole that looked like a gun. He shouted: "Sviat, Sviat", fled and slammed the door behind him.

We went to the groves. Our plan was to spend the night in the young forest, and the next day, to observe and figure out where Stas Jurezko's house was located behind the forest, so that we could go to talk with him the next night.

In the meantime, it was impossible to remain. Wet snow was falling. We could not lie down and could not stand – it broke all the bones. We shivered cold and our teeth clattered. It was dark, and we did not hear any sound. We went up from the groves, snuck toward the river and went into the covered garden of the yard that extended the length of several houses, and came to a certain house. Meirke told me: "Mosko lives in part of this house." Meirke stood with his loaded gun, and I knocked lightly on the window. The face of a girl that I did not know appeared at the shutter. She opened the door and told me to enter. I was not certain, and asked her who lived there. She said that it was the home of her uncle Mosko Jagelavitz.

Even though I looked loathsome and unkempt, he recognized me and knew where I had been. They did not think that any of us had survived in the Dolina forest after the raids.

I gave our password from the forest (a click of the tongue), and Meirke entered. They knew each other. Stefka took us into the warm house, and within a moment, placed a large plate with hot soup, meat and bread on the table. What a good person! When had we last seen such things? Not for years already! I controlled myself and also restrained Meirke – we should eat slowly so as not to injure our innards that had been withered from such a long period of hunger.

Stefka gave us tobacco, and we smoked. She invited us to go to sleep on a divan that was spread out over a foot bath. They would wake us up at dawn and tell us what we should do next.

I lay down with Meirke, embraced him, kissed him and wept. The next morning, Stefka took us into the kitchen in the second part of the house. We were surprised to see Idzi, the daughter of Hirsch Landsman, in front of us. I had not known that Mosko had mounted the wagon that was about to transport her to a work camp in Germany, removed her, and brought her to hide in his house.

She kissed us and wept profusely. After breakfast, she prepared for us a warm bath. After cutting our hair, shaving and casting off so much filth from us, it seemed that only half of our mass was left. We were given clean linens and a true bed with bedding. I will never forget that experience.

Mosko was still in Stanislawow, and the people in the house were afraid of searches by the tax collectors who searched the houses for tobacco and liquor. Therefore, Meirke and I spent a few days hiding in a different place. We thought that we would go to Rozniatow for a few days. However, we did not want to set out too far, so that we could come back to the warmth at night. Like a cat, Meirke went to a haystack at the home of a close neighbor Pankowski Matigewicz, lifted up a few sheathes of straw from the stack, and made a hole. We entered the haystack, and hid deep in the hay.

We returned to Mosko late Friday night. We again parted. Meirke returned to the forest on Sunday night to bring back a doctor, and Dozia brought me to Stas' haystack.

On Monday at dawn, Stas appeared in the haystack, and removed a few bundles of hay from a specific place, which opened into a tunnel through which I crawled into a bunker. With the light of a kerosene torch, I saw Aharon Weidman and Meir Ungar the husband of Dora Gelobter, sitting on sheets.

I cannot describe to you my feelings upon this sudden meeting with Jews who were close friends, after what each of us had experienced until this time.

After talking from the hearts, I fell asleep for an entire 24 hour period, and I woke up with a great desire to eat. There was nothing to eat there. Stas brought into the bunker a spoon, and a cup, as well as a bottle for my physiological needs.

Jews, suffering from great tribulations and sufferings, were able to raise themselves to great levels of morality and even greater levels of heroism. I will only relate to you one episode: There was never enough food in the bunker, and everyone suffered greatly. When Stas brought us our food in one large pot, Meir Ungar would take the first spoonful, then Aharon Weidman, and then I. When they got to the end, Ungar began to make a grimace with his lips as if he was saying that he does not want anymore, he has had enough. He dried off the spoon and waited. Aharon did the same thing, and said: "Do you want it Shaike? Finish it!"

After a few days, I realized the truth. They themselves were deathly hungry, but gave me their last bites, so that I could renew my strength.

After some time, Meir moved to Miski's bunker, where his wife Dora and her sister Sasi Gelobter were located. The Ungar's son Harold came to us.

From time to time the Ungars would send Dozia to sneak a package of food to us. Mendel Landsman, who with his wife Chana was also in Miski's bunker, sent me from time to time a package with bread, a few onions, some garlic and a bottle of liquor. I cannot describe to you what this meant to us.

Good deeds such as these strengthened our spirit and will to continue to survive until the salvation.

However, we endured difficult days of suffering. I do not know how to describe the suffering of lying or sitting in a crowded, smelly hiding place, and not seeing G-d's world for long months. Aharon suddenly became sick, and lay down without moving, and without being able to eat even the little bit that we received. It came to the point where Stas advised Harold and I how to find a place in the stable for a grave.

{442}

## Winds of Freedom

Immediately after Passover 1944, good new began to arrive from the fronts. The end was nearing. At the beginning of August 1944, when we heard the explosions of bombs and machineguns, it was to us like the finest musical symphony. The echo was so loud at the time of the destruction of the bridge in the old city that our haystack shook and our air hole was became covered with earth. We understood that this must be the final German retreat. Within a half an hour, the Red Army was already near us.

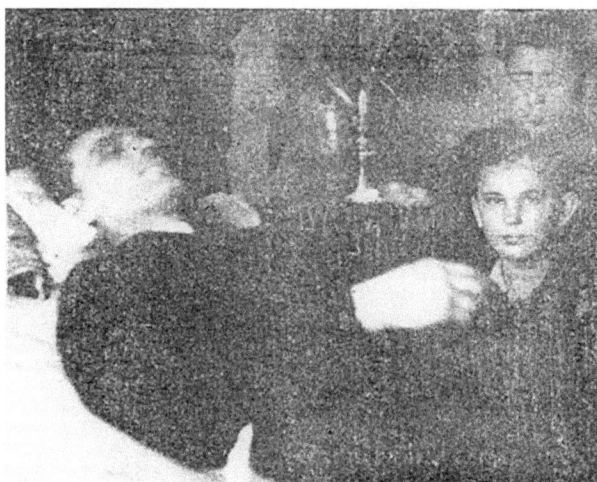

{Photo page 443: Stas Jurezko, one of the righteous gentiles who saved Jews at the risk of his own life. In this picture, we see Jurezko on his deathbed. Over him stands Yeshayahu Lutwak, one of the surviving Jews of Rozniatow.}

On Friday night, Meirke appeared with a Red Army soldier, and brought Harold to Mosko. Throughout Saturday, there were heavy battles in the area of Dolina and Rozniatow. We no longer remained in a bunker, but rather in a hay shed.

On Sunday morning our joy was indescribable, when we saw through the cracks the throngs of gentiles were fleeing with great fear into the forests to hide from the bullets. Our Stas also took his family and cattle and went into the forest. We no longer wanted to risk remaining there. When we saw all of those who were hiding in Mosko's got into a truck to go to Stanislawow, Aharon and I went out through the back door of the stable, walked through the fields, went along the Rivnia and set out on foot in the direction of Stanislawow. When we reached the hill at Krasna, we met other Jews who had left the forests and bunkers: Hirsch Ratenbach, David and Tzili Keish, Hesio and Muni Packer, Klara Segal, and Wilech Knoll. We all walked together in a group, until we arrived at the home of Wilech in Nadworna. There I stayed for two or three weeks. When I returned home, I spent a few days in Stanislawow and then in Kalush. I then returned to Rozniatow late in the night.

The next morning I went to see my parents' home, in which I was born and raised. When I arrived at the synagogue and caught a glimpse of my lane, it became dark before my eyes. No sign remained of any of the houses, including those of Ytzchak Shaya Katzman, Avraham Hoffman, Hinda, Zisa Ziring, Rikel Schwalb's children Chaya and Esther and their families, Kuni and Leib Kartshman, Chaim Shimon Lutwak, Avrahamcha Mark, Yossel Rubinfeld, Avraham Itzik and Mendel Landsman, Sima Zimmerman and Shmuel Hirsch Wechter. They were ploughed over with earth and divided up into plots in which potatoes were growing. Opposite, the house of Shmuel Rosenberg and the bathhouse stood. Through these, I was able to get my bearings and figure out where our house had stood.

With great heartbreak, I leaned on a post of the garden that overlooked our house, wept, and my voice shouted out: Yitgadal Veyitkadash Shmei Raba...

{444}

Yitgadal Veyitkadash[4]

Small were you my town,
Consisting of relatives, friends and acquaintances,
For you, dear martyrs,
I recite Kaddish, as if for a mother,
A memorial and a yahrzeit for you,
Pained and sorrowful am I.
Brutally annihilated and destroyed,
We will always remember you,
Until our end.

Zechariah Friedler.

## TRANSLATOR'S FOOTNOTES

1. The opening verse of the Book of Lamentations.

2. From Psalm 23.

3. The 'tochacha', reproof or reprimand, refers to two chapters of the Torah which outline the punishments awaiting the Jewish people if they do not follow the word of G-d. The two chapters of tochacha are in Leviticus 26, starting from verse 14 (Bechukotai Torah portion), and Deuteronomy 28, starting from verse 15 (Ki Tavoh Torah portion).

4. The opening phrase of the Mourner's Kaddish.

{445}

### Through Fire and Blood in the Years 1939-1956
### by B. Z. Horowitz

{Translator's Note: This is essentially the same as the Hebrew article that starts on page 207. There are some additional facts and nuances in the Yiddish section that are not included in the Hebrew section. One was translated from the other, and my guess is that the Yiddish is the original, as the Hebrew is clearer, more concise, and without some of the embellishing facts. I translated both independently, except for name lists, which I copied from the Hebrew translation.}

When the "father" of all peoples freed us from oppression and poverty, arrests, persecution and a general pursuit of Zionist and bourgeois began. Houses and rooms that had more than two rooms became nationalized. Jewish shops of leather, shoes, manufacturing, gallantery, confectionery, and food lay empty. All organizations, with the exception of Communist organizations, were "voluntarily" closed. All radio equipment had to be brought to the N.K.V.D. We were "free people", free from earning a livelihood and from human life.

On June 22, 1941, Hitler invaded the Soviet Union without declaring war. On June 28, we were evacuated  The Hungarian army marched in from one side and the German army from another side. They barely encountered any resistance from the Russian army, who were not prepared for the illegal war. The Russian party leaders in Rozniatow warned the Jews that they should evacuate to Russia, for all Jews who remained were living under mortal threat. All horses and wagons were with the Rozniatow landowners. Therefore they had to be obtained from the surrounding villages in order to transport the evacuated Jews to Stanislawow, so that they could travel further on from Stanislawow by train. Very few Jews took advantage of this opportunity. Each one had his own reason.

When we arrived in Stanislawow, a portion of the town was in flames, and there was no locomotive. Russian party members who had worked in Rozniatow traveled with us. They succeeded in locating a locomotive from a nearby station, where there were a few open platform wagons loaded with boards. Not paying attention to the heavy rain that was then falling, we sat down on the boards and set out on our way.

At a few places through which the train traveled, we were shot at by Ukrainian bandits. We were fiercely shot at in Przeworsk. However, there, the train station had a large train of soldiers and artillery, which opened cannon fire upon the church from where we were being shot. The church was hit, and the firing upon us was silenced.

As we continued on further, we were bombarded by the Hitlerist airplanes. The train upon which we were traveling from Stanislawow became longer in the meantime. At each station that we passed there were evacuees, and new wagons with people were added to the train. After being bombarded from the air, we arrived in Husyatin on Saturday, July 5, at 8:00 a.m.

**The Events in Husyatin**

More trains, both military and for evacuees, stood at the station. A German bombardment began a sort time after our train stopped. No alarm signal was sounded. The airplanes flew low, dropped bombs, and shot with guns and cannons.

There was a great panic at the stations. Both soldiers and civilians fled. The panic was so great that not one Russian soldier shot his gun. Were the Russian soldiers to have opened fire with their guns and machine guns from the platforms upon which they were sitting, they would have been saved because the airplanes were flying very low. However, not one shot was fired. The bombardment lasted for several minutes, and the situation was very terrible. The area near the station looked like a ploughed up field, adorned with dead bodies, body parts, people without heads, badly wounded and bloodied people. There was no medical assistance available. The victims, as far as I can remember, were as follows:

The Dead:

Chaitzi the wife of Yaakov Laufer, Mordechai Segal the husband of Beila, the son-in-law of Shmuel Rosenberg, Yehoshua the son of Aharon Zamel, Shmuel Zamel, Rosa Kalman the wife of Adlersberg, her brother Meshulam Kalman, Baruch the son of Aharon Zimmerman, Chana the daughter of Moshe Pares (her head was torn off), Hirsch Friedenberg the son of Leibche and Malchi, Meir Rabinowicz from Perehinsko (his head was torn off), and Bronia the daughter of Chanina Brand.

All of the above were traveling on one platform.

Wounded:

Perel Horowitz – wounded very badly, Yechezkel the son of Meir Zimmerman, Leib Laufer the son of Yankel Laufer, and Chana (Meir Rabinowicz's daughter) Rabinowicz from Perehinsko. I was lightly injured in my left knee. As I was busy helping my sister who had been badly wounded, I did not realize that I had been wounded. People were concerned about me, seeing blood streaming from my wounded leg

Many were killed and wounded, and it was impossible to find acquaintances.

Many of our acquaintances who were not immediately found decided to return to their homes. No argument could convince them that returning home was hopeless. On the other hand, proceeding with the evacuation was the only chance to stay alive. This had no effect.

The following acquaintances returned:

Shalom Rechtschaffen along with his wife and two children, Yechezkel Zimmerman, Leib Zimmerman, Yankel Zimmerman, Chaya Rivka Zimmerman, the children of Meir and Mirchi our cousins, and others.

The train upon which we were traveling to Husyatin continued on its way after the bombardment, leaving behind the missing people. The train was again attacked by air bombardment at the next station. There were many missing people. Our brother Baruch, Hirsch Frost and his wife were killed (we heard the news along the way from the survivors).

After the second bombardment, when it calmed down somewhat, the N.K.V.D and the police came aboard and began to sort out the badly wounded and the dead. The dead were buried in a communal grave, soldiers together and civilians together. A sanitary car was set up for the wounded. The wounded soldiers occupied all the beds of the wagons. The civilian wounded were left standing. My sister was very badly wounded. The wound did not stop bleeding, and she had to be satisfied with a place to sit.

The wounded were given no help. The wounded soldiers were able to bandage their wounds with their own first aid kits. The civilians remained bloodied.

Before the journey, pieces of bread and drinks were bought aboard the train. My sister refused food. However she requested a drink, for she was very feverish.

It was impossible to breath in the wagon. Fever, a foul smell and the groaning of the wounded did not allow us to sit down. All of the wounded were bloodied.

Along our further journey, a group of doctors and nurses from an evacuated hospital of Kiev came aboard our train. They examined all of the wounded. They diagnosed gangrene in my sister's wound and advised my sister that her hand should be amputated. Weeping, my sister categorically refused to have her hand amputated. The head of the group immediately began to clean the wound that had turned green, and declared that if she could hold out for 12 hours, she would be saved.

The fever finally went down, and the doctor declared that the danger had passed provided that there were no complications. But he was not sure if she would be able to move her hand.

After eleven days of travel, our train arrived in Karmonchik, and all of those who were seriously wounded were taken to the large local hospital. I was released after three days, but my sister had to remain in the hospital for longer. However, she absolutely refused to remain, fearing that she would not know where fate had taken me. The civic authority sent us to a village where there was a hospital, 15 kilometers from Karmonchik and arranged that my sister could remain there until she was cured. I was set up in the local kolkhoz (collective farm), and I drove to the hospital every day in a wagon from the kolkhoz.

The situation in the kolkhoz was very good. I was able to obtain products in the kolkhoz for my sister as well, even though she was in the hospital. I requested work for the director of the kolkhoz. I was put to work in the office that distributed produce to the members on their workdays: wheat, barley, vegetables. However, we did not remain there for long.

A short time later, we found out that the Hitlerist danger was already at Kharkov, and our village was 60 kilometers from Kharkov. I informed my sister that we had to prepare to set out on our way once again. The doctor did not wish to release my sister from the hospital, assuring her that if the Hitlerists arrive in the village, he would protect my sister as a relative. The director of the kolkhoz also assured me that nothing would happen to me, for if the kolkhoz was evacuated, I would be taken along with them.

I turned to the accommodations committee and inquired about the possibility of being evacuated deep into Russia. We decided to travel in the direction of Stalingrad. We did not know then that our brother had been killed, and we hoped that we might meet him, for there were many of the evacuated people in Stalingrad. We were taken from the kolkhoz to the train station, and given food for our way.

Finally, we set out for Stalingrad. There were thousands of evacuated people with sacks and bedding at the evacuations office. Our few belongings which we took along the way were lost in Husyatin, so we were light "travelers". My sister had to continue on with her wounded hand and with the splints that were stuck in her wounded feet. Lists with the name of the evacuated people hung around the offices. We searched for names of acquaintances and found none.

Food rationing and bread cards were instituted in Russia on the day that we arrived in Stalingrad. We were to be sent to a kolkhoz called Lipovka in a steppe 100 kilometers from Stalingrad. The only way to travel to that kolkhoz was with horse and wagon. Since several families were being sent to that kolkhoz, wagons hitched to oxen were already waiting for us. It was a long trip, and the oxen got tired. It dragged on for a long time, and we were hungry. In that area, the nights were already cold, and we were wearing light clothing. Finally, we arrived in our Garden of Eden which was called Lipovka

## In the Kolkhoz

We were put up with a local family, members of the kolkhoz. We slept on the floor. Each day, we were given a bottle of milk and bread. My first task was to drive through the field with harnessed oxen. My sister lay down sick.

I went out to the field at 6:00 a.m. At noon, we cooked unpeeled potatoes. We worked until the sun went down. Nobody went hungry in the kolkhoz. They divided up the last morsels. The people there were poor, but indeed they were good people. Each Sunday they brought us baked and cooked items, milk, sour cream, and sometimes butter.

I was called up to the military in October, at the age of 46. First, they sent me to a commission near the Volga, guarding large war storehouses. The work was not difficult, and I was able to visit my sister.

The good days did not last for long. Hitler's aviators also attacked here. The storehouses with all their contents burnt down.

In November 1941, I was sent to Saratov. This was a military collection point. From Saratov, I was sent to a military unit in a nearby kolkhoz to work, for winter had already fallen and there were not enough working hands to harvest the crops from the fields. I was never hungry while working in the kolkhoz, and I was able to sleep through the night.

Thus did they send me to various work assignments, easy and difficult, until I reached Stalingrad at the end of 1941. There I felt that I was a true member of the Red Army. I participated in various exercises, and 40 kilometer marches with full equipment or with bricks weighing 16 kilograms. The exercises were conducted at a fast pace.

At the end of February, 1942, my unit was led from Stalingrad to Beketovka, 12 kilometers from Stalingrad. There, there were large arms factories and a chemical plant.

The first days were peaceful. One night, all of the factories were bombarded and wiped out, more from being torn apart inside than from the bombs. The survivors returned to Stalingrad.

The first large scale bombardment by 300 German airplanes ruined a large part of the city. Things got more difficult each day. The Hitlerists tore into the city and began their difficult campaign. I was struck unconscious and taken to the hospital.

When I recovered, I was drafted into Zhukov's army, which was called "The Second White Russian Front". I joined on the difficult march to Berlin.

## At the Ruins

On July 15th, 1945, I set out from Poznan to Rozniatow. I arrived on July 21st. The picture of the city was terrifying. All of the Jewish wood houses were destroyed. The Jewish houses made of brick, half in ruins, had been taken over by Russians for dwellings or offices. The Jewish sheet metal houses were sold by the Hitlerists on open auctions to the Ukrainians from the villages, who transported the houses to the villages where they were re-erected. Ukrainians told me that the Hitlerists asked the Ukrainians who purchased the Jewish houses, "Who will again purchase your houses when the time comes again?"

I found the following Jewish survivors in Rozniatow: : Dr. Karpf and his wife, Meir Ungar and his wife, Dora Gelobter and her two children, Soshia Gelobter, Shaya Lutwak and Meir Turteltaub. All of them registered to transfer to Poland. I could not accustom myself to the tragic scene. The Great Synagogue was turned into a warehouse. The Large Beis Midrash, without doors or windows, with its beautiful paintings on its half fallen walls, had not lost its charm. Unfortunately, it had turned into a latrine. I asked the city administrator if we could take out the remnants, and he permitted this. The brick kloiz had turned into the office of the local newspaper, but was not desecrated. I had the rights to not work for a month as a demobilized soldier, and was provided with a dwelling and food cards from the regional office.

In August 1945, the registered Rozniatowers left for Poland. I remained the only Jew in Rozniatow. At that time, gangs raged around our neighborhood. It was very uncanny to remain alone as the only Jew, but above all else, I was alive. I did not become involved in any politics. I often traveled through the forests and met up with armed gangs. They did no harm to me. On the other hand, when Lehrfeld came to Broszniow, demobilized from the army, he was shot by the gangs. I warned Lehrfeld not to play with politics, for it was dangerous. Apparently, he did as he wanted.

In the interim, my sister returned to Rozniatow. Berish Friedler (Leib Friedler's son) also returned, set himself up with work, and lived with us for four years. Nechemia Shapira also returned as a demobilized soldier, as did Chaim Goldmintz, Shemaya's son. Since he was a member of the party, he obtained a party position. We were no longer so lonely. Time passed without any problems until 1953.

## The Libel Against Jewish Doctors

At that time, a geological group came to Rozniatow to investigate the possibility of digging for oil. Their bookkeeper, a hooligan but with only one foot, appeared in the center of the city one morning at 7:00 a.m., as people were going out to work. He announced, "Comrades, the Jews, our enemies in white robes, want to poison our leader. Beat the Jews. Free Russia!"

As I was going out to work and noticed a militiaman, I remarked to him that the hooligan is inciting against the five Jews who live in Rozniatow and work for the government offices. I then received his answer:

"We have full freedom of speech, and we cannot do anything about it."

Since that day I thought about how to extricate myself from the Red Garden of Eden.

In 1955, Berish Friedler told me that Jews were traveling to Israel from Chernovitz, and that at a certain time every evening one could hear Kol Yisrael (and Israeli radio station) from Jerusalem in Yiddish. It was dangerous to listen to a foreign radio station, so I placed my sister outside on guard as I listened to Kol Yisrael, where they listed the names of those who had arrived from Chernovitz.

I decided to travel to Israel. We had to go through strict procedures. We obtained the needed documents through the intermediation of a cousin in America.

As soon as the documents arrived , the N.K.V.D. found out about it. The first result was that I was fired from my job. Then we began to make hasty efforts to request permission to leave Russia. We had to provide 12 photographs, 8 biographies, a declaration that we did not owe any money, as well as other declarations. All of these preparations took weeks.

When all the enclosures were ready, we had to travel to the Avir in Stanislawow. With pounding hearts, we set out for Stanislawow. There, we were told that our request had been confirmed and they would send us the needed documents to obtain a visa to Austria, for our journey would leave from Austria. Of course, our hearts lightened up, but we had to remain serious in order not to display our joy. We returned from Stanislawow as if we were newly born.

Indeed, I was not certain that they would permit us to extricate ourselves from the Red Garden of Eden, and how long it would take until we would obtain our passes. After a month were received official words that we should go to the Has Bank in Rozniatow, pay 1,600 rubles for two passes with the certification of the bank, and then go to the Avir in Stanislawow in order to obtain our passports.

We were received in the Avir in Stanislawow in a friendly manner, wished a good trip, and told that we should register with the Russian embassy in Israel. If we were not happy or if we encountered difficulties, the Russian embassy would defend us, for we would remain Russian citizens until October 1958. After that, we could extend our passports for as long as we desire. If we were not happy in Israel, the embassy would assist us to return to Russia, where we would be assured of a dwelling and work.

As we left the Avir and returned home, I still was afraid that they would call us back and revoke our passes, for the political situation had sharpened as Nasser had nationalized the Suez Canal.

Nevertheless, our passes were valid to cross the Russian-Hungarian border for one month. One week later, at the beginning of September 1956, we left Rozniatow. We arrived in Vienna on September 7. We remained in Vienna for a week. We arrived in Haifa on August 21[1], and went to Ramat Gan, to people who we had never met in our lives, but to whom we are eternally grateful.

Thus ended our wanderings in the exile

{Photo page 454: Idzia and Miszko Jagielowicz.. With their help, the following Jews were saved:}

Max, Dora and Harald Ungar, Frumeis, Sashi Gelobter, Aharon Widman, Shalom, Salka and Imek Shapira, Kuzin, Mendel and Henia Landsman, Buma Horowitz, Yaakov Laufer, Buchi and Salka Widman, Stach Sokol, Yehuda Frisher, Mauka Turteltaub, Shaya Lutwak.

## TRANSLATOR'S FOOTNOTES

1. I expect that the month listed here is an error, and September was intended.

{455}

## Our Mighty Ones

### by Shaya Lutwak

With the conclusion of the memoirs of my life and the death of our martyrs, I wish to disprove the incorrect notion that Jews went like sheep to the slaughter. Such allegations are like salt on an open wound. Those making such allegations should have respect for the memory of our martyrs, for their heroic spirit as they died in sanctification of the Divine Name. They should look with open eyes at the events of that time, and see and understand the great heroism of their lives and deaths.

With great honor and love, I will mention in brief the heroic stories and good deeds of the following Rozniatower lads: Meir Turteltaub the son of Itche Leizer of Rozniatow, and Hirsch Ratenbach, the son of David and Meirche of Dolina.

Meir the Mighty, whom we all called Meirke; and Hirsch the Mighty known as Hershke – they are etched in the memory for eternity as great Jewish heroes not only for us, the Rozniatow and Dolina Holocaust survivors, but also for everyone who heard of their deeds.

To write about Meirke's experiences from the beginning of the war in 1939 until the liberation in 1945, one must be a talented writer who has the power to portray step by step the fantastic events that took place with those exceptional people who exemplified so much typical humanity and great bravery. I will give over only the following facts in the simplest words.

At the outbreak of the war, Meirke served in the Polish army in an artillery unit. He was wounded in the foot, and he returned home and took over the leadership of the sports organization in Rozniatow from the Soviets. When Germany attacked the Soviet Union, Meirke was mobilized in the Red Army, and was wounded in the foot for a second time. When he came home, he met his exiled parents in Dolina. Life became progressively more difficult. Meirke could not make peace with the new decrees. When the Kalusher Ordenungs Kommandant came to Dolina, he met Meirka and saw that the Jewish armband was too low on his arm. He took him to the Judenrat for a punitive lecture…

A few days Moshe Ziring, who happened to be present at the Judenrat at the time, described the scene. He saw how Meirke was hauled there in anger and beaten with a chair from all sides.

Meirke was very industrious and never sat idly. He always made plans as to how to escape from this hell. He tried to cross the Hungarian border, but was captured in Vishkuv and brought back to Dolina in chains. After spending a few days in prison in Dolina, he was sent to Stanislawow (today called Ivano-Frankovsk) in a transport. There, the well-known murderer Krieger was active. He conducted his murder activity in a place called Rudolf's Mill. After a brief time of hard labor, Meirke succeeded in jumping over the barbed wire fence and fleeing to Kalush. The Jews in Kalush were afraid to keep him. They gave him a box of cash and a sack with farming implements over his shoulder. Thus, he dressed himself up like a farmer and set out on foot for Rohatyn, where his cousins, the grandchildren of Mendel Nemlich, lived.

At the beginning of June 1943, when they began to liquidate all of the ghettos and concentration camps of eastern Galicia, Meirke fled from Rohatyn to Stryj. However, they soon began to liquidate the ghetto there as well, and Meirke fled from there. The guard noticed this and shot at him. Without looking back, he jumped over the Stryj Bridge into the water, hid among the reeds, and miraculously succeeded in arriving in Bolekhov alive

He did not remain for long in Bolekhov, for he found no place to rest there. As they were fleeing from the Bolekhov ghetto, the following people were shot: Shimshon Katzman the son of Shaya Katzman and Herman Laufer the grandson of Efraim Rechtschaffen of Rozniatow. Miraculously, Meirke arrived at Heryn Babi's camp in the Dolina forests. I was already a resident there, and was very happy to see him. Meirke became a resident, a beloved friend of everybody without exception.

Given that the main problem of the fighters in the lack of weapons and ammunition, Meirke was given the task of searching for a source of weapons. He decided to set out for Rozniatow, where he had many gentile friends. He hoped to solve this difficult problem with their help. According to his plan, he was to return in eight days at the latest. However, more than two weeks passed, and we did not hear from Meirke. Everyone was very concerned, until Stach Babi came to the camp on one occasion and said that a youth from Dolina had murdered a Gestapo man, but nobody knows who that youth is.

A few hours later, a panic broke out, and Heryn brought to us the heroic youth who had killed the Gestapo man. From all sides, people came out to greet the hero. Before us stood a human personage with torn and dirty clothes, but on his face there was no sign of a human form. His face was covered with a swollen blue mass. His voice sounded familiar, but it was only when he called me Shaike that I realized that he was Meirke.

It is difficult to describe what we felt at that time.

I wish to describe briefly Meirke's further heroic battles. In Rozniatow, he met up with a few of his gentile friends. He discussed with them about weapons, and then went to the bastard Vasyl, who worked for Baron Walisz. Vasyl advised Meirke to hide in the storehouse of the mailman Jagelavitz. There he would shortly being him something to eat.

Instead of food, the bandit summoned the officer Jarasch with a full band of police and Ukrainian militiamen. The surrounded the storehouse. Meir surrendered and was arrested. He was murderously tortured for several days. Then he was sent to a prison in Dolina. In the prison, he removed a brick in the wall with a nail, and hoped to be able to escape in that manner. Unfortunately, the guards captured him during his work. He beaten harshly and his hands were bound with iron chains

His sixth sense for ingenious ideas, which often appeared as supernatural, helped Meirke this time as well. He had a bit of wire in his pocket, which he used to open the chains. In the forest, he showed us how he did this. Then they took Meirke from the jail to the Gestapo. Aside from the driver, there was a Gestapo man with a loaded automatic gun pointed at Meirke. As the car drove on the hills on the

Harishe on the way to the Dolina cemetery, Meirka took the opportunity, opened the chains, jumped out of the car, and started running through the houses. He arrived in the field.

The driver stopped the Gestapo car and the Gestapo man started to run after Meirke. When Meirke arrived at a tall barbed wire fence, he started to climb up. A bullet hit him in the foot. The Gestapo man took the bloodied Meirke down from the fence and began to beat him profusely with his gun. With his last strength, he began to beat the Gestapo man with the chains that were still in his hands. He succeeded in delivering a strong blow to his eye. The Gestapo man fell over, dying and bleeding. Meirke took his gun and attempted to shoot him on the spot, but there were no longer any bullets. He beat him to death with the gun, dragged him to the fence, and hung him on the barbed wire. He removed his cap. Then he hid among the bushes with the gun in his hand, and later went to a garden between the tall stocks.

Of course the Gestapo immediately sounded an alarm, and dozens of policemen and Gestapo men gathered in the area. They set out for the cemetery, and spread out among the monuments through the entire night.

Meirke remained silent in his hiding place. He did not make a move with any limb until the Gestapo men and police departed and left the forest.

Months again passed, in which we suffered from need and hunger. Finally returned to Rozniatow, where Meirke had survived with Mosko Jagelovitch.

After the liberation, Meirke, like all the rest of the partisans, had the right to remain in Rozniatow. However, the modest youth, who was the embodiment of Jewish strength, decided to voluntarily enlist in the Red Army. He went out to the front, and fought heroically against the murderers of his people.

Today, Meirke lives in America with his wife Irke and their only son Yankele. They live a peaceful and modest life.

## Hirsch Lutwak

Dolina and Bolekhov were already Judenrein. Only a few Jews survived and were hiding in the Dolina forests. Hershke was one of those who arranged the bringing of saved Jews to the forests. Hirsch had often sneaked into the Stryj Ghetto and told the Jews that Jewish divisions are being set up in the Dolina forests under the leadership of the brothers Stach and Heryn Babi. He would also often go into the Bolekhov camps and bring Jews to the forests from there.

His great struggle to find a way to remove the Bolekhov Rebbe, Rabbi Shlomo Perlow, from the Stryj ghetto, forms an interesting chapter. However, unfortunately, this proved to be impossible.

Hirsch Ratenbach was noted for his strong desire to help. He had a good word and a loving smile for everyone. On the other hand, he showed no mercy during his battles with the enemy during the partisan penal actions against them, in which they murdered Jews.

After the liberation, when a few surviving Jews settled temporarily in Dolina, they went to a Christian girl who displayed great self sacrifice by hiding Jews during the difficult times. The surviving Jews knew that they must not leave her alone in Dolina, where the murderers will take revenge upon her and murder her. Here as well, Hershke displayed his ideal character and magnanimous heart. Without concern for all the difficulties, he took her with him on his following journeys.

When he was in Lemberg, he found out that there was a Jewish child who had been hidden in a church. He took her with him so as to save her from gentile hands. He arrived in the displaced persons camp in Berlin with a rescued Jewish child and a Torah scroll. His gentile wife Mani converted in Berlin, and they got married according to Jewish law. Aside from the rescued child, they have a fine son David. They conduct a Jewish household, and live happily and contentedly in Buenos Aires. May they live until 120.

{460}

## The Priest and the Rabbi
### by Yehuda Har-Zohar

During their tour of the Land in the spring of 5624 (1964), someone from the family of Yehuda Axelrad-Hamerman-Weitzner, today living in the United States, came to spend a night with us. We sat with them until the early hours of the morning, and listened attentively to their war experiences in Czechoslovakia.

Among the other stories that he told us, I wish to bring down one story that Mr. Axelrad told me about what happened to his only son, 8 years old, during the terrible days.

After the conquest of Czechoslovakia by the Nazis, after they moved their place of residence several times so that the neighbors will not recognize them, and seeing that the place was becoming more and more difficult by the day, they suspected that one day they would be captured and their fate would be like the rest of the Jews. The parents decided among themselves that at least their only son should remain alive. Perhaps he would be able to be saved from death.

Despite the fact that he was very young, an 8-year-old child, he knew very well what was going on around him and the danger that was flying over their heads. They knew about the persecutions and tribulations that came to them solely because they were Jewish, despite the fact that he knew nothing about Judaism other than the few words that his parents taught him, which symbolized his entire Judaism. These are the few words of Shema Yisrael. He did not understand their meaning, but with his child's knowledge, he knew that he was ready to give his life for them.

The parents took counsel about how to ensure that their only son would remain alive. The thought and decided not to put their faith in the good will of the gentiles by giving over their son to one of the gentiles so that he could be hidden, raised and educated, for at a time of difficulty he would not be able to stand up to this, and the fate of the child would be sealed. Therefore, the only sure place would be in a church. However, how does one get him in there? In what manner and by what means? They decided to approach the priest of the nearby church. Mrs. Axelrad would dress up as one of the gentiles of the neighborhood and explain that when she was a maid of a noble Czech family, she raised and reared this child. Then, one day, the Nazis took the parents to an unknown place. Since she had to earn her living by the work of her hands, she begged the priest to accept this child under his care. She would be willing to give of her money to the church for the kindness that they are doing.

The priest agreed to her request, dressed him in the clothes of young priest apprentices, and entered him into the children's choir of the church. Mrs. Axelrad would go to the church on occasion, apparently to worship, but actually to snatch a glance at her child, the apple of her eye. She saw him wearing a white robe over his clothes, with an incense container in his hands, bringing the goblet of sacred wine to the priest.

The child always found an excuse to steal away during the prayers in order to snatch a brief conversation with his mother, who always waited for him in a dark corner inside the church or at the gate. Since the child was wise, he knew how to fit himself in with the rest of the children in the church with his abilities, and especially with his knowledge of the Czech language. On account of his talents, he became the right hand man of the editor of the church bulletin. This enabled him to be freer with his movements. Since he was busy with the bulletin, he was sent out to obtain paper, to go to the printer, or to do other such tasks. This enabled him to meet up with his mother almost every day at a set time in the public gardens.

After the war, the child went with his parents to the United States. He began to study the language of the country, to attend a primary school, and later high school and university. He excelled in his studies and attained great success. One day, he was called to lecture on his profession at one of the venerable and well known universities in the State of Ohio. He was forlorn in the purely gentile environment, and he searched around to see if he would find at least one Jewish student with whom he could forge a connection. He was about to give up, and then suddenly a veteran professor of Jewish origins came to him and told him that there were several Jewish students there who hid their Judaism. He somehow found out their names, and invited them in a private fashion to his room. During a friendly conversation and with an open heart, he asked them if they would be willing to meet with him one day and to have a free and open discussion. If they were going to meet already, would it not be easiest on the Sabbath eve? One of the students immediately revealed that he knew that there was a wealthy citizen in town of Jewish origin. When they turned to him and explained that there were several Jewish students who wished to meet once a week, he was very happy to hear this and offered his home. He offered his fine parlor for a meeting place. George was the living spirit of this small group. He immediately contacted the national Hillel Foundation, the organization of Jewish students. They sent him the needed material for conducting activities of a Hillel House.

At first, they gathered in the parlor of that Jew on Sabbath eves. The wife of the host was honored with the lighting of Sabbath candles. First she did this unwillingly and with fear, but after several Sabbaths, she became accustomed to the candle lighting ceremony in the Hillel hall. Then, the female students took turns at this, and the lighting of the Sabbath candles was thought of as a great honor, with each person waiting patiently for her turn.

George received all sorts of material for the national organization about leading discussions on various Jewish and religious topics. Debates developed, and life became quite interesting. On occasion, another hidden Jew joined up, and another Jewish heart began to beat. The light of the Sabbath candles ignited the hidden Jewish spark, and the Jewish heart was opened wide. The small circle expanded and grew. It became necessary to rent a hall for special gatherings, and of course everything was done by that Jew who had originally hidden his Judaism and was now so proud of his deeds, and gave himself over to the success of this matter with his whole heart.

One day, another professor appeared at the Hillel house and revealed that he was Jewish. He had heard about the lovely activities at the Hillel House, and since his son was approaching the age of Bar Mitzvah, he requested that this large celebration could take place there. He asked George to organize the celebration as he best saw fit. George immediately contacted the headquarters and received guidance and appropriate materials. He prepared a sermon for the event. The celebration took place with great success, and there was a great resonance among all the Jews from the sermon and the celebration.

Once it happened that one of the local Jewish students lost his father. He immediately turned to "Rabbi" George to arrange the funeral. Once again, George was perplexed. How do you bury a Jew? How to arrange a Bar Mitzvah he had already learned, but he did not now how to arrange a Jewish burial. It would be in the Christian cemetery, but the ceremony must be Jewish. He immediately contacted me and asked me what is said during a burial, and how does one conduct the ceremony. Of course I guided him, and the ceremony took place in peace. Without other options, and with the passage of time, my son George became the "Rabbi" who conducted the prayers from an English translation, and obtained Jewish books in order to not become confused at any time of need. Slowly but surely, my son George, instead of turning into a priest or a cardinal as had been prophesied about him, turned into the local rabbi, without whose advice nobody would make a move.

This is the story of our friend Mr. Aleksander-Hamerman-Weitzner.[1]


{463}


## And Thus it Was...
## by Z. Friedler


And it was... And there was a city called Rozniatow, which expanded with its firm Jewish reality, with its Torah scholars and Zionist dreamers, its people who sat and studied all day and its simple Jews, who bore the anguish of all the exiles and the tumult of the various businesses and commerce, with all its weekday concerns and festival joy. Everyone had faith that there was an order in the world, until the black night came and wiped everything away.

Only the few who survived weep by the rivers of the world over the great destruction. Every fact that I mention here, every photograph of a Rozniatow Jew, of individual personalities and entire family, all of them are a brick in the monument to the former life in our old home, a remembrance to the fine lives of our fathers and grandfathers before them, who split the heavens with their Torah and prayer, with singing and dance – and at the same time with the songs lectures and readings that led to a modern expression of Judaism.  It is also a memory to the horrors that all the Jews went through.

{Photo page 463:  At the memorial ceremony in 5731 / 1971.}

{Photo page 464 top:  At the memorial ceremony of 5731 / 1971.}

{Photo page 464 bottom:  At the memorial ceremony of 5731 / 1971.}

{Photo page 465:  At the memorial ceremony of 5731 / 1971.}

To you, Jewish Rozniatow, all of our children until the farthest generations should know how beautiful you shine in our hearts and memories.  We loved your poor soil, Rozniatow, the marketplace that bustled with business, the cheders and Beis Midrashes that radiated with holiness.  Only few remain alive in various corners of the world.  Everyone bears with themselves not only the black anguish and pain of the horrible destruction, but also the desire that their children and grandchildren will concern themselves with elevating the souls of their grandparents.  They should read these simple words that are told in this book about that life and about the terrible destruction.  They should understand and feel how many tears and how much weeping lies among these letters.

These photographs that we include here are from our gatherings on the anniversary of the destruction of Rozniatow and its environs.

We gather together every year to unite ourselves with the memory of our martyrs.  We see before us all of those who are near and dear, and we feel that for which the human language does not yet have a name.  We dredge up memories that we cannot comprehend until this day.

We indeed sense the grandeur of our gatherings, and we always express the ancient command that remains still with us, written with letters of fire and blood:

Remember and do not forget, never forget!

Our lips never cease to utter:

Yisgadal Veyiskadash, Jewish Rozniatow, Perehinsko, Swaryczow, and Broszniow.

{Photo page 466 top: Rozniatow natives in the United States at the memorial service of 1971.

First row, sitting from the left: Louis and his wife Eva Rizak, Olive and Shimon Lieberman, Klara Diamant, Anda Sternkler, Blima Eigenmacht, Blima Laufer.
Second row: Rosa and Feivel Ginsberg, Kalman Katz and his wife, Esther Teffer, Max Stromwasser and his wife, Chana Landsman, Moshe Lutwak, Fami Axelrad, Dora Unger.
Third row: Mendel Landsman, Yeshaya and Esther Lutwak, Leo and Adela Teffer, Bronia Klein-

hammer, Sala and Munek Enis, Samuel Kirshenbaum, Yehuda Axelrad.}

{Photo page 466 bottom: At the memorial ceremony of 5731 / 1971.}

{Photo page 467:  Nechemia the son of Herzl and Henche Shapiro.}

The book of Rozniatow is concluded, the gathering of material for the book is finished, however we know that everything that was written did not recreate either the life or the workings of our community.  It was impossible to transmit everything, and it was also impossible to include everything that our natives recorded.

We hope that when this book is published, it will serve as an incentive for further gatherings for our natives, and further encounters to perpetuate the value of the great task that has been performed.  We hereby thank all of the people who did everything within their power to ensure that this book would appear in the finest and most complete manner, so that it will serve as a literary monument for our destroyed Jewish community.

Zecharia Friedler

{468}

### In Memoriam

### Yitzchak Spiegel

His path of life was not paved with roses, but its entire path was a line of simplicity in approach to life, cordiality in his relationship to all people, and the internal essence of someone who knows what suffering is.  These traits stood with him to overcome all struggles of life.  In every situation, he had a smile on his face, beaming from him whenever one would meet him.  He was a man of a simple path, honest, doing good, and with a pure heart.  Wherever he went and whatever he did, he was straight with himself and with the faith that dwelt in his midst.  His simplicity drew its source from the deep spiritual foundations of the Jewish town of Rozniatow in the Diaspora;  from the sublime character traits of the family with many children who already spread out to different lands and places during their youth in order to find sustenance for their souls.

He was full of energy, blessed with strength, quiet in his demeanor, and everyone who met him on his path of life became a friend. His thirst for knowledge knew no bounds. He excelled in his great patience and his rational sense of judgement. People placed their faith in him and trusted him.

When he arrived in the Land as the pioneer of his family, his first actions and purpose for his efforts was to bring over his family to the Land despite the conditions of those times – to the shore of promises, to this poor and meager land regarding which he knew the conditions of those years very well.

The man did not rest until he was able to say to himself that he did whatever was possible within human power, and even more so. Upon this altar he offered up the greatest sacrifice that a person could offer, his personal life, for he did not establish a family but rather dedicated his entire holy effort to other members of his family.

Photo page 468: Yitzchak Spiegel

Only later did he build up his own family with Freda, may she live long. Then, he continued his effort at nurturing family relations with those near and distant with great-er energy, forging links with acquaintances, friends, and workmates, in both joy and sorrow. They all regarded him as a faithful friend.

His heart stopped on the 14th of Av, 5731 (1971).


{469}

## Shmuel Leib the son of Yoel Rosenbaum

He was an interesting and complex personality. He was an only son to his parents, and was nurtured by the judge Reb Yehuda Hirsch Koren. He spoke calmly and politely. It was indeed a pleasure to sit in his home and listen to his conversation, that was always spiced with words of the sages. His jokes that he told had a special charm. His statements of opinion were measured, weighed, and calm, with-out fire. He and his father worshipped in the Beis Midrash, but when he studied in the kloiz he would also remain there for prayer. His service and dedication made him appreciated by everyone.

There was a period when his wife's family took him to Germany, but his longing for the town and its people gave him no rest. He returned to Rozniatow and dedicated himself to his desires, to swim in the sea of Talmud. Once again he sat in the kloiz and occupied himself with Torah. His Torah was his faith.

He made aliya in 1934. Despite his depressed economic situation, he was always content with his lot. He did not change his customs. He performed all types of difficult labor, and he dedicated every free hour to the study of Torah.

When his brothers-in-law Yisrael Horowitz of blessed memory and, may he live Tzvi Fesberg built the theater in Petach Tikva, he was hired by them as a cashier. As always, he excelled in his honesty, uprightness and modestly. He was generally appreciated, and everyone treated him with honor and respect.

When he died in Petach Tivka in 5632 (1972) thousands accompanied him on his final journey.

### Reb Yechezkel the son of Reb Avraham Nussbaum

He was born in the village of Knizisk near Rozniatow. He was the grandson of Tzvi Yaakov Stern and Reb Mordechai Stern. He was the son of the sister of Reb Yosef Shimon Stern. He studied Gemara with Reb Yitzchak Branik. At the age of 16, he worked for Leizer Yitzchak Leib.

He left home and traveled to Vienna prior to the First World War. There he completed studies as an accountant, and later worked in one of the banks. He was diligent in studying Torah in the evenings.

He was a faithful friend to his Torah and his people. He absorbed rooted and traditional Jewish culture.

During one of the memorial gatherings for the martyrs of our city, he lectured about the Jews of our city from the previous generation, about the great and important ones of that time.

At one memorial gathering, he guided the gathering and spoke about a memorial book for the martyrs of our city, and even promised to take part in the writing of the book. He poured out his bitter heart with pain and anguish over what the Nazi enemy did to us. He expressed his great joy that he merited to see Jerusalem built up. He requested that Yad Vashem demand that the enemies Kruger and Muller be tried.

He was a member of the committee for the publication of this book. He was greatly anguished that he could not write his memoirs on account of his illness.

He passed away before his time. He was an illustrious man, a man of truth, graced with Torah and wisdom.

May his memory be a blessing!

### Reb David Glass

(He was born in the city of Kalusz in 1875 and died in Jerusalem in 5700 / 1940.) He was accepted as a shochet in the community of Rozniatow in 1903. He was graced with many talents. He was a veteran Torah reader, a prayer leader for the High Holidays, with a pleasant voice and a pleasant demeanor. He endeared himself to the community, which eased his absorption into his community.

The community of Strettiner Hassidim, who were a small minority in Rozniatow in comparison to the Hassidim of Dolina (Zidichow) but strong in their faith to the Strettin dynasty, found him to be man of like mind, which greatly eased his integration into society. He was numbered among the chief scholars of the Chevra Shas. He gave a class to the Or Hachayim circle of young married men on Sabbath eves. He was the rabbi of a number of youths, friends of his sons, who studied Talmud every morning before the Morning Service.

He raised his family throughout a number of years. He was blessed with a family of ten sons and daughters. The needs of his household and yoke of debts that were related to building his house brought the family to economic straits. This was the reason that they left Rozniatow and moved to Germany in 1912, where they lived until the entire family made aliya to the Land of Israel in 1931-1933.

This organization would arrange an annual completion of the Talmud ceremony with festivities, joy and large crowds. This was an important event among the scholars of the city. That night, they would divide up once again the tractates among the members for the next year. This took place each year.

{471}

## The Children From Whom We Were Bereaved

Even though our community is small, the angel of death has already succeeded in snatching from us the best of our sons through the manner that is unique to them: war and accidents.

### Eliahu Hausler

{Photo page 471: Uncaptioned. Apparently Eliahu Hausler.}

He was the son of Leah and Baruch, the only child to his parents. He was born in Germany on June 5, 1930. From his youth, he was educated in a school under the supervision of Dr. Rothschild, and was a good student. However, the Second World War interrupted his studies. When he was eight years old, the Nazis broke into the school where he studied, and snatched him and his friends. That year, he arrived in the Land with his parents, and they settled in Petach Tikva. There, he studied in the PIK"A School. He quickly mastered the Hebrew language and excelled in his studies. He also excelled in sports. He worked in a garage after he finished his studies, for he was attracted to mechanics. He was a member of the Haganah from the age of 14. He participated in the defense of the Shefiim Kibbutz which was attacked by the British.

Photo page 471: Uncaptioned. Apparently Eliahu Hausler.

He enlisted in the army when the War of Independence broke out. He was only 17 and a half years old. He fulfilled his duty as "a guard of the people", and from there he was sent to a sniper's course.

He excelled at that course, and was transferred to an active unit where he served as a sniper. He was very successful at sniping, and was the assistant and right hand man of the captains. He participated in the battles of Tantura and Kakon, and endeared himself to his comrades as a friend and a fighter. He participated in the conquest of Migdal Tzedek, and he fell when he was defending it against a fierce attack.

On July 12, 1948, Eliahu was shielding the machine gunners of his division with his targeted sniping, as he was leaning against a rock. A bullet shot him in the heart, and his friends found him dead while he was still leaning against the rock.

The next day, he was laid to eternal rest in the cemetery of Petach Tikva.

### Mordechai Shnitzer

The son of Yosef and Chana. He fell while standing guard in the south of the country during the War of Independence in 1948.

### Yosef Friedler

The son of Yisrael and Chana. He was born on July 24, 1922 in Hamburg, Germany. He fought in the British army against the Nazi enemy and fell in a sea battle near Malta. His boat sunk in the sea. 138 Jewish soldiers died along with him.

### Yoel Friedler

The son of Yisrael and Rivka. He was born in 1928 in Germany, the son of a religious family. He was the only son in a family with three sisters. He joined the machteret (underground army) of the Irgun Tzvai Leumi and was very active in it. His parents wished to send him to relatives in America to remove him from the constant danger that threatened him both externally and internally. However, he conducted his life in accordance with his response: "We have been drafted for all of life. Only death frees us from duty." When the disturbances broke out again, he was among the first who went to the Old City and organized its defense. This was a small group of youths who stood their stand.

On January 20, 1948, he went to Bikur Cholim with two friends to transmit a message by telephone. Along the way, they were snatched by members of a gang who were accompanied by a British policeman who had given his weapons to one of the Arabs. He shot the three of them. Yoel remained there injured for approximately three quarters of an hour, as the Arabs tortured him. When the members of the Irgun Tzvai Leumi broke through to the place, they found him dying.

His last words were: "Tell them that they beat us… I feel that this is my end, but it was worthwhile."

### Eliezer Lipa (Eli) Sternberg

The son of Yaakov and Miriam. The grandson of Reb Lipa Tanne of Rozniatow as well as of Yosef Sternberg who served in the court of the Admor of Chortkow of blessed memory.

He was born on the 11th of Tishrei, 5707 (October 6, 1946). He studied in the Bilu School. After he concluded his studies in the Bar-Ilan School, he studied diligently in City High School A. His desire was to merge Torah and work. He worked in the security unit in the mornings, and he dedicated his evenings to studies. On the eve of his draft in February 1965, he managed to write several matriculation exams, at which he was highly successful. He intended to complete the rest of them during his army service. He was a youth of many interests, and was involved in various hobbies (chess, stamp and coin collecting, and autograph collecting). He was interested in sports, and participated in races, among other things. He loved to read books, and delved into them until his final day.

His boundless love for his family, his dedication and faithfulness to them, and his concern for every one of them, exudes from his letters to them while in the army.

He was prepared to help his fellow, and therefore, he was loved by all of his acquaintances. His modesty and righteousness were among his traits that endeared him to everyone.

He was able to delay his enlistment until his older brother finished his service. However, he refused to do so. He enlisted in the Israel Defense Forces when the time came. He was placed in a battle unit, and he said: "It is a great honor to serve in such a unit".

He did not even manage to serve for a half a year, for on the 13th of Av 5625 (August 11, 1965), he fell. He was brought to eternal rest in the army cemetery in Kiryat Shaul. May his soul be bound in the bonds of eternal life.

### Michael Dingut

He was born on January 7, 1918 in Hamborn, Germany. He served as a guard. He fell on his guard on the 7th of Nissan 1939, as he accompanied a postal bus in Haifa. His parents, Moshe and Sara (nee Adler) Dingut died in Haifa.

Perpetuated by his uncle Binyamin Adler and his sisters Tova and Ruth

{474}

# A Memorial for Those Who Left Us

## The son of Eliezer Yitzchak of Perehinsko
## Baruch Hausler

He was born on September 1, 1898 in Perehinsko, Poland. He lived in Germany from 1926, and was a merchant of furniture and confectionery. He made aliya to the Land with his family in 1938, at the beginning of the Second World War. In the Land, he volunteered to serve as a guard in the Israel Police force during the time of the British Mandate. He participated along with his son and many others in the defense of Kibbutz Shefiim, at the time that the British were searching for arms. He earned his livelihood from managing a restaurant, until the time that tragedy struck, when his only son fell during the War of Independence in 1948 during the conquest of Migdal Tzedek. The tragedy crushed him deeply, and he was not able to continue managing the restaurant. He accepted a job in the office of commerce and manufacturing. He was a member of the Committee of Bereaved Families in Petach Tikva from the day of its founding.

Photo page 474: Uncaptioned[2]

He bore the pain of the memory of his son for 20 years, and on the eve of Yom Haatzmaut (Israel Independence Day), 4th of Iyar 1968, during the memorial at the monument of Migdal Tzedek, he fell to the ground as he was walking up to lay a wreath for the fallen. Immediately upon his arrival home after the memorial service, he did not even have a chance to say a word, and he died. He suffered a heart attack.

May his memory be a blessing.

## TRANSLATOR'S FOOTNOTES

1. The double hyphenated triple name at the end does not match that which is at the beginning.

2. It is not clear if the name in the title and the uncaptioned photo is that of the father or the son. From the entry on page 471, it appears that the son is Eliahu Hausler, the photo is the father whose name is Baruch, and Eliezer Yitzchak would be Baruch's father.

{475}

# MEMORIAL LIGHTS

{476}

Family Tree of the Weinfeld Family

Drawn by Zeev Weinfeld

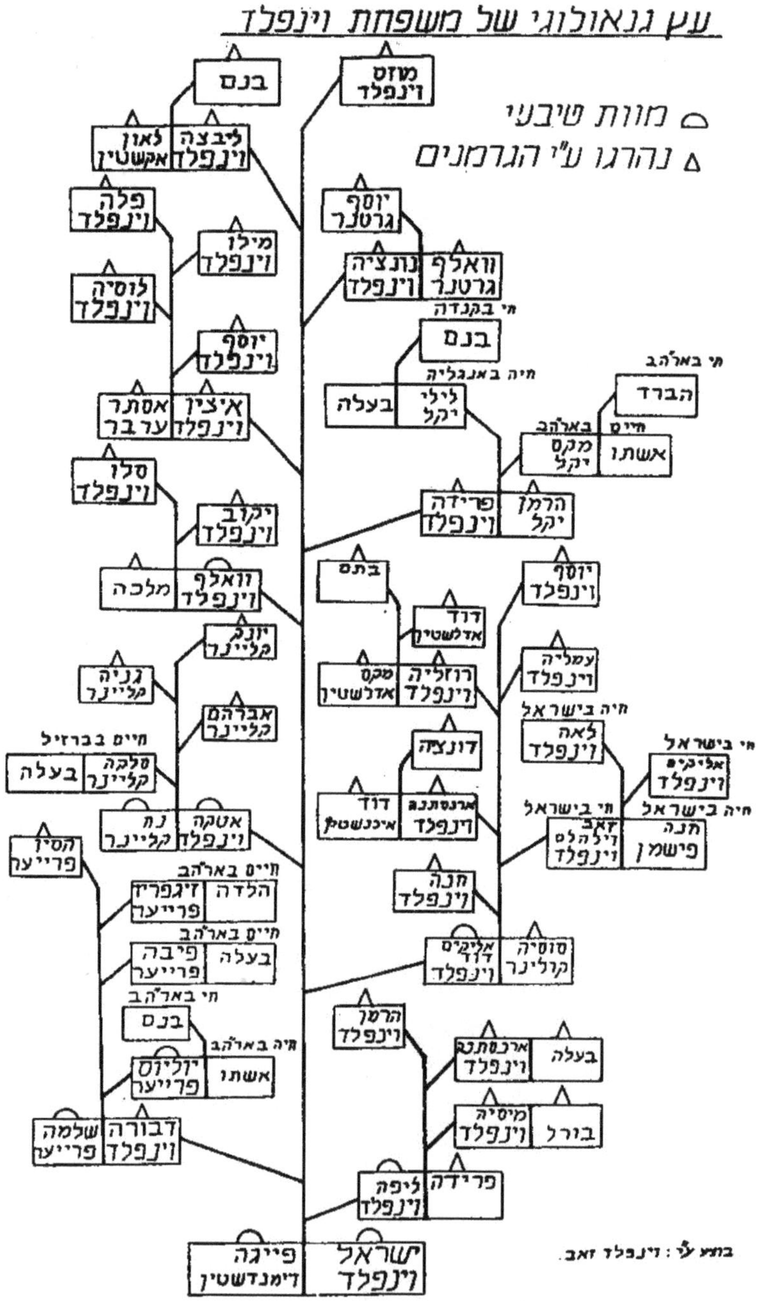

עץ גנאולוגי של משפחת וינפלד

ם מוות טיבעי
א נהרגו ע״י הגרמנים

{Page 476: Family Tree of the Weinfeld Family. Translator's note: The page is a finely drawn family tree, with the roots at the bottom, and ten branches coming from the root. I will render it here as a list.}

An asterisk * signifies natural death
A double asterisk ** signifies that the person was murdered by the Germans
{Root}
Yisrael Weinfeld  *      married Feige Diamandstein  *

{Bottom left branch}
Dvora Weinfeld **  married Shlomo Freier *
Julius Freier *  married his wife who is living in the USA
Son  living in the USA
Fiveh Freier and her husband, living in the USA
Zigfried Freier married Hilda, living in the USA
Hasin Freier **

{Second from bottom branch on left}
Itka Weinfeld *  married Noach Kleiner *
Malka Kleiner and her husband, living in Brazil
Avraham Kleiner **
Genia Kleiner **
Yona Kleiner **

{Third from bottom branch on left}
Wolf Weinfeld *  married Malka **
Yaakov Weinfeld **
Salo Weinfeld **

{Fourth from bottom branch on left}
Itzio Weinfeld **  married Esther Erber **
Yosef Weinfeld **
Lusia Weinfeld **
Milo Weinfeld **
Fela Weinfeld **

{Fifth from bottom branch on left}
Libcha Weinfeld **  married Leon Ekstein **
Son **

{Top branch}
Mozes Weinfeld **

{Bottom branch on right}
Lipa Weinfeld *  married Frieda **
Misia Weinfeld **  married Borel **
Archstana Weinfeld **  and her husband **
Herman Weinfeld **

{Second from bottom branch on right}
Elyakim David Weinfeld *  married Susia Karliner **
Chana Weinfeld **
Archstana Weinfeld ** married David Eichenstein **
Donchia **
Rozalia Weinfeld **  married Max Eidelstein **
David Edelstein **
Daughter**
Yosef Weinfeld **
Emelia Weinfeld **
Zeev Wilhelm Weinfeld  married Chana Fishman,  living in Israel
Elyakim Weinfeld, living in Israel
Leah Weinfeld, living in Israel

{Third from bottom branch on right}
Freda Weinfeld **   married Herman Yokel **
Max Yokel and his wife, living in the USA
Heberd living in the USA
Lili Yokel and her husband living in England
Daughter living in Canada

{Fourth from bottom branch on right}
Nunchia Weinfeld **  married Wolf Gertner **
Yosef Gertner **

{477}

## Memorial Dedications

### In Eternal Memory

For the Weinfeld family of the village of Swaryczow
My father Reb Elyakim David the son of Yisrael HaLevi and Feiga
My mother Susia the daughter of Zeev Wolf Karliner and Chana
Sisters Chana, Esther and her husband David Eichenstein and their daughter
Sister Shoshana-Rozalia and her husband Max Edelstein, their son David and their daughter
Sister Emelia, and brother Yosef

Uncle Lipa and his wife Freida Weinfeld
Their children Misia and husband Borl;  Esther, husband and son Herman

Aunt Dvora Freier (nee Weinfeld) and husband Salomon
Their sons Julius and Herman

Uncle Zeev Wolf and his wife Malka of the family of Reb Itzikel of Rozniatow
Their sons Yaakov and Salin

Uncle Itzio-Yitzchak and his wife Esther nee Archer
Their children: Yosef, Lusia Milo, Fela

Uncle Mozes-Moshe Weinfeld

Perpetuated by Wilhelm-Zeev Weinfeld of Hadera, Israel

———

In Eternal Memory

Of the Fishman family of Wygoda

My father Godel the son of Reb Hersh and Rachel
My mother Leah the daughter of Shalom and Chana
My brother Izik the son of Godel and Leah
My sister Gittel the daughter of Godel and Leah
My brother Berl the son of Godel and Leah
My brother Yeshaya the son of Godel and Leah

Photo page 477: Leah Fishman, mother-in-law of Zeev

Perpetuated by Chana the daughter of Godel and Leah, nee Fishman, today Weinfeld, of Hadera, Israel

{478}

## In Eternal Memory

My father Shmuel Rosenberg
My sister Bina Kassner and her 4 children
My brother Ezriel, his wife and their 4 children
My cousin Ezriel Wasserman, his wife and children
Shmayahu Goldschmidt and his entire family
Anchi Strassman and family
Pesil Buchwalter and her 5 children
Avigdor Diamand and family
Avraham Strumwasser and family
Sheinchi Kassner and family

{Photo page 478: Ezriel Rosenberg and family}

Perpetuated by Beila Sabel nee Rosenberg

{479}

## Remember

{Top left photo:  Ezriel Wasserman}

{Top right photo:  Chani the daughter of Ezriel Diamant}

{Lower photo: Itka Goldschmidt}

Perpetuated by Beila Sabel  nee Rosenberg

{480}

## We Weep Bitterly for our Dear ones

In memory of my dear mother Mrs. Chaya Adler
My sister Gittel Adler
My sister Bilha Adelstein
My sister Roza Langer
My sister Chana Strassman
My brother Shmuel Adler and his wife Freida
My brother Zeev Abba Adler
My brother David Adler and his family
My brother-in-law Leo Langer
  Tuni Langer
My brother-in-law Moshe Strassman

{Photo page 480: Chaya Adler}

{481}

{Photo page 481 left:  David Adler}

{Photo right:  Zeev Abba Adler}

Bluma Milstein
Moshe Milstein
Sara Horowitz and her husband Mendel
Bunchi Rubin
Betzalel Rubin
Mendel Turteltaub
Fishel Friedler
Sara Friedler
Max and Roza Adelstein and their son
Leah Manheim, her husband Nathan and their
son Henry
Shimon Adler
Tzvi Mark
Mordechai Mark and her husband Ita
Gittel Yungerman
Moshe Yungerman
Tzvi Yungerman
Yosef Kassner
Ben-Zion Kassner
Netanel Kassner
Yisrael-Leib Artman and his wife Sheva

His children:
Yosef Strassman
Dvora Strassman
Frieda Adler nee Fesberg and their son Shmuel

Yaakov Strassman the son of Zeev Abba
Zeev Abba Strassman
Bunchio Strassman
Leah Strassman
Mordechai Strassman
Sara Strassman
Chaya Gittel Strassman
Katriel Strassman
Sara Tzirl Strassman
Yehoshua Strassman
Mordechai Strassman
Bluma Strassman
Levi Strassman
Mordechai the son of Yaakov Strassman
Aryeh the son of Yaakov Strassman
Zeev the son of Yaakov Strassman

Perpetuating their relatives and friends:  Binyamin Adler of Kiryat Yam, Esther (Itka) Zimri

{482}

**For These We Weep**

{Top photo: Rashi Fruchter the daughter of Meshulam}

{Bottom photo:  Yaakov Fruchter the son of Meshulam, his wife Yenta the son of Meir Frenkel.  His sister Itzi the son of Meir Frenkel, and their children}

Perpetuated by Moshe Fruchter of the USA

{483}

## Their Memory Will Not Depart From Us

The family of Reb Shmuel Wirt of Rozniatow, who was murdered in the Dolina Ghetto by the Nazis may their names be blotted out on the 17th of Elul 5702 (1942)

The father of the family Reb Shmuel, his wife Frieda and their descendents

{Photo page 483:  Yosef Shimon Stern}

Mamchia married to Reb Yosef Shimon Stern
and their children:
Bracha and her husband Zeida and 5 children
Yechezkel and his wife Leah and 2 children
David and his wife Gittel and 2 children
Sushia and her husband Yitzchak Bauer and 2 children
Mordechai and his wife Pnina and 2 children
Reizl and her husband Yehuda
Esther and Yaakov

Sara Rivka married to Reb Binyamin Spiegel
And their children:
Mordechai and his wife Rachel and 5 children
Shlomo and his wife Sheindel and 2 children
Chava and her husband Shmuel Leib and their children Belchia and Eliezer

{484}

Feiga Leah married to Reb Kalman Halperin
Their children: Gitele, her husband and 2 children
Weizer and 2 children
Chana and her husband
Her children Yaakov and Yitzchak
Yisrael Wirt, his wife Malka and their 5 children

Tila married to Reb Avraham Tzvi Zauerberg, and their children: Chana, Yossi and Pinchas
Malka married to Reb Yisrael Kornbluet and their 5 children
Finkel married to Reb Berish Weiss and their children Reizel and Yaakov
Ronchia married to Reb Ben-Zion Strassfeld, and their children Yaakov and Chana

### In eternal memory

All of them were Hassidim and people of good deeds, involved in charitable deeds at all times. Their homes were wide open. They were a wide branched family. They were murdered by the enemy through all sorts of strange deaths.

Weeping bitterly over the great loss
The only grandchild, the brand plucked from the file:
Miriam the daughter of Avraham Tzvi and Tila Zauerberg
And her husband Yehuda Zauerberg Har-Zohar
Chibat Zion, Israel

{Photo page 484: Kalman Halperin}

{485}

**In eternal memory**

**To the Berger family of Rozniatow**

My father Reb Josef Berger
My mother Mrs. Leah Berger
My sister Bronchia Berger-Widman and her family
My brother Mishel Berger and her family
My brother Yissachar Berger and his family

{Photo page 485 right: Archie Berger}
{Photo page 485 center: Bronchia Widman-Berger}
{Photo page 485 left: Mrs. Leah Berger}

Perpetuated by Tinchia Bronstein-Berger

{486}

**In eternal memory**

{Photo page 486 top right:  Avrhamche Kohen Friedler}

{Photo page 486 top left:  from the right: the granddaughter of Lipa Tanne, Binyamin the son of Blimchi and Rotka Schwalb}

{Photo page 486 bottom:  Blimchi Rechtschaffen}

Perpetuated by Mordechai, Zecharia, and Yaakov Rechtschaffen

{487}

**An Eternal Flame
In Eternal Memory**

My mother Sobel Rosenbaum
My sister Rozchia Sperling
Esther Rosenbaum
Shlomo Rosenbaum and their children

{Photo page 487  From right:  Shlomo Rosenbaum, his wife, and son Rochchi}

{488}

**We Will Always Remember**

{Photo page 488 top:  Shlomo Rosenbaum}

{Photo page 488 bottom:  Sobel Rosenbaum}

Perpetuated by  Blumka Schwartz, nee Rosenbaum

{489}

We Weep Bitterly for our Dear Ones

The family of Leibish Friedler of Rozniatow, murdered in the Dolina ghetto by the Nazis may their names be blotted out on the 17th of Elul 5702, September 8, 1942.

Our father Reb Leibish Friedler the son of Reb Alexander
Our mother Heni-Leah the daughter of Reb Yitzchak Geller
Our sister Frieda-Miriam, her husband Avraham Friedler
Our sister Sara and her husband
Our sister Gittel and her husband
Uncle Mordechai Geller, his wife Gittel from Spas
Uncle Yitzhak Yones, his wife Tauba nee Geller and their children from Spas
Uncle Binem Geller and his wife Gittel
Cousin David Geller and his family
Cousin Eschi Freitag nee Yones and her family
And all of our relatives of the Bitkower family of Spas

Perpetuated by the brothers Sender, Zecharia and Yisrael Friedler

{Photo page 489: Sitting from right: Frieda and her daughter Heni may she live, Leibish and his wife Heni-Leah. Standing Sara and Gittel.}

{490}

**Land, Do Not Hide Their Blood**

The family of Reb Yaakov Yankel Saraf, murdered in the Dolina ghetto by the Nazis may their names be blotted out on the 17th of Elul 5702, September 8, 1942.

Our mother Sara Saraf the daughter of Reb Sender Friedler
Our father Yaakov Yankel Saraf
Our sister Frieda and her husband Shimon Diamand

{Photo page 490 top right: Yankel}
{Photo page 490 top left: Sara}
{Photo page 490 bottom:  Frieda}

Perpetuated by the brothers Sender and Hirsch Baruch Friedler-Saraf

{491}

## In Eternal Memory

In the family of Mordechai-Mottel Friedler of Rozniatow, perished in the Holocaust
Our father Mordechai and mother Sara Friedler
Our sister Chana and her daughter Chaya
Our sister-in-law Chana and her children Yosef, Shmuel, Tova and Tzvia
The children of our sister Rivka: Yaffa, Yaakov, Dvora
Uncles Moshe and Yisrael and their entire families
Cousins Rashi, Miriam, their husbands and children
Cousins Bendet, Moshe, Tzvi and their families
Cousins Uri, Fishel and their families

May their names be blessed forever!

{Photo page 491: Chana Friedler nee Weissman, the wife of Uchi, with her children Tova Shmuel, Tzvia and Yosef.}

Perpetuated by Miriam, Max, Chanina Friedler, and Esther Friedler Miller

{492}

# An Eternal Flame

{Photo page 492 top:  Mordechai, Chana and his wife Sara Friedler}

{Photo page 492 bottom right: Chana and her daughter Chaya}

{Photo page 492 bottom left:  Shmuel Friedler}

Perpetuated by Miriam, Max, Chanina Friedler and Esther Friedler Miller

{493}

## We Weep For Our Dear Ones

{Photo page 493 top right: Moshe Zimmerman}

{Photo page 493 top left: Yaakov Yampel, fell as a partisan in the forests of Stryj}

{Photo page 493 bottom: Yosef Gelobter and his wife}

Perpetuated by Dvora Ungar and Sushi Widman

{494}

Reb Meir Aharon HaKohen Londner. He was born in Stryj.  He lived all his years in Rozniatow. He was a scholar, great in Torah and wisdom, and enthusiastic Strettiner Hassid.  He made aliya in 1908 and settled in the Old City of Jerusalem, where he was the president of Kolel Galicia.

{Photo page 494 top:  Reb Meir Aharon HaKohen Londner}

{Photo page 494 bottom: his grave, dated on the 29th of Shvat 5684 / 1924}

He died at an old age in Safed, the city of the Kabbalists.

{495}

Reb Elyakim Getzel the son of Reb Shimon Spiegel, the son-in-law of Reb Meir Aharon HaKohen Londner.  Born in 1872. Perished on the 17th Elul 5702, September 8, 1942.

{Photo page 495 top:  Reb Elyakim Getzel Spiegel}

Gittel the daughter of Reb Meir Aharon HaKohen Londner. Born in 1872.  Perished on the 17th of Elul 5702, September 8, 1942.

{Photo page 495 bottom:  Gittel}

{496}

**In Memory of My Loved Ones and Dear Ones**

Reb Eliezer the son of Elyakim Getzel Spiegel
And his wife Zalmi nee Getzel
Yitzchak Spiegel and his wife Sheindel, who are buried in the Holy Land
Chana the daughter of Elyakim Getzel
Eliezer the son of Elyakim Getzel
Mordechai the son of Elyakim Getzel
Shalom the son of Elyakim Getzel
Yisrael Tzvi Londner and his family
Avraham Londner and his family
Dov Berl Londner and his family

Who perished at the hands of the German enemies in the Holocaust

Perpetuated by Yehoshua and David Spiegel

{497}

**An Eternal Flame in Memory of:**

{Photo page 497 top:  My brother Yisrael Klinger and his wife}

Our father Yosef Leib Klinger
Our mother Rivka nee Steigman-Szwarc of Kalusz
Our brother Yisrael

Who were murdered in the Holocaust by the Nazis, may their names be blotted out

{Photo page 497 bottom:  Reb Yosef Leib Klinger and his wife Rivka.}

Perpetuated by Baruch and Dov Klinger

{498}

## In Eternal Memory

My Uncle Mordechai Spiegel
And his wife Rachel nee Krigel
Hendel Krigel and her children Baruch, David, Pepa and Sara

{Photo page 498: Mordechai the son of Binyamin Spiegel and his wife Rachel}

Perpetuated by Tzila Fetman nee Krigel

## A Candle for the Soul

In memory of my father Moshe Michael Kornbleut
Brother Yisrael, his wife Malka and their children
Brother Avraham, his wife and children

Perpetuated by the sister Chana Hoffman nee Kornbleut

{499}

## In Eternal Memory

In memory of my sister Klara Chaiche, her husband Yitzchak Kacman, their children Heni, Yaakov, Tzvi

In memory of my brother Shimon, his wife Bronchia nee Fesberg, and their children Yaakov, Esther, Mendel

In memory of my brother Reuven, his wife Tinchia, and their two children

In memory of my sister Fanny, her husband Leo Rappaport, and their children Ala, Hirsch, Yaakov

In memory of my uncle Avigdor Diamand, his wife Chava, and their children Leah, Anshel, Eliezer, Refael, Rikel

In memory of my uncle Ezriel, his wife Sara Wasserman, and their children Heni, Golda, Malka, Tzvi

Who perished in the Holocaust at the hands of the German enemies may their names be blotted out

Perpetuated by A. A. Diamand, Raanana, Rechov Hameyasdim

## In Eternal Memory

To those of our family who perished, as follows:

My mother Roze Heisler the daughter of Shlomo Yungerman
My sister Miriam Heisler
My sister Perel Heisler
My sister Sara Heisler
My brother Hirsch Heisler
My aunt Gittel Meiseles
Her children Moshe Meiseles, wife and children, Hirsch Meiseles, Herzl Meiseles
Her daughter Dina stern (Meiseles)
My cousin Moshe Branfeld
My aunt Perel Roth, her husband and children
Aharon and Eliahu Friedler and their families

My neighbors and friends:
Aharon and Pesia Zamel and family
Dvora Zisser
Ruth and Bluma Schwalb
Hirsch Friedenberg the son of Leib

Perpetuated by Yehudit Heisler-Friedman
{500}

### In Eternal Memory

Our father Levi Auslender
Our mother Chaya Auslender
Our sisters Perel, Adela, Yona
Our brother Yisrael
Our sister Chana and her husband Yitzchak Geltstein and their daughter Bunia
Our uncle Yitzchak Auslender, his wife Rachel and children
Our uncle Avraham Auslender, his wife Dvora and their children
Our uncle Tzvi Lieberman, his wife Chana and their children
Our uncle Shlomo Lieberman, his wife Klara, and their children
Our uncle Herman Schnied, his wife Dvora and their children
Our uncle Yisrael Klinger, his wife Roza and their children
Our uncle Ochs, his wife Berta and their children
Our uncle Moshe Spiegel, his wife Roza and their children
Our uncle Yisrael Putzer, his wife Esther and their children
Our uncle Yoel Szwarc, his wife Adela and their children
Our uncle David Gartenberg, his wife Susia and their children
And all the rest of our relatives who perished in the Holocaust

Perpetuated by Meir and Moshe Auslender

### An Eternal Flame

### In memory of my parents and my family

My father Reb Yosef the son of David Leib Rubinfeld
My mother Mamchi the daughter of Reb Yaakov Meir Nussbaum
My sisters Chaychi, Batya, Echi, Esther
My brother Yehuda Hirsch

Perpetuated by David Nussbaum of Rishon Letzion

{501}

## Their Fine Souls

{Photo page 501 top: Shmuel Leib and his wife Sheindel nee Witzman}

Perpetuated by Yehuda Witzman-Axelrad, USA

## An Eternal Light

In memory of our parents and family who were murdered by the Nazis

Father Reb Shmuel Nussbaum
Mother Rivka
Sister Esther, her husband and their children
Sister Chana
Brother Yitzchak
Uncle Yosef Shimon and the entire family
Uncle Shalom, our aunt, and the rest of the family, may G-d avenge their souls

Perpetuated by Mordechai and Aryeh Stern-Nussbaum

{502}

{Photo page 502 top:  Dr. David Weissman during his presentation}

Perpetuated by Sima Litochovski-Weissman

{Photo page 502 bottom:  Standing:  Gittel, Moshe, Shmerel, Yaakov, Shlomo Avraham, Rachel, Klara.
Sitting from the left: Fruma Winkler, Pinchas Knoll, and Zeev Winkler.}

Perpetuated by Avraham Winkler of Nazareth

{503}

## In Eternal Memory

Our father Baruch Diamand
Our mother Beila Diamand
Our sister Mali
Our brother Mordechai
Hinda
Chana
Simcha
Menachem

Perpetuated by Yehuda Diamand of Haifa

## May G-d Remember

Mrs. Mattil the daughter of Shimshon-Chaim
My daughter Sushia
My son Yisrael
My daughter Mamchia

Who perished in the Holocaust at the hands of the Nazi enemy, may G-d avenge their souls

Perpetuated by Yehoshua Steigman

## An Eternal Light

In memory of my parents

Eli Horowitz and his wife
Sisters Arka and Salka
Brother Yisrael
Reb David Tzvi Horowitz, his wife Esther, and their children Rivka, Mali and Zindel
Yosef Rotenberg, his wife Esther, their daughter Rivka and her children

Who perished in the Holocaust

Perpetuated by Leichi the daughter of Shlomo Shmerel Horowitz

{504}

## An Eternal Light

In memory

Michael Berger and his wife Janet
Chaim Zeinfeld and his wife Rachel nee Laufer

Perpetuated by Dr. Chaim Berger of blessed memory, Bnei Brak

## May G-d Remember

My father Hersh Leib Weinrib
My mother Eti
My sister Sara
My uncle Moshe Wohl
My aunt Matil Wohl
Their daughter Leah Wohl
Their son Avraham Wohl
Their son Yaakov Wohl

Perpetuated by Yaffa Rozenstrauch nee Weinrib
Tel Aviv, Yad Eliahu

———

## In Eternal memory

My mother Fanny Stein
My brother Avraham Stein

Perpetuated by Shoshana Sherel
Miriam Zohar

{505}

### In Eternal Memory

Father Avraham Tanne
Mother Tulchu Tanne
Sister Ita Tanne-Diamandstein

And her family

May their memory be preserved forever!

Perpetuated by Aryeh Tanne
Tel Aviv, 8 Rechov Lilan

---

### In Memory of the Horowitz Family

(Of the Brifni-Ripner flour mill)

Our father Reb Yitzchak Horowitz
Our mother Mrs. Rachel the daughter of Shimon Horowitz
Our brother Tzvi, his wife and two children
Our sister Leah Zissel and her husband Yitzchak Turteltaub and their Falchi and Gita
Our ant Miriam the daughter of Shimon Horowitz and our uncle Chaim Asher
Our aunt Gittel our husband Eli and daughter Pesia

Perpetuated by Felix and Shimon Horowitz

{506}

## May G-d Remember

The pure souls and the merits of our family members who were murdered by the Nazi enemy may their name be blotted out during the days of murder, along with the rest of the community of Perehinsko in Galicia

My revered father Reb Zelig Leib Fishbein may G-d avenge his blood
My revered mother Susia
My brother Yehoshua the son of Reb Zelig Leib, his wife Rozia and their children
My brother Nachman the son of Reb Zelig-Leib
My brother Mendel the son of Reb Zelig-Leib
My brother Yechezkel the son of Reb Zelig-Leib
My sister Luba Fingerhut and her husband Leib Fingerhut
My sister-in-law Roza Fishbein
My sister-in-law Frumchia Fishbein
The children of my brothers and sisters:  Mordechai, Shimon, Chanan, Yisrael, Berl, Leah, Hirsch, Rivka, Wisia

Perpetuated by Ania Nirenberg nee Fishbein,
Herzliya, Neve Emil

## In Eternal Memory

Of Dr. Wasserman of Rozniatow

Dr. Shlomo Wasserman
His wife Gizela nee Spiegel
Their daughter Orna and her husband Richard Witlin

Who were murdered n the Holocaust by the enemy may they be blotted out

Perpetuated by Helena Goldman, nee Wasserman
Nahariya, Yitzchak Sadeh 27

{507}

## An Eternal Flame

In memory of my parents and family members of blessed memory who were murdered by the Nazis

Father Yehuda Berelfein the son of Hirsch Matis
Mother Ruchcha Berelfein the daughter of Zeev Yager
Brother Chaim-Yisrael Berelfein
Sister Chana Berelfein
Sister Finka Berelfein
Sister Dvora Berelfein
Sister Henia Berelfein
Sister Etia Berelfein
Sister Rechtzia Isserlis
Brother-in-law Shimon Isserlis
Nephew Naftali Isserlis
Uncle Sender Bergman
Auht Genia Bergman
Cousin Regina Bergman
Cousin Andza Bergman
Uncle Shmuel Wallach
Aunt Arta Wallach
Cousin Junia Wallach
Cousin Salchia Wallach

May their memories be blessed!

Perpetuating the memory of her dear parents and family members:  Genia (Berelfein) Yungerman

{508}

## In Eternal Memory

Of the Eliahu Spiegel family of Rozniatow


Father of the family Reb Eliahu the son of Yisrael-Avraham Spiegel
Mother of the family Chaya the daughter of Reb Yitzchak Geller of Kalusz
Eldest brother Moshe, his wife and 3 children: Yisrael-Eliahu, Aliza, Fanny
Sister Berta married to Nathan Hirsch
Sister Sushia married to Baruch Rechtschaffen of Perehinsko and their children Yisrael and Esther
Sister Yuga married to Herman Melzer of Stanislawow, and their children Tuni and Esther
Aunt, the sister of my father, Malka and her husband Zisha-Aryeh Kuperberg, and their children Belchi, Hersch, Munia
Uncle, brother of my father, Shlomo Spiegel of Uhrynów, and his entire family
Uncle, brother of my father, Bendet Spiegel of Broszniow
Aunt Sheindel Spiegel and her children Zushia and Tindi
Aunt Bracha Lustig and her entire family
Aunt Esther Geltstein, her husband Yisrael, and their children Zalman, Yitzchak, Fruma and Yeche-zkel
Yosef Helfgut, his wife Tzipa and their children Feiga Frieda
Our neighbors Mordechai-Moti Strassman and Rivka, and their children Nessi, Esther, and Rachel
Our neighbor Yehuda Weissberg and his wife Fruma


All of them were murdered in sanctification of the Divine Name by the Nazis may their names be blotted out on the 17th of Elul 5702 in the Dolina Ghetto


Perpetuated by Chana Spiegel of Holon

{509}

May G-d Remember

The soul of my revered father Herzl Nirenberg
My revered mother Beila
My sister Mrs. Breina Zachmetz
My brother-in-law Yaakov Zachmetz
And their children Binyamin and Miriam
My sister Dvora and her husband Chaim Trop
My brother Yeshayahu and his wife Luba
My sister Leah
My sister Feiga
My brother Meir

Who all perished during the Holocaust with the rest of the community of Perehinsko

Perpetuating their memory:  Dov-Karol Nirenberg
Holon, Mikve Yisrael 14

---

## May G-d Remember

My revered father Reb Avraham Finkelstein
My revered mother Rivka Finkelstein
My brother Dov-Velvel and his wife Chaya
My sister Sara and her husband Yisrael Steigman

Who perished in the Holocaust along with the rest of the community of Perehinsko, Galicia

Perpetuating their memory:
Mordechai Finkelstein, Tel Aviv, Ramat Hatayasim, Rechov Halevavon 1

{510}

### An Eternal Flame

In memory of my parents and family members of blessed memory who were murdered by the Nazis.

My father Yaakov the son of Pinchas Heisler of Nebylov
My mother Tova the daughter of Asher Zelig (nee Yungerman) of Nebylov
My sister Malka the daughter of Yaakov (nee Heisler) Winterfeld of Nebylov
My brother-in-law Zerach Winterfeld
My sister's three children
My wife Pnina Yungerman nee Spiegel-Auslender
My daughter Musia Yungerman
My daughter Lusia Yungerman

The memory of my parents and family members is perpetuated by the son Pinchas.
The memory of my wife and daughters is perpetuated by the husband Pinchas.

May their memories be a blessing!

Pinchas Yungerman
Sdemot Dvora, Doar Na, Lower Galilee

{511}

### In Eternal Memory

Of my good friends and relatives from Rozniatow

Taube-Lea Hausler
Moshe Hausler
Golde Hausler
Nechama Hausler
Shabtai Hausler

Who were murdered in sanctification of the Divine Name.
Honor to their memory!

Perpetuated by Louis Risack, N.Y., USA

### In Eternal Memory

Our dear parents
My father Reb Meir Roth
My mother Mrs. Perel Roth the daughter of Shlomo Yungerman

Perpetuated by their son Kuni Roth, USA.

Our dear parents
My father Reb Yosef the son of Reb Feivel Laufer
My mother Mrs. Rachel-Leah the daughter of Efraim Rechtschaffen

Perpetuated by their daughter Elza Roth, USA

{512}

## In eternal Memory

Reb Aron Enis
Mrs. Mina Enis
Munio Enis
Emma Enis-Eisman
Henryk Enis
Herman Enis and family
Dr. Josef Enis
Janina Enis-Werber
Max Enis
Fanny and Marzu's and Emanuel
Tony, Dunio and Lena Jupiter
Kuba Enis
Berishcha Freilich
Sara Freilich
Jetty Haber-Herman

May G-d avenge their blood of those who were murdered in Sanctification of the Divine Name.

Perpetuated by Harry, Munek, and Salo Enis, USA

---

Reb David Rozenborn

Perpetuated by:
The Yuner family of Perehinsko, Stanislawow region
Berl Fein of Broszniow
Berl Nirenberg of Broszniow
Meir Auslender of Broszniow
Zeev Weinfeld of Swaryczow

{Translator's note, there may be some mix-up in this particular memorial box, as it appears as the list of perpetuators may actually be the list of those memorialized. The name Reb David Rozenborn is preceded by the acronym Shin Yud"Beit – and I am not sure what that means.}

{513}

**In Eternal Memory**

Brancia Wolkentreiber
Aron Wolkentreiber
Sara Wolkentreiber
Dobby Wolkentreiber and her family
Regina (Rivka) Wolkentreiber
Chaim Wolkentreiber
Chancia Turteltaub
Max Turteltaub
Lea Turteltaub
David Wernik
Lotty Wernik
Chaja Wernik

Perpetuated by Nathan Berger, USA

{514}

## In Eternal Memory

To our family members who were murdered in sanctification of the Divine Name during the Holocaust.


Sara Tepper
Ester Kurz
Josef Kurz
Shlomo Widman
Riva Widman
Shiko (Yehoshua) Widman
Eisig Artman
Chaje-Beile Artman
Julek and Mishel Artman
Moshe Artman
Dvora and Yitzchakl Artman
Maier Artman
Rachel, Fridzia and Kuba Artman
Perel (Pnina) Lustig
David Lustig
Baruch and Meir Lustig
Sara Lustig
Sisie-Arie Kupferberg
Malka Kupferberg
Hersh Kupferberg
Rosa Kupferberg
Balcia Kupferberg
Munio Kupferberg
Sala Kupferberg


Perpetuated by Leon-Bernard Tepper and Bernard Widman, USA.

{515}

**Blessed be G-d**

In eternal memory of the souls of my parents, brother, sister and other holy family members who were murdered by the Nazi beast during the Holocaust, may G-d avenge their blood.

My father Berchi Drimer
My mother Esther Drimer
My sister Yutzi Drimer
My sister Fanchi Drimer
My nephew Mordechai Rozenthal, Fanchi's son
My son Yehuda Drimer who was born in Israel
My uncle Yudel Drimer
My aunt Cayla Drimer
Their son Fishel Drimer
Their son Muni Drimer
Their daughter Henche Drimer
Their daughter Tauba Drimer
Yuta Schwindler
Chuka Schwindler
Avraham Schwinder
And the children

{Photo page 515 top:
A photo of my father of holy blessed memory Reb Berchi Drimer, known to all. He was a well-to-do Jew, an honest merchant, upright, seeking truth and performing good deeds. He was always known for participating in a blessed manner in any charitable and beneficial deed. His children are in the photo, as well as my dear mother Esther, the pious woman who was my father's mate. Our house was always open to anyone – and food and support was given to anyone in need who visited the home. May their merit protect us. Amen.}

{Photo page 515 bottom: Uncaptioned. Apparently the perpetuator's son, mentioned above.}

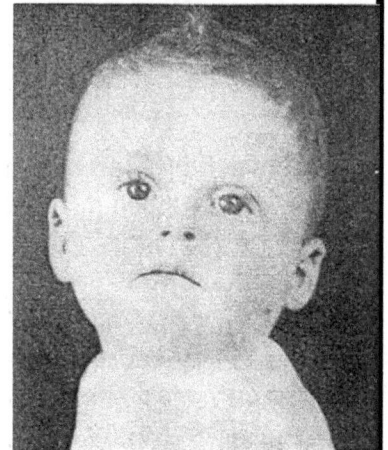

Perpetuated by Michael Drimer

{516}

## In Eternal Memory

Grandfather, grandmother, parents, uncles and aunts, cousins, brothers, sisters, and family members.

Vove-Zeev and Paula Hoffman
Chaicha and her husband Leib-Aryeh Polik
Their daughter Leichi-Leah and her husband Leizer Geller
Their son Shabtai and his wife Nusia nee Tanne
Their son Kubtzi
Their son Max and his wife Rachel nee Mark

Ethel and her husband Yisrael Trau
Their daughters Rashi and Malchi

Shalom Hoffman and his wife Leah
Their son Mottel-Mordechai and his wife
Their son Meir

Perel and her husband Elia Yona Koral
Their daughters Tinchi and Dzoni
Their son Archie

Chana and her husband Shmuel Friedler
Their daughter Lotty and her husband Dr. Avraham Fried
Their grandchildren and great grandchildren Adela and Bodzi-Baruch Geller, and Paula Fried

Perpetuated by Mundzi Trau and Meir Polik of Antwerp,
Esther Trau-Shpak, Mordechai Trau, Rozi Polik Stern, Meir and Shmuel Hoffman of Israel

{517}

**In Eternal Memory**

Our father Shlomo the son of Reb Mordechai HaLevi Stern
Our mother Esther the daughter of Meir HaKohen Fruchter
Our sister Leah, her husband Yitzchak, and their children Rashi, Yosef and Meir
Our sister Miriam, her husband David Axelrad, and their children Tzila and Meir
Our brother Yehuda Tzvi, his wife Hinda nee Graulich and their children
Our uncle Moshe the son of Meir HaKohen Fruchter and daughter Alta


Perpetuated by Moshe, David and Mordechai Stern of Israel
Rachel Stern Horowitz of the USA

---

**In Eternal Memory**


Our father Efraim the son of Katriel Rechtschaffen
Our mother Perel the daughter of Yisrael Frisch



Perpetuated by Sherl-Katriel Rechtshaffen of Antwerp
Reizi and Yaer Rechtschaffen of Antwerp

---

**In Eternal Memory**

Mendel Horowitz and his wife Sara
His sister Recha Horowitz and her husband



Perpetuated by Rachel Horowitz and her children

{518}

## An Eternal Flame

In memory of the dear ones who perished in the Holocaust

Mother Soshia the wife of Reb Chaim Szwarc HaKohen
Sister Hinda
Sister Ruchama, her husband Eliezer Kenigsberg and their children
Brother Leib-Yehuda-Yosef Szwarc and his wife

Perpetuated by Bendet, Chana, Sheinchi, and Shmuel

---

## In Eternal Memory

Father Shmuel the son of Reb Michael Adler

Mother Frieda the daughter of Reb Yisrael Frisch

Perpetuated by Max and Sloma Adler of Antwerp
Roza Shubert nee Adler of Paris

# YIZKOR-BOOK IN MEMORY OF

# ROZNIATOW

## Perehinsko, Broszniow, Swaryczow

## and environs

Edited by SIMON KANZ

PUBLISHED BY: ASSOCIATION OF FORMER
INHABITANTS OF ROZNIATOW, PEREHINSKO.
BROSZNIOW & ENVIRONS

TEL-AVIV & NEW YORK, 1974

Editors:
Sh. Liberman, P. Kaner
J. Har-Zohar, Z Fridler,
B. Shvarz, M. Shtern

**SIMON LIEBERMAN**

# ROZNIATOW!

### "How to value thee
### He could only learn who had lost you"

Thus spoke Adam Mickiewicz of his native Lithuania -- thus I feel about Rozniatow.

Although I left Rozniatow in 1922 for Vienna, Paris and ultimately New York, I have often returned. Those visits to my home town were always exciting events that I looked forward to lovingly. Ever time the train would pull into Stryj -- the home ground -- my excitement would grow and as the train wound its way past Morszyn, Bolechów, Dolina, Rachyn to stop at Krechowice the railroad station for Rozniatow, my heart would beat faster. Part of my family will have met me in Lwow, others in Stryj, many would be waiting for my arrival in Krechowice. There, waiting would also be Mailech Landsmann, the Baalaguleh.

"Baruch habuh, Shimkaleh" Mailech would exclaim in a hearty welcome. I would then be led by him to the horse drawn carriage that would take me and some of the members of my family who had come to meet me on the seven kilometer trip from Krechowice to Rozniatow. The rest of the family for whom he had no room would take the carriage belonging to either Hersh-Luzer Wechter or Alter, also known as 'the Toiber' for he was deaf and almost dumb. He could not speak articulately, he couldn't say much anyway, but words were not necessary, his pleased, cordial face expressed the warmth of his welcome.

Mailech would usually wrap me in rugs, for "you are not used to our climate anymore", he would say, and then at the crack of the whip the last lap of the journey would start. The road was stony and at times very muddy. This trip took an hour. It was the end of a long journey yet it was the most exciting part. It was the return to my family, to old friends, to the little town that I was born in, where I spent my childhood and my first adulthood, the return to the long wooden frame house at the bottom of the hill. There in my memory had lived my great-grandfather, Schmiel-Arie Loew, my grandfather Leizer Itsik and grandmother, Gitl-Libe Loew. There, in the end part of the house, lived Pessel Hoffmann, my grandfather's sister who had been widowed at an early age and who supported herself in a dignified way by supplying yeast to the town. There lived my parents, Scharie Duvid and Ester Lea Liebermann. There from the age of five to eighteen I had lived and been raised along with my five sisters. My sixth sister Loncia, the oldest, had been married while she was still very young and she lived with her husband, Jankiel Loew, in a house built for them right next door.

Every person we passed on the trip from Krechowice was a friendly acquaintance of old who welcomed me cheerfully and wholeheartedly; every spot that we passed was a landmark packed with memories. As we passed the hill called Monastyr at the edge of the river Czeczwa I always remembered Bendit Helfgott who lived there and who for years had been employed by my grandfather. I had often climbed up to their mill and he and his family were always glad to see me. How beautiful that little bridge over the Czeczwa always looked to me! The happy, carefree days of school vacations always came vividly to my mind when after a walk in narrow paths, cutting through wheat fields and corn fields we would gather a group of friends at the Czeczwa for a swim. (See enclosed picture).

There were usually my friends and colleagues, Wilek Adlersberg, Dolek Lusthaus, Edzio Safier, Leon Horwitz, Moishe Lutwak, Milo Turtletaub, Lolo Wassermann, Pinio Kanner, Izio Bermann, all home from Stryj where we studied either in 'Gimnazjum Glowny or Filia' and the girls, Muszka and Hala Wassermann (daughter of the first Jewish lawyer in town), Andzia Kanner, Zonia and Irenia Feuer, Jadzia Safier, Adela Weinlos, Muszka Horwitz, Tyncia Berger, Dora Gelobter and my sisters, Dora, Sabina and Anda. Sometimes when the weather was very warm, the lawyers Wassermann, Safier, Feuer with their wives would join us on these pleasant excursions. Most of the other Jews of the town rarely went swimming though it was rumored that Bernard Londner and Lipe Tanne were marvelous swimmers and could swim the entire length of the town pond back and forth! But it was considered undignified for Jews, once they were married, to indulge in such frivolous activities.

Directly past the Monastyr there ran the path to the left to Swaryczow where the Weinfelds, Gut-Be-sitzers, lived and also in my memory and as we Jews would say, 'lchavdel', Rozia Huminska, who was a maid in our house when I was a child; she had often rocked me to sleep, singing folk songs, or telling me fairy-tales. Then on the left the first house in Rozniatow proper, the home of Zisie Arie Kupferberg whose daughter Adele had married Bucio Tepper and is now living in Bridgeport, Connecticut. Then on the right the house of the town painter, Schnitzer, the home of Bendit Jampel, the house of Leizcr Turteltaub (the Cohen and Matrikel Fuehrer). On the left for a long stretch there were no homes but the vast meadow belonging to Mrs. Goldasz and her son-in-law, the future town post-master, Aroniec. In the house of Widow Goldasz lived Mr. Erber, the father of my friends Fania, Hanka and Lonek. Then again homes on both sides of the street, the home of Bernard Londner, Lipe Tanne Leib Fallik, Jonas Koral, the castle of Baron Walisz, the home of Chaim Schloime Halpern, whose daughter Pepka had been my sister Sabina's close friend, the home of Schulim Laufer who supplied the newspapers to the town, Chwila Gazeta Poranna, Gazeta Wieczorna from Lwow and Die Neue Freie Presse from Vienna; facing him lived Schimschon Strassmann, the forwarding agent, then on the left, the Greek-Orthodox Church and on the right lived the Lusthauses, Bendet Horwitz and Doctor Salomon Wassermann, a leader and supporter of the Zionist movement in our town. Then again across the street lived the barber Philip Ferscht who was the only one in town to own and ride a bicycle.

Next came the prominent sign 'Hotel Weissmann' which would cause my heart to leap. In this house I had spent many happy days and evenings talking, singing, arguing, reading poetry or playing cards with a group of friends. This was also the gateway to the Ringplatz. There, in my early youth lived Chanineh Weissmann, the owner of this brick building. Chanineh was known as a learned Jew and in intelligent Jew. Of him they used to say: the difference between him and most others in town is that he can think of the right answer right on the spot whereas others can do so only on second thought, for to be somebody in Rozniatow one had to be not only pious, but also bright and erudite. One was often challenged for the right answer right on the spot in Rozniatow for by this one was judged, esteemed or looked down on. Nothing was so highly valued as education -- a learned man' was the highest praise that could be bestowed on anyone.

The house of Chanineh Weissmann was an establishment, a hotel, a restaurant, a tavern and in addition it had a hall for weddings and balls and dramatic amateur performances. Chanineh and his two daughters, Mrs. Esther Muntz with her husband and sons and Mrs. Rifkeh Kanner with her son Pinio and daughter Andzia. They were also known for excellent "marinierte Fisch" which they exported in specially built wooden boat-like boxes, hermetically sealed so as not to spill any of the delicious juice. After Cbanineh's death Mrs. Kanner had inherited this two-story structure. She always welcomed and encouraged all the young boys and girls to gather there. I often sunned myself on their balcony in the company of Pinio and Andzia and other young friends, viewing the Ringplatz and the life of its merchants. I especially liked to be there on market days to watch the hustle and bustle, the colorful folk dress of the peasants from Strutyn, from Rownia, from Kamien, Petranka, Perehinsko, Spas other neighboring villages and to listen to the voices of the peasants calling attention to their produce -- sounds which grew into a lusty din and finally a loud roar. Adjoining the Weissmann Hotel was another brick two-story house on the left where lived Leibcie Jackel and on the right a big two-story building belonging to Josel and Pinie Berger. Leibcie Jackel and his wife ran a stationery store which provided them with a living and enabled them to send their son to the University of Vienna where he became a doctor and for a while practiced in Rozniatow. But one could not think of this building without thinking of the 'Keller'. Mrs. Surester Horwitz, a widow, rented the cellar from the Jackels and distributed fruit, usually such exotic ones as oranges and peaches from far away corners of the Austro-Hungarian empire. The cellar was not heated and the winters were harsh; to keep herself warm she would sit over a pot of burning coals held between her legs. It wasn't easy for a widow to support herself in Rozniatow, but, as Pessel, Surester did it and retained her self-respect and enjoyed the respect of the town besides. Before Chamishu-Usr her business was a thriving one and I still remember that delicious, sweet, juicy 'boxer', St. John's bread.

In the Berger building Herman Horwitz ran a candy store, a real 'gourmet' shop also selling choice imported grocery items There we used to buy our cocoa in red tin wagons on wheels and I used to wait anxiously for them to become empty so that I could add them to my train collection. In 1919, right after the first World War one epidemic after another hit the town. Herman Horwitz succumbed to typhoid fever at the same time as the Jewish Judge Hopfen and Doctor Bard who had treated them. The whole town mourned the untimely death of these three respected citizens. Mrs. Horwitz and her four daughters, Musia, Hania, Leicia and Blima continued to run the shop after Mr. Horwitz's death and it prospered. Before the Christmas holidays it was a veritable beehive of activity as the judges, teachers, lawyers, notaries, priests chose from a big variety of delicatessen for their holiday celebrations. There too, of course, lived the owners of the building, Josel Berger and his children, Tyncia, Bronia and Arcie. Tyncia was a good friend of mine and of my sisters. We took dancing lessons together taught by Sender Friedler and we danced at many a ball which we never organized just for entertainment but always for charity: the receipts were always distributed to worthy causes. Frivolous enjoyment per se was frowned upon in Rozniatow, but enjoyment with a good motive was highly approved of. In the same building there was the 'Yatkeh', butcher shop of Pinio Berger and the apartment and 'Kanzlei' office of the lawyer Dr. Szymon Safier. In the afternoons his wife, Dora was usually sitting on the balcony and as Mailech's horses conducted me to my home she would call out excitedly 'Szymek, Szymek!' and greet me with generously thrown hand kisses. Their son Edzio was among the first victims of the Nazi beasts; he had established himself as a doctor and already in 1938 was struck down by this wave of inhumanity. His sister Jadzia had married my cousin Leon Horwitz, who, too, was cut down by the barbarians in his prime of life. He was a very able and promising young lawyer. There were many outstanding and talented young fellows in Rozniatow, there was Dolek Lusthaus a university professor under Soviet occupation of Lwow, Wilek Adlersberg a very capable doctor and innumerable other fine and gifted young men. The world will never know of what service they could have been to humanity. Luckily Jadzia and their daughter Nina survived. Adjoining Berger's house was the home of Pinkas Rechtschaffen, who in association with Chaim Schwartz had conducted the town bank. Then followed another brick house belonging to Sosie Heller. She and her daughter Babele emigrated to Germany. The two downstairs apartments were occupied by my uncles and aunts Schmiel and Malke Horwitz and Mates and Sluveh Willner. Uncle Mates ran a kerchief and linen store and uncle Schmiel a flour and grocery shop. Their daughter Clara Biegeleisen had just given birth to a son when I was in Rozniatow for the last time in February 1939. 1 well remember the joy of the parents, the festive spirit mixed with futile hopes and forboding that was already thick in the air. My cousins Toncia, Etka and Cyla Willner were very bright and alert, from them too, one had a right to expect great promise. But their lives, too, were curtailed abruptly and savagely. On the second floor lived the lawyer Dr. Izidor Feuer. His charming wife, a most hospitable friendly lady, often welcomed me to their home. Their daughter Zonia was my first love and at least to me she seemed the most beautiful, full of joie de vivre. Their daughter Trenia married Nunick Lusthaus, another brilliant young man, just before the Nazi onslaught. I had seen him and Zonia Feuer Landesberg in Sosnowice in February 1939, as I was leaving Poland after my last visit to Rozniatow. They came to the train to bid me good bye. "Do widzenia", "à bientôt" they called to me hopefully as the train pulled out of the station. But we never saw each other again. In Sosie Heller's building there was also a room reserved for the Zionist Verein, where we often met, gave and listened to lectures. Then followed store after store, another kerchief store by Schaie Frisch a variety store by Chaim Usher Jaeckel, a pots and pans store owned by other Horwitzes-Chaim and Mendel, a leather goods store by Feiwel Reisler one flour store after another one for exowned by Josef Shimon Stern in competition with similar stores run by his brother in law and one by his father in law Schmiel Wirt. On Simchas Torah Schmiel Wirt used to dance in the town circle with a bakers shovel high in the air. There was also a flour and maize store run by Mishel Artman and after his death by his widow Blime. Up to my age of 5 when my family had moved to my grandfather's house, we lived next door to them. We were friendly neighbours indeed. Mishel Artmann would give me, my sisters and cousins licence to jump up and down in their tremendous bin full of dried corn, a privilege granted to few other children. Blime Artmann who knew me as a baby always showed me great fondness and I always felt in a friendly atmosphere when visiting her. Then around the bend again a kerchief and linen store by Leib and Chane Friedler, a flour store by Leizer and Udale Geller then another candy store run by Meier Fraenkel. I was a child when Meier Fraenkel had pneumonia and was in great danger. A veritable pall of sadness hung over the whole town. I remember how depressed I as a child had also felt and the great joy as the doctor pronounced him safe on this side of the river Styx. "He passed the crisis" spread through the town and smiles began to appear on people's faces again. Life was precious and valued in Rozniatow!

In the center of the Ringplatz stood (the brick house known as the "Mauer". This too, was a hotel, Hotel Rosenmann. There, too, was a hall for weddings and balls and staged dramatic performances. Sender Friedler was an ex-cellent comic and provided the town with much appreciated diversion. Facing us was the 'Traffic' run by Josl Kassner. This, often, was a gathering place and in front of it usually stood Wewcie Tanne, Juda Weissberg, Shulem and Leibele Hoffmann, Josel Kassner,

Shabse Spiegel, Hersh Londner, Meshilem Fruchter, Meier Frisch, Chaim Schloime Meisels, Shulim Rechtschaffen, Josio Rosenberg and others, all busy, hard working business men -- just a break from their work and having a friendly chat. They would all greet me in a chorus most heartily and Leibale Hoffmann who had mar-ried my aunt Jetti would leave the crowd and run after the horses to join the family in greeting the returning native -- me! Then we would pass the brick house of Hersh and Ethel Rechtschaffen where after her marriage to Doctor Moritz Diamand my sister Clara lived and where the Doctor prac-ticed medicine for several years before they emigrated to the United States.

Across the street from them stood the home of Wewe Hoffmann who for a time had been both mayor of the town and its Kultuspresident. He was the distributor of the naphtha that lit the little lamps in Rozniatow and the surrounding country places. Nearby, but off the main street lived Srul Trau and his wife Ethel. They too had a flour store. Luckily their children emigrated early to Antwerp and Palestine.

Recently I had the pleasure of a visit in my home in New York from Lonek Lusthaus and from Mordche Rechtschaffen from Australia. When all the news has been bad and tragedy and heartbreak the rule, how wonderful to be able after all to report the safety and wellbeing of the few who escaped the barbarous cruelty which was the fate of so many of ours! It is with thankful joy that we record the good life of the survivors who continue in America and Australia and Europe and Israel the traditions of Rozniatower good neighborliness throughout the world.

Across the road from Wewe Hoffmann lived the Rosenbaums, the Barnicks -- a teacher of modern Hebrew whose father, a great 'lamden' was an excellent melamed. I had been a student at his Cheider, and at Simon Lutwak's Cheider and studied with Mechel Fassberg. I also studied with Yidale Melamed, the strict disciplinarian who was feared by all the young Jewish boys in town.

Then the Nisen Schindlers, Nussbaums and Hersh Mendel Artmann's homes and at last the horses came to a halt as the rest of the family who had not met me on the way burst out to greet and welcome me. My wife, Olive, had accompanied me on several visits to Rozniatow (and once she had come alone) and it was always a source of pleasure to me to see the love and affection given her, the daughter in law from a foreign and far-away land. Once my little son Donald came with us to meet his family and though he was but five years old he still has many pleasant memories of the trip.

Now came Grandfather Leizer Itsak Löw who always walked with such dignity and deliberation but this time running to welcome me. In later years he was bedridden and one of my first acts was to run to see him. I have still an almost tangible feeling of love for him and for my grandmother, Gitl-Libcie, always carefully dressed well upholstered with pillows inside -- always vivacious. She died at the age of eighty-eight and on her deathbed when she noticed tears on her daughter's face she said: "Nu, you don't cry when an eighty-eight-year-old mother dies. This is to be expected". These were her last words.

There would be assembled our entire family. Loncia and Jacob Low, their daughters Bronia and Dozia and later the husbands Waldek Reiter and Stanislaus Spiegel, my second sister Rechcia and Zisie Willner and their son Julek from Nadworna and Clara and Doctor Moritz Diamand and their son Richard and Dora and Dr Izio Ginsberg with their daughter Irenia from Tarnopol, Sabina and Dr Milo Dresdner with their little girl Iruchna from Lwow and Anda and Sammy Sternklar with their boy Teddy from Vienna and also my aunts, uncles and cousins, the whole family reunited and at the head of the table beaming with pleasure and approval my beloved father and mother, Scharie Duvid and Esther Leah. My mother would repeat frequently, patting my hand contentently, "Thank God, thank God".

All my dear people in this closely knit family except my two sisters Clara and Anda and their families who had just in the nick of time emigrated to America, are no more.

As I write this I am oppressed not only by pain and heart-ache but also by remorse and shame. Somehow, we in America failed to rouse the world -- Jewish and non-Jewish -- to an uproar of protest, to an outcry of the whole civilized world. But who could believe such things?

But it is in order to resuscitate the happy moments that often prevailed when Rozniatow was a living Shtetl that I'm writing this article, to remember the town's scenic beauty, the magnificent pine forest, the hills -- the beginnings of the Carpathian mountains, the medieval structure on top of the hill that served as the court-house, the pond and the mill run by Froim Rechtschaffen, supplied with water from the pond and then the water coming out into a waterfall where as children we spent many happy hours, but mainly to remember its people, hard-working, friendly, God-fearing, charitable and great believers in education. Past the pond the road was known as "alter Dorf", an exotic street, along rivulets, old homes connected by quaint bridges facing the rising hills. There lived Shloime Shmerl a man of great humor, there was the beautiful home of Alter Bermann, the homes of the Deutschers and finally the last house in town along the river Duba, the home of Mrs. Chaje Adler.

Rozniatow was detached from a railroad line and from any industry. Almost all businessmen sold the same wares as their nearby neighbours, competing and fighting for parnuseh. Yet, despite this struggle for survival and keen competition there always was a strong bond of friendship of compassion and understanding. On Saturdays when I had been visiting at home in Rozniatow a real procession of children would string out during the afternoon with wine or mead from neighbours: "Zu lieb dem Gast" (to welcome the guest) they would say. There was great misery in town, too many shoemakers competing for but few feet that could afford to be shod, too many tailors vying for the limited prospects of customers, too many stores selling flour, too many selling kerchiefs and linens. Every sale made by one was a sale that a neighbour missed and couldn't afford to miss, nevertheless a feeling of good neighborliness prevailed. Of course, there were some animosities, but even deadly enmities were forgotten when trouble or sickness struck and erstwhile enemies gladly joined others with a helping hand. I well remember Purim, grandfather in his home and father in ours sitting at the head of the table on which lay a tremendous Chaleh, "Purim Koiletsch" and a stock of change in front of them. All visitors were given food and money. I, when still a child hardly able to walk, covered the town on Purim to collect charity for the poor. On Fridays I distributed chales that my mother had baked; we could enjoy no festivities and not celebrate the Sabbath lest we shared with (the unfortunate neighbours.

When I walked through the town on my visits home I was always greeted with many warm welcoming handshakes. Whether I walked on the alten Dorf, or the Ringplatz many of whose inhabitants I mentioned before or through the other half of the circle where lived the Gelobters the Axelrads, the Ruv of the town Rabi Hemerling the Schoichet Mojshe Weiser, the Grosses, the Mechl Weissmanns,

Duvid Melamed who taught me the Hebrew alphabet I was always met by amiable welcoming faces, by sympathetic people, by friends.

Thus I chose to remember our town, my town, for wherever I went I felt at home I felt part of it, to remember its spirit of charity, forgiveness and understanding the spirit of warm friendship that molded us into a unit.

Alas. They perished almost as a unit. Rozniatow as we knew it is no more, but this spirit will live and live forever. This is why the Jewish culture remains indestructible.

Neither the inquisition nor the wild excesses of the crusaders in ancient and middle ages can measure up to this methodically organized and executed beastly brutality in the century of progress -- the 20th. Century.

We can't bring back to life our loved, ones. We can't -- wish as we may, turn back the clock but we can and we must remember to hate and fight fascism or any brutal system of government that breathes hatred and discrimination against any minority.

OLIVE L. LIEBERMAN

# MY FIRST VISIT TO ROZNIATOW.

This happened forty years ago. We had been married less than two years, but my husband could, not (because of certain immigration regulations) come to Europe with me. So I went alone to Poland, to Rozniatow, to meet his family.

On the way there were Paris and Vienna, all full of wonder to a girl on her first trip abroad. They were -- and are -- beautiful cities and they looked just as I had thought they would, just as they were described in all the books. But how could I possibly imagine Rozniatow?

Of course, I knew a few things; a homesick boy had told me about the Ringplatz, the names of all his sisters and uncles and aunts and nephews and nieces, the taste of the fresh sour cream on freshly baked crisp potato pancakes -- the wonderful smell of good things always cooking. I knew too about the parents, worrying about their only son, so far from home, married to heaven only knows whom. I knew the names too of boys and girls who used to dance and go to school and have picnics at the river side, and ride on a little train to the mountains of Podlute and Osmoloda.

How strange and wonderful it all seemed when I came there, on the Orient Express, train of movie romance, flying along silver tracks from Vienna to Lemberg.

Newly married sister-in-law Sabina and her doctor husband, Milo Dresdner, met me at the station and drove me through the lovely old city to their apartment. I think that they were surprised that I thought it fun to go there by horse-drawn fiacre and I was puzzled to realize that they would have preferred to ride in a taxi!

Certainly this was a happy, friendly weekend with this merriest of the sisters that I would meet; we stopped here not only for me to rest from my journey (was I ever tired then?) but really so we would not have to travel on the Sabbath bath, a matter I had never considered when I planned the trip.

On Sunday morning we left from the big busy station oh the train to Krechowice, which is, of course, the town Rozniatow is "bei". The train was jammed; it was a time in March when Easter and Passover came together and the school children who studied in the cities, but lived in the country, went home for vacation. Sabina and Milo kissed and embraced several boys and girls -- they smiled at me shyly (Etka Willner and her younger sister Cyla and Bronia Low) and then disappeared into the third class carriages while we rode in state in second.

Everybody left the train at Krechowice -- I watched it speed away through the waving wheat fields and wished that I were still safely inside it. I was young, eager to see and learn all the new things, missing my not -- present husband -- and very frightened too. Of meeting the in-laws!

I turned from the vanishing train to be greeted by the vanguard of the family -- a whole bevy of laughing welcoming sisters and aunts who bustled me into the wagon on high wheels drawn by two horses which stood there waiting for us to come. There I met Clara who had brought scarves to warm my delicate New York throat (it was colder in New York than Poland that winter) and off we went, the baggage piled high in the back and a whole long line of boys and girls and men and women following, walking through the muddy, deeply rutted roads.

It was an unusually warm month for March. The snows had melted and the mud was knee high. The horses could not always pull our wagon with its load of people and bags and three times on the way we all had to get out and walk a way up-hill while the men heaved the wheels out of the mud and helped the horses pull their load out of the deepest mire. I looked and looked in wonder -- I could not see enough -- the beautiful, wavy plain stretched out on all sides as far as the eye could see; dark blue mountains and green forests rimmed the horizon. In the fields stood cattle and on the farms I could observe the peasants in their picturesque dress, working to prepare the land for sowing, while others, barefoot, but carefully carrying their shoes well out of the muddy rain water walked down the road.

And on the roof of each peasant house stood a stork -- delicately balanced over his nest on one ballet poised foot! The air was brisk and the sun bright and a biting wind made me glad to tuck the extra scarf into my coat collar.

At last we were there -- and my moment had come! Now I would meet the parents -- would they like me? Would I like them? We climbed down from the wagon (was that little square we clattered through a moment before really the great, big, coliseum of a Ringplatz that Simon had talked of so often? I couldn't believe it; it must be somewhere else). And we entered the doorway of a house I could not see for all the people crowded into it. What a milling about! -- and greeting and kissing and introducing and how is Simon and how was the trip? -- till suddenly a silence fell upon the whole lively, noisy company. They fell back and made way for a pair of twinkling eyes shining above a snow white beard and Father made his way through the throng of family and friends gathered to meet Shimka's wife from America. He came to me -- alone now in the center of the circle, tipped up my chin into his cupped hand and looked smiling into my face. Then he let it go -- placed his hands on my shoulders and announced to the waiting guests, "Sie is keine Schickse!"

Then everybody crowded round and I think no returned hero from the wars ever had a warmer welcome (or a bigger family). They were ready to receive me with full heart no matter who I turned out to be -- but that I was after all, despite rumors to the contrary -- a Jewish girl, made everybody glad.

A long time later when everybody had been sorted out, cousins connected to aunts and children to parents there came the formal visit to grand mother and grandfather, Eliezer Itsak-Loew. He looked regal, his ancient face framed with white hair as he lay propped up on many pillows in his bed and bustling around him coquettish in a white jabot, there was, spry, lively little grandmother, Gitl Liebe.

"Wie gehts Schimkeleh in Ameriku?" they wanted to know. And when I told them in the German that I had so fortunately been taught to speak at home when I was a child, that I left him feeling fine, but that I missed him very much on this day with his people, the old man replied to me, "Meine Hochachtung, meine Hochachtung". I was very touched -- indeed I had never been so splendidly (or more undeservedly) praised in all my life before.

Of course, I had been told before I came that grandmother loved pretty things just like a young girl, and that grandfather had been bedridden for years. So I had brought with me the gayest kerchief I could find in Vienna for a little old lady, and now, in a corner of the room I could see two little boys quite pink in the face from inflating by blowing into it, the great rubber bed I had bought in Paris to rest more easily grandfather's paper thin bones.

The biggest lunch anyone ever heard of followed. There was a much coming and going at the table. I sat next to my mother-in-law and found her loving and easy to talk to. It seemed to me that we were the only ones who remained seated throughout the whole meal. As in a dream it seemed to me that changing groups sat down to one enormous dish or another, and then ran away and others came, for the next course. But everybody wanted me to eat everything -- I think I did!

After lunch came the Bath. My loving husband had written home that in America everybody had a bath every day -- and I believe he intimated that if they didn't I would probably sicken and waste away. At any rate, I remember that after that big dinner among all the sisters and cousins and aunts and visiting towns people, that they all escorted me into the kitchen where stood a big tin tub and two Ukrainian maids filling it up with hot water poured out of pails. Like the queens of France in child -- birth I took the bath in public and then in order to avoid its weakening effects was hustled off to sleep (in the afternoon!) in a deep downy feather-bed.

Wonderful days followed. I learned who everybody was. I could recite the railroad stations on the way

to Stanislawow. I managed to explain that I could wash without the back-breaking work of bringing water from a well for my bath every day just as did everybody else. I discovered that the girls were interested in Paris dresses and American lipstick. I found that our family was just like people everywhere -- only nicer!

I slept with Clara and Moritz -- Anda made me a beautiful peasant dress, all red velvet and spangles (a dazzling success at masquerades back home). I went to dozens of parties. I walked in the woods. We had two marvelous seders -- Father Zachary-David sat propped up on high white pillows with mother assisting when we all sang HadGad-yo. The matzo-balls were a success. The long service seemed short to me -- and how pleased they all were when I knew -- a girl from a reform temple! -- that the extra glass of wine was for the Prophet Elisha!

Some years later I returned with my husband and our then little boy. Now I knew and loved each one -- now I was truly one of the family. But the excitement and wonder of that first visit could never be recaptured. How could it? There was never anything like that again in all the world!

# ROZNIATOW

## PINIO KANNER -- MOSHE DAVID LUTWAK

Stand at a vantage point on the market square and take a view of our township: The balmy weather of a Friday afternoon, the sun receding slowly with a red glow in the skies, and the old bearded shammes -- synagogal caretaker just walking around with the loud call: "IN SHUL ARAIN" -- "TO THE SYN-AGOGUE!". This signalled the approaching Sabbath, 7th Day of Creation, day of rest, prayer, celebration. The cabs and drivers, always in the square on their service to and fro the Railway Station at Krechowice, some 7 Km distant, have terminated their runs by noon. Any peasants with carts, still in the market place, are leaving, the horse's hoofs beating the dry dirt road, dividing the square in two nearly, but not quite, equal halves. Metal roll shutters are being drawn on some of the shops around the square, others are bolting and padlocking wooden, russet or brown painted, doors and gradually quiet is coming to reign over the township. A last cart of a local peasant, returning from the fields, is speedily galloping down the road, soon to disappear over the bend, leading out of the square, and the first lean figure, clad in black satin coat, "Shtraimel" (velvet cap with foxtails around) on his head, feet in white socks and slippers, emerges on the paved walk, on the way to the Friday evening prayers at the chassidic synagogue called the "Clause". It is Faivel Reissler, his thin long beard fluttering like a white flag, while he is vigorously striding with prayer book under his arm. In the opposite direction, a late customer of the communal baths crosses the square in half run, hastening home to dress and be in time again at his place of prayer -- the Synagogue or the Bet-Hamidrash near by. The three places of worship, situated close to another at a small square just off the main market place, are now the aim of all, and you can watch them. Here, at the entry to the market square near the shop of Meier Fraenkel, you see emerging Leisor-Itzig Loew benevolent smile on his face and neatly dressed; Wolf Hoffmann, then president of the Kehilla -- Jewish Community -- proudly coming along as befits his importance; Hersch Mendel Artmann, flour merchant and with Jeckel Spiegel, seller of kerosene, the only two whom I remember for addressing my grandfather, Chanina Weissmann, with the intimate "thou". This was explained by the fact that the three were as children pupils of the same "cheder", the religious boys-school. Except for the residents of the northern suburb, called "Altes Dorf" (old Village) who had a place of prayer in their quarter, all male Jews, old and young down to age of 3-6, assembled in the brightly lit three houses of prayer to celebrate the Sabbath, dressed for the occasion in their best clothes. It was known and accepted that, if any head of family was missing and not at his regular seat, he is either out of town, or laid up by illness, and his neighbours would exchange information on the point, upon conclusion of the prayers, on the way home.

As a youngster I often accompanied my grandfather to prayers, and remember the explanation he offered on my inquisitive wonderment of the haste of Faivel Reissler, of whom I stood in awe. Why, so it should be -- leaving home for the synagogue is for the purpose of attending a blessed function -- and only a fool would not make haste on such an occasion. Prayers are a dialogue with the Creator and submission of requests, therefore respect and good manners demand that one is in good time for this appointment, and is well prepared for this important meeting. Contrariwise, while walking home from prayers all took it easy, going in pairs or groups, chatting friendly among the general exchange of "GOOD SHABBES" wishes, the offering of which was to mark deference and regard in a formal manner, or neighbourly kindness and friendship among equals. With the blessing of "GOOD SHABBES" on the lips, the spouse and family are greeted upon coming home to a prepared dinner: white table-cloth, lighted candles, all dressed for the Sabbath and ready for benediction and subsequent dining. This marked the end of a busy and hardworking week, and the obligatory white bread, finer dishes and enjoyment of life were shared by the family at the table, while work, business and secular occupations rested. So also stillness and calm came to rest over the Jewish Rozniatow.

To many it may have been the religious content of this seemingly idyllic celebration of the Sabbath, to some chassidim even their exhilarating experience of praying and blessing, at which they believed themselves in presence of God, while to the many "small folks" it simply was a day of better food and relaxation -- to all, however, it was the clear, undoubted and proud manifestation of Jewishness. The cohesion of the religion became by long tradition and many usages of the Sabbath the dividing line between Jew and Gentile, and the observance of this day in the small township acquired a deep national significance.

While this is the Jewish Rozniatow in it's essential general features a few words need be mentioned on the secular township in which there lived also Ukrainians and Poles under a political regime that we first remember as the Habsburg Empire of Austria. This changed for the short-lived Ukrainian Republic from fall of 1918 to the summer of 1919 and then it was part of Poland till World War II. During 1940/summer 1941 it formed a part of the Soviet-Ukraine, came in the summer 1941 under German-Nazi occupation, to meet complete extermination and Holocaust of the Jewish community. Rozniatow was again "liberated" in 1945 and -- it forms since a part of the Soviet-Ukraine.

Historically, these parts were Polish in the XVIII. Century, and came to Austria under the name of Galicia when Poland was divided up between her three mighty neighbours -- Russia, Austria and Prussia. Rozniatow might have been a fief during the Polish reign, and during the early Austrian regime it was the property of the Polish family of Skarbek, feudal earls and lords over vast properties in Galicia.

There are records of a feudal contingent of 60 men from Rozniatow, contributed by the Skarbek family in the period 1835/1845 for the building of the Theatre in Lwow/Lemberg, where there was also a street of their name. The Skarbek properties in Rozniatow were still special institutional management up to World War I, and were rented later to the Glesingers, the income devoted for the Internate (College) in Chyrow, where Polish noblemen's children were educated, including children of Baron Walisz, a resident of Rozniatow. There also lived in retirement during the last years of their life an Earl Skarbek and his French wife, who augmented their small pension by giving French lessons to some Rozniatow girls. The turreted building on the hill in which the Court was located, was once the feudal Skarbek residence, of which the best preserved vestiges was the fine avenue of old lime trees, leading to the Catholic Church, on same hill overlooking the town.

Rozniatow lie in a curve of the river Duba where it is joined by the other river, the Czeczwa, and so suffered repeatedly from floods, sustaining much damage during inundations. The necessity to provide a Land Registry when the peasants were liberated in the Austrian reforms of 1948-1849, the founding of the Court and of the Post Office on November 15th, 1850, turned Rozniatow into a township of some importance, as it became the administrative and also economical focal point for many villages, southward to the Carpathians, with a population of well over 50,000. The village of Perehinsko alone had a population of nearly 10,000, and the oil-drilling in Dubno and Rypne and modern lumber industry with two narrow-gauged railway lines from Broszniow to the vast forests in the mountains, contributed much to commercial and economic development of this otherwise backward and infertile region.

Here then, under a benevolent regime of the Austrian Empire but dependent on mostly indolent Polish administrators, who had to implement the policies of Vienna; surrounded by a backward Ukrainian peasantry whom with they continuously traded -- Rozniatow grew into a township of Jews who generally could stand their own.

While born in Rozniatow of an old local family -- my maternal grandfather Chanina Weissmann was born there 1840, and while I can well remember town and people from around 1910, when I was 6, till I left in 1926, there still are many names of which I have no personal memory, and I find a fount of most relevant information in the Reminiscences of our old friend, Moshe David Lutwak of New York. He is indeed the Chronicler of Rozniatow, registrar of types and to him thanks are due from all. I am addressing the English speaking townspeople and their, young generation in English, relying in great measure upon Moshe Lutwak, and so his name is alongside of mine as co-author of the present lines. Much of the intrinsic value and sagacious observation in the following details are the merit of Moshe, while I make an effort to say it in English and try to do justice to the original story of Moshe Lutwak.

Rozniatow had a population of some 8000, of which well over 6000 were Ukrainians, then designated Ruthenes of Unitarian Greek-Catholic creed, possibly a hundred or so of Poles and some 2000 Jews. There were barely 20-30 brick houses, most were wooden frame constructions, many still with thatched roofs, others with roofs of wooden shingles, very few with zinc plated sheets. It was the township's fateful history that when a few years passed without much damage by floods and overflowing rivers, there were conflagrations, in which the fire spread instantly over the roofs and large parts of the town were consumed. The elderly people in town used to calculate local history by the Large Fire, Large Flood -- and considered themselves well deserving of sympathy, pitiable -- in Jewish a "Nebbich" -- and this was the nickname of the Rozniatow Jew in his Eastern Galicia.

While small scale agriculture, poultry and cattle breeding was the main occupation of the region and of the Ukrainian peasantry, the Poles were mostly state employees with a few artisans, while the commerce in every form and manner, free professions, all lines of handicrafts and main communication services were the reserve of the Jews. There were barely three Jewish owners of arable fields, and only one of them, Isaac Turteltaub, son of Leisor, the official Registrar, tilled his soil, the others employing peasants for this work. The "industry" was represented by the water driven sawmill of Tanne (on the "Fiszarka"), two flour mills and the oil-cake press of Rechtschaffen, and by a good stretch of imagination one can add also the two soft-drink "productions", of which only the one of Mihal Weissmann flourished over a period of time.

Two modern industries -- the sawmills of Broszniow-Krechowice of Glesingers and the oil fields at Rypne and Dubno provided much employment for the region, including Jews, and added immeasurably to the economic development of the township. The wide activities of the Jewish owned firm of Glesinger included even the renting of the Skarbek farm in Rozniatow, earlier under administration of Weigel, a vituperate anti-Semitic Pole. The entire region enjoyed the free fare on two narrow-gauge railway lines operated by the Glesingers for the transportation of logs from the forests, deep in the Carpathian mountains to the sawmills, providing a link between Rozniatow and many villages.

Among the Jews of Rozniatow were a few well to do families, quite a number of businessmen, earning fairly well, a large number of smaller traders and peddlers, artisans, cab drivers, porters and manual workers, who toiled hard to cover their needs, and some simply poor, like in many other communities. There were no rich, all standards then being very modest, and possibly 80% or more owned their homes, as plots and building materials were rather low priced and labour cheap and abundant. The houses on the main thoroughfare and the market square had their front parts turned into business premises, many with sign-boards and the commercial contacts with the region's populace were brisk and widest possible. Like in most townships, there was a weekly market-day on Wednesday and large market-days several times a year, to dates known by their saints, like Mihael, John, Peter -- and then town enjoyed its busiest trading by own and thousands of visitors, with a considerable turnover in the cattle-trading, destined mostly for resale to larger towns and even export by rail as far as Vienna. Some agricultural produce, specific of the region, like eggs, dried mushrooms and herbs, poultry were continuously purchased by specializing merchants for export, providing subsistence for many who had their special connections in the villages, or by peddling personally in the villages.

The main basis of daily food was the bread, mostly baked at home for the whole week ahead, and the potato prepared in all manners and forms and consumed with modest additions, of most varied grades from cheese, fried onions and up to a -- salted herring. The main preoccupation of the Jewish population during weekdays being to provide for Sabbath and the festive meals with the family, this was for many also an economically serious commitment, demanding the provision of some white bread ("Challe"), wine or liquor, meat and, if feasible, sweet dessert, and be it a cooked dried prune.

Ideologically and to some extent culturally, the Jews of Rozniatow were affected by the traditional chassidism of an orthodox way of life, demonstrated also by the wearing of the long coat, wide brimmed hat, side-locks ("Payes") and strictest observance of minutest rules, regulations and usages, applied at all times and occasions. On the other side, there appeared the first opposition of "Haskala" (Culture) of the younger generation who recognized the necessity for a more modern way of life and approach to problems. This affected not only the garb, when the coat became a shorter jacket but also the contact to progressive Jewish movements, leading up to and culminating in the political Zionism, as formulated by Herzl and widely propagated in all countries, where there existed established Jewish communities. Sometime around the turn of 1900 the first CHOVEVEI ZION "club" was formed in Rozniatow, the premises serving later also for prayers on Sabbath and holidays. This club was first housed in the house of Jeckel, where later the Lusthaus family lived, and then in the house of Sosie Heller -- on the first floor where Dr. Feuer lived. (See No. 75 of the Map). The attorney, Dr. Wassermann, was an active member of this Zionist nucleus, members of which were Aron Weissmann, Shalom Rechtschaffen, Moshe Barnik, Dr. Berger, Hersh Mordehai Lutwak, brothers Salomon and Isaac Gross, Lasar Tepper, Marcus Kanner, Mendel Horowitz and several others. Many were sympathizers and supporters in one way or another, and it was toward 1906 that national Jewish political activities developed, including collections for the Jewish National Fund and the visit of a delegate of the Zionists from Lwow/Lemberg, capital of Galicia. A theatrical group performed for the first time in the history of Rozniatow the play of Jacob Gordon: "The Jewish King Lear". Actors were: Shalom Rechtschaffen,

Meier Taub, Aron Weissmann, Shaul Schwalb, while Barnik and Issachar Stern dressed tip as women in order to play their female impersonations.

This was still within the traditional limitations of the Jewish morals and manners, and it is noteworthy that the presentation of Holy Scrolls (Sefer Thora, Thora Scrolls) to the Chovevei Zion, in order to establish the premises also as a place of prayer, were part of the activities, alongside with the opening of the Hebrew School, much to the dislike of some chassidim. The first teacher was Reiter, followed by Herzberg and others. Pupils were mostly boys but there were also a few girls who sat separate from the boys, Hebrew was the catalyst for national awakening in Rozniatow, whose Jews -- in addition to religious traditions -- acquired so a new cohesive sentiment and drive to better their life.

Rozniatow Jews may have been typical of the Galician township in their virtues and bad habits, in the earnest and humorous of the time, but it was said that one would have to get up very early and be very smart in order to win a point over a Rozniatower.

The communal life was directed by the official council -- an autonomous body under Supervision of the regional Starosta, Chief of State Administration, in Dolina, and as regards the Jews, by it's own council called the Kehilla. President of the Kehillah was Veve (Wolf) Hoffmann, well to do merchant, selling kerosene and fuel-wood. Of high stature and long beard, serious and vigorous, he served also Mayor of the town, nominated of course, as was usual under the Austrian regime. It was only later, after 1920, under Polish administration that elections were held for communal offices. Some of the Hoffmann family have happily survived, like the Weissmann in U.S.A., then sons of Leo Hoffmann and also the children of Trau and Falik in Israel.

An important position in the communal life of the township was held by Zacharia Liebermann who over many years served as president of the Kehilla, and member of the town council. He was respected by the Starosta in Dolina and very influential on behalf of Rozniatow. Speaking well Polish, Ukrainian and German, he was neatly dressed, with white beard. He lived on the road leading up to the Catholic Church, and the other part of same house was held by one of the townships patriarchs, Leisor Itzik Loew, father-in-law of Liebermann and holder of state monopoly for the sale of liquor, beer and alcoholic beverages. His charity was proverbial and he was held in highest regard for kindness, assistance and help that he never refused. His son Jacob Loew married his own niece, daughter of Liebermann, and for them a new brick house was erected on part of same plot but facing the main road -- see No. 27 29 and 30 of the Map. Of these widely connected families only few, unfortunately, survive and we are happy to know of the Liebermann children, Clara Diamand, Anda Sternklar and my old pal, Simon Liebermann, all living in New York.

Religious and spiritual leader of the Jewish Rozniatow was Rabbi Hemerling, very learned and pious, poor but always civil and obliging, living at a corner of the market square (see No. 88 of the Map). He had a weekly salary from the Kehilla, now and again only augmented by fees for marriages, arbitrations etc. Upon his demise in the 1920s, the Dayan Yehuda Hersh Korn became the provisional office holder but he so remained over a number of years. Not having been ordained as Rabbi, he received but a low salary, a point of some importance for the elders in the Kehilla and so his wife and children helped out by trading, to meet the family's budget, while he devoted all his efforts to the religious needs of the community, both parties being happy at the bargain.

Payments to the Kehilla for services like kosher slaughtering, burial plots, rentals of bath-house, calls to reading of the Thora during Festivals, seats at services etc. were modest, and the total income of the Kehilla was the smaller, as the best seats during prayers and many honours were held by the well to do by inheritance, all the poor were exempted, and the collecting was in general most liberal. The Kehilla never had any free cash, and special levies had to be arranged in frequent cases of urgency.

There were three main places of worship, all situated around a small square off the market-place: the large Synagogue with nearby the "Clause" and the Bet-Hamidrash. A small place for prayers was also in the suburb "Altes Dorf" (Old Village) for those living far from the center, while the young Zionists congregated for prayers in their club. Many of the leading citizens and others prayed in the large synagogue, where to came also the professionals and white collar men during the Festivals, while the "Clause" served mostly for the chassidim, led by the Rabbi. A large number of others prayed at the Bet-Hamidrash, and some citizens came to prayer on given dates to the other places of wor-ship like visitors -- very likely for some reasons of tradition or usage. The synagogue had on the windows the name of the donor, David Weissmann, grandfather of Mihal Weissmann and uncle of my own grand-father Chanina Weissmann, The Beth-Hamidrash was a new building erected after 1900, and two men -- Samuel Schwindler and Haim-Israel Rottenberg devoted many days of manual labour in the building of their prayer-house. The "Clause" burned down in 1920, and was rebuild in brick and much improved. It is significant that the only pavement in Rozniatow run around the market square and out of it to the large synagogue, as befits the building held in highest regards by all.

If the prayer-houses were the focus of communal life of the grown-ups, the youngsters were taken care of from about the age of four in private religious schools -- the cheder, headed by the teacher -- melamed. David Rottenbach, Aba Tanne, Yosel Abraham were so called "dardeke melamdim" -- the designation being part Aramaeic, part Hebrew for children teachers, who started the boys also on writing, of course, of the Hebrew alphabet. Boys of 7 or 8 then entered the "higher" schools, of which Haim-Simon Lutwak, Judale Kaufmann, Itzik Barnik were the principals. Lutwak, the father of our friends Moshe David and Shaiko Lutwak, was the modern educator who laid more stress on the study of biblical texts (Prophets etc.) and general Jewish subjects including letter-writing. Haim Simon Lu-twak was a man of profound general education and progressive views, reading also modern Hebrew periodicals and among the first to give his sons a college education. He is remembered by many as their guide and mentor. Judale Kaufmann was a very strict disciplinarian, who concentrated on the Talmud and was the least popular of the teachers, while his son Meir Kaufmann was a respected owner of a clothing store, of modern outlook and Zionist. Itzik Barnik was a man of great talmudic learn-ing, highly respected by all, and his son, Moshe Barnik was a teacher of Hebrew and educator who later lived in Palestine and accompanied the poet Nachman Bialik on his tour of Poland. A grandson, Barkai, is an active liberal politician in Israel.

Main places for talks, discussion of news and debates were the Bet-Hamidrash after prayers, when Yoel Tanne, just returned from his frequent visits to Vienna, reported on world politics and other top-ics of interest. Joel Tanne held the State Lottery, was a man of culture and dressed with a measure of elegance. Late were the hours when the lively debates ended, if he reported on news at the imperial court and political events. Sometime during World War I. Tanne left with family for Vienna.

The second place of a free debating "convention" was the front room in the house of Josef Kassner, who held the monopoly sale of tobacco and cigarettes, also of postage and revenue stamps, in a corner house on the main road (No. 47 of the Map). Kassner is remembered for his innate kindness, doing favours to many and whoever asked for a loan, was never disappointed. All had free entry to his front room but on balmy summer days, the debates would be held just in front of his house, all standing around until tired. Survivors of his family are Etty Wolter and Deborah Artmann.

A person of importance and enjoying great respect was Chanina Weissmann, owner of hotel and restaurant on the market square (see No. 81 of Map), pious, learned and outspoken. He was the honorary circumcissor (Mohel), performing the requirement as a commandment of the Thora and training several pupils, to take his place after his demise. Despite his personal orthodoxy he daily read a German newspaper and realized the necessity of a liberal secular education. The only survivor of his family is a grandson, Pinio Kanner, in Israel. A most learned chassid was Faivel Reissler, leather merchant, always the first in observing of commandments and performance of religious duty, taking daily ablutions in cold water (Mikve). His equal in piety and popular for his winning personality was Mordehai Meier Beer Kriegel, who devoted long nights to study and during the baking of Matzot before Pessach was the general supervisor of this important work. Much respected were also the ritual slaughterers, Moshele Shochet and two others by name of David -- one with a black, the other, David Glas, with a ginger beard. The sons of David Glas live in Israel.

Well to do and a citizen of importance was Hersh Rechtschaffen, who often led the service in the Bet-Hamidrash, assisted by his own sons in the chanting of prayers, and while strictly observant, his son Shalom was already leaning to Zionism. Three sons of the Rechtschaffen family happily survive in Israel and Australia. Among the respected and popular elders was a patriarchal flour merchant, Hersh-Mendel Artmann, whose son Isaac Artmann lived in Broszniow and was partner of Jacob Rosenthal of Perehinsko in the sawmill of Sliwek. Another son, Josef Artmann, lived in Vienna and surviving grandsons are Leo and Bucio Tepper and Bucio Widmann in America. Another elder of the town was Mayer-Aharon Londner, of great piety, two of whose sons Israel Hersh Londner and Berl Londner funded their own families and were respected merchants. Grandsons of Mayer Aharon are Shiyo Londner in Belgium and Yehoshua Spiegel in Israel.

Living barely 1 1/2 miles from Rozniatow was the family of Weinfeld, owners of a large farm in Swaryczow, who were coming to town in their own carriage. Of this very popular family a grandson survives in Israel.

Like many other townships, Rozniatow was also blessed by a strikingly pathetic type of individual, named Israel-Leisor Bentscher. Tall, without a trace of hair on his face, except for two small sidelocks, always open-shirted and wearing an old sack around his shoulders, day-in, day-out in same worn clothes, he now and again peddled a prayer book or religious treatise, or earned a little by portering. Without wife or relatives, he just had a corner in the living room of Haim, a worker in the flour mill, near the Bet-Hamidrash. Many believed that this strange, ascetic man mourns the destruction of the Temple in Jerusalem -- and gladly gave him on Fridays some Challe (white bread) that he collected for the poor. He was always quiet, unobtrusive, just slipping in during prayers, aloof in a corner and personified "Nebbich" of Rozniatow.

In sharp contrast to the lean and slow Israel-Leisor was another pathetic figure and part of the townships daily activities, always busy carrying sacks of flour -- stout, bulky, with thick beard and uncouth Iczike the porter. Ridiculed by all for his two passions: desire for meat (hence the nickname "Fleisch") and playing the State Lottery. Highly irritable and shrieking at every provocation, he was touted by many and victim of repeated pranks. Iczike will forever be part and parcel of the bustling market-square.

A group of houses inside the square, at the main road, comprised the "Alte Mauer", a large brick building, one part of which was the bar and restaurant of Israel Rosenmann and parents of Sender Friedler, who will be again mentioned. Adjoining was the iron mongery of Benzion Jaeckel and flour business of Samuel Horowitz, father of our unforgotten pal, Leo Horowitz, lawyer and always active in Jewish communal affairs. Completing this group was the bar of Melach Gross, very observant and pious. His son Icio was a Zionist, avid reader of Jewish literature, whose many books formed later the nucleus of the Jewish library. Another son, Mordehai Gross, erected later a two-store brick house, as hotel, bar and restaurant. Two grandsons of Melach, Simcha and Moshe Gross, live in Israel. (See Nos. 83/84 of Map).

Conspicuous in a part of the market-square near the hotel of Weissmann were the cabs and carriages, who provided the passenger service to and from the railway station at Krechowice, some 7 Km distant, and whenever required performed also mixed passenger & goods transportation to other towns, like Dolina, Kalusz or Perehinsko. The cab drivers were hardworking, decent men, taking care of their horses and remembered are Mihal Waechter, who always had a white, clean and well fed horse, Mailech Landsmann, Aharon Zimmermann, and several others. They all lost out in time to the car and autobus.

Leader of the academic professions in Rozniatow was the lawyer Dr. Salomon Wassermann whose house across the road of the Greek-Catholic Church had a nice front garden with flowers (see No. 121 of Map). He was the leading Zionist and served during the Ukrainian regime 1918/1919 as chairman of the Zionist Organization and of the Jewish National Council, organizing the first social services for the poor. His son Carol (Lolek) lives in America and the daughter Halka in Israel.

The second lawyer to settle in town was Dr. Isidor Feuer who rented the upper floor of Sosie Heller's house in the market-square (see No. 75 of Map). Being the legal representative of the Glesinger enterprise, he was very busy and only later, under the Polish regime, he served for a time as President of Kehilla, as Mayor of Rozniatow and was active in communal affairs. Two nephews of Dr. Feuer, Poldek and Rudek Loebl, very often guests in Rozniatow, have also become lawyers and are reported living in Poland. Dr. Simon Safier, earlier employed by Dr. Wassermann, has opened own offices in the house of Josef Berger in the market-square (see No. 91 of Map). He was very popular and served for some time as President of the Kehilla. His son, Dr. Vet. Lolek Safier and daughter Jadzia live in Poland. Employed by Dr. Wassermann as main clerk was also Aharon Meier Lutsthaus who died early. His very gifted son, Don Lusthaus, while on the staff of Glesingers, graduated and won his Ph.Dr., becoming later Professor of Lwow University, He and brother, Dr. Nuniek Lusthaus, met a tragic end by the Nazis. Their youngest brother lives in Australia.

It is a measure of some economic progress of the town that in the period between World War I. and II. several more lawyers settled and open offices in Rozniatow, like Dr. Menkes, Dr. Kahane, Dr. Redisch (a Dolina man) and two local graduates continued in the legal profession: Leon Horowitz, grandson of Leisor Itzik Loew and cousin of Simon Liebermann and Leon Meisels, whose father Haim Salomon had an iron mongery (see No. 58 of Map). Jews were also clerks at the court, like Koerner, Josef Kaczky, later transferred to Stryj and David Blaustein. Meier Taub was a clerk in Dr. Safier's office, while Mordehai Brotfeld and Chaim Karczman were professional scribes who wrote petitions, summonses etc. The office of court usher was held by Prinz, a veteran of 12 years army service, whose daughter Mathilde participated in our amateur theatricals. Rozniatow also had a Jew as judge, Jacob Hopfen, who however held aloof of all Jewish life. There was only one Ukrainian lawyer, Dr. Korbas, a rabid anti-Semite, while the Notary Public was a Pole, Lukaczewski, a most decent man.

The first physicians, Dr. Berwid and Dr. Sokanina, were Poles but then Rozniatow had several Jewish doctors, like, Dr. Barth, Dr. Sabbath, Dr. Diamand -- son-in-law of Liebermann -- and also a local graduate, Dr. Jaeckel, son of Leibcie Jaeckel, whose house adjoined the Hotel Weissmann (see No. 82 of the Map). Jaeckel senior had a stationery ship and operated also a bank.

The first apothecary was Skalka, who was bought out by another Pole, Macierzynski, a smart businessman, who considerably enlarged the dispensary, operated an autobus, and as a side-line was even a money-lender.

The medical profession would be incomplete without the heal health-practitioners  who cured sick by the application of leeches, recommending and dispensing herbs, extracting teeth. Prime occupation of some was barbering, like Mattis Berie, who wife was most popular and respected, being the township's midwife and greatly charitable. Philipp Ferszt had a nice barbershop, extracted teeth, was an ardend lover of our local theatricals and did their make-up as his contribution to the good cause. Another heal health-practitioner  was Hersh Frost who also travelled around the villages. His children and grandchildren live in America.

Generally respected for his learning was Chaim Schwarz who jointly with Pinchas Rechtschaffen held a bank in form of a Loan-Society. His daughter Schanzi was among the first pupils of the Hebrew school, and we are happy to have with us his eldest son, Bendet Schwarz in Israel, while other children live in America.

After the great fire of 1903 the two brothers Josef and Pinchas Berger erected a large brick house at the market square (see No. 91 of Map). Josef Berger was of the leading cattle exporters, and his eldest son, happily surviving in Israel Dr. Alter Berger was with Hersh-Mordehai Lutwak the first local boys to be educated in college (Gymnasium) which necessitated a stay in Stryj. A daughter of Josef Berger, Tynka, lives in Israel while her brother Arcio passed away. A large shop of fine provisions and foodstuff in the house of Berger was bravely carried on by Rivka Horowitz, whose daughters were among our closest friends and of those Lea and her family happily survive in Israel. A little further up from the Bergers was another two-store brick house of Sosie Heller who traded in household and kitchenware, and the other shop in the same building was of Mathis Willner, in-law of Leisor Itzik Loew. Mathis was liked by all for his good manners and kindness. In the same row was also the flour shop of Shlomo Stern, observant and decent, survived by a son Mordehai in Israel. Several other well to do merchants by name of Stern lived on the market square and remembered is Issachar Stern, son-in-law of Chaim Schwarz and also the very observant Josef Shimon Stern, who bought the house of Liebermann and "got" as son-in-law Zajde, son of the shochet Weiser -- the most eligible young hassid of the town. Zajde himself was later a shochet but his wife Bracha implemented the income by trading provisions. Next to Stern lived his father-in-law Shmuel Wirt, an orthodox of the old school (see No. 70 of Map). At the corner of the market-square (see No. 63 of Map). Friedler had a large textile shop, and his sons bought later the Hotel Weissmann. Next was the other leading shop of provisions and foodstuffs of Meier Fraenkel, observant but liberal and modern, a very respected citizen. Leaning on the house of Fraenkel was the stand of Pincio Schwalb, who also held the position of Shammes of the Kehilla.

Across the road in the market-square were the shops of Benjamin Keller and of Mordehai Friedler, whose son Ucio survived Auschwitz and the younger son Chanina lives happily in Israel. In the same row was also the shop of Jeckel Spiegel -- the first to emigrate from Rozniatow to Palestine soon after World War I. in 1920. All the family settled in Israel, where generations thrive happily. At the next corner of the market-square was the house of Rabbi Hemerling, then of the shochet Moshe Weiser (see No. 97 of Map), then of Abraham Groll and there at the corner was the Hebrew School.

In the same row lived also Hersh Landsmann whose daughter Ida married an Ukrainian, Jagiellowicz. At gravest risks to themselves, Mishka Jagiellowicz and wife have assisted Jews during the Nazi occupation, saving their lives, and many survivors remember them gratefully. The adjoining side of the market-square had several larger houses in which dwelled traders and peddlers but then was also the butcher shop of Israel Friedler and of the watchmaker Hersh Axelrad, proud of his nice beard, probably the finest in town. Next to Axelrad was the house of Karczman (see No. 93 of Map) and there it joined to Mihael Weissmann, a part of whose house was held by his sister and niece, Hinka and Malcia Weissmann, glaziers. Many families lived in smaller houses in the lanes at back of the market-square but there was also the fine house and large orchard of Yehuda Weissberg, see No. 79 of Map.

At the main road leading out of the market-square were several shops, among them the barbershop of Philipp Ferszt and then the Greek Catholic Church (Nos. 124 & 126 of Map). At the house No. 128 of Map lived Simon Strassmann, the town's forwarding agent, taking care of goods arriving by train at the railway station Krechowice and arranging transportation to the shops in town. Not far away was the nice house of Baron Walisz (No. 132 of Map), formerly owned by Dr. Berwid, while on the other side of the road, opposite the Church, was the house of Dr. Wassermann (No. 121 of Map), nearby lived Riva Horowitz and daughters, then the Lusthaus family at No. 130 of Map. Before the Pharmacy of Skalka (No. 131 of Map) we had the Newspaper and Stationery shop of Shalom Laufer. One of his daughters was married to Chaim Seinfeld of Perehinsko, while the other had much success in leading roles of our amateur theatricals. Next to the Pharmacy was the house of Shmuel Nussbaum, whose son survives in Israel.

This part of Rozniatow was known as "Unter der Stadt" -- suburb on the road to Krechowice, and there lived many families in roomy houses with gardens and fruit trees. Remembered among them is the house of Leib Falik, well to do son-in-law of Wolf Hoffmann (see No. 134 of Map), and the Falik children happily survive in Belgium and Israel. There lived Meier Kaufmann, Lipa Tanne, Berl Tanne, while across the road lived Dr. Sabath, Berl Londner and Leisor Turteltaub, the official Registrar. Nearby the town ended at the bridge over the Czeczwa, and on the other side there stood the flour-mill (see No. 144 of Map), owned by the Weinfelds of Swaryczow.

On the opposite end of the market-square, the main road was lined by shops on both sides, leading to the tobacconist Josef Kassner (see No. 47 of Map), turning right to pass the houses of Wolf Hoffmann (No. 46 of Map) where across the road was the house of Eisik Rosenbaum, whose son survives in Israel. Next came the house of Rechtschaffen (No 55 of Map) and then the house of Nissan Schindler (No. 53 of Map) where Chaim Schwarz lived. Here the road split at a right angle, one branch leading past the house of Leisor Itzik Loew (No. 29 of Map) and Adlersberg (No. 35 of Map, opposite), up the hill to the Catholic Church (No. 37 of Map) and the Sokol-House nearby (No. 38). At a lower level of the Church was the large house and garden of the Ukrainian family Woloszynowicz (No. 39 of Map) who 1924 served also as mayor.

At the left of Kassner (No. 47 of Map) was a smaller square, remembered for the house of Itzik Barnik, the excellent melamed and opposite lived Abraham Sauerberg, erudite and liberal, whose daughter survives in Israel. Nearby was the large flour-shop of Israel Trau, who like Eli Yona Koral was a son-in-law of Wolf Hoffmann. He was a liberal and most popular man, survived by son and daughter in Israel.

The main branch of the road, passing the corner house of Shlomo Widman (No. 44 of Map) led to the small lake below the hill, a landmark of Rozniatow. This was an artificial lake, at the lower level of which was the flour mill, a Skarbek property held by Efraim Rechtschaffen (see No. 24 of Map). A short canal under a bridge on the road fed the waterfall turning the millstones by way of paddle wheels, and here we had the extensive Skarbek farm under management of Weigel, later on leased by the Glesinger lumber concern. The hill over the lake commanded a fine view of the town, and here stood the Court (No. 20 of Map, former Skarbek residence), Post Office (No. 21), Police Station (No. 23) and the large School (No. 22 of Map).

The main road below led into the suburb "Das Alte Dorf" -- the Old Village -- very likely the original nucleus of Rozniatow, where many Ukrainians lived. Here stood the houses of the bookbinder Nahman Scheiner (No. 17 of Map) and Mordehai Mark (No. 16), and there was also the house of Jagiellowicz (No. 15 of Map) who married a Jewish girl. Not far away stood the fine house of Alter Bermann amidst a large garden (No. 12 of Map) on a hill. They only son of Alter Bermann, Izio, lives in Israel, retired from government service. At the bend of the road stood a small Chapel (No. 11 of Map). Across the road were several houses of Jewish residents, of whom are remembered Sara Esther Horowitz, who had the leading grocery in town. Her daughter Zlate was among the first girls to learn Hebrew, and she happily survives in Israel. Next lived Leibisch Friedler, whose sons Zaharia Sender and Israel share in Israel our memories of Rozniatow. Adjoining was the Prayer House of the Alte Dorf No 10 of Map). The last houses on the road leading out of town to the village of Rowno were of Shlomo Jungermann (No. 4) and the restaurant-bars of Nahum & Israel Leib Artmann and of Chaye Adler across the road (Nos. 2 & 3 or Man), while the house of Eliahu Horowitz (No. I of Man) marked the end of the Old

Village, just before a small bridge and bifurcation of the road to Pereshinsko and Rowno, leading to the Station of the Glesinger Railway.

Unforgettable remain our years at the Elementary School which we entered at the age of six. Classes were held first in a small house, later to become the Municipality (see No 25 of Map) and in several other places until the fine brick building was erected on the hill over the lake (see No. 2 of Map). The teachers were only seldom fit for their profession, using the cane at practically every occasion, and so their efforts at teaching were defeated by the hate of the pupils. Wladvslaw Heinrich, one of the Polish teachers, was also leader of the SOKOL, a Polish patriotic sport organization, but a habitual drunkard like most of the resident Polish officials. Of the Jewish teachers are remembered Mondschein and Stark and foremost of all, our teacher of Jewish religion Adlersberg. Completely blind in his later years, he bravely continued his educatory work and literally all of Rozniatow were his pupils. Remembered are also the Catholic priest Malinowski and the Greek Catholic, Jackowski, both highly respectable men.

At the age of ten those of us who were to enter high school, called Gymnasium, sat for entry examinations, and so were at school in Stryi or other larger towns, being absent from Rozniatow over many months of the year. However, being at home on vacations, often travelling jointly in one or other direction, bonds of friendship were formed between us, and so groups of youth came into being. Except for the very first pupils of high schools, like Dr. Berger, Dr. Jackel, Lutwak sen. who were several years ahead of us, we would like to record as pals and friends: Dr. Bendet Berger, Izio Bermann, Dr. Wilek Adlersberg, Pinio Kanner, Szymek Liebermann, Rudek and Poldek Loebl, Dolek and Nuniek Lusthaus, Moshe and Shaiko Lutwak, Leon Horowitz, Munio Muenz, Milek Turteltaub, Lolek Wassermann, David Weissmann, and there were a number of girls. Joint activities during vacations comprised some dances, but the main energies were devoted to amateur theatricals, collections for the Jewish National Fund, Jewish Library and later, during the elections of 1922, some political work.

Others -- alongside and/or intermingled with the above groups -- who felt the need of a change, contributed one way or another to open up the town to the XX. Century. Remembered are men like Meier Kaufmann, who early joined the Chowewei Zion, Aron Weissmann, Abraham Hoffmann, Benzion Horowitz, Shimon Diamand, Lonek Erber, the brothers Tepper, Jacob Yampel, who joined in general activities.

The Emperor continued his "gracious" reign, the Polish officials regularly coming to the bar of Israel Rosenmann for their long bouts, leaving drunk, and like the thunder during the summer storm, came upon Rozniatow the sudden awakening in the World War I.

Immediately upon outbreak of the War in September 1914, the calling up of men to active military service deeply affected many households. While all Jews professed to be patriots of Austria, and their allegiance was sincere, actual participation in war was a more serious matter, and so a delegation led by Dr. Feuer left urgently on a Saturday for Dolina, coming back with clear instructions as to who was to join the army. A general moratorium was declared on repayment of mortgages and long term debts, and while all local strategists expected otherwise, the Russian army continued the offensive into Galicia. Order in town was still maintained by the gendarmes under their commander Furmankiewicz but the first families took refuge in other towns, considered safer: Dr. Wassermann, Dr. Feuer, Dr. Safir, Dr.

Barth, Mishel Artmann, Shaye Frisch have so left. Stories were told of Russian Kosaks raping women, of massacres and pogroms -- and very soon the first Kosak patrols appeared. Austrian government offices closed down, postal and railway serviced stopped and the Russian town commander sat up his office in the house of Baron Walisz. There and then Peter Woloszynowicz became Mayor of the town, replacing Wolf Hoffmann, who jointly with Haim Schwarz luckily were bought out by ransom from being taken to Russia as hostages.

Sales of alcohol were strictly forbidden, to prevent drinking by Russian soldiers, as Rozniatow lay on the road to the Carpathian range, on the border of Hungary, where the Austrian Army held strong positions. Austrian officials received no salaries, and the severest hardship was so caused to the aging old bachelor Yona Funt, postal official with a silken white beard, who became a "man about town", forlorn and forsaken, like a prediction of the debacle of Austria. During the winter 1915 the Austrians attacked near Rozniatow, and the town came for 7 days under artillery fire but the attack was repulsed. Some of the younger men were taken to dig graves for the fallen soldiers. Gradually conditions became easier, most of the inhabitants still had some food and even Russian tobacco was obtainable.

Rozniatow was liberated by the Austrians in the summer 1915 but just a year later in the summer 1916, a new Russian offensive under Brussilov reached Stanislawow and Rozniatow was again in the frontal zone of fire. While the first refugees of 1914 returned home, in 1916 several other families, like Leisor Itzik Loew, Chanina Weissmann took refuge in towns of Western Galicia, fearing a new Russian occupation. They returned when the Russian front disintegrated in 1917 upon the fall of the Tsar but conditions deteriorated also in all the Austrian Empire. Already all men between 18 and 42 were called up, food was rationed and clothing was becoming a problem. Many dodged military service by hiding or self inflicted wounds, disruption of postal and rail communications caused serious shortages, and there was a general use of substitutes, known as "Ersatz". In the fall of 1918 the defeat of Germany and Austria caused also the falling apart of the Austrian Empire of the nationalities, and one day a group of young Ukrainians, led by Stephen Lapinecki, took over Rozniatow on behalf of the new Ukrainian Republic. A strong, uncouth lad who just a few years before felled and killed a cabman, Nachman Rosenmann, only because be tres-passed over his parents' garden, Lapinecki and his like were hardly the men to organize communal life and build a state. The Ukrainian peasants, mostly illiterate, used the new "freedom" to vent their hate of the Jews, to rob travellers on the roads but the loud acceptance of new slogans, like self-determination of peoples, facilitated some forms of orderly conduct. Rozniatow was spared of open pogroms, a very respectable farmer, Fedorenko, was appointed Mayor. The Jews could for the first time elect a "National Council" as a legal basis for some communal activities. Chairman of the Jewish Council was Dr. Wassermann, and thanks to him social assistance of the poor was set up. A Poalei Zion club was formed in which Shalom Rechtschaffen was very active. The drama of Gordon "Chasie the Orphan" was performed in Yiddish, the amateur actors being Tinka Berger, Shalom Rechtschaffen, Milek Turteltaub, Jacob Erber, Chajka Diamand and prompter was Moshe Lutwak.

Such events were but of small solace for Rozniatow which could hardly maintain communications with other towns, and commerce shrunk to a minimum. Travelling by rail was a major hazard and the Ukrainians were neither able to set up a proper administration, nor deal with any economic problems. Their only measure was the issue of new money, called the Karbowaniec, to replace the Austrian

Krone, and this was a calamity for the Jewish merchant. The shopkeepers could not refuse to accept this legal currency but the wholesalers would rather not part with their stocks for a clearly valueless scrap of paper. As an event of courage and determination in Rozniatow, the renewal of Hebrew classes by Zvi Fassberg deserves to be recorded, and we are happy that Zvi is with us in Israel also today.

Pogroms of Jews in the Ukraine under Heiman Semjon Petlura were the outburst of a hooligan, hopeless regime, and in May 1919 the Polish army "liberated" Galicia, claimed as a part of Poland in the XVIII. Cent. Army units under General Haller appeared in heroic posture with anti-Semitic songs on their lips, cutting beards of Jews trapped on trains and boding little good. Leniency was the slogan as regards the Ukrainians, and in Rozniatow only the younger Lapinecki was shot when resisting arrest, while the older Stefan was left to go free. On the other side, the new Polish Police Commandant Brojanowski demanded, and got, Jewish girls to scrub the floors and do the housework at the Police Station -- an ominous sign of the new regime's intentions.

Gradually orderly administration was re-established but the Finance Office was moved to the county town, Dolina, and the Post Office then got the building on the hill. Zacharia David Liebermann was nominated President of the Kehilla, a hardly enviable task when the official call was: "JEWS TO PALESTINE". Indeed, the Jaeckel family emigrated 1920 to Palestine in toto, while Poland was led by ministers like the Grabski brothers -- one as minister of Finance, the other of Education -- both proudly anti-Semitic "National Democrats".

Rozniatow was first hit by an imposed levy, called Danina, as a special payment to the state, while at universities and colleges the Numerus Clausus was introduced to keep the Jews out from medical, agricultural and engineering studies. Under these conditions the first parliamentary elections were held in 1922, and the Rozniatow Jews recorded over 600 votes for the Zionist list to the Sejm in Varsaw. Bendet Berger and Munio Muenz represented then the Jewish list during the voting at the Municipality.

Meantime the Poles introduced their own currency, the Mark, while the Austrian Krone and Ukrainian Karbowaniec became obsolete. However, the continuing devaluation of the Mark, opening up of contacts with foreign countries and influx of American Dollars from mailings of relatives created a new trade -- the illegal dealing in foreign currency, which only added fuel to the ever burning anti-Semitic fire. While 1919 the Ukrainians made in towns razzias on Jews, to rob them of remade military uniforms and boots, the Poles have in 1922/23 organized even larger razzias, to go over pockets and confiscate Dollars.

The reform of 1924 by the issue of the Polish Zloty caught the Rozniatow Jews unaware, and they again paid a heavy price for the unasked, unexpected blessing. The rapid change caused a sharp economic crisis, unemployment and recession that endured as a long stagnation. As the Zloty was based on gold, the moratorium of 1914 was cancelled, and the mortgages had to be repaid in Zloty -- as most of the debtors did not care to settle the old debts in Mark. The freezing of rents brought house building to a standstill, prompted the house owners to keep flats unrented, and for new rents key money had to be paid "on the side".

While the Rozniatow shopkeeper and trader had more than enough on his shoulders, and constantly lacking cash and seeking credits, the reconstruction in Europe opened up export markets, especially for Polish coal and lumber, and the forests around Rozniatow as well as the oil fields assured a measure of prosperity for the region. This development offered some openings for new lawyers to settle in Rozniatow, where also several dentists have set up offices. Berko Littauer, Shaye Lutwak, Wilek Turteltaub are so remembered Telephone services were introduced and an exchange was set up at the Post Office but the most visible sign of the new times was the autobus service that replaced the old cabs, vehicles and carriages. One of the first to operate a bus service was the Apothecary Macierzynski, on the side also moneylender and usurer, but then also former cabdrivers, Aron Zimmermann and Mejlech Landsmann became partners of Philipp Ferszt in operating a public bus service to Perehinsko. The third was Abraham Hoffmann, whose autobus was providently destroyed by fire, and he could recover the insurance, as the bad roads, lack of technical skill and costs of repairs caused heavy losses, and all these enterprises ended in financial disaster. At the end only owners who could themselves drive and service their buses could make ends meet in the field of public transportation. However, it was a step forward.

So as to remind Rozniatow of their old problems and woes in being between two rivers, the Duba and Czeczwa, the town was practically submerged in the floods of 1928, and the Rozniatower again justified his pitiable name of "Nebbich".

The clearly anti-Jewish system, controlled by the military, left only law and teaching careers open for the Jews leaving colleges, and many had to study abroad. While many of the graduates had to serve in the army with practically no chance to pass officer examinations, government jobs were invariably closed to the Jew. High school teachers found employment only in private Jewish colleges where also Hebrew was taught (some were based on Hebrew), and Rozniatow never had a Jewish medical man who graduated in Poland. This went alongside a taxing system, based on trading patents, or licences, with graded fees of 3 categories, that every shopkeeper and peddler had to obtain. This assured a foolproof registry for the income tax, based on imposition and demand. Enacted like the repeated levys -- Danina -- the official demand of income tax was arbitrary, and appeals against demands had to be supported by documentary evidence, proper account books etc. This was beyond the shopkeeper of Rozniatow who learnt to avoid even the postal parcel service, the registers of which were utilized by the Finance Office to gain intelligence on goods received. The tax collectors, attached to the Finance Office in the county town Dolina employed local court executors to enforce payment of taxes by impounding goods, furniture etc. while a charge of 15% was collected for overdue taxes plus costs for the forced collection. In many a case this meant the ruin of the shopkeeper who also faced much higher housing rates of his municipality, as a result of pressure from government on their local budgets.

Politically, the regime made use of the always potent anti-Semitism of the population, Polish and Ukrainian, and open boycott and the picketing of Jewish shops enjoyed protection by police, because the slogan "ONE TO HIS OWN" (SWOJ DO SWEGO) -- nationalist in content -- was applied to daily economics, to force the Jew out of his livelihood.

It was openly admitted by the Poles that their fiscal policies and measures aimed at the undermining of Jewish predominance in commerce, and indeed the boycotts and resulting in some cases riots strangled the weakest link -- the small man in small town.

Notwithstanding and despite such obstacles, cultural activities continued in Rozniatow and they deserve to be, recorded.

A committee under Dr. Diamand managed to maintain the Hebrew School by local financing, as Jewish minority schools were denied government subsidies. There was a Jew-wish Sports Club, devoted mainly to football, and although no matches were ever arranged with Polish clubs, now and again such matches were held with other Jewish clubs of other townships. There was a workers' club named "YAD CHARUZIM" with Philipp Ferszt as chairman but most of the cultural activities centered in the Civic Club under Dr. Safier and Moshe David Lutwak as secretary. This club operated the Jewish Public Library, in which Leon Horowitz, Benzion Horowitz, Abraham Hoffmann did good work to maintain a high literary level and efficient administration. It is significant for Rozniatow that this club occupied two rooms in the house of Sosie Heller at the market square -- rent free. A number of Jewish youngsters joined the Chaluzim, preparing in Hachscharot groups for emigration to Palestine.

Alongside and all over the years Rozniatow had a most active group of amateur actors, who put on many theatricals, all except two in Yiddish. The only two plays enacted in Hebrew and Polish respectively were failures and never repeated. Among the actors stood out Sender Friedler -- born theatrical talent and excellent comedian, an superb Falstaff. He is remembered also as having been among the founders of the Rozniatow Landsmannschaft Society in New York and one of its presidents. In one of the early plays we had as actors Dora Liebermann, Dr. Diamand, Zvi Fassberg, Dr. Berger but over the years the following appeared on the Rozniatow stage: Wilek Adlersberg, Juda Hammermann-Axelrad, Leon Horowitz, Pinio Kanner, Simon Lieberman, Dolek & Nuniek Lusthaus, Shaye Lutwak, Godel Schwalb and Weinfelds of Swaryczow. The remembered girl-actors were: Hania & Lea Horwitz, Andzia Kanner, Dwosia Kassner, Adela Kupferberg, Tonia Laufer, Nemlich sisters, Matylda Prinz, Lotka Rosenmann, Escia Trau, Escia Widmann, Benzion Horowitz was often directing and prompter was Simon Diamand.
Being away from Rozniatow as from the thirties, we must leave it to others to tell of the events of World War II, when Eastern Galicia, including Rozniatow, became a part of the Sowjet Ukraina, this regime lasting from November 1939 to June 1941. The subsequent occupation by the Germans, the physical extermination of the Jews by the Nazis, assisted in many cases by their Ukrainian stooges, the Jewish suffering in the ghetti camps and Holocaust are known. There were Rozniatow Jews who fought against the Nazis in units of the Red Army and possibly lived to see the township after liberation in 1945. Even today there may be some Jews living among the inhabitants of our township, but the Rozniatow as it was, as we knew it -- is no more.

# MARTYRS OF HOLOCAUST

## (PERSONS & FAMILIES)

A

Adler David
Adler Chaja
Adler Fruma Fassberg
Adler Gitl
Adler Schmuel
Adler Willy
Adlersberg Wilek, Sigi,
  Lonek, Berta
Andacht Abraham
Andacht Itzchak
Andacht Schalom
Arnold, son In law Spas
  of Izchak Schwaeb
Artman Israel Leib
Artman Mosche
Artur son In law
  Goldshmid Shmaja
Axelrad David
Axelrad Schlomo
Axelrad Zvi-Hirsch

B

Barnik David
Barnik Eisik
Barnik Jehuda
Berel Abraham
Berenfeld Moshe
Berger Cbaja Udel
Berger Josef

Berger David
Berger Mlshel
Berger Pinchas
Berger Sucher son Josef
Berger Sucher son Pinkas
Berman of kamin
Bienstok Jehuda
Bienstok Moshe
Birnholz Mirjam
Birnholz Schimon
Bitkower Dwora Spas
Bitkower Mordchai of

Bitkower Zacharla.
Bitkower Zeev-Wolce
Blau Josef
Bleicher Abraham Zwi
Bleicher Jtzchak
Brand Abraham
Brand Chanina
Buchwalter Mordchal
Bunim Mordchai

D

David Frieda
Deutscher Abraham
Deutscher Chana
Deutscher Lote-Scheindel
Deutscher Mirjam

Deutscher Schalom
Diamand Avlgdor
Diamand Baruch
Diamand Bina
Diamand Israel
Diamand Jehuda-Josef
Diamand Reuwen
Diamand Schaje of Ilem
Diamand Schimon
Diamand Schimon
  son Baruch
Diamandstein David
Dornfeld Avlgdor
Dornfeld Chaskel
Dornfeld Nachman
Drach Abraham
Drach David
Drach Mosche

E

Edelstein Belle
Edelstein Lea
Edelstein Max
Edelstein Schlomo of Spas
Eichenstein David
Ekstein Bronci
Ekstein Chaim
Ekstein Gitl
Ekstein Mordchai
Ekstein Reisel
Engelman Bunio
Enis Alter
Erber Fani
Erber Hani

Erber Leib
Erdman Abraham

F

Falik Leib
Falik Max
Falik Schabse
Faasberg Mechel
Feld Michael
Fendel Jakob
Ferscht Philip
Feuer Dr. Isidor
Feuerstein Jakob
Feuersteln Josef
Fink of Swaryczow
Filer Schmuel
Freler Jehuda
Frenkel Meir
Freilich of Luhy
Fried Dr. Abraham
Friedenberg Zwi
Friedler Abraham
Friedler Leibisch
Friedler Abraham
Friedler Uri
Friedler Aron
Friedler Bendet
Friedler Chana
Friedler Chana
Friedler Eisig
FriedIer Ester
Friedler Fischl
Friedler Hirsch
Friedler Israel

Friedler Leib
Friedler Mordchai
Friedler Mosche
Friedler Raschi
Friedler Schmuel
Friedler Schmuel
Frisch Chaim
Frisch Feiwisch
Frisch Godl
Frisch Israel
Frisch Jehuda
Frisch Leibisch
Frisch Meci
Frisch Meir
Frisch Schmuel
Frischman Gold of Wigoda
Fruchter Jakob
Fruchter Meschulem
Fruchter Mosche

G

Ganz Mendel
Geller Buci
Geller Bunem
Geller Chaim
Geller David of Spas
Geller Elieser
Geller Meir
Geller Mordchai of Spas
Gelobter Josef
Gelobter Hirsch
Gelobter Israel
Gelobter Chaim
Gertner Sara

Godner
Goldschmidt Alter
Goldschmidt Schmaja
Groll Abraham
Gross Mordchai
Gruessgott of Rowno


H

Haber Chaim
Halpern Chawa
Halpern Josef
Halpern Kalman
Hammermann Dwora
Hammermann Jakob
Hammermann Schmuel
Hauptman Leib
Hausman Abraham
Heisler Abraham
Heisler Dawid
Heisler Fischl
Heisler Jacob
Heisler Jakob of Dubka
Heisler Mordchai
Heisler Mosche
Heisler Mosche
Heisler Ruben Gecl
Heisler Schaja
Heisler Simcha
Heisler Sucher
Helfgott Ell
Hochman Jakob
Helfgott Schmuel
Heller
Herz Gitel

Hilman Schimon
Hochberg Leibci
Hochman Leibisch
Hoffman Abraham
Hoffman Jakob
Hoffman Jehoschua
Hoffman Leib
Hoffman Mordchai
Hoffman Schalom
Hofman Wewl
Hoffnung Mosche
Horn Josef Zwl
Horowitz Baruch
Horowitz Berl
Horowitz Eliahu
Horowitz Chaskel
Horowitz Eliahu
Horowitz Hersch
Horowitz Jsrael
Horowitz Jzchak
Horowitz Kalman
Horowitz Dr. Leo
Horowitz Malka
Horowitz Mates
Horowitz Mendel
Horowitz Moshe
Horowitz Mosche
Horowitz RIvka
Horowitz Roza
Horowitz Schmuel

J

Jaeckel Ben Zion
Jaeckel Chaja-Batja

Jaeckel Chaim Ascher
Jaeckel Elieser
Jaeckel Frieda
Jaeckel Lea
Jaeckel Schalom
Jaeckel Tila
Jampel Bendet
Jampel Godl
Jampel Hersch
Jampel Jakob
Jampel Mechel of Spas
Jampel Menasche
Jampel Mosche
Jonas Eti of Spas
Jonas Jtzchak of Spas
Jungerman Schlomo

K

Kohn Abraham
Kahane Dr.
Katz Dr. Isidor
Katz Strutin
Kalman
Kartschman Baruch
Kartschman Chaim
Kartschman Jakob
Kartschman Juda
Kartschman Kunie
Kartschman Rachel
Kartschman Wolf Ber
Kassner Alte
Kassner Aron
Kassner Bunim
Kassner Bendet

Kassner Bendet

Kassner Ell

Kassner Josef

Kassner Natanel Sant

Kassner Scheinci

Katzman Elieser

Katzman Itzchak

Katzman Ita

Katzman Schaja

Katzman Schimschon

Kaufman of Pohorilec

Kaufman Chaim Hirsch

Kaufman Josef

Kaufman Meir

Kaufman Menasche Ber

Keller Benjamin

Keller Godl

Kilstok Jehuda

Kirschenbaum Chaim

Kirschenbaum

Kirschenbaum Leib-Arie

Kleinbrod Jakob Juda

Klinger Ester

Klinger Israel

Klinger Leib Josef

Klinger Leiser Ber

Klinger Malka

Klinger Mordchai

Klinger Mosche Josef

Klirsfeld Zwl

Koenigsberg Ruhama &
  Husband

Kopf Ester

Kopf Josef Hirsch

Koral Eli-Jona

Korn Juda Zwi Dajan

Kopf Pini

Kopf Sara

Kornbbluet Abraham

Kornbluet Jsreal

Kornbluet Meir

Kornbluet Mosche Mechl

Kreiter Leib

Kreiter Schalom

Kriegel Baruch

Kriegel David

Kriegel Hensel

Kriegel Pepci

Kuker Baruch

Kuperberg Sischi Arie

Kuperberg Zwl

Kurz Josef

Kurzberg

## L

Landsman Benzion

Landsman Dunio

Landsman Hirsch

Landsman Issar

Landsman Meilech

Landsman Mendel

Landsman Mosche

Langer Leiser

Laufer Jakob

Laufer Josef

Laufer Nachum

Lehrer Jakob

Lehrer Taube

Leiner Mosche

Lichtman Herman
Lieberman Zacharia David
Lindenwald Schmuel
Litauer Bernard Dentist
Loew David
Loew Jakob
Loew Josef
Loew Mordchai
Loew Schalom
Loew Schmuel
Londner Alte
Londner Breinci
Londner Dwosi
Londner Israel-Hirsch
Dr. Lusthaus Dolek
Lusthaus Ester
Dr. Lusthaus Nunek
Lustig David of Spas
Lustig Mosche Jakob
Lustig Sische
Lutwak Chaim Schimon

### M

Mansfeld
Margulis
Mark Abraham
Mark Dwora
Mark Hirsch
Mark Mordchai
Rabi Matzner
Meier, Robbi's Widow
Meiseles Chaim Schlomo
Meiseles Chaim Schlomo
Meiseles Gitel, Hirsch, HerzI

Meiseles Leib
Meiseles Mosche
Meiseles Natan
Meiseles Schlomo
Dr. Menkes
Mensch Bernard
Menschenfreund
Milstein
Milrad Menasche
Milrad Mosche
Milstein Mosche
Muenz Baruch
Muenz Mosche

### N

Nemlich Mendel
Nemlich Schmuel
Nussbaum Israel
Nussbaum Israel Gezl
Nussbaum Schalom
Nussbaum Schmuel
Nussbaum Schmuel Rlvka

### P

Pineles Mendel
Pohoriles
Press Aron
Press Leib
Press Mosche
Presser Abraham
Presser Schaje
Prinz

## R

Radler Feiwusch
Rappaport Fani
Rattenbach David
Rechtschaffen Bluma
Rechtschaffen Efraim
Rechtschaffen Etel
Rechtschaffen Schalom
Rechtschaffen Schimschon
Reiner David
Reiner Leibusch
Reinharz Schmuel
Reiss Itzchak
Rosenbaum Belle
Rosenbaum Ester
Rosenbaum Eli Rivka
Rosenbaum Hirsch Meilich
Rosenbaum Joel
Rosenbaum Leib
Rosenbaum Schlomo
Rosenbaum Sobel
Rosenberg Alexander
Rosenberg Asriel
Rosenberg Eisik
Rosenberg Josef
Rosenberg Menasche
Rosenberg Mendel
Rosenberg Mosche
Rosenberg Mosche
Rosenberg Schabse
Rosenberg Schmuel
Rosenberg Wolf Ber
Rosenman
Rosenman
Rosenman Israel

Rosenman Itzchak
Rosenman Mosche
Rosenman Schmuel
Rotenberg Chaim
Rotenberg Chune
Rotenberg David
Dubschera
Rotenberg Eli
Rotenberg Jsrael
Rotenberg Jakob
Rotenberg Josef
Rotenberg Meir
Rotenberg Rivka
Roter Marek
Rotfeld Abraham
Roth Bezalel
Roth Chaim David
Roth Meier
Roth Schmuel
Rubin Bezalel
Rubin Hirsch
Rubin Mosche of Rowno
Rubinfeld Jakob
Rubinfeld Josef
Rubinfeld Juda

## S

Sobel Itzchak
Dr. Sabat Schmuel
Dr. Safir Schimon
Samet Mirjam
Scharf Jekel
Schenkler Berci
Schindler Sosie

| | |
|---|---|
| Schlosser Josef | Spiegel Schabsi |
| Schnitzer Chaim | Spiegel Schlomo |
| Schnitzer Herman | Springier Perez |
| Schnitzer Sara | Stein Josef |
| Schumer Itzchak | Stein Nachman |
| Schumer Will | Stein Sara |
| Schwalb Chaim Ber | Stern Alter |
| Schwalb Hirsch Mordchai | Stern Benjamin |
| Schwalb Israel | Stern Chaskel |
| Schwalb Itzchak | Stem David & Slmha |
| Schwalb Josef | Stern David |
| Schwalb Pini | Stern Dina |
| Schwalb Schimon | Stern Golda |
| Schwarz Leibele | Stern Jtzchak |
| Schwarz Mordchai | Stern Josef Schimon |
| Schwarz Natan | Stern Juda |
| Schwarz Susie & Hinde | Stern Juda Hirsch |
| Schweinfeld Rivka | Stern Mendel |
| Schwindler Baruch | Stern Mordchai |
| Schwindler Elci | Stern Mordchai Monti |
| Schwindler Israel Juda | Stern Schlomo & Perl |
| Schwindler Itzchak | Stern Schlomo |
| Schwindler Mordchai | Stern Sosie |
| Segal Mordchai | Stern Sucher |
| Seinfeld Chaim | Stegmann Malcie |
| Semel Aron | Sternbach Juda |
| Sindler Ester | Sternbach Josef |
| Sindler Rivka | Sternbach Schaje |
| Sittler | Strassberg Benzion |
| Sperling Ruchcia | Strassman Benjamin |
| Spiegel Bendet | Strassman Sam |
| Spiegel Benjamin | Strassman Henci |
| Spiegel Eli | Strassman David |
| Spiegel Mordchai | Strassman David & Leni |
| Spiegel Mosche | Strassman Frieda |
| Spiegel Sara Rivka | Strassman Jakob |

Strassman Keile

Strassman Mordchai

Strassman Mosche

Strassman Sara

Strassman Surcie

Strassman Schije

Strassman Wowi

Strauchler Chaim

Stromwasser Abraham

Schnee of Luhy

Spiegel Eliezer

Spiegel Chana

Suesser Breindel

Suesser Dwora

Suesser Meir

Suesser Rachel

Suesser Zacharia

Suesser Zalman


T

Tanne Aba

Tanne Hirsch

Tanne Jehoschua

Tanne Juda Hersch

Tanne Lipe

Tanne Meir

Tanne Schula

Tanne Wewci

Taub Meir

Teitelbaum Schlomo

Tepper Sara

Tisch Mordchai

Trau Israel

Turteltaub

Turteltaub Itzchak

Turteltaub Leiser

Turteltaub Meir

Turteltaub Psachja


V

Vogel Leib

Vogel Abraham

Vogel Breinci

Vogel Noach Israel

Vogel Hirsch Zwi

Vogel Rivka

Vogel Bendet


W

Waechter Abraham

Waechter Aron Leib

Waechter Aron Wolf

Waechter Berl

Waechter Chaim

Waechter Hersch

Waechter Hersch Luser

Waechter Itzchak

Waechter Mechel

Warnik

Wasserman Asriel

Wasserman Chaim Zwi

Wasserman Feiwel

Wasserman Gdalja

Wasserman Juda

Wasserman Meir Ber

Wasserman Mosche

Wasserman Schaul
Dr. Wasserman Schlomo
Wasserman Zelda
Weber Feiwel
Weber Gdalja
Weinfeld David
Weinfeld Itzchak
Weinfeld Lipa
Weinfeld Munik
Weinfeld Rost
Weinfeld Wolf
Weinloes Schmuel
Weinreb Josef
Weinreb Mosche
Weinstok
Weiser Itzchak
Weiser Mosche
Weiser Seide
Weiss Berisch
Weiss Jehoschua
Weissberg Juda
Weissberg Wolf
Weissman Aron
Dr. Weissman David
Weissman Michael
Weitzner Dwora
Weitzner Leib
Weizman Rachel

Widman Broncl
Widman Jeschaja
Widman Schlomo
Wigdorowitz Mates
Wilner Mates
Wirt Israel.
Wirt Schmuel
Wittlin Richard
Wohl Benzion
Wohl Dawid
Wohlbeschaffen Alte
Wohlbeschaffen Esther
Wolfrom Josef
Wolkentreiber Aron
Wolkentreiber

Z

Zimmerman Aron
Zimmerman David
Zimmerman Meir
Zimmerman Mosche
Zimmerman Nachum Leib
Zimmerman Schalom Dawid
Zimment Dawid
Zwang-Gelobter Mendel
Ogrodnik & Wife